LIBERTY
AND
PROPERTY

LIBERTY
AND
PROPERTY

BY

R. V. COLEMAN

ILLUSTRATED

CHARLES SCRIBNER'S SONS, NEW YORK
CHARLES SCRIBNER'S SONS, LTD., LONDON

1951

Foreword

IN *The First Frontier*, published three years ago, we followed the adventures, hopes, failures and successes of the early English settlers in America.

The present volume carries the story forward a century—from the 1660's to the eve of the Revolution. It was a period of great expansion and fateful decision.

We see new colonies being added along the Atlantic coast—sugar planters from Barbados settling in Carolina; Quakers creating a "Holy Experiment" in Pennsylvania; professional philanthropists founding Georgia.

We see great tobacco and rice plantations arising in Maryland, Virginia and the Carolinas—operated by slave labor—the masters living in homes that are still the admiration of all who view them.

We see the forests of New England being turned into ships that roved the Seven Seas—bringing to their owners wealth that established colleges, libraries and hospitals.

We see pirate captains hobnobbing with royal governors of New York—Connecticut and New Jersey farm boys returning from illicit voyages to the Indian Ocean, their pockets bulging with Arabian Gold.

We see hard-bitten traders pushing their packtrains ever farther along the Indian paths—southward toward the Spanish in Florida, westward over the mountains toward the French forts on the Ohio River.

We see French explorers sweeping down the mighty Mississippi; La Salle falling by an assassin's bullet on the plains of Texas; fur traders working up the Missouri, up the Kansas, up the Platte—clashing in a battle to the death with Spanish soldiers from Santa Fe.

We see thousands upon thousands of newcomers to the English colonies—Scotch-Irish, Germans, Swiss—driving the frontiers westward, colliding with the eastward-pushing French. And then, war—a struggle for the continent—with England the victor but at a cost that threatened the jealously guarded rights and liberties of every American.

We see the colonists rise in protest under the watchword of "Liberty and Property." Under that watchword we see the King's taxmasters roughly handled and forced to resign. We see the hitherto separate, individualistic colonies come together as a unit in defense of their liberties and properties. We see the foundation laid for the future United States.

R. V. C.

February 26, 1951

Contents

CHAPTER | PAGE

1. BIRTH OF AN EMPIRE — 1
2. THE KING SPEAKS — 14
3. CAROLINA — 21
4. NEW FRANCE — 31
5. A DUTCH INTERLUDE — 40
6. KING PHILIP — 43
7. LOW PRICES–HIGH TAXES — 56
8. QUAKERS — 67
9. LA SALLE — 77
10. PENNSYLVANIA — 93
11. *QUO WARRANTO* — 105
12. ALONG THE TRADING PATHS — 119
13. TEXAS — 127
14. REVOLUTION — 140
15. THE VISIBLE AND THE INVISIBLE WORLD — 157
16. PATENTS AND PIRATES — 187
17. BROTHERLY LOVE — 218
18. TOBACCO — 240
19. SKINS AND SLAVES — 287

CHAPTER   PAGE

20. LOUISIANA   318

21. THE PHILANTHROPISTS FOUND A
    COLONY   347

22. AN ANGRY GOD   367

23. ABLE MEN AND FINE HOMES   385

24. PEOPLE   425

25. THE HINTERLAND   445

26. OHIO   474

27. COLONIAL UNION FAILS   499

28. THE KING'S REGULAR AND
    DISCIPLIN'D TROOPS   506

29. COMMITTEES OF CORRESPONDENCE   517

30. SONS OF LIBERTY   523

31. THE ROAD TO UNION   532

    BIBLIOGRAPHY   539

    INDEX   589

ACKNOWLEDGEMENTS

To Joseph G. E. Hopkins who, day in and day out during the three years that the book was being written, lent a sympathetic but critical ear to the author's problems and made many a constructive suggestion.

To Ethel M. Watson who, day in and day out, searched for fugitive facts—at the New York Public Library, the New-York Historical Society and other depositories.

To Edna M. Werry and her staff who, with never failing interest, made available to the author the unique historical collections of the Pequot Library at Southport, Connecticut.

To Mary Wells McNeill, Grace Tobler and Irma Wyckoff who, over and over again, typed the manuscript and pointed to spots that needed clarification.

To LeRoy H. Appleton who directed the drawing of the maps.

To James T. Hoar and all those at the Scribner Press who helped in bringing the volume into physical being.

Illustrations and Maps

	PAGE
Map of New Netherland, 1664	3
Map of Duke of York's Proprietary, 1664	5
Map of the English Colonies, 1664	11
Map of Carolina, 1669	25
Map of Iroquois Country, 1666	33
Map of the Discovery of the Mississippi, 1673	37
Portrait of Josiah Winslow	47
Portrait of King Philip	47
Map of New England, 1676	49
Portrait of John Leverett	54
Map of the Southern Colonies, 1670–1680	63
Map of Niagara, 1679	80
Portrait of Henri de Tonti	87
Map of La Salle's Exploration, 1679–1682	89
Map of Pennsylvania and Lower Counties, 1681–1686	99
Map of Carolina and Virginia, 1680–1686	123
Map of Texas and New Mexico, 1685–1690	133
The Whipple House, Ipswich, Mass.	159
Kitchen of the Daniel House, Salem, Mass.	159
Portrait of Increase Mather	165
Portrait of William Stoughton	169
Map of New England, 1690–1704	175
The Stebbins House, Deerfield, Mass.	177
French Soldier on Snowshoes	177
Portrait of Sir William Phips	179
Portrait of Joseph Dudley	179
Map of Madame Knight's Route, 1704	182
Comfort Starr House, Guilford, Conn.	185

PAGE

North Room, First Floor, Comfort Starr House,
    Guilford, Conn.   185
Map of New York, 1704   189
Portrait of William Vesey   191
Dutch House, Pearl Street, New York, 1697   193
Vechte-Cortelyou House, Gowanus (Brooklyn), New
    York, 1699   193
Portrait of Peter Schuyler   197
Portrait of Caleb Heathcote   199
Map of East and West Jersey, 1664–1702   209
Portrait of Lewis Morris   211
Map of Pennsylvania and Maryland, 1684–1712   223
The Slate Roof House in Philadelphia   227
William Penn's Writing Desk   231
Portrait of James Logan   235
Portrait of Hannah Penn   238
Map of the Tobacco Colonies, 1680–1720   243
Portrait of William Fitzhugh   248
The State House, or Capitol, at Williamsburg   259
Portrait of William Byrd, II   267
Portrait of Alexander Spotswood   273
Bed Chamber of Governor's Palace at Williamsburg   275
Portrait of Robert Carter   283
Map of Charleston, 1702–1729   291
Interior of Goose Creek Church   293
Map of the Carolina Hinterland, 1702–1729   296–297
Portrait of Captain Teach   313
Portrait of Sieur D'Iberville   319
Map of Louisiana and New Mexico, 1699–1733   331
Portrait of Don Diego de Vargas   333
Portrait of Tomo Chichi and His Nephew   349
Savannah in 1734   355
The Georgia Trustees Receiving Tomo Chichi and
    His Delegation   359
Map of Georgia, 1732–1755   361

PAGE

Portrait of Jonathan Edwards 369
Yale College in the 1740's 372
Portrait of Timothy Cutler 372
Portrait of George Whitefield 377
Nassau Hall and President's House, College of New
    Jersey, 1764 383
"Stenton," the Country Home of James Logan 389
"Fairhill," the Country Home of Isaac Norris 389
"Berkeley," Charles City County, Virginia 393
"Westover," Charles City County, Virginia 393
"Drayton Hall," Ashley River, South Carolina 402
Interior View "Drayton Hall" 402
Detail of the Wentworth House, Little Harbor, N. H. 409
Home of Thomas Hutchinson, Boston, Mass. 411
Thomas Hutchinson's Country House at Milton, Mass. 411
Redwood Library, Newport, R. I. 415
Portrait of Ezra Stiles 415
Philipse Manor House, Yonkers, N. Y. 417
Mantel, East Parlor, Philipse Manor House 417
Portrait of Sir William Pepperrell 420
Portrait of Cotton Mather 435
Portrait of Samuel Sewall 437
Self-portrait of John Watson 439
Self-portrait of Gustavus Hesselius 439
Portrait of William Bowdoin 441
Map of New York-Pennsylvania Hinterland, 1710–1750 449
Map of Pennsylvania-Virginia Hinterland, 1730–1750 457
Portrait of Conrad Weiser 461
Map of Virginia-Carolina Hinterland, 1730–1756 471
Map of Ohio and the Northwest, 1740–1754 478–479
Map of the Forks of the Ohio, 1755 511

LIBERTY
AND
PROPERTY

Birth of an Empire

I T WAS DAWN of a hot morning, late in August, 1664. Down a rough path, darkened by the forest that crowded on either side, came a gang of negroes, the men chained together, the women and children trailing behind. At their head, leading the way, was a single white man. They splashed through the Raritan River and at a brisk trot turned southward—on past the spot where today Princeton University rears its towers to the sky. Behind them came a similar gang similarly led, and behind that yet another. They had left New Amsterdam, on the Hudson River, the previous evening. Before nightfall they would be across the Delaware River at the Falls where Trenton, New Jersey, stands today. Their destination was the Dutch town of New Amstel, seventy miles farther down the Delaware. In charge of the operation was Peter Alricks, buying agent for Alexander Hinnoyossa, the Governor at New Amstel.

If Alricks forced a fast pace down the road from New Amsterdam, there was good reason for his hurry. Two days earlier he had been engaged in transferring a herd of cattle from the western end of Long Island to the head of the path leading to the Delaware. One or two boatloads had been put ashore—on Staten Island—and another load was crossing the Narrows when four English frigates unexpectedly arrived on the scene. Any question as to the good intentions of the visitors vanished as they put off longboats filled with soldiers who not only intercepted the Dutchmen's ferry but took possession of the cattle already landed. The commissary problem of the invading fleet was quickly solved, but New Amstel was doomed to be short of beef.

In addition to the cattle, Alricks had fifty or sixty negroes at New Amsterdam. They had cost a pretty penny from a Dutch West India slave trader, and they would bring many hogsheads of tobacco from the English planters in Maryland. It was up to Alricks to deliver them to Governor Hinnoyossa if possible. Accordingly, after nightfall on that same day, he slipped the negroes down the harbor, divided them into three groups for safety, and started them for New Amstel as we have seen.[1]

But Alricks might as well have saved his effort. A month later two of the English frigates sailed into the Delaware River and anchored above Fort Casimir, the Dutch stronghold at New Amstel. The Dutch and Swedish farmers, scattered along the western shore of the river, quickly submitted, but Governor Hinnoyossa held out.

The crisis came on Sunday, October 12. With less than fifty soldiers Hinnoyossa crouched behind the walls of the fort. The frigates stripped for action. A company of soldiers was set ashore. Slowly down the languid Delaware the warships eased toward the fort, paralleled by the land party. There was a burst of fire from the frigates; a rush by the storm troops; and all resistance was over. Hinnoyossa fled into Maryland. His slaves, his cattle, his farms, everything he had, became booty for the conqueror—won "by the sword." The English, not the Dutch, sold the slaves to the tobacco planters along the Chesapeake. Some of the Dutch townspeople fared little better; they were stripped "to a very naile." Even the name of New Amstel disappeared. It became New Castle.

Such was the final act by which the Dutch colony of New

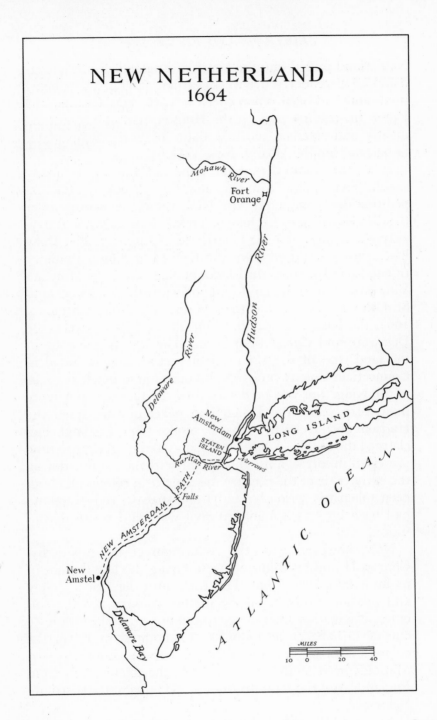

NEW NETHERLAND
1664

Mohawk River

Fort
Orange

Hudson River

Delaware River

New
Amsterdam

LONG ISLAND

STATEN
ISLAND

Raritan River

Narrows

NEW AMSTERDAM PATH

Falls

New
Amstel

A T L A N T I C   O C E A N

Delaware Bay

MILES
10 0   20   40

3

Netherland passed into the hands of England. New Amsterdam had surrendered five weeks earlier, without a shot being fired, and had been renamed New York. Fort Orange, the Dutch fur-trading post up the Hudson, had also submitted quietly and received the new name of Fort Albany, later to become simply Albany, New York.[2]

It was but natural that the names of York and Albany should have appeared in this new English colony. The expedition that conquered New Netherland was acting under the direction of James, Duke of York and Albany, the thirty-year-old brother of King Charles II of England. The Duke had already acquired from the Earl of Stirling a shadowy title to Long Island, to the islands of Nantucket and Martha's Vineyard, and to the land lying between the Kennebec and St. Croix rivers in presentday Maine, when, on March 12, 1664, the King also granted him all the land between the Delaware and Connecticut rivers. The fact that a part of the land west of the Connecticut was already included in Connecticut Colony probably did not even so much as occur to the King. Nor was he deterred by the fact that, for more than forty years, the Dutch had peacefully occupied the Hudson and Delaware rivers. Since 1606 England had claimed the middle Atlantic coast and had from time to time protested mildly against the Dutch settlements. But during the early years of the century the American colonies had not been taken too seriously, and from 1640 to 1660 England had been busy at home with civil wars and political confusion.[3]

Now, however, with the restoration of the monarchy, Charles II and his ministers were laying the foundations of an imperial trade system. This program called for a closely knit relationship between the mother country and the colonies. Navigation laws closed the more profitable trade to outsiders. Tobacco and similar commodities raised in the colonies must be shipped to England and to England only. Manufactured goods could come into the colonies only from England. And the customs due the King were to be strictly collected.

Naturally this affected the profits of the tobacco planters,

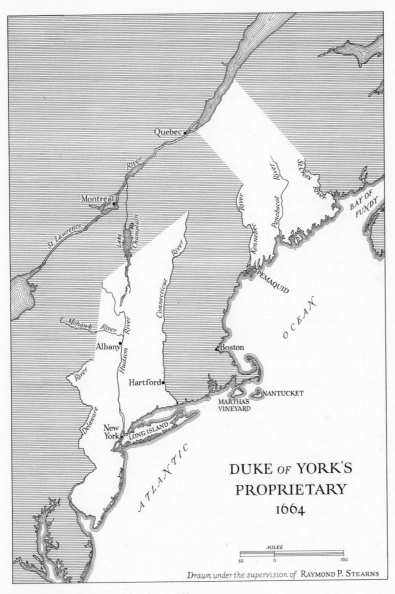

DUKE OF YORK'S
PROPRIETARY
1664

MILES

50   0   100

Drawn under the supervision of RAYMOND P. STEARNS

From the *Atlas of American History*.

5

who had been accustomed to an open market, especially with the Dutch traders. Naturally, too, ways of avoiding the laws were found. One of the simplest of these ways was to send the tobacco up Chesapeake Bay and, by a slight portage between the heads of creeks, deliver it at New Amstel whence it went to Holland. In return the planters received much needed negro slaves, brought into New Amsterdam by the Dutch West India Company and sent overland to New Amstel. Those negroes brought down to New Amstel by Alricks were a part of this illegal trade. The trade was, in fact, doubly illegal. Not only was the sale of the tobacco a smuggling operation; the purchase of the negroes was also a smuggling operation. Through a monopoly recently granted by the King, the English colonists could legally purchase negro slaves only from a company headed by the Duke of York.[5]

New Netherland, reasoned the King's ministers, must be added to the British colonial empire or the colonial program would fail, together with the customs needed by the hard-up King, the profits needed by the merchants who supported his throne, not to mention the income from the slave trade needed by the penniless Duke of York. Accordingly, four ships of the royal navy and a body of soldiers were put at the disposal of the Duke, who placed Colonel Richard Nicolls in command of the expedition. It was given out that the purpose of this armed excursion into the New World was to bring recalcitrant New England to terms. However, Nicolls had a secret commission directing him to seize the Dutch colony for the Duke.[6]

So New Netherland was taken, and from Nova Scotia to Carolina England ruled the coast of America. Thus was realized a colonial empire visioned fifty-eight years earlier by the statesmen and merchants of England. At that time, in 1606 to be exact, the most northeasterly point claimed was 45°, approximately the St. Croix River. Now, in 1664, the St. Croix became the northeasterly boundary of the widely scattered lands granted to the Duke of York. England was re-establishing her territorial claims along the American coast.[7]

The area from the St. Croix to the Kennebec had hitherto known only trader government. There, on the Penobscot, the men of Plymouth had collected furs only to be looted by the French who in turn were looted by the Puritans. There, at Pemaquid, English merchants had developed trading posts from which fishing boats scoured the northern waters, and to which the Indians brought their beaver skins.[8]

Next along the coast lay the former Province of Maine, reaching from the Kennebec to the Piscataqua River. It had been granted by the King, in 1639, to Sir Ferdinando Gorges as a proprietary, which is to say that not only did the land belong to Gorges to dispose of as he wished, but the privilege and duty of governing the inhabitants were also his, subject only to the laws of England. Gorges, however, had proved unequal to managing his province; and since the 1650's it had been ruled by Massachusetts, who claimed the area under a liberal interpretation of her own charter of 1629.[9]

Below Maine came New Hampshire. There the legal right to the land was presumably vested in the heir of Captain John Mason, through a grant from the Council for New England in 1629. But, since Mason had not confirmed his title by a patent from the King, his colony was, in effect, a tenant of the Council for New England; and since the Council was now defunct, the right of government had reverted to the King. However, New Hampshire, like Maine, had been gobbled up by Massachusetts during the civil wars in England.[10]

Massachusetts, by the terms of its charter, extended from three miles south of the Charles River to three miles north of the Merrimac. These bounds had been given, and accepted, on the supposition that the two rivers ran approximately in an east-west line. However, when the disordered conditions in New Hampshire and Maine, and the confusion in the mother country, made the annexation of the two northern provinces feasible, the Massachusetts leaders ran their survey up the northern reach of the Merrimac and insisted that an east-west line through that most northern point was their proper boundary, thus taking in their weaker neighbors. And no one, short of the King, could successfully challenge their action. Massachusetts was a corporation, duly created by the King; its officers were invested with the duty of governing the corporation; they exercised that authority with vigor and according to their own lights.[11]

Adjoining Massachusetts on the south was the little colony of Plymouth, founded by the Pilgrims in 1620. Like New Hampshire, Plymouth existed only by a patent from the Council for New England. With no real authority to govern itself, it had from the beginning done so. Technically the King should have taken charge of the colony. As a matter of fact, Massachusetts largely dominated it.[12]

To the westward were Rhode Island and Connecticut, both originally squatter colonies, self-governing by their own good right. Recently, by charters from the royal hand—Connecticut in 1662, Rhode Island in 1663—they had become corporate colonies similar to Massachusetts, their lands and their right to govern themselves confirmed. New Haven colony no longer existed; it had become a part of Connecticut; and now, by the King's grant to his brother, a large part of Connecticut seemed destined to be annexed to the Duke of York's proprietary.[13]

Between the Connecticut and Delaware rivers lay the larger and most important part of the Duke's proprietary. It was his by a title and authority similar to that by which Gorges had held Maine. The Duke was the proprietor—the landlord and the government. He could command such rents (the land tax of the seventeenth century) as he deemed proper; he could appoint the governor; he could make the laws, without any advice from the people or their representatives.[14]

South of the Duke's province was Maryland, held by Lord Baltimore as a proprietary under much the same terms as those by which the Duke held his lands. Curiously enough New Amstel actually lay within the limits of Maryland. But Baltimore had allowed the Dutch to trespass, and the Duke's expeditionary force had orders to oust the Dutch, which it did at New Amstel as well as at New Amsterdam. Thereafter the Duke's officers retained control—and a new colonial division came into being—later to be known as Delaware.[15]

Across the Potomac from Maryland was Virginia, first of England's permanent colonies in America. It had been founded by a trading company, but in 1624 the King had taken it under his direct control, appointing the Governor and the Council. A House of Burgesses, elected by the freemen, however, continued to provide a large measure of self-government. During the civil wars in England it had been, of all the colonies, the most loyal to the King. Now, with the King's restoration, it was receiving the least favorable treatment. The navigation acts were bearing heavily on the profits from its tobacco; the area between the Potomac and Rappahannock rivers, known as the Northern Neck, had been given to a group of the King's friends, with the privilege of selling the land and collecting the rents for themselves; its southern part had been lopped off and added to the newly created colony of Carolina.[16]

There had been an attempt, as early as 1629, to establish a colony of Carolina, but nothing had come of it, and the patent had lapsed. Then, shortly after the restoration of the King, two men, both in London with a view to bettering their fortunes through claims on the royal favor, agreed that a colony south of Virginia might be profitable. These two men were Sir John Colleton, lately a sugar planter on the English-owned island of Barbados, and Sir William Berkeley, Governor of Virginia. They easily interested Anthony Ashley Cooper, just created Lord Ashley, who also had sugar plantations on Barbados. To aid in financing the project, as well as to bring pressure on the King, five other men, among whom were Sir George Carteret and Lord Berkeley, a brother of Sir William, were persuaded to join in asking for the desired land. The King, ever willing to oblige his friends when it cost him nothing, approved the request and on March 24, 1663, these eight men became the lords proprietors of Carolina, which included a large slice of the then southern part of Virginia and stretched down the coast almost to the presentday northern boundary of Florida. Like Lord Baltimore in Maryland and the Duke of York in his far-flung province, the proprietors of Carolina owned the soil and were the government in their colony. Up to the autumn of 1664, they had done little beyond providing for the collection of quitrents from, and a slight government for, the few planters already operating in the Albemarle Sound region.[17]

Such was the odd assortment of colonies—royal, corporate, proprietary and tenant—scattered along the Atlantic coast of America in 1664. There were perhaps a hundred thousand inhabitants in all, some seven thousand of them in the Duke of York's proprietary. There were few settlements beyond tidewater, practically none without access to navigable water. Fort Albany was the farthest inland but it too had open-water communication with the sea.

In this patchwork the former trading colony of Holland now took its place as a dependency of the crown of England, to be managed and governed for the benefit of the Duke of York and the imperial program then being fashioned by the King and his ministers. Upon Colonel Richard Nicolls, commander of the expedition that captured New Netherland, fell the responsibility of managing it, as Governor under the direction of the Duke.[18]

At New York, Albany and New Castle the majority of the inhabitants were Dutch with a sprinkling of Germans, Swedes and Finns. They took the oath of allegiance to England to save their property, Peter Alricks among the rest; but most of them looked forward to the day when Holland might reassert her authority. On Long Island there were many English who had moved into the liberal Dutch colony from illiberal New England; and the eastern end of the Island, which had formerly been joined with Connecticut, was wholly English.[19]

The source of Nicolls' power lay not in the will of the people, nor yet in the respect for proprietary authority. It lay in a company of professional soldiers at his beck and call. This was something new in the American colonies. Never before had their governments been based on the power of the sword. Well may the "brethren" of New England and the tobacco planters of the South have wondered what might be in store for them.

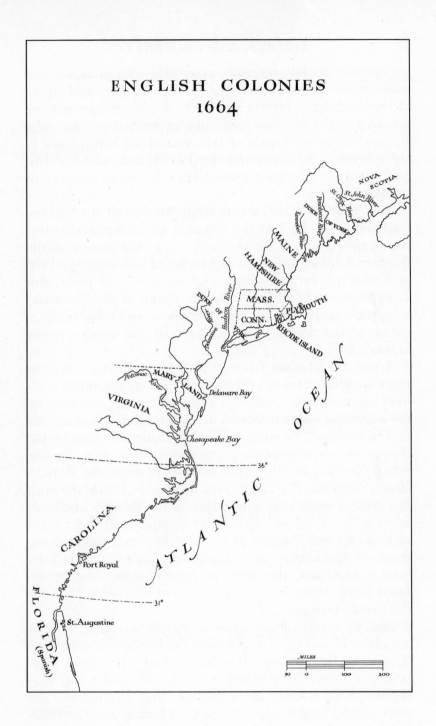

ENGLISH COLONIES
1664

NOVA SCOTIA

St.John River

St.Croix River

Penobscot River

Kennebec River

DUKE OF YORK

MAINE

NEW HAMPSHIRE

MASS.

CONN.

PLYMOUTH

RHODE ISLAND

DUKE OF YORK

Delaware River

Hudson River

Potomac River

MARYLAND

VIRGINIA

Delaware Bay

Chesapeake Bay

36°

CAROLINA

ATLANTIC

OCEAN

Port Royal

31°

FLORIDA (Spanish)

St.Augustine

MILES

50   0   100   200

Governor Nicolls, however, proceeded with prudence and moderation. He respected the property rights and many of the established institutions of the Dutch inhabitants; he put together, from the legislative experience of the New England colonies, a code of laws reasonably satisfactory to the English inhabitants of Long Island; and with the Iroquois Indians adjoining Fort Albany he made a treaty of friendship.[20]

New York City itself was in what Nicolls called a "meane condition," but he had the foresight to recognize the strategic importance of the place. ". . . within five years the staple of America will be drawn hither of which the brethren of Boston are very sensible . . .," he wrote the Duke. But Long Island looked like a complete deficit to the Governor; the people there, he said, "are very poor and labor onely to get bread and clothing, without hopes of ever seeing a penny of monies."[21]

Across the Hudson from New Amsterdam were two or three huddling Dutch villages, cramped in the rear by almost impenetrable swamps. To the southward, however, on the mainland opposite Staten Island, the soil was excellent and in demand. Prospective settlers made the most of the change of government to get grants in this area. To one group Nicolls gave the lands northward from the Raritan River; to another a large tract, known as the Monmouth Purchase, along the southern side of the Raritan and eastward to Sandy Hook. This latter group, composed largely of Quakers and Baptists from New England, founded the towns of Shrewsbury and Middletown after the New England manner and, also after the New England manner, refused to pay quitrents—causing no end of trouble later for the proprietary authorities.[22]

But, as it turned out, Nicolls had been acting without authority in making any grants of land west of the Hudson River. On June 23–24, after Nicolls had sailed from England but before he reached America, the Duke had subdeeded to his friends, Lord Berkeley and Sir George Carteret, all the land lying between the Hudson and the Delaware rivers. It was to be a separate province, known as New Jersey.[23]

News of this transfer of title reached New York in June, 1665, and the following month Philip Carteret, the new Governor of New Jersey, arrived with thirty men to form the nucleus of a settlement. After a brief survey, he selected a spot on the western side of the bay above Staten Island and there proceeded to build a town to which he gave the name of Elizabethtown. As he led his followers ashore, Governor Carteret held a hoe on his shoulder to symbolize his resolution that agriculture should be the basic industry of the new colony.[24]

Berkeley and Carteret, the proprietors of New Jersey, were, as will be recalled, also members of the group of men who had recently acquired title to Carolina. They now adapted for New Jersey a prospectus, called "Concessions and Agreement," that had been prepared for the southern colony. Land was offered subject to a small annual quitrent; freedom of conscience was guaranteed; a representative assembly was provided for.[25]

This document, widely circulated throughout the adjoining colonies, soon brought many permanent settlers. One compact group came from the former colony of New Haven. Strict Congregationalists, they objected to being exposed to the more liberal constitution of Connecticut and envisioned the establishment of a new Bible commonwealth in New Jersey. Securing a tract of land five miles north of Elizabethtown, they founded the town of Newark where, they agreed, none should become freemen except such as were "members of some or other of the Congregational churches, nor shall any but such be chosen to Magistracy or carry on any part of Civil Judicature."[26]

The King Speaks

"MEMBERS of some or other of the Congregational churches." That requirement, if disregarded in Connecticut, and only optional in New Jersey, was strictly enforced in Massachusetts. No man voted, no man held office in that colony unless he were a member of the Congregational church. And that was a situation the King had in mind putting an end to.

As will be recalled, the projected attack on New Amsterdam had been concealed under an explanation that the purpose of the Nicolls expedition was to exact from the New England colonies a proper respect for the restored monarchy. In part that statement was true. With Nicolls had come Samuel Maverick and two other commissioners, under orders from the King to investigate and correct conditions in New England, particularly in Massachusetts. Maverick had been a trader at Massachusetts Bay five years before the vanguard of the Puritans arrived there in 1629. For seventeen years he had managed to get along with the "saints," as they modestly called themselves. In 1646, when he joined with some other Church of England men in protesting against the continued exclusion of non-Congregationalists from any part in the government of the colony, he was forced to depart or suffer the consequences. Now, as a member of the Nicolls Commission, Maverick was back in America to bring Massachusetts to heel and to clear up various problems affecting the other New England colonies.[1]

One of the most immediate of these problems was that having to do with the territorial extent of Connecticut. By a patent given under the King's hand in 1662 Connecticut extended to the Pacific Ocean; by the grant made by the King to his brother in 1664, Connecticut extended only to the Connecticut River; Hartford, Wethersfield, New Haven, Stamford and many other towns fell within the Duke's proprietary. Also, there was the question of Long Island, all of which Connecticut claimed and the eastern end of which she had long controlled. That, too, had been granted to the Duke.

Shortly after the capitulation of the Dutch, and while the commissioners were still at New York, they received a call from John Winthrop, Governor of Connecticut. He did not come to argue with the representatives of the brother of the King; he was much too wise in the way of the world to attempt that. He presented the commissioners with five hundred bushels of wheat and some horses—and made the best bargain he could. Connecticut's western boundary was set at a line twenty miles east of the Hudson, but she lost Long Island irrevocably.[2]

With this Connecticut business settled, Nicolls went ahead with his pacification of the Dutch at New York while Maverick and the other two commissioners proceeded to New England. Rhode Island and Plymouth were respectful enough, but at Boston came the real test of the commissioners' authority. Massachusetts had been practically in rebellion against England when, in 1640, the civil wars broke out in that country. Throughout those disturbances she had sided with the Parliamentary faction against the King. At home she had extended her rule over New Hampshire and Maine; she had coined her own money—the Pine Tree shillings; she had, in effect, looked upon herself as an independent commonwealth. With the restoration of the King in 1660, she had provided an asylum for the regicides; she had openly flouted the navigation laws; she had successfully evaded the royal demand that the Church of England be at least tolerated within her bounds.[3]

All of this the King now commanded the commissioners to correct. But they got just nowhere with the stiff-necked magistrates at Boston. While professing allegiance to the King, neither the Governor nor the General Court would recognize the authority of his commissioners. Not even the presence of Nicolls, who came to Boston in April, 1665, could budge them. They excused themselves in a letter sent directly to the King—followed by a present of two large masts, greatly needed by the royal navy. The purpose of the masts was frankly explained in the minutes of the Massachusetts court; it was "in order to the continuance of our precious liberties without interruption, through the Lord smiling upon our endeavours."[4]

Nicolls, in disgust, returned to New York. Maverick and his two fellow commissioners continued northward to New Hampshire and Maine, both of which it was believed would welcome separation from Massachusetts. On July 10, 1665, they summoned the inhabitants of Portsmouth, Dover, and other New Hampshire towns to meet within the week and listen to a letter from the King. The selectmen of Portsmouth sent a communication "Hast! post hast!" to the "Much honored Governor & Council of the Massachusetts" asking what to do. The express reached Boston at midnight on the 11th. Governor Bellingham crawled out of bed, got his council together, and the following morning the answer was on its way: Pay no attention to the letter from the King, "Surely it cannot but be accounted a figg-leafe." The meetings were held, however, and a few people, doubtless under the encouragement of the commissioners, signed a petition praying the King to release them from the government of Massachusetts. But all that came of it was that the principal malcontent was dragged down to Boston "to answer for his tumultous & seditious practises." New Hampshire remained an appanage of Massachusetts.[5]

In Maine the commissioners had better luck. There the right to govern rested on a royal patent to Sir Ferdinando Gorges, whose grandson and heir, also Sir Ferdinando, had sent, with the Nicolls expedition, a proclamation asserting his proprietary rights and appointing various men, most of them well known in the province, as deputies to govern in his behalf. In addition, the King had sent a letter to the inhabitants of the province confirming Gorges' rights and directing that his deputies be accepted as the government of Maine.[6]

Despite all this the Governor and Council of Massachusetts still maintained that Maine was a part of their colony. The King, they insisted, had placed their northern boundary at three miles above the Merrimac River; they had surveyed the Merrimac; an east-west line three miles north of its northern source included Maine. And they would govern Maine.[7]

In accordance with this decision, Massachusetts, as early as May, 1665, had appointed justices to go into Maine and hold courts, and if anyone "under any pretense of any other authority whatsoever," by which they meant the King's commissioners, bothered them, they were to bring such persons to trial, or sentence them as "the merit of their offences" might require. But when the time came the justices had thought better of forcing the issue, and the King's commissioners, on their arrival, had little more to do than confirm the officials already installed by Gorges' agents. After a careful consideration of the conflicting claims, however, and of the wishes of the people, the commissioners did not take any definite action as to Gorges' proprietary rights; rather they placed the province under the direct protection of the King—and the King, along with a gentle rebuke to Massachusetts, commanded that the government as established by his commissioners be not disturbed.[8]

The population of Maine—scattered along the coast from the Piscataqua River to the Kennebec—numbered perhaps a thousand people. Almost to a person they were of British origin, Protestant with a leaning toward the Church of England. They lived by fishing and farming. There were among them none of great wealth. William Leighton was probably somewhat more than average well-to-do. His personal clothing was valued at twenty-five pounds, eight shillings. His homestead—land and buildings—was worth eighty pounds. He had two oxen, five cows, three heifers, two calves, two steers, a bull, a three-year-old horse, nineteen sheep, and thirteen pigs. Among his household goods were eleven pewter dishes, two chamber pots, a pewter basin, pewter candlesticks, a "suckeing bottle." In his main living room, which may have been a part of the kitchen, there were two chairs, a table, and a considerable supply of table linen. There was a four-poster bed with curtains and valance; the tick was filled with feathers. There were many sheets and pillow cases, and a considerable supply of blankets and bearskins. There was a trundle bed, with its own feather-filled tick, sheets, blankets and covers. In an upstairs room there was another four-poster, similar to the one downstairs, together with many sheets, covers, and cushions. In the kitchen there were many brass and iron kettles, a cheese press, wooden trays, pails, candlesticks, chairs, and a couple of spinning wheels. The cellar was filled with barrels and tubs, fish hooks and lines, and other supplies. There was a lean-to, and a separate milk house. All in all, Mr. Leighton seems to have been quite comfortably fixed.[9]

The majority of people doubtless lived less well, and compensated for their lack of worldly goods by ephemeral pleasures. Take, for example, the accumulation of moral dereliction awaiting the justices at York, Maine, on the morning of July 12, 1666: Elias Grible, drunk—five shillings; Francis Breaster, drunk—five shillings; John Start, drunk and telling a lie—ten shillings; Richard Downe, absenting himself from "the Publique meeteing where the worship of god is dispensed on the Lords day"—five shillings; Richard Downe's wife, "scoulding & abuseing of her neighbors"—five shillings. Joan Andrews, notorious for her disrespect of authority, got ten lashes "on the bare skine" for breaking the King's peace.[10]

Frequently these hard bitten sons and daughters of the Maine coast added to their normal delinquencies by resenting correction. Thus Rowland Young, upon being brought to account "for travelling between Kittery & Yorke on the Lords day" became irritable and "retorted approbrious languidg aganst the graynd Jury in the face of the Court." [11]

Neither sex nor social position saved a sinner from public condemnation. When Eleanor Bonython, daughter of Mr. John Bonython, declined to certify the paternity of her child, she was charged with "haveing a bastard" and sentenced to stand in a white sheet at church during service—unless her father paid a fine of five pounds, which he, remembering his own youth,* of course did. [12]

Sadly different was the fortune of Goody White who, in better days, as the wife of Mr. William Hilton, had been addressed as "Mistress." She now got into a row between her second husband, "Goodman" White, and Francis Morgan, Gentleman, and was sentenced to "receive 10 stripes at the poast" unless her husband paid a fine of three pounds forthwith—and he apparently ducked out and let her take the whipping. [13]

Mr. Francis Morgan had his problems, too. On July 9, 1667, a young woman arose in court and read the following: "I, Ann Lynn, through the suggestion of Satan & my own corruptions do acknowledge that I have sinned against god & my mother Morgan in saying shee was a whore, for which words soe spoken by mee I am heartily sorry for it, that should abuse my mother in Law in this kind for which I hope it shall bee a warneing to mee for tyme to come." Offhand it would appear that from this point on everything was to be peaceful in the Morgan family, but alas, some three months later we find Mr. Morgan being haled into court by his wife, on a charge of "abusive speeches & Actions." There he readily admitted that "hee had strucke his wife & would doe it, for it was below him to Complayn to Authority aganst his wife, & after the testimony aganst were read & sworne, the said Morgan obstinatly sayd that hee repented not of what hee had done. . . ." [14]

Thus, not uninterestingly, life went on in Maine. In 1667, England and France decided to end their current war. By the treaty of peace "Acadia" was returned to France. The

*See Coleman, R. V., *The First Frontier,* pages 250, 309.

area of Acadia had never been very exactly defined but there was no question that it included Nova Scotia. France claimed that it extended to the Kennebec, and actually took possession to the Penobscot. Thus a large slice of the Duke of York's land between the St. Croix and the Kennebec became the property of France, and the rest was subject to controversy. True, the region seemed hardly worth holding. The King's commissioners had visited it in 1665 and found only three small plantations including Pemaquid. The largest did not contain more than twenty houses, and, said the report, "they are inhabited by the worst of men. They have had hitherto noe government and are made up of such as to avoid paying of debts and being punished have fled thither: for the most part they are fishermen and share in their wives as in their boats." The Duke probably would not miss them.[15]

But to Puritan Massachusetts this approach of Catholic France was disturbing. If the Duke, himself a Catholic, could not take care of his proprietary, Massachusetts could. If the King could not protect his Protestant subjects, Massachusetts could. On April 29, 1668, the Massachusetts General Court directed that a whole shipload of masts be sent to the King; he appreciated such gifts—and New Hampshire was permitted to help pay the freight. At the same time the members of the Massachusetts General Court declared "their resolution againe to exert their power of jurisdiction" over the inhabitants of Maine. Writs were dispatched announcing this decision. Justices were appointed to carry it out. And early in July these officials, accompanied by a substantial body of horse and foot soldiers, arrived at York, the capital town of Maine.

The existing magistrates of Maine—those appointed by the King's commissioners—protested this invasion; they exhibited their own commissions; they presented a letter from Governor Nicolls, as one of the King's commissioners, warning Massachusetts not to go against the royal command. But to no avail. They were pushed out of their own courtroom. Those who resisted were arrested. New officers were appointed for the various towns. And Massachusetts again ruled in Maine—the King's commands to the contrary notwithstanding.[16]

Carolina

WHAT THE EVICTION of the King's officers in Maine lacked in humor was, at about the same time, made up for on the coast of Florida. At least Captain Robert Searles' fellow Englishmen explained his descent upon St. Augustine as a "prank." The Spanish governor did not view it in just that light. Nor did the good fathers of the Franciscan mission see anything funny in it; they lost a likely convert to the Faith.[1]

This affair at St. Augustine was one of the many odd coincidences that played a part in the settlement of Carolina, the second largest grant of land ever made by an English king in America. As described in the original patent of 1663 the province stretched from 31° to 36°, nearly five hundred miles along the Atlantic coast, and extended westward to the Pacific. Two years later the area was further enlarged —half a degree northward, to take in another slice of Virginia, and two degrees southward, to take in a large piece of Spanish Florida including even St. Augustine.[2]

There remained, however, the problem of attracting

enough colonists to make the huge province profitable. The
first settlers came from Barbados, through the activities of
Sir John Colleton, the former sugar planter of that West
Indian island. In November, 1665, they made a preliminary
settlement on the Cape Fear River, but soon realized that
neither the soil nor the climate fitted their needs. In the
following summer Robert Sandford, with a few men in a
small ship, was sent to explore the country to the southward.
In Port Royal harbor, so named by Frenchmen in 1562, he
found a location that seemed suitable. The soil was good;
the Indians were friendly. As he was preparing to leave, on
the afternoon of July 7, 1666, a native chief came aboard
his boat and asked him to take a young Indian with him
and bring him back upon his return. Evidently the Indians
wanted to find out what sort of people they were dealing
with, and had anticipated an idea that was in Sandford's
mind. In fact, Henry Woodward, a member of his party,
had already expressed a wish to be left with the Indians in
order to learn their language and customs.

So the following morning Sandford and Woodward went
ashore to the Indian village. There the chief "placed Woodward by him uppon the Throne and after lead him forth
and shewed him a large field of Maiz which hee told him
should bee his, then he brought him the Sister of the Indian
that I had with mee telling him that shee should tend him
& dresse his victualls and be careful of him. . . ." Thus
Sandford told the story, adding, "I stayed a while being
wonderous civilly treated after their manner and giveing
Woodward formall possession of the Whole Country to hold
as Tennant att Will of the right Honorable the Lords Proprietors. . . ." And then Sandford sailed away.[3]

News of Woodward's presence at Port Royal had soon
reached the Spanish Governor of Florida. A few soldiers had
been sent to investigate and he had been taken to St. Augustine. There he had quickly picked up the Spanish language
and ingratiated himself with the friars by expressing a wish
for instruction in Catholicism. He was getting along nicely
when in 1668 Searles and his piratical crew fell upon the
town, and when they left, Woodward went with them.

Somewhere in the West Indies Woodward transferred to another privateering ship, in the hope of getting back to England. But in August, 1669, along came a hurricane and landed the privateer high and dry on the tiny island of Nevis —two hundred and fifty miles east of Puerto Rico. For four months Woodward had to make the best of the situation. Then, early in December, ships were seen approaching from the south. They turned out to be the *Carolina,* the *Port Royal* and the *Three Brothers*—all English and crowded with Englishmen.⁴

From Captain Joseph West, commander of the little fleet, Woodward learned that the Cape Fear settlement of Carolina had failed; that the lords proprietors had decided on another try; that they had chipped in £500 apiece and equipped three ships; that with a hundred or so colonists these ships had left England in September. At Barbados the fleet had picked up additional colonists together with Sir John Yeamans, who was to be their Governor. While lying at Barbados, one of the ships had foundered and the Colleton family had provided the *Three Brothers* to take its place. The expedition was on its way to Port Royal, where Woodward was supposed to be waiting and where Governor Yeamans had orders to establish a new colony. So Woodward climbed aboard the *Carolina* and off they went, west and nor'west, winding through the islands.⁵

But it was a troubled sea into which they sailed. Another great storm whipped up. The *Port Royal* was wrecked in the Bahama Islands. The *Three Brothers* rode it out and got into Chesapeake Bay. The *Carolina,* with Governor Yeamans among its passengers, took refuge at Bermuda. The Governor had had enough of pioneer life; he appointed William Sayle, "a man of noe great sufficiency," as his successor and went back to Barbados. The *Carolina,* after considerable refitting and re-provisioning, again turned her prow toward Port Royal, and in March, 1670, she sailed into that harbor.⁶

The colonists were welcomed by friendly shouts from the natives. But even those shouts—*Bony Conraro Angles* (presumably meaning: Welcome English comrades)—brought

misgivings. Those words *Bony Conraro* suggested the presence of Spaniards in the neighborhood. Woodward's experience may have added to the misgivings. At the same time
the leaders heard favorable reports of Kiawah, some fifty
miles up the coast, and with evident relief moved on to that
place. There they found a commodious harbor formed by
the meeting of two rivers, one of which Sandford had already named the Ashley and the other of which they named
the Cooper. Both names were in honor of Anthony Ashley
Cooper, the most active of the lords proprietors of Carolina.[7]

The point of land between the rivers was an attractive
location but too exposed to Indian attack. Accordingly they
pitched upon a site directly opposite—on the southerly side
of the Ashley—and there began their settlement. With a
creek on one side and a marsh on the other, the place was
easily defensible. They first called it Albemarle Point, but
it soon came to be known as Charles Towne.[8]

This first settlement was shortly reinforced by the people,
or most of them, who had sailed on the *Three Brothers*. That
ship, in returning southward from Chesapeake Bay, had over-
shot Port Royal and found itself at St. Katherine's Island,
off the coast of present-day Georgia. A trade had been struck
up with the Indians; the captain had gone ashore to buy
provisions; and he and a few others had been captured by
a Spanish garrison on the island. The ship, however, got
away and from Indians along the mainland the people
learned that other Englishmen were at Kiawah, to which
place they sailed.[9]

All in all, the summer of 1670, there were something over
a hundred colonists at Charles Towne—mostly men, but
some women. Among them twenty had an actual investment
in the enterprise; they were the freemen—the only ones who
had a voice in the management of the colony. The rest were
servants of one degree or another. There was one negro
slave, and there may have been others but certainly not
many.[10]

The colony arrived too late in the season to hope for
crops that first year, and food was getting low. So the *Carolina* was sent off to Virginia to buy what it could; also to

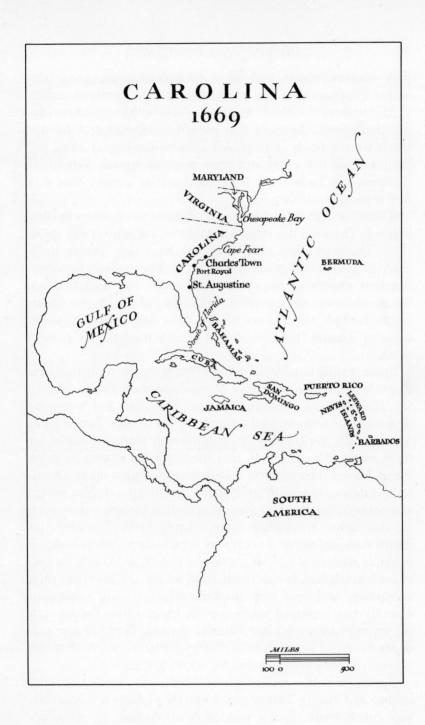

CAROLINA
1669

MARYLAND

VIRGINIA

Chesapeake Bay

CAROLINA

Cape Fear

Charles Town
Port Royal

St. Augustine

BERMUDA

ATLANTIC OCEAN

GULF OF
MEXICO

Strait of Florida

BAHAMAS

CUBA

SAN
DOMINGO

PUERTO RICO

LEEWARD
ISLANDS
NEVIS
St.

JAMAICA

CARIBBEAN SEA

BARBADOS

SOUTH
AMERICA

MILES

100 0   500

pick up some cows and hogs for breeding purposes. The *Three Brothers* was sent to Bermuda on a similar errand.[11]

Meanwhile the colonists set to work building and fortifying their town. Lumber was plentiful. Houses and storage sheds were quickly put up. A palisade was begun along the land side of the town and guns were mounted. When the *Carolina* got back from Virginia, Charles Towne was in a fair state of livability.[12]

Thus far the local Indians had been both friendly and helpful. Through the efforts of Woodward, who could speak their language, they supplied what food they could in return for knives and other trade goods. There were, however, constant alarms of impending attack by the Indians from the south, who were believed to be egged on by the Spaniards. In fact the return of the *Carolina* probably saved Charles Towne from an assault which might have proved fatal.[13]

Spain could hardly have been expected to wish this new English colony any success. It was uncomfortably close to the Florida Straits through which the rich and tempting Spanish plate fleets had to sail on their way home from Mexico and the Caribbean. Englishmen were notorious for their piratical proclivities, and there was no reason to think that Charles Towne would look too critically upon an enterprising captain with gold and silver to spend. Nor was it any secret that the Carolina proprietors claimed that even St. Augustine lay within their colony. True, England and Spain had just made a treaty by which each recognized the colonial possessions of the other in the New World, but no exact bounds had been drawn—and where the frontiers met, manpower and guns were the only arbiters. Still, Spain had scarcely two hundred soldiers at St. Augustine—not enough for an expedition against Charles Towne. Nor did the colonists have the strength or authority to attack St. Augustine. So each fenced itself in and stood on guard.[14]

Naturally some sort of government was needed for the colony at Charles Towne; as a matter of fact, it had available much more than it needed or could use. In 1669, before the expedition left England, a very detailed form of government had been approved by the lords proprietors. This document, in one hundred and eleven sections and known as the "Fundamentall Constitutions," was drafted by John Locke, private secretary to Lord Ashley and later one of England's outstanding philosophers. The intent was to establish "the interest of the lords proprietors with equality and without confusion, & that the government of this province may be made most agreeable unto the monarchy under which we live, & of which this province is a part, & that we may avoid erecting a numerous democracy." [15]

The Fundamental Constitutions provided for a semifeudal organization of the government and of the social life of the colony—with an hereditary nobility and an hereditary serving class. The nobility were to be known as landgraves (an old Germanic title) and as cassiques (a title borrowed from the Indians and meaning chiefs). These, together with the deputies of the lords proprietors, were to sit as a matter of right in a colonial Parliament. In addition, those who owned fifty or more acres of land were to be entitled to vote for representatives in the Parliament. And this Parliament, sitting as a single body, was authorized to make laws for the colony, subject however to veto by the lords proprietors. But in that autumn of 1670 there were, as we have seen, scarcely twenty men eligible to vote. The Constitutions had to be temporarily suspended, and, as a matter of fact, they never were wholly put into effect, though their existence had a marked influence on the character of the colony during the years to come. [16]

Land and the wealth that might come from its cultivation were the prizes that induced men to venture their money and effort in Carolina. The colony was to be a new Barbados, filled with great plantations operated by white servants and slave labor. The lords proprietors reserved to themselves seigniories of 12,000 acres each. Landgraves and cassiques, by bringing in servants or slaves or by proportional assistance to the colony, might receive similar acreages. To the ordinary freeman who paid his own expense to the colony a hundred and fifty acres would be allotted, with an additional one hundred and fifty acres on account of each able male servant which he brought at his own expense, or one hundred acres on account of each female servant or male servant under sixteen years of age. To the indentured servant, when he or she had served out his or her time, one hundred acres were promised.[17]

But the land was not to be taken up in a haphazard manner. The allotments were to adjoin each other. Nor were the people to live on scattered plantations as in Virginia. They were to live in compact towns as in New England. From the towns they would go forth in the morning to work on the plantations, and at night they would return to the towns from the plantations. Lord Ashley was very definite about that, and his injunction left its mark upon the manner of life that developed in southern Carolina.[18]

All allotments of land were subject to a quitrent of a half-penny per acre, payable annually forever, to the lords proprietors. This rent was in accordance with the established custom in England, and was a proper repayment to the lords proprietors for the outlay which they had made in securing their patent, for equipping ships, and for getting the colony started.[19]

Just what crops the soil of southern Carolina would produce was something that only experimentation could prove. At Barbados the fleet had picked up various seeds, plants, and trees—cotton, indigo, ginger, olive, and orange. These were planted in small plots to see what they would do. The immediate need, however, was to provide "for ye belly." Nor with the few colonists available could large plantations be established. So during this first year ten-acre plots were allotted in a semicircle around Charles Towne, and the principal crop planted was corn.[20]

It was Henry Woodward who opened a trade that made Charles Towne and southern Carolina profitable. Hardly was the town established before he made a trip inland to visit the Indians—fourteen days' travel to the northwest. It was rumored that he had discovered gold, but not even gold would have done for the colony what Woodward's contact with the inland Indians accomplished. He had opened a trade in furs that brought ready money in England.[21]

The colonists got through the first winter comfortably enough. The climate was a bit sharper than the Barbadians were accustomed to, but they were all remarkably healthy. The houses were tight. The palisade had been finished. There was ample food. In addition to grain and dried meats there was some milk and cream from the cows that had been bought in Virginia the previous summer. Probably there were also eggs for the more fortunate; Captain Brayne reported to Lord Ashley that, on his ten-acre plot, he had six geese, eight turkeys, and twelve chickens along with six head of cows, seven hogs, and three sheep. There would have been more hogs if someone had not developed an uncontrollable appetite for pork. The Barbadian servants had evidently come prepared for a cold winter. ". . . they are soe much addicted to Rum," complained Captain West, "that they will doe little [else] whilst the bottle is at their nose." [22]

In the late autumn the *Carolina* had been sent to Barbados with glowing reports of the settlement at Charles Towne. A proclamation was issued throughout the island by the representative of the lords proprietors of Carolina. All those who had put up money for the exploring trip of 1666—when Woodward had been left at Port Royal—were now entitled to land in the new colony. Others might secure land by going themselves or by paying for the transportation of servants. In February, 1671, the *Carolina* was back at Charles Towne with seventy new colonists. At the same time another ship, belonging to the Colleton family, came in from Barbados with forty people. [23]

The colony was a going enterprise. The credit for this was in a large measure due to Lord Ashley, soon to become the Earl of Shaftsbury. His was the energetic and capable mind back of the preparations in England. In carrying out Ashley's directions, and in actually establishing the settlement, Captain Joseph West was the strong man. Governor Sayle had proven a weak vessel. He was old and feeble and not very practical. While the settlement was still in a critical stage and there were grave doubts as to a supply of food, Sayle was writing Lord Ashley asking for "a Godly and orthodox Minister." Captain Brayne summed him up as being "hardly Compus mentes." In March, 1671, shortly after the new colonists arrived, the Governor died, and the freemen, unanimously if not officially, elected West as his successor. There was no longer any question as to the success of the settlement.[24]

After eight years of hesitation and failure, the lords proprietors of Carolina had, by their own efforts, founded a permanent colony within their broad grant of land. True, they had a well-rooted settlement on Albemarle Sound, but that they had inherited from Virginia. Between Albemarle and Charles Towne, a distance of three hundred miles, not even a foothold existed; the Cape Fear colony had vanished. Thus in 1671 we find two, and only two, centers of settlement in Carolina—the one on Albemarle Sound, destined to be the mother of North Carolina, and the one at Charles Towne, destined to be the mother of South Carolina.

New France

ENGLAND WAS NOT the only country engaged in pushing forward its colonial frontier in America. France was preparing for an advance westward from her posts along the St. Lawrence River. For years she had been blocked by the five nations —Mohawk, Oneida, Onondaga, Cayuga and Seneca—of the Iroquois Confederacy, whose towns stretched across present-day central New York. Not only had the Iroquois warriors held the French in check; they had exterminated the Huron and Erie Indians, whose habitants gave name to two of the great lakes, and had driven other weaker tribes to seek safety beyond Lake Michigan; either the Iroquois had to be humbled or the fur trade that supported New France would pass to the English at Fort Albany.[1]

In the summer of 1665 a heavy reinforcement of troops arrived at Quebec; the Mohawks and the Oneidas, most easterly of the Iroquois nations, were to be wiped out in order to clear a road for French traders through Lake Champlain to the Mohawk Valley. In preparation for their

thrust southward the French engineers built a series of forts
—Chambly, St. Theresa and others—on the Richelieu River,
between Lake Champlain and the St. Lawrence (see map
on page 33). This show of strength impressed the western
members of the Iroquois Confederacy—the Onondagas, the
Cayugas and the Senecas—who sent embassies to Quebec to
sue for peace. The resulting treaties were interpreted by the
French as meaning that the three nations placed themselves
under the protection of the King of France.[2]

With the Iroquois Confederacy thus split, the French
launched their offensive against the Mohawks. In the dead
of winter—January, 1666—they marched southward over the
frozen surface of Lake Champlain. On they went, through
snow four feet deep, the veterans of European battlefields
struggling with snowshoes, dogs pulling sleds, over Lake
George, along the course of the upper Hudson. And then,
when they should have turned west to the Mohawk towns,
they got lost. Their Algonquin guides had gone on a big
spree and no one else knew the way. On February 19, not
knowing where they were, they encamped near the frontier
Dutch town of Schenectady, fifteen miles northwest of Fort
Albany. At that moment the Mohawks attacked. A few
French heads displayed by the victorious Indians gave the
English officers at Albany their first inkling of the presence
of the French force. A deputation tramped across to the
encampment of the demoralized army and inquired by what
authority French troops were in the Province of the Duke
of York.

It was a delicate moment. France and England were practically at war in Europe. And here, in the backwoods of
America, French and English troops stood face to face. However, neither side wanted trouble and the English took care
of the wounded French soldiers while the rest, with "great
silence and dilligence return'd toward Cannada."[3]

If the Mohawks felt that they had put an end to French
attack, their neighboring tribe, the Oneida, had doubts. And
on July 7, 1666, the day on which Sandford was exploring
Port Royal harbor in Carolina, a delegation of Oneida chiefs
appeared at Quebec where they, like the Onondaga, Cayuga

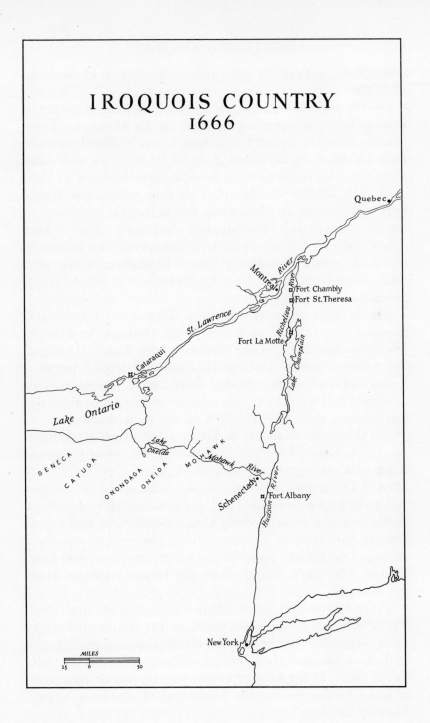

IROQUOIS COUNTRY
1666

Quebec.

St. Lawrence River

Montreal

Fort Chambly

Fort St. Theresa

Richelieu River

Fort La Motte

Lake Champlain

St. Lawrence

Cataraqui

Lake Ontario

Lake Oneida

SENECA

CAYUGA

ONONDAGA

ONEIDA

MOHAWK

Mohawk River

Schenectady

Hudson River

Fort Albany

New York

MILES

25   0   50

33

and Seneca, apparently accepted the protection of the King of France.[4]

Hardly was this treaty signed before the French prepared to launch another and larger attack on the Mohawks. Their line of offense was advanced another step by the erection of Fort LaMotte on an island in Lake Champlain, and from there three hundred canoes, carrying more than twelve hundred men, glided southward. This time they knew where they were going. The Mohawks fled before them, abandoning their towns and their supplies. And the English at Fort Albany stood helplessly by while it happened. The Mohawks had had enough and shortly placed themselves, along with their fellow Iroquois, under the protecting arm of the French governor of Canada.[5]

The way to the west was open. French fur traders and missionaries streamed up Lake Huron, through the strait of Michilimackinac, to Lake Superior and Lake Michigan. From those strategic positions, in the very heart of America, it was but natural that France should have striven to erect a barrier that would halt the western expansion of the English colonies already established on the eastern seaboard.[6]

"In the name of the Most High, Mighty and Redoubted Monarch, Louis, Fourteenth of that name, Most Christian King of France and of Navarre, I take possession . . .," intoned Daumont de Saint-Lusson. As he spoke he stooped and picked up a handful of soil, symbolizing his words. Back of him stood a great wooden Cross; beside him was a post bearing the arms of France; before him surged the river through which Lake Superior discharges its waters into Lake Huron. The place already bore the French name of Sault Ste. Marie.[7]

There had been a Jesuit Mission at the Sault since 1668. Three hundred miles to the west, on the southern shore of Lake Superior, was the Mission du St. Esprit, presided over by Father Jacques Marquette. Two hundred and fifty miles to the south, at the head of Green Bay, on the western shore of Lake Michigan, was the Mission of St. Francois Xavier, founded in 1669.[8]

From the priests of these missions the Governor of New

France had been hearing increasingly attractive accounts of the vast unexplored western country—rich in furs, rich in copper. Most interesting of all, there was said to be a great river running southward or perhaps southwestward—no one knew just whither. Perhaps this river emptied into the Pacific Ocean and would provide a waterway to China and the wealth of the East. In any case the upper Lake region was worth possessing.[9]

Accordingly, Saint-Lusson was sent to take formal possession. With him went fifteen men, and they together with four Jesuits of the western missions were the only European witnesses of the picturesque pageantry at the Sault that June day of 1671. "Vive le Roy," shouted Saint-Lusson as he finished his speech, and from the nineteen Frenchmen the shout echoed back, "Vive le Roy," to the accompaniment of a thin volley of musketry. Father Allouez, who had come up from St. Francois Xavier, preached a sermon, which the Indians found entertaining, and the ceremony was over. France had extended her sovereignty over what today we call the Middle West.[10]

Among those with Saint-Lusson at the Sault was Louis Jolliet. Two years earlier he had visited Lake Superior. No Frenchman knew the upper lake region better than he or had heard more about the great river that ran southward somewhere below the lakes. Shortly after his return to Quebec, Jolliet was commissioned by Count Frontenac, Governor of New France, to find and explore that river. The late summer of 1672 saw him again pushing up the lakes. At the meeting place between Lake Huron and Lake Michigan he found Father Marquette. The priest had given up at St. Esprit and, on the northern side of the strait known as Michilimackinac, had established a new mission to which he gave the name St. Ignace. The site is at present occupied by a Michigan city of the same name.[11]

At St. Ignace, Father Marquette had hopes of instilling his message of salvation into the hearts of the Indians who visited Michilimackinac to fish and trade. However, he had long cherished a wish to visit the savages who lived on the great river, many of whom he had met while at his mission on Lake Superior. Accordingly he welcomed an order to join Jolliet as chaplain of the exploring expedition. Through the long winter months, while they waited at St. Ignace, Jolliet and Marquette studied maps and made their plans.[12]

At last the ice broke up. On May 17, 1673, in two birch-bark canoes manned by five paddlers, they started their momentous voyage. Hugging the western shore of Lake Michigan they entered Green Bay, and guided by the Indians threaded their way up one of its tributaries—the winding, sluggish Fox River. At a point where the Fox approached within a mile of another river, they carried their canoes across the slight divide and again embarked—on the westward flowing Wisconsin. A few days later—the date was June 17, 1673—they rounded a headland, and there before them was a great river, rolling southward. It was the Mississippi.[13]

For three weeks they floated down the great river—as it grew ever wider. They saw the Illinois come in from the east, and the boiling Missouri come in from the west. They passed the mouth of the Ohio, whose upper reach was already known to Frenchmen as La Belle Riviere. They had met a few Indians here and there along the way, and found them mostly friendly. At a village opposite the outlet of a river called the Arkansas they halted. It was now evident that the Mississippi emptied into the Gulf of Mexico. If they went on they might fall into the hands of the Spaniards. They were told that the natives whose villages lined the banks below were particularly bloodthirsty. All in all, Jolliet felt that it was wiser to get back and report what he had found.[14]

So on July 17 they began the long weary paddle upstream. They had learned that Lake Michigan could be reached more easily through the Illinois River than through the Wisconsin and Fox. Accordingly, when they came to the Illinois, they turned in. From the Indians they received a friendly welcome and further information about the route. Continuing on up the river they branched left into the Des Plaines, portaged across into the south branch of the Chicago River, and soon found themselves on the shore of Lake Michigan

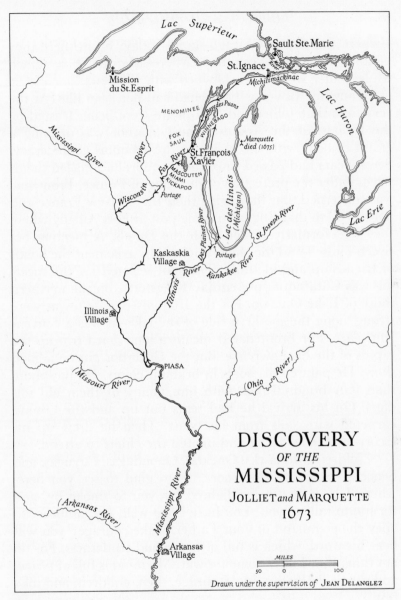

DISCOVERY
OF THE
MISSISSIPPI
JOLLIET *and* MARQUETTE
1673

MILES
50   0   100

Drawn under the supervision of JEAN DELANGLEZ

From the *Atlas of American History.*

—where the city of Chicago stands today. From there they paddled back to Green Bay, where Marquette remained while Jolliet went on to Quebec with his news.[15]

Meanwhile Govenor Frontenac had not been idle. At the very time that Jolliet and Marquette were being feasted by the Indians of the Arkansas the Governor was opening a grand council with the chiefs of the Iroquois confederacy. Seven years had passed since the Iroquois had placed themselves under the protection of the King of France. Frontenac was concerned that they bring their furs to New France and not slip off to that English trading post at Fort Albany where they had formerly traded with the Dutch. A meeting between himself and the chiefs might help to cement the bonds of friendship and of trade. The spot selected for the meeting was Cataraqui (presentday Kingston), on the northern shore of Lake Ontario. For the Iroquois—whose towns were strung along the southern side of the lake—it was a convenient place. For Frontenac it meant a long, hard trip up the rapids of the St. Lawrence. But the Governor put on a good show. He painted his boats in brilliant colors. He had more than four hundred men with him, many of them old soldiers. On his arrival he had tents put up and the ground carpeted with sails from his boats. Then he drew up his escort in martial array and invited the chiefs to attend.

"Children! Mohawks, Oneidas, Onondagas, Cayugas, and Senecas," said the Governor, "I am glad to see you here, where I have had a fire lighted for you to smoke by, and for me to talk to you. You have done well, my children, to obey the command of your Father. Take courage: you will hear his word, which is full of peace and tenderness. For do not think that I have come for war. My mind is full of peace, and she walks by my side. Courage, then, children, and take rest."

Frontenac was the first white man to call the fierce Iroquois his children, and they liked it. They liked the Governor himself; they liked the presents he gave to them and to their women and children; they liked his promise to build a permanent storehouse at Cataraqui from which they would be supplied with guns and other goods in return for their furs. The storehouse, called Fort Frontenac, was being erected by the French engineers even as the conference proceeded; and it was to have its part in the report that was, at that very moment, being brought up the Father of Waters by Jolliet.[16]

France had found her line of expansion. She would push westward along the lakes and southward down the Mississippi. She would hold England to the Atlantic seaboard. For near a century this clash of imperial interests would affect the life of the English colonists. Fear of France would cause England to hold a tight control over her American colonies; fear of France would cause the colonists to accept that control.

A Dutch Interlude

AS GOVERNOR FRONTENAC turned homeward from Cataraqui that summer of 1673, fate temporarily threw a shadow across his plans. As competitors for the Iroquois trade he might have the Dutch, old friends of the Indians, rather than the English. England and Holland were at war. A Dutch fleet was known to be in the West Indies. There were rumors that it was coming up the Atlantic coast. But Francis Lovelace, who had succeeded Nicolls as Governor of New York, did not take the story too seriously. He was busy trying to establish an inter-colonial postal service—between New York and Boston. He had left the command of the fort and the military forces of New York in the hands of a subordinate, Captain John Manning. No preparation had been made to resist a possible attack.[1]

At that very moment, July 21, 1673—while Lovelace was in Connecticut, while Jolliet was paddling up the Mississippi, while Frontenac was on his way from Cataraqui to Quebec —the Dutch war fleet sailed into Chesapeake Bay. A number of ships loaded with tobacco made the visit profitable, but even better, the Dutch commanders learned from some of their prisoners that New York would be an easy prey. On up the coast went the fleet. As nine years earlier the English frigates had bottled up the Dutch, so now the Dutch bottled up the English. And, as nine years earlier, Alricks' cattle had supplied beef for the English sailors, so now Governor Lovelace's sheep on Staten Island provided "breakfast" for the Dutchmen.[2]

To a query from Captain Manning as to why they were there, the Dutch commanders replied that they had come to take the place, "which was their own, and their own they would have." In confirmation of this avowed intention the fleet moved up the harbor and anchored opposite the fort, which stood on the lower tip of Manhattan Island. A few shots were exchanged and the Dutch, without opposition, put a land party ashore. The situation of the English was hopeless. Captain Manning sent a deputation, headed by John Carr, to ask for terms. The terms offered were surrender as prisoners of war. But Carr, who had led the ruthless land assault on Fort Casimir in 1664 (see page 2), was not among the prisoners; he took to his heels and, like Hinnoyossa nine years earlier, did not stop until he got to Maryland.[3]

The flag of Holland replaced the flag of England over the fort on Manhattan Island—originally built by the Dutch as Fort Amsterdam. New York, New Jersey and Delaware again became New Netherland. The English garrison at Fort Albany gave way to a Dutch garrison; and the Iroquois chiefs, who had just finished their council with Count Frontenac, called to express their satisfaction. Elizabethtown, Newark, Shrewsbury and the other recently founded towns of New Jersey sent delegates to swear allegiance to Holland. Peter Alricks promptly repudiated his loyalty to England and was placed in command on the Delaware River. He probably experienced no great sadness in carrying out an order to seize the estate of John Carr. The towns on the western end of Long Island—Brooklyn, New Utrecht and others largely populated by Dutch—welcomed the return to their old flag. The towns of the eastern end of Long Island

—Southold, Southampton and others populated by English —again associated themselves with Connecticut, despite threats of dire penalties by the new Dutch Governor. And Connecticut sent men to back up their resistance.[4]

Thus, with some slight opposition, the Dutch ruled again in their old colony of New Netherland. But their day was short. In May, 1674, a New Englander arrived at Manhattan Island with news of a treaty of peace between England and Holland. New Netherland, asserted the caller, was to be returned to England. He was promptly sentenced to hard labor on the repair of the fort—this for spreading false information. However, the story was true. On November 1, 1674, Major Edmund Andros arrived at New York aboard an English frigate and accompanied by a company of English soldiers. He held a commission from the Duke of York to receive New Netherland from the Dutch and to govern it. Not until the colonies themselves revolted a century later was England's authority on the middle coast again challenged.[5]

6

King Philip

THE LEADERS of Massachusetts evidently detected a certain "providence" in the capture of New York by the Dutch. The event confirmed their already active suspicion that the Duke of York could not take care of his American provinces. In fact, for some time the Massachusetts General Court had felt a growing compassion for the Duke's neglected subjects in that thin remaining slice of his proprietary eastward of the Kennebec. As usual, when planning expansion northward, Massachusetts caused the much-stretched Merrimac River to be surveyed. It was now found that an east-west line three miles north of its most northern part reached practically to the Penobscot. The surveyor suggested that, "If the honoured Court were pleased to goe twenty minitts more northerly in Merrimack River, it would take in all the inhabitants & places east along, & they seemed much to desire it."[1]

At the moment the "honoured Court" hesitated, but, shortly after the capture of New York, orders were issued for the appointment of justices "within our jurisdiction to the eastward" by which was meant the Duke's land between the Kennebec and the Penobscot. Within the area lay the old trading post of Pemaquid and a few other communities —perhaps five hundred people in all, mostly supported by fishing. That they seriously "desired" to be taken in by Massachusetts may be questioned. All they had asked in the past was to be let alone. However, they were too weak to oppose the will of their powerful neighbor.[2]

Puritan Massachusetts at last stood face to face with Catholic France. Over Fort Pentegoet, on the easterly side of Penobscot Bay, waved the French flag. But beyond surreptitiously aiding a Dutch pirate in looting the furs stored in the fort, the Bostonians entered into no contest for possession east of the Penobscot. Nor did they long retain authority east of the Kennebec. Pemaquid was laid in ashes by the Indians in 1676 and reclaimed by the Duke of York shortly thereafter.[3]

Thus the eastward expansion of Massachusetts halted at the Kennebec. To the south, however, there were still possibilities. For more than forty years the magistrates at Boston had looked longingly toward Narragansett Bay as another outlet to the sea. Several times success had seemed within their grasp only to have some untoward incident balk them. Providence Plantation and the Rhode Island squatter settlements were particularly irritating obstructions. And just when, in 1644, Massachusetts was preparing for a southward push, Roger Williams had secured from Parliament a charter that legally established Rhode Island as a colony. In 1663 the King confirmed this charter.[4]

There were, however, flaws in the Rhode Island boundaries; they overlapped or were overlapped by Plymouth on the east and by Connecticut on the west. And as these two colonies were joined with Massachusetts in a confederacy known as the United Colonies of New England, from which Rhode Island was excluded, it seemed reasonable that the latter colony could be squeezed out. The area west of Narragansett Bay was especially in controversy, so much so that Nicolls and his fellow commissioners of 1664 had been specifically directed to straighten out the situation. They had solved it by creating a separate colony to be known as the King's Province, but under the jurisdiction of Rhode Island.[5]

Within and adjoining the King's Province lay the lands of the Narragansett Indians, who, prior to the landing of the Pilgrims, had dominated all the neighboring tribes. In fact, it was probably fortunate for the Pilgrims that their first contact was with the Wampanoags, a milder tributary tribe that welcomed a chance to break away from its overlords. In any case, Massasoit, the chief of the Wampanoags, had readily entered into a treaty of friendship with the Pilgrims; and so long as he lived that treaty had been observed by his tribesmen. In 1661 the old chief died and was succeeded by his son Alexander. The new chief recognized that peace with the crowding white men had not been altogether to the advantage of the Wampanoags. Of their original lands there remained only a small piece along the eastern side of Narragansett Bay. Alexander not unnaturally looked back to the good old days when the Wampanoags were associated with the Narragansetts—and was promptly charged by Massachusetts with forming a conspiracy against the English.[6]

On the advice of the Boston magistrates, the Governor of Plymouth Colony sent Josiah Winslow with a military escort to arrest Alexander. Curiously enough, it was Josiah's father, Edward Winslow, who in 1621, when the Pilgrims were weak, had sought the treaty of peace with Massasoit. Now, forty-one years later, we see Massasoit's son being dragged, at the pistol's point, to Plymouth by the son of Edward Winslow. On the journey Alexander suddenly died—due probably in part to rage and in part to overheat from having to keep up, on foot, with the mounted soldiers. The Wampanoags, however, suspected that Alexander had been poisoned. Philip, a brother of Alexander, succeeded to the chieftainship and turned even more definitely toward an alliance with the Narragansetts. Nor were his advances repelled by Canonchet, chief of the Narragansetts; he, too, had good reason for distrusting the white men. His own father had been knocked in the head at the behest of the commissioners of the United Colonies of New England for venturing to act contrary to their wishes.[7]

For thirteen years Philip, or "King" Philip as he was commenly called, nursed his wrath while the Plymouth people crowded him out of more and more of his land. Then, in the spring of 1675, he could stand it no longer. "I am determined not to live until I have no country," he declared, as he began assembling his warriors at his town of Mount Hope (presentday Bristol, Rhode Island, but at the time within the bounds claimed by Plymouth). Swansea, an English settlement four or five miles to the northward, felt the first blow. The Indians robbed some unprotected houses. An English boy shot an Indian. And the fury broke loose. Troops hurried westward from Plymouth, but all they found was a trail of slaughtered whites and burned buildings. When they thought they had the Indians cornered, they suffered a sharp defeat. Philip led his band into Massachusetts, killing and burning as he went.[8]

During the early stages of the war many Indians wished to remain neutral. Considerable numbers came into Plymouth town and put themselves under the protection of the magistrates. Their fate was to be shipped off to Spain where they were sold as slaves. This did not encourage other Indians to trust themselves with the English. The alternative was to join with Philip. Even the "praying Indians," those who had accepted Christianity and lived among the settlers, joined with the marauders. The frontier towns along the Connecticut River—Springfield, Hadley, Deerfield and others —were attacked. Armed parties that went to the aid of the townspeople were ambushed and wiped out.[9]

By September the war had extended to Maine. As in Plymouth colony, the first offenses were mere insolence and robbery. Twenty Indians visited the home of Thomas Purchase on the Androscoggin River. They pretended a wish to trade, but when they found only Mrs. Purchase and other women at the house they took what they wished and warned that "others would soon come and treat them worse"—which proved all too true. Incidentally, forty-five years earlier Mrs. Purchase herself had been the central figure in quite a furore at Boston. She had been altogether too good-looking for that sober community. The story is told on page 200 of *The*

JOSIAH WINSLOW

Courtesy, Pilgrim Society, Plymouth, Mass.

PHILIP *KING* of Mount Hope.

From the engraving by Paul Revere.

First Frontier. But now, in 1675, the furore was one of life and death; and for many families—from York to Pemaquid —it was death at the hands of the savages.[10]

Meanwhile Philip's warriors were becoming too much for Massachusetts alone. The war was recognized as a common danger that concerned all New England, and the commissioners of the United Colonies took charge. An army of a thousand men was raised and equipped by the joint efforts of Connecticut, Massachusetts and Plymouth.[11]

Rhode Island, although not a member of the United Colonies, was forced into the fight against the Indians, somewhat reluctantly since many in that colony suspected that the blow was aimed at themselves as well as at the savages. But between the blood-maddened Indians and the land-seeking whites there was but one choice for the men of Rhode Island. Even the aged Roger Williams, than whom the Indians had no better friend, served as a captain in defense of Providence. The story runs that when Williams tried to dissuade the Indians from continuing the war they scornfully refused but added, "As for you, brother Williams, you are a good man; you have been kind to us many years; not a hair of your head shall be touched." [12]

And as Rhode Island was forced into the war on the side of the whites, so the Narragansetts were forced in on the side of the Indians. They had tried to remain neutral, fearing that Massachusetts was only looking for a chance to seize their lands. However, when the Commissioners of the United Colonies demanded that Canonchet deliver up those of Philip's people who had found refuge in his country, the Narragansett chief replied, "Not a Wampanoag nor the paring of a Wampanoag's nail." [13]

That settled it. The combined forces of the colonies marched against the Narragansetts. Canonchet hastily sought refuge, with a large number of his people, on an island in the midst of a great swamp—near presentday Kingstown, Rhode Island. The women set up their flimsy wigwams while the men constructed a tangle of fallen trees around the camp. Ordinarily the place would have been impenetrable for an English armed force, but on the night of Saturday, Decem-

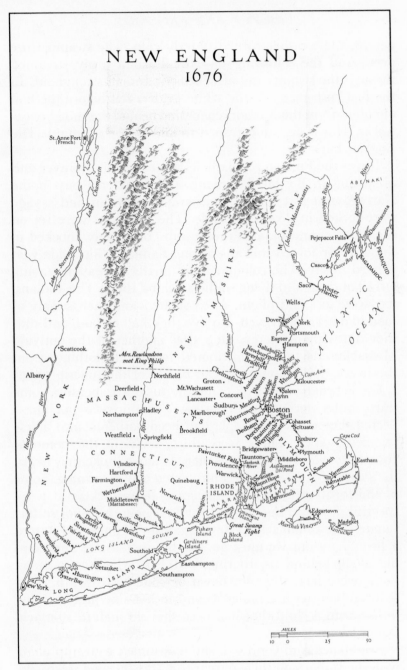

NEW ENGLAND
1676

St. Anne Fort
(French)

Lake Champlain

Lake St. Sacrement

(Claimed by South New Hampshire and New York)

MAINE (joined to Massachusetts)

ABENAKI

Pejepscot Falls

Casco Casco Bay

SAGADAHOC

PEMAQUID

Androscoggin River

Kennebec River

Damariscotta

Saco Winter Harbor

Saco River

Wells

Dover Kittery York

Exeter Portsmouth

Scaticook

Mrs. Rowlandson met King Philip ✕

Albany

NEW YORK

Hudson River

Salisbury Hampton
Newburyport
Haverhill Rowley
Bradford Ipswich
Andover Wenham Cape Ann

NEW HAMPSHIRE

Merrimac River

Northfield

Chelmsford Lowell

Deerfield Groton

Mt. Wachusett Concord

Salem Lynn

MASSAC H U S E T T S

Lancaster

Sudbury Medford Cambridge

Gloucester

Northampton Hadley

Marlborough Watertown

Boston

Connecticut River

Westfield Springfield

Brookfield

Dedham Roxbury
Dorchester Braintree Hull
Weymouth Cohasset
Bingham Scituate

Duxbury

Cape Cod

CONNECTICUT

Windsor
Hartford
Farmington
Wethersfield

Pawtucket Falls
Providence
Warwick

Bridgewater
Taunton Middleboro
Seekonk River

PLYMOUTH

Plymouth

Sandwich Yarmouth Eastham

Quinebaug

RHODE ISLAND

Barnstable

Middletown
(Mattabesec)

Norwich

Swansea
Mount Hope
Dartmouth

New London

NARRA G A N S E T T S

Newport

Connecticut River

New Haven
Derby
(Paugasset)
Stratford
Fairfield

Guilford
Saybrook
Branford

LONG ISLAND SOUND

James Printery

Conanicut Island

Aquidneck Island

Edgartown

Madeket
Nantucket

Martha's Vineyard

Fishers Island

Gardiners Island

Great Swamp Fight

Block Island

Greenwich
Stamford
Norwalk
Setauket
Oyster Bay
Huntington

Southold

Easthampton

Southampton

New York LONG ISLAND

ATLANTIC OCEAN

MILES
10 0   25   50

Based upon Plate 26 of the *Atlas of American History.*

ber 18, the weather turned bitterly cold. The swamp froze over. And the following day the Puritan army streamed through the swamp and attacked the Indian stronghold. In the first rush many of the white leaders fell before the hail of bullets from the warriors concealed behind the rude breast-works. However, an entrance to the fort was found. The English burst in.

It was the Puritan Sabbath, a day for rest and prayer and preaching in Boston, Plymouth and Hartford, but in the Narragansett fort in the great swamp Puritan and savage were locked in deadly struggle. The wigwams were set on fire. Squaws and papooses were indiscriminately knocked in the head or forced into the raging flames. Which side won is hard to say. The colonial army finally retreated, leaving a trail of dead and dying soldiers behind them. The Indians, too, were in a bad plight. Their shelters and their supply of food had been destroyed. To live they had to raid, and that they did without mercy. One after another of the outlying Massachusetts towns contributed food and clothing—from the barns and houses and dead bodies of the townspeople."

On February 10, 1676, came the turn of Lancaster, some thirty miles northwest of Boston. The raid was not unexpected. For days the people had been gathered into a few fortified houses. There were thirty-seven in the home of Joseph Rowlandson, the preacher. As dawn broke they heard the sound of guns and saw unprotected houses burning. Some of the fortified houses were keeping the attackers at a respectful distance, but the Rowlandson house was not so fortunate. The Indians piled straw against the walls and started a fire. ". . . out we must go, the fire increasing, and coming along behind us, roaring," Mrs. Rowlandson tells us. Some were instantly shot down or clubbed to death. Mrs. Rowlandson, with a bullet wound in her side and carrying in her arms a child that had been shot through its stomach, was made a captive.

Frightened and confused, she was forced to tramp along with the Indians on their retreat from the burning town. She suffered from her own wound. She had to carry the wounded child, who cried continuously from its hurt. The weather was cold. Mrs. Rowlandson had little clothing. For three days she had nothing to eat, though the Indians made a great feast from the cattle, sheep, hogs, and chickens they had taken at the town. However, they offered her no violence, and some kindness. When she could no longer struggle along on foot, they placed her on a horse, with the starving and dying child still in her arms. When she fell off they laughed. She slept sitting doubled up on the ground, her flesh raw from exposure. The child died and she had to leave it lying on the frozen earth.

Occasionally she had a word with a daughter and a son who had also been captured and who, with several other captives, were being driven along with the straggling horde. Through it all she comforted herself by reading bits from a Bible that had come into her hands by a special providence; it was given to her by an Indian who had acquired it as part of his loot from a raid on the town of Medfield. When she had to climb aboard a rickety raft to cross a river, she opened her Bible and read, "When thou passeth through the waters I will be with thee, and through the Rivers they shall not overflow thee," Isaiah 43:2.

The route taken by the Indians led northwesterly toward the Connecticut River. There they met Philip, who had spent the winter near the Mohawks in an attempt to enlist their aid in the war. He received Mrs. Rowlandson at his wigwam and offered her a smoke, which she declined because, as she expressed it, one "may be better employed than to ly sucking a stinking Tobacco-pipe." Her employment at the time was that of doing what her Indian mistress told her to do, and this mistress turned out to be none other than the widow of Alexander.

Within a month of her capture Mrs. Rowlandson had adapted herself to the Indian way of life. When ordered out of her mistress' wigwam at night—guests having called —she tried other wigwams until a kindhearted Indian took her in. When she could get food no other way, she foraged or begged, and usually got something. She ate things that would have turned the stomach of a less hungry white person—boiled horse hoofs, raw liver—and found them good.

Sometimes she got extra food by knitting socks or making shirts for the Indians. Often she fared better than her captors—sleeping in a dry wigwam while they lay in the drenching rain outside. She even ventured to talk back to her mistress. "As I was sitting once in the Wigwam here, Phillips Maid came in with the Child in her arms, and asked me to give her a piece of my Apron to make a flap for it, I told her I would not: then my Mistress bad me give it, but still I said no: the maid told me if I would not give her a piece, she would tear a piece off it: I told her I would tear her Coat then, with that my Mistriss rises up, and takes up a stick big enough to have killed me, and struck at me with it, but I stept out, and she struck the stick into the Mat of the Wigwam. But while she was pulling of it out, I ran to the Maid and gave her all my Apron, and so that storm went over."

The Indians were well aware that Mrs. Rowlandson was worth more alive than dead. "Two Coats and twenty shillings in Mony, and half a bushel of seed Corn, and some Tobacco" was Philip's price for her release. Arrangements were finally made, and after three months of captivity Mrs. Rowlandson was returned to the settlements—as were many other captives whose families were able to pay satisfactory ransoms.[15]

But "King" Philip's power was waning. Constant harrying by the colonial troops was bringing hunger to his followers. There were no more towns to raid. The Indians tried to plant crops along the Connecticut River but failed. Canonchet, while leading a party to Rhode Island for seed corn, was surprised and captured. He was turned over to the Pequots and Mohicans, Indian allies of the English, for execution. They cut off his head and sent it to the Connecticut magistrates "as a token of their love and fidelity."[16]

On August 12, 1676, Philip, skulking near his old home at Mount Hope, was shot and killed. His head was sent to Plymouth as a memento—long exhibited to the curious. His followers broke into small bands. Some were hunted down and killed; some were captured and hanged at Boston for the edification of the families of those who had suffered at his hands. In one case, at least, an Indian was turned over to the mob and lynched. At Marblehead, two Indian captives were brought in just as the people were leaving the meetinghouse on the Sabbath day. The women "in a tumultous way, very barbarously murdered them." [17]

Most of the captives were sold as slaves—to die miserably on the West Indian sugar plantations. Some of the Boston magistrates may have recalled Emanuel Downing's advice to Governor Winthrop thirty years earlier: "If upon a Just warre the Lord should deliver [the Narragansetts] into our hands, wee might easily have men and woemen and children enough to exchange for [negroes], which wilbe more gayneful pillage for us than wee conceive. . . ." The Narragansetts had now been delivered into their hands, but the price had been high, very high. A tenth of the male adults of Massachusetts had been killed or captured in the war. Most of the outlying towns had been ravaged. The settlements along the coast of Maine had been wiped out. A staggering debt hung over the colony. In winning the war Massachusetts had lost the abounding manpower and the wealth which, in the past, had enabled her successfully to defy the King. [18]

And at this very time the King again moved to assert his sovereignty. On June 10, 1676, Edward Randolph stepped ashore at Boston. He bore a letter from the King to "The Governors and Magistrates of Our Towne of Boston In New England." This letter he was to deliver and cause to be read in his presence. In addition he carried instructions directing him to inquire into the character of the government of Massachusetts, its military power, and its attitude toward the navigation acts. [19]

Randolph promptly presented his credentials to John Leverett, Governor of Massachusetts, and was as promptly invited to a meeting of the Governor and his Council. The King's letter was presented. It was signed, as was usual with such documents, "By His Majesties Command, H. Coventry." Governor Leverett inquired, "who that Mr. Coventry was." Randolph, fully alive to the implied insult, replied that Coventry was the King's principal secretary of state. As the Governor began reading the letter, Randolph removed

GOVERNOR JOHN LEVERETT
of Massachusetts.

Courtesy, The Essex Institute, Salem, Mass.

his hat as a symbol of respect for the King. Three of the Massachusetts magistrates followed suit, but the Governor and the rest of the magistrates kept their hats on.[20]

The letter set forth that Robert Mason and Ferdinando Gorges, the legal proprietors of New Hampshire and Maine respectively, complained that they were being kept out of possession of their provinces "by the violence and strong hand" of Massachusetts. The Governor and magistrates were directed to send agents to England to present their side of the case.[21]

When the reading of the letter was finished, Governor Leverett coolly remarked that "the matters therein contained were very inconsiderable things and easily answered, and it did in no way concern [Massachusetts] to take any notice thereof." But the Governor had underestimated his caller; Edward Randolph was a very persistent man.[22]

Low Prices -- High Taxes

IRGINIA, TOO, suffered from Indian out-
breaks in 1675 and 1676. However, she suffered much more from a clash between her
own people—a clash brought on by the conduct of the Indian war but rooted in a mass
of grievances long accumulating.

Tobacco was the life of Virginia, as of Maryland and the
Albemarle settlement in northern Carolina. For several years
the price had been low, due in part to the navigation laws
and in part to overproduction. The Virginians had suggested
to the Maryland and Albemarle planters that they all join
in a program for the limitation of tobacco planting, but had
received no co-operation.[1]

The uncertainty of making a living from tobacco had
caused many former indentured servants to hesitate about
taking up land when their terms of service expired. Instead
they had taken what jobs they could get as free laborers, and
consequently had no real stake in the colony. Their position
had been made even less responsible when, in 1670, the Virginia General Assembly passed a law practically limiting
the franchise to those who held land.[2]

Nor were the small landowners too happy. The General Assembly had sat continuously for fourteen years; its membership no longer represented the views of the people—and the people had no opportunity to express themselves through an election. All of the more remunerative offices were in the hands of a small clique of large landowners who were subservient to the Governor. Taxes of various sorts ate up what little profit there was in raising tobacco.[3]

On top of all this the King had treated Virginia as a negotiable property useful only for paying off his personal or political debts. In 1649 he had granted the Northern Neck, that is the land between the Rappahannock and Potomac rivers, to a group of his noble friends as a proprietary in perpetuity. In 1673, he assigned the crown rights in the soil of all the rest of Virginia to the Earl of Arlington and Lord Culpeper, the latter prominent among the proprietors of the Northern Neck. The assignment was to run for a period of thirty-one years. Thus these English lords, who had never been in Virginia and who had no interest in Virginia other than what they could get out of it, were vested with the right to collect quitrents from the landowners of Virginia, to convey vacant lands, and otherwise act as proprietors of the soil of Virginia. The actual government of the colony of course still remained in the hands of the King through the appointment of the Governor and other higher officers.[4]

These grants greatly disturbed the Virginians. They prided themselves on being the most loyal of the King's American colonists, but they objected to being farmed out to his favorites. Agents were appointed to go to England and do what they could to have the grants annulled. To pay the expenses of these agents, still further taxes were laid on the already overburdened tobacco of the planters.[5]

Such was the uneasy situation in Virginia when, in the summer of 1675, Indians from Maryland raided across the Potomac into the plantations of the Northern Neck. The county militia promptly took up the pursuit. The Maryland Indians fled westward and joined others on the upper waters of the Rappahannock, York and James rivers in Virginia. From these hide-outs they began a series of bloody attacks on outlying plantations. To the demand of the planters for protection, Governor Berkeley responded slowly. The suspicion arose that he was more interested in preserving the fur trade with the Indians than in taking care of the tobacco planters. "No Bullets would pierce Bever Skins," growled the unemployed laborers, themselves itching for a chance to loot the Indians—whether hostile or friendly.[6]

At this point a popular leader arose. Colonel Nathaniel Bacon, twenty-nine years old, a member of the Governor's Council and a planter on the upper James River, had, like many others, felt the fury of the Indians. His plantation had been raided and two of his servants killed. All about him, men were gathering in armed groups and demanding to be led against the savages. Bacon accepted the command of this motley army and without a commission, in fact contrary to the expressed command of Governor Berkeley, marched up the James beyond the Falls (presentday Richmond), killing any Indian that came within his reach.[7]

To the hot-tempered Governor Berkeley this army and its leader were nothing less than rebels, and he so proclaimed them. At the same time he recognized that there was widespread discontent in the colony and called for the election of a new General Assembly. And just as the election came on, the "rebel" army returned from its successful foray against the Indians. To the voters of Bacon's home county (Henrico, some forty miles up the James River from Jamestown) the leader of the army was a hero; they elected him as their representative in the new Assembly. Bacon, however, had some misgivings as to his reception by the Governor, and when he started down the river for Jamestown he was accompanied by forty of his adherents. But the Governor did not wait for Bacon's arrival; he sent an armed boat up the river to meet the oncoming hero. Bacon was captured and brought as a prisoner to Jamestown where, after a lecture by the Governor, he was released and restored to his place in the Council.[8]

Among the members of the Assembly were many who agreed with the rebels on the Indian question, and pressure was put on the Governor to give Bacon a commission that would legalize his scouting operations. When the Governor still refused, Bacon slipped out of town, put himself at the head of his army, and marched into Jamestown. Placing his men in military array around the State House, he called on the Governor. "God damne my Blood," he announced, "I came for a commission, and commission I will have before I goe." He got the commission; also an order to raise a thousand men for service against the Indians.[9]

With his conduct thus approved, Bacon returned to the Falls and began organizing his army. Scarcely had he got under way before word arrived that Governor Berkeley was raising another army in the eastern counties—presumably for the purpose of attacking Bacon. Back down the river came Bacon and his army. The supporters of the Governor faded away and he himself fled across Chesapeake Bay to Accomack on the Eastern Shore. Sending an armed ship to capture the Governor, if possible, Bacon turned back westward, harrying the Indians on a wide arc from the Falls of the James to the tributaries of the York River.[10]

Meantime, the expedition sent to capture the Governor had itself been captured, and Berkeley returned in triumph to Jamestown. Back to Jamestown came Bacon and his men. For a week there was skirmishing between the opposing forces, but day by day the number willing to face Bacon's wild crew became fewer. Again the Governor fled to Accomack. Into the town marched the army of servants, field hands, and small planters. Jamestown was the oldest permanently settled English town in America. It was the capital of Virginia. It was the only town in Virginia. There stood the State House. There stood the church. In addition there were twelve brick houses and several of frame construction. The town was the symbol of government in Virginia; to it Bacon and his men applied the torch. On the night of September 19, 1676, only blackened walls and smouldering logs remained to mark the site.[11]

Bacon was now supreme in Virginia. Just what he had in mind doing next will never be known. He professed complete loyalty to the King, but he was actively preparing to resist the King's troops—then on their way from England to put down his rebellion. There is some reason to view the insurrection as part of a general plan—hatched by the discontented elements of Virginia, Maryland and Albemarle —to establish popular governments in the tobacco-raising colonies.[12]

Whatever the plan, if any, it came to an end with the death of Bacon, from a camp malady, in October, 1676. With no competent leader the army fell to pieces. Most of the insurgents simply went home. Some surrendered to the Governor's officers, and were pardoned. Others were captured, and, with very perfunctory trials, hanged. When William Drummond, one of Bacon's principal supporters, was brought before Governor Berkeley, he was received with a deep bow and the greeting, "Mr. Drummond! You are very welcome, I am more Glad to See you than any man in Virginea, Mr. Drummond you shall be hang'd in half an hour." The trial probably did not take half an hour, but it required two hours to erect a suitable gibbet.[13]

In all, some twenty-three of Bacon's followers were hanged, and more would probably have suffered the same fate had not the King recalled Governor Berkeley—of whom he remarked, "that old fool has hanged more men in that naked country than I have for the murder of my father."[14]

The consequences of the insurrection were disastrous for Virginia. The expansion of the colony was halted by the ravages of the Indians. Looting had destroyed much property. Confiscations of estates did not make for progress. The agents who had been sent to England in the hope of having the grant to Arlington and Culpeper annulled, had no success with the King; the best they could do was to buy off the grantees—at the cost of still more taxes on the tobacco of Virginia.[15]

In Maryland, as in Virginia, the low price of tobacco, together with mounting taxes, had created discontent—constantly expressed through the representatives of the people in the lower house of the provincial Assembly. With a view to throttling these complaints, Lord Baltimore, the Proprietor, followed the same course that Governor Berkeley had adopted in Virginia; he limited the franchise to those who owned fifty acres of land or who had substantial personal estates. This naturally irritated the disfranchised class and placed the representatives of the smaller planters at a disadvantage as against the Governor and his Council.[16]

In addition there was a religious cleavage in Maryland. Lord Baltimore—who had never even seen Maryland—was a Catholic. His son, Charles Calvert, who acted as Governor in Maryland and in 1675 succeeded to the proprietorship, was a Catholic. The members of the upper house, or Council, appointed by Lord Baltimore, were largely Catholics. The population of the province was overwhelmingly Protestant.[17]

The Indian war, it will be remembered, began in Maryland. The people of Maryland had watched the course of affairs in Virginia with keen interest. On September 3, 1676, while Bacon was making his final march on Jamestown, a group of Marylanders met at a plantation on the Patuxent River and protested against high taxes, against the disenfranchisement of poor people, and even against the proprietary authority. When ordered to disperse they organized as a military body, beat drums, and defied the Governor's Council. There was among them, however, no Bacon and the proprietary authorities made short work of them. The leaders fled up Chesapeake Bay and overland to New Castle, the former New Amstel, where they were captured. Their fate was to be brought back and hanged on the shores of the Patuxent. Rebellion in Maryland had failed.[18]

In the Albemarle settlements of northern Carolina there was a faction that apparently not only sympathized with Bacon's rebels but personally joined with them. John Culpeper, for one, was in Virginia in 1676. He seems to have been of a turbulent nature, in trouble wherever he went. He had first showed up at Charles Towne, southern Carolina, in 1671—among the settlers from Barbados. Shortly we find him charged with having "sett the poore to plunder the rich." He escaped punishment only by a hurried departure. In 1677, the year following the collapse of the Bacon rebellion, Culpeper was the central figure in a minor rebellion in Albemarle.[19]

This Albemarle region was, as will be recalled, originally

a part of Virginia, and had first been settled by people from that colony. The plantations were strung along the Chowan River and the northern shore of Albemarle Sound. There were perhaps two thousand inhabitants and no effective government. Tobacco was the staple crop and, under the provisions of the navigation acts, could legally be shipped only to England. However, the inlet to the Sound was too shallow for English ships. Nor would Virginia permit the shipment of Carolina tobacco through her landings. The consequence was that practically all the trade of the Albemarle settlements was monopolized by small coastwise boats from New England. The captains of these broadbeamed, flat-bottomed craft, built at Salem or Gloucester, readily negotiated the sandbars, bringing in the merchandise needed by the planters and carrying away their tobacco—for reshipment from New England ports without payment of the King's duties, as Edward Randolph was learning in Boston.[20]

In the summer of 1677 things were going on as usual on the Albemarle plantations when there arrived from England one Thomas Miller. He held a commission from the Commissioners of Customs directing him to collect the King's duty on all tobacco exported from Albemarle; also he claimed authority to act as governor of the colony. A few weeks later the good sloop *Carolina* of Boston—Zachariah Gillam, master—slid over the bar into the Sound. "Old Zach" was there to trade his New England hoes, shovels, axes, and guns for the casks of tobacco in the planters' sheds.[21]

Trouble soon started. A group of planters, led by John Culpeper, descended upon Miller's house, held him a prisoner, seized his papers, and "sent abroad up and down the Country their seditious libells drawn by the said Culpeper to put all in flames." Worse yet, "they did cause the deponent [Miller] by beat of Drum and a shout of one and all the rabble to be accused of blasphemy, treason and other crimes, and so, upon a shout of one and all of the said rabble, was the deponent ordered to be clapt in Irons, which was accordingly done." In short, Culpeper and the planters organized a "Government of the Country by their owne authority and according to their owne modell."[22]

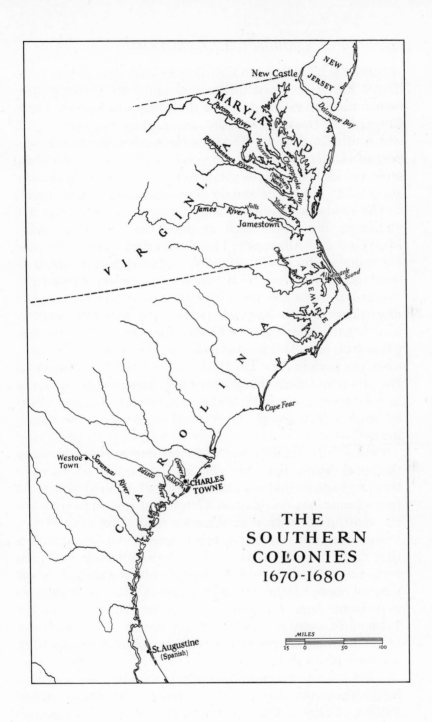

NEW
JERSEY

New Castle

Delaware Bay

MARYLAND

Potomac River

Chesapeake Bay

Rappahannock River

Pawtuxent

Northern Neck

York

VIRGINIA

James River   Falls

Jamestown

Chowan River

Albemarle Sound

ALBEMARLE

C A R O L I N A

Cape Fear

Westoe Town

Savannah River

Edisto River

Ashley

Cooper

CHARLES TOWNE

St. Augustine
(Spanish)

THE
SOUTHERN
COLONIES
1670-1680

MILES
25   0   50   100

"Old Zach" sailed back to Boston with his cargo of tobacco. Miller returned to England and laid his complaint before the Privy Council, and that august body convicted Culpeper of treason. However, the Earl of Shaftesbury—to which title Lord Ashley had been elevated—came to the support of Culpeper and got a reversal of the verdict. Shaftesbury and his fellow lords proprietors of Carolina sent a new governor to Albemarle and the dissatisfaction quieted down.[23]

The southern Carolina colony escaped any serious insurrectionary movement such as those that swept Virginia, Maryland, and Albemarle. This was, in part, due to the capable management of Governor West and, in part, to the fact that the planters were not dependent upon a single crop such as tobacco. None of those exotic seeds and slips—cotton, indigo, ginger, olives—had done particularly well in the experimental gardens at Charles Towne. But almost from the beginning there had been exportable surpluses of humbler sorts: corn and pork to New England; barrel staves and lumber to Barbados. In return the colonists had imported negro slaves in ever greater numbers, and this manpower enabled them to operate increasingly large plantations along the rivers' banks.[24]

One of these plantations was Ashley Barony, lying between the upper Ashley River and the Edisto. It consisted of twelve thousand acres and belonged to the Earl of Shaftesbury. At that plantation, one day in October, 1674, appeared ten strange Indians with deer skins for trade. Not even Henry Woodward could understand their speech, but he did gather that they would be happy to have him visit their town. An invitation of that sort always appealed to Woodward. So off they all tramped, the ten Indians and the one white man, in a drizzling rain. The route led up the Ashley, across the Edisto and westward. For food they shot an occasional deer or a fat turkey. At night the Indians would throw together a shelter of brush and bark.

After a week of travel they came to the high, chalky banks of the Savannah River—not far from the presentday city of Augusta, Georgia. There they were met by other Indians with a canoe, and paddled up the river three or four miles to the

Westoe town—for the Indians turned out to be of that tribe. The town stood on the western bank almost encircled by a loop in the river's course. Across the open neck of land back of the town ran a double row of palisades. Even along the high banks facing the river there was a single palisade, and below it were nearly a hundred canoes ready for instant use. The town itself was a disorderly affair mostly made up of long houses covered with bark. Over the houses, on poles, floated the scalps of the Westoes' late, unsuccessful enemies.

News of Woodward's visit had preceded him. He was welcomed by several hundred Westoes, "drest up in their anticke fighting garbe," by whom he was escorted to the house of the chief. The chief made a long speech which Woodward could not understand except that it was friendly. As many Indians as could crowded into the house to listen; the others pulled the bark off the top and peered down on the strange-looking visitor. When the speech was over, Woodward's hosts oiled his joints with bear's grease and set before him "sufficient of their food to satisfy at least half a dozen of their owne appetites."

Woodward found the Westoes well supplied with guns, ammunition, and other European goods which they had gotten by trading deer skins to "the northward"—probably Virginia, possibly Fort Albany on the Hudson; the Indian trading paths ran all the way to Canada. And this makes clear why a year later Governor Berkeley and his fur-trading friends were loath to exterminate the savages in the western part of their colony. There were tremendous profits in the fur trade: the wants of the Indians provided an outlet for British manufactured goods; the skins and furs which the Indians gave in exchange were in steady demand in Europe. Once the Indians were driven from their accustomed trading paths this business dried up or went elsewhere. It is of interest to note that while Woodward was at Westoe two Shawnee Indians from western Florida dropped in with Spanish beads for barter. The trading paths ran southward, too.[25]

When Woodward went home he was escorted by a delegation of Westoes who promised to come again shortly with skins for trade. Woodward had tapped this new business at a propitious moment. Within a few months Bacon's army broke the northern Indian path. The Westoes turned to Charles Towne with their deer skins and for the guns, knives, and cloth which they had learned to need. So important did this trade become that the lords proprietors decided to monopolize it for themselves. Accordingly in 1677 they forbade the colonists to trade with the Westoes and other distant tribes except under license from Shaftesbury. At the same time they subscribed a hundred pounds apiece to a fund which was put at the disposal of Woodward for carrying on the trade, he being allowed a twenty per cent commission on all the business done.[26]

The planters were far from happy about being thus excluded from this rich source of income, yet the colony prospered and grew. More and more planters arrived and took up land; more and more shiploads of produce went out; more and more shiploads of goods came in. For some years it had been evident that the original site chosen for Charles Towne was not adequate. A number of families had already settled on Oyster Point, the tongue of land where the Ashley and Cooper rivers meet. In 1679 the lords proprietors wrote to Governor West, "We are informed that the Oyster Point is not only a more convenient place to build a town on than that formerly pitched on by the first settlers, but that people's inclinations tend thither; we let you know that the Oyster Point is the place we do appoint for the port town, of which you are to take notice, and call it Charles Town."[27]

The new Charles Town was regularly laid out with wide streets; plots were reserved for a church, town house, and other public buildings; some thirty new houses were built; and in the spring of 1680 most of the people moved across. At their landings or riding in their harbor were fifteen trading ships. The promising young city that today bears the shortened name of Charleston had started on its career as one of the great ports of America.[28]

Quakers

THE COLONIZATION of Carolina was costing the proprietors a pretty sum—for ships, for supplies, for wages. Perhaps this was taking all the money that John Lord Berkeley cared to risk on American ventures. Perhaps the Dutch recapture of the former New Netherland left him in doubt as to his title in New Jersey. In any case, in March, 1674, he sold his half interest in that province to one James Fenwick, an English Quaker who was acting as agent for Edward Byllinge, a London brewer and also a Quaker. The other half interest remained with Sir George Carteret.[1]

Whether Fenwick and Byllinge knew exactly what they had bought may be doubted. It does not appear that even Berkeley and Carteret realized that, in receiving New Jersey from the Duke of York, they got only the soil; the right of government, not being transferable, remained with the Duke. Ignoring, or ignorant of, this limitation, the two original proprietors had proceeded as though they had full power of government. They had issued the "Concessions and Agreement." They had sent over Philip Carteret as their governor.

They had encouraged the election of provincial assemblies —which shortly got out of hand on the subject of quitrents and elected James Carteret, an erring son of Sir George, as "President of the Country." The Dutch invasion had, mercifully, put an end to this wrangle.[2]

With the return of New Jersey to England in 1674 Philip Carteret returned as Governor, under a commission from Sir George; in fact, he came over on the same ship that brought Edmund Andros, who was commissioned by the Duke of York to act as his deputy over the proprietary granted to him by the King—and certainly that included the government of New Jersey, even though the ownership of the land may have been transferred. Andros must have eyed his young fellow passenger with some question.[3]

The situation was further complicated when, in the summer of 1675, Fenwick, as a joint proprietor by purchase from Berkeley, sailed into the Delaware River. With him came his family, his servants, and a small group of settlers. At a place known to the Dutch as Varckens Kill he founded a town to which he gave the name of Salem, meaning peace. But there had not been, nor was there to be, much peace for John Fenwick. He and Byllinge had quarrelled over their respective shares in the New Jersey venture. To settle the controversy, William Penn, a prominent convert to the Quaker conviction, had been called in as arbitrator. Penn allocated a one-tenth share to Fenwick and nine-tenths to Byllinge. Furthermore, since Byllinge lacked capital for financing a program of settlement, Penn and two other Quakers took over his shares as trustees.[4]

Penn was thirty-one years of age at the time. He was the son of a British admiral to whom the King was indebted for a sizable loan and to whom the Duke of York was indebted for staunch service during the Dutch war. Young Penn's conversion to Quaker doctrine had been a shock to his family and to his aristocratic friends. For his open support of Quaker practices he had suffered imprisonment, and while in the Tower of London had written a pamphlet entitled *No Cross, No Crown,* which brought him added fame. As a trustee for nine-tenths of an undivided one half of New Jersey, he made his first appearance in American history.[5]

Joint ownership by such diverse characters as Sir George Carteret and this group of Quakers was, of course, unworkable. Accordingly, in 1676, New Jersey was divided physically. A line was run from Little Egg Harbor, on the Atlantic seaboard, north by west to the Delaware River. The territory on the easterly side went to Carteret, and became known as East Jersey. That on the westerly side of the line went to the Quaker group, including Fenwick, and became know as West Jersey.[6]

But division of the province in no way added to political rights of the several proprietors. Whether as New Jersey or as East Jersey and West Jersey, Andros still looked upon himself as the governor—just as he was of New York, New Castle or Pemaquid. The first to feel his authority was Fenwick who, considering that he owned the land in his one-tenth of West Jersey, began offering acreage for sale. Andros, not having been consulted, charged the new proprietor with distracting "the mindes of the Inhabitants, thorow out the whole River and Bay, not having any Lawfull Power or Authority," and ordered him to appear at New York for trial. When Fenwick, not unnaturally, ignored the summons, the sheriff at New Castle paddled across the river, seized him, and sent him off to New York, where he was found guilty as charged and detained for several months.[7]

Meanwhile, Penn and his fellow trustees for the other nine-tenths of West Jersey, knowing nothing of Fenwick's troubles, had also assumed that they held the right of government in their part of New Jersey. Accordingly, they had worked out a scheme for the distribution of the land and a basis for the administration of justice. This instrument, called, in the language of the time, "The Concessions and Agreements," practically placed the government of West Jersey in the hands of the inhabitants, subject to some fundamental rights such as freedom of conscience.[8]

At the same time the Penn group offered parcels of their land for sale—primarily through Quaker societies in London and Yorkshire—and appointed commissioners to select and lay it out. With these preliminary arrangements made, the good ship *Kent* sailed for America with some two hundred actual settlers aboard.[9]

Fortunately, the *Kent* put in at New York and there the leaders discovered that Governor Andros would have a word to say. By prudently agreeing to hold the "Concessions" in abeyance and otherwise acting subject to the Governor's approval the colonists were allowed to proceed, and in the late summer of 1677 the *Kent* turned into Delaware Bay. Sailing on past Fenwick's colony at Salem, the newcomers disembarked forty miles farther up the river at a place which they named Burlington. The first and second "Tenths" of land were laid out; more ships came with more settlers; and West Jersey soon took on the appearance of an inhabited country.[10]

It was on the question of customs collections that Andros attempted to bring the Governor of East Jersey to terms. If all incoming and outgoing ships could be forced to clear at New York, the importance of that port would be enhanced; also the likelihood of getting all the customs would be greater. Hence, Andros insisted that ships destined for Elizabethtown, the capital of East Jersey, should first make their declarations and pay their dues to the port of New York. And when Carteret, backed by his assembly, threatened resistance, Andros took drastic action. Soldiers were quietly loaded into boats and told to bring the Governor of East Jersey to New York. Reaching Elizabethtown about midnight, the soldiers broke into Carteret's house "siezed him naked, dragged him through a window, struck and kicked him terribly, and even injured him internally. They threw him, all naked as he was, into a canoe, without cap or hat on his head, and carried him in that condition to New York."[11]

Having thus unceremoniously secured his prisoner, Andros formally put him on trial charged with exercising "jurisdiction and government over his Majesty's subjects" within the bounds of the Duke of York. But despite all the pressure that could be brought to bear on the jurors, and Andros sent them back twice, they returned a verdict of "Not Guilty." This decision the Duke shortly confirmed by the recall of Andros as governor over his proprietary.[12]

In the midst of this uproar two visitors arrived at New York. They were Jasper Danckaerts and Peter Sluyter, members of a communal religious sect then flourishing in Holland but looking for a haven in the New World. They had sailed from Amsterdam on a ship belonging to Margaret Philipse, wife of Frederick Philipse. This husband and wife were a remarkable pair. Frederick had emigrated to New Nether-land as a young man, probably in 1647. He was first known as a carpenter; soon he was a contractor; then he engaged in trade and began accumulating land. In 1662 he married Margaret de Vries, a widow of some wealth and with an unerring instinct for profit in trade. When New Netherland came under the English, the Philipses adjusted themselves and went right on making money. By 1679 they were the richest family in New York. Frederick was a member of the Governor's Council, and from that advantageous position took care of the family affairs in the province. Margaret travelled back and forth across the Atlantic—with cargoes of tobacco and other products for England and Holland—with European goods for America. No space was wasted on her ships; where she could not stow merchandise she carried pas-sengers. When Danckaerts and Sluyter brought aboard one more package than was contracted for, she made them pay the extra freight—"unblushing avarice," grumbled the irri-tated Danckaerts. The ship touched at Falmouth, England, as under the navigation laws it was required to do. There Margaret bought another ship, transferred to it some of the goods she had brought from Holland, and sent it off to Bar-bados. More cargo was loaded aboard the original ship, and with it and her passengers she went on to New York.[13]

Danckaerts and Sluyter found themselves quite at home in New York; the majority of the people spoke Dutch; the manner of life was Dutch. They readily got rooms with a Dutch family, and for almost two months wandered around the city and its environs. Calling one day on their friend Monsieur de la Grange, they found that in one part of his house he "had a small shop, as almost all the people here have, who gain their living by trade, namely, in tobacco and liquors, thread and pins and other knick-knacks." At another time they found La Grange "busily employed in his little shop, packing and marking a parcel of ribbons which he was going to send to Barbados, because, as he said, he could not dispose of them here to advantage." [14]

They attended services at the Dutch Reformed Church but were not edified; the minister, said Danckaerts, "was a thick, corpulent person with a red and bloated face, and of very slabbering speech." Still less were they edified when, after church, some of their friends took them to a tavern beyond the city wall to "taste the beer of New Netherland." The place turned out to be a low pot-house, "resorted to on Sundays by all sorts of revellers." [15]

They made several trips to Long Island. Sometimes they crossed on a ferry boat and sometimes in a row boat. At Brooklyn village they noted "a small and ugly church." Everywhere the landscape was dotted with farms whose Dutch owners hospitably offered milk, cider and a Barbados brandy known as *kill-devil*. The ground was covered with ripe peaches, very delicious but left for the hogs to eat. At Gowanus they were feasted with oysters roasted in the open fireplace. There was a considerable trade in these oysters— pickled for shipment to Barbados. The Delaware River settlements provided a good market for the surplus horses and sheep raised on the Island. Mutton was taken across to New York and peddled. [16]

Most of the houses in the Brooklyn area were of frame construction, and seldom large enough to accommodate overnight guests, as Danckaerts and Sluyter discovered. "After supper, we went to sleep in the barn, upon some straw spread with sheep-skins, in the midst of the continual grunting of hogs, squealing of pigs, bleating and coughing of sheep, barking of dogs, crowing of cocks, cackling of hens, and, especially, a goodly quantity of fleas and vermin. . . ." Small-pox was prevalent; in one house "there were two children lying dead and unburied, and three others sick." In general, the visitors travelled on foot; once a considerate host hitched up his team of horses and drove them back to the ferry. [17]

One weekend Danckaerts and Sluyter made an excursion to the upper part of Manhattan Island. The city proper ended at Wall Street; beyond that the country was more or less open. On either side of the road, known as the Broadway, they saw shanties inhabited by negroes and mulattoes—former slaves of the West India Company. At the village of New Harlem they stayed the night at a house "constantly filled with people, all the time drinking, for the most part, that execrable rum." Among these people was James Carteret, who seven years earlier had taken the job of "President of the Country" in New Jersey. He had subsequently married the daughter of the Mayor of New York and had been created a landgrave of Carolina. But he could not behave himself. "He runs about among the farmers, and stays where he can find most to drink, and sleeps in barns on the straw," Danckaerts tells us.[18]

These side trips around New York were all very interesting to Danckaerts and Sluyter, but the real purpose for which they had come to America was to view the land in northern Maryland. They had tried several times to secure transportation or guides but without success. Finally, Cupid came to their rescue. Ephraim Herrman, of New Castle, had recently married a young lady in New York and was preparing to take her home. He was glad to let Danckaerts and Sluyter travel with his party.[19]

They left New York by boat at ten o'clock in the morning, November 14, 1679. Their course lay down the upper harbor, through the Kill van Kull, and along the western side of Staten Island. It took them two days to reach Woodbridge, near the mouth of the Raritan River, where the land journey began, and where Danckaerts and Sluyter procured horses. However, as Danckaerts observed, *"Our* horses, like the riders, were very poor." The party spent another day and a half in getting to the Falls of the Delaware (Trenton). There they found a grist mill, recently erected by the Quakers who had settled in that part of West Jersey. They had to spend the night at the miller's house. It was very small; Herrman and his wife took the only bed; and the others got what rest they could sitting upright, "not being able to find room enough to lie upon the ground." There was a fire, but the wind howled through the clapboards.[20]

From the Falls the river was navigable, and they continued their journey by boat, reaching the new Quaker village

of Burlington shortly after dark. Apparently business was
booming; there were no rooms to be had at the tavern; and
they were lucky to be taken in by a Swede on the western
side of the river. However, the house was much more comfortable than the frame and clapboard houses of the English.
After the Swedish custom, it was built of logs, squared and
one laid above the other, with the ends notched for joining,
and without a nail or spike being needed.[21]

The next day, which was Sunday, they returned to Burlington and attended the meeting of the Quakers, "who went
to work very unceremoniously and loosely. What they uttered
was mostly in one tone, and the same thing, and so it continued, until we were tired out, and went away," recorded
Danckaerts, who did not like Quakers.[22]

Continuing on down the river, past the place where Philadelphia was to be founded three years later, they came to the
village of Upland, soon to become Chester, Pennsylvania. In
1679 the inhabitants were largely Swedes, survivals of the
vanished colony of New Sweden. But even here, to the irritation of Danckaerts, there were transient Quakers. One of
them, a prophetess from Maryland, while seated at a table
next to him, "began to groan and quake gradually until at
length the whole bench shook. Then rising up she began
to pray, shrieking so that she could be heard as far as the
river."[23]

On November 24, ten days after having left New York,
the party arrived at New Castle, a town of forty or fifty
houses directly on the Delaware River. To Ephraim Herrman it was a homecoming—and with a new wife fresh from
the metropolis of New York. Nonetheless he accepted Danckaerts and Sluyter as guests in his home. The leading men
of the town, including Peter Alricks, called to pay their respects and to offer assistance to the travellers on the remaining leg of their journey. John Moll, who had a plantation
on the road to Maryland, guided them part way and put
them on a wide wagon trail which led over the divide from
the Delaware to the head of Chesapeake Bay. After a walk
of some twenty miles, lugging their travelling bags with them,
Danckaerts and Sluyter arrived at the home of Augustine

Herrman, Lord of Bohemia Manor and father of Ephraim Herrman.[24]

Twenty years earlier Augustine Herrman, then past middle age, had first tramped over that same divide as an ambassador from the Dutch Governor of New Netherland to the English Governor of Maryland. Subsequently he had made a map of Maryland which so pleased Lord Baltimore that he granted Herrman twenty-four thousand acres of land. Herrman located his acres in the fertile northern section of the province, established it as a manor, built a large manor house, and for many years lived in considerable magnificence.[25]

But Danckaerts and Sluyter found the Lord of Bohemia Manor a sick old man, with a nagging second wife, his plantations in a run-down condition for lack of attention, and with no one to help him except negro slaves. However, he received them cordially enough and offered to sell them as much land as they needed for their religious colony. The offer was ultimately accepted and within a few years the Labadists—for such was the name of the sect—were established in Bohemia Manor.[26]

With the purpose of their trip accomplished, Danckaerts and Sluyter were ready to go home. They hurried back to New York but discovered that there were no ships leaving for Europe before spring. While waiting they improved their time by making a visit to Albany. As they started up the Hudson, they found themselves, Danckaerts recorded, among about twenty other passengers "of all kinds, young and old, who made a great noise and bustle in a boat not so large as a common ferry-boat in Holland; and as these people live in the interior of the country somewhat nearer the Indians, they were more wild and untamed, reckless, unrestrained, haughty, and more addicted to misusing the blessed name of God and to cursing and swearing." When we learn that "these people" got off the boat at Esopus, presentday Kingston, New York, but then a palisaded town of about fifty houses, we get an inkling of what Danckaerts meant by "the interior of the country."[27]

Sixty miles above Esopus the boat came to anchor at Albany. The old Dutch fort, situated on the river's bank, had been abandoned and a new one built high on the hill overlooking the town and the river. The town itself lay on the hillside and consisted of eighty or ninety houses, surrounded by a palisade. In it lived the merchants who, under license from Governor Andros, traded with the Indians. Outside the palisade were houses in which the Indians stayed while carrying on their trade. And here we will bid farewell to the two visiting Labadists and turn westward into the country from which these Indians got the furs which they offered to the merchants of Albany.[28]

La Salle

IN GENERAL, THE INDIANS who came to Albany with their packs of furs were members of the Iroquois Confederacy. Their towns stretched westward through presentday central New York State. Their trade relations extended much farther. Into their hands came furs from the more distant tribes, and from their hands European trade goods went to those distant tribes. They were the middlemen between the English traders at Albany and the western Indians. They aspired to be the middlemen between the French traders at Montreal and those western tribes.

In the late 1660's and early 1670's it had seemed certain that the Iroquois would become permanent allies of the French. They had placed themselves under the protection of the King of France; they had accepted Count Frontenac as their "Father"; they had welcomed the establishment of Fort Frontenac as a trading post on Lake Ontario. But that fort was the entering wedge that turned the Iroquois from the French to the English.[1]

The fort had from the first been viewed with jealous eyes by the fur traders of Montreal. Whoever held control of it was bound to have an advantage over the traders two hundred miles down the St. Lawrence. Count Frontenac solved the problem by recommending to the King that the fort and the land around it be granted to Robert Cavelier, Sieur de la Salle, whose background was that of an explorer rather than a trader. The King approved, and within two years Fort Frontenac was the center of a thriving community of farmers, canoe-men, skilled laborers, hunters, and soldiers. Two Franciscan friars ministered to the spiritual needs of the settlement. Four small ships lay at the dock or ranged up and down the Lake. Indians brought in their furs and carried away guns, powder, lead, knives, cloth, and gewgaws. The profits were undoubtedly large.[2]

But to La Salle, and probably also to Frontenac, this fort on Lake Ontario was only a starting place for greater enterprises. Jolliet's report on his voyage down the Mississippi had shown conclusively that that mighty river flowed into the Gulf of Mexico. There were populous Indian villages along the river and its tributaries—vast potential sources of wealth. Particularly, not far below the southern tip of Lake Michigan, there was the great Illinois village which Jolliet had visited on his way home.

From *coureurs de bois,* unlicensed wandering traders, came stories of still other tribes—Sioux in the north, Osage in the southwest—rich in hides of the buffalo. All of this La Salle pondered. The prospect beckoned to his ambition. If the King would grant him this western country, as he had already granted him Fort Frontenac, he would make of it a prosperous, profitable colony—for France, for Count Frontenac, and for himself. From the Indians he would secure buffalo hides and other skins. His boats, plying along the Mississippi and its tributaries, would carry these goods direct to France through the Gulf of Mexico, and by the same route would bring back the manufactured goods of France. In time the natives would become civilized and christianized. Hurrying to Paris, La Salle laid his proposal before the King, and in 1678 returned with a patent authorizing him to go ahead —at his own expense and with the provision that he not interfere with the fur trade already established on the upper Lakes.[3]

Autumn was well advanced as La Salle started his men and supplies westward from Fort Frontenac across Lake Ontario. In the van went fifteen canoe-men with trade goods to buy furs with which to finance the cost of the expedition. On November 18, sixteen more men left the fort in a ten-ton ship loaded with tools and supplies; their job was to establish a temporary post on the lower Niagara River. La Salle, with the rest of the men and supplies, brought up the rear, late in December.[4]

It was a motley crew that gathered at the foot of Niagara Falls that winter of 1678–79. Side by side with common laborers born on the St. Lawrence were carpenters and blacksmiths fresh from France. There was Father Hennepin, already familiar with frontier life. There was Henri de Tonti, a veteran of European battlefields, on one of which he had lost his left hand, and as a substitute wore a formidable-looking iron hook. And in charge of everything was La Salle, thirty-five years of age, bursting with energy, very sure of himself.[5]

Before them, from a plateau three hundred feet high, roared and tumbled the outflowing waters of four great lakes. Above the Falls lay an open waterway to those lakes. A stiff climb to the plateau, a walk of five miles, and the Falls were behind them; they were on the comparatively quiet waters flowing in from Lake Erie. Three or four miles farther on they found an inlet suitable for building a small ship. There they established a camp, and, while the carpenters began laying a keel, the others lugged up from the lower landing the forge, anvil, tools, anchors, rope, sails, equipment, and supplies.[6]

La Salle had taken the precaution of asking permission from the Seneca chiefs before starting his operations at Niagara, and they had grudgingly consented. But as the work went on, the Indians viewed both the fort and the ship with growing dislike. Niagara was their door to the western trade; they neither wished to share it with nor to have it controlled by others. As a token of their disapproval they refused to sell corn to the Frenchmen; and as the ship grew on the ways, they threatened to burn it. However, in the spring of 1679

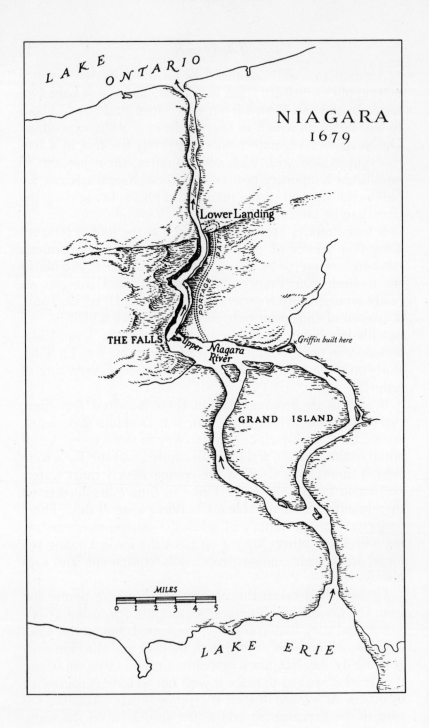

LAKE ONTARIO

NIAGARA
1679

Lower Niagara River

Lower Landing

PORTAGE PATH

THE FALLS

Upper Niagara River

×Griffin built here

GRAND ISLAND

MILES
0 1 2 3 4 5

LAKE ERIE

the *Griffin,* as La Salle christened it, slid into the upper Niagara River. She was of forty-five tons capacity, equipped with sails and armed with five small cannon. On August 7, fully rigged and loaded, she started on her maiden voyage —through Lake Erie, through the narrow strait known as *d'étroit,* through Lake Ste. Claire, and up Lake Huron to Michilimackinac where, on August 27, she came to anchor before the Jesuit mission of St. Ignace.[7]

But it was a troubled call. The Jesuits did not like La Salle and his Franciscan missionaries. They looked upon the west as their own field of endeavor and wished no interference. They may have tampered with the loyalty of some of La Salle's men; he suspected as much.[8]

Nor, at Michilimackinac, were any of La Salle's traders waiting with packs of furs. Instead he heard stories of their being at Ste. Marie and other places where they had no business being. It was said that some had wasted his goods; others were trading on their own accounts. In any case there was no cargo for the *Griffin,* and La Salle turned southward into Lake Michigan. There he had better luck, as it seemed. Near the entrance to Green Bay were a few of his men with a large stock of skins. Just where they had got them La Salle did not enquire too closely. The King had definitely specified that he was not to trade at Green Bay, but he needed furs desperately to satisfy his creditors at Montreal and Quebec. Loading the packs aboard the *Griffin,* he ordered her captain to deliver them at Niagara and hurry back—rejoining the expedition at the foot of Lake Michigan.[9]

Meanwhile La Salle, with thirty-three men, with his forge and with his lighter tools, paddled southward in canoes. Through raging storms they pushed on, down the western shore of the Lake, past the Indian town called Milwaukee, past the entrance to the Chicago portage. At the mouth of the St. Joseph River they unloaded their canoes and put up and fortified a building which they named Fort Miamis.[10]

For more than a month they waited, anxiously scanning the waters of the Lake, for the arrival of the *Griffin,* but in vain. Aboard her were the anchors and rigging for a ship which La Salle planned to build on a tributary of the Mis-

sissippi. Thinking that the captain might have misunder-
stood the rendezvous, La Salle sent two men to circle the
Lake while he, with the others, in eight canoes—still carrying the forge and tools—started up the St. Joseph River. Near
the presentday city of South Bend, Indiana, they lifted the
canoes out of the water, shouldered them, and trudged five
miles over the almost imperceptible divide to the westward-
flowing Kankakee, which soon joined the Des Plaines River
to form the Illinois.[11]

Here, at last, La Salle was within those "western parts of
New France" which the King had authorized him to explore
and possess. But as the long line of canoes, creeping down
the ice-clogged river, came in sight of the Great Illinois Village, all was silence. Along the bank of the river stood four
or five hundred cabins, framed with poles and covered with
grass mats. Everything was in good order. There was plenty
of corn in the *caches*. But there were no inhabitants. It was
as though everyone had gone on a visit. And such was really
the case. The Indians were at their winter encampment sixty
miles farther down the river, near presentday Peoria, Illinois.
There La Salle found them a few days later.[12]

The Indian chiefs received their French visitors with some
suspicion. Rumors had been passing from tribe to tribe that
the dread Iroquois were preparing an attack on the Illinois.
Vaguely the Indians had gathered that La Salle had something to do with the impending trouble. They were more
inclined to look upon him as an enemy than as a friend. The
situation was bad. Six of La Salle's men, fearful for their
scalps, sneaked out of the camp one night and hurried back
to Michilimackinac. French eloquence and French presents,
however, prevailed, and the Indians agreed that La Salle
might establish a fort among them and build his ship.[13]

Selecting a site slightly below the Indian encampment, La
Salle put his men to work. Those axes and saws, that forge
and anvil, which they had so patiently carried in their canoes
all the way from Green Bay, now came into use. Bunk houses
and storage houses were quickly framed and covered. Around
them, on the land side, arose a sturdy palisade, which must
have interested the Indians, whose own villages stood open

to all comers. On the river's edge the carpenters began laying a keel for the ship. Fort Crevecœur, as the place was named, buzzed with activity; and La Salle, as always, began thinking of the next step.[14]

From Fort Crevecœur to the Mississippi the distance was less than a hundred and fifty miles. Southward from that point La Salle would make the trip in his ship, but the stretch from the mouth of the Illinois northward might as well be explored while the ship was building. There were possibilities of trade in buffalo hides from the Indians along the way.

Accordingly, La Salle fitted out three men, including Father Hennepin, with a variety of trade goods and ordered them to drop down the Illinois to the Mississippi, at which point they were to turn north toward the mouth of the Wisconsin. They started on their voyage late in February, 1680, while the rest of the men worked away on the ship and La Salle probably did a bit of profitable fur trading at the fort.[15]

By the first of March the ship was well advanced, but where was the *Griffin*? She was long, long overdue at the foot of Lake Michigan. La Salle decided to investigate. Leaving Tonti in command at Fort Crevecœur, he returned with two or three men to Fort Miamis, hoping against hope that the *Griffin* had shown up. He found the men he had sent to look for her, but they had neither seen nor heard of the missing ship. In fact, the fate of the *Griffin* remains to this day one of the mysteries of the Great Lakes. She was probably lost in the furious storms that swept the west during the autumn of 1679.[16]

Griffin or no *Griffin*, La Salle had to have anchors and rigging if his new ship were to sail down the Mississippi and across the Atlantic. The nearest place to get them was Fort Frontenac—five hundred miles eastward as the crow flies, twice that distance by the Lakes. He chose the shorter route. Trudging through slushy snow, wading icy streams, making rafts where necessary, he and his companions pushed across southern Michigan. At the western end of Lake Erie they made a canoe and paddled on to Niagara, where a few of his men still occupied the temporary fort. On May 6 he was at Fort Frontenac.[17]

When he left Fort Miamis, La Salle ordered the men at that post to report to Tonti at Fort Crevecœur. They did so—and in addition reported to the other men that La Salle was broke. The story had its natural result. One day while Tonti was absent most of the men walked off their jobs, took what supplies they could carry, and headed for Michilimack-inac. Tonti sent word of the disaster to La Salle, and with the three remaining men and two Franciscan friars moved up to the Illinois village, where he did some trading for furs while the friars endeavored to instruct their savage charges in the way to salvation.[18]

Whether the Indians learned anything from the friars, or wished to, may be doubted. But Father Membre, one of the friars, learned a good deal about them. The men were "tall of stature, strong and robust," he tells us. In the summer time they went entirely naked except for ox-hide moccasins; in the winter they wore dressed skins. They were idle, thievish and cowardly. They were polygamous and lewd, "even unnaturally so, having boys dressed as women, destined for infamous purposes." Hermaphrodites were common among them.[19]

At about the same time, Father Hennepin, also, was learning something about the western Indians. He and his two companions had turned up the Mississippi as directed—paddling northward over the route down which Jolliet and Marquette had floated seven years earlier. It is possible that they expected to meet French traders working westerly through the Fox-Wisconsin waterway from Green Bay. Instead they met a war party of Sioux Indians and were forced to accompany them to their villages on the upper waters of the Mississippi—opposite the western end of Lake Superior.

These Sioux villages did not consist of cabins such as those made by the Illinois Indians. The houses were tepees—lodge poles converging to a center at the top, and covered with skins. By the master of one of these tepees, Hennepin was adopted as a son, and found that he had five mothers. He was treated well enough but almost starved—or so he felt—on the meager fare which, during most of the year, sufficed for the Indians. He could "gain nothing over them in the way of salvation, by reason of their natural stupidity," he tells us. The Sioux evidently felt much the same about the friar, but they put him to work—shaving the children's heads, treating the grown-ups for colds, and dosing everybody with "orvietan," a cure-all which he seems to have carried with him in large quanities.

As the summer wore on, Hennepin and his fellow explorers began to think of ways to get home. It was seven or eight hundred miles back to Fort Crevecœur. It was about five hundred miles to the mission of St. Francois Xavier on Green Bay, and for that place they apparently headed.

However, the great, unknown west of 1680 was a smaller place than is usually realized. In 1678 Daniel Greysolon, Sieur Duluth, accompanied by several well-armed men, had left Quebec with orders to pacify the Indians about Lake Superior and open that region to French trade. His mission had been eminently successful and he was preparing to return eastward when word reached him that there were white men among the Sioux. Hurrying southward he rescued Hennepin and his companions and guided them safely to Michilimackinac, where they barely missed meeting La Salle—on his way from Fort Frontenac with men and supplies for the post on the Illinois River.[20]

News of the desertion of his men at Fort Crevecœur had reached La Salle at Fort Frontenac during the summer. But Tonti had assured him that he and the few men with him would hold on until relief came. La Salle got together a new party—carpenters, masons, laborers—and again started west on August 10, 1680. While his cavalcade of canoes was working its way through the lakes, the long-rumored blow fell on the Illinois towns.[21]

The Iroquois had been unhappy about La Salle's fort at Niagara. They had eyed the *Griffin* with distrust. Duluth's embassy to the Sioux, and La Salle's fort on the Illinois River both threatened their control of the western fur trade. Possibly their fears were whetted by the Jesuits, who also resented La Salle's incursion into the west. Certainly they were egged on by the English merchants at Albany, whose profits depended upon the packs of furs brought in by the Iroquois.[22]

On September 10, 1680, scouts from the Great Illinois Village sighted an Iroquois war party led by old Tegantouki, a Seneca chief who, two years earlier, had grumbled at Niagara. Tonti did his best to stop the fight but only got himself suspected by both sides. Tegantouki suggested it would be a good idea to burn him, but an Onondaga chief interposed. The Illinois lived up to the character given them by Father Membre. After some slight resistance most of them retreated across the Mississippi; those that did not get away furnished the usual savage entertainment for the victors— tied to stakes and tortured as long as there was life in them.

After the Illinois had fled, Tonti was invited to a council with the Iroquois chiefs. They placed before him six packs of beaver with the explanation that the first two were to inform Count Frontenac that they would not "eat his children," meaning the Illinois. The third pack was a plaster for a slight wound Tonti had received. The fourth pack was oil with which to rub his limbs in preparation for a long journey. The fifth pack was to show that the sun was bright. The sixth pack was to suggest that Tonti and his men should profit by the fact that the sun was bright and depart the next day for the French settlements.

Tonti states that he kicked the presents away. Be that as it may, he and his men departed early the following morning, taking with them a considerable stock of furs. When they came to the fork made by the junction of the Kankakee and Des Plaines rivers, they followed the latter and crossed by the Chicago portage to Lake Michigan (see map on page 89). Paddling onward, up the western side of the lake, they were wrecked and continued on foot. Only after great suffering did they reach the Potawatomi village at Green Bay.[23]

Had Tonti travelled by the Kankakee and St. Joseph rivers he might well have met La Salle, who was coming down the eastern side of the lake. La Salle arrived at Fort Miamis on November 4, left his heavy stores, and with a few men pushed on to the Illinois. He needed no human reporter to tell him what had happened. He saw the burned village— inhabited only by wolves, buzzards, and crows. He found where the Illinois Indians had made their camps as they fled.

HENRI DE TONTI.
From a painting by Nicholas Maes, said to
have been made in 1685.

Courtesy, J. E. Maryon-Daulby, London.

He found where the final orgy of torture had been celebrated by the Iroquois. But he found no trace of Tonti and his party.[24]

Returning to Fort Miamis, La Salle spent the winter of 1680–81, but it was not a wasted winter. Near the fort were the Miami Indians, a wandering tribe. Also, there were many refugee Indians from New England and Virginia—some perhaps wearing shirts made by Mrs. Rowlandson; others with guns looted from plantations along the James River. From these diverse elements La Salle formed the nucleus of a western confederacy. Later he added some Shawnees who were unhappy on the Ohio. And as the Illinois Indians began returning to their ruined homes, they, too, were included. La Salle taught them how to protect their villages with palisades. He supplied them with guns. With their help he would be able to resist the Iroquois. From them he would get the packs of furs with which to pay off his creditors at Montreal and Quebec, and to continue his explorations. This time, however, he would use the easily replaceable canoe rather than again attempt to build a ship.[25]

By the late autumn of 1681 La Salle was ready to make the long-delayed trip down the Mississippi—the final exploration that would place him in legal possession of those "western parts of New France" granted to him by the King. He had made another trip to Fort Frontenac and had brought on more men and supplies. Tonti and Father Membre had rejoined him. His Indian confederation had grown.

Early in January, 1682, the expedition was streaming down the Illinois River. In the canoes were twenty-three white men, eighteen Indians, ten squaws and three papooses. They passed Fort Crevecœur, falling to ruin, the unfinished ship still standing, like a skeleton, on its props. On February 6 they floated out on the broad Mississippi.

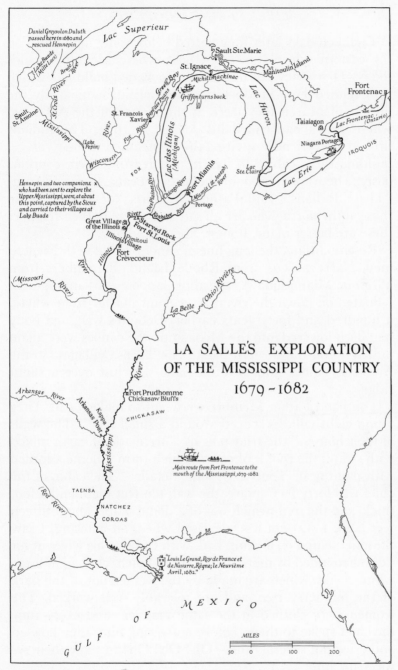

Daniel Greysolon Duluth
passed here in 1680 and
rescued Hennepin

Lac Superieur

Sault Ste.Marie

(Lake Buade
(Mille Lacs)

Brule River

St.Croix River

St. Ignace

Manitoulin Island

Michilimackinac

Green Bay

Bay des Puans

Griffon turns back

Fort
Frontenac

Sault
St.Antoine

Mississippi River

St. Francois
Xavier

Lac Huron

Taiaiagon

Lac Frontenac
(Ontario)

Fox River

(Lake
Pepin)

Wisconsin

Lac des Ilinois
(Michigan)

Niagara Portage

IROQUOIS

FOX

Des Plaines River

Chicago River

Fort Miamis

Miami (St. Joseph) River

Lac
Ste.Claire

Lac Erie

Hennepin and two companions, x
who had been sent to explore the
Upper Mississippi, were, at about
this point, captured by the Sioux
and carried to their villages at
Lake Buade

Kankakee River

Portage

Great Village
of the Illinois

Starved Rock
Fort St.Louis

Illinois Village

Pimitoui

Fort
Crevecoeur

Illinois River

(Missouri River)

La Belle (Ohio) Riviere

LA SALLE'S EXPLORATION
OF THE MISSISSIPPI COUNTRY
1679 ~ 1682

Arkansas River

Fort Prudhomme
Chickasaw Bluffs

Arkansas Post

Kappa

CHICKASAW

Mississippi River

Main route from Fort Frontenac to the
mouth of the Mississippi, 1679-1682

(Red River)

TAENSA

NATCHEZ

COROAS

"Louis Le Grand, Roy de France et
de Navarre, Regne; le Neuvième
Avril, 1682."

M E X I C O

G U L F   O F

MILES

50   0   100   200

Based upon Plate 33 of the *Atlas of American History*.

Eighteen days later they halted below some high bluffs on
the eastern side of the river, near where Memphis stands
today. There they put up a small stockaded building—which
they named Fort Prudhomme—and left a few men. By the
middle of March they were at the mouth of the Arkansas,
where Jolliet had ended his voyage in 1673. The Indians
proved most friendly, inviting the Frenchmen to their village,
building them cabins to live in and feasting them continuously. The women brought them corn, beans, flour and fruit.
"These Indians," said Father Membre, "do not resemble
those at the north, who are all sad and severe in their temper;
these are better made, honest, liberal and gay."

Re-embarking, the long line of canoes—filled with Frenchmen, Narragansetts from Rhode Island, Pamunkeys from
Virginia, Miami squaws, squealing papooses, Arkansas guides
—floated on down the river. At a point not far from where,
a hundred and forty years earlier, DeSoto's weighted body
had been lowered into the Mississippi, the canoes were again
pulled up on the western bank. The Taensa villages—so the
Arkansas guides informed La Salle—lay just over a slight
ridge.

Tonti and Father Membre were sent to make a call. They
found eight villages spaced around a small lake. "The walls
of their houses," the friar tells us, "are made of earth mixed
with straw; the roof is of canes, which form a dome adorned
with paintings." Tonti adds some details: "The cabin of the
chief was forty feet square, the wall ten feet high, and a foot
thick, and the roof, which was of a dome shape, about fifteen
feet high. I was not less surprised when, on entering, I saw
the chief seated on a camp bed, with three of his wives at his
side surrounded by more than sixty old men, clothed in large
white cloaks, which are made by the women out of the bark
of the mulberry tree, and are tolerably well worked. The
women were clothed in the same manner; and every time
the chief spoke to them, before answering him, they howled
and cried out several times—Oh! Oh! Oh! to show their respect for him. . . ."

Tonti also tells us that the Taensa worshiped the sun.
"They have a temple opposite the house of the chief, and

similar to it, except that three eagles are placed on this temple who look toward the rising sun. The temple is surrounded with strong mud walls, in which are fixed spikes on which they place the heads of their enemies whom they sacrifice to the sun." Inside the temple was an altar at the foot of which "three logs are placed on end, and a fire is kept up day and night by two old medicine-men. . . ."

When the Taensa chief returned the Frenchmen's call, he did not scramble through the underbrush along the river as Tonti and Father Membre had done. On the contrary his people cleared a path for him and provided a cane mat on which he sat during the visit. "He was preceded by two men carrying fans of white feathers. A third carried a copper plate and a round one of the same metal, both highly polished."

But La Salle was impatient to be on his way. Everything indicated that the journey's end was near. From the frozen prairies of the Illinois he and his band had descended into a tropical country. Strange, luxuriant trees lined the river's banks. Alligators splashed into the water as the canoes approached. On April 6 the river separated into three channels. La Salle took the western one; Tonti took the middle one; and another party took the third. In each channel, as they advanced, the water became more and more salty. And then the wide expanse of the Gulf of Mexico opened before them. La Salle had completed the exploration that Jolliet had begun.

On April 9, near the river's mouth, a great cross was set up and beside it a post bearing the arms of the King with an inscription reading, "LOUIS LE GRAND, ROY DE FRANCE ET DE NAVARRE, REGNE. LE NEUVIEME AVRIL, 1682." The Frenchmen sang the *Te Deum,* and La Salle, holding aloft his commission, took formal possession in the King's name—of the Mississippi, of all the rivers that flowed into it, of all the land watered by those rivers, and of all the people living therein. To this vast region he gave the name of Louisiana.

Only La Salle's wild crew witnessed the ceremony, and none of them, not even La Salle, cared to linger at the river's mouth. It was a desolate spot, and they were short of provisions. When they found some dried meat left by wandering Indians, they readily appropriated it—until they discovered that it was human flesh. Still, Father Membre later recalled that "It was very good and delicate."

Half famished, the expedition pushed back up the river. Progress was slow. Malaria lurked in the steaming banks. For two months La Salle lay sick at Fort Prudhomme, nursed by Father Membre and a few men. Tonti and the others struggled on, and La Salle followed as his strength permitted. In October he joined Tonti at Michilimackinac. He had seen the great river and he had reached a decision. No longer would he attempt to colonize Louisiana from Canada. He would make his next approach by sea—from France through the Gulf of Mexico.[26]

10

Pennsylvania

WHILE LA SALLE was recuperating at Michilimackinac, that autumn of 1682, William Penn stepped ashore at New Castle, on Delaware Bay.

Seven years had elapsed since the courtly Quaker first interested himself in colonial affairs. They had been fateful years—for Penn and for America. From being incidentally concerned with West Jersey, Penn was now a dominant figure in England's New World—a trustee for West Jersey, a joint proprietor of East Jersey, sole proprietor of the Delaware Counties, and sole proprietor of Pennsylvania.

Penn's outstanding position in American colonization was due primarily to the favor of the Duke of York. Why the Duke thus heaped his favors upon Penn is less easy to understand. It was a strange friendship, this between the autocratic, unbending, Catholic Duke and the easy-going, impractical, idealistic Quaker. But there it was; whatever Penn asked for, the Duke granted or persuaded the King to grant; so it seemed, at least. The thought arises that Penn may have been the intermediary through which Quaker money, and there was plenty of it, flowed into the pockets of the needy Duke in return for privileges and opportunities. On the other hand, it may well be that the Duke adroitly used Penn to forward his own colonial program.

Be the explanation what it may, the Duke's favor grew as Penn's activity increased, and Penn's success grew as the Duke's favor increased. Thus when Penn became a trustee for West Jersey and found the authority of his commissioners challenged by Governor Andros, he appealed to the Duke, and the jurisdictional rights of the colony were promptly acknowledged. A similar confirmation of Carteret's authority in East Jersey was shortly followed by the purchase of that colony by Penn and a group made up mostly of Quakers and Scottish friends of the Duke. At about the same time Fenwick sold his one-tenth interest in West Jersey to Penn.[1]

His experience with the West Jersey venture had opened new spiritual vistas to Penn. Like the Puritans a half century earlier, he saw in America a refuge from the doom that was, he felt sure, impending over Europe. He would found a colony where his fellow Quakers and other persecuted Protestants might live in peace. He doubtless knew something of the lay of the land west of New Jersey. The Duke may have advised him as to a suitable location for his "holy experiment." In 1680 he petitioned the King for the unpatented land lying between Maryland on the south and New York on the north—to be granted to him as a proprietary on terms similar to those by which Lord Baltimore held Maryland.[2]

The King readily approved Penn's request, particularly since it could be counted as an offset to £16,000 which the royal purse had overlooked repaying to Admiral Penn for funds advanced to the navy. The Lords of Trade, however, had a few words to say about the terms of the patent before it received their approval. Under a proprietary grant such as that requested, there were two separate features—the land and the government. The land, for all practical purposes, became the property of the proprietor, to dispose of to whom and on what terms he saw fit. That presumably was a profit. In return the proprietor accepted the job of bringing in people and governing them. That was a responsibility and an expense. But within his own province the proprietor was the final authority, barring only such limitations as the patent placed upon him. The idea back of a proprietary grant was that it relieved the King of expense and responsibility while he retained his sovereignty through the allegiance of the proprietor. This had worked satisfactorily in the early days of colonization. But with the development of a trade empire in which customs were an important item in the support of the government, it became essential that the colonies should be more immediately dependent upon the King, as the Lords of Trade expressed it. What they really meant was that they wanted no colonial governors standing between their collectors of customs and the rich cargoes that entered and departed from the American ports. They were having enough trouble with corporate Massachusetts and proprietary Maryland where the collectors were as apt to be in jail as were the captains who evaded customs—and where evasions were encouraged by governors from whom there was no appeal. Such was the problem, and to meet it proper safeguards were written into Penn's patent. He was required to "admitt and receive" at his ports the collectors appointed by the Commissioners of Customs. Cases having to do with the laws of trade and navigation might be appealed to England. The inhabitants of the province were to owe their allegiance to the King rather than to the proprietor.[3]

And so the patent passed the Great Seal on March 4, 1681. Penn wished to name his province Sylvania on account of the vast forests with which it was filled. To this the King prefixed the name of Penn, in memory of the proprietor's father.[4]

The bounds of Pennsylvania started from the arc of a circle drawn at a distance of twelve miles north and west from New Castle, and ran up the Delaware River to 43°, thence due west five degrees, thence south to intersect the southern boundary. The description of this southern boundary was ambiguous to say the least. It was to start from the circle around New Castle, and run west on the fortieth parallel—Maryland's northern boundary. The ambiguity becomes evi-

dent when we note that the fortieth parallel lay more than
ten miles north of the most northerly point of the circle. Ignorance of this geographical difficulty can hardly be claimed
in view of the fact that in drawing his boundaries Penn must
have had before him Augustine Herrman's map of Maryland in which the fortieth parallel was placed even farther
north than it actually lies. Cecilius Calvert, the second Lord
Baltimore, had given Herrman a vast grant of land for "doing
him right" in that map; Charles Calvert, the third Lord
Baltimore, would hardly fail to charge Penn with doing him
wrong in ignoring it.[5]

However, in the spring of 1681 Penn apparently worried
little about impending boundary troubles. The Duke would
take care of any misunderstandings. Penn had more pressing
problems. He sent William Markham to Pennsylvania to ex-
tinguish Indian titles and establish good relations with the
Swedish farmers who had lived along the Delaware for more
than forty years. They would not be at the mercy of a "governor who comes to make his fortune," Penn assured them.
Meanwhile, his main concern was to sell land and get people
into his province. To forward this objective he issued a prospectus: "Since (by the good providence of God) a country
in America is fallen to my lot, I thought it not less my Duty
than my honest Interest to give some publick notice of it to
the World. . . ."[6]

He gave a temperate description of Pennsylvania; he explained how the inhabitants were to be governed; he listed
the occupations that would presumably find financial rewards
in the province; he estimated the costs involved in going
there. He set forth the terms on which land might be acquired: five thousand acres for a down payment of one hundred pounds and an annual quitrent (payable forever, of
course) of one shilling per hundred acres; or two hundred
acres at a quitrent of a penny per acre, with no down payment.[7]

This prospectus was widely circulated in England and
Wales; translations were sent into Holland, western Germany, and France. As a result, applications for land began
pouring in. One of the largest buyers was a stock company

known as the Free Society of Traders, with more than two hundred shareholders. It bought twenty thousand acres of Pennsylvania land.[8]

To further stimulate sales, Penn promised special concessions to the "first purchasers." With each five-hundred-acre purchase made before a specified closing date there would go a bonus of ten acres in a city that was to be founded at some suitable place in the province.[9]

This proposed city took on additional importance as the character of the province became known and the possibilities for a profitable trade were recognized. In October, 1681, Penn sent over three commissioners to assist Markham in laying out the city and in assigning land adjoining it, but the final selection of its location probably was not made until the spring of 1682 when Thomas Holme arrived with a commission as surveyor-general.[10]

With land sales going nicely, with a goodly number of people already in the province and many more preparing to sail, Penn settled down to the congenial task of drafting a Frame of Government within which his "holy experiment" might function. He would be the Governor—with a treble vote in the Council. The Council would be elected by the freemen of the province and together with the Governor would exercise the executive power. The Council would formulate and propose laws which a representative Assembly, also elected by the freemen, might approve or disapprove. Such, in brief, was Penn's Frame of Government as issued on April 25, 1682.[11]

Appended to the Frame were forty laws, intended to serve as a basis for a Pennsylvania code. One of these laws directed that those who believed in one eternal God and felt obliged "in conscience to live peacefully and justly in civil society, shall, in no ways, be molested or prejudiced for their religious persuasion. . . ." Another limited the franchise to those who owned upwards of fifty acres of land or who paid personal taxes of a proportional amount; in short, only those who helped to support the government were to have a voice in it.[12]

As Penn received more and more detailed reports from Markham, he doubtless began to realize that the water approach to his province and his city was controlled on one side of Delaware Bay by West Jersey and on the other by the land lying southward of that semi-circle above New Castle. Legally, New Castle and all the rest of the land on the westerly side of Delaware Bay, southward of 40°, lay within the province of Maryland. But Lord Baltimore had made no effective protest when the Swedes settled there, nor when the Dutch displaced them, nor yet when the Duke of York succeeded the Dutch. Accordingly the Duke claimed the land and exercised jurisdiction, although by a title which, as his secretary admitted, "to an ordinary person would not be very secure." Such as the title was, however, Penn wanted it, and as usual got his way. On August 24, 1682, the Duke gave Penn a quitclaim to New Castle and the Lower Counties on the Delaware.[13]

All that spring and summer of 1682 ships and settlers had been leaving England for Pennsylvania. The Welsh pioneers, representing a very sizable land purchase, were on their way. Nicholas More, president of the Free Society of Traders, was preparing to sail, with his family and some fifty servants. Problems were sure to arise, particularly about the assignment of land and lots, which only Penn could settle. It was high time for him to be in his province. Early in September he was one of many passengers aboard the three-hundred-ton ship *Welcome* bound for Delaware River.[14]

It was an unhappy voyage—smallpox took a heavy toll of both passengers and crew. On October 27, however, the *Welcome* anchored off New Castle. Penn sent a messenger ashore to inform the Duke's commissioners of his presence; also that he was the new proprietor of the town and the Delaware Counties. The following day the Duke's commissioners, who interestingly enough turned out to be John Moll and Ephraim Herrman, put Penn in possession of the province. Moll records the picturesque ceremony. They gave Penn the key to the fort "to lock upon himself alone the door, which being opened by him again, we did deliver also unto him one turf, with a twig upon it, a porringer with river water and soil, in part of all what was specified in the said indenture."[15]

A few days later Penn pushed on up the river and landed

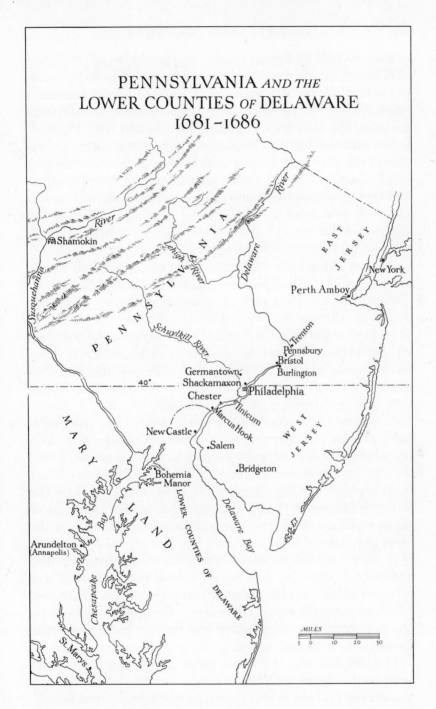

PENNSYLVANIA *AND THE*
LOWER COUNTIES *OF* DELAWARE
1681–1686

Shamokin

Susquehanna River

River

Lehigh River

Delaware River

EAST JERSEY

New York

Perth Amboy

PENNSYLVANIA

Schuylkill River

Trenton

Pennsbury
Bristol

Germantown
Shackamaxon
Burlington

40°

Chester
Philadelphia

Tinicum
Marcus Hook

New Castle

WEST JERSEY

Salem

MARYLAND

Bridgeton

Bohemia
Manor

Arundelton
(Annapolis)

LOWER COUNTIES OF DELAWARE

Delaware Bay

Chesapeake Bay

St. Marys

MILES

5   0   10   20   30

in his province of Pennsylvania—at the old Swedish village
of Upland, which he rechristened Chester. There for some
weeks he made his residence; and there, at a hastily convened
Assembly of the freemen, a temporary code of laws was
adopted, the Delaware Counties were joined with Pennsylvania, and the Swedish inhabitants were naturalized as citizens of the province. It may well be that at this time he met
the Indians in council under an elm tree at Shackamaxon
and there, by his philosophy of mutual goodwill and understanding, won from them a promise of peace so long as the
sun and moon should shine—even as a persistent, though
unsubstantiated, tradition has long insisted.[16]

Around the middle of December, Penn journeyed southward into Maryland and met Lord Baltimore. Whatever
illusions he may have nursed as to his ability to fix up the
boundary dispute between himself and the Proprietor of
Maryland suffered a bad setback. Baltimore stood squarely
on the terms of his patent: his northern boundary was the
fortieth parallel; and it appeared that Penn's new city—between the Delaware and Schuylkill rivers—lay within Maryland. The rival proprietors parted stiffly.[17]

However, Penn went ahead with his city. Nor was Baltimore's claim the only one with which he had to deal. The
site of the city had been far from a wilderness when Holme
decided upon it earlier in the year. Along the Delaware River
front lay the Swedish village of Wicaco, surrounded by the
well-tilled farms of the inhabitants. Holme had to buy them
off to make room for the city lots promised by Penn to the
"first purchasers"—and evidently the Swedes made the most
of it. In return for their old homes they got eight hundred
and twenty acres on the westerly side of the Schuylkill and
other valuable considerations. Penn found them charming,
"a plain, strong, industrious People." But a less sympathetic
observer remarked that "since the English came they [the
Swedes] have gotten fine Cloaths and are going proud."[18]

Philadelphia was the name given to the new city. However, in the winter of 1682–83, it was a city of streets, systematically laid out in rectangles, rather than a city of homes.
High Street, a hundred feet wide, ran from river to river.

Broad Street, of the same width, crossed High at right angles, dividing the city into quarters. The other streets, paralleling High or Broad, were fifty feet in width. In the center of the city, where High and Broad intersected, a ten-acre plot was reserved for a meetinghouse, townhouse, market, and other public buildings. Similar plots were reserved in each of the four quarters of the city.[19]

Some of the people, that first winter, lived in caves on the river bank; others had houses of sorts. One was being built for Penn, with doors and porticoes said to have been brought from England in the *Welcome*. Thomas Paschall, who had arrived in September, 1682, and been assigned land on the westerly side of the Schuylkill, rented a small house in which he and his family lived. It was fairly rough going—"people that come must work." Still they had plenty to eat, and the Indians sold venison for a trifle. In any case, it was better than making pewter in England. "I never wisht my self at Bristol again," Paschall reported to a friend back home.[20]

As spring came on, more people arrived and demanded their land. Some began clearings for farms; others started building on lots within the city. By July, Philadelphia boasted eighty houses, "such as they were." The Free Society of Traders had been assigned one whole street and half of another as its bonus of city lots; it was operating a tannery, a sawmill, and a gristmill; down the Bay it had boats catching whales.[21]

Cattle and sheep were plentiful. Horses were bred in such numbers that the surplus was being shipped to Barbados. Wheat, barley, oats, and other crops were being raised not only on the farms but within the bounds of the city. Where Fairmount Park stands today, Andrew Doz was beginning a vinery. From England came shoes, cloth, grindstones, kettles, axes, and other necessities. From Barbados came sugar, rum, and negro slaves. All found a ready market. What the people could not get at Philadelphia or Chester they sometimes found in the fairs at the West Jersey town of Burlington, twenty miles up the river from Philadelphia.[22]

A weekly post was established that carried letters from Philadelphia southward to Chester, New Castle, and Mary-

land; also northward to the "Falls" (presentday Trenton),
whence the overland road ran to the new port town of Perth
Amboy, East Jersey, named in honor of one of Penn's associate proprietors of that province.[23]

Nor was education overlooked. The Provincial Council
arranged with Enoch Flower, an experienced teacher, to
open a school in Philadelphia. For teaching a child to read
English, Flower charged four shillings per quarter; for both
reading and writing, the charge was six shillings; and if arithmetic was included, the charge was eight shillings.[24]

Church spires did not dominate the scene. The early settlers of Pennsylvania were overwhelmingly of Quaker conviction. Their first meetinghouse "was nothing else than a
Lodge or Cottage, nailed together of Pine-boards imported
from New York."[25]

In the late summer of 1683 there arrived at Philadelphia
the vanguard of a new immigration, that of Germans. In
numbers the newcomers were not impressive—only nine people. But among them was Francis Daniel Pastorius with a
power of attorney from a group of Germans at Frankfort
who had bought fifteen thousand acres of Pennsylvania land.
The land was to be on a navigable river, and Pastorius demanded the bonus of lots in Philadelphia even though the
purchase had been made after the list of "first purchasers"
was closed. Penn was in a tight place; he did not have enough
city lots to go around as it was. Still, he wanted those German settlers, and to keep them happy he signed over the
requisite number of lots from some he had reserved for his
son.[26]

A few weeks later, on October 6, another group of Germans—thirty-three in all—arrived from Crefeld, Germany.
They, too, had warrants for several thousand acres of land.
Both of these German groups insisted that their land should
lie in a solid block so they could perpetuate their language
and their ways of life. Penn preferred granting the land in
small, separate plots until more settlers were on hand, but
compromised by giving the Germans six thousand acres on
the east side of the Schuylkill north of the limits of Philadelphia. And there the city of Germantown came into exist-

ence—along a single street with three-acre home lots. In 1684 there were twelve families and a total population of forty-two persons.[27]

If Penn had unhappy moments with dissatisfied land purchasers, he had equally unhappy moments in his attempts to establish a government for the province. The fact was that his Frame of Government, which seemed so perfect in England, would not work in America. Penn himself had violated it almost from the beginning, and at a meeting of the Council and Assembly held at Philadelphia during the early part of 1683 the Frame was revised amidst an uproar that boded no good for the future. Nicholas More, president of the Society of Free Traders, spoke his mind so freely as to be disqualified from public office.[28]

With all the wrangling and disappointments, Penn had ample reason to be proud of Pennsylvania. As he journeyed about, on horseback or in his six-oared galley, he saw land being cleared and crops springing up. The city was growing by leaps and bounds—three hundred and fifty-seven houses in the summer of 1684, many of them substantially built of brick. On Front Street, Samuel Carpenter was finishing a quay large enough to accommodate ships of five hundred tons capacity. Penn estimated that there were more than eight thousand people in the province.[29]

But there was one threat to his province that Penn could not overlook—and that was Lord Baltimore. The Proprietor of Maryland had definitely established the position of the fortieth parallel—at a point just north of the growing city of Philadelphia. There was no question as to where the line lay, and that line was the northern boundary of Maryland according to the patent given Baltimore's father in 1632. To back up his claim Baltimore sent Colonel George Talbot to the Schuylkill River to demand possession of all the land south of the fortieth parallel. Worse yet, Talbot built a small fort within five miles of New Castle, and announced that he was there to stay.[30]

The boundary controversy had gone beyond a point that could be settled by compromise between the two Proprietors. In the spring of 1684 Lord Baltimore sailed for England to lay his case before the Lords of Trade. Penn dared not leave his own claims undefended. He wrote to the Duke of York informing him of Baltimore's departure and added, "I am following him as fast as I can." In August Penn, too, was on his way to England.[31]

Providence favored Penn. Within a few weeks of his arrival in England his friend, the Duke of York, succeeded to the throne as James II. Nor did the news that came out of Maryland improve the position of Lord Baltimore. In line with the developing imperial policy, the Commissioners of Customs had stationed a collector at the Maryland ports. To Baltimore this was an invasion of his proprietary rights, and the collector's activities were resented if not hindered. In the autumn of 1684 the collector was aboard a ship lying in Chesapeake Bay off the mouth of the Patuxent River. Colonel Talbot came aboard. A violent quarrel ensued, and Talbot fatally stabbed the collector, who, of course, was the King's agent.[32]

Whatever chance Baltimore might have had for a fair decision was at an end. The Lords of Trade forced a compromise on the title to the Delaware Counties, and the question of the boundary between Maryland and Pennsylvania was temporarily lost sight of in a *quo warranto* against Baltimore's patent. It was desirable, reported the Lords to the King, that Maryland be brought to "a nearer and more immediate dependence upon your Majesty."[33]

Quo Warranto

THE LORDS OF TRADE, before whom Penn and Baltimore argued their respective claims, were a committee of the King's Privy Council. Their authority and functions stemmed from the problems incident to a colonial empire. The colonies had been created by the King, that is, they existed by virtue of patents issued by him. It had become an accepted constitutional principle that such dependencies were the immediate charges of the King rather than of Parliament. Thus, colonial administration lay exclusively in the hands of the King and his personally selected advisers, namely, the Privy Council.

As the colonies grew and administrative problems increased, special committees were, from time to time, directed to study these problems and make recommendations to the Privy Council. In some cases the committees were made up entirely from the membership of the Council; again, leading merchants might be included. Such a committee had, in 1664, directed the Nicolls Commission to bring New England into line with the imperial program—and had failed as we have already seen—on pages 14 to 17. Later the Earl of Shaftesbury, one of the proprietors of Carolina, had headed a Council of Trade and Plantations. In 1675 the committee was reconstituted as the Lords of Trade and Plantations. It was this latter committee which, in 1676, sent Edward Randolph to Massachusetts with a letter from the King questioning that colony's annexation of Maine and New Hampshire, and directing that agents be sent to England to justify its actions. In addition, Randolph had been ordered to investigate the form of government established in Massachusetts, its commercial and military strength, and particularly its observation of the trade and navigation laws of England.[1]

These trade and navigation laws, like the committees on trade, had their genesis in the problems created by colonies beyond the seas. In 1619 the Virginia Company had found itself faced with severe competition in marketing the tobacco raised in its colony. The King stepped in and saved the situation by practically giving Virginia-grown tobacco a monopoly of the home market. In return, however, the King ordered that "henceforth all Tobacco and other commodities whatsoever to be brought and traded from the foresaid plantation shall not be carried into any forraine partes until the same have beene first landed here and his Majesties Customes paid therefore." In other words, if the Mother Country had to support the market, it intended to control the market—and collect the customs.

Such was the theory of colonial trade as laid down by James I in 1621, but forty years were to pass before the program was systematically worked out. Nor was it enforced with any regularity. Even under royal governors, Virginia shipped much of its tobacco directly to Holland in Dutch ships.[2]

Meanwhile Massachusetts, Maryland, Connecticut, Rhode Island, and Carolina had been created under corporate or proprietary patents which placed them beyond the immediate supervision of the King and in a manner gave them grounds for questioning the application of the navigation acts. Massachusetts, especially, had openly disregarded the acts, basing her action on the principle that laws passed by

Parliament extended only to the seas bounding England and did not "reach America. The subjects of his Majesty here being not represented in Parliament so wee have not looked at ourselves to be impeded in our trade by them. . . ." [3]

And certainly the trade of Massachusetts had not been "impeded." Ketches ranged up and down the coast picking up cargoes of anything that would sell. Larger ships, built at Boston, Salem, and other towns, carried this produce to Europe and Africa where it was traded for other commodities, often including negro slaves, that would bring a price in the West Indies. There in turn molasses, sugar, cotton, and iron were bought and carried back to the American colonies. In 1676 Randolph reported to the Lords of Trade that there were two hundred and thirty ships, of from fifty to two hundred and fifty tons capacity, owned in Massachusetts, while several new ships were built each year for sale abroad. "There is no notice taken of the act of navigation, plantation, or any other lawes made in England for the regulation of trade," he said. "All nations having free liberty to come into their ports and vend their commodities, without any restraint. . . ." [4]

It was, however, on the question of jurisdiction over Maine and New Hampshire rather than of shipping that the Lords of Trade first came to grips with Massachusetts. Both Gorges and Mason, the claimants respectively of Maine and New Hampshire, were insistent upon restitution of their colonies. Massachusetts, in compliance with the King's command (see page 55), had sent agents to justify its action in annexing these colonies, but their evasive tactics had irritated rather than persuaded the Lords. Nor had Randolph, back in England from his unhappy visit to Boston, any kind words for the magistrates of Massachusetts; in addition to their seizure of Maine and New Hampshire, he charged them with having protected the regicides; with having illegally coined money; with having "put his Majesty's Subjects to death for opinion in matters of Religion" and so on through a long indictment. [5]

On July 20, 1677, the Privy Council gave its verdict, and the King concurred: The government and the soil of Maine

belonged to Gorges as heir of his grandfather, Sir Ferdinando
Gorges. Mason had a valid claim to proprietorship over the
soil of New Hampshire, but since his grandfather's patent
from the Council for New England had not been confirmed
by the King, he had no rights in the government of the
province. Neither colony fell within the bounds or under the
jurisdiction of Massachusetts. And that seemingly settled the
long controversy. Not even a present of ten barrels of cranberries, two hogsheads of "special good" samp (hominy),
and three thousand codfish, which Massachusetts sent to the
King, had any effect. A few masts might possibly have saved
the day; they had done so when crises had arisen in years
past (see pages 16 and 20).[6]

Still, if cranberries, samp, and codfish did not appeal to
King Charles, the magistrates at Boston were aware that
cold cash would appeal to Gorges—and from him they quietly
bought the patent of Maine. The Privy Council and the King
had just got through certifying that the patent was good—
that it granted the right to govern the province and to dispose
of the land within its boundaries. Now, those rights presumably became the property of Massachusetts, and in accordance with them Massachusetts continued her authority in
Maine.[7]

This piece of sharp action did not contribute to the popularity of Massachusetts with the King and his Council. Nor
did Randolph permit the King to forget the other sins of the
magistrates at Boston: They made laws that were repugnant
to the laws of England; they did not permit the Church of
England service; and always the old refrain that they violated the laws of trade and the navigation acts. So serious
were his charges that the Lords of Trade began talking about
a *Quo Warranto* against the Massachusetts patent. The
agents of the colony made the best defense they could, and
tried to excuse where they could not defend, but each time
Randolph came back with more charges.[8]

The policy of Massachusetts had been to spin out the hearings, to put off any definite decision, to wear the Lords down.
That had worked in the past. But this time it did not. Whenever things seemed to be quieting down, Randolph bobbed

up with still more charges. For two solid years he dinned into the ears of the Lords the various misdemeanors of Massachusetts, and in the end he got action. He was authorized to proceed to America and establish New Hampshire as a royal province, wholly separate from Massachusetts. Also he was given a commission as Collector of Customs for New England and directed to enforce the navigation acts. But his demand for the issuance of a *Quo Warranto* against the Massachusetts patent was ignored.[9]

In December, 1679, Randolph was back in Boston. He was, as he reported, and without exaggeration, received "more like a spy, than one of His Majesty's servants." A local rhymester accurately summed up the feeling of most of the people toward the royal official:

> "Welcome, Sir, welcome from ye easterne Shore,
> With a commission stronger than before
> To play the horse-leach; robb us of our fleeces,
> To rend our land, and teare it all to pieces;
>
> .   .   .   .
>
> Boston make roome, Randolph's returned, that hector,
> Confirm'd at home to be ye· sharp Collector"

and so on for many uncomplimentary lines.[10]

Randolph's first important job—that of establishing the new royal government in New Hampshire—went off without mishap, though it was amply evident that the people of that colony did not wish to be separated from Massachusetts and that they were fearful of the claims that Mason, as proprietor, might make on their lands. John Cutt, "a very just and honest man, cast out of all Publick Employment by the Government of Boston," according to Randolph, accepted the office of President of the province, and several of the leading men somewhat reluctantly took places on the Council. A General Assembly put together and approved a body of laws —and New Hampshire was started on her way as a self-governing, separate colony. In the commission to Cutt, however, was the ominous statement that future land titles would be subject to the payment of quitrents to be arranged with Mason.[11]

As Collector of Customs for New England, Randolph was not so successful. In that job he was, of course, primarily dependent upon the Massachusetts magistrates for police assistance—and he did not get it. When he tried to condemn illegal shipments, the goods or the ships were removed under his nose; and if he brought suit in the local courts, he found himself faced with counter damage suits. No one dared help him; his deputies were beaten up and their families turned out of their houses. "I expect hourly to have my person seized & cast into prison," he reported to the Lords of Trade in June, 1680.[12]

By the following March, Randolph realized that Massachusetts was too much for him, and returned to England. On the basis of past experience, that should have been the end of it, but not with Randolph. No sooner was he in England than he again bombarded the King and the Lords of Trade with complaints against the Governor and magistrates of Massachusetts: They had no regard for the King's commands; they constantly violated the navigation acts; their behavior amounted to "no lesse than High Treason"; only a *Quo Warranto* against their patent would bring them to reason. The Attorney-general, to whom the complaints were referred, was inclined to agree with Randolph. But the King was not yet ready for such drastic action; he temporized by writing a letter to the Massachusetts authorities in which he scolded them for their past actions, told them to observe the navigation laws, and ordered them to send over new agents with sufficient powers to settle the points at issue. With this letter Randolph again sailed for Massachusetts in the autumn of 1681.[13]

Even with Randolph on the high seas the Lords were not permitted to forget New England. News began flowing in from New Hampshire. Mason had arrived and, by the King's order, been admitted as a member of the Council. But the people, and even the Council, refused to recognize him as Proprietor of the province. The crux of the trouble was Mason's demand for quitrents, which he needed desperately, but which the settlers could ill-afford to pay and did not feel they should pay. Mason complained that some members of the Council asserted that "neither His Majesty nor [himself] had anything to doe in the province or right to any land therein. . . ." He asked the Lords to "require and command the inhabitants to acknowledge and receive him as their true and lawful proprietor." The King, who was probably thoroughly weary of Mason, met the situation by appointing one Edward Cranfield as governor, and sending him over in the vain hope that he might straighten out the situation.[14]

Hardly had the King and his Council thus settled the New Hampshire business, before a flood of new complaints against Massachusetts came pouring in from Randolph. He had arrived at Boston—for his third visit—in December, 1681. .This time the Massachusetts magistrates really made things hot for him. Not only did he get no help in collecting customs, but he was charged with being a "Subverter of their Government"—a crime punishable by death under the Massachusetts laws. ". . . if they can by any meanes they will take away my life," he wrote to the Lords, adding, "Nothing will serve but bringing a Quo Warranto against their Charter: which may save my life & reform this Government."[15]

Incessant reports of this sort, overdrawn though they were, stirred the Lords of Trade to greater activity than the Massachusetts magistrates realized. Grudgingly they again sent agents to defend their patent against the growing attack. And, at about the same time, the Lords ordered Randolph home "to attend the further progress of the business of New England, either in the Regulation of the Government upon the receit of the powers which his Majesty has directed to be sent over to the Agents here, or in default thereof, in the prosecution of the Quo Warranto intended to bee brought against their Charter."[16]

The issuance of a writ of Quo Warranto against a colony was not without precedent. The Virginia patent had been annulled in 1624 through such an action. A Quo Warranto had been brought against Massachusetts in 1635 but had failed to take effect. Now, in the early 1680's the Quo Warranto assumed great political importance as an instrument for breaking down all sorts of chartered liberties and privi-

leges. *Quo Warrantos* were brought against the charter of
the city of London, against Oxford and against many other
corporations throughout England. Some stood trial and lost;
others submitted without trial. The purpose of the actions
was to concentrate power in the hands of the King. And, for
the moment, the King had it all his own way. What he asked
for, the judges gave.[17]

It was in this atmosphere that the Massachusetts agents
arrived in England. Make what defense they might, their
patent seemed doomed. "We stand in need of help from
Heaven," one of them wrote back to Boston, and the practical men of that town took the hint. In June, 1683, we find
John Hull, he who minted the Pine Tree shillings, directing
his London man of business to make funds available to the
agents. The purpose, said Hull bluntly, was "to buy our peaceable enjoyments of men."[18]

But the bribe, if a bribe would have served, came too late.
In that same month of June, a *Quo Warranto* against the
Massachusetts patent was issued by the Attorney-general of
England. In October Randolph was back at Boston where
he served the writ on the colony.[19]

It had been hoped by the Lords of Trade that Massachusetts would submit and ask for terms rather than attempt to
defend herself at the King's Bench. As a matter of fact, some
of the magistrates were for yielding, but dared not stand
against the violent opposition of the ministers. And considering the background of the colony, the ministers were right.
Massachusetts had been founded as a refuge from the "corruptions" of the Church of England. A new form of church
organization—the Congregational—had been established in
the colony. The civil government existed primarily as a
means of perpetuating that church organization. In all matters of importance the magistrates called upon the ministers
of the churches for advice, and from their Bibles the ministers provided the guidance needed. During the first thirty
years of the colony it was a frankly accepted fact that only
those who belonged to one of the Congregational churches
could vote for magistrates or members of the General Assembly; and, despite all the admonitions of the King since

1660, that practice still continued. The right to govern their colony in their own way was guaranteed in the patent received from King Charles I in 1629. If that patent fell, the church-state government of Massachusetts would fall. ". . . do not sin in giving away the inheritance of your fathers," thundered the ministers.[20]

The decision was to contest the writ. A London lawyer was engaged to appear at the King's Bench for the colony. But all to no avail. The Lords of Trade shifted the suit to the Court of Chancery; no time was allowed for an answer; and on October 23, 1684, the patent was annulled. Massachusetts as founded by John Winthrop, Thomas Dudley, and the old leaders legally ceased to exist.[21]

In fact, Massachusetts, which at one time seemed destined to expand throughout New England, was now to be swallowed up in New England. With it, under a single government, were to be combined Maine, New Hampshire, and the King's Province on Narragansett Bay. Plymouth, Connecticut and Rhode Island would soon be brought under the same government either by submission or by *Quo Warrantos.*[22]

Still Massachusetts clung to hope. She had not been officially advised of the change. Her General Court continued to rule as in the past. A revolution in England might save her as it had in 1640. The easy-going King Charles was growing old. The Duke of York was heir apparent, and the Duke was not popular in England. As an advocate of unlimited royal power he was disliked; as a Catholic he was distrusted. On February 6, 1685, Charles died and the Duke ascended the throne under the title of James II. Instantly rebellion raised its head. The Duke of Monmouth, illegitimate son of Charles, made an armed bid for Protestant support—and lost. For the moment James, who more than Charles had been back of the move to reorganize the colonies, was supreme.[23]

These disturbing events had interrupted the activities of the Lords of Trade. Even Penn and Baltimore, in England with their boundary controversy, were forced to cool their heels and their tempers; Randolph heard that both of them were apt to lose their provinces through *Quo Warrantos.*[24]

However, as the year 1685 wore along, the Lords again

settled down to the problem of how New England should be governed, and arrived at a decision. In place of governors, magistrates, and assemblies, elected by the freemen of the colonies, New England would receive, by appointment from the King, a General Governor and Council who would make the necessary laws and administer justice. In the main, these new officials were to be selected from men of standing in the various colonies. But Randolph saw to it that he himself was appointed Secretary. Also, he got a place on the Council for his friend Mason, though he did suggest that the Lords "advise him to moderation." [25]

And well might Randolph have worried about Mason's moderation. His deficiency in that grace was keeping New Hampshire in a constant turmoil. He insisted that the inhabitants of the province were his tenants and as such must pay him quitrents for their land. Governor Cranfield, upon his arrival, gave wholehearted support to Mason's claim—in consideration of a financial interest. Collecting, however, was a different matter. For example, Goodwife Cotton, of Strawberry Bank, informed the Provost Marshal that "he was a Rogue & a Rascall & all that he was concerned with were Rogues and Rascalls." Furthermore she threatened to scald him with hot water if he came into her house. Seabank Hog set forth that "the governor and the rest of the gentlemen were a crew of pitiful curs." Through packed juries the Governor and Mason could get verdicts of dispossession, but no constable cared to serve the writs. One tried it at Dover and was knocked down by a Bible in the hands of a young girl. [26]

Governor Cranfield soon found that, although he was invested with authority by the King, he lacked the power to carry out his mercenary projects. His Council turned against him; the elected assemblies were against him; the inhabitants of the towns signed petitions against him and sent them over to the King. Even the Lords of Trade refused to support him. At that point the Governor realized that the cold winters of New Hampshire did not agree with his "thinn constetution" and retired to a job in Barbados, leaving as his deputy a local character with the intriguing name of Walter Barefoot. [27]

Mason stayed on, living as a boarder at the Barefoot home. There, on the evening of December 30, 1685, Thomas Wiggins and Anthony Nutter called. They were invited to stay for supper, and accepted. After supper, which was served in the kitchen near the open fireplace, Wiggins not too politely informed Mason that he did not belong in New Hampshire, did not own any land there and never would. Mason, thereupon, ordered Wiggins out of the house, and when Wiggins declined to go, took him by the arm to hurry him along. "Whereupon," as Mason told the story, "Wiggins took hold of my cravat, and being a big, strong man, pulled me to the chimney and threw me upon the fire, and lay upon me, and did endeavor to strangle me by grasping my windpipe, that I could hardly breathe. My left foot was much scorched and swelled, my coat, periwig and stockings were burnt, and had it not been for the deputy governor, who was all that time endeavoring to pluck Wiggins off from me, I do verily believe I had been murdered. I was no sooner got out of the fire but the said Wiggins laid hands on the deputy governor, threw him into the fire, and fell upon him so that two of the deputy governor's ribs were broke. I did with much difficulty pull Wiggins off the deputy governor. Wiggins being risen upon his feet did again assault me and the deputy governor, and threw the deputy governor down; whereupon I called to a maid servant to fetch my sword, saying the villain would murder the deputy governor. The servant coming with my sword in the scabbard, I took hold thereof, but it was snatched out of my hands by Anthony Nutter. . . ." All in all, the proprietor and Deputy-governor seemed unable to cope with the situation in New Hampshire.[28]

On May 14, 1686, Edward Randolph arrived at Boston. It was his fifth visit to New England. Ten years had passed since that day in 1676 when Governor Leverett informed him that the complaints of the King against Massachusetts were "very inconsiderable things." Now Randolph came bearing commissions by which the government of Massachusetts was to be taken from the officials elected by the freemen and placed in the hands of officials appointed by the King.[29]

Joseph Dudley was to be the new President of New England. He had lately served as one of the agents of Massachusetts in the hearings before the Lords of Trade. He had been one of the magistrates who, in 1676, had listened to the reading of the King's letter. He was a graduate of Harvard University. He was, in fact, a native-born New Englander, the son of Thomas Dudley, one of the leaders among the founders of Massachusetts. While Joseph was still a child, his father died; his mother subsequently married John Allen, minister at Dedham; and young Dudley grew up in the Allen household—all of which brings up an interesting incident. Back in 1648 Allen was delivering a sermon before the ministers at the Cambridge synod when into his vacant chair crawled a snake. Governor Winthrop commented at the time, "Nothing falling out but by divine providence, it is out of doubt, the Lord discovered somewhat of his mind in it." Whether or not anyone remembered the portent, certain it is that in 1686 the people of Massachusetts looked upon Joseph Dudley as a snake in the vacant chair.[30]

It was a somber meeting that took place in the Town-House at Boston on May 17. Present was Simon Bradstreet; for fifty-seven years he had served the Massachusetts Bay Company in an official capacity; he had been Governor since 1679; he was now eighty-three years of age. Present were the Massachusetts magistrates; some had been included as members in the new Council; most of them had been ignored. Present was Joseph Dudley, the new President. Present was Robert Mason, a member of the new Council—with a new periwig, we will hope. Present was Edward Randolph, the new Secretary. Present was Captain George, resplendent in his naval uniform; he was master of his Majesty's frigate, *The Rose,* which had brought Randolph to Boston and was lying in the harbor. Samuel Sewall, John Hull's son-in-law, dropped in. Governor Hinckley, of Plymouth, was an interested spectator.

Addressing himself to Governor Bradstreet and the magistrates, President Dudley spoke:

"And first I must acquaint you that we may now take you only for such as you are (viz.) considerable gentlemen of this place and Inhabitants of all parts of the countrey, and so a proper assembly to have his Majesties commands communicated to you, and under that notion we treat with you. We may not deal with you as a Governour and Company any more."

He then went on to explain the reasons for the change in government. When he had finished, former Deputy-governor Danforth inquired:

"I presume you expect no reply from the Court?"

to which Dudley answered,

"I know no Court here in being till the Kings court be in order and settled."

And that was the end of the Massachusetts Bay Company, the end of the government which President Joseph Dudley's father had helped to found in 1629. Silently most of the company filed out. Some stayed a few minutes to talk in groups —wondering what they could do. But they could do nothing. It had been done.[31]

The change in government brought no immediate change in the everyday life of the people. There was the novelty of a Church of England service on Sundays—conducted by the Rev. Robert Ratcliff, who came over with Randolph. The majority of the inhabitants had never seen such a show and they flocked to it out of curiosity. But when Randolph and Mason suggested that one of the three Congregational meetinghouses of Boston be made available for Ratcliff's services, there was a quick refusal by the members.[32]

Randolph had brought along with him a pocketful of *Quo Warrantos*—against Rhode Island, Connécticut, East Jersey, West Jersey, and even Delaware. The first two he promptly served. Rhode Island agreed to submit without a suit; Connecticut gave a receipt for the writ and said nothing. The fact was that none of the writs were any good; the dates for delivery had expired; but they served their purpose. Those to whom they were addressed knew what was intended and that resistance was useless. The American colonies were to be knit into a unified dependency of the King.[33]

It was recognized that the Dudley regime in New England was temporary—paving the way for a royal governor. Several names had been considered by the Lords of Trade, but the choice fell upon Sir Edmund Andros, formerly Governor at New York. He was a soldier and a capable administrator, a man who would carry out faithfully the King's program, but not a man likely to understand the Puritans of New England or to be understood by them. In June, 1686, he was commissioned as Captain-general and Governor of the Territory and Dominion of New England, which included Massachusetts, Maine, New Hampshire, the King's Province, and Plymouth. The area eastward from the Kennebec, commonly called Pemaquid, was added a short time later. Connecticut and Rhode Island still retained their separate corporate existences—but not for long.[34]

On the Sabbath morning, December 19, 1686, while reading the Bible to his family, Samuel Sewall heard a great gun or two, and correctly surmised that Sir Edmund Andros had arrived at Boston. Mr. Willard, in his sermon at South Church, later in the morning, said he "was fully persuaded and confident God would not forget the Faith of those who came first to New England, but would remember their Posterity with kindness."[35]

The following day Sir Edmund and several of his officers came ashore. Their bright scarlet coats interested the townspeople. Former Governor Bradstreet and other leading men met them at the landing. Eight companies of the Massachusetts militia stood at attention as the new royal governor proceeded to the Town House where members of the Council awaited him. Samuel Sewall wrote in his diary, "The day was serene but somewhat cold."[36]

Along the Trading Paths

CAROLINA, LIKE THE other colonies not already under royal control, was threatened with a *Quo Warranto* but escaped—partly because the proprietors were men of high station in England and partly because they readily offered to surrender their patent, for a consideration.[1]

The fact was that the Carolina proprietors probably would have welcomed an opportunity to sell out to the King. The Earl of Shaftesbury was dead and the other members of the group had no great interest in colonizing America. Individual planters and merchants, actually living in Carolina, particularly in the Charleston area, were laying firm foundations for future fortunes, but the absentee proprietors were not reaping profits commensurate with their investments or their hopes.[2]

Not even the monopoly of the Westoe trade had turned out as the proprietors expected. The merchants at Charleston, excluded from this most profitable business, easily found grounds for a war against the Westoe—largely carried on by instigating other Indians to make the attack. By 1682 a wan-

dering band of Shawnee was in possession of the Westoe town
on the upper Savannah River. Such of the Westoe as survived, and could be caught, were brought down to Charleston by their Indian masters and sold as slaves to the enterprising English merchants—for shipment to the sugar islands.[3]

In these events we may view the ever recurring cost of
civilization. For the sake of their own well-being in England
—perhaps a new coach or coat—the proprietors, by presents
of guns and offers of coveted trade goods, had encouraged a
favored tribe of natives to kill and skin deer in numbers far
greater than had been their custom or need. The upland
forests were fetid with the rotting carcasses of animals slaughtered only for their hides. The Westoes rolled in wealth—
knives, axes, bright cloth, beads. Envy quickly found takers.
The colonists wanted a part in the trade; other Indians
wanted a part in the English merchandise. The bodies of the
Westoe joined the carcasses of the deer or sweated out a few
short years on the sugar plantations of Barbados. First the
deer, then the Indian, paid the price of progress.

With the Westoe thus wiped out, Henry Woodward, who
directed the Indian trade for the Proprietors, began pushing
his operations southward and westward from the Savannah
River. Soon he collided not only with the Spanish in Florida
but with a Scottish colony recently established at Port Royal,
near presentday Beaufort, South Carolina.[4]

Port Royal had been the site of a short-lived French colony
in 1562–63. It was there that the Carolina expedition of
1669 had been directed to plant its colony, but fear of the
Spaniards had caused the leaders to move on up the coast
to Ashley River. Now, in 1684, a company of Scotchmen,
under arrangement with the Carolina proprietors, selected
this place as a refuge from religious persecution in their
homeland. Stuart's Town, as the colony was named, did not
come under the government established at Charleston, which
irritated the older settlement. The fact that the newcomers
were Scotch also made for strained relations with their English neighbors. Robert Quary, acting governor at Charleston,
refused to provide the arms known to be needed and requested by the Stuart's Town people. On their part the

Scotch acted without much regard for the welfare of Charleston. Lord Cardross, the leader at Stuart's Town, placed Woodward under arrest for presuming to trade with the Indians on the lower Savannah River. He encouraged Indian raids against the nearby Spanish. And retaliation came quickly.[5]

In September, 1686, three Spanish galleys came creeping up the coast. Aboard were perhaps a hundred Florida Indians led by a few well-armed Spaniards. Some of the Scots were killed outright, their buildings were burned, their property carried off. And that was the end of Stuart's Town. Spain had called a halt to British expansion toward St. Augustine.[6]

With Woodward and his skin traders the Spaniards were not so successful. Peddling his kettles and beads along the Indian path, Woodward heard constantly of richer trade ahead. Two hundred miles beyond the old Westoe town he came to the Chattahoochee River. On its western bank stood Coweta, one of the principal villages of the Lower Creek Indians. A few miles down the river was the recently abandoned Mission of Savacola, from which Franciscan friars had vainly striven to Christianize the Creeks and bring them within the sphere of Spain. The Indians had shown little interest in the spiritual message of the friars but they were keenly alive to the value of Woodward's trade goods. It was not long before the deer skins collected at Coweta were being packed along the path to Charleston rather than southward to the Spanish traders at Apalache (see map on page 123).

News of this invasion naturally reached Antonio Matheos, commander of the Spanish garrison at Apalache. With a mixed force of Indians and soldiers he marched northward to expel the English. But all he found was a deserted Indian village and an impudent letter from Woodward expressing his regret at being absent. Back to Apalache marched Matheos—and back to Coweta came Woodward. This was too much, and again Matheos marched northward. Again he found no one home—the Creeks were all on a hunt, or so he was told by the few old people he overtook. He did, however, discover Woodward's storehouse and took out his wrath on it. A considerable amount of English merchandise along with several hundred deer skins went up in smoke. Similar vengeance was meted out to the town of Coweta, as a suggestion that it did not pay to deal with Englishmen. But that was all Matheos could do, and hardly was he on his way back to Apalache before the Indians were rebuilding their flimsy town and Woodward was refilling a new storehouse.

In the late summer of 1686—at about the time that the Spaniards were attacking Stuart's Town—Woodward started his caravan eastward from Coweta. Pack horses and pack-laden Indians stumbled along the rough, narrow path, forded Flint River, waded the Ocmulgee and the Oconee, rafted the Savannah. Woodward himself, too ill to walk, was carried on a litter. Twenty years had passed since that day in 1666 when he had voluntarily remained with the Indians at Port Royal—to learn their languages and their ways of life. Well may he have reflected, as he jolted along, that the young city of Charleston owed its prosperity, if not its existence, to his success in developing a trade in skins with the Indians.

He probably did not know that, even as his long caravan toiled eastward, the Scotch settlement at Port Royal was being destroyed. However, a few of his men, following a path near the coast, fell into the hands of unfriendly Indians. They lost their packs and their lives—unfortunate, but a part of the risk assumed by those who engaged in the Indian trade.

Woodward brought his main caravan safely into Charleston. The wages paid to his traders brought prosperity to the town. The customs paid to the collector brought revenue to the King. The freight paid for transportation helped to increase England's seapower. The wages and profits which came from the finished leather added to England's growing commercial strength. What was more, Woodward had opened a path into the interior of America—a path along which there would be a market for English manufactures— a path along which English traders would compete with Spaniards and Frenchmen not only for business but for the sovereignty of a continent.

To the northward of Carolina the trading path was controlled from Virginia. As early as 1670 Governor Berkeley

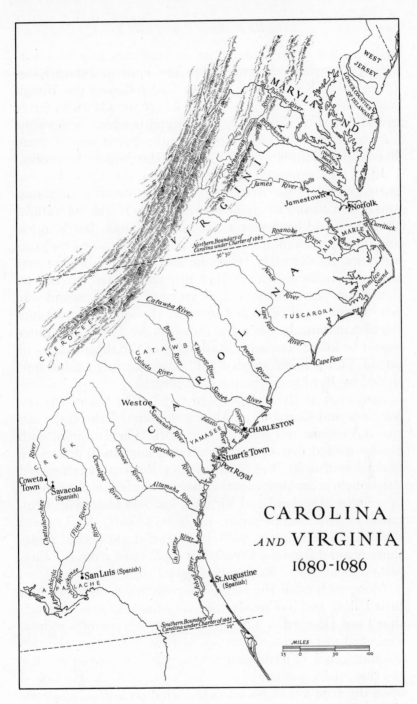

WEST
JERSEY

LOWER COUNTIES
OF DELAWARE

MARYLA
ND

Potomac River

Rappahannock

V
I
R
G
I
N
I
A

Shenandoah

Northern
Neck
River

James River Falls

Jamestown

Norfolk

Roanoke River

Currituck

ALBE MARLE
Chowan River

Northern Boundary of
Carolina under Charter of 1665
36° 30'

Neuse River

Pamlico Sound

C
H
E
R
O
K
E
E

Catawba River

C A R O L I N A

TUSCARORA

Cape Fear River

C A T A W B A

Broad River

Wateree River

Saluda River

Cape Fear

Westoe

Santee River

Pee Dee River

Savannah River

Edisto River

Ashley River

Cooper River

CHARLESTON

River

C R E E K

Ogeechee River

YAMASEE

Stuart's Town

Coweta
Town

Savacola
(Spanish)

Ocmulgee River

Oconee River

Altamaha River

Port Royal

Chattahoochee River

(Flint River)

St. Marys River

Ochlockonee River

San Luis (Spanish)

A
P
A
LACHE

Apalachicola

St. Johns River

St. Augustine
(Spanish)

Southern Boundary of
Carolina under Charter of 1665
29°

CAROLINA
AND VIRGINIA
1680 · 1686

MILES
25 0   50   100

123

had sent one John Lederer on an exploring trip into Virginia's hinterland. Starting from the Falls of James River (presentday Richmond) Lederer had followed the Indian path southwestward to the region where the Catawba River breaks out of the Blue Ridge. The reports which he brought back showed the possibilities for trade. But it was William Byrd rather than Governor Berkeley who reaped the profits.[8]

Byrd had extensive land holdings at the Falls. He imported merchandise from England for his own plantations, and he ran a store where he sold to others. It was but natural that he should have sent a few packs of cloth, beads, guns, and other merchandise down the path to be traded for skins and furs. By the early 1680's he had a flourishing business with the Indians. There were ups and downs, of course. Sometimes the cloth which he received from England was not just the shade of color desired by the squaws; sometimes Barbadian brandy flowed a little too freely and a trader would be killed; but with it all, most of the ships that went out of James River carried a few hogsheads of skins consigned by Byrd to his factor in England.[9]

And even as Byrd dominated the Indian trade between Virginia and Carolina so Albany dominated the trade between Virginia and central New York. The Iroquois, with guns provided first by the Dutch and later by the English, had pressed down the Susquehanna River and conquered the doughty Susquehannocks. Before them lay the valleys of western Maryland and Virginia, sparsely filled with weak bands of Indians. In return for beaver skins, the Iroquois supplied those Indians with European trade goods, sometimes secured from the French but more often from the English merchants at Albany (see map on page 33).

Along with trade the young Iroquois braves indulged in a little killing and looting. In fact, they made so much trouble that Lord Howard of Effingham, the Governor of Virginia, suggested to Governor Dongan, of New York, that the two colonies join in exterminating them. This, of course, was the last thing the Governor of New York wished to do. He looked upon the Iroquois as his particular charges and as an essential buffer between New York and the French settlements along the St. Lawrence River. Accordingly, he invited the Governor of Virginia to accompany him to Albany for a talk with the Iroquois chiefs.

When the treaty opened, late in July, 1684, the two governors were faced by representatives of the Mohawk, Oneida, Onondaga, and Cayuga. The Seneca were too far away to attend, and were, in any case, not involved in the outrages. The Mohawk also disclaimed any part in the southern raids. The Oneida, Cayuga, and Onondaga admitted that their young men might have behaved badly and offered a present of beaver skins as a token of repentance. For the future they promised that the covenant chain between themselves and the people of Maryland and Virginia should be kept "bright as silver." The treaty was concluded by the burial, in the courtyard at Albany, of five axes—one each for the Oneida, the Onondaga, the Cayuga, Maryland, and Virginia.[10]

Throughout the conference the Iroquois addressed Lord Howard as "Big Knife," confusing his name with a Dutch word meaning cutlass. Thus was coined a designation by which for more than a hundred years Virginians were to be known among the northern Indians.[11]

Governor Dongan took advantage of the Albany meeting to trick the Iroquois into signing a statement—written on "two white dressed deer skins"—admitting that they were the subjects of the King of England. This was thought to be a neat offset to the claim of the French that the Iroquois were the subjects of the King of France. But when it came to an issue, the Iroquois refused to recognize either claim. Chief Outreouati, of the Onondaga, addressing the English later in the summer of 1684, stated the Iroquois position: The French were their Father; the English were their Brother—this because the Indians themselves "willed it so," he said. "Neither the one nor the other is my master. He who made the world has given me the land I occupy. I am free."[12]

To the Governor of New France Outreouati voiced a similar message: "We are born free. We no more depend upon Onnontio [their French Father] than on Corlaer [their English Brother]. We can go where we will, to take there what we think proper, and buy and sell as we please." This was a

point of view that the French refused to accept. Either the
Iroquois should behave as the dutiful Children of their French
Father or they should be eliminated altogether. King Louis
thought it would be a good idea to have the braves sent over
to France, there to pull oars in the royal galleys. But when
the Governor of Canada tried to put this policy into effect
the results were not all the King anticipated.[13]

For example, in 1687 the Senecas, most westerly of the
Iroquois nations, were marked for punishment. Governor
Denonville, with some two thousand regular troops, militiamen and voyageurs, moved up the St. Lawrence River to
Fort Frontenac, opposite the Indian towns. Re-enforcements
were ordered in from the west. Tonti and his Indian allies
hurried overland from the Illinois country. Duluth and other
officers came down from the upper lakes, joining Tonti at
Detroit. As the combined party paddled eastward along Lake
Erie they picked up a convoy of English fur traders under the
command of Major Patrick MacGregorie—headed for Michilimackinac and carrying enough brandy to have seriously
weakened French control at that strategic place.[14]

But, despite this preliminary success, the French campaign
proved a fizzle. Denonville burned a few Seneca towns, cut
down a few acres of growing corn, built a flimsy fort at Niagara, and then stopped. The Indians had been more irritated than hurt. They rebuilt their towns and planted more
corn, but their packs of furs went to Albany rather than to
Fort Frontenac, nor did the other members of the Iroquois
Confederacy feel too kindly toward their French Father. The
English made the most of the situation by offering aid and
comfort to their distressed Brothers. Tonti returned to the
west where at Fort St. Louis, perched high on an eminence
overlooking the Illinois River, he found La Salle's brother
awaiting him with a strange story.[15]

Texas

AFTER HIS RETURN from exploring the Mississippi in 1682, La Salle had spent several months with Tonti in the Illinois country. He had made grants of land to his followers; he had directed the building of Fort St. Louis on a high rocky bluff facing the Illinois River; he had assured the Indians of protection against Iroquois raids. Then, in the autumn of 1683, leaving Tonti in charge, he departed for Quebec, and sailed for France. There he laid before the King his proposal to go by sea and plant a new colony at the mouth of the Mississippi, a colony which, among other advantages, would enable France to wrest northern Mexico from the Spanish.[1]

The project appealed to King Louis. Four ships—a man-of-war and three smaller vessels—were put at La Salle's disposal. Soldiers and mechanics were assigned to the expedition. As usual, a number of adventurers volunteered, as did also several missionaries among whom were Father Membre, who had accompanied La Salle on the trip down the Mississippi, and Abbé Jean Cavelier, La Salle's brother. Around the first of August, 1684, the little fleet was on its way to the Gulf of Mexico.[2]

The voyage was long. Misunderstanding and distrust developed between La Salle and the commander of the fleet. In the West Indies one of the small ships was captured by the Spaniards. December was well advanced when they rounded Cuba and turned northward into the Gulf. Soon they sighted the coast line, and day after day followed it westward. But La Salle could not identify the mouth of the Mississippi. They may, in fact, have been west of it when they first sighted the coast. Utterly confused, La Salle decided to land his colony. In the operation one of the two remaining small vessels was wrecked and much-needed supplies were lost. Still, enough food, clothing, tools, and guns were put ashore to keep the colony going, and in March, 1685, the man-of-war sailed for France.[3]

And there they were—the colony that was to people the Mississippi and conquer Mexico; there they were—piled up on a sand bar at the entrance to what today we call Matagorda Bay, a hundred and twenty miles west of presentday Galveston, Texas, four hundred and fifty miles west of the Mississippi.[4]

The one remaining small ship had been left with the colony, and it was now used to move the people and supplies to a more healthful spot—on a small river entering the top of the bay. A substantial building was erected, cannon were mounted, a palisade was put up, and the settlement was given the name of Fort St. Louis. We call it St. Louis of Texas to distinguish it from the fort on the Illinois River where Tonti was awaiting word from La Salle.[5]

About one hundred and eighty people had been landed, but dysentery and heat had taken their toll. Hostile Indians had picked off a few here and a few there as opportunity offered. Rattlesnakes had struck and their victims had succumbed. Constantly men had deserted or simply disappeared. Less than a hundred remained as the year 1685 wore along.[6]

They were a strange lot. There were the Abbé Cavelier and the other priests. There was Henri Joutel, whose father had been a gardener for La Salle's uncle. There was Duhaut, who had a considerable investment in the enterprise. There was Liotot, a surgeon. There was one Hiens, a German, formerly occupied as a buccaneer. There was Nika, a Shawnee hunter, who had accompanied La Salle when he returned to France. There were soldiers and laborers, picked up from the streets of French towns. There were women and children, even a few damsels who had come along in the expectation of finding husbands.[7]

Within the palisade were some hogs and chickens that had been brought in the ships, but the real meat supply came from the herds of buffalo that grazed nearby. The Frenchmen were amateurs at buffalo hunting and it took them some time to learn that the great shaggy beasts lived, and resented familiarities, for a considerable time after being fatally shot. Father Membre, while accompanying the men on one of their hunts, made the mistake of poking a "dead" buffalo with the butt of his gun. He was knocked down and badly trampled.[8]

With the fort in a liveable condition, La Salle left Joutel in command while he, with a number of men, started out to explore the surrounding country. Just where he went or what he learned is uncertain, but in March, 1686, he was back at the fort. Six weeks later he started out again, with twenty men. This time he travelled northeast, and at least reached the villages of the Cenis Indians, within fifty miles of the present eastern boundary of Texas. There he must have learned definitely that the Mississippi lay to the eastward.[9]

Had La Salle done his exploring by boat, he might well have met Tonti, who at that very time was hunting for him. The faithful captain had received word of La Salle's landing and in February, 1686, had started down the Mississippi, accompanied by thirty Frenchmen and a number of Indians. At the mouth of the river he had sent men east and west along the coast in canoes. For a hundred miles in either direction they had searched the shore and the inlets, but of course found no sign of the missing colony. Reluctantly Tonti turned back up the river. However, at the mouth of the Arkansas he left Jean Couture and a few men, to wait in the hope that some word might come.[10]

In August, La Salle was back at his fort above Matagorda Bay. He brought five horses that he had acquired from the

Cenis, but of the twenty men who went out with him only eight returned. The rest had died or deserted. Nor had things gone too well with the colonists during his absence. Duhaut had been busy stirring up discontent; the one remaining ship had been wrecked; death and desertion had left their mark. Scarcely thirty men, women, and children greeted the returning travellers. It was evident that relief must be sought. La Salle's decision was to try, with some of his men, to reach Tonti in the Illinois country, while a few others, with the women and children, held the fort. Twenty people, including Father Membre, were picked to stay. Seventeen, among whom were the Abbé Cavelier, Joutel, Duhaut, Liotot, and Hiens, were to accompany La Salle on the desperate journey. On January 12, 1687, the rescue party filed out of the fort and headed northeast toward the Cenis villages. With them went the five horses, well loaded with axes, knives, beads, and other trade goods.[11]

It would have been better had La Salle chosen his companions with more care. Among them were several who bore him no good will. Duhaut, especially, had gathered about himself a faction that felt, perhaps honestly, that La Salle had mismanaged the whole enterprise, that he was, even in the conduct of the present march, jeopardizing the lives of his followers and those left at the fort. Surely there was ground for such a conclusion. In two months scarcely a hundred and fifty miles had been covered. It was quite a different record from that made by La Salle in 1680 when he went from the Illinois to Fort Frontenac in practically the same length of time. Now he seemed confused, irresolute. More and more the irresponsible element in his party listened to the mutterings of Duhaut.[12]

A very small incident—hot words over a division of buffalo meat—brought the dissension to a climax. Three of La Salle's loyal supporters, including Nika, were knocked in the head by Liotot while they slept. When La Salle came to inquire for the missing men, Jean L'Archeveque, Duhaut's servant, was the only person in sight. He gave an insolent answer to La Salle's greeting and walked toward an ambush where Duhaut and Liotot crouched with their guns. As La Salle came within range two shots rang out and he fell dead. His body was stripped by Hiens and left for the wild beasts of the prairie. Thus, on March 19, 1687, along the bank of the Navasota River in eastern Texas, died the man who aspired to conquer the Mississippi.[13]

Duhaut and his fellow conspirators were now in full control of the expedition. Cavelier, Joutel and the others had no alternative but to accept the situation, unless they too wished to die. Duhaut's intention, apparently, was to return to the fort, salvage one of the ships, and get away by sea. However, since food was running short, Joutel, Hiens, and a few others were sent on easterly, to the Cenis villages, to trade knives and hatchets for corn.

They were received by the Indians in a friendly way; bowls of boiled corn were proffered by the women; a corner was cleared for them and their goods in one of the houses. These houses, Joutel tells us, looked more like large beehives or hayricks than buildings. They consisted of long poles set in a circle with the tops so drawn together that there was an opening only sufficient for the escape of smoke. This framework was then covered with hay or weeds. Some were as much as sixty feet in diameter, and the average housed from fifteen to twenty families, each having its private set of bunks, though all used the common fire always burning in the center of the house.

At this village Joutel found two Frenchmen who had deserted from La Salle on former expeditions. They had "gone Indian," discarded clothing, and collected several wives. One of them even had his face and body tattooed after the fashion of the natives. Nor, except for the tattooing, were the Indians themselves uncomely. In fact, the Frenchmen found the Indian women quite attractive, so much so that additional men came up from Duhaut's camp to do a bit of trading of one sort and another.

Thus seven weeks passed while Duhaut tried to make up his mind what to do. He had agreed to let Cavelier, Joutel, and whoever else wished, continue onward to the Illinois country, and in the end he decided that the whole party should go that way. This was too much for Hiens, the former

buccaneer and accomplice in the murder of La Salle; he had
no wish to risk his neck in a French settlement. Accompanied
by one of the deserters, he hastened over to the camp and
after a brief argument shot Duhaut while his companion extended the same treatment to Liotot.

Hiens was now in control. And as he strutted among the
beehive houses of Cenis, arrayed in La Salle's best scarlet
coat, the cynosure of all feminine eyes, he might well have
felt satisfied. His was the life to which any conscientious buccaneer looked forward. But if others wanted to travel to the
Illinois country, he had no serious objection. Nor was he un-
fair about the trade goods. To those who were leaving he gave
thirty or forty axes, four or five dozen knives, some powder
and shot, and three horses. About the first of June they started
—Cavelier, Joutel and five others.[14]

Their course lay north by east, across the Red River and
into southwestern Arkansas. Indians guided them from one
village to the next and were on the whole friendly and helpful. In fact they were sometimes too friendly. At one village
they put on a special show for the travellers. Singing at the
top of their voices, they selected Father Cavelier as the guest
of honor, probably on account of his clerical garb. They led
him to an especially prepared spot, laid handfuls of grass at
his feet, and washed his face. Then the real entertainment
began. The women joined in the singing; gourds filled with
pebbles kept the measure, while an Indian stationed behind
the priest dandled him from side to side in unison with the
music. The next scene was even better. The master of ceremonies brought two maidens and, says Joutel, "made them
sit down in such a posture that they looked one upon the
other, their legs extended and intermixed, on which the same
master of ceremonies laid M. Cavelier's legs in such manner
that they lay uppermost, and across those of the maids." At
that point the good Father rebelled, to the disgust of the
Indians and the evident disappointment of the non-clerical
Frenchmen.[15]

A few days later—July 24, to be exact—they came to a
large river, and looking over to the opposite side saw a wooden
Cross and a house built after the French fashion. They fell

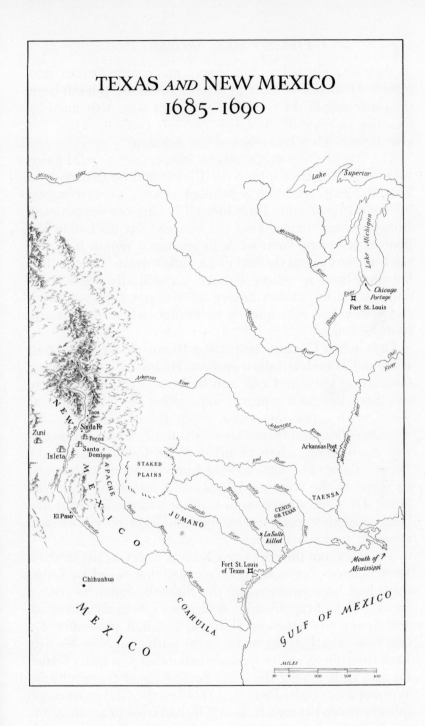

TEXAS *AND* NEW MEXICO
1685-1690

Lake Superior

Missouri River

Mississippi

Lake Michigan

River

Chicago Portage

Fort St. Louis

Illinois River

Missouri River

River

Ohio River

Arkansas River

NEW

Taos

Santa Fe

Zuni

Pecos

Arkansas River

Isleta

Santo Domingo

Mississippi River

Arkansas Post

STAKED PLAINS

APACHE

Red River

TAENSA

M E X I C O

Pecos River

Brazos

Trinity

Sabine River

JUMANO

Colorado

River

CENIS OR TEXAS

El Paso

Rio Grande

River

La Salle killed

Chihuahua

Fort St. Louis of Texas

Mouth of Mississippi

Rio Grande

COAHUILA

GULF OF MEXICO

M E X I C O

MILES
50 0   100   200   300

on their knees, lifted up their hands and eyes to heaven, and returned thanks to the Divine Goodness. Canoes put out from the other side of the river and soon they were welcomed by Couture and one of the other men left there by Tonti the year before. They had reached the Arkansas.[16]

The rest of the journey was by canoe, over a well-known route—up the Mississippi to the Illinois and up that river to Fort St. Louis, where on September 14 they were welcomed by Tonti's lieutenant, Tonti himself having not yet returned from the campaign against the Seneca. But neither to the lieutenant nor to Tonti when he arrived a month later did the travellers reveal the fact of La Salle's death. Instead they led their hosts to believe that he was still alive, and in his name asked for enough beaver skins to pay their way back to Quebec and subsequently to France, where they finally told the story.[17]

Only when Couture visited the Illinois in the autumn of 1688, did Tonti learn the true story. He immediately ordered Couture to visit the Cenis and find out if the French were still there, but the trip proved impossible. The following year Tonti, with a few men, went down the Mississippi to the Taensa village and thence westward to the Cenis villages. It was April, 1690, when he arrived. He found none of the French there. The Indians told him conflicting stories and he came to the conclusion Hiens and the others had been killed. He wanted to go on to La Salle's fort to see what had become of the people there, but could get no guides, and returned to the Arkansas.[18]

Tonti was not the only one who was worrying about those Frenchmen in Texas. It will be recalled that one of La Salle's ships had been captured by the Spanish. From its crew a general idea of the intended settlement was easily extracted, and Spain was naturally alarmed. She had just suffered a crushing setback at the hands of the natives in New Mexico. Loot from the desecrated mission churches was being traded far and wide among the nomadic Indians of the southwest. Word of a successful French foothold on the Gulf coast would quickly sweep through from one Indian tribe to another, and might be fatal; in fact, that was just what La Salle had in mind.[19]

For more than eighty years Spanish governors had ruled in New Mexico—a somewhat indefinite area along the Rio Grande from El Paso to Taos, and extending westward to Zuni (see map on page 133). The pueblo-dwelling natives, perhaps sixteen thousand in number, had grudgingly accepted a thin veneer of Christianity. Catholic churches, presided over by Franciscan missionaries, had taken the places of the Kivas where of old the Indian medicine men had conducted their heathen ceremonies.

Living in the province, widely scattered among the pueblos, were about three thousand Spanish ranchers, soldiers, and officials. Stock raising was the principal industry. Each year a long train of wagons creaked up the river from Mexico with manufactured goods and other supplies, and creaked back loaded with hides. Santa Fe was the capital, and there Governor Antonio de Otermin made his headquarters with a few officials and soldiers. Alonso Garcia acted as lieutenant-governor over the southern pueblos.[20]

Early on the morning of Saturday, August 10, 1680, Father Juan Pio, accompanied by Pedro Hidalgo, rode northward from Santa Fe toward the pueblo of Tesuque where the priest was to celebrate the Mass. But no Indians were waiting at the church. Instead, painted for war and armed with lances, bows, and arrows, they were marching out of the pueblo. Father Pio hurried after them, calling, "What is this, children, are you mad?" He was promptly murdered, and Hidalgo, getting away with difficulty, rode for his life to Santa Fe where he told his story.[21]

A similar story might have been told of all the northern pueblos. Unheard by the Spaniards, the spirit voices of the Indians' ancestors had spoken: God, the father of the Spaniards, and Santa Maria, their mother, were to die. The pueblos were to return to a religion and a way of life that was old before Spain existed. With the utmost secrecy the Indians had laid their plans—and all struck at practically the same moment.[22]

At most of the pueblos and unprotected ranch houses the surprise attacks were completely successful. Priests were knocked in the head at their altars. Ranchmen were shot in the fields. Women and children were murdered in the houses. Churches were burned. Cattle and horses were driven away. Within three days it was all over except for Santa Fe, and then the savage victors turned all their fury on that town. Prolonged defense was impossible and on August 21, with about a thousand refugees, many of them women and children, Otermin began a precarious march down the Rio Grande, hoping to find safety with Garcia at Isleta.[23]

The Indians bothered the marching Spaniards very little, satisfied apparently with seeing them depart. But along the way the refugees saw grim evidence of what had occurred. At Santo Domingo, on the east side of the Rio Grande, thirty miles below Sante Fe, they found the bodies of five Spaniards behind the church; three priests had been dumped into a common grave nearby. A little farther along they came to the house of Captain Augustin de Carbajal. The doors stood open; everything had been stolen; in the parlor and an adjoining room lay the bodies of the Captain, his wife, a grown daughter, and another woman. Much the same was the condition at the home of Cristobal de Anaya: he and his wife, six children, and some others—twelve in all—lay dead by the door, their bodies stripped.[24]

Well may Otermin and his band have counted the leagues to Isleta and the reinforcements which Garcia would bring. But when they got to Isleta it was completely deserted. Garcia had seen something of what was going on; he had been told that all the Spaniards to the northward were dead; and he too had started down the river with some fifteen hundred poorly armed refugees.[25]

However, succor for both Garcia and Otermin was at hand. For the better part of a year, a wagon train had been plodding up the road from Mexico City—with supplies for New Mexico. At just this time it arrived at El Paso, escorted by a company of soldiers. Men and food were hurried northward to meet the refugees, and shortly the entire surviving Spanish population of New Mexico was encamped at El Paso. Many of them stayed there, creating a permanent settlement. Some futile efforts were made to recover the lost province, but for a decade the pueblo dwellers of the upper

Rio Grande maintained their independence. The traders began looking for new fields from which to recoup their losses.[26]

A profitable trade in buffalo hides had long existed between New Mexico and the Jumano, a tribe of Indians who followed the migrations of the great herds as they passed southward along the Staked Plains (see map on page 133). The Pueblo uprising had, of course, broken Spanish contact with this nomadic people. In 1683, however, a few Jumano appeared at El Paso and asked that the trade be resumed. The Spaniards were willing enough, but a new road had to be found—one that would avoid both the hostile Pueblos and the wild Apache who had joined with them. With the Jumano emissaries as guides, an expedition pushed down the Rio Grande a hundred and fifty miles and more, turned northward across the Pecos, and then east to the upper waters of the Colorado River of Texas. There they found the Jumano encampment. So promising were the prospects, both for hides and for converts to the Cross, that plans were made for a trading post and a mission.[27]

At just this time came news that La Salle, with three ships and two or three hundred people, had sailed into the Gulf of Mexico with the intention of planting a colony somewhere along its northern shore. The Viceroy of Mexico was ordered to find the Frenchmen. Ships from Vera Cruz searched the coast in 1686 without results. The following year more ships engaged in the hunt. The wrecks of La Salle's two vessels were discovered at Matagorda Bay, but the fort up the river escaped detection.[28]

In 1688 Alonso de Leon, Governor of Coahuila, on the lower Rio Grande, heard that a Frenchman was living among the Indians on the easterly side of the river, and ordered him brought in. He turned out to be a deserter from La Salle's colony, and with him as a guide De Leon led an expedition against the French fort. On April 2, 1689, the Spaniards crossed the Rio Grande not far from presentday Laredo. For nearly three weeks they floundered through the region we now call southern Texas—fording streams, cutting underbrush and asking questions of the Indians. By the 22nd they knew they were approaching the fort, and then it loomed up before them across a level plain beside a small river or creek—a crude structure two stories high, built from ship lumber. Nearby were a chapel and five smaller houses, made of adobe and roofed with buffalo hides. But there was no challenging roar from the fort's cannon. All was silence—and confusion. Scattered about were broken guns, broken chests, torn books. Everything that could not be carried away, or that was not wanted, had been destroyed. Three bodies, one that of a woman, lay among the ruins. The devastation was evidently the work of Indians.[29]

A few days later two Frenchmen, under a promise of safety, came into the Spanish camp. They were "streaked with paint" and clad only in skins after the Indian manner. We have already met both of them. One was Jean L'Archeveque, who had acted as the decoy when La Salle was shot; the other was one of the men who had "gone Indian" at Cenis. They stated that the massacre at Fort St. Louis had happened only a short time previous to the arrival of the Spaniards, perhaps a month; that they had been at Cenis when it occurred; and that, when the story reached them, they had come down, together with two other Frenchmen, and buried fourteen of the victims. With this information, and the two French witnesses, De Leon marched back to Coahuila.[30]

But the probability that there were still some French among the Indians bothered the Spanish authorities, and in the spring of 1690 De Leon made another trip to La Salle's former fort. He found it much as he had seen it the year before, and this time he applied the torch. From various bands of Indians living in the vicinity he rescued five French children. Also he pushed on to the Cenis, whom he called the Texas. He had already heard of Tonti's visit, only a few days earlier. He doubtless hoped to find the two other Frenchmen known to have been living with the Texas Indians, one of whom may well have been Hiens. But, whatever the fate of the old buccaneer, he does not appear to have fallen into the hands of the Spaniards.

De Leon entered the principal Texas town in considerable state despite the fact that the road was knee-deep with mud and water. A lay brother led off with a linen banner on which was displayed a picture of the Blessed Virgin. Behind him, on foot, came four priests carrying their staffs and singing the Litany of Our Lady. De Leon and his officers followed on their horses, and the rest of the soldiers waded along. At the chief's house they were feasted on tamales, frijoles (beans), and corn mush.

A couple of days later a high mass was celebrated in the village "with all solemnity and a procession." That being completed, De Leon caused the flag of Spain to be raised while he delivered to the chief "a staff with a cross, giving him the title of governor of all his people, in order that he might rule and govern them." Particularly, the new governor was admonished to "make all his families attend Christian teachings, in order that they might be instructed in the affairs of our holy Catholic faith so later they might be baptized and become Christians."

Father Massanet, spiritual leader of the expedition, had already made up his mind to establish a mission among the Texas. A church and a house for the priests were quickly erected—San Francisco de los Texas it was named. Three soldiers were detailed to remain as a guard, and the rest of the expedition returned to Mexico. Thus did Spain establish her first mission and armed post in the present state of Texas, a name then applied only to a small area southwest of the presentday town of Nacogdoches.[31]

Revolution

THE INDIANS OF TEXAS may have glimpsed salvation in the mission placed over them by Father Massanet, but the Puritans of New England had seen only "the great Scarlet Whore" of Rome in the rulers set over themselves by their Catholic King, James II.

The fact that Governor Andros was a communicant of the Church of England did not save him from suspicion; in the eyes of the Puritans he was only a Papist in disguise. In fact, everywhere they turned the New Englanders saw "the wild Beasts of the Field" waiting to devour them. Governor Dongan, at New York, was an avowed Catholic; Lord Baltimore, Proprietor of Maryland, was a Catholic; even William Penn, the new Proprietor of Pennsylvania, was altogether too friendly with King James. And to the north were the French, Catholics of course, whose King was believed to have an unwholesome influence over the King of England.[1]

However, all this was a punishment that the Puritans could bear because it was presumably temporary. King James was in his fifties; his daughter Mary, the wife of William of

Orange, would succeed him—and she was a Protestant. So the people stood silent while Andros and his Council took over the government which hitherto had been administered by their own elected officials.

The first real resistance to the new regime came over taxes. The rate laid by Andros and his Council was not higher than customary, nor was it to be collected in an unusual manner. What irritated the people was that a tax of any kind should be laid by officials not of their own selection; in other words, they objected to taxation without representation—and several Massachusetts towns refused to comply. Notably the selectmen of Ipswich declined to act under the Governor's warrant because it "did abridge them of their liberty as Englishmen." A town meeting backed up the selectmen; and John Wise, their minister, joined in the protest. Andros promptly caused Wise and the selectmen to be hauled down to Boston and put on trial. When, in his defense, Wise asserted "the priviledges of Englishmen according to Magna Charta," Joseph Dudley, who sat as the presiding judge, is reputed to have replied, "Mr. Wise, you have no more priviledges left you, than not to be sold as slaves." A jury, picked for the purpose, brought in a verdict of guilty, and on October 24, 1687, sentence was passed. All were given heavy fines, and in addition Wise was suspended from the ministry.[2]

The result of this trial, and the remarks of Chief-justice Dudley, were commonly known in Connecticut when, on October 31, word reached Hartford that Governor Andros was approaching that town for the purpose of adding Connecticut to the Dominion of New England. Three *Quo Warrantos* had been served on the colony; two had been invalid because their time limits had expired; the third had not been pressed by the Lords of Trade because they assumed that the governor and magistrates would yield without a trial. But thus far Connecticut had ignored the Dominion government. She had held courts of election as usual, and the officials thus chosen had continued to make the laws, lay the taxes, and administer justice in the colony.[3]

Governor Andros evidently had serious misgivings as to how he would be received at Connecticut, and came prepared for any emergency. At his heels was a company of mounted grenadiers, some sixty of them. In his train were eight members of his Council. Trumpeters announced his progress. But there was no opposition. The soberly clad local militia met the red-coated cavalcade at the Wethersfield ferry and escorted it to Hartford. Governor Treat and his fellow magistrates received Andros with all courtesy. The Governor called a special meeting of the General Court, at which, according to the colony record, Andros "took into his hands the Government of this colony of Connecticut, it being by his Majesty annexed to the Massachusetts & other colonys under his Excelencies Government." Following that brief record the secretary of the colony wrote the single significant word "Finis." [4]

The record kept by Andros gives practically the same account of this transaction. Later there grew up a pretty story to the effect that Governor Treat remonstrated at length against the loss of the colony's charter rights; that while the charter, that is the royal patent of 1662, lay on the table, "The lights were instantly extinguished, and one captain Wadsworth, of Hartford, in the most silent and secret manner, carried off the charter, and secreted it in a large hollow tree." Early versions differ as to whether the tree was an elm or an oak, but in time the latter triumphed and as Charter Oak has become a symbol for bold resistance to tyranny. [5]

One reason why Connecticut had not earlier been forced into the Dominion of New England was that the Lords of Trade had in mind uniting her with New York and the two Jerseys. Such a concentration of power would, it was hoped, make the French less belligerent in the Iroquois country— and help the fur trade at Albany. However, with Connecticut's submission to Andros, this plan for a second dominion was dropped, and on April 7, 1688, New York and the Jerseys were also added to the Dominion of New England. [6]

Thus Andros became Captain-general of the territory from the St. Croix River (the present northeastern boundary of the United States) to Delaware Bay. It was an unwieldy unit; in fact, it was anything but a unit. The problems of New York did not interest the people of Massachusetts; the fishermen of Maine had nothing in common with the Quaker farmers of West Jersey. Nor could Andros hope for real co-operation from those he governed. They had no voice in public affairs, and for the most part wished him and his Council no good. The members of his Council were, of course, selected by the King. In general, they were men of ability—some from Massachusetts, some from New York, some from each of the colonies—but it was seldom that all could meet at the same time. The result was that a small clique usually managed even the most important affairs.[7]

Naturally, too, there gathered about Andros a group of under-officials, not members of his Council, not even natives of the colonies, whose only concern was that of lining their own pockets. ". . . of all our Oppressors," said a spokesman for Massachusetts, "we were chiefly squeez'd by a Crew of abject Persons fetched from New York . . . by these were extraordinary and intollerable Fees extorted from every one upon all Occasions, without any Rules but those of their own insatiable Avarice and Beggary."[8]

Even more serious, for the inhabitants of Massachusetts, was an attack on their land titles. Grants by the Massachusetts Bay Company had not followed the established English procedure by which a quitrent, though only of token value, was demanded and paid annually. Instead the General Court made grants to groups of leaders who held the land in trust for their towns and parcelled it, in fee simple, to the inhabitants. Always a considerable area was held as common land, belonging to the town and used as pasture until such time as the growth of population called for a further division. To Andros and his land lawyers this procedure gave no title at all. To get firm titles new grants would have to be taken out —at the cost of sizeable fees, of course, and perhaps with the payment of quitrents. Quite as disturbing were the assaults made on the common land by Randolph and others of the governing group. Wherever they saw a desirable piece of pasture or village green they would enter a petition for it on the assumption that it was ungranted land, and sometimes they were successful in getting possession.[9]

By the spring of 1688 Massachusetts had had about all she

could take. Increase Mather, teacher of the Second Church of Boston and Rector of Harvard College, accepted the responsibility of personally appealing to King James for a restoration of the charter which had been annulled four years earlier. News of Mather's intended journey soon reached Edward Randolph, busybody of the Governor's Council. To him such a mission meant only trouble, and he set himself to block it. Raking up a charge of libel against Mather he attempted to have him put under arrest. When the minister did not appear on the street a constable was set at his door. But Mather was equal to the situation. Donning a wig and a long white cloak, he walked by the waiting officer, unrecognized. For a week he lay concealed, two days being spent in a little boat off Plymouth Harbor. On April 7, well out to sea, he climbed aboard the good ship *President* and was on his way to England.[10]

Andros, also, doubtless feared the influence that Mather might bring to bear in England, but he was too busy in America to worry much about possibilities of that sort. In fact, at the time of Mather's departure he was aboard the frigate *Rose*, visiting the settlements along the Maine coast. The region to the eastward of Pemaquid had long been claimed by France, and at the mouth of the Penobscot stood the old French fort named Pentegoet. For some years it had been occupied by the Baron de Saint-Castin and his Indian wives, Indian brothers, and Indian followers. The Baron was a Frenchman who liked Indian ways of life, and the Indians liked him. His establishment at Pentegoet lacked some of the orderliness of civilization, but it attracted furs from the Indian hunters, and Saint-Castin had made a fortune trading with merchants of Boston.[11]

Pentegoet, however, lay within the limits claimed by the Dominion of New England; Andros may have had it in mind when he sailed eastward; in any case he included it among his calls. But he did not meet the Baron. To English trading ships, with cloth, kettles, and knives, Saint-Castin was ever ready to extend a welcome; to ships of war, with cannon, redcoats, and gold braid, he was not at home. He and his Abenaki followers took to the woods and stayed there despite fair words and threats. Andros retaliated by stripping the fort of trade goods, furs, and everything movable except a small altar. He then left word that Saint-Castin might recover his property at Pemaquid by taking the oath of allegiance to England. This made the Baron very unhappy; also it irritated the French Governor at Quebec.[12]

Five months later, while Andros was at Albany renewing the covenant chain with the Iroquois, the savages of Maine began raiding outlying English settlements from Pemaquid to Kennebunk. To every Indian that took part in the attacks Saint-Castin is said to have promised a pound of powder, two pounds of lead, and a supply of tobacco. The inhabitants were shot down or carried away—often to afford sport at the wild frolics of the savages. Houses were burned. Cattle were wastefully slaughtered. Saint-Castin was taking his revenge.[13]

Andros, who had hurried back to Boston, at first tried to soothe the Indians, and then turned what should have been a punitive expedition into a small war. Sending two companies of regular soldiers eastward, he shortly followed with seven or eight hundred men drafted from the colonial militia. Samuel Sewall escaped service by hiring a substitute, price five pounds. As any experienced Indian fighter would have known, the troops found no foe with which to fight, and the best Andros could do was to establish a number of garrisons where the men shivered through the cold Maine winter, the colonial troops becoming more and more discontented.[14]

Early in January, 1689, Andros, at Pemaquid, received a disturbing message from King James. England was threatened by an invasion from Holland; it might be extended to the colonies. The Governor-general of New England was warned to be on his guard against an attack by William of Orange, the husband of James' Protestant daughter, Mary. Andros accordingly issued a proclamation to the officials and people of the Dominion directing them, in the name of King James, to resist the Prince of Orange.[15]

A month later the captain of a ship arriving at New York from Virginia related to Francis Nicholson, Andros' Deputy-governor, a piece of news he had picked up in the southern colony. William, Prince of Orange, had landed in western England. Nicholson did not believe the story, and remarked that even if it were true, "the very prentice boyes of London will drive him out againe." However, he passed the rumor along to Andros at Pemaquid.[16]

The facts were that Old England, like New England, had had all of King James that it could take. His arbitrary government was bad enough; his insistence upon toleration for Catholics was contrary to everything that Protestant England stood for. But perhaps what tipped the scale was a tiny baby. In June, 1688, the King's second wife, Catholic Mary of Modena, gave birth to a son. This child would, of course, be reared as a Catholic and would presumably succeed his father. The King's Protestant daughter Mary, wife of the Prince of Orange, was no longer heir to the throne. The people of England refused to face the prospect of a Catholic succession. Their thoughts turned to Protestant Mary, but to get her they had to take her Dutch husband also. Secret negotiations resulted in an agreement by the English leaders to support William upon his landing in England. In early November the Dutch fleet went scudding down the Channel on a brisk east wind, some called it a Protestant wind, while the English fleet lay helplessly hooked in the sands at the mouth of the Thames. William made his landing at Torbay, and the great men of England flocked to his standard. James, deserted even by his trusted followers, fled to France where Louis XIV accepted him as the King of England and promised to help him regain his throne.[17]

Andros must have known a good deal about what was going on in England, but, like Nicholson, he may have felt that James would win out in the end. Three years earlier the Duke of Monmouth had landed in the west of England with the intention of ousting James, but had lost his own head. William's attempt might go the same way. In any case, until he was officially advised otherwise, Andros owed his allegiance to the King who had appointed him—and he had received no official notification of a change. As March wore along, still without any instructions from London, Andros, doubtless worried, returned to Boston. There he found "a general buzzing among the people, great with expectation of their old charter, or they know not what." This buzzing, which Andros did not fully understand, was Boston's response to a message from Increase Mather indicating that the old charter would be restored.[18]

It was Mather, in fact, who had blocked the sending of any royal instructions for Andros. The preacher had been very busy in England. He had even made some progress with King James; then had come the revolution, and he had to start all over. But with the advent of King William, he found himself on closer terms with those in power. Through the good offices of the King's secretary he was permitted to see an advance copy of a circular letter addressed to the colonial governors and directing them to hold their offices until advised otherwise. That, of course, would have continued Andros in power, and Mather asked that it not be sent to New England. To this request the King acceded. Thus Andros was left without official instructions and placed in a most embarrassing position.[19]

By the middle of April the facts of the revolution in England were common knowledge in all the colonies; some had already proclaimed the new sovereigns. But Andros' only proclamation was the one of January 10, issued at the command of James and warning the people of New England to be on guard against William. Curiously enough William Penn and Lord Baltimore, the one bound to King James by friendship and the other by religion, had also failed to proclaim William and Mary in their colonies. With considerable justification the colonists suspected that their governors were sticking by King James, and that Louis XIV, as the protector of James, might take over in America. The people of Massachusetts began muttering that their militiamen were being held on the Maine coast simply to make the French conquest easier.[20]

About April 12, one of the militia companies, stationed at Kennebunk, mutinied and the men started for Boston, where they arrived on the 17th. Andros gave orders that they were to be marched back, under guard, the following morning. But that morning, namely the 18th, distracting events occurred.

Young fellows armed with clubs began running through the streets. Soon the town was swarming with armed men. Captain George, commander of the royal frigate *Rose,* was seized as he came ashore on an errand. All of the governing clique that the mob could catch were clapped into jail. Andros, Randolph, and a few others prudently took cover at the Fort, in the hope of getting aboard the *Rose;* but the boat that came for them fell into the hands of the mob.[21]

Meanwhile, former Governor Bradstreet and a number of the other magistrates who had been ousted by Dudley in 1686 gathered at the Town House and constituted themselves a Council of Safety. Andros and Randolph were sent for, and when they arrived were placed under arrest.[22]

The Fort, however, still held out. Accordingly the mob, now organized into companies under the command of officers of the Massachusetts militia, began an assault. One of the batteries was captured and its guns turned on the garrison. The situation of the redcoats was hopeless; one of them, evidently of Dutch origin, aptly expressed it: "What the Devil should I fight against a tousand men." But the officer in charge wanted an order from Andros before he gave up, and Andros, a prisoner at the Town House, would not give the order. Randolph was more compliant. With guns poked in his ribs he hustled across town and took responsibility for the surrender. His reward was to be lodged in the common jail along with several of his former associates in power.[23]

The following morning, while additional hundreds of armed colonials poured into Boston from the outlying towns, the garrison of the Castle, a fortified island in the harbor, surrendered. Later in the day the lieutenant in charge of the *Rose* agreed that the sails of his ship might be taken ashore as a guarantee of its good behavior. And to make the revolution complete, Joseph Dudley, who had been holding court at Southold, Long Island, was shortly picked up and sent to join Randolph in the Boston jail where, according to the latter, they were "in danger to be stunk up by the Goal being filled up with poor prisoners, especially wounded men who rott & perish for want of one to dresse their wounds."[24]

The people of Massachusetts were again in control of the

government of Massachusetts. Governor Bradstreet together with the magistrates and deputies who had been elected in 1686 again took their places. The laws in force in 1686 were restored. An address was sent to King William thanking him "for casting off the yoke from our brethren of England and from ourselves."[25]

Mather, in England, made sure that King William got the proper interpretation of the outbreak. "I presume," he said, "your Majesty has been informed of the great service which your subjects in New England have done for your Majesty, & for the nation, & for the Protestant interest. . . ." The King expressed his gratitude and wrote a letter to the New Englanders approving their action.[26]

With the overthrow of the Andros regime in Massachusetts, the Dominion of New England came to an end. The General Court of Connecticut reconvened on May 9, 1689, and took up where it had left off—with the word "Finis"—only eighteen months earlier. Rhode Island took similar action.[27]

In New York the situation was complicated. The people, predominantly Dutch, had little in common with the New England colonies and had not relished being joined with them in the Dominion. They had no such background of self-government as the New Englanders. With them a royal governor was to be taken for granted. Any resentment they may have felt toward their English King was changed to joy as word seeped in that their own beloved Prince of Orange was to occupy the throne of England.

But as month succeeded month and they found themselves still being ruled under the name of King James they became restive. Why did not Colonel Nicholson, Deputy-governor under Andros, proclaim William and Mary? Why did the Church of England chaplain at the Fort still read prayers for the success of James II and for the welfare of that Catholic baby of his? The reason, of course, was that the Deputy and the chaplain had not been directed otherwise. But the people suspected the worst: Nicholson was a Catholic, they whispered; he was holding out for King James; they were to be delivered to the French. The news of what had happened at

Boston added to the tension. Only an incident was needed, and that incident soon occurred.[28]

On May 30 there was a clash of authority between a captain of the local militia and the regular soldiers. Nicholson flew into a rage at the captain and said, "I would rather see the town on fire than be commanded by you." Soon word spread that the Deputy-governor had threatened to burn the town, perhaps massacre the inhabitants. Drums beat on the street. The militiamen seized control of the fort. Nicholson fled. William and Mary were formally proclaimed. And a Committee of Safety was formed to keep order and govern the colony.[29]

Out of this discord and readjustment there arose a popular leader. Jacob Leisler, a German, had come to New Amsterdam as a common soldier in 1660. Through marriage with a rich widow he had acquired the capital for a successful career in trade, and in 1689 was accounted one of the leading merchants of New York. As a captain of one of the militia companies, he had taken a prominent part in bringing the Committee of Safety into being, and on June 28 was appointed by that body as Captain of the Fort. He was, in fact, at the head of the temporary government, and as such wrote a letter to the new sovereigns explaining the departure of Colonel Nicholson and giving an account of his stewardship. He subscribed himself as the "dutiful and obedient subject" of their Majesties.[30]

The delivery of this letter, and any necessary verbal amplification, was entrusted to one Joost Stoll, who had taken an active part in the rougher aspects of the late uproar at New York and who was described by one of Leisler's enemies as "famous for nothing, unless his not being worth a groat." Unfortunately for Stoll's success, Nicholson had preceded him to England, and as between the testimony of the late Deputy-governor and the ambassador of the self-constituted Committee of Safety, the King was far from convinced that Leisler was serving any useful purpose in New York.[31]

For a King who was primarily interested in organizing a European coalition against France, William was doubtless somewhat bored, that summer and autumn of 1689, with the mounting letters and addresses from America. In addition to those from Massachusetts, Connecticut, Plymouth, Rhode Island, and New York, there now came one from Maryland. As will be recalled (page 103), Lord Baltimore had gone to England in 1684 to fight out his boundary controversy with William Penn. So long as James II was on the throne, Baltimore, of course, got the worst of the argument; not alone was his boundary in danger; a *Quo Warranto* was issued against his patent. This action fell with the fall of King James, but a popular movement, similar to that in New York, did the business quite as effectively.

As in New York, the outbreak in Maryland headed from the failure of the proprietary government to recognize the revolution in England, and the conviction among the overwhelmingly Protestant population that their Catholic Proprietor and Council had joined in a conspiracy to destroy them. The upheavals in Massachusetts and New York doubtless had their influence. And in July, 1689, a Protestant Association was formed under the leadership of John Coode, the least of whose bad habits was said to be a "love to amaze the ignorant and make sport with his wit." St. Mary's, capital of the province, was captured, together with the provincial records; and the Association rather than Lord Baltimore ruled in Maryland—"without the expense of a drop of blood," as King William was dutifully informed.[32]

From the Potomac to the St. Croix the colonies were being ruled by questionable *de facto* governments—and this at a time when the growing French threat called for political and military strength. The task of re-establishing stable government was the responsibility of the Lords of Trade, whose first idea was to restore the Dominion of New England. This point of view received considerable support from the testimony of Andros, Dudley and Randolph, now in England after almost ten months imprisonment at Boston. In April, 1690, they appeared before the Lords of Trade and so well justified their administration in New England that not even the Massachusetts agents were willing to appear against them. Nonetheless the New Englanders were firmly opposed to a reconstitution of the Dominion and King William declined to force the issue.[33]

The policy of colonial consolidation, so dear to King James and his advisers, was, for the time being, at an end. Connecticut and Rhode Island were allowed to continue under their old charters. New Hampshire was again made a royal colony. East and West Jersey were returned to their proprietors. But in most other respects the re-establishment followed the imperial plan worked out over the past thirty years by the secretariat of the various committees on trade and plantations. Kings and Privy Councillors might come and go but the secretaries stayed on, and they were the men who directed England's colonial policy.

In general, private colonies, whether corporations such as Massachusetts had been under her old charter or proprietaries such as Maryland and Pennsylvania, were not viewed with favor by the Lords of Trade in 1689. The fact that there had been a revolution in England did not at all mean that there should be a change in the policy of bringing the colonies to a closer dependence upon the King. Without so much as a *Quo Warranto* Lord Baltimore was stripped of his right to govern Maryland. The province became a royal colony under a governor appointed by the King.[34]

William Penn might well have fared even worse than Baltimore had he not prudently disappeared from public view. Suspected on account of his close association with King James, and caught in what appeared to be a treasonable correspondence with his old master, the proprietor of Pennsylvania spent two years hiding from the officers of the law while his colony was governed by the royal governor of New York.[35]

The Puritan leaders of Massachusetts strove valiantly to recover their original charter, but without success; instead, on October 7, 1691, the colony received a new charter under which the freeholders, qualified by property rather than church membership, elected their representatives, but the King appointed the Governor. In the matter of territory, however, the charter was liberal. Plymouth colony, long under the dominance of her stronger neighbor, was legally and permanently joined with Massachusetts. Maine, which Massachusetts had bought in 1678, also became a part of the enlarged colony. And to all this was added "Nova Scotia," which might have meant a good deal but which came to mean the area lying between Sagadahoc and the St. Croix River, formerly a part of New York but henceforth a part of Maine.[36]

New York, which of all the disturbed colonies should have been King William's first concern, became in fact the victim of a sequence of misadventures. Since its capture by the English in 1664 the province had been ruled by the sword. It was at New York that America had first seen redcoats. It was from New York that regular soldiers could be quickly moved to any danger point in the colonies—as they had been by Andros when trouble flared in Maine. With the deposition of King James and the rising tension between England and France it was even more important that the province should have been reinforced and in able hands. The rumor that France planned to capture New York was no idle tale. The advisers of Louis XIV proposed just that—by an expedition through Lake Champlain to Albany and down the Hudson River.[37]

Of this French scheme the Lords of Trade were well aware, and shortly after receiving news of the overthrow of the Andros regime they caused the appointment of a new governor, Henry Sloughter, who was to sail for New York with a sizeable body of regular troops. But at that point fate intervened in the form of a rebellion in Ireland, headed by the former King James and encouraged by King Louis of France. Until that was settled, there were no troops or ships available for America.[38]

And in the meantime Jacob Leisler directed the government of New York. From being Captain of the Fort he created himself Lieutenant-governor of the province. He appointed local officers for the counties, and directed elections for other offices. Most noteworthy of all, he issued a call for a meeting of representatives from the various colonies, with a view to forming a confederation for defense and offense against the common enemy.[39]

This call was generally accepted by the New England colonies. From Massachusetts went Samuel Sewall and William Stoughton. They left Boston on April 21, 1690, by horseback, and proceeded to Newport, Rhode Island. There they left their horses and hired a sloop—at twelve shillings per day—in which they sailed westward through Long Island Sound to Oyster Bay, Long Island, where again taking to horses they rode by way of Hempstead and Jamaica to Brooklyn ferry and crossed over to New York. Leisler met them with considerable pomp, and they on their part made no question about recognizing him as the Governor.

Under Leisler's leadership the delegates decided upon a plan of action. New York, Massachusetts, Connecticut, Plymouth, and Maryland would each provide a quota of troops; Rhode Island promised money in lieu of men. The troops were to be assembled at Albany, whence they would march against Quebec, which city would at the same time be attacked by a war fleet operating through the St. Lawrence River.[40]

This first real inter-colonial effort failed. It failed in part, and in a large part, because Leisler was unable to get along with those who did not agree with him. He could lead by rough, bold action, but he lacked the gift which turns opposition into support. When some of the more prominent men of the province refused to co-operate with him, he could think of no better means of persuasion than to put them in jail. Thus he created powerful enemies who undermined him by their reports to England. In May, 1690, the principal merchants, traders, and other inhabitants of New York addressed a petition to William and Mary asking relief from the "burthen of Slavery and arbitrary Power executed over us by the inraged fury of some ill men among us . . . ruling us by the sword at the sole Will of an Insolent Alien"—by which latter term they meant the German Leisler. Among the signers of this document was Elias Boudinot, an elder of the Reformed Church, who, according to Catherine Dubois, found even more personal ways of expressing his disapproval of Leisler. Catherine set forth that, while calling at Boudinot's house, "there being also severall persons in company, the said Elias Boudinott did then and there boast and relate that he had affronted the Lt. Govr. Leisler, by putting his finger in his nose and then pointing at the said Lt. Govr. and that the said Govr. asked him why he mocked him, and that he had answered, may I not clean my nose, and is my nose not my own, and that he had done the same over again before his face." [41]

At about the time these pleasantries were taking place in New York, the Irish army was defeated at the battle of the Boyne; and in December, 1690, Governor Sloughter, with four ships and two companies of soldiers, one of them under the command of Major Richard Ingoldesby, left England. On January 29, 1691, Ingoldesby and the redcoats arrived at New York—ahead of the Governor. But Leisler stubbornly refused to surrender the Fort until the Governor arrived. Ingoldesby on his part assumed a little too much authority in allowing soldiers to be assembled in the city for what looked like an attack on Leisler. As the redcoats paraded down the street, there was a shot from the Fort. Two men were killed, and Ingoldesby's men in attempting to answer the fire exploded a cannon, killing six more men, one of them being Major Patrick MacGregorie, whom we last met convoying a cargo of brandy up Lake Erie. [42]

What might well have been a serious situation was saved by the timely arrival of Governor Sloughter. Still stubborn, Leisler demanded "orders under the King's own hand, directed to him" before he would surrender the Fort. But his followers were not ready to back him that far, and Major Ingoldesby took control without resistance. Inside the Fort, prisoners in chains, the Major found two men whom the King had designated as members of the Council of the new Governor. The story goes that the chains were struck from their legs and put on Leisler. [43]

In any case Leisler and his councillors were put under arrest charged with treason and murder "for holding with force the King's fort against the King's Governor." Joseph Dudley, sometime President of New England, late of the jail at Boston, was one of the presiding judges, by virtue of appointment by the King as a member of Sloughter's Council. Eight of the prisoners, including Leisler of course, were convicted. All but Leisler and Jacob Milborne, his son-in-law, were pardoned. [44]

Sloughter hesitated to sign the death warrants, and claimed

he did so only to quiet the "clamour of the People." A persistent story, however, has it that Leisler's enemies got the Governor gloriously drunk and that the warrants were signed and the executions over before he sobered up. Be that as it may, on Saturday, May 16, 1691, in a pouring rain, at a spot which may be identified as in the vicinity of the presentday City Hall, Leisler and Milborne were hanged and beheaded. Domine Selyns, who in his sermons had done all he could to bring about the condemnations, offered spiritual consolation. The bodies were buried at the foot of the gallows. Four years later the Parliament of England reversed the sentences.[45]

15

The Visible and the Invisible World

A VISITOR TO MASSACHUSETTS in the late 1680's would scarcely have realized that Zion was crumbling. Godly ministers presided over the churches in the more than fifty towns grouped in a semicircle about Boston and extending westward to the Connecticut River. In Boston itself, a city of perhaps seven thousand inhabitants, there were three churches. The First Church had been founded in 1630 by John Winthrop and other "saints"; since 1668 Mr. James Allen, "very humble and very rich," had been its minister, and with him was associated Mr. Joshua Moodey, a militant servant of the Lord. At the Second, or North, Church, Mr. Increase Mather, son of the revered Richard Mather, was minister, assisted by his son, Cotton Mather, a promising young man who had been graduated from Harvard at the age of sixteen and ordained at twenty-three. At South Church, Mr. Samuel Willard, "well furnished with learning" and of "natural fluency," served without an assistant. By their moral and spiritual characters these men molded and dominated the religious and social life of Boston.[1]

157

There was, to be sure, another so-called church in Boston, recently established and known as King's Chapel, where the Church of England service was conducted—for some few obscure merchants and undesirable royal officials. The organist was known to give dancing lessons for a fee. So far as the better-class people were concerned, this semipopish institution could be ignored.[2]

At its upper level the social life of Boston embodied a high degree of culture, well tinged with religion. Samuel Sewall, for example, was a graduate of Harvard College. He had thought of taking up the ministry but instead had married the daughter of the very wealthy John Hull and added to his fortune by commercial enterprise. Similarly there was William Stoughton; after graduating from Harvard he had gone to England and taken a degree at Oxford University. In his younger days he had preached, both in England and New England. Large land holdings, sometimes secured through official favor, enabled him to live well and give much of his time to public service. It was he who set forth that "God sifted a whole Nation that he might send Choice Grain over into this Wilderness."[3]

This "Choice Grain" was bountifully watered by Sabbath-day sermons and Thursday lectures, delivered by the ministers and often printed for wider distribution by the Boston booksellers of whom there were several. In addition the published sermons and discourses of English ministers poured into New England in a steady stream—being offered for sale at the bookshops and carried to the outlying towns by itinerant salesmen.[4]

Occasionally, too, the established book business was spurred by free-lance competition. Thus in the winter of 1685–86 John Dunton arrived at Boston from England "with a great number of books" which he had in mind selling direct to individual buyers. He had counted on the preachers as his most likely customers but was in the beginning a little puzzled by the proper aloofness of the Boston clergy. He was, he said, "as welcome to them as sour ale in summer." Still Cotton Mather took him in; showed him his library, "very large and numerous"; and introduced him to several of the

The Whipple House (*above*) was standing in Ipswich at the time of Dunton's Visit.

From Whitefield, *The Homes of Our Forefathers.*

Kitchen of the Daniel House, Salem, Mass.

Courtesy, Library of Congress, Washington.

students at Harvard, who proved ready customers. With this start Dunton was soon doing so well that the regular Boston booksellers offered to buy up the remainder of his stock, but he refused, not wishing to lose the thirty per cent which they would have expected as a discount.

Boston was the principal market for Dunton's books but he knew that there were many prospective customers in the smaller towns. Accordingly he made a visit to Salem. He found the town "about a mile long, with many fine houses in it." Samuel Sewall's brother, who lived there, asked him to his house for supper, "and had I staid a month there, I had been welcome gratis," Dunton tells us. But he did not need to stay a month or to visit other towns. Salem took all the books he had left. Still, he could not resist a trip to Ipswich, twenty-five miles north of Boston. He went on horseback, of course. With him, for an outing and sitting sidewise on a pillion behind his saddle, went his landlord's daughter. That even the strictest of the Puritans saw nothing wrong in such a jaunt is indicated by the fact that the minister at Wenham, a village on the way, welcomed them with "a noble dinner," and when they arrived at Ipswich the girl's uncle took them in for the night, giving them "fat-pig and a bowl of punch" for supper. The next day the minister of Ipswich invited the visitors to his house and provided "handsome entertainment." Dunton improved the opportunity by checking through his catalogue with the preacher—and probably picked up enough mail orders to pay his horse hire.[5]

In addition to the importations by the booksellers, many colonists, during their occasional visits to England, bought books according to their personal interests. When Samuel Sewall was preparing to leave London in the summer of 1689, he seems to have spent most of his time haunting bookshops. Single volumes, sets, folios, presents for his friends, mostly books of a theological character, went into his baggage aboard the ship bound for New England.[6]

These books brought home by Sewall in 1689 might be looked upon as symbols of New England's deliverance from a Catholic king. James the Second was in exile; William and Mary, Protestants both, were firmly seated on the throne of England.

King William, however, was to prove an expensive luxury for England and for England's American colonies. Scarcely was he sure of the throne before he plunged the country into a war with France, a war that, with intermissions, was to continue for three quarters of a century. To finance this military effort William's ministers were forced to the expedient of creating a Bank of England, from the deposits of which the needed funds might be borrowed on the credit of the state. Thus was England, for the first time, saddled with a national debt—which easy way of meeting expenses appealed to the colonies when they, too, spent more than they had.

Naturally the hostilities in Europe extended to America, and from 1689 to 1763 there was raid and counter raid between the French settlements and the English colonies, with Indian allies used by both sides and with all the horrors of savage warfare.

Within a few weeks of the withdrawal of the militiamen from the eastern coast, following the overthrow of Andros, the Indians had fallen upon the unprotected towns. At Dover, New Hampshire, in June, 1689, twenty-three people were killed and twenty-nine made captive. Among the victims was Major Richard Waldron, against whom the Indians had a particular grudge. During King Philip's War he had, through sheer treachery, captured two hundred of their fellow tribesmen, some of whom had been executed and the rest sold as slaves in the West Indies. Now, after thirteen years, the Indians had Waldron in their hands. One by one they slashed him with their knives, recording their long-delayed vengeance with cries of "I cross out my account." The following August, Pemaquid fell before an Indian attack, its slight garrison and the inhabitants butchered or carried off to Canada. And this was but the beginning.

Late in February, 1690, Samuel Sewall, of Boston, gave a dinner party. Among the guests were Governor Bradstreet and his lady, Mr. William Stoughton, Mr. Samuel Willard, Mr. Joshua Moodey and his wife, Mr. Cotton Mather, and twelve others, all prominent in the religious and social life of the town. Mr. Mather "Returned Thanks in an excellent manner," and they all joined in singing part of "the Six and fiftieth Psalm." But, said Sewall, "the bitterness in our Cups was . . . the Massacre at Schenectady by the French." [9]

The attack on Schenectady was one of three offensives planned by Count Frontenac, Governor of New France. The purpose was primarily to create in the minds of the Indians a proper respect for the wrath of Onontio, as the savages called the Governor. The expedition had started from Montreal. There were about a hundred Frenchmen. Among them was Pierre le Moyne, Sieur d'Iberville, later to be the Father of Louisiana. With the French went perhaps a hundred christianized Iroquois who had left their brethren to live near the Catholic missions on the St. Lawrence River.

Trailing southward along Lake Champlain and Lake George, the party reached the vicinity of Albany without being detected. But there the French leaders lost their courage; Albany, with its fort and garrison, was no easy prize. Fifteen miles westward lay Schenectady, founded by Dutch traders and farmers in 1662. It contained about sixty houses surrounded by a strong palisade. The inhabitants, however, had long lived in peace with their savage neighbors, and on the cold, snowy night of February 8 the palisade gates stood wide open as usual. Not a soul was on guard or awake as, about midnight, the French and their savage allies slipped into the enclosure. A wild screech and an instant of terror were all that many of the people ever knew. Others were not so fortunate. Sixty lay dead the following morning. The town was burned. The French and their Indians, with twenty-seven captives and much loot, tramped back to Montreal. [10]

This was the story that Sewall heard at his dinner party in Boston on February 24. A month later, just as Mrs. Sewall, Madam Bradstreet, Mrs. Mather, and Mrs. Moodey were starting, in a hired coach, to have dinner with Mr. Stoughton at Dorchester, there came "the dolefull news . . . that between 80. and 100. persons were kill'd and carried away" at Salmon Falls in New Hampshire. Frontenac had delivered his second blow. The situation was becoming serious; Massachusetts issued a call for volunteers; the defenses of

Boston were put into order; and Leisler's invitation to join in an inter-colonial conference was accepted.[11]

As will be recalled (page 154), the plan agreed upon at New York was to attack Canada by land from Albany and by sea through the St. Lawrence River. While preparations for these moves were under way, Massachusetts underwrote an expedition to wipe out, perhaps at a profit, the French settlement of Port Royal in the Bay of Fundy. In command was Sir William Phips, a picturesque native son of New England. Born at the frontier post of Pemaquid he had, as a young man, moved to Boston where he became a successful ship carpenter. From roving seamen he learned that somewhere off the Bahama Islands there lay at the bottom of the sea a Spanish treasure ship—long forgotten even by the Spaniards. He organized a salvaging expedition, found the ship, and fished up a vast fortune in gold and silver. In honor of his exploit he was knighted by the King, and returned to Boston a wealthy man, admired by everybody and particularly by the Mathers, whose church he soon joined. And now, in May, 1690, Phips led a fleet of seven ships, filled with militiamen, into Port Royal harbor (presentday Annapolis, Nova Scotia). The French, in the presence of overwhelming force, attempted no defense. From a journal kept by a member of Phips' staff we get a picture of what went on: "*May* 11. The fort surrendered. *May* 12. Went ashore to search for hidden goods. We cut down the cross, rifled the Church, pulled down the high altar, and broke their images. *May* 13. Kept gathering plunder all day."[12]

But even as Phips counted his loot at Port Royal, Count Frontenac's third blow descended upon the English. Fort Loyal, on the site of presentday Portland, Maine, was captured and its garrison killed or tortured by the Indian allies of the French officers who led the attack.[13]

Nor did Quebec fall before the combined assault of the English colonies. Fitz-John Winthrop, of Connecticut, in command of the army gathered at Albany, found himself short of men and supplies. The Iroquois, whose help had been counted on, proved backward. Smallpox broke out. And before the troops reached Lake Champlain they had ceased to be an army. Winthrop led the survivors back to Albany. In the meantime the naval expedition, under the command of Phips, reached Quebec but, lacking the assistance of the land troops, could accomplish nothing and returned to Boston with only a staggering bill of expense to show for its effort. The bill was met in much the manner that England was preparing to meet those of King William, by an issue of paper money. And the Indians continued their attacks—at York, Wells, and other settlements along the eastern coast.[14]

That God was angry with the New Englanders was amply evident to their leaders. ". . . shall our Father spit in our face and we be not ashamed," asked Governor Bradstreet. This conviction of God's displeasure was doubtless an influence in bringing to a head at this time an assault upon the outworks of spiritual doubt. The ministers had long recognized that rationalism, that is, the refusal to credit things that could not be proved, was but a step removed from questioning the existence of God. Therefore things that ordinarily could not be proved must be proved. "Witchcrafts, Diabolical Possessions, Remarkable Judgements upon noted Sinners, eminent Deliverances, and Answers of Prayer," were, in the opinions of the ministers, "to be reckoned among Illustrious Providences"; in short, these phenomena were "Demonstrative evidence that there is a God, who judgeth in the Earth, and who though he stay long, will not be mocked alwayes."[15]

At a general meeting of the Massachusetts ministers in 1681 Increase Mather was commissioned to collect and record some of these illustrious providences. The result was a small volume published in 1684 and filled with accounts of strange and vexatious experiences suffered by people in New England. There were stories of boys who barked like dogs; of chamber pots that lifted themselves out from under beds and poured their contents over sleeping victims; of hot stones that flew around inside houses breaking windows and doing other damage; of trousers that beat their owners during the dark hours of night; of pinches and pin pricks that came out of thin air.[16]

But this book, said Mather, was only a beginning; ". . .

INCREASE MATHER.

Courtesy, The Massachusetts Historical Society, Boston.

having (by the good hand of God upon me) set this Wheel a going, I shall leave it unto others, whom God has fitted, and shall incline thereto, to go on with the undertaking." [17]

The next turn of the wheel came five years later—from the pen of Mather's son Cotton and under the title of *Memorable Providences, Relating to Witchcrafts and Possessions. A Faithful Account of many Wonderful and Surprising Things that have befallen several Bewitched and Possessed Persons in New-England.* The volume contained an endorsement by four leading ministers among whom were Samuel Willard and Joshua Moodey. The author plainly stated the purpose of his book: "Go tell Mankind that there are Devils and Witches." [18]

And Mather knew whereof he wrote. He had personally observed the bewitchments of the children of John Goodwin. With his own eyes he had seen them at one moment so stiff "that not a joint of them could be stir'd," and the next moment "so Limber that it was judg'd every Bone of them could be bent." With his own ears he had heard their piteous cries as an invisible tormentor cut them with knives. He had even taken one of them, a girl, into his household where he had noted that in her bewitchments she could not pronounce the name of God, could not read from *Milk for Babes,* a pious primer prepared by Mather's own grandfather, John Cotton, and memorized by every Boston school child. But she could read from a ribald book of *Jests* and descant wittily upon its contents.

These strange afflictions of the Goodwin children were easily recognized as the doing of a witch who, through a contract with the Devil, was able to visit and torment them without being visible to the ordinary person, though sometimes plainly seen by the sufferers. Suspicion soon pointed to an old woman who had quarrelled with the Goodwin family about some missing linen. She was charged with witchcraft, convicted, and hanged. [19]

The story of the Goodwin children spread through the New England towns. Mather's book was widely read and talked about. Other books with similar accounts of witchcraft came in from England. And the inevitable soon happened.

In February, 1692, two children, members of the family

of a minister at Salem Village, became afflicted in much the same manner as the Goodwin children. Under questioning they named their tormentors—a negro slave woman and two other old women of the community. Soon other children and even some grown women became afflicted—and the number of accused persons grew. The magistrates took a hand. The treatment accorded Goodwife Corey, one of the accused, was typical. She was examined in the presence of her accusers. She was asked why she afflicted the children. She answered that she did not. Thereupon the children insisted that her answer had been dictated by "the Black Man" whom they saw whispering in her ear as she testified. When she "bit her Lip, they would cry out of being bitten, if she grasped one hand with the other, they would cry out of being Pinched by her." It was obvious to the magistrates that she was a witch and they clapped her into jail along with several others.[20]

By this time the Salem cases were attracting wide attention. On April 11 Samuel Sewall wrote in his diary: "Went to Salem, where in the Meeting-house, the persons accused of Witchcraft were examined; was a very great Assembly; 'twas awfull to see how the afflicted persons were agitated." A less sympathetic account speaks of "hidious clamors and Screechings" by the complainants.[21]

Before the end of May there were about a hundred persons in jail charged with witchcraft. A special court was created to try them. At the head of this court was William Stoughton. Samuel Sewall was a member. The other members were similarly prominent in the public affairs of the colony.[22]

Some of the suspects confessed—said anything the judges wanted them to say—and in that way saved their lives. Others stood by their denials and thereby convicted themselves, since in the eyes of the judges denial of the existence of witchcraft proved collusion with the Devil. When juries failed to bring in verdicts of guilty, they were sent back to try again. When a defendant seemed to be making a good case for himself or herself, the afflicted children would swoon or cry out that the accused was torturing them. When Giles Corey refused to plead either guilty or innocent, he was, by due process of law, pressed to death—stretched on his back under heavy weights. During the somewhat lengthy execution "his Tongue being prest out of his Mouth, the Sheriff with his Cane forced it in again, when he was dying." [23]

On August 19 five of the convicted witches were hanged at Salem. Cotton Mather, sitting on a horse, watched the show and assured the other spectators that the culprits "all died by a Righteous Sentence." In all, nineteen suspects were hanged and one pressed to death before public doubt brought the trials to a sudden end. [24]

From the mass of depositions and statements we get a glimpse of how the Devil operated. For example, on September 8, when failure to confess meant death, Mary Osgood stated that, some years earlier, she had seen "the appearance of a cat, at the end of the house, which yet she thought was a real cat. However, at that time, it diverted her from praying to God, and instead thereof she prayed to the devil; about which time she made a covenant with the devil, who, as a black man, came to her and presented her a book, upon which she laid her finger and that left a red spot: And that upon her signing, the devil told her he was her God, and that she should serve and worship him, and, she believes, she consented to it. She says further, that about two years agone, she was carried through the air, in company with deacon Frye's wife, Ebenezer Baker's wife and Goody Tyler, to five mile pond, where she was baptized by the devil, who dipped her face in the water and made her renounce her former baptism, and told her she must be his, soul and body, forever, and that she must serve him, which she promised to do. She says, the renouncing her first baptism was after her dipping, and that she was transported back again through the air, in company with the forenamed persons, in the same manner as she went, and believes they were carried upon a pole." [25]

From Mercy Short we get a reasonably good description of the Devil himself. He was "A Short and Black Man . . . no taller than an ordinary Walking-Staff; hee was not of a Negro, but of a Tawney, or an Indian colour; hee wore an high-crowned Hat, with strait Hair; and had one Cloven-Foot." He was often accompanied by "Spectres," that is, the

WILLIAM STOUGHTON.
Courtesy, Harvard University.

immaterial forms of such converts as Mary Osgood; and these spectres did the pinching, biting, and other things complained of by the afflicted ones.[26]

In the records of the trials Cotton Mather found material for a new and convincing account of witchcraft which, under the title of *The Wonders of the Invisible World,* was published at Boston in 1693 "by the Special Command of His Excellency, the Governour of the Province of the Massachusetts-Bay." The book carried an endorsement by William Stoughton and Samuel Sewall stating that they found "the Matters of Fact and Evidence Truly reported." [27]

His Excellency, the new royal Governor of Massachusetts, had arrived at Boston in the midst of the witchcraft excitement. He turned out to be none other than the former Pemaquid carpenter, Sir William Phips—appointed at the solicitation of Increase Mather, who returned with him from his political mission in England. Presumably, the elder Mather and the Governor accepted the facts of the witchcraft epidemic as they heard them from Cotton Mather. It was, in fact, Phips who created the special court for the trial of the suspects. But as the summer wore along, the Governor felt less sure about the procedure of the judges and in October called a halt.[28]

The prosecutions were, as it proved, at an end. Slowly the jails were emptied of suspects. Witnesses recanted their confessions. Jurymen expressed regret for their verdicts. In January, 1697, Samuel Sewall stood in his pew at South Church while a "petition," written by himself, was read by Mr. Willard, the minister. In this document the former judge noted "the reiterated strokes of God upon himself and his family"; he recognized his "Guilt" in connection with the trials and desired "to take the Blame and shame of it, Asking pardon of men, And especially desiring prayers that God . . . would pardon that sin and all other his sins" and "Not Visit the sin of him, or of any other, upon himself or any of his, nor upon the Land." It would appear that in making this statement Sewall was moved about equally by contrition and by the fear that God would make him sweat if he failed to clear himself. Nonetheless it was a courageous action, and one could wish that Giles Corey and the nineteen who were hanged might have been there to hear it.[29]

Cotton Mather apparently did not feel called upon to admit any blame for his part in the witchcraft affair. But he did quiver under the strokes which the Lord permitted Robert Calef, a mere merchant, to lay upon him. For several years Calef was known to be preparing a book in which the injustices practiced at the witchcraft trials were exposed and the Mathers, father and son, exhibited in a not too favorable light. Curiously enough, one of the passages in the book to which young Mather took particular exception was a description of himself seated on the bed of an afflicted damsel, comforting her by rubbing her stomach. Calef intimated that the damsel was not too modestly covered. Mather denied both the lack of covering and the impropriety of the ministerial massage.[30]

Calef was, of course, refused a license to publish his book in Boston, but finally did so in London—under the suggestive title of *More Wonders of the Invisible World*. On November 15, 1700, Cotton Mather recorded in his diary that copies of Calef's book had arrived in Boston—and sadly added, ". . . tho' I had often and often cried unto the Lord that the Cup of this Man's abominable Bundle of Lies, written on purpose, with a Quil under a special Energy and Management of Satan, to damnify my precious Opportunities of Glorifying my Lord Jesus Christ, might pass from me; Yett, in this point, the Lord has denied my Request." Increase Mather, then president of Harvard College, took more direct action; he ordered Calef's book burned in the college yard.[31]

But Increase Mather's authority at Harvard was soon to end; in 1701 he was forced out of the presidency. His former dominant position in the affairs of the colony was waning also, as was that of his fellow ministers. Their part in the witchcraft excitement had not helped their prestige. The provisions of the new charter had broken their power over the General Assembly. No longer was membership in one of the Congregational churches or approval by one of the Con-

gregational ministers the sole qualification for voting. Now,
any man who paid taxes on a reasonable estate had the right
to vote for his representative in the assembly or to hold office
himself.

And as religion ceased to be the main aim of the colony,
so its enjoyment ceased to be the principal pleasure of the
people. The Thursday lecture-day, second only to the Sabbath among the older generation, could be spoken of as
"Whore Fair, from the Levity and Wanton Frollicks of the
Young People, who when their Devotion's over, have recourse
to the Ordinaries, where they plentifully wash away the re-
membrance of their Old Sins, and drink down the fear of a
Fine or the dread of a Whipping-post." [32]

Even the serious Samuel Sewall occasionally allowed himself and his family a "treat." In 1699 we find him taking two
of his sons and three of his daughters in a coach to the Turk's
Head Inn at Dorchester, where they ate sage cheese and
drank beer and cider. But when some low jokester strewed
a deck of playing cards over his front lawn, Sewall suspected
he was being mocked. [33]

Always there hovered over the colony the grim threat,
often translated into reality, of Indian raids instigated or led
by the French of Canada. In July, 1694, some ninety people
had been killed or captured in a surprise attack near Portsmouth, New Hampshire. Among the dead was Mrs. Cutts,
widow of the former President of the province. A few days
later the Indians struck at Groton, Massachusetts. Forty people were killed or captured. And so it went at every frontier
town. [34]

In 1696 the great, new fort at Pemaquid, New England's
strategic eastern outpost, fell before a combined French and
Indian attack. Reared on the ashes of the old stockade that
the Indians burned in 1689, this new fort was constructed
of stone, with walls six feet thick, and was thought to be impregnable. But to the Sieur d'Iberville, he who had taken
part in the raid on Schenectady, the strength of Pemaquid
was only a challenge. Sailing from Quebec with two warships and a considerable number of soldiers, he picked up
some fifty Indians at Port Royal. St. Castin and his Abenaki

warriors joined the expedition at Penobscot, and they all moved on Pemaquid, which suddenly found itself invested by land and by sea. *Surrender or you will have to deal with savages* was the message sent into the fort by St. Castin— and the fort surrendered. Iberville reduced it to rubble and returned eastward. English settlements and English authority disappeared from the Maine coast.[35]

The morale of the New Englanders was somewhat restored by Hannah Dustin. She, along with many others, was captured by the Indians at Haverhill, Massachusetts, in the spring of 1697. She was practically pulled out of a bed in which she had very recently given birth to a child. She saw the child brained as a useless encumbrance and knew that the same fate awaited herself if she failed to keep up with the retreating Indians. Day after day she tramped along with her savage captors who, as good Catholics, mocked her Protestant God: a poor God that could not protect his children. Still Hannah clung to her faith and searched her memory for a Biblical text that would fit her situation. Finally she remembered the story of how Jael had driven a tent pin through Sisera's head while he slept—and that gave Hannah an idea. There were in the party two other white captives, a woman and a boy, together with about a dozen Indians. One night while all the others were asleep Hannah communicated her idea to her fellow captives, and the three of them went to work with hatchets. They returned to Massachusetts with ten scalps worth five pounds apiece in bounty money offered by the General Court.[36]

As New England exulted over Hannah's exploit, the diplomats of England and France were patching up a treaty of peace, signed in September, 1697, and known as the Treaty of Ryswick. But four years later, with Queen Anne on the throne of England, the long drawn-out struggle for power again flared into war. And again New England became the target for French-inspired Indian raids. ". . . we must keep things astir in the direction of Boston, or else the Abenakis [the Maine Indians] will declare for the English," said the French Governor of Canada.

In line with this policy of keeping things "astir," Hertel

de Rouville led a war party from the Montreal area in February, 1704. With fifty Canadians and two hundred Indians —crunching along on snow shoes; with dogs pulling sleds loaded with supplies—Rouville headed southward over the ice-covered surface of Lake Champlain. It was the old road to the Iroquois country, but long before they reached the head of the lakes the straggling groups of men and dogs turned eastward, toward the Connecticut River.

Most exposed of the Massachusetts settlements on the Connecticut River was the town of Deerfield. It consisted of about forty houses, fifteen of them enclosed with a palisade to form a defensible center. There had been warnings of an impending French attack and some twenty volunteer militiamen were quartered in the houses within the enclosure—presumably on guard but in reality not letting their duties interfere too much with their sleep.

On the night of February 28, with the snow drifted nearly to the top of the palisade, the townspeople and the soldiers of Deerfield went early to their warm beds, blissfully ignorant of the fact that within two miles of the town Rouville's French and Indians lay hidden—shivering and hungry. Two hours before dawn Rouville gave the order to move and with hardly more noise than the wind in the trees his band advanced over the crusted snow and dropped inside the palisade.

The houses stood plainly outlined against the surrounding snow. Most of the doors yielded easily to the blows of the invaders. Whoever resisted was killed or subdued. Those who submitted were tied and herded into groups. One house only, that of Benoni Stebbins, withstood the attack. With the town in flames; with over a hundred captives, including the minister, John Williams, and his family; and with such loot as could be carried, the raiders started the long trip back to Montreal, two hundred and fifty miles to the northward.

Some of the captives died on the march; others, Mrs. Williams among them, were tomahawked because they could not keep up. Side by side with acts of cruelty the Indians showed their usual kindliness, carrying children on their shoulders or pulling them on sleds. Nor was any woman subjected to

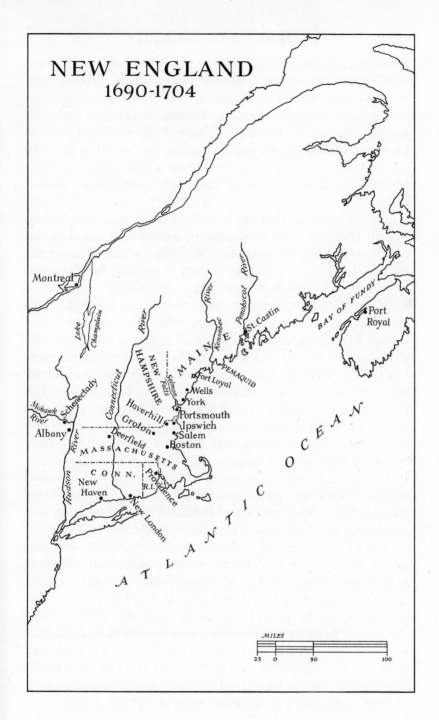

NEW ENGLAND
1690-1704

Montreal

Lake Champlain

River

Mohawk River

Schenectady

Albany

Hudson River

Connecticut River

NEW HAMPSHIRE

Salmon Falls

Haverhill

Groton

Deerfield

MASSACHUSETTS

CONN.

New Haven

New London

Providence

R.I.

MAINE

Kennebec River

Penobscot River

St. Castin

PEMAQUID

Fort Loyal

Wells

York

Portsmouth

Ipswich

Salem

Boston

BAY OF FUNDY

Port Royal

ATLANTIC OCEAN

MILES

25 0   50   100

175

violence or insult. Of the captives who reached Canada some
were ransomed and returned to their families. Others, particularly children, were converted to Catholicism by the mission priests and remained in Canada. Several of the girls
married young Frenchmen. Eunice Williams, daughter of
preacher Williams, not only became a Catholic but married
an Indian and became the mother of a large brood of half-
breeds who took the family name of their Puritan grandfather.[37]

Attacks such as that on Deerfield unquestionably served
to halt the westward expansion of Massachusetts; they did
not, however, appreciably affect its economic life. The wealth
of New England came from the sea coast and the sea—from
lumbering, ship building, shipping and fishing.

But as the seventeenth century gave way to the eighteenth
the shipping business of New England was experiencing a
slump. Fewer ships were being built at Salem and along the
Piscataqua than twenty years earlier. Of those that were
built many were for sale in England rather than for use by
the merchants of Massachusetts and New Hampshire. The
free trade upon which New England shipping had prospered
was a thing of the past. No longer could the navigation acts
be blandly ignored. Since 1691 Edward Randolph had been
Surveyor-general of Customs for North America; his collectors were stationed in every important port. Nor could
these collectors be circumvented by the old device of hauling
them before a local court and having their rulings reversed;
since 1697 all cases having to do with customs fell within the
jurisdiction of Vice-admiralty Courts, and the judges of those
courts were appointed on the recommendation of the Surveyor-general of Customs. Moreover, the colonial governors
—whether appointed by the King, as in Massachusetts, or
appointed by the proprietors, as in Carolina, or elected by
the freemen, as in Connecticut—were required to cooperate
with and assist the customs officers and the Vice-admiralty
Courts. Thus, whatever the rights or privileges granted to the
various colonies by their charters, all were brought under a
uniform, and unified, imperial control.

Canadiens en Raquette allant en guerre sur la nege

Above. The Stebbins House. Deerfield, Mass.

Courtesy, Pocumtuck Valley Memorial Association of Deerfield.

Right. French soldier on snowshoes.

From Bacqueville de la Potherie, *Histoire de l'Amérique Septentrionale.*

Sitting at the center of this network of imperial control, and administering it, was the Board of Trade, a committee of the Privy Council created in 1696 as successor to the Lords of Trade. And back of this committee, providing practical advice, stood the great merchants of London—men whose wealth supported the throne, men whose enterprise made jobs for the King's subjects, men who looked upon the colonies as of value only in so far as they made a profit for the Mother Country. Giving continuity to the program and rigidly maintaining it, regardless of what sovereign occupied the throne or what great nobles held places on the committees of trade, was a permanent secretariat that did the actual work. Randolph was but one who served, and guided, the committees during the reigns of Charles II, James II, William III and Queen Anne. And, like his fellow bureaucrats, Randolph never changed his mind, never backed down, never gave up.[38]

Such was the tightly controlled trade empire of which Massachusetts had become a part by the end of the seventeenth century. It is difficult to see how she could have done otherwise, but what a change from the day, only twenty-five years earlier, when her governor could dismiss the complaints of the King as "very inconsiderable," scarcely worthy of notice (see page 55).

Still, it must be recognized that in losing her independence Massachusetts had gained the assurance of aid against annihilation by the French. Nor had the first royal governors proved hard masters. Governor Phips was a native New Englander and had lived most of his adult life at Boston. His Pemaquid manners were sometimes a little realistic, as, for example, when he used his fists on a disrespectful ship captain, but he had the interests of New England at heart. And upon Phips' death in 1694 the executive administration of the colony fell into the hands of Deputy-governor William Stoughton, also native born and sympathetic to the colonial point of view. Even during the regime of the Earl of Bellomont—appointed Governor of Massachusetts, New Hampshire and New York in 1697—Stoughton continued as Deputy

SIR WILLIAM PHIPS.

Courtesy, Wm. Tudor Gardiner,
Gardiner, Maine.

Right, JOSEPH DUDLEY.

Courtesy, Massachusetts Historical Society, Boston.

in Massachusetts while his lordship spent most of his time struggling with the problems at New York.[39]

Only after 1702 did Massachusetts face the full impact of royal control, or, to be exact, control under the rules laid down by the Board of Trade. Bellomont and Stoughton had both died. Joseph Dudley, renegade native son of Massachusetts, one-time President of New England, and prominent member of the Council in the unhappy days of Andros, aspired to Bellomont's job. For ten years Dudley had lived in England. There he had held various offices, there he had reconciled himself to the Church of England, there he had made influential friends. Nonetheless, his great and abiding ambition was to return to America, in a position of power, and that ambition was now in a measure satisfied. He got the appointment as Governor of Massachusetts and New Hampshire, but he failed in his efforts to have New York and New Jersey included.

Dudley was commonly known as a "prerogative man," which is to say that he stood for bringing all governmental rights, including those of the colonies, into dependence upon the King. His reception by Massachusetts was somewhat less than cordial. Sewall noted with disapproval that he wore a wig—evidence of susceptibility to European notions. The General Assembly expressed its estimate of his value by voting him exactly one-half the salary formerly granted to Bellomont.[40]

A teamster, hauling a load of wood, probably expressed the feeling of the average New Englander toward Dudley. Meeting the Governor's big, shiny chariot on a narrow road, and being ordered to pull over, he replied, "I am as good flesh and blood as you . . . you may goe out of the way." And when the Governor angrily drew his sword, it was jerked out of his hand and broken.[41]

Dudley should have been content with the enemies he had in Massachusetts without adding the ill-will of Connecticut and Rhode Island. Possibly a sense of duty to the King, more probably personal ambition, prompted him to charge the two neighboring colonies—both self-governing under royal charters—with evasions of the navigation acts, with failure to co-operate in the war against Canada, with any irregularity that might bring about annulments of their charters and place them under his general governorship. The scheme did not work, but that Dudley should have attempted it shows the persistence of the plan for uniting the colonies into groups, or perhaps a single group, under a single royal governor. Equally, the resistance of Connecticut and Rhode Island reveals the tenacity with which the original colonial units clung to their individuality.[42]

One inter-colonial enterprise that even Connecticut and Rhode Island found unobjectionable was a postal service. Established in 1697 under the management of Andrew Hamilton, Governor of East Jersey, the service extended from New Castle through Philadelphia, Burlington, and Perth Amboy to New York, thence eastward through New Haven, New London, and Boston to Portsmouth, New Hampshire. Post riders travelled in both directions, in relays, on weekly schedules.[43]

Often the post riders served as guides or escorts for timorous or lonesome travellers. Thus in October, 1704, when starting on a trip from Boston to New Haven, Madam Sarah Knight rode out a few miles and spent the night, not too comfortably, at an inn where she knew the postman would stop. The next morning she jogged along with him, relieved of worry about forks in the road. A little above Providence they met the rider from the west; the two postmen exchanged letters and each turned back the way he had come, while Madam Knight jogged along behind the western man.

At Providence they crossed the head of Narragansett Bay on a ferry. A little farther on they came to a river which travellers usually forded, but Madam Knight dared not risk it. The good-natured postman found a boy who took her across in a canoe, leading her horse, and on they went. Soon it began to get dark; bushes and overhanging limbs of trees became real hazards on the narrow path that served as a road; Madam Knight could not keep up with her guide and feared that she was lost. She might have been even more frightened had she realized that she was approaching the

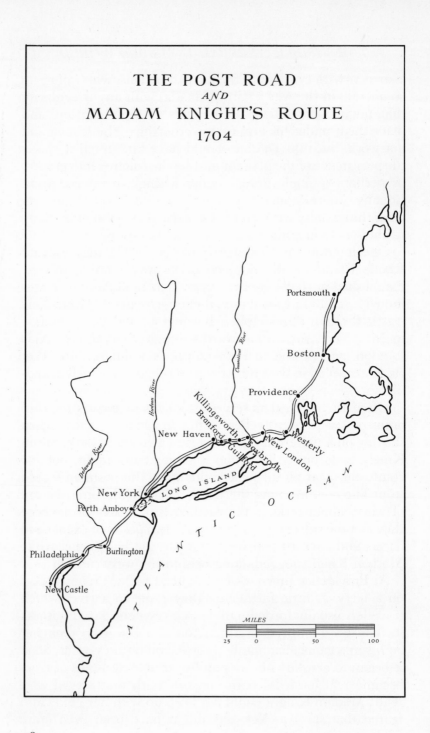

THE POST ROAD
AND
MADAM KNIGHT'S ROUTE
1704

Portsmouth

Boston

Connecticut River

Providence

Hudson River

Killingsworth
Branford   Saybrook
New Haven   Guilford   New London
Westerly

Delaware River

New York

LONG ISLAND

Perth Amboy

ATLANTIC OCEAN

Philadelphia   Burlington

New Castle

MILES
25   0   50   100

site of the Great Swamp Fight over which still hovered the angry ghosts of the hundreds of Narragansett Indians slain there twenty-eight years earlier by white-skinned people like herself. It was sweet music to her ears when she heard, not too far ahead, the notes of the postman's horn and judged that he was arriving at the inn where they were to spend the night. We can appreciate her feeling when we consider that she was a heavy woman, thirty-nine years of age, and had ridden near fifty miles that day, on a sidesaddle.

At four o'clock the next morning Madam Knight and the postman were again on their way. But when they came to the Pawcatuck River (presentday Westerly, Rhode Island), her courage was not equal to fording it. So the postman sped on with his letters, and she sat by the river's bank until the tide went out, after which she crossed over—into Connecticut colony, where, a few miles down the road, she spent the night with relatives. The next morning she had the good luck to meet an old man and his daughter on their way to New London, and rode along with them. As the father urged his lean nag into a hard trot, the girl, seated behind him and with only a bag for a pillion, protested: "Lawful Heart, Father! this bare mare hurts mee Dingeely,* I'me direfull sore I vow."

At the ferry over the Thames River the poor girl got a chance to rest her weight on her feet, though both she and Madam Knight were well scared by the tossing of the boat. On the western side of the river lay the village of New London where they arrived at about nine o'clock at night. Despite the hour Madam Knight looked up the local minister and accepted an invitation to spend the night at his home.

The following morning she was again on her way—guided by a young man recommended by the minister. The Con-

---

Dingeely is an obsolete adverb derived from the same root as the word *dingdong*. The general meaning is that of striking something with force. For anyone desiring more detailed etymological data the present author suggests a ride of thirty miles, as this girl had just taken, sitting sidewise, with only a bag as protection against the sharp backbone of a lean mare. Then put the mare into a hard trot. A description of the resulting physical sensations will be a proper definition of the word *Dingeely* as here used.

necticut River was crossed by a ferry at Saybrook, and the night was spent at Killingsworth. Probably Madam Knight did not know or give much thought to it if she did know, but in this village, at this time, the institution that later became Yale University was beginning its fourth year—in the home of Abraham Pierson. For many years Pierson had served as minister at Newark, New Jersey, of which Puritan town his father had been one of the founders (see page 13). In the early 1690's he had returned to Connecticut and accepted the call to Killingsworth, where in 1701 he joined in establishing the "Collegiate School within his Majesties Colony of Connecticut." We will hope that it was not one of Mr. Pierson's students who, when Madam Knight and her guide inquired the road to New Haven, told them to "Ride a little further, and turn down by the Corner of uncle Sams Lott."

Be that as it may, Madam Knight found the right road, continued on through Guilford and Branford, and early in the afternoon of her sixth day of travelling arrived at New Haven—one hundred and fifty miles from Boston. From her Journal we get some interesting sidelights on the life of this town, founded sixty-six years earlier by Theophilus Eaton and John Davenport as a Bible commonwealth. One day, while Madam Knight was at the house of a merchant, a "tall country fellow" came in, his mouth full of tobacco—"for they seldom Loose their Cudd, but keep Chewing and Spitting as long as they'r eyes are open." The caller "advanc't to the middle of the Room, makes an Awkard Nodd, and spitting a Large Deal of Aromatick Tincture, he gave a scrape with his shovel like shoo, leaving a small shovelfull of dirt on the floor, made a full stop, Hugging his own pretty Body with his hands under his arms. Stood staring rown'd him, like a Catt let out of a Baskett." At last he inquired, "Have You any Ribinen for Hatbands to sell I pray?" The merchant inquired how his customer expected to pay: if in silver coin, there was one price; if in provisions, as grain, beef or pork, there was another price; and if on trust, the price made up for the risk. This detail being settled, "the Ribin is Bro't and opened. Bumpkin Simpers, cryes its confounded Gay I vow;

Above. Comfort Starr House, Guilford, Conn., much as it appeared when Madam Knight passed through the town in 1704.

North room, first floor, Comfort Starr House, Guilford, Conn.

Both pictures are shown by the *courtesy* of the Library of Congress, Washington.

and beckning to the door, in comes Jone Tawdry [presumably his wife], dropping about 50 curtsees, and stands by him; hee shows her the Ribin. *Law You*, sais shee, *its right Gent,* * do You take it, *tis dreadful pretty."* "

When Yankee Doodle made himself dandy in 1704 his wife saw to it that he had something more Gent than a feather for his hat.

* Elegant or genteel.

Patents and Pirates

DINNER AT NORWALK—"Fryed Venison, very savoury." Madam Knight was again on the road. After two months in New Haven—apparently settling an estate—she had found that a trip to New York was necessary. With her, and like herself on horseback, went a male relative and a man she had hired to "wait on" her. After dinner they rode on through Stamford, "a well compact town"; toiled up the steep hill to Greenwich; and crossed into New York province. Supper, at Rye, turned out badly and Madam Knight went hungry to bed—in an upstairs lean-to room which she shared with the two men. She had a bed by herself but the tick was filled with corn husks that rattled and the covers were thin. The men fared even worse; their bed was so short that their feet stuck out. All of them were glad enough to be on their way by daylight the next morning, Thursday, December 7, 1704.[1]

It was still early when they passed through the village of Mamaroneck; otherwise they would have noted and been duly impressed by the manor house of Colonel Caleb Heathcote, Lord of the Manor of Scarsdale, member of the Governor's Council and prosperous merchant of New York. The Colonel's manorial title was comparatively recent, and after the fashion of newcomers he was striving to improve the community, his particular interest being the development of a Church of England parish. Perhaps a little spiritual leaven was desirable. Some of the oldtimers could have told stories of a "quiet" but "nimble" trade carried on with certain Barbadian merchants whose ships found relief from Mr. Randolph's prying customs inspectors in the lonely inlets along Long Island Sound.[2]

Four or five miles down the road Madam Knight and her companions came to New Rochelle. There they had a good breakfast at the house of a Frenchman. In fact, the town, as the name would indicate, was largely made up of French Huguenots who had settled there, in 1690, as a refuge from religious persecution in their homeland. Among them was a four-year-old boy named Peter Faneuil.[3]

From New Rochelle the road bore westerly to Kings Bridge, over which the travellers crossed Spuyten Duyvil creek to the northern end of Manhattan Island. This bridge, the only land connection with the Island, had been built ten years earlier by Frederick Philipse. We have already met him and his remarkable wife, Margaret (page 71). Both had now gone on their last great trading venture, and their grandson, nine years of age, was Lord of the Manor of Philipsborough, a domain stretching northward more than twenty miles along the Hudson River. Madam Knight made a note of the bridge toll, three pence for each horse and rider.[4]

There still remained a ride of nearly fourteen miles along a narrow highway between farms and farm houses, barns and leafless peach orchards. Less than halfway down the Island they passed through the village of Harlem. Six or seven miles farther on they came to the farm (*bouwerie* in the Dutch tongue), formerly belonging to Governor Peter Stuyvesant. A few houses stood along the road and the tiny village was commonly spoken of as The Bowery. A mile and a half beyond was the place where Jacob Leisler had been hanged in 1691, though his remains were no longer buried at the foot of the gallows—Governor Bellomont having caused them to be re-

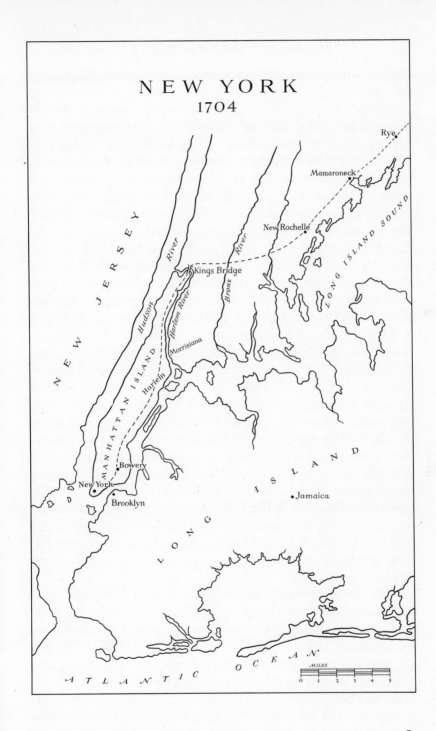

NEW YORK
1704

Rye

Mamaroneck

New Rochelle

LONG ISLAND SOUND

NEW JERSEY

Hudson River

MANHATTAN ISLAND

Harlem River

Bronx River

Kings Bridge

Morrisiana

Harlem

Bowery

New York

Brooklyn

LONG ISLAND

Jamaica

ATLANTIC   OCEAN

MILES
0   1   2   3   4   5

moved, with pomp and ceremony, to the Dutch Church in the city.[5]

Another five minute ride—along a road known as Broadway—brought the visitors abreast the still somewhat new Trinity Church—"very fine," Madam Knight thought it. Almost every New Yorker of any consequence had contributed to its building. Caleb Heathcote had furnished lime and other materials. Captain William Kidd, a well-to-do shipmaster, had "lent a Runner & Tackle for hoising Stones." The edifice stood just outside the northern city gate—on land formerly a part of the King's Garden and used to supply the Governor's table. The grant had been made by Governor Fletcher after he knew that his term of office was at an end; his successor, the Earl of Bellomont, complained that the loss of this land deprived him of a place to pasture his cow.[6]

Trinity differed from the other churches of New York in that it was the *established* church, supported by public taxes and, through the Bishop of London, subject to the Anglican hierarchy. When, in 1693, the provincial Assembly passed a vague law authorizing a "settled Ministry," its members had no thought of creating an established church, much less of establishing the Church of England in the province. However, Governor Fletcher so interpreted the act and Trinity was the result. Its first rector was William Vesey, a native son of Massachusetts. He had graduated from Harvard College under Increase Mather. But he had a leaning toward the Anglican discipline, and with the financial backing of the Trinity vestrymen he went to England, received ordination, and, returning to New York in 1697, was formally inducted as rector at Trinity.[7]

The "gate" by which Broadway entered the "walled" part of the city was a street sign rather than an obstruction. Nor was there much left of the wall; most of the stones had been used to build a new city hall at the upper end of Broad Street, the city's only paved street. Broadway itself was still a dirt road, and in bad weather pretty difficult. Ordinarily, however, an effort was made to keep the streets clean; John Vanderspeigel had been hired for that job in 1695—at a yearly wage of £30. A few coaches lumbered about the streets. Gov-

THE REV. WILLIAM VESEY

Courtesy, Trinity Parish, New York, and the New-York Historical
Society, New York.

ernor Fletcher had one in 1697. Bellomont used a calash, which was a somewhat lighter vehicle than a coach. For the convenience of the thirsty there were three wells on Broadway and four on Broad Street. And for the safety of those who had to be out after dark there were scattered street lights.[8]

Most of the houses were of brick, sometimes of various colors laid in checkered designs. Madam Knight was struck with the neatness of the rooms—the woodwork "very white scowr'd," the hearths and stairways laid with tile and kept clean. "The English go very fasheonable in their dress," she noted. "But the Dutch, especially the middling sort, differ from our women, in their habitt go loose, wear French muches which are like a Capp and a head band in one, leaving their ears bare, which are sett out with Jewells of a large size and many in number. And their fingers hoop't with Rings, some with large stones in them of many Coullers as were their pendants in their ears, which You should see very old women wear as well as Young."[9]

Madam Knight found the people friendly and sociable, "they'r Tables being as free to their Naybours as to themselves." Sleigh-riding to places of entertainment was a popular winter diversion. Madam Knight was one day a guest at a farm house near The Bowery, where she shared in a "handsome Entertainment of five or six Dishes and choice Beer and metheglin [fermented honey and water], Cyder, &c." —all of which the hostess said was the produce of her farm. The traffic, too, impressed Madam Knight; she estimated that on the way out and back her party met between fifty and sixty sleighs—travelling "with great swiftness and some so furious that they'le turn out of the path for none except a Loaden Cart."[10]

The total population of New York City in 1704 did not exceed five thousand people, most of them living within the half-mile-square area south of the wall. It was a very mixed population. The Dutch still predominated in number though the English were gaining on them. There were many French or Flemish people. Perhaps every seventh person was a negro; many of these were house servants, but others worked

Right. Dutch House, Pearl Street, New York, 1697.

From *Valentine's Manual,* 1847.

Vechte-Cortelyou House, Gowanus (Brooklyn), New York, 1699.

From *Valentine's Manual,* 1858.

in the fields on the upper part of Manhattan Island. Across the Harlem River, in 1698, Attorney-general James Graham had thirty-three slaves working the farm land of Morrisania Manor, which he rented from Lewis Morris.[11]

This strange medley of humanity was a survival from the Dutch beginnings—beginnings in trade rather than in a quest for new homes by spiritually or racially related people. New York was a "foreign" city when, by the sword, it was added to England's growing colonial empire. For a quarter of a century it was ruled as conquered territory, the inhabitants having no voice as to how they were governed.

With the "glorious revolution" of 1688, however, a new day dawned for New York. Among the instructions given Governor Sloughter when he departed from England to take up his official duties in the province was one authorizing him to call a representative Assembly "according to the usage in our other Plantations in America." New York had joined the ranks of the royal colonies; its government would be in the hands of a governor, a council, and an assembly. The governor would be appointed by the King, and usually would be a professional royal servant; the Council would be formed from leading men of the province, often upon the recommendation of the Governor but always with the approval of the King; the Assembly would be elected by the qualified voters of the province and would presumably express the popular point of view.[12]

It was a fair prospect for a well-ordered government and a contented people. But when Governor Sloughter sailed into New York harbor, he found himself facing guns and being asked for his credentials. Unquestionably it was an irritating reception, but the execution of Leisler did not solve the problem. The people simply divided into two factions—the Leislerians and the anti-Leislerians. And Governor Sloughter dodged the issue by dying.

Thus in the critical year of 1691 the government of New York was in confusion; the provincial treasury was empty; the already scanty population was being drained away to the adjoining colonies. This in face of the fact that New York's frontier was the door through which a French attack might be expected. The Lake Champlain waterway provided a natural approach from Montreal to the upper Hudson, as the charred walls of Schenectady made all too evident. Except for its military strength Albany would have shared the fate of Schenectady, and with Albany gone, the way would have been open to New York city and the Atlantic seaboard. Upon Albany depended the safety of New England, New Jersey, Pennsylvania, Maryland, and Virginia, as well as the province of New York. Leisler had seen this clearly enough, but his effort to get the colonies to co-operate had failed. The Lords of Trade saw it clearly enough, but they were not willing to attempt another Dominion of New England. That experiment had turned out badly.[13]

There was, to be sure, a touch of the ever-present idea of colonial consolidation in the two commissions given to Colonel Benjamin Fletcher in 1692. He was made Governor of both New York and Pennsylvania, though the commissions were separate and each colony retained its individual existence. The ostensible reason for the dual appointment was to provide Pennsylvania with a Governor in the place of William Penn, still under suspicion of attachment to the exiled James II. But the appointment did not pass without challenge; from his hiding place in London Penn wrote Fletcher, ". . . that Country and [the] Government of it [are] inseperably my property . . . tread softly and with caution."[14]

But if the idea of a political union of the colonies was quiescent, a plan of military union was very much to the fore. Shortly after Fletcher's appointment, Queen Mary, doubtless on the advice of the Lords of Trade, sent a circular letter to Massachusetts, Pennsylvania, Maryland, and Virginia. directing them to assist the Governor of New York with men or money for the protection of Albany. At about the same time Connecticut and the Jerseys were ordered to place their militia under Fletcher's command.[15]

The scheme, however, did not work out as well as might have been hoped. The Jerseys furnished a few men. Connecticut stood squarely on her charter rights in regard to her militia; she was willing to give aid, but she would command her own troops. Maryland and Virginia voted money for supplies, but the funds failed to materialize. The peace-loving Quakers of Pennsylvania would "rather dye than resist with Carnall weapons," Fletcher discovered. Massachusetts had no scruples about war, but when Chidley Brooke, Governor Fletcher's messenger, arrived at Boston late in July, 1693, with a demand for troops, Governor Phips was not receptive. "What he said was loud & angry" and it was summed up in the statement: "I will not send a man nor a farthing of money to the assistance of N. York," and, doubtless thinking of the Indians lurking on his own frontiers, added, "Tis a monstrous thought to suppose I should." The fact that the Queen had had the thought did not interest Phips. When Brooke complained to a member of the Massachusetts Council that the Governor had been "very hot," he was told, "Sir, you must pardon him. Tis dogg-days. He cannot help it." [16]

To a professional civil servant such as Fletcher, with no roots in American soil, the attitude of the colonies was incomprehensible. He could not grasp the fact that the group individualism which had enabled them to create their separate settlements, each with its distinctive life, would cause them to fear union or even close relationship with their neighboring colonies. He could not understand that each of them preferred to take care of itself—with the aid of the Mother Country in an emergency, of course—and that they expected their neighbors to do the same. Colonial union might be ever so reasonable, ever so advantageous materially, but it broke against the dogged resistance of the colonists themselves. Fortunately there was no well-organized French attack from Canada, only sporadic raids; and Peter Schuyler, commander of the Albany militia, took care of those. Equally important, Schuyler saw to it that the covenant chain between the Iroquois and the English was kept bright. The Canadians had no wish to become involved in trouble with those merciless savages. [17]

If Governor Fletcher did not understand New England or Maryland or Pennsylvania, he did understand New York. There was in that province a group of men of wealth and ability who thought of America primarily in terms of the

PETER SCHUYLER.

Courtesy, Erastus Corning, 2nd, Mayor, City of
Albany, New York.

British empire and their own financial advancement. They were, by instinct and background, anti-Leislerians. With them Fletcher aligned himself. From them he demanded support for his policies, and got it both in the Council and in the Assembly. In return he gave them what they wanted. Caleb Heathcote, for example, was a rich young merchant recently arrived from England; he was made a member of the Governor's Council; soon he was receiving fat contracts for supplying the military forces with clothing and firewood.[18]

Or, take the case of Frederick Philipse. He, too, was a member of the Council. He had a great deal of land along the Hudson. Fletcher erected the land into the Manor of Philipsborough. The old Dutchman probably cared very little about the honor, but there were more solid advantages. To the lord of the manor went the monopoly of operating mills and other profitable enterprises. The right to build Kings Bridge was an item of the manorial grant, and, as we have already seen, every horse and rider that passed over that bridge paid toll to Philipse. Every ship that in passing under it required the bridge to be raised paid toll to Philipse. Those tolls must have paid for the bridge and its upkeep many, many times over.[19]

Substantial, too, was Fletcher's aid in the acquisition of wide acres, sometimes wide miles, of land in the as yet unsettled parts of the province. As Governor, he had the authority to dispose of unpatented land provided the applicant had a deed from the Indian owners, which latter could usually be secured without too great expense. To men who voted right in the Council and Assembly or who contributed generously to the Governor's private pocket, land patents were readily available. Thus a comparatively few men came into possession of vast tracts which they held subject to ridiculously small quitrents.[20]

One of the more impressive of these land grants was that made to Captain John Evans of His Majesty's Navy; it was five hundred square miles in area and located in Ulster County. The consideration, according to Evans' own testimony, was a quitrent of forty shillings annually to the King and a present of £500 to Governor Fletcher. Adolphus Philipse, a son of Frederick Philipse, received a patent for 135,-

CALEB HEATHCOTE.

Courtesy, New-York Historical Society, New York.

ooo acres on the eastern side of the Hudson opposite present-day Newburgh. For this he paid an annual quitrent of twenty shillings. Caleb Heathcote, in partnership with eight other men, applied for and received a patent to an even greater tract north of Poughkeepsie; it came to be known as the Great Nine Partners Patent. A group of five Albany speculators, including Peter Schuyler and Godfrey Dellius, minister of the Dutch church, were given a vague title to a narrow strip of land running for fifty miles on each side of the Mohawk River. Others received similar grants, some larger and some smaller.[21]

The consequences of these grants were very great. Since they contained no provision requiring the patentees to bring in settlers, great areas remained vacant. Since the annual quitrents were not large enough to force the owners into selling a part of their land in order to hold the rest, they could hold it all, and did. They would lease the land, not sell it. Thus whoever settled on their land must do so as a tenant rather than as a fee simple owner. "What man," observed the Attorney-general of New York, "will be such a fool to become a base tenant to [these great landlords] when for crossing Hudson's river that man can for a song purchase a good freehold in the Jersies?" Many others had arrived and would arrive at the same conclusion. The tide of settlement that should have created farms and villages in New York province flowed to the Jerseys and Pennsylvania.[22]

Probably Governor Fletcher did not realize the harm that his exorbitant land grants would do; probably he honestly believed they would advance settlement of the right kind. True, in making the grants he lined his own pockets, but that was the custom of the day. Nor were aspiring landlords the only source of income for an enterprising governor. Ship captains seeking commissions as privateers often paid handsomely, particularly if their destination was known to be the Indian Ocean rather than the usual French shipping lanes. For more than three quarters of a century the rich merchandise and gold coins of the Indies had attracted English pirates. Perhaps the business had deteriorated socially since the days when it was dominated by the Earl of Warwick, but under the merchants of New York and Rhode Island it was better organized. The pirates now had their own ports—on the island of Madagascar, off the eastern coast of Africa. To these ports they could return after their forays; at them they could refit their craft and recruit their crews; there, in stores supplied by ships from New York, they could buy clothing, food, drink —everything a pirate needed, though at staggering prices. Wine that sold for £19 a cask in New York brought £300 at Madagascar. This business of supplying the pirates laid the foundation of many a New York fortune.[23]

When a Madagascar ship returned to New York, Arabian gold, as the coins of the East were called, flowed freely. Usually there came back with each ship a few men or boys who had seen a little more than merchant service; their easily won wealth and the stories they told awakened the envy of their friends. To the farm boy of New Jersey or Connecticut the Indian Ocean was the Wild East, a place of adventure where a brisk lad might make his stake—enough to enable him to buy a farm of his own, marry the girl of his choice, have a pew in the Congregational church. To the experienced ship captain it was a place where he might acquire enough Arabian gold to settle down as a respectable merchant, perhaps be named to the Governor's Council. All the captain needed was a commission from the Governor—the New York or Rhode Island merchants would furnish the rest. Thus when Captain Tew, "a most notorious Pirate," applied to Governor Fletcher for a commission to despoil the French "in the mouth of Cannada River [the St. Lawrence]," the Governor was very happy to comply—at a price. There was no secret about where Tew was going—he publicly announced that his real objective was the Indian Ocean. Nor did this announcement dampen the Governor's regard for his pirate friend. The two dined and supped together; took rides in the Governor's coach, drawn by six horses; exchanged presents. And when Tew returned from his voyage—having made £8000 as his own share—the Governor was waiting for him —with open pockets.[24]

What Fletcher collected from Tew we do not know, but it may be estimated from his fees in the case of the good ship *Jacob,* which in April, 1693, arrived off New York after a successful voyage to the Indian Ocean. With the loot turned into ready money and divided among the fifty-five veteran pirates aboard, Captain Edward Coates, who was in command, prudently went into Long Island Sound and sent a messenger to New York to clear up any difficulties about getting the men safely ashore. For "protections" (certificates of good character) for the men, the Governor was offered £700, which offer was readily accepted. In the meantime, however, a number of the men had jumped ship with their loot, and the amount could not be made up. The deal was finally settled by Captain Coates giving the ship to Governor Fletcher in return for clearance and "protections." The Governor sold the ship to Caleb Heathcote for £800, considerably less than it was worth, and everybody was happy.[25]

In general, the Governor asked a hundred dollars per pirate for ordinary "protections," and from the master or owner he seems to have taken what the traffic would bear. Captain Coates claimed that he paid Fletcher £1300 to get himself clear. In addition, the more courtly pirate captains usually gave presents to the Governor's wife and daughter.[26]

All in all, it was estimated that from gratuities of one sort or another—"he left no trick or fraud unpractised to get money"—Fletcher put some £30,000 in his pocket during the five and a half years he served as Governor of New York. This could be estimated as having a value of about a half million dollars, as money went two hundred and fifty years later.[27]

Partly on account of his land grants and partly on account of his encouragement of pirates, Fletcher was dismissed in 1697. His successor was the Earl of Bellomont, who, as will be recalled (page 178), also held commissions as Governor of Massachusetts and of New Hampshire; in addition he was given the command of the militia of Connecticut, Rhode Island, and the Jerseys. The idea of military unity was growing. However, Bellomont spent very little time in New England and he had no occasion to put the militia question to the touch. He was very busy in New York—uncovering Fletcher's misdoings. He was, in fact, under specific instructions from the Lords of Trade to have the more exorbitant land grants

annulled. In the future no such extensive grants were to be
made, or any at a quitrent of less than two shillings six pence
for each one hundred acres, with a requirement that settlement of the land must be under way within three years.
Piracy must be stopped.[28]

Bellomont doubtless did his best, but even as he poured
out to the Lords of Trade story after story that he had collected about Fletcher, the Lords passed along to him one that
they had picked up in Germany. It appeared that shortly
after Bellomont's own arrival at New York a sloop belonging to Frederick Philipse, and under the command of his
son, Adolphus, had sailed out of New York. Somewhere along
the coast it had met a ship returning from Madagascar. Into
the sloop had gone everything aboard the Madagascar ship
except some negroes. Then the sloop sailed into Delaware
Bay and lay concealed while the Madagascar ship proceeded
to New York and landed its negroes. That done—all in strict
compliance with the navigation laws—the Madagascar ship
sailed back down the coast, met the sloop, reloaded the East
India goods, and went around the north of Scotland to Ham-
burg, Germany—without Governor Bellomont or Mr. Randolph's customs collectors having been any the wiser.[29]

Worse yet was the trick played on Bellomont by Captain
Kidd. It all went back to an agreement made in 1696—in
London—between Bellomont, Kidd, and Robert Livingston.
Kidd will be recalled as one of the contributors to the building of Trinity Church. He had served with distinction as a
privateer against the French; he owned considerable property in New York, and lived in a pretentious house in the city.
Livingston was a Scotchman who had settled at Albany in
1674; twelve years later he was Lord of the Manor of Livingston. Governor Fletcher characterized him as a man who
had "made a considerable fortune by his employments in the
Government, never disbursing a six pence, but with the expectation of twelve pence, his beginning being a little Book
keeper, he has screwed himself into one of the most considerable estates in the province."[30]

Under the contract of 1696, Kidd agreed to attack and
make prizes of the New York and New England pirates in the

Indian Ocean, thus putting an end to piracy in that region, a service very acceptable to the King and the East India Company. Bellomont undertook to get Kidd a commission from the King and to supply four-fifths of the cost of buying and fitting a proper ship, Livingston and Kidd supplying the other fifth. Kidd was to secure his crew, a hundred or so men, who were to receive as pay not more than one-fourth of the value of any prizes taken—and no prizes, no pay. Of the remaining value of the prizes, four-fifths was to go to Bellomont and one-fifth was to be split between Kidd and Livingston. To finance his share of the expense, Bellomont took in five partners, one of them being His Grace, the Duke of Shrewsbury, King William's Principal Secretary of State.[31]

Kidd bought his ship in England and sailed it to New York, where he completed his crew. "Many flockt to him from all parts, men of desperate fortunes and necessitious in expectation of getting vast treasure," reported Governor Fletcher, and added, "Twill not be in Kidd's power to govern such a hord of men under no pay."[32]

Fletcher's prophecy proved only too accurate. Failing to catch any pirates, Kidd's crew became mutinous and demanded prizes be they what they might. According to Kidd's story, they locked him in his cabin while they robbed a few ships. As a result of these breaches of discipline, Kidd found himself in possession of the *Quidah,* a richly loaded Moorish merchant ship, and with her he started for America. In the West Indies he learned that he had been proclaimed a pirate, and leaving the *Quidah* there, he came on northward with a small sloop in the spring of 1699. Just how much and what of his loot he carried along is uncertain; one of his men stated that he brought "several Bailes of East India goods, three score pound weight of gold in dust, and in Ingots about a hundred weight of Silver and several other things which he beleived would sell for about ten thousand pound." Anchoring at the eastern end of Long Island, Kidd got into touch with a lawyer who in turn got into touch with Kidd's partner, the Earl of Bellomont. Interestingly enough Bellomont was found at Boston, where according to the contract of 1696 Kidd was to deliver his prizes. Interestingly, too, Robert

Livingston, the other partner in the venture, came riding posthaste across country from Albany to Boston. There was considerable dickering; one of Kidd's men presented Lady Bellomont with some jewels; it was pointed out that the *Quidah,* with a cargo worth £30,000, would remain in the West Indies if there were any difficulties; seemingly Bellomont promised to protect Kidd. In any case Kidd came into Boston—and was shortly under arrest.[33]

The rest of the story is shrouded in some mystery. Kidd was sent to England for trial. The interest of the Duke of Shrewsbury and other prominent men was concealed, as were other pertinent pieces of evidence. It appears that the English public was aroused against pirates; Kidd had made himself particularly noticeable; and he was offered up as a vicarious sacrifice for the sins of all the pirates who had reduced the dividends of the East India Company. On May 23, 1701, he was hanged at Execution Dock, London—just ten weeks after the Earl of Bellomont died a natural death in New York.[34]

Later generations have so embellished the story of Captain Kidd that his name has become synonymous with piracy in its most romantic form. Much sand has been moved on the eastern end of Long Island by people hunting for treasure presumably buried by Kidd or his men; Bellomont heard that "Arabian Gold is in great plenty there." However, among the pirates of the day Kidd would have been looked upon as a rank amateur; ready money, not contracts or promises, was what brought forgiveness to a pirate.[35]

At about the time Kidd was trying to make terms with Bellomont at Boston, Captain Giles Shelly arrived at New York. He, too, had come from the Indian Ocean, but whatever part he had taken in actual piracy was well covered up. Moreover, he had cleared from Madagascar as all honorable men engaged in the business always did. As he sailed slowly along the Jersey coast, he dropped off a man with a letter addressed to Stephen De Lancey, a rising New York merchant and one of the backers of the voyage. Governor Bellomont reported the homecoming: they "so flushed them at New Yorke with Arabian Gold and East India goods, that they set the government at defiance." De Lancey and his partners made a profit of £30,000 on the voyage. How much Captain Shelly got for his share we do not know but we do know that in later years his house was furnished with considerable luxury—brass glittered at his hearths, seventy-four pictures hung on his walls, his furniture was painted in gay colors, and in an era when chairs were not common he had seventy. He was one of the respected merchants of New York, even as Kidd had been before his clumsy venture in a business that he did not understand. What the ordinary pirate-seaman made during a term of service in the Indian Ocean may be estimated from the contents of the chests of two who came home on Shelly's ship. The inventory showed "about seaven thousand eight hundred Rix dollars & Venetians, about thirty pounds of melted Silver, a parcel of Arabian & Christian Gold, some necklases of Amber & Corrall, sundry peaces of India silkes." [36]

The execution of Kidd, and the extension to the colonies of an act of Parliament providing death penalties for piracy, marked the end of the Madagascar trade. Also, Bellomont had seemingly been successful in annulling some of the more exorbitant grants of land, such as that to Captain Evans; but Lord Cornbury, who succeeded to the governorship in 1702, joined with Fletcher's old friends in annulling the annulments. In addition, Cornbury made a few grants on his own account. A tract known as the Wawayanda Patent, consisting of one hundred and fifty thousand acres in Orange County, was given to Chief Justice John Bridges and eleven partners. A huge block of land extending twenty-five miles along the north bank of the lower Mohawk River and reaching northward twenty-two miles—squarely in the heart of the Indians' hunting grounds—was confirmed to thirteen Albany speculators; the Kayoderosseras Patent it was called for short. A *Little* Nine Partners Patent supplemented the already large Nine Partners Patent in Dutchess County. [37]

Lord Cornbury, like Fletcher, expected gratuities for approving these land grants. Even in the most personal transactions he made the public purse pay his bills. When Lady Cornbury died, Elias Boudinot, he who had thumbed his nose at Governor Leisler (see page 154), advanced money for the funeral expenses; his lordship paid the debt by granting some public land to Boudinot. When funds were appropriated for military expenses, Cornbury put them in his own pocket. In fact, he found no bribe too small and no situation unworthy of a bribe. Nor was avarice his only fault. In 1707, Lewis Morris, writing to the Secretary of State of England, in behalf of the Assembly of New Jersey, had the following to report: ". . . I must say something which perhaps no boddy will think worth their while to tell, and that is, his [Cornbury's] dressing publicly in woman's cloaths every day, and putting a stop to all publique business while he is pleaseing himselfe with that peculiar but detestable magot." By the word *magot* Morris meant *fantastic notion*—and, at that, the word is perhaps a more suitable one than some applied today to those afflicted with Cornbury's *peculiarity*.[38]

In paying their respects to Lord Cornbury, the people of New Jersey knew whereof they spoke. Since 1702 he had been Governor of their colony as well as of New York. The long separation between East Jersey and West Jersey had come to an end. It had been a separation marked by more than a surveyor's line or a stretch of rough country. From its beginning East Jersey had looked eastward to New York, while West Jersey, due to its Quaker origin, had become closely associated with the growing province of Pennsylvania. Both were proprietary provinces, which is to say the soil and the right of government had been granted by the King to proprietors who, in effect, were the King in their own proprietaries. As will be recalled, the Duke of York was the original proprietor; he had transferred his title to Berkeley and Carteret; Berkeley had sold his divided half (West Jersey) to a group of Quakers; Carteret's heirs had sold his half (East Jersey) to a group of English and Scottish merchants. The power of a proprietor to transfer title to the soil within his proprietary was beyond question; his power to transfer the right of government was very questionable, and all proprietors of New Jersey subsequent to the Duke of York had to face a challenge of their governmental authority. However, except for the short period during which the Dominion of New England functioned, the proprietors in each of the Jerseys had exercised and continued to exercise the right of government; they, rather than the King, appointed the governors and the governors' councils.[39]

The Quakers who bought West Jersey divided the purchase into one hundred shares, each share being rated as a "propriety" and backed by 13,000 acres of land, which acreage they estimated as being one one-hundredth of the total of West Jersey. Edward Byllynge, the principal man among the purchasers (see page 67), owned several proprieties, while others had but a fractional interest in a single propriety. There are records of as little as a thirty-sixth of a propriety, which meant that the owner had one thirty-sixth voice in the distribution of the land within his "hundred" (the 13,000 acres covered by his share), and in the selection of a governor or in the general management of the affairs of the province he had one thirty-sixth voice in one among a hundred shares or proprieties.[40]

Following the death of Byllynge in 1685 the majority of the proprietary shares of West Jersey were purchased by Doctor Daniel Coxe, of London, who assumed the government of the province through Deputy-governors. As the principal land owner (he estimated his holdings at a million acres), Coxe made every effort to attract new settlers; he encouraged the cultivation of fruit in the Cape May area; he established a pottery industry at Burlington. But the good Doctor discovered that the job of running even a small colony was too much for one man, and in 1692 he sold the larger part of his shares to a group of London merchants—most of whom were not Quakers, and one of whom, incidentally, was later a partner with Stephen De Lancey in Captain Shelly's profitable voyage to Madagascar. These new proprietors, operating under the name of the West Jersey Society, continued the land-selling program. New settlers flowed in from England and the neighboring colonies, and within a few years the formerly dominant Quakers were but a fraction in the growing population.[41]

Burlington, on the east side of Delaware River a few miles above Philadelphia, was the principal town. There, sawmills

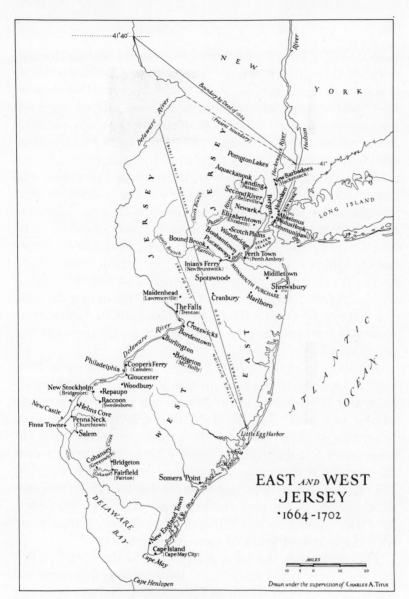

EAST *AND* WEST
JERSEY
·1664-1702

From the *Atlas of American History.*

turned timber into lumber. Brewers, bakers, and clothwork-
ers plied their trades. A large markethouse provided a center
around which several fairs were held each year. Bread, beer,
beef, pork, butter, cheese, and fruit were offered for local
consumption or for export to Barbados in the ships swinging
at the wharves. Small boats went to and from Philadelphia.
Children attended schools supported by rents from land set
aside for educational purposes. Above the markethouse was
a spacious hall in which the Assembly of the freeholders held
its sessions. Surrounding the town were the "fair brick houses"
of such men as Samuel Jennings, a Quaker who had come
over in 1680, and Jeremiah Basse, agent of the West Jersey
Society. John Tatham, the one-time Deputy-governor, lived
on the north side of town in a "Great and Stately Palace"
with a "delightful Garden and Orchard." Bordering the eastern shore of Delaware River, from the Falls to Salem, were
plantations whose surpluses and needs made the province
prosperous.[12]

The manner of life in East Jersey was quite different. New
England had early put its impress upon that region. Middletown and Shrewsbury, in the Monmouth Purchase (see page
12), were typical New England towns, self-contained even
to settling in their town meetings many matters which the
proprietors felt should have come within the jurisdiction of
the provincial Assembly. After a quarter of a century they
still insisted that they owned their land in fee simple and that
the collection of quitrents by the proprietors was a grievance.
Newark, holding to its Connecticut traditions, sympathized
with the anti-rent point of view of its neighbors.[13]

The grain that the land produced and the cattle that it
pastured were what made East Jersey worth quitrents and
effort. ". . . a man who lives here needs go no where to buy
any things," wrote one of the settlers, adding, "Here he can
have Corn and Cattle and every thing that is necessary for
mans use, if he be Industrious; only the thing that is dearest
here is Cloathing, for there are but few sheep to this Country. . . ." The credit balance that enabled the settler to get
his clothing, and a few other things such as kettles and axes,
came mostly from the sale of surplus cattle. Ordinarily the

LEWIS MORRIS.

From a portrait by John Watson.
Courtesy, Brooklyn Museum, Brooklyn, N. Y.

cattle roamed at large; town brands proved their regional origin; private brands proved their actual ownership; and the calf took the brand of the cow it followed. After the spring roundup, beef was on its way to Barbados, and the farmer could pay for his clothes.[14]

Side by side with small farms operated by the owners and their families, were a few estates such as that owned by Lewis Morris. At the age of twenty he had inherited three thousand acres in the Monmouth Purchase, near Shrewsbury, and another two thousand acres in New York. The latter land lay easterly of the Harlem River and included Jonas Bronck's old farm—destined to give its name to the Bronx. Not even the honor of having his New York estate erected into the Manor of Morrisania—for which Governor Fletcher unquestionably expected something—could keep Morris in that province. He rented his new manor to his father-in-law, Attorney-general James Graham, and made his own residence in East Jersey. Along with the usual overseers and indentured servants he had sixty or seventy negro slaves working on his farms. He operated an iron mill from ore dug on his own land. He served as judge in his county, and was a member of the Governor's Council.[15]

Elizabethtown had been the seat of government under the Carteret regime, and the first deputy-governors for the new proprietors—the twenty-four English and Scottish merchants who bought the proprietary in 1682—made their residence there. They found the inhabitants "a sober professing people, Wise in their Generation, Courteous in their Behaviour, and Respectful to us in office among them." Elizabethtown, however, lacked the depth of water required for shipping, and the proprietors were intent upon having a port town. At the mouth of the Raritan River they found a suitable location, on a point of land where a ship of three hundred tons could "easily ride close to the Shoar, within a planks length to the houses of the Town."[16]

All that was needed was the town, and that they began building—frame houses thirty feet long by eighteen wide and eighteen high. In spacing the houses it was directed that they "be not Crowded one upon another, but that Each House

have backwards a considerable void for a Yard and Garden."
And in front of the houses, along the river bank, a row of trees
was left "for shade and shelter exceeding pleasant." The
place had been called Amboy by the Indians; to this the
proprietors prefixed the name of Perth, in honor of the Earl
of Perth, one of their Scottish associates. There, at Perth
Amboy, the proprietary officers made their homes; there the
merchants and traders conducted their businesses; there, from
1686 onward, the provincial Assembly held its sessions. Perth
Amboy had displaced Elizabethtown as the capital of East
Jersey.[47]

Through the activities of the Scottish proprietors many of
their fellow countrymen—farmers, merchants, overseers—
came to East Jersey subsequent to 1682. Prominent among
these Scots was Andrew Hamilton, a merchant, who settled
with his family at Perth Amboy in 1686. The following year
he was made Deputy-governor, and after the demise of the
Dominion of New England he was appointed Governor of
both East and West Jersey.[48]

Along with his official job, and perhaps as a part of it,
Hamilton often acted as agent for the absentee landlords.
When William Dockwra, of London, got the idea that he
would make his East Jersey land pay a profit by raising cattle,
Hamilton advised against it—"it is the greatest cut throat in
the world to medle in any thing toutching a plantation if a
man is not his own overseer upon the spot . . . *servants eats
a man up if he is not Constantly over their heads,"* wrote the
canny Scot.[49]

One commission that Hamilton undertook had long consequences. In 1691 Thomas Neale, Master of the Royal Mint
in London, had received from the King a monopoly for the
carriage of letters at a profit in the colonies. In quest of someone to handle the business for him in America, Neale hit upon
the Deputy-governor of New Jersey. By 1697 Hamilton had
his relays of post riders organized and the colonies were
getting their first real postal service—on a strictly business
basis. The postmen with whom Madam Knight rode through
Rhode Island in 1704 were employees of the organization
founded by Hamilton and were expected to make a profit

for Neale. They were not paid to loiter along with females in distress. So successful was the enterprise that in 1707 the British government bought out Neale's monopoly and placed the colonial service under the General Post Office.[50]

Unquestionably, Hamilton was one of the most competent men in the province, but the position of Deputy-governor was a thankless one. Hamilton and his official associates necessarily represented and worked for the proprietors, while the majority of the inhabitants objected to being governed by the appointees of a group of merchants more interested in quit-rents and profits than in the welfare of the people. They— the people, the freeholders of Middletown, Shrewsbury, Newark and other lesser towns—felt that they were entitled to a governor and council appointed by the King, as in New York. And the Board of Trade agreed with them; to the members of that all-powerful body the proprietary form of colony was an anachronism—a step above a trading post but not a proper government for a colony in England's growing trade empire.[51]

To pacify the people of the province and thereby avoid the wrath of the Board of Trade, the proprietors, in 1697, had ousted Hamilton and installed Jeremiah Basse as Deputy-governor. And in one respect the change had been advantageous. For several years the proprietors had striven to have Perth Amboy declared a free port, that is, a port at which ships might enter and clear. To this New York had objected vehemently—had insisted that all ships entering the area at the mouth of the Hudson must declare at and clear from New York, otherwise that port would lose its commercial importance along with revenue needed for the defense of Albany. In this contention the Board of Trade backed New York. Basse decided to put it to a test. The ship *Hester,* of which he was part owner, was lying at Perth Amboy. Basse had her loaded with barrel staves, and cleared her for departure. At that point Governor Bellomont sent a party of soldiers over to the Jersey town and seized the ship on a charge of failure to clear from New York. Perhaps this incident had something to do with Bellomont's characterization of Basse as "the most a scowndrel that ever I knew; he will bragg and lye with any man living." Be that as it may, in a suit at the King's Bench in England Basse not only won a verdict recognizing Perth Amboy as a free port, but was awarded damages against the Governor of New York for the loss of the *Hester*.[52]

This was a most important victory for the proprietors of East Jersey, but they did not have long to enjoy it. Their authority was nearing an end. Basse, strangely enough, aligned himself against the proprietors in the matter of quitrents. The freeholders took the hint and refused to pay. In desperation the proprietors ousted Basse and re-appointed Hamilton as Deputy-governor, but it was too late. The people were in open resistance to the proprietary authority.[53]

In March, 1700, William Sandford, President of the Essex County Judiciary, prepared to open court at Elizabethtown —where a former governor had noted the sober, courteous and respectful character of the people. Now, however, Samuel Carter, speaking "in behalfe of himself and his Neighbors," called President Sandford, "President Rascall," and challenged him "and the rest of the Justices out of the Court severall times, often giving the President the Lye and Bidding him Kiss his arse. . . ." In fact, according to the record, Carter "used and uttered words and Actions wholly unfitt to be mentioned," and the court was forced to adjourn amid "a Generall noise and hollowing with unseemly actions and Insolent Gestures."[54]

Later in the year Judge Sandford tried to hold a court at Newark. Some fifty or sixty men, including Samuel Carter, rode up from Elizabethtown and again challenged the procedure. The judge was pulled off the bench; "his hatt and wigg halled of his head"; his sword was taken away and broken; and, for good measure, he received "Three blows, Two of which ponches in the brest & one in the face." His fellow judges were "grosely abused, some of their clothes torn of their backs with many other abusefull words & actions Received from the Rabbell." The constable was "pulled by the haire & his staff Taken from him & Thrown out of doore."[55]

In Monmouth County, where the freeholders had consistently opposed the proprietary authority, Lewis Morris was President of the County Court. He had no intention of being pushed around by the "Rabbell," and when the people of Middletown and Shrewsbury flouted his authority he sent the sheriff to make a few arrests. "This the people tooke Greaviously," we are told, and when the officer persisted, they "went & met him, banged him, broake his head and sent him packing." [56]

With East Jersey thus in turmoil, the Lords of Trade stepped in with a demand that the proprietary patents for both Jerseys be surrendered. The proprietors had no alternative but to comply, and in April, 1702, East and West Jersey were united as the royal colony of New Jersey. Queen Anne, who had just succeeded to the English throne, commissioned her cousin, Lord Cornbury, the newly appointed Governor of New York, to act also as Governor of New Jersey. In recognition of the dual nature of the colony it was arranged that the Assembly should meet alternately at Burlington and Perth Amboy. [57]

Five years passed—of misrule and corruption. The New Jersey Assembly was in session at Burlington. Lord Cornbury was present—in male attire presumably. In the Speaker's chair was Samuel Jennings, the old Quaker. "May it Please the Governour," said the Speaker, "We her Majestys loyal subjects, the Representatives of the Province of New Jersey, are heartily sorry, that instead of raising such Revenue as it is by the Governour (as we suppose by the Queens directions) required of us, we are obligded to lay before him the unhappy Circumstances of the Province." Point by point the Speaker spread before the Governor his shortcomings, bluntly charging him with favoring those who paid him best. "And we cannot but be very uneasy," continued Jennings, "when we find by these new methods of Government our Liberties and Properties so much shaken, that no man can say he is Master of either, but holds them as Tenant by Curtesie, and at Will, and may be stript of them at pleasure." The address ended with some sage advice. "We conclude," said the Speaker, "by advising the Governour what it is that principally engages the Affections of a People, and he will find no other Artifice needful, than to let them be unmolested in the enjoyment of what belongs to them of Right." [58]

Nor did Cornbury get off with merely listening to this lecture. Lewis Morris, as we have seen (page 207), summed up the whole sordid story in a letter to the Secretary of State; and with his letter Morris enclosed a copy of Jennings' address, a petition from the Assembly, and a Remonstrance of the people—which latter Robert Quary, Judge of the Admiralty Court at Philadelphia, called "a most scandalous libell." However, the documents had their effect; within the year Cornbury had ceased to be Governor of New York and New Jersey, though the sheriff held him in New York until he settled up with his creditors. [59]

In surrendering their patents to East and West Jersey, it was understood by the proprietors that the rights to the soil would be restored to them, and this was done. Thus the proprietors or their agents continued to collect quitrents on land previously granted and to dispose of undeeded land. In fact, the proprietary title to the Jerseys survived the American Revolution, when the Baltimore, Penn, and Fairfax titles fell, and exists to this day. Each year at Burlington and Perth Amboy those who own a share in a proprietary, or their representatives, meet to transact business. There is, to be sure, little business to transact, since practically all of the land of New Jersey has long since been deeded. An occasional sand bar, appearing where none existed, is at the disposal of the proprietors; a quitclaim deed for an unquiet title sometimes justifies a search of the vast mass of records still in the custody of the two proprietary groups, but that is all that is left of the patent that once included every acre of land in New Jersey. [60]

Among the records stored at Burlington is one, we will hope, showing the assignment to Mahlon Stacey, in 1680, of eight hundred acres of land at the Falls of the Delaware. Jasper Danckaerts had spent a miserable night there in 1679 (see page 73). In 1714 William Trent, a Philadelphia merchant, bought the land and laid out a town which in his honor was called Trent Town, and which, seventy-six years later, superseded Burlington and Perth Amboy as the capital of the State of New Jersey. [61]

Brotherly Love

"FOR THE LOVE OF GOD, me, and the poor country, be not so *governmentish,* so noisy and open in your dissatisfactions," begged William Penn, from London, of the quarrelling leaders of Pennsylvania.[1]

The bickering had started with Penn's departure from Pennsylvania in 1684 (see page 104). Soon it had reached a point where even Chief-justice Nicholas More, one of the Quaker founders of the province, was being cited for impeachment by the Quaker dominated Assembly.[2]

With a view to bringing some order into the government, Penn, in 1688, appointed as Deputy-governor his kinsman John Blackwell, a soldier, a Puritan, and a resident of New England. The Quakers made short work of him. Samuel Richardson, a member of the Council, insisted "that William Penn could not make a Governor," and when Blackwell in anger ordered him out of the Council room, he replied, "I will not withdraw, I was not brought hether by Thee, & I will not goe out by thy order; I was sent by the people, and thou hast no power to put me out." Even more contemptuous of the Deputy's authority were Thomas Lloyd, Keeper of the Great Seal, and David Lloyd, Attorney-general of the province. Those two men, though not closely related, were both originally from Wales. Thomas had come to Pennsylvania in 1683; David had arrived three years later. Both were Quakers and both refused to take orders from the Deputy. It was with evident relief that Blackwell accepted dismissal by Penn, but his parting remark about the Philadelphia Quakers lived on. "Each prays for his neighbor on First Days [Sundays] and then preys on him the other six," he said.[3]

Penn, still in England, needed the prayers of his fellow Quakers seven days a week. The revolution that swept James II from the throne left Penn without friends in high places. As against the possibility of being called upon to answer charges of treason, proprietary rights in Pennsylvania seemed unimportant, and Penn authorized the provincial Council to elect its own executive head. The choice fell upon Thomas Lloyd, and it was to him that Governor Sloughter of New York, in 1691, directed a plea for help against the French, who were momentarily expected to be streaming down the Hudson valley. Lloyd replied, "While retaining a good regard for your difficulties we are unable to answer your requirements." When this was reported to England, the Lords of Trade not without reason came to the conclusion that Pennsylvania would not fight even if attacked.[4]

An attack on Quaker principles, however, found the Pennsylvania Quakers quick to resist—with their own weapons, of course. Fundamental among the teachings of the founders of the sect were a disregard for ritual and a dependence upon the Inner Light. These fundamentals were now challenged by George Keith, headmaster of Penn's school in Philadelphia and a former close associate of the Proprietor. In part Keith was probably moved by ambition to succeed to leadership of Quaker thought; in part he probably recognized that many Quakers actually hungered for the mystical element in religion. In any case he questioned the sufficiency of the Inner Light and he commended the ceremony of the Lord's Supper. So attractive were his teachings that full half of the Philadelphia Meetings accepted his point of view. But to Thomas Lloyd and the older group, the Keithians were merely agents of disunity, and at the Yearly Meeting of 1692 they were vigorously censured. Keith sailed for England where he was "disowned" by the London Quakers. His followers, however, remained as a disturbing element in the colony founded as a haven for Quakers.[5]

One unhappy consequence of the Keithian controversy was the loss by Pennsylvania of its first printer. William Bradford had learned his trade in London as an apprentice of Andrew Sowl, whose imprint appeared on much of the Quaker literature of the day. In 1685 the former apprentice married the daughter of his master and sailed for Pennsylvania—with his new wife, a printing press, and enough type to do small jobs. For some years he made a precarious living from provincial contracts, from a bookstore which he established, and from a paper mill in which he had a part interest. Whether or not he agreed with Keith's teachings Bradford did a good business printing and selling the pamphlets that resulted from the differences of belief. But with Keith's condemnation the young printer found himself without official patronage and under arrest. A timely offer, from Governor Fletcher, of the New York public printing was gratefully accepted, and thirty years later we find Bradford the publisher of New York's first newspaper.[6]

As will be recalled, Fletcher was, from 1692 to 1694, Governor of Pennsylvania as well as of New York. Lloyd's refusal to help in the defense of Albany had been too much for the Lords of Trade, and disregarding Penn's proprietary rights, they had advised the King to take charge through his own Governor. For two years Pennsylvania was practically a royal colony. But so far as getting the Quakers to vote money for war even a royal governor found himself powerless. "We may and doe commiserate you," said Lloyd for his fellow Quakers, "but supply you at this juncture we can not." In other words the Quakers of Pennsylvania would not "dip their money in blood." In the end they saved their principles by voting money to "feed the Hungry and clothe the Naked" Indians; that the money was used to buy guns and scalping knives was something they could not help and need not know.[7]

What the Pennsylvania leaders wanted above everything

was the return of Penn—to accept the responsibility for defending his province. By 1694 he had cleared himself of conspiring with the exiled James II and was in a position to demand the return of his proprietary, which he did. The Attorney-general and the Solicitor-general of England gave opinions in favor of Penn, and the Lords of Trade had no alternative but to accede. Before doing so, however, they called Penn before them and made him promise to go personally to Pennsylvania as soon as possible; in the meantime he was to direct the provincial Assembly and Council to provide men or money for the general defense of the American colonies; and particularly he was to supply men or their equivalent for the aid of New York. To all of this Penn agreed, and pending his own arrival in America, appointed William Markham, who had been his deputy back in 1681, to again serve as Deputy-governor.

Had Penn been a little less worldly he well might have cast aside his proprietary claims and joined with a group of some forty men and women who arrived in Pennsylvania in the spring of 1694. They devoutly believed, and their faith was based upon the most exact mathematical calculations, that the Millennium was to begin that autumn. They had journeyed all the way from Germany to meet this event on the banks of Wissahickon Creek—in presentday Fairmount Park, Philadelphia. At their head was twenty-one-year-old Johann Kelpius, graduate of the University of Altdorp in Bavaria, theologian, mystic and near saint. Many of the others were of the same type. When the Millennium failed to start on schedule, they still hoped on, living in caves, often without food, devoting their lives to meditation and prayer. They may be commemorated as pioneers among the many strange religious groups attracted to early Pennsylvania.

While Kelpius, on Wissahickon Creek, prayed for the day of perfect peace, and Markham, in Philadelphia, struggled to secure from a stubborn Assembly the funds for prosecuting a war, Penn, in London, worked out, on paper, a scheme of colonial union which, had it been adopted, might have saved a future conflict. What he proposed was a congress made up of two representatives from each of the colonies, and presided over by a commissioner appointed by the King. He suggested that the meetings might be held at New York and that the Governor of that province might be the commissioner. All problems of intercolonial justice, commerce, and defense should be within the jurisdiction of the congress. Not even Edward Randolph, in his constant and voluminous recommendations to the Lords of Trade, had submitted a program equal to this.[10]

But Randolph was still on the job. Nineteen years of unpopularity and insult had in no way lessened his adherence to what he conceived to be his duty. He was now Collector-general of Customs and as such roamed from colony to colony gathering information, supervising his deputy-collectors, often personally making arrests. Sometimes he had a royal frigate at his service; at other times he got about as best he could. Thus, on Sunday, April 14, 1695, he was coming up the Delaware River aboard a hired sloop when his attention was attracted to the brigantine *Dolphin,* of Boston, lying quietly at anchor off Chester, Pennsylvania. He had the sloop put alongside and climbed aboard. After a few inquiries of William Trout, master of the *Dolphin,* Randolph scratched "a broad Arrow on the Mast and said he would & did seize the said Brigantine for the King." The broad arrow was a symbol of royal ownership traditionally placed on trees reserved as masts for the King's ships. Thus, the *Dolphin* was under arrest on suspicion of evasion of the Navigation Acts. The next morning Master Trout petitioned Governor Markham for a prompt trial, which petition the Governor granted. A jury was summoned; the case was heard; a verdict was given in favor of the *Dolphin;* and she was allowed to proceed to Boston with her cargo of wheat and flour. At the same time damages in the amount of forty-four pounds eighteen shillings were awarded Master Trout as recompense for his trouble; and when Randolph refused to pay, a warrant was issued for his arrest.[11]

Experiences of this sort were what caused Randolph to insist upon the establishment of Vice-admiralty courts in the colonies. And, as we have seen (page 176), such courts were created in 1697. For the Philadelphia district Robert Quary

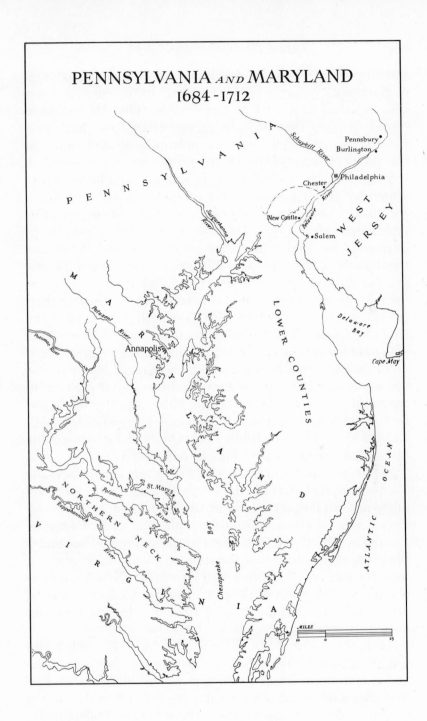

PENNSYLVANIA *AND* MARYLAND
1684 - 1712

P E N N S Y L V A N I A

Schuylkill River

Pennsbury
Burlington

Chester
Philadelphia

New Castle
Salem

WEST
JERSEY

Susquehanna River

M A R Y L A N D

Patuxent River

Potomac River

Annapolis

LOWER COUNTIES

Delaware River

Delaware Bay

Cape May

St. Mary's

Potomac River

NORTHERN NECK

Rappahannock River

V I R G I N I A

Chesapeake Bay

A T L A N T I C   O C E A N

MILES
10   0   25

was appointed as judge, doubtless on the recommendation of Randolph. Quary was no newcomer to America. We met him as acting Governor of Carolina in 1685. He had been dismissed from that position on the charge of "harboring pirates," which would indicate a familiarity with some of the problems involved in illegal trade.[12]

In the case against the *Dolphin* Randolph had been represented by David Lloyd—acting probably as a lawyer for a fee rather than in an official capacity or because of any principle involved. Three years later Lloyd took a prominent part in a case against the Vice-admiralty court. It appears that goods of considerable value had been seized on the ground of illegal importation and stored at New Castle in the custody of the Marshal of the Admiralty. Action for their release was brought before a local court. In the midst of the trial Lloyd asked the marshal by what authority he had acted. The marshal produced his commission—an impressive document embellished with a picture of the King. Lloyd took the commission, held it up "in a scornful way," and pointing to the picture jeered, "This is a fine baby, a pretty baby, but we are not to be frightened by babies." The justices thought Lloyd's remarks were funny, but Quary failed to see the humor, and reported the incident to London.[13]

Sometimes, to the irritation of Randolph and Quary, the Vice-admiralty Court did not get jurisdiction over cases having to do with illegal trading. In 1698, for example, the *Loyal Factor* was caught evading the regulations while taking on a cargo at New Castle. But when Markham stayed her under his proprietary authority, the difficulty was easily adjusted by a gratuity of £80 from Caleb Heathcote, New York merchant and part owner of the ship. Thus the Collector-general of Customs and the Judge of Vice-admiralty lost fees that ordinarily would have gone to themselves.[14]

More serious were the charges brought by Randolph and Quary against Markham on the ground that he "supported and Encouraged" pirates. Ships fitted out in Delaware Bay had, they said, taken part in notorious piracies in the Indian Ocean; returned pirates walked the streets of Philadelphia. Markham's son-in-law, according to Randolph, was a veteran of the fleet in which Captain Every, in 1693, raided Moorish shipping on the Red Sea. It was common knowledge that Captain Kidd, on his way up the American coast in 1699, lay off the mouth of Delaware Bay and received supplies from Philadelphia. And when Shelly was off Cape May, clearing for his arrival at New York, Quary had asked Governor Markham for a boat and forty men with which to go out and capture the pirate ship. Markham had refused, which probably was just as well for Quary's physical welfare, but the Governor's failure to comply provided telling criticism when the story was laid before the Lords of Trade.[15]

So damning were these complaints that Penn realized the time had come for him personally to take charge of his proprietary if he did not wish the King to do so. On September 3, 1699, he sailed for Pennsylvania. With him were his young wife, Hannah, and a grown daughter, Letitia, the child of his first marriage. Also accompanying him was James Logan, a twenty-five-year-old Scottish lad destined to become his secretary and trusted advisor. During the voyage, so the story goes, the ship was attacked by pirates. Penn, as became one of Quaker principles, went below, but Logan joined with the crew in standing ready to beat off the assailants. When later the young man was reproved by Penn, he replied, "I being thy servant, why did thee not order me to come down? But thee was willing enough that I should stay and help fight the ship when thee thought there was danger."[16]

It was a thriving, prosperous, and happy province that Penn found awaiting him on the shores of Delaware River, if we may wholly believe an account written at the time. The soil brought forth grain in abundance. Mills along every creek turned the grain into flour. Bakeshops offered tarts, pies, and cakes as well as bread. In Philadelphia there were hundreds of "Noble Houses"; there were rope-walks, breweries, and other industries. At Germantown the inhabitants manufactured paper and linen. Spacious country homes of the gentry, surrounded by gardens and orchards, dotted the landscape. Beggars were unknown in the province; lawyers and physicians were in little demand—the people being "very Peaceable and Healty." "Barrenness among Women hardly to be heard of, nor are old Maids to be met with; for all commonly Marry before they are Twenty Years of age, and seldom any young Married Woman but hath a Child in her Belly, or one upon her Lap." So wrote Gabriel Thomas, who had lived in Pennsylvania since 1681.[17]

Making due allowance for local pride, Philadelphia had made mighty strides in the fifteen years since Penn had last seen it. It had changed from a straggling settlement to a busy city, the capital of a province containing more than twenty thousand inhabitants who consumed English manufactured goods to a value of perhaps £14,000 annually and exported an even greater value in tobacco, furs, grain, horses and other products of the soil. But not all the inhabitants of Philadelphia lived in "Noble Houses"; many of them lived in tenements above tightly packed warehouses or stores.[18]

For Penn, one of the noblest houses in the city, the home of Samuel Carpenter, was made available, and there he and his family lived for a few months. With the coming of spring, however, they deserted the city for their country home of Pennsbury, twenty-five miles up the Delaware and somewhat opposite the West Jersey town of Burlington.[19]

The Pennsbury house was two and a half stories high, of brick construction. Downstairs there were a Little Hall, a Great Hall (dining and living room), a Best Parlor, and an Other Parlor. In the Great Hall there were a long table, a little table, six chairs, a napkin press, and a collection of dishes, mostly pewter; also in this room, and stored in a Great Red Trunk, were tablecloths, napkins, and bed linen in considerable quantity. The Best Parlor contained two tables, two great cane chairs and four smaller ones, seven cushions, and the usual brass andirons, fire shovel and tongs. Most of the rooms were equipped with fireplaces.[20]

Upstairs there were four bedrooms and a nursery—Mrs. Penn had given birth to a son shortly after her arrival in the province. The Best Chamber was furnished with a bed and bolster, two pillows, two blankets, a silk quilt, a table, a looking glass, six cane chairs, a water stand, and a chamber chair. The other rooms were somewhat similarly equipped. In the garret there were four extra bedsteads, a quilt, blanket, rug,

THE SLATE ROOF HOUSE IN PHILADELPHIA

was built by Samuel Carpenter as a home for his
family. Upon the arrival of the Penns in 1699 it was
put at their disposal and was occupied by them for
some months. Upon their retirement to Pennsbury,
Logan continued to live in the house and it was
looked upon as the proprietary center in the city.
Even after the Penns returned to England in 1701
Logan retained the house as a residence and office.
In 1703 financial reverses forced Carpenter to offer
the house for sale and it was bought by William
Trent at a price of £850, which might be estimated
as equivalent to $17,000. Later the house was
owned by Isaac Norris, though he appears to have
preferred "Fairhill," in the Northern Liberties of
the city, as his permanent home.

and other necessities including three sidesaddles, one of which belonged to Mrs. Penn.[21]

The kitchen and laundry were separate from the main house. There was a small brew-house. And there was a stable for twelve horses. Penn fancied himself somewhat of a judge of horse-flesh; he had brought over with him a young stallion named Tamerlane—said to be out of Godolphin, a famous Arabian sire. In addition to the family coach Penn kept a calash for the use of his daughter Letitia, and a sedan-chair for Mrs. Penn.[22]

As a matter of course there were a number of indentured white servants and negro slaves about such a place as Pennsbury. And, as from the days of Eve, washday presented its troubles. With a big wash piled up, it was discovered that the houseboy's wife, Parthenia, had been "sold to Barbadoes" and he wanted to go down to Philadelphia for a last visit before she was shipped. Mrs. Penn suggested instead that Parthenia should come up to Pennsbury and help with the wash, but had some misgivings: linen had a way of disappearing in Parthenia's vicinity.[23]

The road between Pennsbury and Philadelphia left a good deal to be desired; at times it was impassable for the Penn coach. A surer means of conveyance was the family barge; and when the needs were small, though urgent, a message could be sent down to Logan by the Burlington boat and back would come the "great stew pan" that had been left in the house at Philadelphia, or a sack of corn meal needed in making mush for visiting Indians, or some coffee berries, if the guest merited that tasty new beverage. Of course, the Burlington boat did not bring small articles up to Pennsbury; it dropped them off at Samuel Jennings' where a boat from the Penn place picked them up. Chocolate was often on Mrs. Penn's list of wants, which perhaps explains the Proprietor's growing waistline.[24]

Unfortunately we have no authentic portrait of Penn at this time but we know that he was plump; also, from the fact that he bought wigs, we may assume that he wore them; and from the concern which he showed over a pair of misplaced leather stockings, we may judge that he used them, but whether because of fashion or as a protection to his gouty leg is uncertain. The wonder is that he did not have rheumatism; the roofs leaked and the house was often damp.[25]

One of the compensations for the hardships of Pennsbury was the proximity of Samuel Jennings and other Quaker friends at Burlington. There is a pretty story of one such visit. It appears that Jennings and a few of his friends were sitting in his house smoking their pipes when they saw the Penn barge coming up the river. It pulled in at the wharf and the Governor climbed out. It was evident that he was making a call—and it was a fact known to all that he detested the use of tobacco. Jennings and his friends hastily laid their pipes out of sight and as the Governor entered the room, thick with smoke, not a man was smoking. Sensing the situation Penn said, "Well, friends, I am glad that you are at last ashamed of your old practice," to which Jennings replied, "Not so, not so! We thought it best to lay down our pipes sooner than give offense to a weaker brother."[26]

This friendly banter with his fellow Quakers of West Jersey was all very pleasant, but Penn had soon discovered that not all the people of his own province were as peaceable as Gabriel Thomas had pictured them; and there were altogether too many lawyers—Robert Quary for one, and David Lloyd for another. Logan characterized Lloyd as "extremely pertinacious and somewhat vengeful." But the immediate vengefulness came from Quary. He complained to Penn against Lloyd for his "pretty baby" remarks, and Penn, not daring to disregard the implied insult to the King, dismissed Lloyd from his place as Attorney-general.[27]

As a result of this reprimand Lloyd put himself at the head of a discontented popular party which demanded a new and more liberal Frame of Government. Penn, always inclined toward democracy in government, told the members of the Council and Assembly, both of which bodies were chosen by the electors, to go ahead and draw up a Frame that would suit them. ". . . if there be anie thing that jarrs, alter itt," he said, "if you want a law for this or that prepare itt." And "prepare itt" they did. By the Charter of Privileges agreed upon in 1701 the Assembly became the sole lawmaking body, and except for the right to appoint a Deputy-governor and some few other officers the Proprietor was divested of any part in the government of the province.[28]

Penn was not too happy about the Charter of Privileges but accepted it. When, however, David Lloyd drew up a Charter of Property, Penn balked. The land was his and he proposed to make the most of it—to recoup his expenses in founding the province, to supply his living costs, and to provide for his children. His fellow settlers, the voters, might control the Assembly and make the laws, but he would control the Land Office, and he did. The income from quitrents was slight—people would not pay; the income from the sale of land little more than met the expense of surveys and the salaries of the Commissioners; but as a long-term investment Penn's faith in the land was justified. Consistently he saw to it that when a new area was opened, choice parcels of land were reserved for himself—parcels that would rise in value as the settlers improved their adjoining acres.[29]

Just when it seemed that Penn had solved the more pressing problems of his province, and that he might look forward to spending the rest of his life happily at Pennsbury, he had to face an attack from England. The Lords of Trade, doubtless on the recommendation of Edward Randolph, had presented to the House of Commons a report on the proprietary and corporate colonies, namely, Pennsylvania, East and West Jersey, Maryland, Carolina, Connecticut, and Rhode Island. These colonies, according to the report, did not conform to the laws of trade, they harbored pirates, they neglected their defenses, and so on. The uproar then going on in East Jersey (see page 215) well illustrated the charge of proprietary weakness. Voluminous complaints against Pennsylvania, gathered by Colonel Quary and filed with the Lords of Trade, further supported the recommendation that all the colonies be placed directly under the Crown.[30]

Penn realized that if he were to retain his proprietary he would have to fight for it personally in London. He had already made Logan Secretary of the Province; in addition, he now made him Commissioner of Property and Receiver-general—in other words, Logan became responsible for the

William Penn's Writing Desk.

Now in possession of The Library Company of Philadelphia, Ridgway Branch, by whose *courtesy* it is here shown.

231

sale of land and the collection of quitrents. To act as Deputy-governor during his absence, Penn appointed Andrew Hamilton, who was still hanging on as Governor of the Jerseys. Pennsbury was put into the hands of a caretaker; Logan was authorized to look after all loose ends; and in November, 1701, Penn and his family sailed for England. Close behind them went Quary—to do Penn "all the mischief" he could. The surrender made by the Jersey proprietors in the spring of 1702 was, Penn felt, "an ugly preface" for his own defense.[31]

It was serious business for Penn, this struggle for his proprietary. He had spent a great deal of money on the venture; he had received little in return—not enough to feed his horses and pay his servants, he said; he had lived high, probably too high, and he was hard-up—"I never was so low and reduced," he wrote to Logan early in 1703. Logan advised him to make a bargain with the Lords of Trade, "if to be had on any good terms," and let the Crown take over the government of the Province. The "most knowing" among the Pennsylvania Quakers admitted that government was "so ill-fitted to their principles" that it had best be in other hands; they did not want the responsibility for defending the province. Penn, apparently, was inclined to agree with them, for in the summer of 1703 he was pressing the Lords to buy him out.[32]

Quaker principles were again on the defensive in Pennsylvania that summer of 1703; George Keith, the one-time Philadelphia schoolmaster, was back. In the eight years since he had been "disowned" by his fellow Quakers, Keith had gone over wholeheartedly to the Church of England. In 1700 he was ordained by the Bishop of London, and the following year was chosen as American agent for the newly organized Society for the Propagation of the Gospel in Foreign Parts. The purpose of this organization, commonly called the S. P. G., was that of missionizing for the Anglican Church. In the American colonies it was particularly concerned with assisting in the formation of new parishes and in supplying and supporting ministers.[33]

As the agent of the S. P. G., Keith roamed back and forth through the colonies from New England to North Carolina.

It was due to his encouragement that Caleb Heathcote organized a parish covering his manor of Scarsdale. From one
of the ministers supplied to that church we get an interesting
insight into the thinking back of the S. P. G. It was, said the
minister, "a great and glorious design of propagating the
faith, and settling the church as well in this, as in others of
Her Majesty's plantations, thereby rescuing them from the
grossest ignorance, stupidity and obstinacy; and therein right-
ing them in those damnable and dangerous positions and
tenets which have been imbued and instilled into those poor,
unwary, deluded souls in their minority, by blind, ignorant,
and illiterate guides." That was something for the Mathers
to think over.[34]

The wavering Quakers of New Jersey and Pennsylvania
were the especial targets of Keith's exhortations, and a considerable number were won back to the Church of England
by his efforts. Occasionally he met his match, as in the case
of a Seventh-Day Baptist who, during a dispute in a Philadelphia meetinghouse, forced Keith "to quit the field to his
great dishonor." Royal officials, such as Colonel Quary, naturally supported the Church of England crusade, but Logan
probably expressed the sentiments of the great majority of
the Pennsylvanians when he reported to Penn, "That lump
of scandal, G. K., has left us for Virginia."[35]

The Charter of 1701 had made a governor more or less
unnecessary, and on his part Deputy-governor Hamilton had
spent little time on Pennsylvania. In March, 1703, while with
his family at Perth Amboy he was seized with "a violent
fever," and a month later was dead. As his successor, Penn
selected a twenty-six-year-old Welshman, John Evans—"He
shows not much, but has a good deal to show," wrote the
Proprietor to Logan. And so it proved.[36]

With Evans came the Proprietor's eldest surviving son,
the child of his first wife, twenty-three years of age, and also
bearing the name of William. "Watch over him for good,
qualify his heats, inform his judgment, increase his knowledge," wrote Penn to Logan. The purpose of the visit was
that the young man might "improve his study . . . with in-
tervals in the woods and upon the waters, where," said the

father, "I should be glad such company as Isaac Norris, Samuel Preston, and sometimes Samuel Carpenter . . .," all very respectable Quaker gentlemen, the last named being fifty-six years of age."

Logan probably did his best to guide young Penn along the right path. He rented the Clarke mansion, the finest house in Philadelphia—located at Chestnut and Third streets—and there he and young Penn and Governor Evans and a young English lawyer named Roger Mompesson set up housekeeping. But the son of the Proprietor did not always spend his evenings with his books or in grave converse with Samuel Carpenter. Rather "his natural sweetness and yielding temper" led him to join the Governor in unseemly revels. On one occasion there was a gay masquerade where women ran about in breeches and men in skirts, "contrary to nature and decency." At another time, while he and the jovial Governor were visiting Enoch Story's tavern late at night, a riot broke out. Young Penn called for pistols (that from the son of the Proprietor and in the City of Brotherly Love) ; the lights went out; and the chief offenders, among whom was Penn, were hauled before the Mayor's Court. Said Isaac Norris, "I wish things had been better or he had never come." Even young Penn realized that it was time for him to be going home. To pay his bills and finance the trip, he had to sell the manor set aside for him by his father years earlier. The buyers were William Trent (for whom Trenton, New Jersey, is named) and Isaac Norris. The price reflected the seller's need. Today a part of the area is occupied by a city named Norristown."

Logan, always loyal to his employer, blamed young Penn's difficulties on his father's old enemy: "He was barbarously treated by that rascal David Lloyd." And the Proprietor, like any good father, rose to the defense of his son: "if those illegitimate Quakers [meaning his former friends in Pennsylvania] think their unworthy treatment no fault towards me, they may find that I can, upon better terms, take their enemies by the hand than they can mine," by which he meant that he might surrender the province to the Queen; which, after their brief experience with Fletcher, was the last thing the Quakers wanted."

JAMES LOGAN.

From H. B. Hall's engraving reproduced as a frontispiece in
Volume II of the *Correspondence between William Penn
and James Logan.*

235

All that the Quaker leaders of Pennsylvania asked was to be allowed to live peaceably under their new Charter—with a powerful Assembly, a shadowy Council and a weak Governor. But they were already discovering that success has its price. The people of the Lower Counties (later known as Delaware) did not care to continue their union with Pennsylvania under a government such as that adopted in 1701; they realized that they would be swallowed up in their growing neighbor. New Castle, the chief town of the Lower Counties, had been a place of importance before Pennsylvania was even thought of; the people were different from those of Pennsylvania. Isaac Norris, in 1700, had referred to them as "Frenchified, Scotchified, Dutchified"—and our minds wander back to the 1660's and 1670's, when Peter Alricks and Ephraim Herrman and John Moll were the leading men there (see pages 74 and 98). When the Charter of 1701 was under consideration, the Lower Counties had insisted upon the inclusion of a clause permitting them to separate from Pennsylvania if, after a three-year trial of the existing union, they did not care to continue it. Now, in 1704, they exercised this option; in the future they would share the governor appointed for Pennsylvania but they would have their own assembly and their own way of life.[10]

With Pennsylvania and the Lower Counties separated, a promise of peace seemed to settle over the hitherto warring factions. Even Quary stopped agitating against the proprietary government. "Only that lurking snake, David Lloyd, keeps and is kept at a distance," said Logan. And so the winter of 1704–05—the coldest that anyone could remember—passed by, and spring gave place to summer. On July 10 Logan received a request to meet with David Lloyd and two associates "upon a business they had to communicate." The business proved to be a letter from young Philip Ford of London informing them that he and his family, rather than Penn, owned Pennsylvania and the Lower Counties.[11]

The name of Philip Ford, father of the writer of this letter, was well known to the old settlers of Pennsylvania. Back in 1681, before there was any land office in Philadelphia or even any Philadelphia, it was Ford, at his house in Bow-lane,

Cheapside, London, who took the down payments for land in Penn's new colony. In fact Ford appears to have been the banker for Penn's venture, and when Penn needed money he drew on Ford. As security for these loans Penn gave Ford a mortgage on Pennsylvania and the Lower Counties. Naturally Ford charged interest on the balance due from Penn, which balance grew constantly larger. About 1696 Parliament laid a tax on money at interest. This would have added an appreciable amount to the charges which Ford would have made against Penn, and Ford suggested a way to avoid it. If Penn would give him a bill of sale for Pennsylvania and the Counties, Ford could exhibit that instead of the mortgage note and the tax would not be applicable. Penn at first demurred, but he, like his son, had a "natural sweetness and yielding temper." Ford was a fellow Quaker. Penn had no reason to suspect him, and he signed the bill of sale.[42]

For some years all went well; Penn was freed from financial worries; undoubtedly he lived beyond his means; and Ford compounded the interest semi-annually at 8 per cent. Then, in 1702, Ford died and shortly his son and widow presented Penn with a bill for over £14,000—much more than he could raise. The alternative to payment was a threat by the Fords to exercise their equity in Pennsylvania and the Counties under the fake bill of sale. Penn, charging that he was being defrauded, took refuge in the London debtor's prison until the Chancery Court reduced the Fords' claim to a more moderate figure. At that point a group of Quaker friends stepped in and, assuming the mortgage, made it possible for Penn to continue as Proprietor of the province.[43]

Still, the sale of his right of government or of his entire proprietary to the Crown seemed the only way out for Penn. And in 1712 he had practically arranged such a deal when an apoplectic stroke resulted in loss of memory. He lived on for six years but in a state of mental uncertainty. During this critical period and until her own death in 1727, Mrs. Penn, remaining in England, managed the proprietary' for herself and her young sons, John, Thomas and Richard. William, Junior, having been provided for by his father's Irish estates, had no interest in Pennsylvania.[44]

HANNAH PENN.

William Penn's second wife.
Courtesy, National Museum, Independence Hall, Philadelphia.

Meanwhile a new generation grew up in Pennsylvania to whom the name of Penn meant only a vague, impersonal absentee landlord who insisted on quitrents. James Logan had become old and rich; "Stenton," his home near Germantown, was one of the show places of the province. Isaac Norris, too, had continued to grow in wealth, some of which he had used to help release Penn from the London debtor's prison. With all their own worldly advancement these two men stood loyally behind the proprietary interest and gave Hannah Penn the support that enabled her to hold the title to Pennsylvania until her boys, known as the "Young Proprietors," were old enough to take charge. In 1732, John Penn, who had first seen the light of day in the Slate-roof House at Philadelphia, wrote to Norris acknowledging "the many and great obligations I am under to you for your constant good advice and friendly assistance for many years, both to my late Father and since his decease to us his children." [45]

Tobacco

ON THE MORNING of June 14, 1709, the roar of heavy guns drifted up the James River of Virginia. To young William Byrd at Westover, twenty-five miles above Jamestown, the distant sounds brought a message: the tobacco fleet was in. Other outlying planters—on the York River, on the Rappahannock, and along Chesapeake—heard the news in the same way.

Virginia and Maryland leapt to life. With the fleet would come news from England, home some of the planters still called it. There would be letters from friends and relatives —with their messages of good or ill. There would be communications from the merchants—about the price of tobacco. There would be shipments of the goods ordered the year before—saddles for the men, dresses for the women, pots and pans for the kitchen, shoes for the servants, shirts for the slaves, all the things that white men considered necessary and that were not made in Virginia.

The next morning a longboat pulled up at the Byrd landing. The captain of one of the ships was calling—cap in hand

—with letters for "Colonel" Byrd. Soon another longboat and another captain arrived with more letters. Naturally the captains were invited to stay for breakfast or dinner, and naturally the subject of cargo came up—how many hogsheads of tobacco would Byrd put aboard the ships? How much per ton would the captains expect for freight? Twelve pounds (perhaps $240.00) was the rate being asked by most of the captains that spring, and a stiff charge it seemed to the planters, particularly since all of the letters from London forecast a low price for tobacco that year.

Byrd did not quibble over the charge for freight, but the sailors earned their wages getting his tobacco aboard. Even the 200-ton ships of the day found it impossible to get up the James as far as Westover. Thus, the big hogsheads of tobacco, weighing about five hundred pounds each, had to be rolled out of Byrd's warehouses onto flatboats and floated down to the ships. The sailors protested that "rolling" tobacco was not part of their jobs, but the captains assured Byrd that it was no trouble at all.[1]

After all, Byrd was one of the big tobacco shippers and no captain or merchant could afford to quarrel with him. He owned the plantation at Westover; he owned plantations up the Appomattox River; he owned plantations at the Falls of the James, where Richmond stands today. All this he had inherited from his father, whom we met in the early 1680's —living at the Falls, keeping a store, sending pack-traders down the Indian path, and shipping hogsheads of furs to England. Life at such a frontier trading post was necessarily rough, and the Byrd children, like those of many other planters, were sent to England for their education. Young William, born in 1674, had been put in an English school before he was ten years of age. And while he was learning to be an English gentleman, the Virginia enterprises of his father prospered.[2]

Most of the overseas business of Byrd, senior, was carried on through the London firm of Perry & Lane, of which Micajah Perry was the guiding genius and so remained for nearly forty years. To that firm Byrd sent most of his tobacco and furs, and from them he ordered much of the goods required in his trade or for his own use. Typical was his admonition, "Let mee not faile of all my Indian Trucke betimes, the want of Beads, or some other traffic being often times a great prejudice." Sometimes shipments of goods turned out badly. "I have had many complaints about my stockings this year," reported Byrd to Perry & Lane in 1683, "as allso of Hats, threds & Some of the Linnen, iron worke & nails the worst ever saw, Which I hope will hereafter bee mended."[3]

To other merchants Byrd was not always so polite. To one he wrote, "The Saddle you sent mee for my Selfe, I find the Stirrup of a Side Saddle which I suppose was Sent instead of a Curb bitt which I find Wanting." To another, regarding a somewhat personal shipment, he observed, "I wonder you should Send mee 2 Close stools (which to mee or any else I thinke are uselesse) without pans."[4]

As the years passed by, Byrd's fur traders had to go ever farther into the hinterland to collect their pelts. In 1686 he reported, "My traders have all Mett with ill Successe, two of them I heare are kill'd about 400 miles of, & the rest have lost all their Horses, & forced to leave their goods abroad. . . ." He shipped but seven hogshead of furs that year.[5]

But of tobacco, in 1686, Byrd shipped four hundred and sixty-one hogsheads. Some of it was the product of his own plantations, but a good part was doubtless acquired in trade from small planters. And, like others, he began to worry about the risk involved in a single crop. "I cannot imagine," he confided to Perry & Lane, "what this trade will come too Since as wee increase there will bee certainly greater quantity of Tob'o made, but the case hath been the Same these 40 or 50 years. I could wish we had Some more certain Commodity to rely on but see no hopes of itt."[6]

Despite Byrd's misgivings about the future of tobacco he joined in the importation of negro slaves—whose labor added to the quantity of tobacco raised in Virginia. These importations were made under license from the Royal African Company, which company held a monopoly of the colonial slave trade. The actual shipments, however, were often made by London merchants. Thus, in 1684, Byrd had written Perry & Lane that if they brought in a cargo of negroes he would

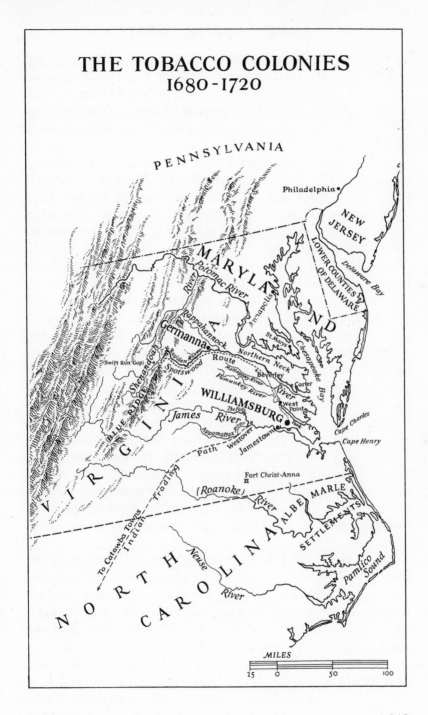

THE TOBACCO COLONIES
1680-1720

PENNSYLVANIA

Philadelphia•

NEW JERSEY

Delaware Bay

LOWER COUNTIES OF DELAWARE

MARYLA ND

Potomac River

Annapolis•

Chesapeake Bay

Rappahannock River

Germanna•

St. Marys

(Swift Run Gap)

Rapidan River

Spotswood

Route

Northern Neck

Beverley

Carter

SHENANDOAH

BLUE RIDGE

Mattapony River

Pamunkey River

WILLIAMSBURG

The Falls

West Point

James River

River

York

Cape Charles

V I R G I N I A

Appomattox River

Westover

Jamestown

Cape Henry

Path

Fort Christ-Anna

(Roanoke)

River

ALBE MARLE

SETTLEMENTS

To Catawba Towns

Indian Trading Path

N O R T H

Neuse River

C A R O L I N A

Pamlico Sound

MILES

25   0   50   100

take about five hundred, between twelve and twenty-four
years of age. He further directed that if the slave ship came
by way of Barbados he wanted 1,000 gallons of rum, 3,024,-
000 pounds of sugar and 200 pounds of ginger. Evidently the
negroes, like the rum, sugar, and ginger, were for re-sale as
merchandise.[7]

But the venture did not turn out well. "I have been mighty
unhappy in the Negroes," wrote Byrd to Perry & Lane, "All
that had the small pox (itt seems) hapned into my lott. One
dyed on board & another in the Boat. My people that went
for y'm caught the distemper & brought itt into my family,
whereof poor Mrs. Brodnax & 3 of my Negros are allready
dead, and about fifteen more besides my little daughter have
them. Pray God put a Stop to itt."[8]

It was the smallpox, not the slave trade, that Byrd prayed
God to put a stop to. The importation of slaves continued at
such a pace that within twenty-five years leading men of the
colony were convinced that "the Country is already ruined
by the great number of negros imported of late years." In
part the acceleration in the slave trade was due to the demand
by the planters for a cheap and stable labor supply; in part
it was due to increased activity on the part of the Royal
African Company. Slave ships became frequent callers at the
James and York rivers; often there were several riding in the
rivers at the same time. Prices were reasonable—£25 to £30
for a prime negro, male or female—and there was no lack
of buyers. By the end of the century there were about seven
thousand negroes in Virginia as against two thousand in
1670.[9]

For William Byrd the growing importation of slaves meant
more tobacco, both from his own plantations and from the
planters to whom he sold his English merchandise and his
negroes. In addition to these profits there fell to him the head
rights due whoever brought *people,* free or slave, into the
colony. The old Virginia Company had established the custom of allowing fifty acres of land for each person who came
to Virginia, the right to the land, however, being vested in
the person who paid for bringing in the newcomer. These
rights to land became known as head rights. The intention

had been to encourage the bringing in of poor families or servants who would become *bona fide* settlers, but the system had been extended to include slaves, and as slaves were imported in increasing numbers the head rights became increasingly valuable. They could be used for the acquisition of more acres by a planter such as Byrd or they could be sold, like any other property, to anyone who wanted to acquire land.[10]

So more land was opened, with more labor to cultivate it, and each year more tobacco was raised. There were ups and downs in the business, of course. The crop of 1688 was so bad that it was hardly worth shipping and the price so low it hardly paid to ship it—even with freight at £6 a ton. Naturally local trade was dull and Byrd could order little from the London merchants. "The most I want is plain Shoes & Hoes," he directed. But the following year things were booming and the problem was to get enough cargo space for the endless hogsheads of tobacco ready to be rolled to the landings.[11]

Evidently Byrd shared bountifully in the general prosperity. Writing to a relative in England he said, "I designe (God willing) to remove downe the River about 20 or 30 Miles where I am now building & hope you will Send us (according to your promise) your, with your fair Lady's Picture to adorn my new house." To Perry & Lane he wrote, "I am now building att Westopher & desire you to Send mee One Bed Bedstead Curtains, with all manner furniture, Chairs, table, Looking Glass for a Chamber to bee Handsome & neat, but cheap, also 1 doz. best Rushia Chairs, 1 Small, 1 Middleing & 1 large Ovall table."[12]

That same summer of 1690 Byrd requested Perry & Lane to take his son William into their offices and there "lett him Learne what may bee wanting" to fit him for a business career. To young William himself, then sixteen years of age, the father expressed the hope that he would so acquaint himself with business "that you may bee no Stranger to itt when necessity will require you to attend itt. . . . But above all be mindfull of your duty to Heaven, and then you may bee assured God will bless you in all your undertakings."[13]

Nor was young William a disappointment to his father.

When he returned to Virginia in 1692, he was not only a polished Englishman but, as time was to prove, a competent man of business. The fur trading family of the Falls had come up in the world. Byrd, senior, was a member of the Governor's Council; his home at Westover compared favorably with the homes of the neighboring planters on the James River; his acres and his slaves compared favorably with those of young Robert Beverley, great landowner on the Rappahannock River and soon to be Byrd's son-in-law. Not even Robert Carter, beginning to be known as "King" Carter, and living across the Rappahannock in the Northern Neck, could claim a greater material well-being; nor could William Fitzhugh, proprietary agent for the Northern Neck, boast a higher position in the colony."

The Northern Neck, as the region between the Rappahannock and Potomac rivers came to be called, was an anomaly. It had been split off from Virginia in 1649 as a proprietary, somewhat as Maryland had been split off in 1632 and as Carolina was to be split off in 1663—except that in the Northern Neck the proprietary rights had been restricted to the soil, and carried no authority to govern the inhabitants. Thus the planters of the Northern Neck sent their burgesses to Jamestown, just as did the planters of any other part of Virginia, but their quitrents were legally payable to a group of proprietors rather than to the King. The impecunious Charles II had intended the grant as a reward to his friends. It remained for many years, however, an unprofitable property, the planters refusing to recognize the rights of the proprietors and declining to pay either purchase price or quitrents for their lands. One by one, the original proprietors sold out until, by 1688, sole title was vested in Thomas, Lord Culpeper, from whom, by his daughter, it passed to the Fairfax family.¹⁵

At this point the proprietors, namely Lord Culpeper's widow and Lady Fairfax, his daughter, adopted a more vigorous policy. The land office was placed in the hands of two substantial planters of the Neck who were expected to see to it that quitrents were paid for land already settled, and that new land was granted only under tenancy from the proprietors. As might have been expected, however, the agents, in making grants of unoccupied lands, often became their own "best customers," picking up choice tracts for themselves as opportunity offered.[16]

One of these agents was William Fitzhugh. Born in England in 1651, and educated for the law, he had come to Virginia when about twenty years of age and acquired land along the Potomac River. By the 1680's he was a successful planter and was shipping tobacco in considerable quantities. It is probable that, like Byrd, he acquired some of his tobacco through trade, and that he bought and sold slaves. In 1681 he heard that a slave ship was expected in York River and asked a friend to buy five or six of the negroes for him. That same year he directed his agent in New York to buy negroes on his account—mostly men, and not to pay over £20 apiece. When a tramp ship from Piscataqua River, New Hampshire, wandered into the Potomac, Fitzhugh suggested that the master go to Barbados and bring back a cargo of negroes. If he would do so, Fitzhugh agreed to buy to the value of fifty thousand pounds of tobacco under the following schedules: 3,000 pounds of tobacco each for boys or girls between seven and eleven; 4,000 pounds each for boys or girls between eleven and fifteen; 5,000 pounds each for men and women between fifteen and twenty-four.[17]

Along with managing his plantation, Fitzhugh engaged actively in the practice of law and charged good fees for his services. From one English client, a lady whom he suspected of being short of ready cash, he offered to accept "Tapestry hangings for a room twenty foot long, sixteen foot wide and nine foot high, and half a dozen chairs suitable"—and she could take her time about paying the rest.[18]

When, three years later, that is, in 1686, Fitzhugh gives us a description of his house we see why he was willing to take hangings, the equivalent of panelling or wallpaper, as part of his fee. His house was, he said, "furnished with all accomodations for a comfortable & gentile living . . . four of the best [rooms] hung & nine of them plentifully furnished with all things necessary & convenient."

Adjoining the main house there was the usual kitchen,

WILLIAM FITZHUGH

Courtesy, Mr. Henry Fitzhugh—without whose permission further
reproduction may not be made.

a dairy, a dovecot, a stable, a barn, and a hen house, all "pallizado'd in with locust Punchens, which is as good as if it were walled." Also there was a garden one hundred feet square, and an orchard of about twenty-five hundred fruit trees, both well enclosed with locust fencing.

His home plantation consisted of a thousand acres and was operated by a "choice crew of negroes"—twenty-nine in all, most of them Virginia-born, living in three separate "quarters." In addition there was, according to Fitzhugh's description, "a good Stock of Cattle, hogs, horses, mares, sheep, &c., and necessary servants belonging to it, for the supply and Support thereof. About a mile & half distant a good water Grist miln whose tole I find sufficient to find my own family with wheat and Indian corn for our necessities & occasions." [19]

Farther up the river Fitzhugh had three more tracts of land, one of 21,996 acres, one of 500 acres and one of 1,000 acres, "all good convenient & commodius Seats"—and this was prior to his appointment as land agent for the Proprietors; in 1701 he had 54,000 acres. As it was, in 1686, he figured that his up-river land would in a few years "yield a considerable annual Income . . . besides sufficient of almost all sorts of goods to supply the family's & the Quarter's occasion for two if not three years. . . . The yearly crops of Corn & Tobo together with the surplusage of meat more than will serve the familys use, will amount annually to 60000 lb Tobo . . . & the negroes increase being all young & a considerable parcel of breeders will keep that stock good for ever." [20]

Fitzhugh, like Byrd, grumbled over the bad prices of tobacco in 1688. ". . . at lowest as ever I knew it," he recorded, "Crops hardly furnishing the Servants with cloaths and working tools that make it." Still, that very year we find him ordering from a London merchant

   1 doz. silver hafted knives
   1 doz. silver forks
   1 doz. silver spoons, "large and strong"
   1 set silver castors
   1 3-qt silver tankard

1 silver salvator plate
4 silver porringers
1 silver basin
1 doz. silver plates
4 silver dishes "2 pretty large for a good joint
    of meat"

all to be marked with a coat of arms as supplied.[21]

When the silver did not arrive with the 1689 tobacco fleet, Fitzhugh wrote in wrath to the delinquent merchant, charging him with having deliberately failed to fill the order, "perhaps esteeming that I had been extravagant in sending for those things, and you by your great judgment would moderate by forbearing to send. I must tell [you] it is a factor that I require, not a Director or Superadvisor, & expect one to follow orders not to dispute the necessity or Inconvenience of them, especially considering it was my own money to be disposed & neither desired nor Requested to run in debt for a farthing." Needless to say the order was transferred to a more understanding merchant, and in the summer of 1690 the silver arrived—just as the new Governor of Virginia paid a visit to Fitzhugh's home, and—as the owner proudly recorded—it was the Governor who "first hanscell'd* it." [22]

This new Governor was Francis Nicholson. We last saw him (page 150) departing rather hastily from New York, where he had been in command for Andros. He now came to Virginia as Deputy under Lord Howard of Effingham, who had been practically forced out of the colony but still clung to the office and its £2,000 a year salary (say $40,-000). It was an inauspicious beginning for the Deputy-governor. Fitzhugh, a member of the House of Burgesses, must have looked his guest over with some misgivings. William Byrd and the other members of the Governor's own Council unquestionably viewed him with suspicion. Nicholson, however, joined in the popular activities of the colonists and soon won their goodwill. Particularly his wholehearted backing of the movement to establish a college in Virginia assured him the support of the influential men of the colony.[23]

*Hansel is an obsolete word meaning *to initiate.*

The idea of a college, for the training of pious ministers, had developed in the fertile mind of the Rev. James Blair, who the previous year had been appointed by the Bishop of London as his Commissary, or Deputy, in Virginia. Nicholson's backing was all that was needed to make the project a success. The Council and Burgesses joined with him in sending Blair to England to solicit a charter for the College, to be called William and Mary in honor of the King and Queen. The Commissary was also authorized to solicit funds and to hire teachers.[24]

In this mission Commissary Blair was eminently successful. The Bishop of London gave the enterprise his blessing. Even the self-centered King William was enthusiastic and contributed approximately two thousand pounds—out of the Virginia quitrents. Only the Attorney-general was unpleasant. He thought the money might be used for a more practical purpose, England being then at war with France. To Blair's plea that the people of Virginia had souls to be saved, Mr. Attorney replied, "Souls! damn your souls!—make tobacco."[25]

In 1693 Blair returned to Virginia with a royal charter for the college, and with endowments in money and land sufficient to build and support it. Properly enough, Blair was made president for life. William Byrd was one of the trustees. Several sites were considered, but the decision fell upon Middle Plantation, seven miles northeast of Jamestown, between the James and the York rivers. Brick, stone, and ordinary lumber for the building were secured locally; the contract for other materials went to Perry & Lane, the London merchants.[26]

On his return to Virginia, Commissary Blair missed one face among those who welcomed him. Nicholson was no longer Governor; in his place was Sir Edmund Andros, late head of the late Dominion of New England. None of the charges against Andros had been made good by the New Englanders, and in recognition of his steadfastness in a difficult situation he had been given the well-paid governorship of Virginia, while Nicholson was shortly compensated with the governorship of Maryland.[27]

Maryland, as will be recalled, had experienced in 1689 a revolutionary movement somewhat similar to those that took place in Massachusetts and New York. A Protestant Association, led by John Coode, had seized the government from the Catholic proprietor—and in 1690 the Lord Chief-justice of England had made the seizure official. To Lord Baltimore was left the proprietary right to the soil of the province; he might dispose of unsettled land; he would still collect quitrents from settled land—estimated by James Logan as worth £700 annually; but the government of the province was vested in the crown. Lionel Copley, a soldier who had been helpful to King William, was sent over as royal governor—the first such official that Maryland had seen.[28]

At just that time Edward Randolph, newly promoted to the job of Surveyor-general of the Customs in America, also arrived in Maryland, full of business as usual. "I know there is a great deal to doe in your parts, especially in the Eastern Country adjoining New Castle," he had written in advance to Copley. And sure enough he found the inlets infested with the ships of what he called "New England rogues and doggs and pitifull damned Scotch Pedlars" whom he promptly put under arrest on charges of illegal trading. But this was before the establishment of Vice-admiralty courts in the colonies, and the cases had to be tried before local juries which proved sympathetic to the traders. The verdicts in every case went against Randolph and he accused Copley of having packed the juries. This was too much for the Governor, who wrote to the Lords of Trade complaining against Randolph for "disturbing the peace and tranquility of the Province, so that he hath indeed effected here what he hath done in all other parts of the world (where ever he set foote) made the whole country weary of him, boastingly vaunting that he thanks God he has lived these five and twenty years upon the curses of the people." In the end Copley practically chased Randolph out of Maryland—but the effort was too much for the Governor; in September, 1693, he died and Nicholson, as Deputy-governor, succeeded him.[29]

When Nicholson arrived in Maryland, the provincial capital was still at St. Mary's on the Potomac. Established by

Leonard Calvert in 1634, this town was the home of many
of the great Catholic landlords; but always there had been
an impermanence about the place; even the pretentious
state house built in 1676 was falling apart by 1694. Lord
Baltimore's loss of power had dealt the Catholic founders
and their town a fatal blow. The dominant political strength
of the province lay at the Puritan settlement of Ann Arundel
Town, up Chesapeake Bay; and thither Nicholson removed
the provincial records and built his new capital—renamed
Annapolis in honor of Princess Anne, sister of the Queen.[30]

Maryland, like Virginia, was a tobacco producing colony.
The same ships that picked up Fitzhugh's hogsheads on the
Virginia side of the Potomac picked up the hogsheads of
the Maryland planters on the other side of the river and
along the shores of Chesapeake Bay. Many of the Maryland
planters lived in a style similar to that of Fitzhugh or Byrd,
but in Maryland, as also in Virginia, there was often a less
attractive side of plantation life. This was vividly, perhaps
a little too vividly, revealed by a visiting rhymester of the
day. For supper he was given, as he told the story,

> ". . . Pon* and Milk, with
> Mush well stoar'd,
> With homine† and Syder-pap
> (Which scarce a hungry dog wou'd lap)
> Well stuff'd with Fat from Bacon Fry'd,
> Or with Mollossus dulcify'd."

After supper the host lugged out a keg of rum and assured
his guest that Maryland was a great place to live in.

> "This said, the Rundlet up he threw
> And bending backward stoutly drew,
> I plucked as stoutly for my part
> Although it made me sick at Heart."

Sleep proved impossible. A cat and a pig fought in the chimney corner; the dog barked; geese and ducks were chased
into the house by a fox; and a rattlesnake sent the poor ten-

---

*Corn pone.   †Hominy.

derfoot up a tree, where mosquitoes bit him. Escape to an inn brought little relief—

> "A Herd of Planters on the ground,
>   O'er-whelmed with Punch, dead drunk, we found."

The home of a gentleman seemed the only refuge, and there, sitting himself down by the fireplace, he joined "a jolly Female Crew" in playing cards.

> "We scarce had played a Round about,
> But that these Indian Froes* fell out.
> D——m you, says one, tho' now so brave,
> I knew you late a Four-Years slave;†
> What if for Planter's Wife you go,
> Nature designed you for the Hoe.
> Rot you replies the other streight,
> The Captain kiss'd you for his Freight;
> And if the Truth were known aright,
> And how you walk' the Streets by night
> You'd blush (if one could blush) for shame."

Across the Chesapeake Bay, on the Eastern Shore, where Randolph had found the New England rogues and damned Scotch peddlers, the visitor

> ". . . met a *Quaker, Yea* and *Nay;*
> A Pious Consientious Rogue,
> As e'er woar Bonnet or a Brogue,
> Who neither Swore nor kept his Word
> But cheated in the Fear of God;
> And when his Debts he would not pay
> By Light within‡ he ran away." [31]

Governor Nicholson got off to a good enough start in Maryland. He aided in the establishment of King William's

---

*By Indian Froes is meant American Fraus, or housewives.

†Indentured servants were commonly bound for four years. Thus the meaning is that the planter's wife had come over as a servant, which was often the case.

‡Quaker manners, convictions and speech are being mocked. Thus Quakers would not take an oath by swearing on the Bible; by "Light within" is meant the Inner Light on which Quakers placed so much trust.

School at Annapolis—later to become a part of St. John's College. In the beginning the members of the Puritan group that had overthrown Baltimore gave their support to the new Governor, and he in return backed them for places of authority and profit. By 1696, however, a rift had developed. Whether John Coode and his followers were hatching a conspiracy against the Governor is impossible to say, but Nicholson suspected that they were and he launched a campaign of vilification, perhaps amply deserved, against the old revolutionary. Randolph, as usual, was involved; he charged Coode with having failed to turn over some £500 of duty money which, as deputy collector on the Potomac River, he had taken in. In addition to this the Governor acquired a sheaf of depositions charging Coode with blasphemy; he had denied that "God Almighty ever begat a son"; he had said that "the Priests of both the Churches, Roman and Protestant, were Rogues; and that it was all one to serve God or the Devil, for Religion (said he) is but policy." Worse yet, according to other accusers, there was reason to think he was a disguised Catholic priest.[32]

Laying his depositions before the provincial House of Burgesses, the Governor demanded that Coode be expelled from that body. The House flatly refused, and the Governor was furious. It was, he said, contrary to law and understanding that the House should protect a man such as Coode, who "in his life and conversation" was "so haniously flagitious and wicked scarce to be parrelled in the province."[33]

Coode, anticipating the Governor's attack, had "privately Removed all or most part of his Goods and Chattells & himself into the Colony of Virginia," but the Governor stripped him of all appointive offices, issued a proclamation offering a reward for his arrest, and caused his house to be searched for incriminating evidence. Maryland was "Govern'd by an Arbitrary Sort of Power," grumbled the people of the province—and unpleasant stories drifted across the Potomac to Virginia.[34]

As an offset to the fury of the Governor or the hainous flagitiousness of John Coode, Maryland became the principal recipient of an unique contribution by the Reverend

Thomas Bray. In 1696 Bray was appointed by the Bishop of London as his Commissary in Maryland, a position similar to that held by Blair in Virginia, but a much more difficult one. In Virginia the Church of England was, and from the beginning had been, the established church. In Maryland, thanks to the Catholic Lord Baltimore, there was no established church and each religious group was free to worship as it pleased. The Proprietor and the great landlords were Catholics; the servants and small planters were generally Church of England adherents from habit rather than from any evangelical fervor; the Puritans in the Annapolis area were the aggressive religious faction. In addition there were a goodly number of Quaker converts along the Eastern Shore.

Such a setting was not attractive to Church of England clergymen, and Commissary Bray soon found that the only ministers he could interest in going to Maryland were those who could not get livings otherwise and who usually were desperately poor. This gave Bray an idea. Partly with a view to attracting ministers and partly with a view to making such as he got more serviceable, he undertook to provide them with parochial libraries. Funds were raised by solicitation among the friends of the Church in England, and by 1699 enough money was available to equip a number of libraries with the sort of books needed by clergymen.

The following year the project was enlarged to provide for Laymen's Libraries, the books "to be Lent or Given at the Discretion of the Minister." Nor was the good work limited to Maryland; Bray's organization was soon supplying libraries to Church of England parishes from Carolina to Massachusetts. Back of these benefactions was, of course, the purpose of evangelizing for the Church of England, and out of it developed the Society for the Propagation of the Gospel in Foreign Parts, which we have already seen in operation in New York, New Jersey, and Pennsylvania (pages 232 and 233) and which throughout the colonial period exerted a great influence upon religious thought and practice.[35]

Meanwhile, in Virginia, Commissary Blair was finding Governor Andros less co-operative than his predecessor. Per-

haps the reception which the Commissary had received in
England, from the Bishops and the King, had caused him
to have an exalted opinion of his position; his appointment
in 1694 to a place on the Governor's Council had probably
added to his self-appreciation. Naturally this attitude irritated the Governor, and when the Commissary denied the
authority of the Governor to pass on the credentials of the
clergy, things had reached an impasse. The Governor solved
the problem by suspending Blair from the Council. Blair
retaliated by hurrying to England with complaints against
the Governor, and won. Andros resigned and was, in 1698,
succeeded by his former subordinate, Governor Nicholson
—to the relief of John Coode and other Marylanders.[36]

At Jamestown, Nicholson found a situation that must have
reminded him of St. Mary's five years earlier. The town had
never consisted of more than a few houses. Plantation life
did not encourage the development of towns; and not even
its position as capital of the colony could make Jamestown
thrive. In 1676 the town had been burned by Bacon, and
when Nicholson arrived in 1698, there were but three or
four houses and a ruinous church, standing in the midst of
charred rubble; the State House had just burned down. At
the Governor's suggestion the Burgesses and Council agreed
that the capital should be moved to Middle Plantation,
where the first building of William and Mary College had
been completed.[37]

The new town, to be called Williamsburg in honor of
King William, was planned with great care. Some two hundred and eighty acres of land were assigned for building lots,
roads, and other town uses. The lots were one-half acre each
in size, and the purchasers were allowed two years in which
to erect their dwellings—twenty feet wide by thirty feet long,
and to stand six feet back from the highway. Failure to comply with these specifications would deprive the purchaser of
a title to his lot. A purchaser might, however, buy two lots
and comply with the building code by putting up a single
proportionately larger house.[38]

For the State House a site was selected a mile eastward
of the College. The building—constructed of brick with shin-

gle roofing—was in the form of two wings connected by a
gallery surmounted by a cupola. One wing was designed for
the use of the House of Burgesses and the other for the Governor's Council. To pay for this new public building a tax
of fifteen shillings was placed on each Christian servant, except English, imported into the colony, and of twenty shillings on each negro—to continue for three years.[39]

The State House was completed within a few months, but
six years later Robert Beverley, the Rappahannock planter,
tells us that "This imaginery City is yet advanced no further, than only to have a few Publick Houses, and a Store-
House, more than were built upon the Place before. And by
the Frequency of Publick Meetings, and the Misfortune of
his Residence, the Students are interrupted in their Study,
and make less Advance than formerly."[40]

However much or little advance the students of William
and Mary made in their studies it must be admitted that
neither in 1705 nor for many years to come was the college
more than a grammar school. Nor did the more prominent
planters send their sons to William and Mary. Thus when,
in 1698, William Fitzhugh's son was eleven years of age, his
father did not consider putting him in the new college of
Virginia. Rather he sent him to England. ". . . by this
comes a large & dear consignment from me, the consignment of a son to your Care & Conduct," wrote Fitzhugh to
a merchant of Bristol. The merchant was to put the boy into
a boarding school and supply him with suitable clothing—
"what is fit and decent, as befits an honest Planter or farmer's Son, not with what's rich or gaudy," directed Fitzhugh.
In addition to clothing, the boy was to be provided with
books "or now & then a little money to buy apples, plums
&c . . . do by him as if he were a child or relation of your
own," wrote the father.[41]

In the same letter in which he consigned the boy to the
Bristol merchant Fitzhugh ordered—

2 large silver dishes	1 pair silver candle sticks
1 doz. silver plates	1 pair silver snuffers
2 silver bread plates	and stand;

The State House, or Capitol, at Williamsburg,

as restored by Colonial Williamsburg, Inc., by whose
courtesy this photograph is shown.

also a calico quilted morning gown for himself. The old planter was indulging his taste for silver and allowing himself some of the luxuries of life. And it was high time he was doing so, if ever; his sands were almost run. In 1701, at the age of fifty, worn out with hard work, he died.[42]

Three years later William Byrd, the Elder, died—at the age of fifty-two. He, too, had sacrificed years of life on the altar of worldly success. Byrd and Fitzhugh were among the last of the great planters who, born in England, had come to Virginia and built up large estates. Their sons, like Robert Carter and young Robert Beverley and many others, were native-born. Even though educated in England, they thought of themselves as Virginians. Governor Nicholson well stated the change in a letter of 1701. Said he, "There is little or no encouragement for men of any tolerable parts to come hither. Formerly there was good convenient land to be taken up and there were widows who had pretty good fortunes which were encouragements for men of parts to come. But now all or most of the good lands are taken up, and if there be any widows or maids of any fortune, the natives for the most part get them; for they begin to have a sort of aversion to others, calling them strangers."[43]

But the turn of the century brought no recognition by the Board of Trade or other royal commissions that the American colonies were coming of age. The policy of an imperial trade empire had been accepted—the colonies were a property to be exploited for the enrichment of the Mother Country. The secretariats that administered the policy had been established—little men with fixed ideas—and the advisability of adapting to changing conditions did not apparently so much as occur to them. Not even the Revolution of 1688 and its repercussion in New England freed the colonies from the formula of ever greater "dependence upon the King," by which was meant dependence upon the merchants of England. Nor did the passing of Edward Randolph, visible symbol of the policy and its enforcement, bring any change in its application.

For a quarter of a century Randolph had striven to break down the special privileges that had been granted to the corporate and proprietary colonies by King Charles I and King Charles II. Ignored, scorned and insulted, he had none the less, and almost singlehandedly, brought Massachusetts under royal control. Imprisonment and fines, laid upon him by the infuriated colonists, had been taken as part of his day's work. Neglect and poor pay by his home government had in no way deterred him. Year after year he had stuck doggedly to his job—a slave to his duty as he interpreted it. In 1700 and 1701 he was in England pressing the attack against the proprietary colonies, the attack that took Penn hurriedly back to England in the latter year (see page 232), and that actually forced the proprietors of East and West Jersey to surrender their patents (see page 216).[44]

The result had been less than Randolph wished, but he had brought two more proprietary colonies to dependence upon the crown; there remained to be broken only Maryland, Pennsylvania, Delaware and Carolina, besides the chartered colonies of Connecticut and Rhode Island. Late in 1702 Randolph sailed for America; it was his seventeenth trip across the Atlantic; he was seventy years of age but evidently still vigorous. The following spring he was on the Eastern Shore of Virginia, again searching out those "New England rogues" and "Scotch Pedlars," probably being cursed—without a friend, old and alone—when he died. Governor Nicholson, who had known him since the days of the Dominion of New England, announced his death to the Board of Trade—in eleven words. Joseph Dudley, recently appointed royal Governor of Massachusetts, may have paused long enough over the news to recall that except for Randolph he would not have been occupying the position he did.[45]

Robert Quary, formerly Judge of the Court of Vice-admiralty at Philadelphia, succeeded to Randolph's place of Surveyor-general of Customs and roving agent for the Board of Trade. He, and an ever increasing host of royal officials, acting under instructions from the secretaries of the various royal commissions in England, increasingly exercised authority over an ever increasing number of colonial activities. Too often they carried out their duties rather like police officers than like business partners; there was too much of the "Damn your souls! Make tobacco!" attitude. Doubtless they believed that they were loyally serving their King and their country. Probably they felt that the curses of the colonists only proved that they, the agents and the secretaries, were doing their work efficiently. What they did not realize was that before the century had run, those curses would swell to a volume that not even the rattle of musketry could still.

As a rule the royal governors and officers of the various royal boards or commissions worked harmoniously together; they were expected to do so and it was to their interest to do so. Governor Nicholson had consistently supported Randolph, and in 1703 Quary reported to the Board of Trade that Virginia "was never under better or happier circumstances since it was a province than now. Her majesty's revenue never better managed with more justice, care and judgment than at this present, nor ever augmented and improved to that height as now it is, and yet the public taxes were never easier or lighter than now, and consequently the inhabitants never better pleased or satisfied. . . . And yet after all this, which is a matter of fact, I am obliged to acquaint your lordships that there are some uneasy, factious and turbulent spirits (though few in number), that do envy this happiness and endeavor to distract and disturb the peace and quiet of this government." [46]

This was a very nice encomium for the Governor, but Robert Beverley, the blunt-spoken native son of Virginia, must have been one of the factious and turbulent spirits. He accused Quary and Nicholson of being a pair of dangerous troublemakers. In their reports to England, according to Beverley, they had slandered a number of the leading planters and had characterized the House of Burgesses as "a pack of rude, unthinking, willful, obstinate people, without any regard to her Majesty or her interest, and it's laid as a crime to them that they think themselves entitled to the liberties of Englishmen." [47]

Beverley's charges against the Governor were particularly severe: He commonly fell into "excessive Passions"; he "uttered abusive Language"; he "often commits Gentlemen to Gaol, without the least Shadow of Complaint against them, and that without Bail. . . . Some of those have taken the Liberty to tell him, that such Proceedings were illegal, and not to be justify'd in any Country that had the Happiness to be govern'd by the Laws of *England*. To whom he has been heard to reply, *That they had no Right at all to the Liberties of* English *subjects, and that he wou'd hang up those that should presume to oppose him, with* Magna Charta *about their Necks.*" [48]

Beverley's remarks cost him his public offices in the colony, but Nicholson also lost his job. The Governor had been too abusive to too many influential people. His friend Quary was not the only one who could get the ear of the Board of Trade. Old Micajah Perry, of the London firm of Perry & Lane, counted on receiving the bulk of the hogsheads of tobacco from the great planters of Virginia and, when they became sufficiently unhappy, he could always be depended on to say a few pointed words to William Blathwayt, the strong man of the Board. And when in addition, as soon occurred, the Bishop of London's appointee, Commissary Blair, sent a petition to the Queen asking for the Governor's removal, it was time for the Board to act. Nicholson was recalled in 1705. The governorship of Virginia went to George Hamilton, the Earl of Orkney, as a reward for unique gallantry in the service of his sovereign. Naturally, his Lordship had no intention of coming to America, but he liked the salary— around $40,000 a year as we have already estimated it. For some years the general government of Virginia was left largely to the genius of the House of Burgesses and the Council.[49]

The House of Burgesses was the representative body of the General Assembly. Its members were elected from the various counties on summons by the Governor. Prior to 1670, the franchise had been extremely liberal, but in that year it was restricted to those who owned land and, except for a short time during the period of Bacon's uprising, so remained. Even with this limitation, the electoral base seemed a little broad to some royal officials. Governor Spotswood, in 1712, complained to the Board of Trade, ". . . the Mob of this Country, having tryed their Strength in the late Election and finding themselves able to carry whom they please, have generally chosen representatives of their own Class, who as their principal Recommendation have declared their resolution to raise no Tax on the people, let the occasion be what it will. This is owing to a defect in the Constitution, which allows to every one, tho' but just out of the Condition of a Servant, and that can but just purchase half an acre of Land, an equal vote with the Man of the best Estate in the Country." [50]

The Council had a multiple function. Its members counselled and advised the Governor, and in many cases their concurrence was necessary to his action. During the Governor's absence the Council acted in an executive capacity. In the General Assembly, it sat as an upper chamber. As a court it took jurisdiction in certain cases. The members of the Council were appointed by the King and were, in general, men of ample estate and recognized ability. Estate was important since Councillors often handled large sums of public money; ability was desirable since they customarily appropriated to themselves all the more responsible, and lucrative, colonial offices. Typical of the members of the Council was young William Byrd, appointed in 1708 when he was but thirty-four years of age. [51]

Upon the death of his father, in 1704, the day had arrived for which young Byrd had been trained by Perry & Lane in London and by practical experience in Virginia. We have already glimpsed him as a tobacco planter in 1709 (page 240). He owned broad acres of land at Westover, up the Appomattox, at the Falls and elsewhere, or rather he *held* these acres subject to payment to the King of an annual quitrent of two shillings for each hundred acres. These quitrents—payable, of course, in tobacco—were collected by the sheriffs of the various counties, who incidentally were appointed by the Governor upon the advice of the Council, of which body, Byrd was, as we have seen, a member. The sheriffs, after deducting their fees, paid the balance over to the Receiver-general who also was allowed a fee for his services. Pleasantly enough Byrd was the Receiver-general. [52]

Always there was a question as to whether quitrents were payable on unimproved land, and in general, no serious effort was made to collect on such land. Had every acre of patented land paid the rents the total would have been very large. As it was, the King had at his disposal a considerable amount of annual income which could be used in any way he wished. Sometimes it was applied to Virginia projects, as in the case of the college; sometimes it was used for general colonial defense or offense, as when, in 1711, Byrd was directed to remit the entire amount to the Governor of New York to help pay for an attack on Canada.[53]

Except for the quitrent, land bore no tax burden. The ordinary cost of government—as administered in the parishes, in the counties and in the colony—was combined into an assessment against those who were known as tithables. At the time with which we are dealing, these tithables included all white men upward of sixteen years of age; all white women employed in field work, and all slaves over twelve years of age if born in Virginia, or over fourteen if newly imported. Thus the tax was on the basis of heads, or polls; it was an assessment against human power. A great planter such as Byrd, with perhaps a dozen indentured white servants and with scores of negro slaves, paid a poll tax proportional to his producing power. A small planter might well pay only on himself. Allowing for fluctuations in the value of tobacco, and the purchasing power of money, the poll tax may be estimated at about ten dollars per person.[54]

In addition to the quitrent and the poll tax, there were several indirect taxes, the most important of which was one of two shillings on every hogshead of tobacco exported to England. Estimating the content of a hogshead at five hundred pounds this tax was slight as against the charge for freight, averaging, say, £10 per ton or fifty shillings per hogshead, and an import duty of somewhat more than forty shillings per hogshead payable immediately upon arrival in England.[55]

The prices which the planters received for their tobacco varied from year to year according to the demand and the type of leaf. In the later years of the seventeenth century it is probable that the planters did not receive more than two

pence per pound. When, in 1711, Byrd received £5 per hogshead, for hogsheads that probably averaged six hundred
pounds, we may assume that this amount was clear of the
freight and import duty, which charges were commonly paid
at the end of the voyage; also this price of two pence was considered low; more usually during this period the price appears
to have averaged between four and five pence a pound.[56]

And with these prices the planters, particularly those who
bought up and shipped their neighbor's tobacco as well as
their own, were doing very nicely. Young William Byrd, living at Westover in the house built by his father in 1690, was
able to gratify tastes and enjoy a culture unknown to the
elder Byrd. A room that the older man might have used to
store furs was now a library. The works of the great writers
—Greek, Latin, Hebrew, and French as well as English—lined
its walls. The young planter usually started his day by reading a chapter in Hebrew or a few verses in Greek from Homer,
Thucydides or other masters of language. Also, each morning, he went through a sort of physical exercise which he
called his "dance." The elder Byrd would have gotten the
same exercise by sorting sacks of Barbadian sugar in his store
room; but he had sent his son to England to acquire refinement, and surely he had gotten his money's worth.

Westover was probably typical of the homes of the well-
to-do Virginia planters. The main house and its dependencies (smaller flanking buildings) were well removed from
the "quarters" where the negro field hands lived, as well as
from the barns where the tobacco was cured and stored.
Byrd and his wife and their infant daughter, Evelyn, had
their apartments in the main house. The nursemaid, a white
woman, and some few young negroes, personal servants, also
lived in the big house. The white male servants—young
fellows who looked after the stores, acted as secretaries or
handled odd jobs about the place—lived in one of the dependencies. Another dependency would provide living accommodations for the negro house servants, who were seldom
housed with the field workers at the "quarters."

Through the house there passed a constant stream of visitors—neighboring planters and their wives and daughters,
relatives, hungry clergymen, ship captains, overseers, sheriffs

WILLIAM BYRD, II.

From the portrait by Sir Godfrey Kneller, now in the possession of
William Byrd, New York City, by whose *courtesy* it is here reproduced
from a print supplied by the Valentine Museum, Richmond. Further
reproduction may not be made without Mr. Byrd's permission.

with quitrents, lately-freed servants with money to buy head-rights. Some stayed only a short time, some stayed for days at a time. To each a suitable hospitality was extended—cider for any, wine for the socially elect, dinner, supper or lodging for those who arrived at mealtime or late at night. A turn at billiards or a session at cards, always for stakes, whiled away many a pleasant hour.[57]

Byrd's dining table carried many delicacies, and well it might. His orchards supplied apples, peaches, quinces, and cherries. All the usual vegetables grew in his gardens. There were watermelons, muskmelons and grapes. In his enclosures or roaming at large were chickens, sheep, hogs, and cattle. Partridges, wild ducks, and geese could be had for the shooting, and fish for the catching. Still, some directing mind must have supervised the selection and preparation of the available food; credit for that apparently goes to Mrs. Byrd—young, pretty, tempestuous but capable. And capable she needed to be, for Byrd was the sort of husband who knew what he was eating; on one occasion he gave Moll, the negro cook, some stripes because she had not boiled the bacon sufficiently. In fact, Byrd frequently took a hand in disciplining the house servants. He beat Anaka for letting little Evelyn wet the bed; time after time he beat Jenny for slight offenses; once he beat her too much. Mrs. Byrd also applied physical punishment to the house servants according to her judgment. On one occasion, when she was using the fire tongs on one of the negro maids, Byrd interfered and very nearly got beat up himself. These paternalistic punishments were not limited to the negroes. When Billy Wilkins, an indentured white boy, committed the double offense of telling a lie and not writing well, Byrd personally chastised him, as he did also his young nephew and niece when the occasions required.[58]

But the supervision of a well appointed, and disciplined, home did not exhaust Byrd's talents for management. Practically every afternoon he took a walk about the Westover plantation—directing the work, seeing that it was being done properly, correcting either his white foremen or the negroes as seemed necessary. Nor was he afraid to put his own hands to work; when he figured that he could prune the young peach trees better than anyone else, he pruned them.[59]

At the Falls and on the Appomattox, his plantations were under the care of overseers, but Byrd kept constantly in touch with them. Almost daily some of his servants tramped up the rivers with messages from Byrd to the overseers, or down the rivers with reports from the overseers. Periodically he visited each of the plantations, inspected the crops, examined the negroes and their quarters, saw that such special enterprises as his tannery or one-man coal mine were operating properly, and in fact informed himself on all aspects of his business.[60]

Negro labor was the power that made the plantations produce—and the plantations had to produce if they were to exist. The negroes were a heavy investment. Not only was there the initial purchase price of each negro; there was the importation tax, there was the annual poll tax, there were food, clothing, shelter, and care. A slight error in the application of the labor of the negroes meant the difference between many hogsheads of tobacco or few. For example: On the afternoon of May 9, 1712, there came a cold rain. All the field hands at Westover were rushed out to set tobacco plants —4,000 were in the ground before dark. The next day the cold rain continued; 26,000 plants were set. For more than a week, in the cold rain, the negroes were kept at it, and the tobacco was off to a good start. As a reward, and perhaps as a preventative of bad effects from exposure, Byrd saw that each worker had a stiff drink of liquor after the day's labor.[61]

It was hard work, this rush of getting in the tobacco plants at just the right time, but it must be borne in mind that the small white planter was, at just the same time, working just as hard and perhaps harder, planting his tobacco. Robert Beverley, who lived all his life in Virginia, tells us that "the work of their Servants, and Slaves, is no other than what every common Freeman do's. Neither is any Servant requir'd to do more in a Day, than his Overseer."[62]

The conversation that accompanied the hoeing of the tobacco doubtless lacked some of the refinement that characterized a social gathering in Byrd's library, but the rude jests and songs took the pang of loneliness out of the labor. Also the many hands required for "hanging" the tobacco in the curing barns or packing it into hogsheads must have made the work far from drudgery. Rolling the hogsheads to the landing was heavy labor, but there was an element of competition in it. And the ride down the rivers on the big flatboats, with twenty-five or thirty hogsheads aboard, must have been real fun. True, at the end of the ride the hogsheads had to be rolled into the holds of the tobacco ships; true, the barges had to be rowed back upstream; but even pulling an oar, when done in unison with the wild songs of his fellow oarsmen, was a show dear to the heart of the average negro.

Occasionally a negro would learn a trade—such as carpentry or blacksmithing—and win a place above his fellow slaves at the quarters, but the great majority did only what they were told to do and as little of that as they could. When Byrd found his Westover "people" shirking too noticeably, he ordered several of the worst offenders whipped. The same punishment was extended to a number of negroes at the Falls who had succumbed to a yearning for fresh pork. As a matter of fact, the latter got off easy since the law directed that for hog stealing a negro should have his ears clipped. All in all, it was an age of whipping, beating and other forms of physical punishment—whether as applied to negroes on a Virginia plantation or to seamen in the British Navy—and Byrd did not hesitate to lay on the lash, or even his toe, where such application would make for better order.[63]

On the other hand, when his negroes were sick or in trouble, Byrd, like any other good planter, was quick to have them cared for, often personally giving the indicated treatment. When his man John had the piles, Byrd took care of him. When Jenny needed a midwife, one was sent for. When, in the winter of 1710–11, the usual wave of influenza swept through the quarters, Byrd spent most of his time, day after day, looking after his "sick people." Nor was his concern only that of an owner worried over a possible loss of property. For each of the sick he had a feeling of kindly interest. "God's Will be done," he recorded when an unnamed boy died; and when A-g-y seemed better, his "God be praised" came from the heart. Twenty of his negroes died before the sickness subsided.[64]

Although there were good doctors in Virginia, and Byrd frequently sought their help, he generally preferred his own treatments. For ordinary complaints, a purge or "vomit" served; and he could and did give either or both—to his negroes, to members of his family, to his friends or to himself. Bleeding was always helpful, according to Byrd's theory. One winter he had several of his negroes bled "by way of prevention." When John, his body servant, complained of a pain at the root of his tongue, Byrd caused him to be bled. When his wife was threatened with a miscarriage, he insisted on her being bled, but she, alas—"so much her fear prevailed over her reason,"—held off until too late.[65]

Ague was the bane of Virginia's summers. First a touch of fever and then a chill that reached to the victim's very marrow, repeated two or three times each twenty-four hours. Nearly everyone had it the summer of 1711. In Byrd's case, the ague continued for a month and was accompanied by a jaundice. The doctor finally insisted upon a stiff dose of Jesuit Bark, as quinine was then called. Byrd's best compliment for the medicine was that it made him so deaf that he could not hear the hubbub made by the ladies who called to condole with him. But it cured him.[66]

Perhaps a contributing factor to Byrd's improvement was a message that reached him from his Appomattox plantation. Tony, the Indian trader, had come in with over four hundred skins. That seemed like old times, when furs and skins were building the family fortune. And Byrd could use the extra money. The previous year he had offered Lady Orkney £1,000 for the governorship of Virginia. The lady had been willing enough, but the Privy Council had frowned upon the deal, and Byrd turned his political aspirations to Maryland, doubtless with substantial fees to the right people in England.[67]

But Virginia needed a resident Governor and since Lord Orkney declined to come over, the Queen appointed Colonel Alexander Spotswood, a professional soldier, as his Deputy —and they might divide the salary between them. The arrival of the new Deputy-governor, in the summer of 1710, had brought a flurry of political and social activity to the otherwise quiet capital at Williamsburg. As a member of the Governor's Council, Byrd was naturally in the midst of it all.

Time after time, he made the trip down the river—part of the way by boat or ferry, part of the way by horseback, generally accompanied by a servant with extra horses. Sometimes he stayed only a day or two; sometimes a week or a month."

There, at Williamsburg, Byrd met his fellow planters, present like himself as members of the Council or of the House of Burgesses. For many hours each day he sat as a legislator in the General Assembly or as a judge in cases within the jurisdiction of the Council. He was a frequent dinner guest at the home of the Governor or an overnight guest in the homes of his nearby friends. He spent much of his leisure time at the public coffee house, drinking and playing cards with his cronies. One night he and Robert Carter (later known as "King" Carter), and two other friends, after having partaken liberally of French brandy at Carter's rooms, went to the coffee house and, to an accompaniment of much lewd talk, shook dice until almost four o'clock in the morning. Byrd lost £12, say $240.00; also he recognized, later, that he was "almost drunk." To make the night complete he went to his lodgings and, as he expressed it, "committed uncleanness," for which the next morning he humbly begged God Almighty's pardon. And he made a solemn resolution, with a finger pointing to the entry in his journal, not to spend so much time in gambling."

Byrd and Carter were not the only ones who had to live in rooms while at Williamsburg; practically all those whose homes were at a distance lived that way. The town was too small to provide other accommodations. Commissary Blair was one of the fortunate few. He had been appointed rector of Bruton Parish—within which Williamsburg lay—and could thus fulfill his functions as a member of the Council, as well as of President of William and Mary College, without the hardship of a journey."

Even Governor Spotswood had his residence in a rented house although an official home (the Governor's palace) was then in the process of construction. It was to be "built of brick, fifty-four feet in length, and forty-eight feet in breadth . . . two stories high," and with a "covering of stone slate."

ALEXANDER SPOTSWOOD.

From the frontispiece of *The Official Letters of Alexander Spotswood.*

The total cost was estimated at £3,000. In 1710 the Assembly appropriated an additional £2,195 for the completion of the house—the amount to be raised by a duty on the importation of liquor and slaves. The Governor was not too pleased with all the architectural details of his prospective home, and one afternoon he invited Byrd and several of the burgesses to meet him at the new house, where he pointed out improvements that needed to be made. In 1713, the Assembly appropriated £1,900 for furnishing it, but some years later it was still unoccupied.[71]

Naturally the Governor was interested in the College—which was not progressing too favorably. The building had burned down in 1705, but another had taken its place. Then, too, Mr. Blackamore, the Headmaster of the Grammar School had exhibited a sad failing; he would get drunk. In 1709, the Governors of the College, of whom Byrd was one, had decided to turn him out "for being so great a sot," but he had asked for another chance and received it. President Blair probably had a certain sympathy with the erring headmaster; his own wife was very fond of the bottle, though the family explained it as temperament. Professor Le Fevre too, presented problems. He had been recommended to Spotswood by none other than the Bishop of London, and was supposed to have come over on the same ship with the Governor. He did, in fact, arrive at the dock with a young woman about sixteen years of age who was variously classified as his maid and his wife, and in the resulting confusion both were left behind. And it was better so, reported Spotswood to the Bishop, since "the present Master of the Grammar School is much reformed of late."[72]

But, as usual in such cases, the Frenchman and his "hussey," as the Governor called the young lady, soon appeared in Virginia—still with the recommendation of the Bishop. Spotswood tried his best to persuade Byrd and the other trustees to oust Blackamore and give Le Fevre the job of Headmaster, but in vain. They did, however, appoint the Frenchman to the place of Professor of Philosophy and Mathematics at a salary of £80 a year. A year later, the Governor reported to the Bishop that the Professor had been "so negligent in

Bed Chamber of Governor's Palace at Williamsburg,

as restored by Colonial Williamsburg, Inc., by whose *courtesy* this
photograph is reproduced.

all posts of duty and guilty of some other very great irregu-
larities, that the Governors of the College could no longer
bear with him, and were obliged to remove him from his
Office, tho' at the same time out of Regard to the hon'ble
recommendation he brought with him they continued his
Sallary for four months longer than he officiated." Spotswood thought that most of Le Fevre's trouble was due to the
"idle hussey." As the Bishop, mellow in experience with the
ways of mankind, read this report, he may have recalled
stories that were drifting back to England about a "niece,"
a pretty woman, who had accompanied the Governor to Virginia. And at about the same time, William Byrd, taking
a walk about Williamsburg, met Blackamore. The Headmaster was drunk.[73]

Whether the character of the teachers had a deterrent
effect on the size of the student body, or whether the student
body drove the teachers to drink is hard to say, but in 1712
there were but twenty-two white boys at William and Mary
and about the same number of Indians. These latter were
collegians through the munificence of Robert Boyle, the eminent scientist, who had left a bequest for the purpose of chris-
tianizing the Indians of America. Micajah Perry had seen
that most of the money went to William and Mary College.
The boys were at first recruited through the Indian traders
to the south and west. They were provided with clothing and
lodging, and it became Mr. Blackamore's duty to see that
they learned to read and write and understand the principles
of Christianity. Governor Spotswood discovered that by promises of favors to the straggling Indian groups still living in
Virginia, particularly those south of the James River, he
could get more students than the Boyle foundation could
support, and he suggested to the Bishop of London that the
Society for the Propagation of the Gospel should help out.[74]

The Indians of southeastern Virginia were worthy of a
little special attention just at this time. They served as a buffer
against the Tuscaroras who had been raiding and killing in
North Carolina. Partly to control and partly to aid these
Indians, Spotswood encouraged the Assembly to organize a
Virginia Indian Company, composed of twenty substantial

men of the colony and with a twenty-year monopoly of the
Indian trade. The Company built a fort not far from the
North Carolina line, and named it Christ-Anna, which should
have assured the support of the Bishop of London and of
Queen Anne. Twelve soldiers and a schoolmaster were stationed at the fort; there the Indian children learned the cat-
echism—at the expense of the company; and there the Indian
hunters brought their furs—to the profit of the company. It
was a statesmanlike solution of the problem of frontier defense, but the old-time fur traders did not like it.[75]

On the northwestern frontier most of the trouble had been
caused by parties of Iroquois on their forays southward from
New York. Spotswood blocked these incursions by establishing a settlement of Germans at the crossing of the south
branch of the Rappahannock. These Germans, experienced
miners, had been recruited by Baron Christoph von Graffenried, a visionary Swiss adventurer, to develop a silver mine
supposed to exist somewhere in the American back country.
But all the Baron's fine schemes, including a colony in North
Carolina, had turned out badly and some disposition had to
be made of the German miners, who were stranded in England. Spotswood had long been interested in the possibilities
of profitable mining in Virginia; he arranged to have the
Germans sent over; and they assured him that there were
"divers kinds of minerals" in the upper Rappahannock region. That, together with the element of frontier defense,
settled the matter. In 1714, the Germans were established at
a place called Germanna—on the Rapidan branch of the
Rappahannock some twenty miles west of the presentday city
of Fredericksburg. Spotswood built them a fort, equipped it
with a couple of cannon and they were expected to repay the
cost of their support and make a profit for those who underwrote their transportation.[76]

The year following the establishment of Germanna, a
young French Huguenot, named John Fontaine, visited the
settlement. He had started from Williamsburg, by horseback
of course. At the head of York River, where the Pamunkey
and the Mattapony join, he crossed by ferry to West Point;
there a hospitable planter took him in for the night. A cen-

tury earlier that same point of land had been covered by the Indian town of Machot, one of the homes of the redoubtable Powhatan. Fontaine was to see along the way a few miserably poor Indians but he gave never a thought to the vanished glory of the father of Pocahontas. Another day's journey, up the Mattapony, partly by canoe and partly by horseback, brought him to the plantation of John Baylor, whom he described as "one of the greatest dealers for tobacco in the country." Four years later, when Baylor died, Robert Carter referred to him as "The great negro seller, and in all respects the greatest merchant we had among us." To Fontaine, Baylor extended the best entertainment available, and the next morning the traveller was again on his way, heading for Robert Beverley's house on the upper waters of the Mattapony. It was a thirty mile ride, and he did not get there until ten o'clock at night."

Beverley, since losing his official positions early in the century, had retired to this frontier estate and was, at the time of Fontaine's visit, more interested in his vineyard than in politics. Seventeen years had passed since his seventeen-year-old wife, Ursula Byrd, William's sister, had died in giving birth to their only son. "This man lives well," recorded Fontaine, "but though rich, he has nothing in or about his house but what is necessary. He hath good beds in his house, but no curtains; and instead of cane chairs, he hath stools made of wood. He lives upon the product of his land." Beverley tried to sell Fontaine some land on the Rappahannock River, but the Frenchman disliked the terms and pushed on to Germanna—thirty miles beyond the last settlement—where he spent the night "very indifferently" on a pile of straw at the minister's house. "There are but nine families," Fontaine recorded, "and they have nine houses, built all in a line; and before every house, about twenty feet distant from it, they have small sheds built for their hogs and hens, so that the hog-sties and houses make a street." The town was palisaded and in the center was a blockhouse "intended for a retreat for the people, in case they were not able to defend the palisadoes, if attacked by the Indians." All in all, Fontaine summed up the situation in the statement: "The Germans live very miserably."

From a hill on Beverley's land Fontaine had seen, faintly
in the distance, the forbidding mountain range, blue against
the sky, that marked the western bounds of Virginia as then
known. For half a century that barrier had piqued the curiosity of Virginians. Some few explorers had climbed over it.
But it remained for Governor Spotswood to officially pub-
licize a road into the valley on the other side. On August 20,
1716, accompanied by Fontaine and a few others, and "what
baggage was necessary," the Governor left Williamsburg "for
an expedition over the Appalachian mountains." As far as
Germanna they followed the road taken by Fontaine the
previous year. There "several gentlemen of the country" and
a dozen Rangers joined the party. Four or five days were
spent in examining the settlement, getting the horses shod
and preparing for the rough travelling beyond. Fontaine was
not greatly impressed with the Germans' mine; he did not
believe the mineral was silver; doubted even that it was lead.[70]

At seven o'clock on the morning of August 30, the trumpet
sounded and, as Fontaine put it, "we got up"; but they did
not leap from their beds. Fontaine's head was buzzing from
quinine taken to ease a sharp attack of ague; one of the men
had so high a fever that he went home; all of them had spent
the night in tents, and, said Fontaine, "we found by the pains
in our bones that we had not had good beds to lie upon." It
was two o'clock before they got under way and they made
only six miles.

By easy stages, and getting into the spirit of the jaunt, they
pushed onward, west by south, up the Rapidan. Occasionally
they shot a bear or a deer. Constantly they killed rattlesnakes.
At night they made large fires, pitched their tents, cut boughs
to lie upon, and "had good liquor," as Fontaine assures us.
The list of liquors carried along on the pack horses amply
supports his statement. There were red and white wines,
Irish usquebaugh, brandy, two sorts of rum, champagne,
canary, punch—and the catalogue ends with "&c."

Each morning the mountain barrier reared itself darker
and higher before them. On September 3, they were at its
foot. Two days later, after a stiff climb, preceded by axemen, they reached the crest of the ridge. "We drank King

George's health, and all the Royal Family's at the very top of the Appalachian mountains," said Fontaine. As a matter of fact they were on the top of the Blue Ridge, presumably in Swift Run Gap where today Route 33 runs through from Stanardsville to Harrisonburg.

It was a fair autumn day and before them lay the lush valley of the Shenandoah. Notched trees, marked by Indians, showed the way down, and in the early evening they reached a river which they named the Euphrates; it was, of course, the South Branch of the Shenandoah. The following day, on the banks of the river, a picturesque ceremony occurred which can best be described in the words of Fontaine: ". . . the Governor buried a bottle with a paper inclosed, on which he writ that he took possession of this place in the name and for King George the First of England. We had a good dinner, and after it we got the men together, and loaded all their arms, and we drank the King's health in champagne, and fired a volley, and all the rest of the Royal Family in claret, and a volley. We drank the Governor's health and fired another volley." [80]

Fortunately for the gaiety of the occasion, Spotswood did not know how many ranges still remained to be crossed before the Appalachian Mountains were surmounted. On his return home, it is said, he presented each of his companions of the journey with a gold pin shaped in the form of a horseshoe; and the possessors of these decorations became known as the Knights of the Golden Horseshoe. [81]

Among these Knights of the Golden Horseshoe such men as William Byrd and Robert Carter were conspicuous by their absence. The Governor was losing his popularity among the influential people. The establishment of the Indian Company had cost him the support of the fur traders. The Board of Trade directed him to dissolve the Company. A measure requiring tobacco to be inspected and graded brought him into the bad graces of the House of Burgesses—and the Board of Trade backed the Burgesses. An attempt to reorganize the superior courts resulted in his own Council preferring charges against him. The Governor must have seen the handwriting on the wall, but he stood to it and fought for what he thought was right. Was the Governor, he asked, to be the boss in Virginia, or was the colony to be ruled by "the Haughtiness of a Carter, the Hypocrisy of a Blair . . . the Malice of a Byrd?"[52]

Byrd had been in England since 1715, exerting his "malice," as Spotswood called it, or patriotism, as others would have phrased it, where it would do the Governor the least good. As usual in such cases, there was more to Byrd's attacks than met the eye. The planter had political aspirations. He had, as will be recalled, hoped for the governorship of Virginia before that office went to Spotswood. Subsequently he had schemed for the governorship of Maryland, but in 1715 the fifth Lord Baltimore, by renouncing Catholicism, recovered full control of his Proprietary. Baltimore, rather than the King, would in the future name the deputy-governor of Maryland. There was no honor in such an appointment even if Byrd could have hoped for it, and he accordingly turned all his energy to unseating Spotswood, with a view to getting the governorship of Virginia for himself. Spotswood countered by trying to have Byrd dismissed from his place as a member of the Council. Neither was successful, and in 1720 Byrd returned to Virginia with a message for both factions: They were to stop quarrelling and attend to their business.[53]

The reaction of the Virginia Council to this admonition was expressed in a letter of July, 1720, from Robert Carter to a London merchant: "Politics I hope I have done with for the rest of my days. The essay we made to redress ourselves from some oppressions we thought we had reason to complain under have met with great discouragements from home." There spoke "the haughtiness of a Carter," and well may Spotswood have wondered what was to come. Sure it was that "Robin" Carter was not done with politics.[54]

But for the moment Carter contented himself with raising, buying, and selling tobacco. On his own plantations, along the Rappahannock River in the Northern Neck, he apparently specialized in sweet-scented tobacco which had a better market than the more common Oronoco raised on most of the plantations. Also, he usually had his tobacco stemmed—shipping the leaves only—which naturally gave it a higher price per pound. In 1720, he was getting eleven pence a pound on the London market, which he called "a living price, and truly to have less will make but poor doing with us." Still, as compared with the four or five pence paid for unstemmed tobacco a few years earlier, this price represented a very good return. And Carter took pride in his tobacco. He tried to have it so cured and packed that it would be "nice." When he heard that William Pratt, who picked up tobacco here and there wherever it could be bought, had received a better price than himself, he wrote to Micajah Perry, "I will endeavor to be nicer than ever I have been that I may keep pace with that miscellaneous gent, Mr. Pratt, who fluxes me egregiously."[85]

Carter, too, was a "miscellaneous gent" at times; he bought and shipped much tobacco not raised on his own plantations. His sloop plied up and down the Rappahannock and Potomac rivers, picking up the odd hogsheads produced by the small planters. Also, he had a part interest in a ship, named *The Carter,* which sailed back and forth with the tobacco fleet between England and Virginia; thus if freight was high, Carter won on the profits from the ship, and if freight was low, he made more profit from his hogsheads of tobacco. And, like Fitzhugh and Byrd and Baylor and many another planter of the day, Carter occasionally had a financial interest in the slave trade. In 1720, he brought in a shipload of negroes from Barbados. Doubtless some of them were for his own plantations—he had lost a considerable number by sickness the preceding winter—but many were sold, the buyers giving their notes and Carter guaranteeing them with the London house of Perry.[86]

With all his far-flung and generally profitable business enterprises Carter was careful about his money. When William Dawkins, a London merchant, attempted to raise the planter's standard of spending by quoting what others did, he was informed, "I must cut my coat according to my cloth and bless God I am able to do so well as I do." And when the merchant spent more for a pair of earrings and a tombstone than Carter had authorized, he was tartly told, "I shall be obliged to you to let me be the master of my money."[87]

ROBERT CARTER.

Commonly known as "King" Carter.

Reproduced by the *courtesy* of the present owner, Mrs. J. H. Oliver, "Shirley," Charles City County, Virginia, from a photograph provided by the Frick Art Reference Gallery, New York.

Further reproduction may not be made without the permission of Mrs. Oliver.

Carter had inherited a considerable land estate from his father; he had added to it by energy and attention to his business; but his great opportunity had come when, in 1702, and as successor to William Fitzhugh, he became agent for the Proprietor of the Northern Neck, which position he held until 1711 when he was superseded by Thomas Lee. But now, in 1721, he again received the appointment—through the good services of old Micajah Perry. Tobacco being on the decline, Carter had some misgivings about the money profits from the agency, but as a long-range investment he made no question of its possibilities. "One great perquisite of this estate," he wrote to Perry, "is the granting away the lands that are untaken up." And Carter made the most of it. When he died, ten years later, and was buried under that tombstone —the one purchased for him by Mr. Dawkins and the finest in the English colonies—he owned three hundred thousand acres of land and was able to leave to each of his twelve children enough to assure his or her financial and social position in the colony.[88]

In 1720, Carter's eldest son, John, and at least two of the other boys were being educated in England. John had been in the charge of the Perrys who evidently thought that the wealthy planter was being a bit niggardly in the lad's allowance, especially as he was shortly to be called to the bar. Carter made short work of that idea. He could not afford more, he bluntly told Perry, and added: "That yours may swim in a much greater affluence is the cordial desire of, Sir, Your sincere humble servant."[89]

The younger Carter boys were under the supervision of William Dawkins, he who had paid too much for the earrings and tombstone. In a careless moment, Dawkins had named £40 each, annually, as a sufficient amount for the maintenance and education of the boys. But additional items kept slipping in and expenses mounted. "The world is strangely altered, sure, since I was young," observed Carter. "I lived with old Mr. Baily [evidently his English schoolmaster] six years. I never stood my brother in £30 in any one year of the time."[90]

Still, with all his fussing, Carter wanted the boys to have

the best. He agreed to pay John's back bills, including the tailor's account—some fifty pounds; but for the future he expected him to get along on £150 a year, say $3000.00 as buying power rated two hundred years later. Also Carter wanted the boys brought up with correct religious principles —"as I am of the Church of England way, so I desire they should be. But the high-flown up top notions and the great stress that is laid upon ceremonies, any further than decency and conformity, are what I cannot come into the reason of. Practical godliness is the substance—these are but the shell." [91]

Practical godliness. . . . In the autumn of 1722 Governor Spotswood journeyed to Albany, on the Hudson River in New York province, there to join in a treaty with the Iroquois. The covenant chain forged between these northern Indians and Long Knife in 1684 (see page 125) had grown rusty. Particularly Spotswood wanted the Iroquois, in their forays southward, to pass west of the mountain ridge rather than near the new settlement at Germanna. The Indians were pleased to renew the chain and to make it bright. They called attention to the fact that God made the white people Christians and themselves Heathens, and seemed satisfied with the arrangement. They readily agreed to all that Spotswood asked even though, as they said, "there is a Nation amongst you [the christianized Indians of Christ-Anna] against whom we have so inveterate an enmity, that we thought it could not be extinguished but by a total Extirpation of them, yet since you desire it, we are willing to receive them into this Peace & to forgive all that is past." [92]

It would have been well had the Christian gentlemen of Virginia exercised the same practical godliness. They, however, were intent upon the total political extirpation of Governor Spotswood. Interestingly enough, it was Commissary Blair who counted *coup* on the Governor. The controversy was over the long-disputed right to induct ministers. Doubtless the Commissary was in the wrong and knew it—"the hypocrisy of a Blair"—but the Governor lost both the controversy and his job. [93]

Probably, however, Spotswood would have been dismissed even if Blair had not joined the attack. The Governor had touched the pocketbooks and the pride of a group that, through the relationship of blood, marriage, or business interest, controlled Virginia. And he was not one of them. Like Nicholson several years earlier, Spotswood sensed the reason for his defeat. "These are the men," he said in speaking of his opponents, "that look upon all persons not born in the Country as forreigners, and think that no other quallification is necessary for an employment, or ought to be considered in the disposal thereof, but that of being born in the Country." [94]

And since Spotswood necessarily labored under the handicap of not having been born in Virginia he did the next best thing; he made the colony his home. Out on the frontier, about the settlement of Germanna, he had already acquired, by somewhat questionable methods, many thousands of acres of land, some of which land had once been thought to contain silver but was now found to be fairly rich in iron ore. The former Governor became an industrialist. Negro slaves replaced Germans as laborers. Furnaces were erected. Soon pig iron was being shipped to England; pots, andirons, chimneybacks and other utensils were being made and sold locally; and bar iron was being supplied to blacksmiths in the other colonies. [95]

So promising were Spotswood's prospects that competitors naturally entered the field. Among others, the English owners of the Principio Iron Works, located in northern Maryland, sent their manager on a prospecting trip into Virginia. On Accokeek Creek, a small stream running into the Potomac, near the later city of Fredericksburg, ore was found in what appeared to be paying quantities. The land belonged to Augustine Washington, an enterprising farmer, who entered into a contract with the Principio people to dig the ore and share in the profits from a furnace to be erected at the company's expense. By 1732, in which year Mrs. Washington presented her husband with a new son, christened George, it seemed that the southern shore of the Potomac was destined to be dotted with smoking iron-furnaces rather than with tobacco fields. [96]

19

Skins and Slaves

"FULL OF LICE, Shame, Poverty, and Hunger:—I turned Player and Poet." Thus Anthony Aston described his arrival at Charleston, South Carolina, in 1702. How his plays impressed the Carolinians is unknown, but he had just taken part in one of the minor dramas of American history, namely, Governor Moore's attack on St. Augustine.[1]

England was again at war—with both France and Spain this time; Queen Anne's War, we usually call it. In southern Carolina the governorship was temporarily in the hands of James Moore, an old settler who was deeply engaged in trade with the Indians, particularly in that phase of it by which the Indian tribes were encouraged to war upon each other in order to secure captives for the Charleston slave market. It was even said by some of the Governor's enemies that the expedition against St. Augustine was launched primarily for the purpose of catching and enslaving Indians. Others maintained that the attack was in retaliation for an assault which the Spaniards intended upon Charleston.[2]

The early autumn of 1702 witnessed the Governor's flo-

tilla, with five hundred white men (including Anthony Aston) and about the same number of friendly Indians (largely
Yamasee), sailing southward from Port Royal. At the St.
Johns River a part of the force turned inland and approached St. Augustine from the rear, while the main fleet
assaulted it from the water side. The townspeople, in the
face of overwhelming odds, fled into Fort San Marco, and
though the English and their Indian allies looted at will elsewhere, the stronghold remained impregnable. After a futile
siege of three months and with Spanish reinforcements
blocking the harbor, Governor Moore burned his ships and
led his army, somewhat hastily, up the coast to Charleston.
With him, forced along as captives, went five hundred Indians from the Franciscan missions at and around St. Augustine. There had been no room for them in San Marco and
they were destined for the slave market. Governor Moore
and his captains probably did very well as a result of the
raid, but most of his men returned in the condition described
by Aston.[3]

A year later, having been superseded as governor by Sir
Nathaniel Johnson, Moore was given another opportunity
to show his prowess against the prestige of Spain—as well as
of France which had just established a settlement in Mobile
Bay. With fifty white men and perhaps a thousand Indian
allies Moore headed south and west across the upper neck
of Florida to the rich Apalache region—dotted with Franciscan missions and filled with tame, christianized Indians.
On January 14, 1704, the Carolinian horde was before the
Mission of Ayubale, near presentday Tallahassee (see map
on page 297). Father Angel de Miranda marshalled his followers and made a stubborn defense, but when the day
ended twenty-five Apalache Indians lay dead and a hundred
and fifty were prisoners in the hands of the English. Captain Mexia, with a handful of Spanish troops, rushed to the
Father's defense from the presidio of San Luis, and also suffered defeat. One after another the missions, thirteen in all,
were destroyed. In the early part of March, 1704, loaded
with loot, including church plate and perhaps a thousand
Apalache Indians, Moore retired eastward. At practically

the same time, far to the north, Hertel de Rouville and his Indian allies were herding a group of English captives from Deerfield, Massachusetts to Canada (see page 174).

Many of Moore's captive Indians were sold as slaves; the rest were settled on the easterly side of the Savannah River, within the area controlled by the Carolinians. The expedition had put an end to all danger of a Spanish or French attack through Florida. There remained, however, the constant possibility of an invasion by sea, and in 1706 it materialized. On Saturday, August 24, watchmen sighted five strange war ships off Charleston harbor. The attacking fleet was, in fact, under French command but had been reinforced and provisioned by the Spanish at Havana and St. Augustine. While the invaders felt their way up the channel toward the upper harbor, the people of Charleston came to arms. A battery, erected at a spot still known as Fort Johnson in honor of the governor, pinned the French fleet against Sullivan's Island (see map on page 291). French landing parties were attacked and defeated. And then the Governor took the offensive. Six small merchant ships were armed and sent down the Bay. The French fleet fled, leaving behind two hundred and thirty of their men as prisoners.[5]

Thirty-six years had passed since the Charleston settlement had been planted—"in the very chops of Spain." All of the eight original proprietors had gone to their last rewards; their proprietary shares had passed into the hands of heirs or successors interested in the province only as a source of revenue. No effort had been made by the new proprietors to provide capable governors; little provision had been made for the administration of justice; naturally the navigation laws had been flouted. Constantly Edward Randolph, as Collector-general of Customs, had complained against the Carolina officials for violations of the Acts of Trade, and in 1701 the province was included among those whose governments were to be recovered by the King. But the move failed so far as Carolina was concerned, and the province continued to be ruled by the appointees of a little group of proprietors meeting in London.[6]

Still, despite neglect and selfish exploitation, southern

Carolina had grown, and to many of her settlers the colony
had proved a source of wealth. By 1706 there were more
than six thousand white inhabitants in the settlements clus-
tered about Charleston. More than half of them lived in the
city itself—on the point of land where the Ashley and the
Cooper rivers meet. "The town," said John Lawson in 1709,
"has very regular and fair Streets in which are good Buildings of Brick and Wood . . . The inhabitants by their wise
Management and Industry have much improv'd the Country which is in as thriving Circumstances at this time as
any Colony on the Continent of *English* America." [7]

Rice, "the best in the known World," according to a former governor of the province, had become a staple crop, so
much so that the Board of Trade in London had placed it
on a par with tobacco as a commodity to be strictly regulated under the navigation laws. On his plantation, named
"Silk Hope," Governor Johnson was raising silkworms and
deriving an annual income of £300 to £400 from their industry. Some pitch and tar were being produced. The cattle
industry was growing. [8]

Northward from Charleston, up the neck of land between
the Ashley and Cooper rivers, ran a road "beautified with
odoriferous and fragrant Woods . . . so pleasantly Green
that," said an observer, "I believe no Prince in Europe, by
all their Art, can make so pleasant a Sight for the whole
Year." On either side of this road lay the plantations of the
principal planters—"very courteous" gentlemen, who lived
"nobly in their Houses," and gave "very genteel Entertainment to all Strangers and others" who chanced to visit them. [9]

Farther northward, where the road crossed the Santee
River, many Huguenots, refugees from their own country,
had established themselves on scattering plantations. An
English visitor noted that these French, "being a temperate
and industrious People, some of them bringing very little
Effects, yet by their Endeavours and mutual Assistance
among themselves (which is highly to be commended) have
outstript our English who brought with 'em larger Fortunes,
though (as it seems) less endeavour to manage their Talent
to the best Advantage." [10]

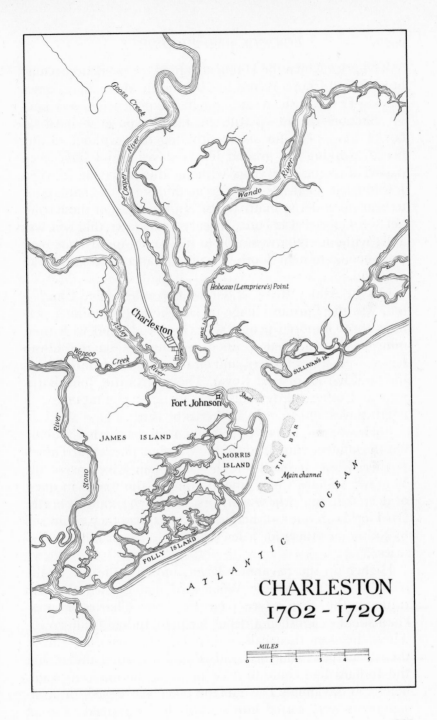

Goose Creek

Cooper River

Wando River

Hobcaw (Lempriere's) Point

Charleston

HOG ISLAND

Ashley River

Wappoo Creek

SULLIVAN'S IS.

Fort Johnson

Shoal

THE BAR

JAMES ISLAND

MORRIS ISLAND

Main channel

Stono River

OCEAN

FOLLY ISLAND

ATLANTIC

CHARLESTON
1702 - 1729

MILES
0   1   2   3   4   5

The price which the Huguenots paid for their success may be gathered from a record left by Judith Manigault. "Since leaving France," she wrote, "we had experienced every kind of affliction—disease—pestilence—famine—poverty—hard labor. I have been for six months together without tasting bread, working the ground like a slave; and I have even passed three or four years without always having it when I wanted it. God has done great things for us enabling us to bear up under so many trials." In the midst of these trials her son Gabriel was born; seventy years later that son was able, without embarrassment to his estate, to advance over $200,000.00 to help South Carolina finance its resistance to England.[11]

On the Ashley River, about twenty miles above Charleston, was the Puritan village of Dorchester, containing perhaps three hundred people who, in a body and with their minister, had arrived in 1696. Southward, on the Edisto River, were a few settlers, and on the southern frontier, near the fatal harbor of Port Royal, Thomas Nairne, John Barnwell and other hardy souls worked large plantations with negro slaves and raised vast herds of cattle.[12]

Such was the extent of settlement in southern Carolina, but the influence and trade of the Carolinians extended much farther. Close at hand, on the Savannah River, were the Yamasee Indians whose hunters ranged the woods in quest of deer skins and whose warriors, after 1703, ranged northern Florida in quest of helpless Indians that they could sell to Nairne or others for a few yards of cloth or other necessities.[13]

Higher up the Savannah River, opposite the site of the old Westoe town where Woodward first opened the skin trade in the 1670's (see page 65), the Charleston merchants had established a depot for their Indian trade goods. There they sent their calico, their bright coats, their knives, their trade guns and the hundred and one other things that the Indians had come to need or might be made to want. There, at Savannah Town as the place was called, the consignments were sorted into suitable lots, strapped in great bundles on the backs of patient pack horses or equally pa-

Interior of Goose Creek Church.
Built in 1711.

The fertile land along Goose Creek, which stream flows into Cooper River ten or twelve miles above Charleston, attracted the early settlers from Barbados. Evidently they were an independent lot, as in 1693 the Lords Proprietors warned Governor Ludwell to "beware the Goose Creek men." Among them were James Moore, who later led the expeditions against St. Augustine and Apalache, and Edward Middleton, whose great-grandson was one of the signers of the Declaration of Independence.

From *Harper's New Monthly Magazine,* Vol. LII.

tient Indians, and started on their various ways under the supervision of adventuresome and generally not too scrupulous traders.[14]

A well beaten path led westerly to the Lower Creek towns on the Ocmulgee and Chattahoochee rivers (see map on pages 296–297); Coweta, where Woodward skirmished with the Spaniards in 1686, had lost some of its importance but was still well worth a call. Branching from this Lower Path was an Upper Path which led to the Upper Creek towns on the Tallapoosa River; there, after 1702, the traders had to compete against Frenchmen from the new settlement at Mobile.[15]

Nor were the Upper Creek towns the end of the path. Some of the traders pushed on to the Chickasaw villages in presentday northeastern Mississippi. What the Chickasaw lacked in skins they could always make up for by a raid on their southern neighbors, the Choctaws; and in fact the traders urged such raids to the end that slaves might be available as exchange for the array of goods unstrapped from the pack horses and spread before the covetous savages.[16]

The opening of a new path from Savannah Town northwesterly to the headwaters of the Savannah River probably was smoothed by a former acquaintance of ours, though a stranger to the Carolinians. It will be recalled that, when in 1687 Joutel and his fellow survivors of the La Salle expedition reached Arkansas Post they were met by two Frenchmen, one of whom was named Couture. Four or five years later Couture appeared in Carolina, having come, apparently, by way of the Tennessee River and through the Cherokee villages which lay in the mountainous region where the upper waters of the Tennessee and the Savannah interlace. Certain it is that Couture later guided a party of English traders from Carolina to the Mississippi by this route and certain it is that from about the time of his arrival at Savannah Town a steady trade with the Cherokees developed.[17]

Of the English goods offered to the Indians those most in demand were guns, powder, and bullets. Knives, scissors, axes, hoes, and kettles were always part of a trader's pack.

Vermilion, for painting the savage anatomy, and looking glasses, for admiring it, were desirable vanity items. Coats of many kinds, petticoats, cloth of many colors, hats for men and girdles for women were necessities.[18]

The Indian currencies most acceptable to the Carolina traders were, as we have observed, skins and slaves. The skins, mainly deer skins, were shipped to England where they were used in a great variety of manufactures. In the ten years from 1701 to 1710 the number of deer skins thus shipped from Carolina averaged nearly 52,000 per year, and their value probably outstripped any other commodity exported by the colony.[19]

As to the number and value of the slaves acquired in the Indian trade we have no definite figures, but they must have been very large. The Indians, encouraged by the traders, accepted it as a part of their economic life that when they could not get enough skins to pay for the things they wanted, then they must make war on their neighbors in order to procure enough slaves to make up the deficit. Thus, slaves became a standard medium of exchange in the Indian towns and in the Charleston markets. Some few of these captive Indians were used on the Carolina plantations, but in general the planters preferred negroes. Most of the Indians were sold to Barbados and other sugar islands where the mortality was high and the replacement demand steady. Some few went to New England and the northern colonies; the *Boston News Letter* often carried advertisements listing Carolina Indians for sale or offering rewards for the recovery of those who had run away.[20]

The one region in which the Charleston traders had been unable to push their operations successfully was that to the northward—among the Catawba and related tribes. Virginia had early pre-empted that trade and held it. In 1700 John Lawson, perhaps under encouragement from the Carolina Proprietors, undertook a voyage of exploration into this part of the province. He started from Charleston accompanied by four or five other Englishmen and three or four Indian guides. About fifteen miles up the Santee they came to the first of the French plantations and were "very courteously

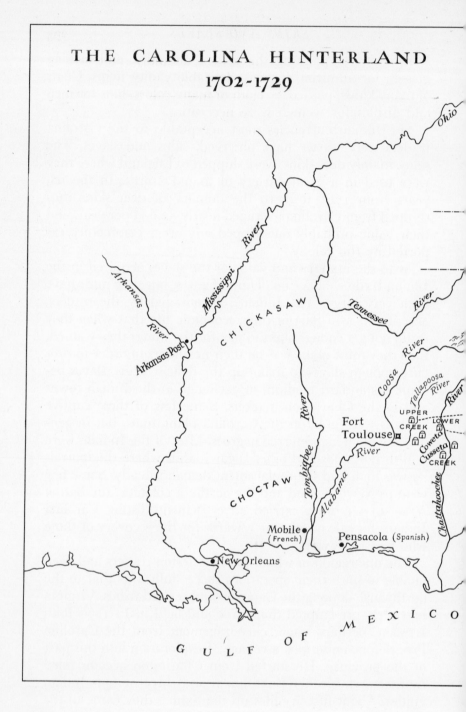

THE CAROLINA HINTERLAND
1702-1729

MILES

25 0   50   100   200

297

received" by the planter and his wife. Lawson estimated that there were some seventy French families on the river, and he was impressed with the fact that they were all "very clean and decent in their Apparel."[21]

Pushing on northwesterly, up the Santee and its Wateree branch, the explorers visited one Indian tribe after another —observing their customs and ways of life. What they saw gave one of the travellers an idea, or as Lawson tells the story, the Englishman "having a great Mind for an *Indian* Lass for his Bed-Fellow" spoke to the guide who easily arranged the matter. The lass, however, affected a becoming coyness until her gallant exhibited the beads, red calico and other treasures with which his pockets were filled, and some slight part of which she might expect to receive. "Then they went to Bed before us all." In the gray dawn of the following morning Lawson was awakened by the gallant of the previous evening; he had a grievance. His lass was gone. His beads and his calico were gone. Even his shoes were gone. And little sympathy he got from his Indian hosts; when they heard the story they laughed until their sides were sore.[22]

From the Catawba towns Lawson and his party turned northeasterly along the path over which for years William Byrd's traders had urged their pack trains. In addition to deer skins the Catawba—and occasionally the Cherokee— had sent Byrd a goodly number of beaver, prizes from the streams flowing out of the Blue Ridge; but of slaves very few apparently accompanied the Byrd caravans. Lawson and his men saw none of Byrd's traders but they followed the Virginia path to a point not far from presentday Durham, North Carolina. From there they circled east and south to the settlements about Albemarle and Pamlico sounds—all that there then was of North Carolina. As they approached the Pamlico River they passed through a village of Tuscarora Indians—pinebark houses set in rows with streets between.[23]

Lawson evidently made his home in North Carolina during the next few years. In 1705 he joined in the founding of the town of Bath and in 1708 he received, from the Lords Proprietors, the office of Surveyor-general of North Caro-

lina. This appointment may have been given as a reward for
a book which he had written and which was at that time
being set in London, under the title of *A New Voyage to
Carolina, Containing the Exact Description and Natural
History of that Country; Together with the Present State
thereof and A Journal of a Thousand Miles, traveled thro'
several Nations of Indians, giving a particular Account of
their Customs, Manners; etc.* The book painted North Carolina in glowing colors: the soil produced abundantly; the
climate was serene; the Indians were docile; white people
who lived there became beautiful; the women were fruitful.[24]

While in London in 1709, seeing his book through press,
Lawson met Baron Christoph von Graffenried who had left
his native Switzerland for two valid reasons, one being to
escape his creditors and the other to recoup his fortune in
America. The fortune was to be made from silver mines already, supposedly, located by Franz Louis Michel, a fellow
Swiss, who had flitted mysteriously through Pennsylvania,
Virginia and Carolina, always leaving behind the suspicion
that he had discovered—somewhere in the hinterland—rich
mineral deposits. On his return to Switzerland, shortly before Graffenried's departure, Michel had generously, for
what consideration we know not, agreed to let the Baron in
on his discoveries—even as he had earlier agreed with young
Governor Evans of Pennsylvania, and even with William
Penn, and probably with others. Graffenried took the enterprise seriously; on his way to England he contracted with
a group of German miners to come to America and work
in the mines.[25]

In London, during his talks with Lawson, Graffenried
doubtless heard much about Carolina. Also, in London, Graffenried found himself again in contact with Michel, there
as the representative of a Swiss company negotiating with
the Lords Proprietors of Carolina for a tract of land in their
province. Somewhat naturally Graffenried was drawn into
the land scheme and shortly, on borrowed money but as a
member of the Swiss company, became the owner of several
thousand acres of land lying between the Neuse and Trent
rivers in North Carolina.

The purpose for which this land had been acquired was that of founding a colony—to be composed of Swiss and Palatines. These "poor Palatines," as they were generally called, were refugees from the devastation then being spread over Germany by the armies of France. Many thousands had fled to England and were being cared for at public expense. Any arrangement by which they could be absorbed into the American colonies was a desirable solution and the Queen had agreed to aid the Swiss company's colonizing venture by paying the transportation of the Palatines to their new home in North Carolina.[26]

After the usual delays, the Palatines—six hundred and fifty of them—sailed from England in January, 1710. They were so tightly packed aboard the ships and the voyage was so long that many died during the passage. The sickness that always went with settlement of new land carried off still more. And by the time Graffenried arrived with the Swiss contingent, in September, 1710, a full half of the Palatines were dead. The rest were huddled in an unhealthy camp along the Trent River, clearing land that happened to belong to Lawson.[27]

Graffenried did what he could to bring order out of chaos. He had the land surveyed and a suitable plot assigned to each family. He laid out a town, called New Berne, on the point of land where the Neuse and Trent meet. And he erected some slight lines of fortification. But winter was upon the settlement and the people had to be fed and clothed until crops could be raised. Additional assistance, promised by the Queen, had failed to materialize. Supplies, expected from the Lords Proprietors, were delayed due to a minor civil war between two rival North Carolina governors. In fact, it was common talk that some of the local officials expected to "get an Estate by these Foreigners."[28]

John Urmston, a minister who had been sent to North Carolina by the Society for the Propagation of the Gospel, reported that Graffenried's people would have starved that winter of 1710–11 had they not been assisted by their neighbors. But not even their neighbors had very much. There were a few wealthy planters but most of the inhabitants were poor. Urmston and his family lived many a day, he said, "only on a dry crust and a draught of salt water out of the sound;" his parishioners, far from supporting him, took the attitude that he was "beholden to them for coming to hear" him. In fact, Urmston had a low opinion of the people of North Carolina. "This is a nest of the most notorious profligates upon earth," he wrote home. "Women forsake their husbands, come in here and live with other men they sometimes followed. Then a price is given to the husband and madam stays with her Gallant. A report is spread abroad that the husband is dead. Then they become Man and Wife, make a figure and pass for people of worth and reputation, arrive to be of the first Rank and Dignity. . . ." [29]

Despite the preacher's estimate of the province, many of Graffenried's new settlers preferred it to Europe. Christen Engel, in a letter to relatives and friends at home, said: "No one has any desire to be back in Switzerland . . . I would also wish that the poor neighbors were with us and then they would not need to suffer hunger if they would only be willing to work a little. Therefore whoever has a desire for it, let him just venture boldly under the protection of the Most High. To be sure they do not give one a ready built house and cleared land. Each one can labor for it and clear it himself. . . . But after the rain comes sunshine. And now we are, the Lord be praised, all as well as we have never been before." [30]

It is evident that none of the members of Graffenried's colony were conscious of the one very real threat that hung over their heads. The land on which they were settled had belonged to the Tuscarora Indians.. Some few of the savages still clung to their homes after the arrival of the Swiss and Palatines. Lawson advised Graffenried to drive them off, but the baron decided to buy them out. A day was set for the ceremony. The Indian king, dressed in his best, arrived with his followers who seated themselves in a circle on the ground. Graffenried, decked out in "whatever would glitter most," had seated himself on a chair, when into the midst of this solemn council staggered Michel, the silver prospector, slightly drunk. He pulled the Indian King's crown off his head and threw it as far as he could and silenced a loquacious native orator by giving him a sound beating. With considerable difficulty Graffenried patched up the peace conference and acquired title to the land in return for the usual presents.[31]

The Indians moved inland, but they did not forget; in fact they may have taken practical precautions against being moved again. We cannot but wonder what was back of that unusually large consignment of skins brought into Appomattox by Byrd's man, Tony, during the summer of 1711 (see page 271). Did Tony give guns and powder for the skins? In any event the Tuscarora seem to have been well supplied with firearms and ammunition that autumn of 1711 and, at that very time, a strange fatality placed within their grasp the two men most responsible for the loss of their former home.

The weather was nice; the grapes were ripe; Lawson and Graffenried were leisurely ascending the Neuse in a small boat rowed by two negroes. Along the river's bank plodded their riding horses in charge of trusted Indian guides. Graffenried said later that the purpose of the trip was to find a new road to Virginia. The nearby Tuscarora Indians, however, put their own interpretation on the outfit; they suspected, and perhaps correctly, that the Surveyor-general and the colonizer were spying out more land for a new settlement. Accordingly, they surrounded the explorers and took them into one of their towns to explain themselves.

At first the Indians seemed friendly enough but when Lawson became abusive the attitude of the chiefs changed. The prisoners were made to sit down on the bare ground; their hats and wigs were pulled off and thrown into the fire; their pockets were plundered; and they were put on trial. In the middle of a great open space, as Graffenried later described the ceremony, they "sat bound side by side . . . upon the ground, the Surveyor-general and I, coats off and bare headed; behind me the larger of my negroes; before us was a great fire and around about the fire the conjurer, that is, an old gray Indian, a priest among them, who is commonly a magician, yes, even conjures up the devil himself. He made two rings either of meal or very white sand, I do not know

which. Right before our feet lay a wolf skin. A little farther
in front stood an Indian in the most dignified and terrible
posture that can be imagined. He did not leave the place. Ax
in hand, he looked to be the executioner. Farther away, before us and beyond the fire, was a numerous Indian rabble,
young fellows, women and children. These all danced in the
most abominable postures. In the middle was the priest or
conjurer, who, whenever there was a pause in the dance,
made his conjurations and threats. About the dance or ring
at each of the four corners stood a sort of officer with a gun.
They beat time with their feet, and urged on the dancers
and when a dance was over shot off their guns. Besides this,
in a corner of the ring, were two Indians sitting on the ground,
who beat upon a little drum and sang so strangely to it, in
such a melody, that it would provoke anger and sadness
rather than joy. . . . Meanwhile there were two rows of
armed Indians behind us as a guard, who never left their
posts until all was over: Back of this watch was the council
of war sitting in a ring on the ground very busy in consulta-
tion."

All night long the trial went on and the following morning
the verdict was reached: Graffenried was to be reprieved;
Lawson was to be executed; the settlements were to be raided.
And these decisions were promptly carried out. The baron
was spared being a witness of Lawson's fate, but he had to
stand helplessly by while five hundred Tuscarora warriors
sped away to attack his colonists. Helplessly, too, he had to
stand by as the raiders returned with their prisoners and their
loot.[32]

Taken wholly by surprise the white settlements were an
easy prey for the Indians and for a time it seemed that they
might be wiped out completely. Between the squabbling political factions no official had sufficient authority to lead an
effective offensive against the Indians. Accounts of the outbreak soon reached Virginia and South Carolina: sixty English and perhaps as many Swiss and Palatines dead; an uncertain number held as captives by the Indians; Graffenried
as well as Lawson reported killed.[33]

Governor Spotswood mobilized his militia—seven hundred

horsemen and nine hundred foot—near the North Carolina border, and threatened the belligerent Tuscarora with dire penalties if they did not release their prisoners. Also ‑he improved the occasion to recruit as many Indian boys as possible for enrollment in William and Mary College; these "students" made good hostages in case of trouble. Most of the Virginia militiamen apparently looked upon the expedition as a lark. William Byrd, who was along as commander-in-chief for Henrico and Charles City counties, tells of his men getting the Indian girls drunk and of "playing the wag" with them; also, when the Governor, yearning for a night's sleep, put a sentry at his tent door to halt the flow of jovial officers, they, in revenge, at around two o'clock of a morning, did a war dance just outside the head of his bed.[34]

South Carolina was more realistic in its aid. Colonel John Barnwell, with a few militiamen and several hundred friendly Indians—Cherokees, Catawbas, Creeks, and Yamasee—marched northward. The Tuscaroras fell back into a fortified town and stood on the defensive. Meantime, Barnwell's Indians, having gathered up a goodly number of stragglers, hurried back with them to the Charleston slave markets. The best that Barnwell could do was to patch up a peace with the hostile northern Indians and follow his warriors home.[35]

Naturally, the Tuscaroras continued their depredations and again South Carolina came to the rescue. In the early weeks of 1713 another punitive force marched northward—across the Santee, across the Peedee, across the Cape Fear, through swamps and floods and bottomless roads. In command was Colonel James Moore, son of the conqueror of Apalache. As in the year previous, the army consisted of less than fifty white men and perhaps eight hundred mercenary southern Indians. This time the Tuscaroras were completely routed; many were killed; several hundred were captured; and, as in the year previous, the captives were marched southward—across the Cape Fear, across the Peedee, across the Santee—to the slave markets of Charleston.[36]

Only those Tuscaroras survived who retreated swiftly into the hinterland. Nor did they dare remain there. In parties of a dozen or so, and over a period of many years, they made their way northward and were welcomed by their Iroquois brothers in the province of New York; the Five Nations became the Six Nations—Mohawks, Oneidas, Onondagas, Cayugas, Senecas, and Tuscaroras. And the land in North Carolina where the Tuscaroras had lived and hunted began to fill up with white men.[37]

Graffenried's colony, however, was at an end. In financial straits before the Indian outbreak, the Swiss company was now bankrupt. Some of the colonists stayed on and finally procured individual title to plots of land. Graffenried himself turned from the ruined colony at New Berne to the glittering silver mines of Michel's prospectus. These mines, according to a map provided by Michel, lay somewhere up the Potomac River, and thither Graffenried journeyed, to meet Michel and some anonymous business associates from Pennsylvania, apparently acting for William Penn. But Michel did not show up. Graffenried and the others ascended the river to the locality of presentday Harpers Ferry. The scenery was charming, but no silver mines appeared, nor did Michel. Slowly it began to dawn upon Graffenried and his associates that they had been duped. The gentlemen from Pennsylvania took their way home "badly satisfied with the tergiversations and strange conduct of Mr. M." And the baron returned sadly to Europe. In England he found his German miners, some forty in all, on their way to join him in America. With neither colony, mines, nor enough money to buy his own food, Graffenried could do no more than recommend them to the Perrys and to Governor Spotswood's agent with the result that, as we already know (page 277), they opened the iron mines at Germanna on the Rapidan River of Virginia.[38]

Whether South Carolina's expeditions against the Tuscaroras should be looked upon as humanitarian efforts to aid a hard-pressed neighbor or as profitable opportunities to gather up some saleable slaves is difficult to determine. But scarcely had the last Tuscarora captive been sold in the Charleston slave market before South Carolina herself needed aid against an uprising by her own Indians.

It was but natural that, with her far-flung Indian trade,

unfortunate incidents and animosities should develop. The misdeeds of her traders—and those misdeeds were both many and widespread—had a tendency to bring all Carolinians into disrepute with the savage victims. For example: In the Apalache towns Captain Musgrove "demanded Indians to goe & hoe his Corn and if they did not answer his demands, he would beat them." Joss Crosley, "being Jealous of a whore of his, beat & abused an Apalache Indian man in a barbarous manner." Philip Gilliard "took a young Indian against her will for his Wife, and Cruelly whipped her & her Brother . . . to the great griefe of the Indians there present." [39]

Tuskenehaus, an Indian of Cusseta in one of the Lower Creek towns, had a touching grievance. He had gone to war in the hope of picking up a few slaves with which to pay his debts and support his family. While he was away it happened that John Pight, a Charleston trader, presented a bill against the town—on account of goods for public purposes no doubt. The head men, being short two slaves of the amount of the bill, gave Tuskenehaus' wife and her mother to Pight to make up the balance. Even the Commissioners of Indian Trade, a body established by the South Carolina Assembly, agreed that Tuskenehaus had been harshly dealt with, and ordered his wife returned. The record is silent as to the mother-in-law. [40]

In most cases it is evident that the Commissioners did their best to protect the Indians against "the head strong unruly Traders." According to their rules no one was allowed to trade with the Indians without a license, backed up by a sizeable bond which could be forfeited in case of violations. A General-agent, John Wright, travelled from one Indian town to another checking on the conduct of the traders and listening to complaints by the Indians. The traders were forbidden to use rum in making their sales, and the Indians were directed to refuse payment for debts claimed on account of spirits. [41]

For some years the Yamasee Indians had been growing increasingly dissatisfied with their lot. Apparently they were heavily in debt to the traders; they had lived beyond their means; they had wanted more guns and calico than they could get skins or slaves to pay with. In the summer of 1711 —at about the same time that the Tuscaroras were nursing their intended vengeance in North Carolina—the Yamasee assured the Commissioners of Indian Trade that they "were preparing to goe to War and a hunting to pay their Debts." Also, they complained, as they had done in the past, that their hunting grounds were being trespassed upon by the English cattlemen of Port Royal.[42]

In addition to the trouble over the debts and the intrusions, there were the usual incidents. Alexander Nicholas, a trader, had "beat a Woman that he kept for his Wife so that she Dyed and the child within her, another Woman he has beat Since, the Chasee Kings Wife who is very ill & another Woman, being King Altimahaws Sister." Evidently, in beating women, Nicholas was partial to royalty. Then there was the case of Thomas Parmiter; he "toock two shee Tuckabugga slaves" from Indian Jack without making proper payment for them. Just what was the occasion for John Frazier's "beating the Tomatly King [chief man]," we do not know, but Stephen Beadon testified that it was common report that "Frazier was apt to Beat & abuse the Indians." So serious were the complaints of the Yamasee that in 1712 Thomas Nairne, one of their cattle-raising neighbors, was appointed as special agent for them. But this move only added to the suspicions of the Indians; they were "mightily dissatisfied," Cornelius Macarty informed the Commissioners, "for fear that Capt. Nairne would cause theire Lands to be taken from them."[43]

Debts, brutal treatment, dread of losing their homes all combined to bring about the inevitable Yamasee outbreak. The first blow was struck at the town of Pocotaligo, some twenty miles north of the presentday city of Beaufort, South Carolina. Thomas Nairne, the local agent, and John Wright, the general agent, had gone there to adjust some routine grievances; also in the town were the usual number of resident traders; everything seemed to be proceeding satisfactorily, and the white men went to bed on the night of April 14, 1715, without any thought of serious trouble. The next morning those who found time to think at all knew that the trouble was very serious indeed. Most of the traders were killed at once. Nairne was burned at the stake, a little at a time, over a period of several days. Some of the nearby settlements were wiped out completely. At Port Royal many were saved by flight to a ship that chanced to be lying in the harbor.[44]

The Creeks, who were commonly suspected of having been at the bottom of the plot so far as Indian strategy was concerned, promptly joined in carrying it out. At Coweta and the other Lower Towns all the English traders were knocked in the head. The same fate was meted out to the traders among the Choctaws, who hopefully reported their action to the French at Mobile. Even the Catawbas, almost unknown to the Charleston traders, joined in the fray—killing, burning and pillaging along the Santee. Soon all the outlying plantations were ruined or deserted and all that remained of the colony of South Carolina lay within a twenty-five-mile circle around Charleston.[45]

Only the Cherokees had remained aloof from the savage attack on the Carolinians, and of them there was doubt. For weeks they wavered between the emissaries from the Creeks and the emissaries from Charleston. In the end the head men of Chota, the capital of the Overhill Towns—on the Little Tennessee where it breaks out of the Blue Ridge—said the deciding words: If they remained neutral, "they should have no way in geting of Slaves to buy amunition and Clothing and that they were resolved to get ready for war." The war was to be against the Creeks. English trading goods had won.[46]

And the Cherokee warriors, together with the men and munitions sent by Virginia and the supplies sent by New England, turned the tide. By the spring of 1716 the hostile Indians had had enough, and the Carolinians could become critical of the price that they had been forced to pay for their salvation. Governor Spotswood, they felt, had driven a hard bargain for his militiamen; it was even suspected, and with considerable reason, that he had taken advantage of the disturbed conditions to advance the fortune of that Virginia Indian Company in which he was so deeply interested. Skins that previously had gone to Charleston were believed to be going to Christ-Anna.[47]

But Charleston's real trade loss was in the south and southwest. The defeated Yamasee fell back into Florida and their future trade went to St. Augustine; their debts to the Carolina traders, estimated at one hundred thousand skins, were lost. The Creeks made peace, but moved westward toward the French, and in the years to come their trade was divided between Charleston and the new French post, known as Fort Toulouse, on the Coosa River. If the Spanish and French had not encouraged the Indian outbreak they had certainly profited by it. The economic consequences of the Yamasee war were reflected in South Carolina's export of deer skins. In 1716 only 4,702 went to England as against 55,806 in 1715, and for the five year period from 1716 to 1720 the annual average was only 20,600 as against an earlier average of 52,000.[48]

The Yamasee outbreak had sent a shiver of apprehension throughout the English colonies—not so much because of the Indians as because it was suspected that the Indians were being directed by the French. True, England and France, and also Spain, were at peace, had been since 1713, but the treaty had left the respective American spheres of England and France to negotiation. France might well be attempting, through savage allies, to improve her position at the council table. Caleb Heathcote, from his Manor of Scarsdale in New York province, wrote a warning letter to the Secretary of State of Great Britain; the situation, he said, was "exceeding dangerous, for the Indians under armes in Carolina are reported to be very numerous . . . and if the French, with whom they have allready too good an understanding, can keep 'em together & steady to their interest, North America must immediately arm itself, unite & be very vigorous, or the whole will be in danger." Similar communications from other leading men in other colonies poured into England.[49]

From Carolina itself the British ministers and Board of Trade were bombarded with demands for royal aid—all of which, of course, were referred to the Lords Proprietors of the province. But the Lords Proprietors could do nothing. "We, the proprietors of Carolina," reported Lord Carteret, "having met on this melancholy occasion, to our great grief find that we are utterly unable, of ourselves, to afford our colony suitable assistance in this conjuncture; and unless his majesty will graciously please to interpose, we can foresee nothing but the utter destruction of his majesty's faithful subjects in those parts." But the Proprietors would not surrender their patent, nor would Parliament force them to do so.[50]

With the Indians and French hovering in her rear, with no adequate support from those whose duty it was to protect her, Carolina was now faced with a new enemy. The conclusion of peace with France and Spain had left a swarm of English privateers without legal employment. Their business, however, had become a vested interest and they went right on raiding commerce—of whatever nation had the fattest cargoes. From being privateers they had easily become pirates. The numerous inlets about Cape Fear (see map on page 297) proved attractive as bases at which to outfit for a raid and to which to return with their loot—and the whole American coast, from Newfoundland to Florida, became their hunting ground. The rich South Carolina ships were especially attractive to the pirate captains. Thus, in June, 1718, the combined fleets of Stede Bonnet and Captain Teach, better known as "Black-Beard," sat down before Charleston Harbor, captured several outward-bound ships and even sent an armed boat into the city with a demand upon Governor Robert Johnson for needed medicines. Failure to comply with their request meant death for several prominent hostages who had fallen into their hands. The Governor complied.[51]

With Governor Eden of North Carolina, "Black-Beard" and Bonnet did not need to be so rough. This official, for whom Edenton was later named, had arrived from England in 1714. He was an ardent churchman and shortly became a vestryman of "the Eastern Parish of Chowan Precinct." Evidently, too, he was a charitable man, for when, shortly after the Charleston episode related above, Stede Bonnet appeared and asked for a pardon, the Governor supplied it—in accordance with a general proclamation issued by the King for the purpose of reforming pirates.[52]

Thus equipped with the King's pardon in addition to a stout ship and a willing crew, Bonnet sailed northward. In

Delaware Bay he captured several rich merchantmen, after which he dropped down the coast to Cape Fear River to recondition his ship. Soon word got about as to the pirate's location and Colonel William Rhett, of Charleston, offered to lead an expedition against him. On September 26, 1718, Rhett, with two heavily armed and well manned ships, entered the Cape Fear River—and promptly grounded, with the masts of Bonnet's ship in plain sight over a sandbar. All night long the air rang with preparations for the battle that would come with the morning tide. Morning brought not only water but a stiff off shore breeze and Bonnet, with all sail set, attempted to break past Rhett's blockade. In their maneuvering, all three ships grounded and, lying almost on their sides, spent the day shooting at each other. Again the incoming tide joined the fray. And when Rhett's ships were the first to straighten on their keels the pirates saw that their chances were hopeless and surrendered. Rhett returned to Charleston with his prisoners; a celebrated trial followed; Bonnet and several of his men were convicted and sentenced to be hanged.[53]

"Black-Beard" came to an even more dramatic end. Like Bonnet he retired to North Carolina after the Charleston raid and secured a pardon from Governor Eden. Then, dismissing most of his men, he started for the West Indies, or such he declared his destination to be. Shortly, however, he returned to Bath, the capital of North Carolina, with a French ship which, as he told Governor Eden, he had found floating around the ocean without anyone aboard, although the ship contained a valuable cargo. The Governor was apparently satisfied with the story, and Tobias Knight, the local Judge of Vice-admiralty, readily condemned the ship as a fair prize. In disposing of the cargo a considerable quantity of sugar and other goods went secretly into the Judge's barn at the little town of Bath.[54]

Jealousy perhaps prompted some residents of North Carolina to tell Governor Spotswood of Virginia what was going on at Bath. In a way it was none of Spotswood's business, but he was a royal official and made it his business. At his own expense the Governor hired two small sloops, fitted them up for a fight and put them under the command of Ellis Brand, Captain of H. M. S. *Lyme* then lying in Hampton Roads. The captain's instructions were to bring in "Black-Beard," dead or alive.

Brand found the pirate ship at Ocracoke Inlet (see map on page 297), with only some twenty men aboard. The fight was short but savage; twelve of the attacking party were killed; about the same number of pirates lay dead on the bloody deck of their ship when the battle was over; among them was "Black-Beard," in whose pocket was found a letter from Judge Tobias Knight, of Bath, containing a covert warning of the impending attack. Captain Brand returned to Hampton Roads with "Black-Beard's" head dangling from his bowsprit.[55]

Another pirate captain, ignorant of what was happening on the southern coast that fall, started operations as usual off Charleston only to be killed on his own ship by a boarding party under the command of Governor Johnson. His crew was added to the already large number who were to swing from the line of gibbets being built along the mud flats at Charleston. Carolina had ceased to be a safe place for pirates.[56]

In suppressing the pirates, as in beating back the Indians or in expelling the French fleet, the South Carolinians had received little aid from their Lords Proprietors. The excuse was that two of the Proprietors were minors and no legal action could be taken. But when the provincial Assembly touched the proprietary pocketbook or authority, the Lords could act quickly enough. They promptly vetoed trade regulations designed to pay off expenses incurred in defending the province, but which infringed upon proprietary profits. Even more irritating was an order to the Governor to dissolve the existing Assembly and call for the election of a new one which would presumably be more amenable to the proprietary authority.[57]

Governor Johnson did as he was directed but apparently neither he nor any other of the proprietary officers knew of a paper that was being passed from hand to hand throughout the province. The signers pledged themselves "to stand by

CAPTAIN TEACH.
Commonly called Blackbeard.

From Charles Johnson, *A General History of the Lives and Adventures of the Most Famous Highwayman etc.* (London, 1736).

and support whatsoever should be done by their representatives then newly chosen, in disengaging the country from the yoke and burden they labored under from the proprietors, and in putting the province under the government of his majesty." [58]

The new Assembly met on December 17, 1719; but instead of proceeding to business in the usual manner its President informed the startled Governor that it could not "act as an Assembly, but as a *Convention,* delegated by the people, to prevent the utter ruin of this government . . . that the lords proprietors have unhinged the frame of government, and forfeited their right to the same. . . ." [59]

The Convention then invited Johnson to continue to act as governor, but under the King rather than the Proprietors. Very properly he declined. "I hold my Commission from the *true and absolute Lords and Proprietors of this Province,*" he said, "In Subordination to them I shall always Act." The Convention took him at his word and chose James Moore, son of the hero of Apalache, as temporary Governor in his place. [60]

As the militia started to escort the members of the Convention to the ceremonies inaugurating the new government, Johnson halted the commanding officer. "How dare you appear in arms against my orders?" he demanded. A line of levelled muskets, all converging upon himself, convinced the former Governor that his orders no longer counted with the armed forces of the province. [61]

There remained one more chance of squashing the rebellion, and Johnson took it. Two British men-of-war had recently arrived at Charleston. To their commanders Johnson was the legal governor and on his appeal they moved up the harbor and anchored in front of the city. Johnson then informed the leaders of the Convention that unless they submitted, Charleston would be blown to pieces. But the bluff failed to work; with seventy pieces of artillery in their own hands the revolutionists were in a position to ignore such a threat. The question of authority in South Carolina was to be settled in London. [62]

In the spring of 1720 Colonel John Barnwell, "Tuscarora

Jack" as he was called in honor of his expedition to the northern colony, arrived in England to lay Carolina at the feet of
the King. Fortunately perhaps, King George, who had succeeded Queen Anne in 1714, was absent—attending to affairs
in his native Hanover—and the plea of the Carolinians fell
almost directly into the lap of the Board of Trade. It was an
opportunity such as the Board had long looked forward to,
and without so much as a *Quo Warranto* South Carolina was
taken into the King's hands. The Lords Proprietors had no
alternative but to acquiesce. There still existed the possibility
that their rights might be restored, and in the meantime they
retained title to the soil—with a claim upon any balance that
might remain from the quitrents after the provincial salaries
had been paid.

The position of South Carolina as a buffer against French
or Spanish attack called for an experienced Governor, and
he would of course be appointed by the King on the recommendation of the Board of Trade. The selection fell upon
our old acquaintance, Francis Nicholson. Since losing the
governorship of Virginia in 1705 he had served as an officer
in two abortive expeditions against Canada, launched from
the northern colonies; he had recovered Nova Scotia for England and been named as its Governor. His heavy-handed
attempts to act as general supervisor of colonial finances,
trade and ecclesiastical affairs—an enlargement of the duties
formerly carried out by Randolph and Quary—had inspired
some lines in the first play written and published in the English colonies. This distinctly coarse production, entitled *Androboros,* appeared in New York in 1714, under the imprint
of William Bradford, the one-time Quaker printer of Philadelphia (see page 220). The author was none other than
Robert Hunter, Governor of New York; and in his literary
effort he was assisted by Lewis Morris whom we have already
met as a landowner and official in New Jersey (see pages
212, 216).

Nicholson was justly famous for his bursts of temper. An
Indian, observing him during a fit of anger, thought that he
had been "born drunk." While Governor of Virginia he was
credited with having set forth that if Miss Martha Burwell

married anyone other than himself, he would cut the bride-
groom's throat, he would cut the officiating clergyman's
throat and he would cut the license-granting justice's throat.
Some say that he included the young lady's father and brothers among those whose throats would be cut. A dozen years
later Samuel Sewall recorded a scene that took place during
a meeting of the Massachusetts Council. Nicholson went into
a rage over a minor difference of opinion and upbraided his
opponents in a tone of voice described as a "Roaring Noise."
Not getting his way, he then stalked out "and walk'd the
Exchange, where he was so furiously Loud that the Noise
was plainly heard in the Council-Chamber, the door being
shut."[65]

But with all his peculiarities, Nicholson probably knew
more about the English colonies as a whole and had a better
first-hand understanding of their problems than any other
one man of his time. As governor of five different colonies—
from Nova Scotia to South Carolina—his experience was
comprehensive. He recognized, had long recognized, that
South Carolina, like New York, was a crucial part in the line
of defense against French encroachment from the west. And
when, in 1728 at the age of seventy-three, the old Governor
died, he had welded South Carolina into an effective barrier
to French advance from Mobile or the Mississippi. Also, it
is of interest to note that he died a bachelor and left the bulk
of his estate to the Society for the Propagation of the Gospel.[66]

During these years—from 1720 to 1728—the legal status of
Carolina was confused to say the least. Technically the patent
of the Lords Proprietors was in full force and effect. Actually,
from Virginia to Florida, the Proprietors still owned the land;
in North Carolina they still exercised the full power of government through a Governor appointed by themselves; but
in South Carolina the government was under a Governor
appointed by the King. It was an impossible situation, and
seven of the eight Proprietors—Lord Carteret alone standing
out—were resigned to selling their rights, if they could make
a satisfactory bargain. In 1729, the year after Nicholson
died, the King offered and seven of the Proprietors accepted
£2500 each for their proprietary interests. Thus for a total

of £17,500 (perhaps $350,000.00) the Crown acquired sev-
en-eighths of the right in the soil and the government of the
two Carolinas.⁶⁷

There still remained Lord Carteret's one-eighth share, and
for fifteen years the lone Proprietor and the King continued
as tenants in common. Then an arrangement was entered
into by which Carteret surrendered all his right of government in both the Carolinas and accepted as his full share
of the land a sixty-mile-wide strip running across northern
North Carolina.⁶⁸

Thus legally in 1744, though actually in 1729, the Carolinas became royal colonies. For each colony the King appointed a governor; for each colony he named the members
of the council; in each colony a representative assembly was
elected by those qualified to vote. Over both colonies—as over
Virginia, New Jersey, New York, Massachusetts and New
Hampshire—the Board of Trade exercised a unifying influence.

Within North Carolina lay Carteret's land, which came to
be known as the Granville Grant, since, just at the time the
arrangement was made, Carteret succeeded to the Granville
title. For nearly forty years every land owner in the Grant,
which included the richest and most populous section of
North Carolina, owed his quitrents to Granville's agents—the
rents that formerly had been payable to the Lords Proprietors
and that in other parts of the colony were payable to the
King. As in the Fairfax Proprietary, which in many ways
Granville's Grant resembled, the proprietary agents had great
latitude in the disposal of unassigned land. Too often their
greediness held back settlement or caused frontiersmen with
defective titles to be dispossessed. Their sharp practices were
in a large measure responsible for the tragic battle between
settlers and militiamen on the banks of the Alamance River
in 1771. A few years later, a new State of North Carolina
put an end, once and for all, and with more satisfaction than
justice, to this last remnant of the vast semi-feudal gift made
by Charles II to his noble friends in 1663.⁶⁹

Louisiana

PROMINENT AMONG the instructions which Francis Nicholson carried to South Carolina in 1721 was one directing him to fortify the mouths of the rivers, particularly that of the Altamaha, emptying into the ocean between Port Royal and St. Augustine (see map on page 297). The purpose was not protection against the Spanish, but rather precaution against the "probability of encroachment by the French . . . from their great settlement upon the river Mobile."[1]

This "great settlement" at Mobile was but part of a network of French towns and trading posts stretching from the Alabama River on the east to the Red River on the west and northward to the Illinois country. La Salle's dream had come true.[2]

The first of these French settlements on the Gulf had been planted in 1699 by Pierre le Moyne, Sieur d'Iberville, a native son of Canada. We have already met him as a volunteer in the attack on Schenectady in 1690 and as the captor of Fort Pemaquid six years later (see pages 162 and 172). In establishing the colony in Louisiana, Iberville was acting as

LE MOYNE D'IBERVILLE

From Pierre Margry, *Découvertes et Etablissements.*

an officer of the King and at the King's expense. With him, aboard two royal frigates, had come some two hundred soldiers, settlers, priests and adventurers. Among the latter was Iberville's eighteen-year-old brother, Jean Baptiste le Moyne, Sieur d'Bienville.[3]

In avoiding La Salle's mistake of overshooting the mouth of the Mississippi Iberville hugged the coast from Apalache westward. At Pensacola (see map on page 331) he found a Spanish captain already in possession—sent there for the specific purpose of blocking a landing by the French. Even after entering the Mississippi, Iberville was not sure that he had actually found the great river. But a letter handed to Bienville by an Indian chief reassured him; written in French, dated thirteen years earlier and signed by Tonti, it had been left for delivery to La Salle upon his arrival in the river.

Still, Iberville did not establish his first settlement on the Mississippi; rather he landed his colonists and built his fort on Biloxi Bay near the present Gulf town of the same name. Then, early in May, 1699, he, with his frigates, returned to France, leaving De Sauvole de la Villantray and Bienville in command.[5]

Even as Iberville's frigates sailed out of the Gulf, one Captain Bond, commanding a frigate armed with sixteen guns and flying the flag of England, was searching for the mouth of the Mississippi. Like La Salle he had missed his objective and made a landfall on the coast of Texas. Beating back easterly Captain Bond entered the river on August 29 and started up its winding course. A few miles below the present city of New Orleans he met, coming down stream in canoes, a party of Frenchmen headed by Bienville. A parley ensued out of which it developed that the English captain had been sent to explore the river preparatory to bringing in a group of colonists for Doctor Daniel Coxe, whom we last knew as the majority proprietor of West Jersey (see page 208). Subsequently Coxe had purchased the defunct 1629 patent of Carolina (see page 9) and by 1698 was seemingly well on the way to establishing his, and England's, title to the lower Mississippi country. King William favored the project and Father Hennepin, whose unhappy wandering through presentday Minnesota we have already observed (page 84), had lent a hand by so rewriting his experiences that instead of being rescued from the Sioux by Duluth, he, rather than La Salle, floated down the Mississippi and became its real discoverer—all for his royal patron, King William of England.

Such was the background of the meeting of the French and English on the Mississippi that late summer day of 1699. Bienville claimed that he bluffed Coxe's ship out of the river by an overstatement as to the strength of the French settlement. Be the reason what it may, the English captain did turn around and sail away—and to this day, the stretch of river where the incident occurred is known as English Turn. Had Captain Bond arrived a few months earlier or been a bit more persistent, the history of the Mississippi valley might have been very different.

If any doubts still lingered in Bienville's mind as to the identity of the river whose lower stretch he held, those doubts were finally dispelled by a voyage made by Pierre le Sueur —who knew the upper Mississippi when he saw it. For fifteen years he had been a trader among the Sioux in presentday Minnesota. In fact, like Duluth and others, Le Sueur had been charged with being a *coureur de bois* (woods ranger), which term was commonly applied to those who lived and traded among the Indians without a license or other formal authorization from Quebec. When, however, in 1696, all the independent traders and *coureurs de bois* were ordered out of the west, on pain of being condemned to the galleys, Le Sueur obeyed—returning to France where he obtained a grant to a mine which he claimed to have discovered in the Sioux country. Arriving at Biloxi in 1700 he equipped a boat with long (lateen) sails and, with a few men, started up the Mississippi. It was a strange rig for the Father of Waters and the startled Indians viewed it with alarm, but it won through. Somewhat below presentday Minneapolis Le Sueur turned into the Minnesota River. There he built a fort and picked up a load of worthless multicolored stones with which he returned to Biloxi. Historians have usually felt sorry for him but there is a reasonable possibility that underneath the stones Le Sueur had enough packs of furs to make the trip profitable. The men he left to hold his fort—L'Huillier, he called it—do deserve our sympathy. They were promptly chased out by the pugnacious Fox Indians, who, holding the portage between Lake Michigan and the Wisconsin River (map on page 37), had set themselves up as middlemen for any European goods going to the Sioux. And they had no intention of letting traders slip in the back door from Louisiana. Le Sueur's venture was at an end.[7]

As news of Iberville's settlement travelled up the Mississippi, scores of *coureurs de bois,* who had ignored the royal edict of 1696 and as a result were practically outlaws in Canada, swarmed southwards. They were a trying lot to the officers at Biloxi. Bienville, himself a Canadian, understood them well enough, but De Sauvole, fresh from France, complained bitterly of their "unruliness and inconstancy." Why, he asked, "do they leave their country and why do we see them wandering about this one and elsewhere unless it is only in order not to work at all and not to be dependent on any one whomsoever?" A letter on its way to Paris from the Governor of Canada would have answered part of De Sauvole's question; it told of over a hundred men who had left Michilimackinac and were on their way down the Mississippi with twenty canoe-loads of furs that should have been sent to Montreal and Quebec.[8]

And the officers at Biloxi bought the furs. If they had not, the English merchants at Charleston probably would have done so. One band of *coureurs de bois* took the precaution of getting competitive bids. Caching their furs on the Wabash River, they followed Couture's old route through the Cherokee towns to Carolina. At some outlying point, probably Savannah Town, they met Governor James Moore and showed him samples. What would he give for more furs like those? Four and a half livres (say $3.00) apiece was Moore's offer. But before accepting this price, the men inquired at Biloxi as to the terms on which they could ship directly to France. The Governor of Canada had already anticipated this possibility and was asking that Louisiana be wholly prohibited from shipping beaver; let the new colony be limited to exporting buffalo hides, he suggested.[9]

Even our old friend Tonti came down from the Illinois country to see what was going on. In February, 1700, he arrived at Biloxi with five canoes, deep-laden with packs of furs and manned by nineteen paddlers. For eighteen years—first as a lieutenant of La Salle and later as a partner of Francois Daupin de la Forest, La Salle's former commander at Fort Frontenac—Tonti had dominated the Indian trade and Indian policy from the foot of Lake Michigan to the mouth of the Missouri. Following La Salle's death, Tonti and La Forest had asked for and received possession of Fort St. Louis with the same rights in the Illinois country that had formerly been granted to La Salle. Soon realizing that the fort—perched as it was on Starved Rock—could not provide a satisfactory base for their operations, they built a new post, consisting of four large buildings enclosed by a stockade, at a place known as Pimitoui—within the limits of the present city of Peoria, Illinois (see map on page 331). There they carried on a profitable trade for furs; there they maintained a small garrison for the protection of the western country; and from there they incited the western Indians to make raid after raid upon the Iroquois.[10]

It was from Pimitoui that Tonti had organized the expedition that, in 1693, broke the Iroquois blockade of the Lakes. For three years not a canoe had dared go down to Montreal and Quebec; Iroquois warriors watched at every portage; furs on which the St. Lawrence merchants had advanced funds lay in evergrowing packs at the western posts; bankruptcy impended for all Canada. Then Tonti acted. Under his direction the western traders rendezvoused at Michili-mackinac, and such a convoy of canoes swept down the Lakes that no Iroquois war party dared challenge it.

All Montreal turned out to welcome the men from the west, and a wild crew they were: gayly bedecked *voyageurs* swinging their paddles in time with their improvised songs; silent, watchful Miami and Kickapoo guides; nervous *coureurs de bois*, more Indian than the Indians; shrewd traders from Fort St. Antoine, from Sault Ste. Marie, from St. Joseph; and among them—as the canoes scraped to their landings—was grim Tonti with the iron hand. They had saved New France, so everyone felt. Even Count Frontenac came up from Quebec to add his plaudits to those of the grateful merchants.[11]

But, like so many brilliant feats, before and since, the reopening of the fur trade had its disadvantages. Within two years there were more furs piled up in Canada and France than the market could absorb in a decade. The edict of 1696 followed: trading licenses were cancelled; the *coureurs de bois* were ordered into the settlements; only Tonti and La Forest were exempted from the royal ordinance, and their operations were severely restricted. The west was returned to the Indians.[12]

The response, however, was not exactly what the King and his ministers had expected. Far from being happy about the removal of the traders and the *coureurs de bois* the Indians protested vigorously. Their point of view was well expressed by Chief Onanguisset of the Potawatomi during a visit to Count Frontenac in 1697. "Father!" said he, "Since we want powder, iron and every other necessary which you were formerly in the habit of sending us, what do you expect us to do? Are the majority of our women who have but one or two beavers to send to Montreal to procure their little supplies, are they to intrust them to drunken fellows who will drink them, and bring nothing back? Thus, having in our country none of the articles we require and which you, last year, promised we should be furnished with, and not want; and perceiving only this—that nothing whatsoever is yet brought to us, and that the French come to visit us no more —you shall never see us again, I promise you, if the French quit us; this, Father, is the last time we shall come to talk with you."[13]

It was evident that the western Indians would not undertake the long trip to Montreal to exchange their pelts for guns, powder and blankets, but guns, powder and blankets they would have. If the French did not supply them, the English would. Still the French ministry was not prepared to sanction a return to the system of trading posts and *coureurs de bois* and a glut of furs. A new compromise policy was worked out. At strategic points, under the immediate control of the King or of companies responsible to him, French colonies would be established, and about these settlements the Indians would be gathered. Thus the French settlers, unlike the *coureurs de bois*, would be under the restraint·of family life and the tight control of church and law; brandy and squaws would not be so readily exchangeable; the priests would have a better chance to reap a harvest of savage souls; and the Indians would have, close at hand, a ready market for the sale of their furs and the purchase of their supplies.[14]

Iberville's settlement in Louisiana was expected to provide an initial opportunity for putting this new policy into effect—the southern Indians, however, preferred to choose their own homes, and few regroupings of these tribes resulted. At Detroit, on the other hand, Antoine de la Mothe Cadillac so succeeded in attracting distant tribes that a new center of trade and savage power was created. Cadillac was a Gascon who had arrived in America in 1683 and secured title to a tract of land in presentday Maine. There, for some time, he had made his home. He also had personal property at Port Royal (now Annapolis, Nova Scotia) some of which was included in the plunder gathered up by Phips' men in 1690 (see page 163). Four years later he was appointed commander of the garrison at Michilimackinac, only to lose that job when the western posts were abandoned in 1696.[15]

From his acquaintance with the western country Cadillac had recognized the strategic significance of the strait (*détroit*) connecting Lake Huron and Lake Erie. And in 1699, shortly after the arrival of Iberville on the Gulf, he went to France and laid before the Comte de Pontchartrain, Minister of Finance, a plan for a similar settlement at Detroit. Pontchartrain approved, and in the summer of 1701 Cadillac led the nucleus of his colony—a hundred men in twenty-five canoes—to the spot which he, to Pontchartrain's amusement, thought might some day become "the Paris of America." A rough fort, surrounded by a palisade, was the first improvement in the future town.[16]

Other colonists, soldiers, priests, and traders followed the pioneers and added to the population of the colony. The Hurons moved to Detroit from the Michilimackinac region.

A part of the Fox nation hovered uneasily about the town. The Miamis left their home at the foot of Lake Michigan to live on the Maumee River in present Ohio—within easy reach of Cadillac's traders. It has been estimated that shortly there were as many as six thousand Indians within the area surrounding Detroit.[17]

Thus by the early years of the eighteenth century the French line of settlement—encirclement it appeared to the English—was established: from the St. Lawrence to Fort Frontenac, through Niagara and Lake Erie to Detroit, thence by portages to the Ohio, and down the Mississippi to Louisiana. Michilimackinac, the former metropolis of the west, was bypassed; only the bells of St. Ignace—and they not for long —recalled the concourse of savages and traders who once gathered there. Trade had followed the Indians.

In the Illinois Country, claimed by both Canada and Louisiana, a marked change also took place. No longer was Tonti's post at Pimitoui needed as a rallying point for attacks upon or defense against the Iroquois. The garrison and the Indians at Detroit took care of that; and among these Indians were many who had previously been attached to Tonti's post. Other Illinois Indians—particularly the Kaskaskias— heeded Iberville's call for removal southward—to act as a bulwark against English penetration by way of the Tennessee and Ohio rivers. By that route Jean Couture had just led a party of Carolina traders to the mouth of the Arkansas River. Le Sueur had met one of them on his way up the Mississippi. From the Chickasaw towns came stories of a regular trade with the Carolinians (see maps on pages 296, 331).[18]

Iberville was thoroughly alarmed. The re-location of the Kaskaskias was but one of his schemes for locking the door against the wide-ranging men from Charleston. Among the Kaskaskias, in their new home on the Mississippi, Father Gabriel Marest established a Mission of the Immaculate Conception; and nearby a few Frenchmen, probably former *voyageurs,* some with French wives and some with Indian wives, formed a village and laid out their farms. At about the same time another French village was coming into being opposite the presentday city of St. Louis where the Mission of the Holy Family ministered to the Cahokia Indians. The center of population in the Illinois Country was moving from the Illinois River to the Mississippi. As Kaskaskia and Cahokia grew, Pimitoui withered and died. Tonti, the veteran of the Illinois, was ordered to report at the new post of Mobile.[19]

The settlement at Mobile was another move in the plan to halt the English advance from Carolina. Iberville wanted a foothold even farther to the eastward and suggested that Spain, then closely allied to France, allow him to occupy Pensacola. That idea, however, did not approve itself to the Spanish, and Iberville had to content himself with a location on the Mobile River. There he erected a fort, named Louis in honor of the French King, and to that place, early in 1702, he moved his headquarters and most of his colonists. Mobile became the capital of Louisiana.[20]

And even as Mobile was being established, Iberville was forging a French-Indian confederation aimed at the Carolina traders. The preliminary negotiations were intrusted to Tonti. Doubtless he already knew that the two most important tribes within southern Louisiana were the Choctaws and Chickasaws. Doubtless he well knew that for years past the Charleston traders had encouraged the Chickasaws to war against the Choctaws in order to get slaves that could be traded for English goods. Doubtless he knew that any attempt by white men to make peace between the two tribes was dangerous. Nonetheless, with an escort of but ten men, Tonti visited both tribes and persuaded their chief men to accompany him to Mobile for a peace talk with Iberville.[21]

There, at Mobile on March 26, 1702, the Indian chiefs faced three of the most able Frenchmen in America. Dominating the talks was Iberville, Canadian born, thoroughly familiar with Indian nature, fearless, cruel as an Indian, the kind of a man that savages respected. Acting as interpreter was young Bienville, cautious, likable, a man they could trust. And in the background was Tonti, the man with the iron hand, who looked through and through them and could not be fooled with double talk (see his portrait on page 87). The proposals made by Iberville were that the Choctaw and

Chickasaw should expel the English traders from their towns; that the French should establish a trading post at which the Indians could buy the goods formerly purchased from the English; and that deer and buffalo skins rather than slaves captured from each other should be the currency used in buying these French goods. The chiefs agreed and Iberville reported, *"La paix est conclue."* [22]

But the peace did not stay concluded. Governor Moore's raid on the Apalache caused the other southern Indians to question the advisability of expelling the Carolina traders from their towns. In fact the Chickasaws were soon engaged in their old practice of capturing Choctaws for sale to the English. Nor could the French live up to their promise of supplying the Indians with the goods they needed; French manufacturing lagged far behind that of England. Fate itself seemed to be working against the French colony. In 1704 Tonti died, at the age of fifty-four; two years later Iberville was struck down by yellow fever, at the age of forty-five. France was at war with England, and Louisiana "was so to speak abandoned to the care of Sieur de Bienville," as he himself phrased it twenty years later. [23]

With soldiers and colonists to feed and clothe, Bienville received very few supplies from France. He was forced to borrow flour from the Spanish at Vera Cruz. The Indians had no alternative but to turn to the English traders for the guns, powder, lead and other things that they had come to depend upon. The situation was clearly revealed in a letter written by Bienville to Pontchartrain: "I know none of our [Indians] that would be willing for a great deal to separate themselves from the French whom they naturally like, and they are on the side of the English only through necessity and interest . . . I am without merchandise. I have no powder." [24]

Except for the attack by the French fleet on Charleston in 1706 (see page 289), it is likely that the Carolina traders and their Indian allies would have captured Mobile. As it was they burned the Spanish town at Pensacola and ranged at will through the territory claimed by Bienville. The Choctaws, who had remained friendly to the French, were the chief sufferers. Typical was a raid led by Thomas Welch, Carolina planter and western trader. With five other Englishmen and three hundred Indians, probably Chickasaws, he descended upon the Choctaws. It was a strictly business arrangement. Welch furnished his Indians with ammunition. In return he received fifteen of the captives of which he gave two to each of his five white assistants. This netted him five slaves for his investment. His Indian followers profited by all captives in excess of fifteen.[25]

Bienville, watching the operations of the English, came to the conclusion that the same system, if followed by the French, might improve the economic condition of Louisiana. He suggested to Pontchartrain that he be allowed to subsidize the Choctaw to bring in Indian captives which could be traded in the French West Indian colonies for negro slaves at the rate of two Indians for one negro. Negroes were preferred to Indians because they did not melt back into the tribes so readily. "The colonists eagerly ask for negroes to clear the land," Bienville reported. With a supply of negroes the colony would flourish; without them agriculture languished.[26]

Louisiana was, in fact, declining rather than going ahead —this despite all attempts to increase the population. The soldiers and settlers sent from France were too delicate for the steaming shores of the Gulf. Yellow fever swept them away almost as fast as they arrived. Occasional shipments of marriageable girls, selected from houses of correction, seem to have found husbands readily enough, though sometimes a girl stubbornly declined all suitors, and too often the lads from Canada preferred Indian squaws as being better looking and more robust. Barrenness or mortality must account for the comparatively few children. In 1708, with twenty-eight women in the colony there were but twenty-five children. The total white population at the time, as reported by the commissary officer, was one hundred and ninety-nine, "plus 60 Canadian backwoodsmen who are in the Indian villages situated along the Mississippi River without permission from any governor, who destroy by their wicked, libertine lives with Indian women all that the missionaries of the foreign missions and others teach them about the divine mysteries of the Christian religion."[27]

The Canadian backwoodsmen were not the only ones who upset the good work of the missionaries. Even at Mobile many of the officers of the military establishment had female Indian slaves who were, as a report expressed it, "always with child or nursing. The priests accuse their masters of it because their children are half-breeds and the masters throw the blame onto the Indian men." Whoever was responsible, the arrangement had its financial advantages for the poorly paid officers; they sold the offspring in the slave markets. Some reforming elements felt that the officers should be compelled to sell the women also, when they could get good bids from the sugar islands, and replace them with male slaves.[28]

All in all, Mobile of the early 1700's seems hardly a place where a lone woman of respectable character would have cared to live, and yet one of the inhabitants of the squalid little town that huddled around Fort Louis was the widow of Pierre le Sueur. She supported herself and her four children by running a store in her home—selling brandy, linen, hats, shirts, shoes, old iron and anything on which she could make a sou. There were those who whispered that the goods which Madam Sueur sold came out of the King's warehouse; she was a cousin of Bienville.[29]

This charge of favoritism to members of his family was constantly levelled against Bienville; also the fact that he acted as Governor without formal commission tended to make his authority questionable. And when, in 1711, Louis XIV recognized his responsibility to the colony by appointing a full-time Governor, the choice fell not upon Bienville but upon Antoine de la Mothe Cadillac who, after ten years of service as commandant at Detroit, had just returned to Paris.[30]

It is likely that Cadillac's appointment was part of a new general plan for the improvement of the colony. In any case, at just this time, Louis XIV granted Louisiana to Antoine Crozat, one of his wealthy subjects, in much the same manner as a half century earlier Charles II had granted Carolina to a group of Proprietors—except that Crozat's concession was limited to a term of fifteen years. In return for bringing in settlers and otherwise developing its resources Crozat was given control over every business transaction in Louisiana.

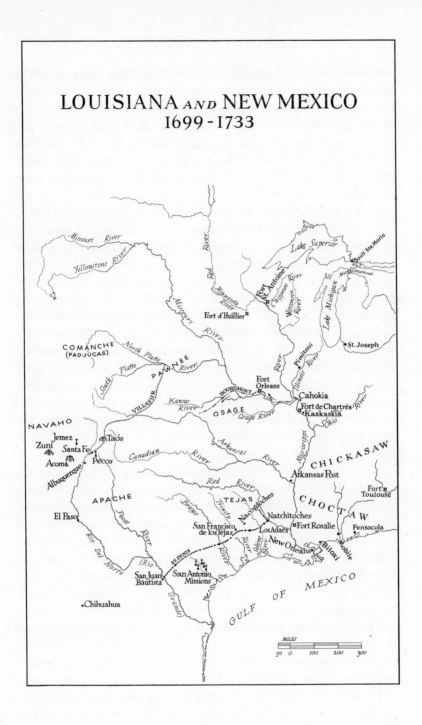

LOUISIANA *and* NEW MEXICO
1699-1733

Missouri River

Yellowstone River

Red River

Lake Superior

Sault Ste.Maria

Minnesota River

Fort St.Antoine

Chippewa River

Mt. Michilimackinac

Missouri River

Fort d'Huillier

Wisconsin River

Lake Michigan

COMANCHE (PADUCAS)

North Platte River

South Platte

PAWNEE

Pinitoui

Illinois River

St. Joseph

VILLASUR

BOURGMONT

Kansas River

Fort Orleans

Cahokia

Fort de Chartres

Kaskaskia

NAVAHO

Jemez

Zuni

Taós

OSAGE

Orage River

Ohio

Santa Fé

Acoma

Pecos

Canadian

Arkansas River

Mississippi River

CHICKASAW

Albuquerque

River

Arkansas Post

Fort Toulouse

APACHE

El Paso

Pecos River

Red River

Brazor

TEJAS

Trinity

Nacogdoches

CHOCTAW

Natchitoches

Fort Rosalie

Pensacola

Rio Del Norte

San Francisco de los Tejas

Los Adaes

New Orleans

Mobile

Biloxi

ST.DENIS

(Rio

Chihuahua

San Juan Bautista

San Antonio Missions

Sabine River

Grande)

GULF OF MEXICO

MILES

50 0   100   200   300

331

An Indian with a deer skin or a *coureur de bois* with a buffalo hide could sell only to Crozat's agent. But deer skins and buffalo hides would not repay Crozat's operating expense. Mines or trade with Mexico were the bait that had caused the French man of business to risk his money. And while Cadillac himself searched up the Mississippi for gold and silver, Louis Juchereau de St. Denis was directed to open the trade with Mexico.[31]

St. Denis, like Iberville and Bienville, was Canadian born, and with them he had come to Louisiana in 1699. From time to time over the years he had explored the Red River and in 1710 had established trading relations with the Natchitoches Indians. Now, in 1713, he selected Natchitoches as his starting point for Mexico. From there he continued westward through the place where, in 1690, Father Massanet had established the short-lived Mission of San Francisco de los Tejas (see page 139). Three or four days farther on he passed by the spot where, in 1687, La Salle's riddled body had been left in the bushes by his assassins (see page 131). Another three hundred miles of hard riding brought St. Denis to the presidio of San Juan Bautista, on the Rio Grande opposite presentday Eagle Pass, Texas. There he was detained pending advice from Mexico City.

Months passed by—but not monotonously for Louis Juchereau de St. Denis. At San Juan Bautista was the Spanish commandant's granddaughter, Manuela Sanchez Ramon, lonely and beautiful we may believe. And the dashing young man from Canada made the most of the situation. When he returned from Mexico City, where he had argued the authorities out of keeping him in prison, St. Denis and Manuela became man and wife, which event certainly did not impair the groom's standing below the Rio Grande.[32]

While at San Juan Bautista, St. Denis doubtless heard many details of the reconquest of New Mexico. As will be recalled (page 136), the Spanish survivors of the Pueblo Revolt of 1680 had ended their flight at El Paso; and there they had remained for twelve years during which time the Indians of the Pueblo Country had lived according to the ways of their fathers, wiping out all traces of Christianity.

DON DIEGO DE VARGAS

Reproduced from the frontispiece of *First Expedition of Vargas into
New Mexico, 1692,* by J. Manuel Espinosa—by the *courtesy* of Professor Espinosa and the University of New Mexico Press.

Then, in 1692, Diego de Vargas, with a small force of soldiers, two priests, and fifty friendly Indians, pushed northward from El Paso. As he approached the former settled area along the Rio Grande, where in 1680 there had been teeming pueblos and prosperous haciendas, Vargas found only desolation. Even at Santo Domingo, once an important town, he found no sign of life. "I entered the square," reported Vargas, "and found that it is strong, with high walls, but with its dwellings and living quarters vacant."

Vargas was now within thirty miles of Santa Fe. He had taken no prisoners, nor apparently did the Indians know that a Spanish army was in their country. The road was washed out and showed no evidence of having been used. It took two days to get within striking distance of the town—and still Vargas was undiscovered. At two o'clock of the morning of Saturday, September 13, the Spaniards started their final march on the former capital of New Mexico. Halting his little army in the gardens just outside the walls, Vargas directed his soldiers to cry out five times, "Glory be to the blessed sacrament of the altar." It was still dark but multitudes of people crowded to the walls to see what was going on. At first they refused to believe that the visitors were Spaniards, and when convinced, were inclined to fight. Vargas, however, persuaded them not to attempt resistance and by sheer nerve—he was outnumbered ten to one—brought them to agree that the Spanish regime might be re-established among them. The same scene was repeated, with slight variations, at Pecos, at Acoma and at other towns. Without the loss of a man, or the shedding of blood, the towns, one after another, yielded. Two thousand two hundred and fourteen Indians, mostly children born subsequent to the destruction of the missions, were baptized.

But when, the following year, the former Spanish landowners appeared, the Indians again rebelled. For four years there was bloody war—hundreds of men were killed, hundreds of women and children were sold into slavery before the Indians finally gave up and accepted, under fear of total extermination, the gentle guidance of their Christian shepherds.[33]

Such, in effect, would have been the facts which St. Denis gleaned in Mexico regarding affairs in New Mexico. Also, he would doubtless have heard something of the Spanish rediscovery of a region first explored by one of Coronado's captains but long neglected. In fact, despite Melchior Diaz's feat of heading the Gulf of Colorado in 1540, it was commonly believed by seventeenth-century Mexicans that California was an island. This fallacy was definitely dispelled in 1701 by Father Eusebio Francisco Kino, a Jesuit missionary to the Pima Indians. Constantly extending his missionary circuits to the northward Kino had, by 1700, reached the Santa Cruz River, a tributary of the Gila in presentday Arizona. There he founded the mission of San Xavier del Bac, which to this day ministers to the faithful. The following year he descended the Gila to its junction with the Colorado River, crossed on a raft, and found himself in California. He had not only reopened a western route to New Mexico but had proved the possibility of a land passage to Monterey and other already explored ports on the California coast.[34]

It is not likely, however, that either New Mexico or California occupied a very large place in the thoughts of St. Denis as. leaving his bride at San Juan Bautista, he started back to Natchitoches in 1716. With him went a small party of Spaniards—not as an escort but to find out where the Frenchmen had come from and to take steps against further encroachment. As a result of their report a Spanish fort and trading post was erected at Los Adaes, about twenty miles southwest of Natchitoches; a hundred and twenty miles farther west a mission, named San Francisco de los Neches, was established on or near the site of the former San Francisco de los Tejas; and another two hundred miles westward, about half way to San Juan Bautista, a mission, with the pleasing name of The Alamo, was founded on the San Antonio River.

Meanwhile, after reporting to Cadillac at Mobile, St. Denis returned to Natchitoches with a new supply of goods for his trading house, now permanently located at that point; the beautiful Manuela joined him; and soon pack horses were plodding between the Red River and the Rio Grande. Thus were forged the links in a trade chain that, despite national friendships or animosities, stretched from Carolina to Mexico. Thus an English coat from a Savannah Town pack might well have found its way to Santa Fe, or a Spanish dollar from Mexico might, and often did, turn up in Charleston.[35]

But this trade, however profitable its details might be to a St. Denis, was not sufficient to appreciably offset the expenses assumed by Crozat. Nor had Cadillac, in his explorations up the Mississippi, found any gold or silver mines; the Governor was, in fact, very frank in his opinion that the colony was "not worth a straw." And in this judgment Crozat evidently concurred; in 1717 he surrendered his concession which still had ten years to run.[36]

What Cadillac and Crozat lacked in vision as to the future of Louisiana was supplied by John Law, a Scotchman who had long lived in France and there acquired a reputation as a wizard of finance. To him the semi-tropical colony on the mighty river with the musical name was an ideal asset around which to organize a stock-selling enterprise that would make everybody rich. Incorporating the Compagnie de l'Occident (Company of the West), Law asked for and received the concession of Louisiana. Alluring prospectuses caused the stock to boom; additional companies were organized and pyramided into the parent holding company, which became known as the Compagnie des Indies. People stood in line to pay fifty times the par value of the stock.[37]

And in Louisiana things were booming, too. Bienville had replaced Cadillac as governor, and was making the most of Carolina's loss of prestige in the Yamasee war. Near the junction of the Coosa and Tallapoosa rivers—between the Upper and Lower Creek towns, squarely astride the Lower Path from Savannah Town to the Choctaws—he established a military post and trading house, named Fort Toulouse (see maps on pages 296 and 331). To this post came many of the skins that previously had been picked up by the wandering traders from Charleston.[38]

Engineers were set to work surveying the entrance to the Mississippi, along which, despite the fact that the French had been in Louisiana for eighteen years, no permanent settlement had been made. It was found that the channel was

feasible for ships, and in February, 1718, Bienville sent men
to clear a patch of land for a new town to which the name
of New Orleans was given.[39]

Actual settlers, convict laborers and negro slaves were
poured into the colony. To further hasten settlement the
Company made large grants of land to wealthy individuals
who would undertake to bring in an agreed-upon number of
people. Law himself took such a grant—twelve miles square
—near the mouth of the Arkansas River. On this land he settled several hundred Germans who had been uprooted from
their native soil by the wars raging in Europe. Farther up
the Mississippi, near Kaskaskia, Pierre Duque, Sieur de Boisbriant, Commandant of the Illinois District, laid the foundations for Fort de Chartres, destined to become the military
and civil center of that area, which was now officially recognized as a part of Louisiana.[40]

Thus from Fort Toulouse on the Coosa River to St. Denis's
trading house at Natchitoches—an east-west distance of almost four hundred miles—and northward from the mouth of
the Mississippi to the Illinois—almost seven hundred miles
—Louisiana reached its tentacles into the heart of America.
Also, by establishing contact with Canada through the new
settlement at Detroit, Louisiana was helping to draw the
French line of military posts ever closer to the western side
of those mountains into whose eastern passes Spotswood's
Knights of the Golden Horseshoe were finding their way.

The pattern of this French advance toward the middle
English colonies was ominous enough to those who had the
sight to see. Joliet and Marquette had opened the St. Law-
rence-Mississippi route by passing up the Ottawa River into
Lake Huron, thence into the upper part of Lake Michigan
and into Green Bay, whence the Fox River led to a portage
into the Wisconsin with an entry into the Mississippi near
presentday Prairie du Chien, Wisconsin (see map on page
37). All of this was very distant from any English colony.
Less than ten years later La Salle shortened the route by
carrying around Niagara and continuing past Green Bay to
the foot of Lake Michigan, where he portaged to the upper
waters of the Illinois River and thence into the Mississippi

somewhat above St. Louis (see map on page 89). Now,
in 1720, Lake Huron and Lake Michigan were both bypassed. Communication between Canada and Louisiana
passed up Lake Erie, at the western end of which stood
Detroit—ascended the Maumee River—portaged into the
Wabash, on which Fort Ouiatenon was established—and descended to the Ohio, whence the Mississippi was entered at
presentday Cairo, Illinois (see maps on pages 478 and 479).
The portage from the Maumee to the Wabash was three hundred miles nearer Williamsburg, Virginia, than was the portage from the Fox to the Wisconsin. And back of Carolina
lay the growing colony of Louisiana.

Such was the French menace when Francis Nicholson arrived in South Carolina in 1721. Momentarily the situation
looked even darker than it was; Bienville had improved a
break in friendship between France and Spain to capture
Pensacola. No wonder Nicholson was ordered to guard against
possible French expansion down the Altamaha River to the
Atlantic. This order, in fact, originated in Carolina—whose
leaders were well informed of what was going on—and the
man who most actively supported the policy, namely "Tuscarora Jack" Barnwell, was given the job of stopping French
expansion. All through the summer of 1721 he and his men
sweated in the swamp at the mouth of the Altamaha, "wading naked up to the waist or sometimes to the neck," getting
together four-inch cypress planks from which a gabled blockhouse, twenty-six feet square, was erected—Fort King George,
they called it."

Whatever influence this tiny fort, lost in the ooze of the
Altamaha, may have had in checking the ambitions of France,
its construction brought an immediate protest from Spain,
and in time Spanish intrigue was responsible for its abandon-
ment. Nor did Spain allow the French to retain Pensacola;
both by force of arms and by diplomacy she defended her
claim to the place and recovered it."

In Texas and the west, also, Spain attempted to uphold
her territorial claims against the encroaching French. We
have already noted how St. Denis' post at Natchitoches was
offset by a Spanish garrison at Los Adaes. Attempts to estab-

lish other French posts in presentday Oklahoma brought sharp protests from Mexico City, and the activities of Etienne Venyard, Sieur de Bourgmont, on the fur-rich Missouri River stirred the Spaniards to punitive action.

Bourgmont had been a minor officer under Cadillac at Detroit. In 1706 he deserted his post because of an unfortunate love affair and joined a dissolute group of *coureurs de bois* on the southern shore of Lake Erie—where Cleveland stands at present. There he was joined by his lady friend but fear of arrest soon sent him on westward to the Missouri River, where he gathered about him a considerable group of fur traders—*coureurs de bois,* in the fullest meaning of the expression. Some of his men pushed their trade up the Osage (see map on page 331); others worked far to the west, up the Kansas, up the Platte,—how far we do not know.[43]

Persistent rumors that there were Frenchmen among the Pawnee Indians began seeping into Santa Fe in 1719 and in the spring of the following year, Don Pedro de Villazur was directed to investigate. As an escort he was assigned forty soldiers and a few civilian assistants. Among the latter was Captain Juan de Archibeque, a man of wealth and social standing in Santa Fe. We will, however, recognize him as Jean L'Archeveque, the French lad who, thirty-three years earlier, had acted as decoy for the assassins of La Salle on the plains of Texas, and who in 1689 had surrendered to De Leon (see pages 130 and 138). Subsequently he had been carried to Mexico and in 1692 turned up in El Paso where he joined the forces led by Vargas in the re-conquest of New Mexico.

Now, in the hot month of June, 1720, Captain Archibeque was an important member of the Villazur expedition—marching northward from Santa Fe. Ten well-loaded horses and six pack mules were required to carry his equipment, including perhaps some trading goods. How many pack animals were needed by Villazur we do not know but among other conveniences he took along a silver dinner service. Father Juan Minquez, too, went well supplied with furniture for the altar.

Trailing through Sangre de Cristo Pass the expedition

turned east and crossed the Arkansas River near the present Kansas-Colorado boundary line. A few miles beyond, at a place known as El Quartelejo, Villazur added a number of friendly Apache Indians and plodded on northward. On August 15, sixty-two days out of Santa Fe, he camped on the south bank of the Platte River just below the junction of the North and South branches (see map on page 331). In the fork of the river, where the city of North Platte, Nebraska, stands today, was the Pawnee village, containing perhaps three hundred and fifty warriors, armed with bows and arrows, and an undetermined number of French traders, armed with muskets.

For days the Pawnee scouts had observed the slow approach of the Spanish force. During the evening they visited the camp, but Villazur apparently anticipated no serious trouble. The following morning, just as dawn was breaking, came the attack—bursts of arrows from the Pawnees, blasts of musketry from the Frenchmen. In a matter of minutes it was all over. Villazur, Archibeque and the greater part of the soldiers lay dead on the ground; some few soldiers and the Apache guides were fleeing southward. The pack train, the silver dishes, the altar furniture all fell to the victorious Pawnee and their French allies.[44]

News of what had happened on the Platte was slow in reaching the French settlements. In February, 1721, a few canoes pulled up at Fort Chartres on the Mississippi. In the pockets of the French paddlers was a considerable amount of newly melted silver. An Indian chief who came with them presented Captain Boisbriant with a chasuble and a chalice. Later that same year, Father Charlevoix saw some of the Villazur loot in the hands of Indians at Green Bay in Wisconsin. From such inarticulate sources the story was pieced together. The few Spaniards who got back to Santa Fe gave their superiors more detailed accounts.[45]

Thus ended Spain's most ambitious attempt to expel French intruders from the plains of Kansas and Nebraska. But at the very time that Villazur's army was crumpling before the arrows of the Pawnee on the banks of the Platte, John Law's financial empire was crumpling on the banks of the Seine. By the end of 1720 he was a penniless fugitive, hiding from the wrath of those who had lost their savings in his venture. The Mississippi bubble had burst.[46]

The Compagnie des Indies, however, remained sufficiently solvent to retain control over Louisiana and its inhabitants. When Law's German tenants from Arkansas came down the river in anticipation of being sent back to Europe, Bienville practically forced them to stay in the colony, though under conditions that proved favorable to themselves. To each family he assigned a piece of land a few miles above the new town of New Orleans, and in time the Côte des Allemands (German Coast) became the truck garden for the growing city.[47]

Still, without Law's driving energy, the activities of the Company, and of the colony, slowed down. In some ways this was an improvement; for example, the transportation of convicts was stopped. Unfortunately, however, prospective wives for the unmarried settlers continued to be recruited from the hospitals and houses of correction. Sieur Chassin, a young officer stationed at Fort Chartres, commented pointedly on this practice. Said he, "The Company has already sent four or five hundred girls, but officers and those who hold any rank cannot make up their minds to marry such girls who in addition to the bad reputation that they bring from France give reason to fear that some also bring remnants of infirmities of which they have been imperfectly healed."[48]

Seemingly Chassin did not know about the Casket Girls, so-called from the *cassettes* (small chests) in which they carried their extra clothing. They were the offerings of the church societies of France and were guaranteed to be virtuous even though they might lack somewhat in pulchritude.[49]

But, despite a shortage of suitable wives, the population of the colony was growing. By 1724 there were about 5,000 white inhabitants. And to feed all these people, let alone make a profit from them, as the Compagnie des Indies had to do if it were to survive, required that they be employed in profitable work. In the Gulf region a plantation system, similar to that of Carolina, was developing. Negro slaves were the heavy manpower; white employees were the administrative power. Many of the plantations belonged to the Company; others were privately owned; Bienville had at least two. The produce was mainly tobacco, with some prospect of rice, indigo and silk. Timber was, as in all new colonies, a constant source of revenue.[50]

The Illinois Country was persistently believed to contain valuable mineral deposits. With a view to the discovery and exploitation of these hidden treasures the Company sent over a Paris banker named Philippe Francois Renault. A considerable force of negro laborers was put at his disposal and he was expected to find and produce silver and copper. What he did find and produce in paying quantities was lead —on the Meramec River west of presentday St. Louis.[51]

But the men who actually made a profit for the Company in the upper country were Bourgmont's *coureurs de bois*. Who they were or how many there were we do not know, but that even a few could have been present at the battle on the Platte in 1720 indicates that the total number must have been considerable. Bourgmont himself was not present at the defeat of Villazur; he was, at that time, in France receiving pardon for his past misdeeds and permission to establish a trading post on the Missouri River. The result was Fort Orleans, built in 1722, ninety miles east of presentday Kansas City—and designed to serve both as a trade depot and a military defense against possible Spanish incursions into the Missouri country. From this post Bourgmont extended French contact with the migratory western tribes, even establishing friendly relations with the fierce Comanche.[52]

In short, as in Carolina so in Louisiana, it was peltries that made the colony go—whether buffalo, beaver, bear, otter and raccoon from the Indians of the Wabash and the Missouri or deer from the Indians of the Coosa and the Chattahoochee. And Bienville knew, none better, how to manage, threaten, cajole, and keep these Indians friendly to France. He had, as we have seen, made the most of Carolina's trouble with the Yamasee; he had brought some of the Creek trade to Fort Toulouse; he had successfully tampered with the Cherokee friends of the English; and he had gripped the powerful Choctaw to himself by an alliance. But, as so

usually happened with colonial governors, he had made enemies among the officers of the Company, and in 1725 he
was recalled to France and removed from office.[53]

Bienville's removal was Carolina's opportunity. English
policy called for a consolidation of Creek and Cherokee
power against the French. Hitherto these two tribes had been
encouraged to war against each other in order to provide
slaves for the West Indian trade. Now such profit appeared
negligible as against the French threat. In 1727 the head
men of the Cherokee and Creek towns were invited to meet
at Charleston. They were profusely entertained and a solemn treaty was staged, with the members of the provincial
Assembly sitting in as interested parties. Long Warrior of
the Cherokee town of Tennessee made the keynote speech.
"Why," he asked of the Creek, "do you goe to the French
[at Mobile] and Spaniards [at Pensacola]? What do you get
by it? . . . This great town [Charleston] is able to Supply
us with everything wee want, more than all the French and
Spaniards."[54]

Cherokee and Creek smoked the pipe of peace, but how
long would it last? Hardly had the Creek emissaries got
back to the Chattahoochee before Perier, the new Governor
of Louisiana, had an ambassador on the way to them—and
the Carolinians had to forestall him, if they could. By one day
the English agent beat the Frenchman to Coweta. His "talk"
went to the heart of the struggle. "There's been several of
you down in Charles Town and seen Ships coming in every
Day, and did you ever hear the English talk of such Things?
We wont get out of our chairs to go and look at so foolish
a thing as one Ship. When a small Spanish Canoe is coming
to your Towns the whoop will be carried to the Abickaws
before she gets to Cowetas, but I can never hear any of
you talk of our Pack Horses coming till you hear the bells
Gingle." And there it was; the Indians accepted it as a
matter of course that the English could supply them with
all the goods they needed; but it was an event when the
French or Spanish brought in a slight supply.[55]

Even the Choctaws, traditional friends of the French, were
beginning to accept the "gingle" of the English packhorses

as a necessity. Red Shoe, of Cushtusha Town, told Governor Perier's ambassador why he dealt with the Carolinians: "I was at the house of a Chickasaw . . . the Englishman was staying there, also. He asked the Chickasaw who I was. He replied to him that I was a Choctaw and the best of his friends. The Englishman said that we must all three be united; that he was ashamed to see me so poor and that he wished to make me a present of a coat and of something else which I took, adding that if the English were coming to trade it was only because the French did not give us what we needed." [56]

Nor did medals, bearing King Louis' picture, and decorative commissions, take the place of coats and guns. Said the Great Chief of the Choctaws, "I know that the English, when they appoint a chief, give him all that he needs, and the French, who could do the same thing, leave me poor. . . . What is the use of this medal and of this big letter? I am still poor." And he threw the medal and commission into the river. [57]

Governor Perier took the hint, and a timely distribution of presents among the Choctaw chiefs halted an Indian conspiracy—probably inspired by the English traders—to drive the French out of Louisiana. As it was, when the Natchez spear-headed what was to have been a general uprising, it failed to spread and the Choctaws joined half-heartedly in its suppression. [58]

The Natchez, located on the site of the later city of Natchez, Mississippi, had developed their own unique social and religious culture long before the coming of the white man. In fact, the son of the Sun had brought civilization to them, and his descendants—those of the Sun caste—still governed the tribe according to the laws and ceremonial customs prescribed by this early visitor. As a symbol of their relationship with the Sun a perpetual fire burned within their temple; there, too, preserved in a sacred stone, resided the son of the Sun. It is quite understandable that the ruling descendant of the Sun should have looked with some question upon the newly arrived white men, and they with some question upon him. [59]

From time to time Bienville had experienced minor difficulties with the Natchez and, to hold them in check, he
had caused a small fort, named Rosalie, to be erected on
the bluffs adjoining their town. Nearby had grown up the
French settlement of St. Catherine. In the early winter of
1729 word spread among the Natchez that they were to be
forced out of their towns to make room for more French
settlers. Fearful of French encroachment, hopeful of a supply of English trade goods, and confident of assistance from
their fellow Indians, the Natchez struck. On the morning
of November 28 the garrison at Fort Rosalie was massacred;
most of the men at the French village were killed; many of
the women, children and negroes were made captive.[60]

Governor Perier was slow in exacting vengeance. In part
he did not know how far the conspiracy extended. With
good reason he doubted the loyalty of the Chickasaw; he
could not even be sure of the Choctaw. Nor were his troops
dependable. In the end he captured a few Natchez, mostly
women, some of whom he burned, others of whom he shipped
as slaves to San Domingo. The rest escaped to the Chickasaw and the Governor dared not force their surrender.[61]

All in all, this first major war of the Louisianians against
a native tribe added nothing to French prestige. For the
Compagnie des Indies it was fatal; that corporation, like
the Proprietors of Carolina when faced with the Yamasee
outbreak, was financially unequal to a prolonged military
effort. In 1731 it surrendered its concession and Louisiana
became a royal French colony much as, a few years earlier
and under similar conditions, Carolina had become a royal
English colony.[62]

Bienville was restored to the governorship and ordered
back to Louisiana. When he arrived, in the spring of 1733, he
found the colony, according to his report, "in a much worse
condition than he had thought it . . . especially with reference to the disposition of the Indians in general." Due
to the slackness with which they had carried on the war
with the Natchez, the natives had "conceived a sovereign
contempt" for the French. "On the other hand," Bienville
continued, "the English have made infinite progress in their

minds; the Chickasaws entirely belong to them, a part of the Choctaws is wavering, the nations on the upper part of the river of the Alabamas are inclining more in their direction than in ours, and the Illinois by the rebellion which they made last year and by the groundless quarrels that they sought with us leave no ground to doubt but that they were instigated by the English." [63]

"Such," concluded Bienville, "is the general state of the colony." He hoped, however, that with a little time, work and application he would be able to restore Louisiana to the state of tranquillity in which he had left it eight years earlier. Optimistic Bienville! [64]

21

The Philanthropists
Found a Colony

AT THE VERY TIME that Bienville was expressing confidence as to the future of the French settlements on the Mississippi, a new English colony was coming into being on the Atlantic coast —with territorial claims that reached westward through the very heart of Louisiana. At the moment, however, this new colony consisted only of a slight clearing on the high southern bank of the Savannah River; and there, in the month of May, 1733, surrounded by pallid Englishmen, late from the debtors' prisons of London, and by tawny Indians, mostly renegades from the Creek towns, James Edward Oglethorpe and Chief Tomo Chichi were holding a treaty.

It was an amicable meeting of minds, this between Oglethorpe and Tomo Chichi, made possible by the fortunate presence of Mary Musgrove, half-breed wife, or one of the wives, of John Musgrove, who, it will be recalled, used to beat the Indians if they failed to hoe his corn (see page 306). Mary, able to speak both Creek and English, was serving as interpreter—happy in Oglethorpe's promise of a regular salary of £100 a year. Oglethorpe, too, was pleased with the outcome of the treaty; a philanthropic man, he wished from the Indians only an assignment of title to the land, and that he readily received from Tomo Chichi, a kindly old savage who had no claim to it anyway. And approvingly over the treaty makers, we may believe, hovered the benign spirit of the late Reverend Thomas Bray.[1]

We will identify Doctor Bray as the founder of a society for the free distribution of libraries to needy ministers and of the Society for the Propagation of the Gospel in Foreign Parts (see pages 232 and 256). These were but a few of many societies—all dedicated to doing good—of which Doctor Bray was the founder or in which he took a prominent part. There was the Society for Promoting Christian Knowledge, there were societies for organizing charitable schools and hospitals; there was even a society for the improvement of manners. Particularly Doctor Bray was interested in the christianization of the negro slaves in the American colonies. Constantly he solicited funds for his various philanthropies, and from time to time received some sizable bequests on account of which he acted as a trustee. Doubtless these contributions helped to finance his activities, but it does not appear that money was his objective; rather he sought the satisfaction that came from doing good, as he understood it.[2]

Nor in his desire to do good was Doctor Bray strikingly different from many of his contemporaries; he was outstanding but not peculiar. Consider, for example, that such a hardheaded business man as Caleb Heathcote, Lord of the Manor of Scarsdale, in New York, gave liberally of his time and means in support of the S. P. G. (Society for the Propagation of the Gospel), and that so cantankerous a public servant as Francis Nicholson bequeathed his estate to it. Or consider the spiritual development of George Berkeley. As a student at Trinity College, Dublin, in the early 1700's, he was deeply influenced by Locke's *Essay on Human Understanding*, the mature summing up of the liberalizing philosophy of the man who in 1669 compiled the Fundamental Orders of Carolina. To young Berkeley the *Essay* opened new vistas of speculation and soon he went a step farther.

Tomo Chachi Mico
oder König Von Yamacran und Tooanahowi Seines
Bruders des Mico oder Königes Von Etichitas Sohn.
nach dem Londischen Original in Augspurg nachgestochen von
Joh: Jacob Kleinschmidt.

TOMO CHICHI AND HIS NEPHEW.

Engraved from a painting by Verelst. Reproduced by the *courtesy*
of the Bureau of American Ethnology.

In a study entitled *A Treatise Concerning the Principles of Human Knowledge* he dismissed the material world as non-existent except as the mind made it real.[3]

But mere speculation did not satisfy Berkeley's spiritual cravings and in 1728, at the age of forty-three, we find him giving up a rich benefice in the Church of England to promote a plan for the christianization of the American Indians. So sure was he of government support for his scheme that, accompanied by a number of literary and artist friends, he took ship for America and established a home near Newport, Rhode Island. Soon there gathered about him a group of inquiring-minded Rhode Islanders, and a Literary and Philosophical Society was formed. We may assume that the discussions carried on by the members of this Society are accurately reflected in a manuscript which Berkeley composed at the time—under the title of *Alciphron, or the Minute Philosopher*. Presented in the form of dialogues, the subjects range from "The Benefit of Drunkenness, Gaming and Whoring" to "Man an Accountable Agent." Three-quarters of a century later Timothy Dwight, President of Yale University, in introducing the First American edition of *Alciphron,* called the book "an able defense of Divine Revelation" and added that Berkeley was "universally considered as one of the first Philosophers, who have appeared in any age, or country." [4]

But the Parliamentary appropriation for the Indian college, cornerstone of Berkeley's missionary scheme, failed to materialize. Even Doctor Bray had condemned the project as impractical, and many others, including William Byrd, of Virginia, and James Edward Oglethorpe, a member of the House of Commons, had been outspoken in their opposition. So in 1732 the philosopher-philanthropist returned to England, there to publish *Alciphron* and to find consolation in appointment to the Bishopric of Cloyne.[5]

Now take the case of Thomas Coram. It is not likely that he was impressed by Locke's *Essay on Human Understanding,* much less by Berkeley's *Treatise Concerning Human Knowledge*. He had gone to sea as a cabin boy when he was eleven years of age, and in the 1690's was operating a shipyard near Taunton, Massachusetts. Being a confirmed Church of England man it is not surprising that he got into arguments with his Congregational neighbors. As a sort of final fling at these theological opponents, Coram placed a tract of land in trust for the erection of an Anglican church, "if ever hereafter the inhabitants of the town of Taunton . . . should be more civilized than they now are." Returning to England he became a parishioner of Doctor Bray and threw most of his energy into philanthropic enterprises. For a quarter of a century he strove for the establishment of a new colony between Maine and Nova Scotia—for the rehabilitation of poor and unemployed Englishmen. In this he was unsuccessful, but he did succeed in leaving one noble memorial to his name, namely the Foundling Hospital of London, which, after two hundred years, is still in existence.[6]

Whence did Coram receive the inspiration to serve humanity? From Doctor Bray? If so, we may ask whence came Doctor Bray's inspiration? The answer might well be: From Henry Compton, Bishop of London. Certainly the Bishop approved of Bray's philanthropic activities and was himself a liberal donor to many worthy causes. Who or what influenced the Bishop? The answer must be that humanitarianism was, at the time, recognized by countless thousands of sincere Protestants, all over Europe, as a means by which their entrance into Heaven was assured. In Germany, among the Lutherans, the Pietistic movement was in full swing. Societies dedicated to good works were being widely organized. At the new University of Halle, center of Pietistic activity, the students were indoctrinated with the conviction that by good deeds rather than by simple faith the ends of Christianity were to be achieved.[7]

And from Halle the Pietistic influence radiated throughout the Protestant world. For example, as a result of his sojourn there from 1710 to 1716, Count Zinzendorf carried back to his home in Saxony a burning desire to serve humanity—which took tangible form when a part of his estates became a sanctuary for an exiled remnant of the once far-flung *Unitas Fratrum* or, as it is more usually called, Moravian Church, the direct spiritual descendant of Huss and Wycliffe.[8]

But Pietism had its limits and its schisms—as is illustrated by the experience of August Gottlieb Spangenberg. While a student of law at the University of Jena, he had become increasingly aware of the new spiritual force abroad in Germany, and turned to theology. Shortly, he organized a society for the care of the sick and the poor only to have it suppressed by the authorities as a "Zinzendorfian institution." An invitation to lecture at Halle also turned out badly. Spangenberg found his Pietistic colleagues too worldly; they found him too lacking in doctrinal discipline. He was ordered to submit to the authority of his superiors or depart. Declining to do either he was, on the King's orders, escorted outside the city gates of Halle and told not to return. Like the Moravians, Spangenberg soon found a congenial home with Count Zinzendorf whose assistant in missionary work he became.[9]

While the Pietists of the University of Halle were losing a Spangenberg to the undisciplined extremes incident to their liberalism, they were gaining, unrecognized by themselves or the recruits, two new converts at Oxford University in England. John and Charles Wesley, sons of a Church of England minister and themselves candidates for ecclesiastical preferment in that Church, felt the Pietistic leaven that was at work in the Protestant world. Binding themselves to a strict method of religious discipline they received, in derision, from a fellow student the nickname of "Methodists." Their new spirit of humanitarianism was visibly expressed in visits to the unfortunates in the city prisons.[10]

The condition of these unfortunate prisoners, most of them confined because of debts, had been under observation by Doctor Bray as early as 1702. A quarter of a century later he had proposed a scheme by which they might be put to some profitable labor in order to earn their release. At about the same time a committee of Parliament, with James Edward Oglethorpe as chairman, began an extensive study of the debtors' prisons, with the result that legislation was passed freeing several thousand poor prisoners. But without employment the former prisoners might as well have been in jail, since there were no jobs for them in England.[11]

At this point Doctor Bray's successors stepped in. The good Doctor himself had gone to his final reward but before doing so he had organized one last, over-all philanthropic society, known as the Associates of Doctor Bray, whose members controlled the trusteeships of the various bequests formerly in the Doctor's hands. On July 30, 1730, these Associates agreed to ask the King for a grant of land southwest of Carolina on which to settle "poor persons of London." [12]

This was not the first project for a new colony between Carolina and Florida. Shortly after the Yamasee outbreak, one Sir Robert Montgomery had come forward with a grandiose plan for a Margravate of Azilia to be located in just that area. The Carolina Proprietors, interested in any arrangement that would let them out of defending their proprietary, had readily encouraged Sir Robert, but his financial arrangements had failed to work. Again, in 1724–26, Jean Pierre Purry, a Swiss, had offered a proposal for colonizing the region with needy Swiss settlers. He had even gathered his colonists together at Neuchatel ready for emigration when the Proprietors welshed on their agreements with him, and the whole enterprise collapsed. [13]

Now however, in 1730, the affairs of Carolina were no longer dominated by a group of Proprietors; seven of the eight had already sold out to the King (see page 316). Also, that summer of 1730, all London was agog over the doings of a delegation of Cherokee Indians who one day were guests of the King at dinner, who another day were posing for portraits by eminent artists, and who, each night, attended a different theater to be stared at by the crowds. [14]

The visit of these Cherokees was not an officially arranged affair. On the contrary, it was a wholly unexpected pleasure originated by Sir Alexander Cuming, a slightly demented Scotsman who, in the early spring of 1730, had been studying natural history along the Trading Path northward from Savannah Town. Learning from the frontier settlers that the Cherokee were wavering in their friendship for the English, Cuming hurried on to Keowee, a native town on one of the upper branches of the Savannah River, and there persuaded the Indians to drink King George's health on bended knees.

The Indians doubtless enjoyed the bit of pageantry; and Cuming interpreted it as a symbol of allegiance to the Crown of England. At the Overhill Towns, on the Tellico, on the Hiwassee and on other streams in presentday eastern Tennessee, the same ceremony was repeated, and shortly Cuming returned to Charleston, where he embarked for England accompanied by a group of seven Cherokees, one of them a boy and none of them very important among their tribes.

On their arrival at London the Cherokees were taken in tow by the Board of Trade and, as guests of the government, shown the sights of the town. After three months of feasting and entertainment the Indians were invited to take part in a treaty with their English ally. Presents were displayed, speeches were made and, all in the best manner of the American forest, the seven minor Cherokees bound their fellow tribesmen to perpetual friendship with England. This event, too, was duly publicized.[15]

It was in this atmosphere of widespread interest in the southern American frontier that a charter was started on its way through the legal machinery, granting the land between the Savannah and the Altamaha rivers to the "Trustees for establishing the Colony of Georgia in America." These Georgia Trustees turned out to be, without exception, members of the Bray Associates, and prominent among them were Oglethorpe and Coram. The terms of the charter were such as a practical government would extend to a group of philanthropists. For twenty-one years the Trustees might manage the new colony—spend their money in building towns, settling colonists, developing trade, defending it against enemies—and then, at the end of the twenty-one years, the colony reverted to the King.[16]

These harsh terms, however, did not dismay the Trustees, interested as they were in making their colony an asylum for the poor of England, particularly for those who had been recently freed from the debtors' prisons. And as usual where a philanthropic cause was concerned, the Georgia project was made the subject of an intensive propaganda. Newspaper articles were written or inspired; sermons were

Savannah in 1734.

Courtesy, Stokes Collection, New York Public Library.

preached; pamphlets were distributed; Parliament appropriated £10,000; collectors were sent out to solicit money from individuals and institutions; Carteret contributed his one-eighth interest in the Georgia area.[17]

At the same time the Trustees were actively selecting their first colonists. All applicants, whether presently in the debtors' prisons or already released, were carefully examined as to their fitness; philanthropy was selective and with good reason since from the funds gathered by the Trustees the colonists had to be transported, fed, clothed, provided with housing, tools, seed and in fact everything required to start an agricultural life. In the late fall of 1732 the first group of settlers—about a hundred and twenty-five "sober, industrious and moral persons"—embarked aboard the ship *Anne,* with Oglethorpe at their head. In January they were at Charleston from whence they went on down the coast to Port Royal. There the colonists were put ashore while Oglethorpe, accompanied by some South Carolinians, went on to the Savannah in search of a suitable spot at which to establish the settlement. About eighteen miles up the river they came to a high bluff along the southern bank, occupied only by Tomo Chichi's small band of Yamacraw Indians. The place suited Oglethorpe; temporary consent for the white settlement was gained from Tomo Chichi; and on February 12, 1733, the colonists were assembled on the bluff. Georgia had, in reality, been founded. Clearings were made in the woods; streets were laid out; rude houses took the places of tents. Yamacraw Bluff became Savannah.[18]

We have already witnessed Oglethorpe's definitive treaty with the Indians. The land would, of course, have been settled whether the Indians agreed or did not agree, but savage good will was an asset. The plan of settlement worked out by the Trustees for their debtor wards was the village-farm type, similar to that of New England. Thus, in Savannah, each head of a family received a town lot of about five acres—for a house, barn, garden, orchard, etc.—and a farm of about forty-five acres, making an allotment of fifty acres in all. The theory was that such a farm was all that a man and his family could operate. Furthermore the land could not be sold, and it was inheritable only by the eldest male heir; failure of a male heir was to result in the reversion of the land to the Trustees. Naturally, charitable cases could not afford to buy slaves, so the ownership of slaves was prohibited in Georgia. Also, probably with a thought to the reason why most of the settlers had originally gotten into debt, the sale of rum was forbidden.[19]

Additional English settlers arrived from time to time as the Trustees raised funds, and in March, 1734, came the first of foreign blood—the Salzburgers, seventy-eight of them, religious refugees from eastern Germany. They were admitted through the influence of two Germans who had become members of the Georgia Trustees. The expense of their transportation was borne between the German Evangical Lutheran Church and one of Thomas Bray's charitable societies. Oglethorpe was on hand to welcome them at Savannah; in fact, when their ship arrived at the wharf, "almost all the inhabitants of the Town of Savannah were gathered together," as John Martin Bolzius, spiritual leader of the newcomers reported; and he added, "they fired off some Cannons and cried Huzzah!" To the home lots and farms assigned to them a few miles above Savannah the Salzburgers gave the name of Ebenezer. More of their countrymen followed and they soon took firm root in the colony.[20]

But in the spring of 1734 the stream of new colonists seemed pitifully small to Oglethorpe and with a view to accelerating activity by his fellow Trustees he sailed for England. With him, as guests of the Trustees, went Tomo Chichi and several other Indians. Their arrival in London created a sensation similar to that raised by the Cherokees four years earlier. They called on the King and the Archbishop of Canterbury; they visited Eton; and when they returned to Georgia they carried with them enough presents to assure their friendship for some time to come.[21]

Meanwhile Oglethorpe was making the most of the renewed public interest in Georgia. Parliament was persuaded to appropriate an additional £26,000 for the project; more colonists were started on their way to America; particularly, a group of Highland Scots, near two hundred in all, were enlisted to settle on the Altamaha. They were chosen because of their good moral characters but also because of their good fighting characteristics. Theirs was the job of holding the southern frontier against the Spanish.[22]

Quite different were the members of another small group of settlers who, at this time, joined in the migration to the new colony. They were Moravians, a part of the sect that had found sanctuary on the Saxon estates of Count Zinzendorf. News of the Georgia project had spread across Europe and in 1733 the Count had asked to be accepted as a "venturer" in the new lands. Under this classification he, like any other person who was able and willing to pay all the expenses involved, was alloted fifty acres for each servant he sent over. Zinzendorf's only exception in sending the Moravians was that they should not be required to bear arms. Pietists and pacifists, they fitted into a humanitarian society but hardly into a colony which more and more was looming as a military buffer against Spain. At the head of these first few Moravians, and as Zinzendorf's agent, came August Gottlieb Spangenberg, the unfrocked Lutheran professor of Halle.[23]

And still more colonists were on the way—two shiploads of them, under the personal charge of Oglethorpe. Most of them were poor people, coming at the expense of the Trustees. Others, like Sir Francis Bathurst, came with their families and servants as "venturers." Also, among these newcomers to Georgia were the Wesley brothers, John and Charles, late of Oxford University. John was to serve as minister at Savannah; Charles was to be Oglethorpe's secretary. All in all the human cargo was a choice addition to an humanitarian colony. But below deck the ships were crammed with such unhumanitarian items as cannon, small arms, and ammunition. On February 5, 1736, the little fleet came to anchor in Tybee Roads below Savannah.[24]

And Oglethorpe knew exactly what he was going to do with both the colonists and the munitions. Leaving John Wesley and a few others at Savannah, he loaded the rest into small boats and started them down the coast. On St. Simons Island, south of the mouth of the Altamaha, and

The Georgia Trustees receiving Tomo Chichi and his delegation. From a painting by Verelst, owned by the Earl of Shaftesbury.

clearly beyond his charter bounds, he built a strong fort and established a town to which he gave the name of Frederica. Farther south, on the same island, he built Fort St. Simons, to protect Frederica. Still farther south, on Cumberland Island, he built Fort William to protect Fort Simons; and at the mouth of the St. Johns River, sixty-five miles beyond the limits given in his charter, he built Fort St. George— only forty miles from the Spanish stronghold at St. Augustine.[25]

It was little wonder that Spain protested; and her protest was taken by Oglethorpe as proof of her hostile intention. Hurrying back to England he appealed to Parliament for military aid against the aggressive attitude of Spain, and was provided with a regiment of soldiers. Humanitarianism apparently did not extend to papistic Spaniards.[26]

Nor was piety always being received at its own value among Oglethorpe's own settlers. Charles Wesley, who had been assigned as minister to Frederica, lasted only a few weeks. It appears that when he admonished, in a ministerial manner, a lady who had been rough with her maid, the lady got a bit rough with the minister. Others took sides, mostly against the minister, and he returned to England, there to compose "Jesus, Lover of My Soul" and other famous hymns.[27]

At Savannah, John Wesley did a little better; in fact, he seems temporarily to have found the place attractive because of the presence of "Sophy" Hopkey, a not untypical daughter of Eve. But even romance went awry for the young preacher. Some say that John jilted "Sophy" on the advice of Spangenberg and some say that "Sophy" jilted John because he was too deliberate in his courtship. In any case the girl married Mr. Williamson. Subsequently, according to John, he took occasion to admonish the newly wedded "Sophy" for some unspecified faults; she flew into a rage and suffered a miscarriage, which her aunt said was John's fault for making her so mad. On top of all this John refused her permission to partake of communion—and that was just too much. "Sophy's" husband sued the minister for defamation of his wife's character; the weight of official influence

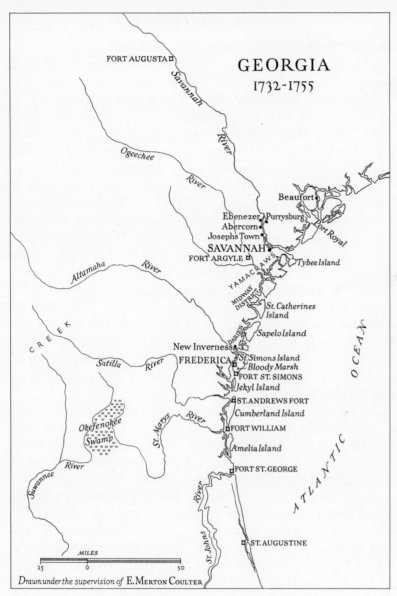

From the *Atlas of American History.*

was on "Sophy's" side; and John discreetly slipped across
the Savannah River to Purrysburg—a new town in Carolina
founded by that Swiss promoter who once wanted to settle
Georgia—and, like his brother, returned to England where
he became the father of Methodism.[28]

As Wesley landed in England, early in 1738, he learned
that George Whitefield, his successor as leader of the "Methodists" at Oxford, and destined to be his successor in Georgia,
was on the point of sailing for Georgia—and wrote him a
letter advising against going. Whitefield, however, twenty-
four years of age, burning with missionary fervor and very
sure of himself, was not to be dissuaded. With him, on this
trip to Georgia, went his twenty-six-year-old friend, James
Habersham, an incipient business man but at the moment
filled with a desire to do good, which he made manifest by
aiding Whitefield in the establishment, near Savannah, of
what was called the Bethesda Orphanage but which was
more properly a school. The institution appears a bit top-
heavy for a frontier community such as Savannah, but it
served as a worthy cause for which, by fiery sermons, to
solicit contributions.[29]

At the time, that is in 1739, the philanthropic experiment
of the Georgia Trustees seemed to be on the way to fulfill-
ing the most optimistic hopes of its backers. Near five thousand people had come to the colony, about half of them at
the charge of the Trustees and the other half on their own
account. New towns—Abercorn, Josephs Town, and others
—had been founded about Savannah. Up the river, near the
site of the vanished Westoe village and opposite the Carolina trading post of Savannah Town, Georgia had established her own fur trading post, named Augusta. On the
Altamaha, the Highlanders were firmly seated at their town
of New Inverness. Frederica, now a formidable fortress, well
garrisoned with regular soldiers, faced St. Augustine. Only
a war with Spain, it seemed, was needed as an excuse for
the capture of Florida—and that war was impending.[30]

The Moravians, however, were not happy at the prospect.
Spangenberg had already left Georgia for Pennsylvania.
His followers watched with dismay as their fellow settlers

—in the colony established to do good to man—marched up and down, stood at attention, and presented implements designed to destroy man. They, the Moravians, had come to Georgia on the promise that they would not be called upon to bear arms, and they stood on their rights—to the irritation of the other colonists who were soon called upon to do more than drill.[31]

A slight incident brought the strained English-Spanish relations to a head. One Thomas Jenkins, an Englishman, tried some smuggling in the West Indies and was caught. The Spanish cut off one of his ears and told him, or so he said, to give it to the King of England. The result was the War of Jenkins' Ear, and Oglethorpe's chance to capture Florida. In anticipation of such an event he had been appointed commander of the militia of South Carolina as well as of Georgia; these militiamen, together with the regular soldiers who were also under Oglethorpe's command, made a force of about nine hundred men, to which were added perhaps a thousand loot-hungry Indians. And with this army Oglethorpe marched on St. Augustine in the spring of 1740. The English navy was to aid in the attack by the establishment of a blockade along the coast, but proved useless in the shallow coastal waters. The upshot was that the Spanish brought in re-enforcements at will. Fort San Marco, the stronghold of St. Augustine, proved too much for Oglethorpe's artillery and, like Governor Moore thirty-eight years earlier, he was forced to march bootlessly home.[32]

And now it was the turn of the Spaniards to have a try at wiping out Georgia. Frederica on St. Simons Island was naturally their first objective. In the summer of 1742 the blow fell. Some fifty vessels of one sort and another landed perhaps two thousand soldiers—riff-raff volunteers from Cuba, negroes, Indians, and a few trained officers. To meet this attack Oglethorpe had only some five hundred men— mostly Highlanders from New Inverness and regular soldiers. Georgia's own population had sunk so low that few militiamen were available, and South Carolina did not respond to Oglethorpe's call. The decisive action was an ambuscade at a spot that came to be known as the Bloody

Marsh. Two hundred of the Spanish forces were killed or captured and the demoralized survivors shortly re-embarked for St. Augustine. Georgia was saved. Said George White-field, who was in England collecting money for Bethesda Orphanage rather than serving as chaplain at Frederica, "The deliverance of Georgia from the Spaniards is such as cannot be paralleled but by some instance out of the Old Testament." [33]

With the Spanish threat removed Oglethorpe soon lost interest in Georgia, and returned to England. His position with the colony had from the first been a peculiar one. He was not the governor; in fact, during these early years Georgia had had neither governor nor a government. In a humanitarian Eden it hardly seemed reasonable that a government should be needed. The Trustees would provide for the colonists and tell them what to do, and presumably, like obedient children, they would do as they were told. [34]

Unfortunately, however, the humanitarians could not all agree as to what was humanitarian; also a certain amount of ordinary human nature had crept into the colony. The peace-loving Moravians, never very numerous, had, to a man, followed Spangenberg to Pennsylvania. Hundreds of the recipients of the Trustees' charity had also departed. And those who remained asked for less paternalistic care and more opportunity to take care of themselves. Particularly, they wanted fee simple title to their land; they wanted slaves to work their acres; and they wanted rum—to drink and to trade to the Indians. [35]

The prohibition against rum was the first of the philanthropic standards to fall. In truth, the removal of the regulation was but recognition of an established fact. For some years rum had been openly sold and as openly bought. Commands from the Trustees to bring offenders to account were disregarded. ". . . from high to low the magistrates drink it and are unwilling to enquire what others use it," reported a Georgian. In 1742 the Trustees yielded; rum might be imported provided it was paid for with the products of the colony. [36]

In the matter of slavery the Trustees held out longer, and

were supported by Parliament when the colonists attempted to go over their heads. The steady loss of able settlers to neighboring colonies, however, forced recognition of the fact that without slave labor, rice and other staple crops could not be raised in Georgia; white men could not stand the hard labor under the broiling sun. And, as in the case of rum, many of the planters had already evaded the rule against slavery by hiring negroes—for periods of as long as a hundred years—from their South Carolina neighbors. James Habersham, the leading merchant of the colony, was outspoken in his demand for the legal admission of slaves; George Whitefield, the spokesman for humanitarianism, seconded the demand—on Biblical authority, of course; even Bolzius, the Salzburg minister, withdrew his objections. And in 1749 the Trustees grudgingly accepted the institution.[37]

In the case of land, also, the colonists had found a way around the limits of ownership set by the Trustees, and a number of fair-size plantations were in operation during the late 1740's. Gradually the Trustees admitted that fifty-acre plots were uneconomical in a climate such as that of Georgia and that without the right to buy and sell as judgment dictated, the land would neither produce crops nor attract capable settlers. In 1750 the old land regulations were dropped.[38]

With the disappearance, one by one, of the paternalistic regulations concerning land, rum and slaves, Georgia began to prosper. Rice plantations, operated with slave labor, brought wealth to the tidewater area. The fur business, pointed up with rum, gave employment to hundreds of traders. Augusta became the great southern fur trading post whence literally thousands of packhorses departed annually with their loads of English goods for the Creek, Cherokee and other Indian towns, and to which they returned with deer skins and other peltries. Many of these skins went to the Savannah mercantile house of Habersham & Harris, whose partners carried on an ever-increasing trade with England and the other American colonies.[39]

But in gaining a bit of the world, Georgia lost her soul, or so it seemed to the philanthropic gentlemen who had sponsored the colony. All in all the experiment had been a

sad disappointment. The subjects of the humanitarian effort
had failed to appreciate what had been done for them. Many
went right on failing in their struggle with the world; those
who succeeded bit the hand that had supported them in
their weakness. Even Mary Musgrove showed a deplorable
lack of ability to profit spiritually from the benefits of civilization. She, in succession to John Musgrove and one or
two others, had married one Thomas Bosomworth, a ne'er-
do-well preacher, who perhaps gave her bad advice. Also,
apparently, Mary in her savage way, not understanding
philanthropy, brooded over the fact that Oglethorpe had
overlooked paying her the £100 a year which he had promised her. In any case, the people of Savannah had a close
call when, in 1749, Mary led a motley collection of Creek
warriors to the outskirts of the city, and demanded justice
according to her lights. And, in the end, she got it—£2,100
in money and title to St. Catherines Island.[40]

What with ungrateful, grasping savages and ungrateful,
rum-drinking, slave-driving colonists, Georgia was nothing
that the Reverend Mister Thomas Bray's philanthropic successors cared to be responsible for. And in 1752, with their
twenty-one-year charter still unexpired, the Trustees surrendered their patent to the King. Georgia became a royal
colony with a governor, a council and an elected assembly
—much like South Carolina, North Carolina, Virginia, New
Jersey, New York, Massachusetts, and New Hampshire.[41]
Of the former proprietary colonies there remained only
Pennsylvania, Delaware and Maryland; and of the still earlier corporate type of colonies only Connecticut and Rhode
Island held their charters. In all there were, as one may
determine by counting them, thirteen English colonies strung
along the Atlantic coast between Nova Scotia and Florida.
Back of them, following the line of the Great Lakes and the
Mississippi River, lay the French settlements. The objective
of both nationalities was the same, namely, possession of
America. In the northern area their frontiers had clashed
for over fifty years. In the southern area they stood face to
face; and in the central area the distance between them was
growing less each year.

An Angry God

"WHEN YOU COME to be a firebrand of hell . . . you will appear as you are, a viper indeed. . . . There is the dreadful pit of the glowing flames of the wrath of God; there is hell's wide gaping mouth open . . . and God is dreadfully provoked. . . . If you cry out to God to pity you, he will be so far from pitying you in your doleful case, or showing you the least regard or favor, that instead of that, he will only tread you under foot. And though he will know that you cannot bear the weight of omnipotence treading upon you, yet he will not regard that, but he will crush you under his feet without mercy; he will crush out your blood and make it fly. . . ."[1]

Such were but a few of the punishments awaiting the unconverted—as revealed to them by Mr. Jonathan Edwards, minister of the Congregational Church at Northampton, Massachusetts. And fear of hell's fire, or of the omnipotent foot, had its effect; scores of people formerly given to "licentiousness" or "lewd practices" sought salvation;

there was, in short, a remarkable "ingathering of Souls."
Even the little ones were moved. Phebe Bartlet, aged four,
while sitting in the privy one day was overheard to lisp,
"Blessed Lord give me salvation! I pray, Beg pardon all my
sins." A query from her mother brought forth the confession
(most grammatical for so young a child), "I am afraid I
shall go to hell." Recognition of guilt was a good beginning,
and soon Phebe not only won assurance of her own spiritual
regeneration but became instrumental in the conversion of
her playmates.[2]

Naturally, the atmosphere in which Edwards conducted
his revivals resulted in a good deal of hysteria among his
listeners, hysteria which many of his fellow ministers felt
was scarcely the equivalent of a spiritual experience. But
under the Congregational form of church organization there
was no way of bringing a minister to censure except by the
action of his own congregation. In separating from the
Church of England the Puritans had separated from all
forms of episcopacy. They had even declined to associate
their churches through presbyteries such as characterized
their fellow-dissenters, the Presbyterians. Beyond subscrib-
ing to a confession of faith—agreed upon at Cambridge in
1648—each congregation was a unit unto itself; that was
why they called themselves Congregationalists.[3]

In one important detail, however, the churches had revised their requirements for membership. Under the Platform of 1648 public confession of "Gods manner of working upon the soul" was required of those who would pass the
narrow door of the church. As time went on, the younger
people had found it increasingly difficult to give convincing
testimony of this regenerative spiritual experience. Accordingly, in 1657, a less rigorous formula had been agreed upon
by a group of the leading ministers. By this so-called Halfway
Covenant one might become a member of the church without confession of spiritual regeneration, though such members were not to be admitted to baptism or to the Communion. Some ministers went even farther; Solomon Stoddard, Jonathan Edwards' grandfather, allowed all professing
Christians to partake of the Communion; and Benjamin

JONATHAN EDWARDS.

From a portrait by Joseph Badger. Reproduced by the *courtesy* of the
Yale University Art Gallery, New Haven, Conn.

Colman, minister of the Brattle Street Church at Boston, did away entirely with public confessions of religious experience.[4]

Elsewhere also among the churches of New England liberalism was rearing its head. Even Harvard College, training-school for the Congregational ministry, was infected, and with a view to restoring the church to a semblance of its original purity a number of the more conservative leaders, including Cotton Mather, joined in founding a new college located at Saybrook in Connecticut colony. As a part of this same conservative movement, the General Assembly of Connecticut directed the churches—Congregational, of course—within its jurisdiction to send delegates to a synod to be held at Saybrook, there to draw up a plan of church discipline. The result was the Saybrook Platform of 1708 by which the Connecticut churches were formed into "Consociations" by counties—an organization so similar to that of the Presbyterians that the latter were easily drawn into the Connecticut Congregational system.[5]

But the Saybrook Platform could not keep Connecticut exclusively Congregational. In fact, the seed of heterodoxy had already been planted in the colony—and by none other than our old acquaintance, Caleb Heathcote, Lord of the Manor of Scarsdale in nearby New York province. As Heathcote reported the situation to the S. P. G. (Society for the Propagation of the Gospel), of which organization he was an honored member, Connecticut was filled with "miserably blinded people . . . many, if not the greatest number of them, being little better than in a state of heathenism, having never been baptized or admitted to the Communion," but all required to pay taxes for the support of the Congregational churches. Also, as he had recently heard, "the passive, obedient people, who dared not do otherwise than obey," were being called upon to contribute to the creation at Saybrook of "a thing which they call a college."

His sense of duty as an Englishman as well as his responsibility to the S. P. G. moved Heathcote to action. In the early autumn of 1706, accompanied by George Muirson, a Church of England clergyman, he rode easterly—across the

New York line and into darkest Connecticut. The little village of Stratford, just beyond presentday Bridgeport, was the objective. In that community lived a few families still loyal to the Anglican church; also it was believed that the resident minister would be receptive. But word of the unchristian purpose of the visitors had preceded them and upon their arrival at Stratford they were informed by the magistrates that any attempt to form other than a Congregational church was contrary to the laws of Connecticut—and Connecticut, being a charter colony, made its own laws, elected its own governor and appointed its own enforcement officers. As for the prospective communicants of the new church, they were assured that fines and jail would be their rewards if they went near the house where Muirson was scheduled to conduct services.[6]

Still, in the face of all threats and discouragements, the church was planted—on a stony field little blessed with sunshine. Fifteen years went by and the Lord of the Manor of Scarsdale was called to his last accounting, an accounting in which the Connecticut parish would hardly have appeared worth mentioning. And yet the harvest was at hand. George Pigot, a missionary for the S. P. G., was in charge of the Church of England activities at Stratford. A few miles to the eastward lay the Puritan town of New Haven whither had been moved the growing college formerly at Saybrook—recently named Yale. At the head of the college was Mr. Timothy Cutler, graduate of Harvard and an outstanding Congregational minister. Among the Yale tutors was Daniel Brown. At West Haven, an adjoining town, Samuel Johnson, a former Yale tutor, was serving as the Congregational minister. With these men and others Doctor Pigot was laboring as only a convinced missionary can labor. On the day following Commencement, 1722, Cutler, Brown, and Johnson announced to the amazed trustees of Yale that they doubted the validity of the Congregational church; that they believed the Church of England to be the only true church; and that they proposed going to England to accept ordination from an Anglican Bishop.[7]

Puritan New England was shaken to its very foundations.

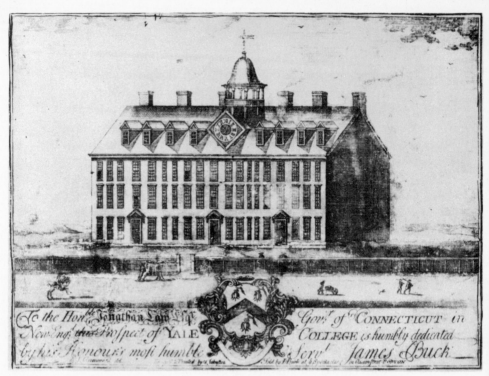

Above. Yale College
in the 1740's.

TIMOTHY CUTLER.

From an engraving
by Peter Pelham.

372

"How is the gold become dim! and the silver become dross! and the wine mixed with water!" cried one disillusioned minister. In the mind of many a Congregationalist the question must have arisen as to whether the once inspired "New England Way" was not dying of dry rot. Cutler's return from England as rector of the newly formed Christ Church at Boston—the second Episcopal church in that city—did not add to the confidence of the Puritan divines of Massachusetts. Nor did Johnson's assignment as S. P. G. missionary at Stratford make for ease in the minds of the Connecticut Congregationalists. The Church of England, which the grandfathers of the New Englanders had fled Old England to escape, was again among them; and it evidently offered something which cold Congregationalism could not give.[8]

But neither the Anglican service nor the Congregational sermons fully satisfied a widespread spiritual craving that had already been recognized by the Pietists in Europe and was soon to be satiated in America. The Dutch farmers and shopkeepers of the Raritan Valley in New Jersey were the first to experience this new spiritual ecstasy. To them, in 1720, as minister of the Dutch Reformed Church came Theodorus Jacobus Frelinghuysen, fresh from Europe and its Pietistic stirrings. His impassioned sermons disturbed many of the more prominent, and spiritually comfortable, members of his church, but others increasingly turned out to hear him. Conversions multiplied, and the ferment extended beyond the Dutch and the Dutch church.[9]

Among those who followed the labors of Frelinghuysen with evident approval were William Tennent, minister of the Presbyterian church at Neshaminy, Pennsylvania, and his son, Gilbert. They, recent emigrants from northern Ireland, were conducting a training-school, later known as "Log College," in which promising young men were being prepared for the Presbyterian ministry. It was a propitious time for such an undertaking. Thousands of Scotch-Irish, that is, Scottish people formerly settled in northern Ireland and now uprooted by economic conditions, were pouring into the American colonies. Many of them were finding homes in New Jersey and Pennsylvania. Almost to a person they were Presbyterians, and they wanted ministers.[10]

In 1726 Gilbert Tennent, then twenty-three years of age, received a call to serve as Presbyterian minister at New Brunswick, New Jersey—where Frelinghuysen's revival was then at its height. It was a situation fitted to Tennent's temperament and he was soon out-evangelizing his Dutch rival. The souls of the Raritan Valley were searched and purified as they had never been before—and even farther into the other colonies the ferment spread.[11]

To George Berkeley, presiding over the Literary and Philosophical Society at Newport while waiting for funds to establish his Indian college, the screamings of Frelinghuysen and Tennent and the moanings of their penitents must have seemed inexpressibly vulgar. But to the physically weak and spiritually gloomy Jonathan Edwards, poring, lonely, over his Bible among the coarse inhabitants of Northampton, the ingathering of souls to the southward posed a challenge. Beginning with a series of prayer-meetings for the young people, Edwards gradually reached out for the more mature sinners. We have already heard typical extracts from his sermons (page 367). Steadily he pointed out that the unconverted person was "held in the hand of God, over the pit of hell," and that God would rather enjoy dropping him in. As in New Jersey there was a mad rush for safety; within three years it was necessary to build a new meeting-house almost twice the size of the old one.[12]

From New England to Pennsylvania the stage was set for a great spiritual awakening. On December 2, 1739, George Whitefield, whom we last met in Savannah establishing Bethesda Orphanage, stepped ashore at Philadelphia. After a short stay in Georgia he had gone back to England, received ordination in the Church of England, and engaged in itinerant preaching to secure funds for Bethesda. His sermons were too popular, in the sense of rabble rousing, for most of his fellow ministers, and their pulpits were closed to him. Accordingly he preached in fields and other outdoor places. Vast crowds came to listen, and the collections were good. His less successful colleagues spoke of him as "a spiritual pick-pocket." He returned to America with complete confidence in his power of persuasion and with £1,000 for his orphanage.[13]

But Whitefield was in no hurry to get to Georgia. He would try his sermons on the people of Philadelphia, though there as in England, and for the same reason, most of the ministers soon refused to let him use their pulpits. So as in England, he preached in the open air—and as usual people flocked to hear him. Benjamin Franklin, a prosperous young printer and newspaper publisher of the city, walked around the field trying out the distances at which he could hear the minister's voice and computed that more than thirty thousand people could easily listen to the sermon. The Philadelphians, however, more liberal than their English cousins, could not bear the thought of anyone with a message being pushed out into the cold. Accordingly they subscribed sufficient funds to put up a building one hundred feet in length by seventy in width —and there Whitefield preached whenever he was in the city. "It was wonderful," Franklin tells us, "to see the change soon made in the manners of [the people]. From being thoughtless or indifferent about religion, it seem'd as if all the world were growing religious, so that one could not walk thro' the town in an evening without hearing psalms sung in different families of every street." [14]

From Philadelphia, Whitefield went to New Jersey where he met Gilbert Tennent and a group of other young preachers trained at the elder Tennent's "Log College." To them he paid a high compliment. They were, he said, "the burning and shining Lights of this Part of *America*." And when Whitefield visited New York he invited Tennent to accompany him, observing that "Hypocrites must either soon be converted or enraged at his Preaching. He is a Son of Thunder, and I find doth not fear the Faces of Men." [15]

After a not too happy call at Savannah, Whitefield again returned north, always preaching and always collecting for the orphanage. In the autumn of 1740 he made his first appearance in New England. At Boston most of the Congregational churches opened their doors to him; at Northampton he met Jonathan Edwards and preached in his church. Everywhere he attracted throngs of hearers. Typical perhaps is an account left us by Nathan Cole, a Connecticut farmer: ". . . one morning all on a suding about 8 or 9 o'clock there

came a messinger and said mr. whitfield preached at hartford and weathersfield yesterday and is to preach at middletown this morning at 10 o'clock i was in my field at work
i dropt my tool that i had in my hand and run home and
run thru the house and bad my wife get ready quick to goo
and hear mr whitfield preach at middletown and run to pasture for my hors with all my might fearing i should be late
to hear him i brought my hors home and soon mounted and
took my wife up and went forward as fast as i thought the
hors could bear, and when my hors began to be out of breath
i would get down and put my wife on ye saddel and bid her
ride as fast as she could and not stop or slak for me except
i bad her and so i would run untill i was almost out of breth
and then mount my hors again and so i did several times to
favor my hors we improved every moment to get along as if
we were fleeing for our lives all this while fearing we should
be too late to hear ye sermon for we had twelve miles to ride
dubble in littel more than an hour. . . ."

As the Coles approached Middletown they found the roads
filled with horses and riders, all like themselves hurrying to
the place where Whitefield was to speak. The dust was ter-
rific. Said Mrs. Cole, "Law! Our clothes will be all spoiled."
When they arrived at the village green, Cole saw ferry boats
bringing crowds of people from the opposite side of the river—
". . . every thing men horses and boats seamed to be struglin
for life."

And then came the great moment. Whitefield ascended
the platform. ". . . he looked almost angellical a young slim
slender youth before some thousands of people & with a bold
undaunted countenance." The sermon, said Cole, gave him
"a heartwound . . . I saw that my righteousness would not
save me." [16]

So successful was the New England tour that Gilbert Tennent was invited to Boston to continue the revival. And he
proved even more effective than Whitefield, both in drawing
hearers and in bringing about conversions. Said Timothy
Cutler, Rector of Christ Church and one-time president
of Yale, there "came one Tennent, a minister impudent
and saucy; and told them they were all *damned, damned,*

GEORGE WHITEFIELD.

From a portrait by John Wollaston.

377

damned! This charmed them; and in the dreadfullest winter I ever saw, people wallowed in the snow night and day for the benefit of his beastly braying." [17]

Worse was yet to come. Itinerant preachers, inspired or impressed by Whitefield and Tennent, went from town to town screaming of hell's fire and damnation. ". . . in every Place where they come," reported the Boston *Post-Boy,* "they represent that God is doing extraordinary Things in other Places, and that they are some of the last hardened Wretches that stand out; that this is the last Call that ever they are likely to have; that they are now hanging over the Pit of Destruction, and just ready, this Moment, to fall into it; that Hell-fire now slashes in their Faces; and that the Devil now stands ready to sieze upon them and carry them to Hell." [18]

Charles Chauncy, minister of the First Church of Boston, was moved to publish a little book entitled *Seasonable Thoughts on the State of Religion in New England.* In this volume are many descriptions of the methods followed by the New Light preachers, as they were called. "They often begin with a single Person, a Child, or a Woman, or a Lad, whose *Shrieks* set others a *Shrieking;* and so the Shrieks catch from one another 'till the whole Congregation is alarmed, and such an awful Scene, many Times open'd, as no Imagination can Paint to the life. . . . This frequently frights the *little children,* and sets them a Screaming; and that frights their *tender Mothers,* and sets them to Screaming, and by Degrees spreads over a good part of the Congregation: and 40, 50 or an 100 of them screaming all together makes such an awful and hideous Noise as will make a Man's Hair stand on End. Some will faint away, fall down upon the Floor, wallow and foam. Some Women will rend off their Caps, Handkerchiefs, and other Clothes, tear their Hair down about their Ears, and seem perfectly bereft of their Reason." [19]

Outstanding among these itinerant preachers was James Davenport, a great-great-grandson of the first minister of New Haven colony. An account of one of his meetings is given in Chauncy's book: ". . . with the *utmost Strength* of his Lungs [he] addrest himself to the Congregation. . . . You poor unconverted Creatures, in the Seats, in the Pews, in the Galleries, I wonder you don't drop into Hell! It would not surprise me, I should not wonder at it, if I should see you drop down *now, this Minute* into Hell. You Pharisees, Hypocrites, *now, now, now,* you are going right into the Bottom of Hell. I wonder you don't drop into Hell by Scores and Hundreds." At this point a number of people began to show the usual signs of emotional distress and the preacher called them into the front seats. "Then he came out of the Pulpit, and stripped off his upper Garments, and got up into the Seats and leapt up and down sometime, and clapt his Hands, and *cried out* in those Words, the War goes on, the Fight goes on, the Devil goes down, the Devil goes down; and then he betook himself to *stamping* and *screaming* most dreadfully."[20]

At the little town of New London, Connecticut, Davenport put on a special exhibition. Directing his converts to bring in such of their books as were by Cotton Mather, Benjamin Colman and other conservative ministers, he made a bonfire of the pile—symbolic of the eternal tortures which the unenlightened authors were presumably destined to suffer in hell. Having thus gotten into the spirit of the thing, the preacher decided to strike a blow at worldly pride. Hoop petticoats, silk gowns, cloaks, cambric caps, red heeled shoes, fans, necklaces, all the most prized possessions of his female followers were heaped up for another bonfire. To top the lot the preacher tossed in his own plush breeches. At that point, and perhaps for obvious reasons, a degree of prudence returned to the celebrants and they decided that salvation might be attained and their clothes retained, which decision, remarked a young blade of the town, "was lucky for Davenport who, had fire been put to the pile, would have been obliged to strutt about bare-arsed, for the devil another pair of breeches had he but these same old plush ones which were going to be offered up as an expiatory sacrifise."[21]

Such were the excesses that cast discredit upon some phases of the Great Awakening. A few of the colonies issued regulations against itinerant preachers. In the eyes of the ordinary man those who professed the New Light were simply "biggots," easily recognizable by their "down hanging" looks;

Tennent was a "fanatic"; and Whitefield preached only for the sake of "private lucre and gain." On the other hand, Benjamin Franklin, who became well acquainted with Whitefield, assures us that he never had the "least suspicion" of the evangelist's integrity; that he was in all his conduct "a perfectly *honest man.*" [22]

Within three or four years the more spectacular aspects of the Great Awakening had run their courses, though the breezes of contention still stirred men's minds. Thus in 1744, a traveller, while waiting for the ferry at Saybrook, Connecticut, was treated to a discussion on justification, sanctification, regeneration, free grace and original sin by a group of natives whom he described as "a rabble of clowns." However, as the traveller rode onward—through one village after another—he was impressed with the meeting-house steeples silhouetted against the sky. Those meeting-houses were the abiding symbols of the religion of New England and into them, unquiet but revived, had retired the spiritual furore of the Great Awakening. [23]

Occasionally, as at Marblehead, Massachusetts, or Newport, Rhode Island, the steeples pointed upward from Anglican churches—ornaments in the celestial crown of Doctor Thomas Bray, whose S. P. G. had, in most cases, brought them into being. The Church of England was slowly winning back the grandsons and great-grandsons of the seventeenth-century separatists. Many, even, of the young Quakers of Pennsylvania, sons of wealthy fathers, were giving up the peculiarities of their sect and returning to the Anglican establishment. [24]

But the communicants lost to the Church of England by the separatists were more than made up by the new converts who poured into the various denominations as a result of the Great Awakening. Observing the number of his hearers who became Baptists, Whitefield remarked, "My chickens have turned ducks." In the Middle Colonies and particularly in New Jersey, where Gilbert Tennent and his fellow graduates of the Log College led the New Light crusade, the Presbyterian Church became the favorite haven for the regenerate. [25]

Log College itself was no more, but its mission was to live

on. In 1746—the same year in which William Tennent died and his college closed—a group of ministers and laymen, sympathetic to the New Light movement, secured from the Governor of New Jersey a charter for a new college. Gilbert Tennent and other Log College men were added to the Board of Trustees, and the College of New Jersey came into being. Jonathan Dickinson, a graduate of Yale and minister of the Presbyterian Church at Elizabeth Town, was named as president; and the beginning class, eight or ten students in all, assembled at his house in May, 1747.[26]

Within a matter of weeks Dickinson died and was succeeded by Aaron Burr, minister of the Presbyterian Church at Newark, to whose house the students were removed. Burr, like Dickinson, was a New Englander, having been born and reared at Fairfield, Connecticut. Also, like Dickinson, he was a graduate of Yale and had readily accepted a call from a Presbyterian church. The fact was that the Congregational and the Presbyterian churches were so nearly alike as to be practically indistinguishable. Jonathan Edwards' first church, after his graduation from Yale, had been under Presbyterian organization. Southerners travelling in New England commonly referred to the Congregational churches as Presbyterian.[27]

Under Burr's administration the College grew in numbers and influence. In 1754 Ezra Stiles, later a president of Yale, but at the time a young lawyer practicing at New Haven, Connecticut, was a guest at commencement. The ceremony was held in the meeting-house at Newark; a proper address was delivered by President Burr; George Whitefield, the revivalist, sat in one of the pews with Governor Belcher, and received an A.M. degree. But, as always, Whitefield stole the show. "About half an hour after the academic exercises," Stiles tells us, "Mr. Whitefield, mounted on a stage by the Court House, preached a sermon in Open air to a large auditory from Luke 1. 15."

The following evening, on his way to Philadelphia, Stiles stopped at the little village of Princeton and "viewed the foundation of the College House"—a hundred and seventy-seven feet long by fifty-three and two-thirds feet wide. This

building was to be the new home of the College of New
Jersey. It had, in part, been made possible by lotteries operated in Connecticut. More important, however, were the
contributions secured in England and Scotland by Gilbert
Tennent and Samuel Davies, the latter a promising young
minister lately in charge of the Presbyterian missions in Virginia. Nor had the degree to Whitefield been an empty ges-
ture; it was he who had paved the way for the success of
Tennent and Davies in the British Isles.[28]

By 1756 the building was ready for use—Nassau Hall it
was named in honor of King William III, of the House of
Nassau. The College of New Jersey had found a permanent
location. It was the fourth institution of higher learning in
the English colonies, having been preceded by Harvard and
Yale, both Congregational, and by William and Mary, which
was Anglican. The new college was, of course, dominated by
those of the Presbyterian persuasion. Interestingly enough—
perhaps 'twas predestined—the College of New Jersey, child
of the Great Awakening, sired by the New Lights, became
the final field of labor for Jonathan Edwards, first of the
New England revivalists. When, in 1757, President Burr died,
Edwards was offered the presidency. He had been ousted
from Northampton as too fervent for his congregation, and
was eking out a living—mostly supplied by the S. P. G.—as
missionary to the Indians in western Massachusetts. With
some misgivings as to his fitness, but to the entire satisfaction
of the trustees, Edwards became the third president of the
college that later became Princeton University.[29]

An English traveller, visiting the College of New Jersey
at just about this time, has left a fleeting picture of the
student life. There were some sixty boys in residence at
Nassau Hall—"two students . . . in each set of apartments,
which consist of a large bed-room with fire-place, and two
studies."[30]

Scarcely less remarkable than Edwards' translation to the
presidency of the New Jersey college was Samuel Johnson's
installation as head master of King's College in New York.
We will recall him as the former Yale tutor who, in 1722,
along with Cutler and others, apostatized to the Church of

Nassau Hall and President's House, College of New Jersey, 1764.

From an engraving by Henry Dawkins.

England. For many years thereafter he directed the Anglican missions in Connecticut. As sentiment mounted for a college in New York province, he took an active part; and when, in 1754, King's College was chartered and came under Church of England control through a grant of land by Trinity Church, he accepted an invitation to become president of the new institution—the fifth college in the colonies, later to be known as Columbia University.[31]

It was an age of college founding. The University of Pennsylvania was germinating at Philadelphia under the initiative of Benjamin Franklin. The future Brown University was taking form in Rhode Island. Other lesser institutions had their faint beginnings during these years. Unquestionably the S. P. G. had prepared the ground; unquestionably the Great Awakening had stirred the soil; but, equally unquestionably, the movement stemmed from a social maturity that provided leisure for cultural interests.

Able Men and Fine Homes

AT THE VERY TIME that the College of New Jersey, later to become Princeton, was starting on its long career, Benjamin Franklin, aged forty-two, was retiring from business to devote the remaining years of his life to "philosophical studies and amusements."

Franklin had arrived at Philadelphia in 1723 as a runaway apprentice boy looking for a job. Within ten years he was master of his own printing shop; he was proprietor of the *Pennsylvania Gazette,* a successful newspaper; and he was publisher of *Poor Richard's Almanac,* which, throughout the colonies, enjoyed a popularity second only to the *Bible.* Almanacs were, at the time, looked upon as necessities in every home and office; they served as calendars; they indicated the times of the tides, the changes of the moon, and the positions of the planets—all of which was of practical interest to farmers, shippers and travellers. In addition to the astronomical data, the almanacs—and there were many different ones published—usually contained a certain amount of miscellaneous information and entertaining material. It was in this latter department that *Poor Richard* excelled. His homely philosophy—"The used key is always bright" or "It is hard for an empty sack to stand upright"—tickled the fancy of the eighteenth-century readers and resulted in large sales.

But Franklin was far from being a mere money maker. As a young fellow of twenty-one he had organized a society, known as the Junto, in which problems concerned with philosophy and natural history were discussed. In 1731 he had taken a leading part in the founding of the Library Company of Philadelphia. Fifty men each had made down payments of forty shillings and agreed to pay ten shillings a year for fifty years. The money in hand went for the purchase of books, which were housed in the Junto club-room. On a given day each week the subscribers might examine the volumes and borrow such as they wished. And that, said Franklin, "was the mother of all the North American subscription libraries."[1]

As the members of the Junto became acquainted with men of similar interests in other cities and other colonies a more ambitious society came into being—dedicated to "the promotion of useful knowledge among the British Plantations in America." Such was the genesis of the American Philosophical Society, founded in 1743, oldest among the still existing learned societies of the United States.[2]

Naturally the members of the American Philosophical Society exchanged data with the members of the Royal Society of London, and in 1746 Peter Collinson, of the London society, presented his American correspondents with a "glass tube" together with directions as to its use in making electrical experiments. The subject, new to Franklin, completely fascinated him. By 1751 he was convinced that the force which he produced with the "glass tube" was identical with the phenomenon known as lightning and in a letter to Collinson suggested that by rods attached to high buildings electricity might be drawn from the clouds. Collinson read the letter before the Royal Society whose members found it amusing, but declined to give it space in their *Transactions.* A London publisher, however, printed it, and a French scientist caused it to be re-issued in France, where the suggested experiment was successfully carried out.

At about the same time, Franklin, using a kite equipped with a silken cord for a conductor and a key as a point, drew enough electricity from a storm cloud to charge a Leyden jar and to satisfy most scientists of the validity of his hypothesis. With his fame thus established, the Royal Society not only printed an account of Franklin's findings but made him a member without fee. At home, Harvard College, William & Mary College, and Yale College each conferred its Master of Arts degree upon him.[3]

In thus using his early financial success to underwrite a maturity given to research and scientific achievement Franklin was but following a pattern already set by many men of his time. Consider, for example, the life of James Logan. We will recall him as the Scottish lad who came over with Penn in 1699 (see page 225). For long years he faithfully served the proprietary family and the province. Simultaneously, through shrewd investments in land and trade with the Indians, he accumulated a comfortable private fortune. And by the time he was fifty years of age he was in a position to indulge his personal tastes. On a five-hundred-acre tract of land near Germantown he built a pretentious country house to which he gave the name of "Stenton"; and there, during the last twenty years of his life, he lived in "princely style," collecting one of the largest and finest libraries in the colonies.

Of his books—he had more than three thousand—Logan said, ". . . they have been my delight and . . . will I believe continue my best entertainment in my advancing years." Later he spoke of reading as his "disease." But he did more than simply read his books; he put his reading to use. His experiments in the impregnation of seeds contributed to the knowledge of sex in plant life and consequently to controlled breeding. From this it seems a far cry to Cicero's dialogue on old age, but in 1744, over the Franklin imprint, Logan's translation of that Latin classic appeared in English—and was, incidentally, one of the nicest pieces ever turned out by Franklin's presses.[4]

Nor was Logan miserly of his library. When John Bartram,

a Quaker farmer living down by the Schuylkill Ferry, showed talent in discovering and propagating unusual plants, Logan not only loaned him books from his library but sometimes gave them to him. Other men, including some members of the Library Company, became interested in Bartram's botanical research and recommended him to Peter Collinson as the best source from which to get American plants and shrubs. Soon Bartram was shipping off to England—at five pounds five shillings per box—consignment after consignment of specimens destined to find places in the great gardens of England. Linnæus and other European scientists recognized his discoveries; the Queen of Sweden wrote him a commendatory letter; the King of England appointed him as his own botanist—with a salary of fifty pounds a year; distinguished visitors wore a path to his garden.[5]

It was an age of country houses—with landscaping taking an ever more important part in the architectural scheme. On the Continent and in England men of wealth vied with one another in formalizing their gardens or in filling them with exotic flowers, shrubs and trees. Naturally all of this was reflected in America. "Stenton" was but one of several ambitious country homes about Philadelphia. It was, in fact, modest as compared with "Bush Hill," the home of Andrew Hamilton—not to be confused with the man of the same name who served as Deputy-governor of New Jersey and Pennsylvania in the late 1600's.

The Hamilton of "Bush Hill" was a lawyer, best known to fame in connection with the Zenger libel trial of 1735. The background of that affair was an adverse decision by Chief-justice Lewis Morris, of New York, in a case where Governor Cosby was concerned. In retaliation the Governor dismissed Morris, who had served for nearly twenty years, and moved the junior justice, James De Lancey, into first place. Naturally, Morris and his friends protested. And when they could get no support from the *New York Gazette*—Bradford not wanting to lose his public printing contract—they subsidized John Peter Zenger, a somewhat illiterate printer, in establishing a newspaper known as the *New-York Weekly Journal*. As was to have been expected Zenger's articles infuriated the

"Stenton," the country home of James Logan.

"Fairhill," the country home of Isaac Norris, a successful
Philadelphia merchant.

Both pictures are by the *courtesy* of the Pennsylvania
Historical Society, Philadelphia.

Governor, and shortly the new editor found himself in jail charged with libel. Worse yet, all the New York lawyers who might have been expected to defend Zenger were practically disbarred. At that point the Morris faction asked Hamilton to come to New York and handle the case. He accepted, and not only secured an acquittal for Zenger but established a legal precedent that went far toward assuring the freedom of the press. Such a lawyer could, of course, afford a show-place in the country, and "Bush Hill" appears to have been one. Ezra Stiles commented on its "elegent" garden with seven statues in Italian marble, and the house with "splendid & grand apartments magnificently decorated & adorned with curious paintings, hangings & statuary, & marble tablets, &c." [6]

Nor was the vogue for fine houses and gardens restricted to Pennsylvania. For fifty years, all up and down the coast from New Hampshire to Carolina, the masons and carpenters and landscape artists were busy.

We have already become well acquainted with William Byrd II—living in a fairly new, fairly impressive house at "Westover" on the James River. We have seen him in his library, its walls lined with Greek and Latin classics. We have watched his barges sweeping down the river loaded with hogsheads of tobacco. In 1715 he went to England on what was said to be a business trip. While there his wife died, and for a decade "Westover" saw little of its master. He took permanent quarters in London, drove about in his own coach, threw himself into the social life of England, with only flying visits to Virginia.

During one such visit—in the winter of 1720–21—word reached Virginia of a new outbreak of the plague in England. Byrd seized his pen and an opportunity. Under the pseudonym of "A Lover of Mankind" he wrote *A Discourse concerning the Plague with some Preservatives against It.* The big folios on his library shelves served him well in developing his subject. Greek and Hebrew quotations embellish the work. But it was in presenting the "Preservatives" that Byrd spoke like a true Virginian. There were numerous preservatives that would help, but one stood forth as the supreme specific. "I am humbly of the opinion," says A Lover of Mankind, "that when there is any danger of a pestilence, we can't more effectually consult our own preservation, than by providing ourselves with a reasonable quantity of fresh, strong scented Tobacco. We shou'd wear it about our clothes, and about our coaches. We should hang bundles of it around our beds, and in the apartments wherein we most converse. If we have an aversion to smoking, it would be very prudent to burn some leaves of Tobacco in our dining rooms, lest we swallow the infection with our meat. It will also be very useful to take snuff plentifully made of the pure leaf, to secure the passages to our brain. Nor must those only be guarded, but the pass to our stomachs should be also safely defended by chewing this great *Antipoison* very frequently. . . ."

Byrd sent his manuscript to Micajah Perry, the old tobacco merchant of London, and Perry got it published—by J. Roberts, near the Oxford-Arms in Warwick-lane—price one shilling. If it did not dispel the plague, we will hope it helped the sale of tobacco. In any case, something improved the market at about this time for in the late 1720's and early 1730's the Virginia planters evidently had ample funds.[7]

In 1726 Byrd, with a second wife, came back to Virginia to stay—and found his young neighbor, Benjamin Harrison, who had just married one of "King" Carter's girls, building a new house—of brick construction and quite showy as it stood on a slight elevation above the James River. Probably "Berkeley," as the new Harrison house was called, made the thirty-six-year-old "Westover" look a bit outmoded to its owner. In any case a new "Westover" was soon under way. Beautifully wrought iron-work, beautifully carved woodwork, beautifully designed plaster-work, all were fashioned in England and shipped over. Skilled workmen, too, must have been imported from England to supervise the laying of the brick walls, the installation of the windows, and the decoration of the interior. Probably two or more dependencies, or flanking buildings, were erected at the same time. Experts doubtless were brought over to design and plant the series of gardens that sloped down toward the river and complemented the great house. The result was one of the fine homes

of America—still so after more than two centuries of time,
.after the ravages of war, after neglect, and after unskillful
restoration.[8]

Other great houses either had appeared or soon were to
appear along the banks of the James, the York, the Rappahannock and the Potomac. "Stratford," the massive home
of Thomas Lee, facing out over the wide Potomac from
Westmoreland County, had been under construction as early
as 1725. Lee had made his fortune as agent for the Fairfax
family, hereditary proprietors of the Northern Neck (see
page 284). True, he lost the job to "King" Carter in 1721,
but he was already a wealthy man, master of thousands of
acres of fine tobacco land worked by hundreds of negro slaves.
He could afford a home such as "Stratford."[9]

And Carter, with the recovery of the Fairfax agency, became even richer. Doubtless his money helped to finance the
building, in 1726, of "Berkeley," whose mistress was his
daughter. His own great house, "Corotoman," on the Rappahannock, burned in 1729, and he apparently never rebuilt it,
but that same year he aided his son Robert in establishing a
home in Westmoreland County. Known as "Nomini Hall"
from its location on Nomini Creek, a small stream flowing
into the Potomac, this new Carter place was one of the fine
homes of the Northern Neck. As described some years later
by a tutor for the Carter children, the house was of brick
construction, "but, the bricks have been covered with strong
lime Mortar; so that the building is now perfectly white; It
is seventy-six feet long from East to West & forty-four wide
from North to South, two Stories high. . . . It has five stacks
of Chimneys, tho two of these serve only for ornaments. . . .
There are four Rooms on a Floor disposed of in the following
manner. Below is a dining Room where we usually sit; the
second is a dining-Room for the Children; the third is Mr.
Carters study; & the fourth is a Ball-Room thirty feet long—
Above stairs, one Room is for Mr and Mrs Carter; the second
for the young Ladies; & the other two for occasional Company."

At distances of one hundred yards from each corner of
the main house stood four other "considerable Houses"—one

"Berkeley," home of the Harrison family,
Charles City County, Virginia.

Photograph by the author.

"Westover," the home of William Byrd, II.
Charles City County, Virginia.

Photograph by Huestis P. Cook.

serving as a schoolhouse, one as a stable, one as a coach house, and one as a wash house. In the schoolhouse were rooms for the tutor, a clerk, and the boys of the family. These flanking buildings, or dependencies, were common to all the great houses of Virginia and to a lesser extent to those of Pennsylvania. And always there were formal gardens, intersected by walks and often embellished with artistically contrived seats and pergolas.[10]

Hardly was the whitewash well dried on the walls of "Nomini Hall" when, in 1732, "King" Carter died. This left the Proprietor of the Northern Neck without a resident agent. Lord Fairfax, who all his life had lived in poverty as compared with the Carters and the Lees, decided that the Fairfax family might well enjoy the perquisites of its own estate. In line with this policy he appointed his cousin, Colonel William Fairfax, as agent, and in 1735 was himself in Virginia.

The forty-two-year-old Proprietor, already somewhat of a recluse, was charmed with the country; especially he was interested in the hinterland. How far did his proprietary extend? To the "first heads or springs" of the Rappahannock and the Potomac, the patent said. But which fork of the Rappahannock? Fairfax claimed the southern, or Rapidan, fork. Such an interpretation carried his bounds across the Shenandoah Valley and into presentday West Virginia—more than five million acres. He returned to England to demand the utmost limits, and in the end made his claim good.[11]

Meanwhile Colonel William Fairfax remained in the Northern Neck as man of business for his noble cousin. About 1740 the Colonel, like the Lees and the Carters, began to yearn for a fine home with gardens and a view across the Potomac. Well up the river, sixty miles above "Stratford," almost on the frontier, Fairfax found the location he wanted. And there, on a sightly eminence, he built "Belvoir," a two-story brick mansion "with four convenient rooms and a large passage on the lower floor; five rooms and a large passage on the second." All in all it was a very nice home, though the Colonel's young daughter, Anne, usually called Nancy, may have feared it would be a bit lonely.[12]

Just above "Belvoir" lay the Little Hunting Creek plantation. It belonged to Augustine Washington, whom we last met digging iron ore on his farm at Accokeek Creek. The iron business had not particularly prospered but Washington was nonetheless a well-to-do man; he owned some ten thousand acres of good land and had some fifty slaves when, in 1743, he died. To Lawrence, his oldest son, he left the Little Hunting Creek plantation, a few slaves, the iron business, and some other assets. To George, a younger son, by a second wife, he left a farm near the new town of Fredericksburg, ten slaves, and some miscellaneous properties. The widow and other children were properly provided for.[13]

Lawrence Washington's presence at the Little Hunting Creek plantation doubtless caused a stir of interest in the neighborhood, since, in addition to being the new master of a sizable tract of land, he was a recently returned veteran of Admiral Vernon's widely heralded though not too glorious expedition against the Spanish Main. As a matter of fact, young Washington's greatest military feat had been that of escaping the yellow fever. But to Nancy Fairfax the solemn-faced Lawrence was a dazzling hero; within a matter of weeks she became his bride and a new, comparatively modest, house, of frame construction, arose on the Washington plantation, which Lawrence, in honor of the Admiral, rechristened "Mount Vernon."[14]

Eleven years went by. Lawrence Washington was in a premature grave; his widow was remarried; "Mount Vernon" was in the possession of his twenty-two-year-old half-brother George, and destined to become another of the fine houses of Virginia.

All of these great Virginia houses were the product of tobacco—a produce over which the planters ever grumbled either on account of quantity or quality or price, but which nevertheless created a manner of living unique in an unique age. William Byrd's *Discourse concerning the Plague* had not caused Englishmen to drape their homes with the leaf. An act, passed by the Virginia Assembly "for amending the Staple of Tobacco, and for preventing Frauds in His Majesty's Customs" had doubtless improved the quality. Under this law all tobacco had to be delivered at public warehouses where the hogsheads were examined, weighed and stamped. Bad tobacco was condemned and burned. For that which passed inspection, the owner received notes that passed current as so much tobacco, and consequently, under the long established custom of Virginia, as money. This regulation was expected to raise the price and stabilize the market, but —as before and since—supply and demand, rain, sunshine and frost all played a part; and twenty years after the warehouses were in operation we find Joseph Ball, George Washington's half-uncle, caustically remarking, "Tobacco is not much better than dung in London," but Uncle Joseph was often caustic.[16]

As tobacco was to Virginia so rice had been, and to a considerable extent remained, to South Carolina. The story goes that the first seed was secured from a Madagascar ship blown off its course and forced to take refuge in Charleston harbor. From what we know of the Madagascar ships we will hope that this one was at Charleston only by mischance. In any case, the seed flourished in the hot, swampy soil of Carolina. Soon planters along the Ashley, the Cooper, the Santee and the Stono were raising rice on land that previously had been looked upon as of little worth. In 1704 an estimated three hundred and forty tons of the exotic cereal were shipped to Holland alone. With good reason the British Treasury sensed a new staple crop similar to tobacco. The export of rice not only was brought within the Navigation Laws but it was made an "enumerated commodity" which meant that it could be shipped only to England whence it would be re-exported by British merchants to the Continent or the Spanish Main. Thus regulated, the production of rice lagged and not until 1730, when the southern European market was again made directly available to the planters, did the acreage markedly increase. In 1740 ninety-one thousand one hundred and ten barrels were shipped as against eighteen thousand a dozen years earlier. By 1754 the annual production was well over a hundred thousand barrels. Rice had become South Carolina's chief export to Europe.[17]

And another staple crop was developing. The introduction

of indigo is commonly credited to Eliza Lucas Pinckney. In 1741, when she was but nineteen years of age and still Miss Lucas, she planted some indigo seed on her father's plantation, situated on the Wappoo River a few miles westerly of Charleston. Frost took that crop. But Eliza tried again, and by 1744, along with becoming the wife of Charles Pinckney, she produced enough indigo to justify an attempt at commercial manufacture. Again there were failures. The mystery of making indigo—in specially designed vats, constantly watched—did not come easily. By 1747, however, a respectable quantity of the blue lumps had been made and were shipped to England where they were wanted desperately, for use as a dye in the growing textile industry.

To encourage these pioneer American producers of indigo, the English government offered a bounty of six shillings a pound. The provincial government of South Carolina offered an additional bounty of five shillings. Naturally the production of indigo became attractive to the planters. Also, the new crop had two advantages over rice: it could be raised inland as well as on the tide-driven rivers; and the value was so high as against the bulk that transportation became a minor item of expense. By 1754, over 200,000 pounds were exported annually; twenty years later the annual shipments had risen to over a million pounds.[18]

With two great staple crops, both of which required heavy labor to raise and harvest—rice had to be threshed by hand—the demand for slaves grew year by year. Captive Indians proved useless for such work, as we have already seen (page 295). White laborers could not stand up to the heat. Negroes, acclimated to the swamps of Africa, could work long hours, under the burning sun, up to their knees in water, and be little the worse for it.

In 1726, Samuel Wragg, who had long engaged in the Carolina trade, stated that there were near forty thousand negro slaves in South Carolina, which doubtless was an exaggeration. "Gambia Men and Women" or "Gold Coast negroes" were preferred by the planters, and the price varied according to the source of the shipments. In general, the retail price for a prime negro was from £30 to £40 sterling.

As a matter of course all Charleston merchants handled slaves, though the outstanding dealer of the time was Henry Laurens, grandson of a Huguenot refugee. Not only did he act as distributor for cargoes sent by London merchants, but he owned or had an interest in ships actually engaged in procuring negroes along the coast of Africa. So extensive was his business that the old system of physically exchanging rice for negroes was abandoned; instead Laurens paid for his negroes, when purchased from other shippers, with bills of exchange, and he sold to the planters on notes dated against the next crop of rice or indigo. Sometimes he had as much as £10,000 outstanding. And when more credit was needed than Laurens could prudently extend, Gabriel Manigault, another prominent merchant, whose mother we have already met (see page 292), acted as banker.[19]

By the time he was forty years of age Laurens was a very wealthy man and, like Franklin and Logan, retired from business. His hobby was land. He bought a plantation along the Santee River where he raised rice and indigo; he acquired a large tract of unsettled land in the back country; he had rice plantations on the Georgia coast; at "Mepkin," a three-thousand acre estate on the Cooper River some thirty miles above Charleston, he developed a beautiful country home.[20]

Manigault, too, attained a position of great wealth at a comparatively early age. In 1739, when he was only thirty-five, he bought "Silk Hope," a 5,518-acre estate on the upper reaches of the Cooper River, formerly the country home of Governor Robert Johnson. Fifteen years later Manigault, like Laurens, retired from business and occupied himself with raising rice and indigo.[21]

In thus acquiring land and establishing homes in the country Laurens and Manigault were striving to place themselves in the social class occupied by the Draytons, the Middletons and others whose plantations lined the Ashley and Cooper rivers and whose homes vied successfully with those that dotted the river banks of Virginia or the outskirts of Philadelphia. Still the mark of the counting house or the office was upon these newer planters; they could not completely give

up their town houses. The Manigault home in Charleston
was itself an impressive, and doubtless comfortable, place.
From Mrs. Manigault's diary we gather that she stayed in
town most of the time and let Gabriel travel back and forth
from Charleston to "Silk Hope"—all of fifty miles the round
trip whether by boat or horse.[22]

The Pinckneys, too—Eliza and her lawyer husband—had
a well-lived-in town house, inherited by Colonel Pinckney
from his merchant father. It was a two-story brick structure,
situated on a large lot facing the harbor. On the first floor
a flagged hall ran from the front to the back of the house.
From this hall there opened, on one side, a diningroom and
bedroom, and, on the other side, a library and housekeeper's
room. On the second floor were a large drawingroom, over
thirty feet in length, a small drawingroom, and three bedrooms. All the rooms were finished with heavy panelling. The
mantelpieces were high, narrow and decorated with carvings
of shepherds, cupids and other figures. In the rear of the
house was a row of small buildings—quarters for the servants,
stables and such. Also there were gardens for flowers and
vegetables.

Five miles up the Cooper River from this town mansion lay
"Belmont," the Pinckney country home. The house, large
and of brick construction, stood on a slight headland from
which there were charming views up and down the river.
More important than views, to Mrs. Pinckney, were the gardens and the opportunity to improve them. To the indigenous
oak, magnolia and other trees she added many exotics. The
same interest that prompted Logan to beautify "Stenton" or
Bartram to tend his garden on the Schuylkill obsessed Eliza
Pinckney on the Cooper River. Nor did she lack understanding friends. Particularly, Doctor Alexander Garden, whose
name and botanical fame is commemorated in the *gardenia,*
must have been a help and inspiration to the mistress of
"Belmont." It may well be that many of Bartram's choice
specimens found their way into Eliza's gardens since the
Pennsylvania naturalist and the Charleston doctor frequently
exchanged their findings.[23]

Occasionally, during the early years at "Belmont," Mrs.

Pinckney's gardening operations were interrupted by messages from the overseer of her Wappoo River plantation. The indigo would not get dry. The rice suffered from lack of rain. The negroes were sick. The barn could not be finished because Sogo (probably the negro carpenter) was busy making barrels. The ladles (used in making indigo) were too short. The boat did not come for the tar. The wild cats and foxes ate the chickens.[24]

Always, as their sloops came down the rivers, loaded with barrels of rice for export, the masters and mistresses of the plantations were faced with stern economic facts: "Tis a melancholy time with poor planters; those that are in debt have no hopes of extricating themselves, for rice was never so low as now," wrote Eliza Pinckney in 1745, while her father echoed the old complaint of the Virginia tobacco planters, "The Extravagance of Freight takes up a great part of the Produce."[25]

The equipment of a plantation, and the establishment of a home on it, involved a considerable investment—as may be deduced from an advertisement which appeared in the January 5, 1759, issue of the *South Carolina Gazette*. "Lake Farm," consisting of 804½ acres between the Ashley and Stono rivers, was to be sold, together with "Upward of Fifty likely strong Negroes, among which is a very good driver [overseer] who understands the management of a plantation, and planting perfectly well; Two coopers, one that makes tight casks; the other has served Three years in the trade; two men cooks, one of which is a professed cook, and the other a very good one; several seamstresses that are also good housewenches; washerwomen, house-wenches, and waiting men; plantation slaves, and handy boys and girls."

The household furniture at "Lake Farm" included mahogany tables, chairs, chests of drawers, beds and bedsteads, a marble table, an 8-day clock, a "variety of good pieces of painting" and a "good collection of books." There was a considerable amount of glassware and fine china. Among the numerous pieces of silver were two candlesticks and a snuffer, two coffeepots, one teapot and stand, many spoons, six salt "sellers," two pepper boxes, and several dishes of various sorts. One can almost see the corner shelf on which were some "curious shells" and "foreign insects in spirits." In the garden was a large roller, five "handsome garden benches" and some "orange and lemon trees in tubs." In the stable was a "chariot" and harness for four horses; also a single horse "chair." And finally there were the plantation tools, the horses, cattle and hogs, indigo seed, etc., etc.[26]

A few days earlier another advertisement had appeared in the same newspaper—giving us additional insight into the nature of a medium-size Carolina plantation. "Ashley Wood and Jerico," on the northerly side of the Ashley River, about ten miles above Charleston, was up for sale. There was, said the notice, "sufficient land to work 50 or 60 Negroes on Corn, Rice and Indico for *One Hundred* Years; and there is now a large Indico-Field under a good substantial new Fence with 5 sets of Indico vats, and a Lime vat; Two Hundred acres of Rice land already cleared, Part of which has been planted, is under a good Dam; a Foot of Water will overflow the whole, and its Foundation is a fine black Soil about 6 inches deep. . . . There is on that Part of the Plantation which fronts the River and the Road, a large two-story Mansion House, with a barn and other outbuildings, all of Brick; the whole a little out of Repair occasioned by the late Hurricane. From this House you have the agreeable Prospect of the Honourable John Drayton, Esqr's Palace and Gardens . . . About a Mile and a Half from the House there is a good Overseer's House, a barn 55 x 20, with a shed, all of brick: The other out Houses, such as Negro-Houses, Kitchen &c. are Wood, but lately built."[27]

". . . the Honourable John Drayton Esqr's Palace and Gardens" were, indeed, an agreeable prospect. The house, situated on the southerly bank of the Ashley, still stands and may best be visualized, outside and inside, by the illustrations on page 402. The gardens were a combination of nature and art. Clumps of live oak with trailing beards of moss punctuated wandering lawns edged with camelias, flowering almond, bridal wreath and crepe myrtle. Hedges of box protected tulips or roses in season. Snowdrops and crocuses peeped from under the leaves at a time when New England

"Drayton Hall," Ashley River, South Carolina.

Interior view "Drayton Hall."

Courtesy, Carolina Art Association, Charleston.

was still under stark winter. Jessamine flamed in wild profusion from its native or exotic hosts. All this and infinitely more in every combination and shade of color.[28]

Another Carolina show place of the time was "Crowfield," located on Goose Creek and belonging to the Middleton family. Eliza Pinckney describes it: "The house stands a mile from, but in sight of the road, and makes a very handsome appearance; as you draw near it new beauties discover themselves; first the fruitful vine mantleing the wall, loaded with delicious clusters. Next a spacious Basin in the midst of a large Green presents itself as you enter the gate that leads to the House which is neatly finished, the rooms well contrived and Elegantly furnished. From the back door is a spacious walk a thousand feet long; each side of which nearest the house is a grass plot ornamented in a Serpentine manner with Flowers; next to that on the right hand is what immediately struck my rural taste, a thicket of young, tall live oaks where a variety of airey Chorristers pour forth their melody, and my darling the mocking bird joyn'd in the artless Concert and inchanted me with his harmony. Opposite on the left hand is a large square boling green, sunk a little below the level of the rest of the garden, with a walk quite round composed of a double row of fine, large flowering Laurel and Catalpas which aford both shade and beauty."[29]

Trees for "shade and beauty" . . . . That thought might occur to a romantic girl in South Carolina, but to the lumbermen of Maine and New Hampshire, a thousand miles up the coast, trees were a product of the soil, to be cut down and sold for a profit, even as tobacco or rice or indigo were by the southern planters. For a hundred years axemen had been hacking at the vast pine forests that stretched north and east from Massachusetts. Countless shiploads of lumber and of barrel staves had gone to England, to the Continent, to the Wine Islands, to the Sugar Islands.

But not all the trees in the woods could—legally—be sawed up for lumber. White pines measuring twenty-four inches in diameter a foot from the ground, standing on land acquired from the Crown since 1691, were reserved as masts for ships of the royal navy. They could be felled only by royal license and could be shipped only to the royal navy yards in England. Authority over such trees was vested in a royal official known as the Surveyor-general of the King's Woods, whose deputies ranged the forests—carving the King's broad arrow on standing pines of the proper dimensions and verifying that no trees bearing that mark were cut by unauthorized lumbermen. Naturally the boss of a logging camp, with his work held up because of the inclusion of a few questionable trees in his raft, had no kindly feelings toward meddlesome deputies of the Surveyor-general of the King's Woods.[30]

Sometimes the deputies were dragged into local courts while the evidence passed under the saw; oftentimes the lumbermen simply took matters into their own hands. Thus, in 1734, at Exeter, New Hampshire, we are told, "a great number of ill disposed persons assembled themselves together and in a Riotous, tumultous & most violent manner came into the house of Capt. Samuel Gilman of said Exeter (who kept a public house in the said town) and did there fall upon Beat wound & terribly abuse a number of men hired & imployed by the Hon. David Dunbar, Esq. as Surveyor General of his Majesties woods. . . ."[31]

Twenty years later, we find another Surveyor-general complaining to the Governor of Connecticut that, while his deputy "was in the Execution of His office, one Daniel Whitmore of Middletown threw him into a Mill pond, whereby his life was endangered, & he otherwise disabled thereby from persueing the Kings business."[32]

But, despite all opposition, year in and year out, the mast ships came over from England, took on loads of white pines and sailed home. Many and many a ship of the Royal Navy was rigged on masts and spars from the woods of Maine and New Hampshire.[33]

Lesser trees than those reserved for the King provided masts and spars for the forty- and fifty-ton sloops, snows and brigantines that every season were built along the New England coast—often to be sold after carrying a cargo of lumber and staves to Europe or the West Indies. In the late 1730's Benning Wentworth, of New Hampshire, entered into a contract with the government of Spain to supply a large shipment of timber. It was later whispered by Wentworth's enemies that some of the logs supplied might have rated the King's broad arrow. To finance the transaction he borrowed considerable sums of money in London, and he personally supervised delivery of the timber in Spain. At that point disaster struck. Spain, drifting into war with England, refused immediate payment. Wentworth's appeals to the English government for redress went unanswered, and Jonathan Belcher, royal Governor of Massachusetts and New Hampshire, sneeringly referred to him as the "Spanish bankrupt." But while Wentworth lingered in London, hoping for relief from his financial embarrassment, strange things happened, not at all to the satisfaction of Governor Belcher.[34]

As will be recalled, Maine, first by annexation and later by purchase, had long been a part of Massachusetts. New Hampshire, also, for many years had been a dependency of its larger neighbor, and, even after its establishment as a royal province, remained tied to Massachusetts through a joint governor. Too often, it seemed, the governor had looked upon New Hampshire as a step child. The leading men of the province wanted a wholly separate government; also they wanted the boundary line between themselves and Massachusetts clarified.[35]

This boundary controversy went back to the contention by the Massachusetts magistrates that the source of the Merrimac River, wherever found, marked their northern line (see page 7). They had not succeeded in making this claim take in the part of New Hampshire east of the Merrimac. but they still could and did claim all the land west of that river. For almost ten years the controversy had dragged along without approaching an agreement, and, at just the time Wentworth arrived in London from his disastrous Spanish venture, the conflicting claims were before the Privy Council for final determination.[36]

To bolster its side of this controversy, Massachusetts had dug up from obscurity one John Tufton Mason, a sailor, whom they satisfactorily proved was the heir of the John Mason to whom New Hampshire had been granted by the

Council for New England in 1629—and therefore the legal proprietor of all the land within that province (see page 7). In consideration of £500 this John Tufton Mason readily confirmed the boundary wished by Massachusetts and further, in return for having his expenses paid, agreed to go to London and support the Massachusetts claim before the Privy Council.[37]

On his arrival in London, however, Mason received a very cool reception from the lawyers handling the case for Massachusetts; in fact, he was given his expense money and told to go along home. At that opportune moment the doubtless disgruntled "Proprietor of New Hampshire," late sailor from Boston, fell into the capable hands of John Thomlinson, London merchant and agent for the New Hampshire Assembly. And on April 6, 1739, Mason, Thomlinson and a group of five New Hampshire men, of whom Benning Wentworth was one, entered into an agreement: If within a year after New Hampshire was definitely separated from Massachusetts, Mason received £1,000 either from the Wentworth group or from the government of New Hampshire, then he would deed his proprietary interests either to the group or the government, whichever paid him the money.[38]

With the proprietary title thus within their grasp, Wentworth and his friends threw all their energies into an effort to have New Hampshire declared a separate province and to secure for it a favorable boundary line. In both objectives they were eminently successful.

Governor Belcher was dismissed and the joint governorship was discontinued. William Shirley, a Boston lawyer, noted for his support of the King's prerogative in colonial affairs, became the new Governor of Massachusetts. And Benning Wentworth became Governor of New Hampshire.[39]

The boundary line between the two provinces, as finally determined by the Privy Council, followed the Merrimac River only to the point where that stream turned definitely northward; thence the boundary was to be a line running due west until it met with "his Majesties other Governments"— a statement so indefinite as to cause much subsequent controversy.[40]

Governor Wentworth arrived in New Hampshire, from London, late in 1741 and in the following January met with the Provincial Assembly. There was no secret about his part in making the agreement with Mason. In fact, the original document was laid before the Assembly "for their Perusal & Consideration"; time after time the Governor and his associates urged the Assembly to take over the contract and require Mason to deed his proprietary interest to the Province; but the Assembly refused to act. Finally, on July 30, 1746, the holders of the agreement, increased to twelve men but with Governor Wentworth not appearing, took a deed from Mason and thus became the Proprietors of all the land comprised within the Province of New Hampshire. At the same time they reassured established landowners by quit-claiming title to all land already settled under charters from New Hampshire.[41]

The determination of the boundary line between New Hampshire and Massachusetts had placed at the disposal of the Masonian Proprietors a vast area of unsettled land—unquestionably theirs as far as the Connecticut River, open to challenge by New York west of that river. Grants were made in township units (usually six miles square) to groups of petitioners, and validated through charters issued by Governor Wentworth in the name of the King. There was no charge for the land but each grantee was required to plant five acres within five years on account of every fifty acres which he received, and—relic of the old feudal title—to pay a quitrent, consisting of one ear of Indian corn, each year for the first ten years, and thereafter one shilling annually forever for each hundred acres of land.

The Proprietors, in lieu of other payments receivable from the grantees, themselves became grantees, each, according to his investment in the purchase from Mason, receiving, along with the actual settlers, shares of land in each new grant or township. And in each charter appeared the following clause: To "His Excellency Benning Wentworth Esq a Tract of Land to Contain five Hundred Acres. . . ." When we consider that between 1749 and 1764 one hundred and twenty-nine townships were granted, and that the value of the land grew as settlement increased, it is not difficult to see that the "Spanish bankrupt" was soon able to pay off his creditors and have an increasing competence left.[42]

Doubtless, too, Governor Wentworth retained an interest in the lumber business carried on by his brother, Mark Hunking Wentworth, who was, above all competitors, the lumber baron of the northern woods. Nor were the family interests harmed by a deal through which, in 1743, Benning Wentworth, in addition to the governorship, acquired the office of Surveyor-general of the King's Woods.[43]

With wealth and position assured, Benning Wentworth, like Byrd of Virginia or Drayton of South Carolina, wanted a country home. The spot he hit upon was Little Harbor, two miles out of the village of Portsmouth, at the mouth of the Piscataqua River. There, hidden from the road by a hill but with a fine water view, he built his house—a rambling frame affair of fifty-two rooms. The architectural scheme has bothered some visitors, but the house met the needs of a climate where, if the "dependencies" were to be reached during the winter months, they had to be under a common roof.

In short, the house is described as being an irregular collection of buildings, in general of two stories in height, joined together to make three sides of a square. Among the fifty-two rooms the so-called Council Chamber seems to have been the most impressive, with its high panelled walls and hand-carved mantel. Up a flight of stairs was a spacious parlor, and other rooms wandered off, even to a stable sufficient for thirty-five horses.[44]

A house of fifty-two rooms called for a sizable staff of servants and among them as maid of all work was the pretty, laughing Martha Hilton, just turned twenty. Something about her, perhaps her innocent smile, attracted the aging Governor, a widower of some years. As the story goes, his Excellency gave a dinner party to which were invited all the dignitaries of Portsmouth, including the rector. When the dinner was finished the host arose; standing beside him was Martha. "Marry me to this lady," commanded the Governor, and the flustered rector complied. Whatever the details, the

A detail of the Wentworth House, Little Harbor, N. H.

From Samuel Adams Drake, *Nooks and Corners of the
New England Coast.*

409

marriage is a matter of record—and Martha became mistress of Wentworth Hall, with its fifty-two rooms.[45]

Despite their provincialism these little New England servant girls seem to have had a way with the men. Take the case of Agnes Surriage—just sixteen—flashing black eyes—barefooted—scrubbing the floor at the tavern in Marblehead. In walked young Charles Henry Frankland, heir to a baronetcy in England, Collector of Customs at the Port of Boston, quite the dandy of Massachusetts officialdom. One look into those dark eyes and Charles knew that it was his duty to buy Agnes a pair of shoes. Another look and he saw intelligence, character and poise—awaiting only his touch to burst into flower. Easily he arranged with the girl's mother—desperately poor —to have Agnes educated in Boston at his expense.

Four years went by, and in 1746, Charles succeeded to the English baronetcy. Agnes had blossomed into a beautiful young woman, and openly became his mistress. That was too much for Boston—which showed its disapproval in no unmistakable fashion. To meet this situation, Sir Charles bought a pretty piece of land—four hundred and eighty-two acres— some fifteen or twenty miles southwest of Boston, and there made Agnes a home. Well back from the public road, and reached by a driveway cut through a grove of chestnut trees, a great house was built and richly furnished. Terraced lawns sloped to gardens bordered with hedges of box and shaded with ornamental trees. Barns and servant quarters— Sir Charles had twelve negro slaves on the place—were spaced with orchards of apple, pear, plum, peach, cherry, apricot and quince. With a well stocked cellar, with music and congenial friends, life went happily on.

In 1755, Frankland—with Agnes along, of course—was visiting Portugal when an earthquake struck. The baronet was buried under the debris; Agnes saved his life; and he married her. The following year Sir Charles and Lady Agnes returned to Boston. He bought a fine house in the best part of the city, and, as husband and wife, the Franklands were readily accepted by Boston society, though Thomas Hutchinson, living in his stately mansion next door, writing a *History of the Colony of Massachusets-Bay,* must sometimes have been

The Home of Thomas Hutchinson in the North End of Boston.
From *The American Magazine*, February, 1836.

Thomas Hutchinson's Country House at Milton.
From *History of Milton, Mass.*, 1640–1887. Edited by A. K. Teele.

a bit annoyed with their noisy parties, particularly when Sir Charles rode his horse up and down his stairway to demonstrate how nicely the risers were designed.[46]

Hutchinson was a native New Englander. He was, in fact, a great-great-grandson of Anne Hutchinson who had been banished from Massachusetts in 1638 and later massacred by the Indians near New Amsterdam. His house, three stories in height, built of brick, facing the street and backed by a large garden, differed only in size and detail from the homes of James Bowdoin or Peter Fanueil or of a score of other rich Bostonians. They were the city homes of merchants; they lacked the open settings, the almost baronial control over their surroundings, that characterized "Westover" or "Drayton Hall." True, Hutchinson and others had country homes at Milton, a few miles out of the city, but such estates were parts of a country village rather than nerve centers of labor and production.[47]

It was trade that had built these fine Boston houses. Hutchinson's father had been a very successful merchant, and Thomas continued the business, along with monopolizing a number of profitable political offices. James Bowdoin, whose grandfather had come to America as a Huguenot refugee, had inherited a fortune from his merchant father; he added to it both by business ventures and by putting money out at interest. Peter Faneuil had been born in the French refugee village of New Rochelle, in New York province, within a short walk of the spot where Hutchinson's great-great-grandmother was massacred. As a young man he had taken service with his uncle, a successful merchant of Boston. On the uncle's death, Peter inherited both the fortune and the business.[48]

The trade of these Boston merchants was as diverse as the wants of mankind, but the steady profits were made in fish, in lumber, in rum and in slaves. The last two were closely related: rum bought slaves, and slaves paid for the West Indian molasses from which rum was made. So essential was rum to the New England traders that it, or rather molasses, attracted the attention of the British Board of Trade. Too much molasses was being bought in the French and Spanish islands while business lagged in the English sugar-producing island of Barbados. In 1733, Parliament placed a prohibitive tax on foreign molasses. For a moment it seemed that the New England trade was doomed, but in one way or another, and mostly by smuggling, molasses continued to pour into Massachusetts, and even increasingly into Rhode Island, where Newport came to rival Boston in what was known as the Triangular Trade.[49]

Typical of this Triangular Trade—between New England, Africa and the West Indies—was the voyage of the *Sanderson*, a forty-ton sloop owned by William Johnson, merchant, of Newport. David Lindsay was master; his crew consisted of two mates and six men. In March, 1752, the *Sanderson* began taking on cargo at Newport. There were 80 hogsheads, 6 barrels and 3 tierce (less than a hogshead, but more than a barrel) of rum, which figured out to 8,220 gallons. There were 79 bars of "African iron"—in great demand on the Gold Coast. There were 19 barrels of flour; 4 tierce of rice; 2 barrels of snuff; 28 iron pots; some lumber, barrel staves, etc., etc., including a supply of shackles and handcuffs.

On February 28, 1753, from Anamaboe, on the coast of Africa, Captain Lindsay reported: "I have Gott 13 or 14 hhds of Rum yet Left abord & God noes when I shall Gett clear of it. Ye Traid is so dull it is actually a nouf to make a man Creasey." His men were sick. His cable had worn out and broken. The timbers of his ship were opening: "We can see day Lite al round her bow under deck." There were five other Rum Ships, that is, New Englanders, in the roadstead. ". . . on the whole," grumbled the captain, "I never had So much Trouble in all my voiges."

Nonetheless, on June 17, 1753, Captain Lindsay and the *Sanderson* were at Barbados. They had had a tough passage but there they were—with fifty-six negroes aboard "all in helth & fatt"; also 40 oz. of gold dust and eight or nine hundred pounds of "maligabar" pepper. There—at Barbados— the captain sold forty-seven of his negroes, together with his lumber and some of his staves (set up as casks) for £1,466/13/6, and bought fifty-five hogsheads of molasses and twenty-seven barrels of sugar. Then he sailed for Newport. The molasses would make more rum, and there was a nice balance—in exchange, in gold, in negroes, in pepper and in other commodities—left for the owners. It had been a successful voyage.[50]

Voyages such as this created wealth that could support public benefactions as well as private homes. Thus when, in 1747, the members of the Newport Literary and Philosophical Society (see page 350) decided that the town needed a public library, there was no difficulty about raising the money. Abraham Redwood, a merchant engaged in the West India trade, gave £500 "to be laid out in a Collection of Useful Books"—and in his honor the new institution was named the Redwood Library. Henry Collins gave a part of his bowling green as a site. Others contributed generously for the erection of a handsome building, of classical design, which today forms a section of the enlarged structure.[51]

The opportunity for study afforded by this collection of books attracted many cultivated people to Newport. It was doubtless a contributing factor in causing Ezra Stiles, the New Haven lawyer, to accept a call to serve as minister of the Second Congregational Church of Newport. Doubtless he profited from the library; also as its librarian, a position which he held for twenty years, Stiles did much to develop the library.[52]

But the library did not exhaust Redwood's thirst for knowledge. On his country estate he experimented with the cultivation of oranges, limes, pineapples and other tropical trees and plants. He even had hot-houses where, as a contemporary reported, "things that are tender are put for the winter."[53]

The one outstanding country house of the Rhode Island region, however, belonged to Godfrey Malbone, wealthy slave trader and privateer. His father had come to Newport from Virginia in the 1720's; perhaps Godfrey had inherited a taste for a home in which he could turn around. Anyway, on a six-hundred-acre tract of land just north of Newport he laid the foundations for his house and began planting his gardens. From land which he owned at Brooklyn, Connecticut, he caused blocks of pink sandstone to be quarried, carted

Redwood Library, Newport, R. I., as built in the late 1740's.

EZRA STILES.

From a portrait by Nathaniel Smibert, son of John Smibert.

Courtesy, Gallery of Fine Arts, Yale University, New Haven.

415

across to Providence and floated down to the place where the construction was under way. In 1744, three years after the house was finished, Dr. Alexander Hamilton, of Annapolis, visited "Malbone" and noted: "It is the largest and most magnificent dwelling house I have seen in America. It is built entirely with hewn stone of a reddish colour; the sides of the windows and the corner stones of the house being painted like white marble. It is three storys high, and the rooms are spacious and magnificent. There is a large lanthern or cupola on the roof, which is covered with sheet lead. The whole staircase, which is very spacious and large, is done with mahogany wood. This house makes a grand show att a distance, but is not extraordinary for the architecture, being a clumsy Dutch modell. Round it are pretty gardens and terasses with canals and basons for water, from whence you have a delightfull view of the town and harbour of Newport with the shipping lying there." [54]

It should be observed that Malbone's house was anything but "a clumsy Dutch modell." It was, in fact, one of the fine houses of eighteenth-century America. But Hamilton was a doctor, not an architect. A month earlier, while sailing up the Hudson River opposite Yonkers, New York, he had noted, off to the right, "a little country house belonging to one Philips." What he had actually seen was the manor house of Philipsborough. And probably it was a "little" house, much as it had been built by Frederick and Margaret Philipse in the late 1600's, before a manorship had even been thought of. In fact, Margaret, shipowner and trader (see page 71), had not lived to enjoy the honor of being a Lady of the Manor, nor had Frederick long survived her. Now, in 1744, their grandson, also named Frederick, was the Lord of the Manor, and the following year, according to tradition, he completely remodelled and greatly enlarged the old house. It became three stories high, of brick construction, facing castward toward the Albany Post Road across a wide terraced lawn with formal gardens on either side. To the west, sloping down to the river, was a park stocked with tame deer. On the south, the Neperhan River, lined with grist mills, flowed into the Hudson—as is shown in the view on page 417.

Philipse Manor House, as seen by an 18th Century artist. The view is from the southerly side of the Neperhan River with the Hudson on the left.

From the original, now in the possession of the Philipse Castle Restoration, Tarrytown, N. Y.

Mantel, East Parlor, Philipse Manor House.

Courtesy, The New York Department of Education.

Photograph by John Vrooman.

As in most of the fine houses of the day the interior finish of the remodelled Philipse home was highly decorative: the walls were panelled and pilastered; the ceilings were ornamented with arabesque relief; the stair rails and balusters were of solid mahogany. Fifty servants, many of them negro slaves, were required to take care of the house and its grounds.[55]

All this grandeur at Yonkers was, to a large extent, based upon rents paid by the hundreds of tenants on the Philipse land—land which the tenant never could hope to own and which, in the case of a life tenancy, always reverted to the landlord. Similar landrents supported the Van Rensselaer manor house at Albany, the Livingston manor house at Clermont near Poughkeepsie, the Cortlandt manor house at Croton, the Van Cortlandt mansion just north of the present New York City line, and many another country seat from the Mohawk to the jaws of Long Island.

These great landlords, all more or less related to each other, controlled New York, economically and politically. They, and in most cases their fathers, and even their grandfathers, had known only luxury. It is not likely that the Philipse girls entertained their suitors with stories of how their great-grandfather worked as a carpenter or how their great-grandmother extracted the last guilder from Jasper Danckaerts (see page 71). Nor would James De Lancey, rising young politician, have wooed his wife, Anne Heathcote, daughter of Caleb Heathcote, with tales of how his great-grandfather Van Cortlandt, sire of all the Van Cortlandts, had come over as a soldier for the Dutch West India Company, and got his start running a brewery. Anne doubtless was well aware that James' father, Stephen De Lancey, had made his fortune in the Madagascar trade. And surely no one would have reminded the stately Robert R. Livingston, Judge of the Vice-admiralty Court, that his grandfather had been a partner of Captain Kidd.[56]

It was a close circle, this landed oligarchy of New York, but not a closed circle. Outsiders could and did break in— sometimes adding color and gaiety to the province. Thus when, in the summer of 1730, Captain Peter Warren sailed

into New York harbor in command of H. M. S. *Solebay,* and
decided to make the city his home station, a long train of
very important events had begun. The Captain got off on the
right foot socially; within a year of his arrival he married
Susannah De Lancey, daughter of Stephen De Lancey, granddaughter of Stephanus Van Cortlandt, and sister of James
De Lancey. Bradford's *New York Gazette* carried a fulsome,
and more or less poetical, notice of the wedding—

> "Their Nuptial Entertainments such have been
> As here before was seldom seen,
> Adorn'd with musick, Dancing and Delight,
> Where-with they pass'd away the wellcome Night."

and much more to the same effect.[57]

The De Lanceys and Van Cortlandts did not have to support the captain's gold braid. No privateer out of Newport
had a better eye for rich prizes than the commander of the
Solebay. And as his prize money grew, Warren judiciously
invested it in New York real estate. Piece by piece, he bought
a three-hundred-acre farm in the area covered today by
Greenwich Village. There, in his spacious house, surrounded
by handsomely designed gardens, he entertained the elite of
the city—with wines intended for the great dons of Mexico
and from silver plate intended for Spain. And like many another farsighted man the captain dabbled in western land.
At four cents an acre he acquired from Governor Cosby's
widow a 14,000-acre tract along the southern side of the
Mohawk River, some thirty miles west of Albany. Of course
he had no time personally to manage this wilderness estate,
but he had a promising nephew in Ireland, William Johnson,
whom he sent for and put in charge.[58]

Warren's great opportunity, however, came with the outbreak of war between England and France in 1744. The
eastern provinces—Massachusetts, New Hampshire, Connecticut and Rhode Island—were intent upon the capture of
Louisburg, a French fortress located on Cape Breton Island
and controlling the northern sea lanes. Through the efforts of
Governor Shirley, of Massachusetts, an intercolonial army
of about four thousand men was assembled. William Pep-

SIR WILLIAM PEPPERRELL.

From a portrait by John Smibert.

Courtesy, The Essex Institute, Salem, Mass.

420

perrell, a wealthy merchant of Kittery, Maine, was placed
in command. And Peter Warren was directed to provide
naval support, which he did so effectively that French re-
enforcements were held at bay while the undisciplined New
Englanders captured the undergarrisoned and unprepared
fortress.

News of this feat of arms sent a thrill of exultation throughout the American colonies. An American army had humbled
the proud citadel of France. The returning troops were
hailed as conquering heroes. Nor did England show a lack
of appreciation. Expenses incurred by the colonies were refunded to them in cold cash. Pepperrell was knighted. Warren was made an admiral and sent against a French fleet
assembling off Cape Finisterre from which engagement he
emerged with added honors, including knighthood. New
York saw Sir Peter no more. He retired from the navy—with
£200,000 in prize money; won a seat in Parliament; and
settled down to the life of a country gentleman in Ireland.[59]

As Warren faded from the American scene his young
nephew, out on the western fringe of settlement, strode onto
the stage. War with France made it vitally important that
the Iroquois be held to their ancient friendship with New
York. Upon that friendship depended the English fort and
trading post at Oswego—on the southern shore of Lake Ontario, just across from the French Fort Frontenac. William
Johnson not only kept the Indians in line but he saw to it
that supplies got through to Oswego. The Mohawks were
ready to follow Johnson anywhere; the rest of the Iroquois
would generally follow the Mohawks. Said Governor Clinton, ". . . none upon the Continent can influence them to
continue stedfast in their engagements, so much as this Gentleman."[60]

We may, perhaps, detect a certain wistfulness in the Governor's regard for a man who had influence over other men;
the Governor himself had little influence over anyone. This
situation was not wholly due to Clinton's defects of character. The royal prerogative, as represented by a governor,
had been declining for many years. As early as 1726 Cadwallader Colden, a member of the Governor's Council, had

reported to the Board of Trade that the New York Assembly had "so often forced the Governor and Council to yield . . . that the Assembly now thinks there is no longer any use colouring their Desire of assuming to themselves the sole Disposal of the Revenue and Public Money by the resolve of their house only." By 1746 James De Lancey's political machine, controlling the Assembly, the Council and the Courts, left the Governor little leeway to do other than acquiesce in what the leaders of the province wished to have done.[61]

Nor was the situation in New York unique. Since the days of Joseph Dudley the Massachusetts Assembly had held its governors in check through the power of the purse; either the governors concurred or they did not get their salaries. Governor Glen of South Carolina, in 1748, complaining of the encroachment of his assembly, said, "Thus by little and little the people have got the whole administration into their hands, and the crown is by various laws despoiled of its principal flowers and brightest jewels." Similarly, Governor Dinwiddie reported in 1754 that the Virginia Assembly was in "very much a Republican way of Thinking," and addicted to "making Encroachments on the Prerogative of the Crown."[62]

It is not to be understood that the colonists, at this time, were deliberately opposing the power of the crown; on the contrary they had the greatest respect for the royal institution. But they looked upon themselves, when acting through their own representatives, as the permanent and proper sources of authority over matters having to do with colonial affairs. Governors, unless elected by themselves as in Connecticut and Rhode Island, were but passing decorations; often the governor's very instructions, received in the name of the King, were actually based upon recommendations made by the assemblies through their own London agents.[63]

These colonial agents occupied a very important function as liaison men between the colonial governments and the Board of Trade. The system of agents had grown up slowly from necessity. From time to time, as special problems arose during the seventeenth century, this colony or that would send a special agent to England to present the colonial point of view. As time went along, not only the colonial assemblies but the home government felt the need for full-time resident agents in London. Said the Lords of Trade, in writing to the Earl of Bellomont in 1698, "There is one thing very usefull, practised by some of His Majestys Plantations, which is: to have some persons here as Agents who we may call upon for further information as may be requisite upon occasion. . . ." Sometimes prominent colonials undertook these missions; William Byrd II thus served Virginia at various times; Benjamin Franklin lived in England several years as agent for Pennsylvania. Usually, however, a London lawyer or merchant was retained; John Thomlinson, acting for New Hampshire in the Massachusetts boundary case, was typical. Ordinarily, a Committee of Correspondence, appointed by the colonial assembly, directed the agent and received his reports. His duties ranged from presenting unimportant petitions to the Board of Trade or Privy Council to appearing personally before the King. Unknown to history, these hardworking and generally conscientious agents played vital parts in the building of the British empire. But by the very nature of this direct contact through their agents the colonial assemblies came to look upon the royal governors and their functions as superfluous. The assemblies could run the affairs of their colonies; the King's prerogative was only flowers and jewels.[64]

Nor was colonial encroachment upon the prerogative always the work of the assemblies. We have seen how Byrd, Carter, Blair and others—all members of the Governor's own Council—joined in ousting Spotswood. The fact was that in Virginia, as in New York, Massachusetts or South Carolina, many men of wealth and ability were adding their weight to a political ground swell designed to place the control of the colonies in their own hands. At the same time other equally able and wealthy men were resisting this so-called "Republican" movement with all their strength. Thomas Hutchinson, with a representation of the British crown over every window in his Boston house, consistently upheld the royal prerogative—and profited through offices bestowed upon him by the King, though he lost in public esteem. Many others, destined to be known as loyalists in the years to come, took the same position as Hutchinson for no other reason than that such was their conviction.

It was a confusing political cleavage, this that developed in the American colonies during the mid-eighteenth century. Confusing too is the term "Republican." Neither Byrd in Virginia, nor De Lancey in New York, nor any responsible colonial of the day, visualized America as a republic, or wanted such a form of government. What they did want was to so control their various provinces that they might exploit the resources of those provinces for their own advantages and for the advantages of other colonials.

People

TO A THOMAS HUTCHINSON the preservation of the royal prerogative was all-important but to a young man bundling with his best girl —the King's rights mattered not at all; at least we have no record so to indicate. As a matter of fact, we have no first-hand accounts of any sort as to what really went on during a bundling; always the participants were someone else, usually "the lower people." From a Church of England clergyman visiting Massachusetts we get the following details: "When a man is enamoured of a young woman, and wishes to marry her, he proposes the affair to her parents (without whose consent no marriage in this colony can take place); if they have no objection, they allow him to tarry with her one night, in order to make his court to her. At their usual time the old couple retire to bed, leaving the young ones to settle matters as they can; who, after having sate up as long as they think proper, get into bed together also, but without pulling off their under garments, in order to prevent scandal. If the parties agree, it is all very well; the banns are published, and they are married without delay. If not, they part, and possibly never see each other again unless, which is an accident that seldom happens, the forsaken fair-one prove pregnant, and then the man is obliged to marry her." [1]

Other authorities insist that the bundlers went to bed with all their clothes on. When we consider further that the bundling probably took place in the same bed with the girl's father and mother and brothers and sisters, or at any rate in the same room, beds and bedroom space being what they were among the "lower people," then—when we think of all that and of the firewood that it saved—the practice seems to compare favorably with other forms of courtship, and doubtless added to the social interests of farm life during the cold New England winters. [2]

Not that life on a New England farm was dull—winter or summer. Take the case of Joshua Hempstead, of New London, Connecticut, for example: On Saturday, December 22, 1733, he was busy carving letters on a gravestone. The following day, being the Sabbath, he was, of course, at church. The minister preached all day. "Wm. Morgan made a open & public Confession of being Guilty of Incontinency before Marriage owened the Covenant & was Babtized & his child William." There was an inch of snow. Monday, Hempstead was in town most of the day where he and Thomas Prentis held a court and sentenced Sambo, Mrs. Christopher's negro slave, to be whipped—"30 Stripes for Striking Samll Beebee with an Iron a piece of a fryingpan handle Cut his head with itt." Tuesday, December 25th, Hempstead again conducted court. (Not a word about the un-Christian holiday celebrated as Christmas in less puritanical colonies.) On Wednesday, it rained and he went into town to attend a session of the Probate Court. Thursday he carted five pair of stones (probably millstones, possibly gravestones) to the dock for shipment to Groton. On Friday he mended a bridge, attended a lecture and was present at a session of the Town Selectmen. Certainly no dull moments for Joshua Hempstead. [3]

Equally active was the life of Timothy Walker, of Pennycook, now Concord, New Hampshire. In the spring he and his negro slave, Prince, set out hundreds of apple trees, sowed grain, planted corn. In the summer they mowed and hauled the hay, harvested the wheat and rye and barley. In the autumn they were very busy making cider, husking and cribbing the corn. Even in the dead of winter Prince, with a yoke of oxen, was hired out to the boss of the mast camp—to help pull the big logs to the river's edge. And every Sabbath day —spring, summer, autumn and winter, sometimes with the snow so deep the horses could hardly get through—Walker preached, for he was also the minister for Pennycook.[4]

Ezra Stiles, the minister of the Second Church at Newport, fared better than Walker; he did not have to run a farm in order to live. His parishioners supplied him with many of the necessities of life. Among the diverse contributions which he received were: a load of hay; a half bushel of onions; a turkey; cider; pork; butter; cheese; pumpkins; six bottles of wine; a coat and breeches.[5]

In addition to the First and Second Congregational churches there were, in Newport, by the middle of the century, a large Quaker meetinghouse, two Baptist churches, and one of the finest Church of England edifices in the colonies. This latter, named Trinity, was equipped with a pipe organ, presented by Newport's erstwhile philosopher-resident, Bishop Berkeley; and from the church steeple there looked out a clock made by William Claggett, local mechanical genius. But, with all its urbanity, Newport was still a part of Rhode Island, and Rhode Island remained Puritan —as visitors discovered when they had in mind passing through on the Lord's Day. There was no travelling on that day; nor was it profitable to swear over the matter.[6]

Boston was even more strict as to observance of the Sabbath. Not only was ordinary travel forbidden, but no one, doctors excepted, was allowed on the streets during the time of meeting. From sundown Saturday night, when the Sabbath began, to sundown on Sunday night, when it ended, no one might so much as walk in the Common.[7]

At other times, however, gayer spirits of the town made up for lost time. In 1750, Francis Goelet, captain of a merchant ship, recorded his experiences. ". . . haveing an Invitation from the Gentlemen to Dine at Mr. Sheppard's,

went Accordingly where was a Company of about 40 Gentlemen, after haveing Dined in a very Elegant manner upon
Turtle &c. Drank about the Toasts, and Sang a Number of
Songs, and were Exceeding Merry untill 3 a Clock in the
Morning, from whence Went upon the Rake,* Going Past
the Commons in our way Home, Surprised a Company of
Country Young Men and Women with a Violin at A Tavern
Danceing and Makeing Merry, upon Our Entering the house
the Young Women fled, we took Possession of the Room,
haveing the Fidler and the Young man with us with the Keg
of Sugard Dram, we were very Merry, from thence went to
Mr. Jacob Wendells† where we were Obliged to Drink Punch
and Wine, and about 5 in the morning made our Excit and
to Bed." [8]

The more staid citizens took their pleasures in a more
sober manner. "For their domestic amusements," we are told,
"every afternoon, after drinking tea, the gentlemen and ladies
walk the Mall [meaning the Common] and from thence adjourn to one another's houses to spend the evening." [9]

A favorite diversion for both the men and the women was
a jaunt to the Sign of the Greyhound or some similar place
of entertainment a few miles out of the city. "When the
ladies ride out to take the air, it is generally in a chaise or
chair,‡ and then but a single horse; and they have a negro
servant to drive them. The gentlemen ride out here as in
England, some in chairs and others on horse back, with their
negroes to attend them." [10]

"And," continued our informant, "the ladies here visit,
drink tea, and indulge every little piece of gentility, to the
height of the mode; and neglect the affairs of their families
with as good a grace as the finest ladies in London." [11]

Doctor Alexander Hamilton, who visited the city in 1744,
tells us that Boston abounded with "pritty women" who were
"free and affable" and dressed "elegantly." "Assemblies of
the gayer sort," he says, "are frequent here; the gentlemen

* "Going on the rake" was a common seventeenth century expression
which may be translated by the twentieth century "Going on a bat."

†The great-grandfather of Oliver Wendell Holmes.

‡A chair was a single-seated vehicle similar to the later sulky.

and ladys meeting almost every week att consorts of musick and balls. I was present att two or three such and saw as fine a ring of ladys, as good dancing, and heard musick as elegant as I had been witness to any where." Nor was this gaiety limited to Boston; the Reverend Mister Andrew Burnaby observed, disapprovingly, that the ladies of Virginia were "immoderately fond of dancing." [12]

Clubs provided social meeting places for strictly masculine society. There was at Boston, for example, the Physical Club which met at the Sun Tavern where the members drank punch, smoked and perhaps occasionally indulged in physical exercise. In Newport, there was, as we know, the Philosophical Club, but, after Berkeley's departure, discussions concerning privateering and ship building seem to have vied with philosophy. At New York the Hungarian Club met every night; among its members were Governor Clinton, Chief-justice James De Lancey, Speaker-of-the-House Adolph Philipse and other worthies. "To drink stoutly" and "talk bawdy" was a prime qualification for membership, according to Doctor Hamilton, who added, "Two or three toapers in the company seemed to be of opinion that a man could not have a more sociable quality or enduement than to be able to pour down seas of liquor and remain unconquered while others sunk under the table." [13]

At home, in Annapolis, Hamilton was a member of The Ancient and Honourable Tuesday Club. Notable among its rules was one that, if anyone at any time brought up the subject of Maryland politics, "no answer shall be given thereto, but . . . the society shall laugh at the Member offending in order to divert the discourse." [14]

In a different strata of society other clubs were coming into being primarily for the purpose of political discussion. In Boston, for example, there was the group commonly referred to as The Whipping Post Club. One of the founders and leading members was a young fellow named Samuel Adams. He had come of a well-to-do family, and had received every advantage that education could give. A clue to his mental outlook may be gleaned from the subject of his thesis for a Master's degree at Harvard, namely: "Whether it be lawful to resist the Supreme Magistrate, if the Commonwealth cannot be otherwise preserved." Adams had argued affirmatively. In business he had proved a failure, frittering away a small fortune advanced to him by his father. Nor were official preferments showered upon him. Only in the field of local politics, as leader of similarly frustrated men, was he a success.[15]

In Massachusetts, as in all the colonies, but a small percentage of the male population was entitled to vote for representatives in the general assemblies. Due to the property qualification required of a freeman, thousands upon thousands of small tradesmen and apprentices were practically unfranchised so far as provincial affairs were concerned. In the New England town meetings, however, it had long been customary to permit all adult males to have a voice—and Boston, large as it was (20,000 inhabitants), still clung to the town meeting form of government. In these meetings Adams and his fellow malcontents ruled supreme, and through the action there taken, they often influenced provincial politics; always they influenced public opinion. To the political organization incident to these meetings Governor Shirley attributed the "Mobbish turn" of the city. A town meeting, said he, "may be called together at any time upon the Petition of ten of the meanest Inhabitants, who by their Constant attendance there generally are the majority and outvote the Gentlemen, Merchants, Substantial Traders and all the better part of the Inhabitants; to whom it is Irksome to attend at such meetings, except upon very extraordinary occasions."[16]

The particular "Mobbish turn" which brought forth these observations occurred in 1747. England was at war with France. A British squadron lay in Boston Harbor. Numerous sailors had deserted, and to make up his complement of men the commodore sent a press-gang along the waterfront. Instantly the town was in an uproar. Officers who happened to be ashore from the fleet were seized by the mob and held as hostages; when Governor Shirley attempted to protect other officers, his house was invaded; the session of the General Assembly was stoned; and the militia failed to respond to the Governor's call. For three days the city was in the hands of the mob, and not until the men who had been taken up by the press-gang were released did the commotion subside.[17]

Such demonstrations may be viewed as manifestations of a democratic upsurge; certainly they were evidences of an incipient revolutionary movement. Back of them lay a deepening conviction, fed by such men as Samuel Adams, that the royal officials and the prerogative men were not to be trusted where the interest of the common man was concerned.

And the common man had many grievances. Most vital was an economic one. Massachusetts, like all the other colonies, but more so, lacked a stable currency. The trouble had all started back in 1690 when Phips failed to take Quebec and the colony had been forced to issue paper money in order to pay the expenses of the expedition (see page 164). This procedure had proved an easy way to pay debts, and when more debts were to be paid, more paper was issued. The other colonies followed suit with varying degrees of depreciation, and by the 1740's a traveller passing from Georgia to New Hampshire found as many rates of exchange as there were colonies. It was all figured in pounds, shillings and pence, but there was a broad spread between pounds sterling and the paper pounds of the different colonies. In Massachusetts the situation had reached a point where it took £550 provincial to buy £100 sterling. There was, of course, no coin in circulation; only tattered paper bills.[18]

The inflation incident to this growing depreciation of the currency had operated to enrich the merchants and speculators, and to impoverish the people of small means. So serious was the situation that in 1741 Parliament forbade the issue by Massachusetts of further paper money. Since the very nature of such a currency required the issue of ever more, the province was practically at a stop economically. To circumvent the parliamentary prohibition, which applied only to notes issued by authority of the province, a group of local financiers organized a private Land Bank whose notes were based on the security of mortgages held on land or products of the land. This project, too, Parliament promptly outlawed. Meanwhile the capture of Louisburg, accomplished by the New Englanders on credit and enthusiasm, brought relief to Massachusetts from its financial tangle. To each of the colonies that had taken part in that glorious exploit Parliament appropriated money sufficient to reimburse them for their expenses. The amount assigned to Massachusetts came to about £180,000 sterling. On the insistence of Governor Shirley and Thomas Hutchinson, then Speaker of the Assembly, supplemented by a practical command from the home government, the Assembly agreed to use this money to retire the paper issues. In 1749 the specie arrived from England—653,000 oz. of silver and ten tons of copper, all in coins, which were exchanged for the well worn paper notes. Massachusetts was on a hard-money basis.[19]

But the deflation, like the inflation, bore harshly on the poorer people and even on the less agile among the wealthy. Samuel Adams' father, one of the directors of the defunct Land Bank, was ruined in the operation. Naturally Samuel, unable to cope with financial affairs, but without peer as a champion of the common man, looked with an ever more jaundiced eye upon Thomas Hutchinson, the wealthy errand boy of the King. And there were many Samuel Adamses, each with a private grudge against the prerogative men of their colonies.[20]

Nor were the new-rich an attractive class. Many had acquired their wealth by a type of privateering little better than piracy. Others had made their profits from the graft that is always incident to war contracts. The result was a distinct lowering of the moral standards of the people. It was a coarse age. There was, in all the colonies and in all walks of life, much drinking, much vulgar conversation, much gambling. In 1709, William Byrd had refused to allow a member of his household to attend a horse race because, as he said, "there was nothing but swearing and drinking there," and yet, as we know, Byrd himself sometimes drank too much and used language of which he was thoroughly ashamed. Forty years later, we find Governor Dinwiddie, urging the members of the Council and Burgesses of Virginia, "to discourage Gaming, Swearing, and immoderate Drinking, par-

ticularly at County Courts." Evidently conditions were getting worse rather than better.[21]

In 1730 a Rhode Island minister recounted a shocking
incident that occurred—of all places—at North Church, Boston. It seems that one Barter had "fallen into *ye prevailing
sin of drunkenness.*" To aid in his reformation he was given
the job of ringing the church bell. But one Sabbath, after
the sacramental vessels were set out for communion, but before the people arrived, Barter was faced with and yielded
to temptation. In fact he yielded so comprehensively that he
lay *dead drunk* in the belfry throughout the sermon and
sacrament time. "Oh, terrible and almost unheard-of wicked
action," exclaimed the narrator.[22]

Rough words and expressions, often lubricated by rich
tobacco juice, enlivened much of the conversation. *Son of
a bitch,* with suitable prefixes and affixes was a favorite
epithet. Profanity was heard everywhere. The Great Awakening had tempered the growing coarseness but the New
Light converts were often as offensive in their affectation of
piety as the sinners in their lack of it. In Massachusetts, the
law assessed a fine for every oath, and yet Doctor Hamilton,
during his visit to that province, tells the story of a Boston
lady who, being informed that he was a physician, burst
forth, "O Jesus! A physitian! Deuce take such odd looking
physicians."[23]

Hamilton was a Scotsman. He had taken his degree at
the Medical College of the University of Edinburgh. In 1739
he came to America and settled at Annapolis in the Province
of Maryland. There he developed a lucrative practice and
inspired a local lad named Thomas Bond to take up the
medical profession. Bond, after studying for a few years under
Hamilton, completed his education in Europe and opened
an office in Philadelphia, where, in 1751, he conceived the
idea of establishing an institution for the reception and cure
of sick persons. He outlined his plan to Benjamin Franklin,
who organized a publicity drive, and shortly the American
colonies had their first public hospital; also, within a few
years, their first medical school.[24]

And a medical school was needed. Some few of the doc-

tors, such as Alexander Garden at Charleston, Thomas
Graeme at Philadelphia, and Cadwallader Colden at New
York, had earned their degrees from European universities,
but the great majority had picked up their knowledge in a
haphazard way, and should not have been practicing. Among
these provincially trained physicians, Zabdiel Boylston, of
Boston, was a shining exception.[25]

In 1721 smallpox broke out in Boston. From a negro slave
which he owned, Cotton Mather heard a strange story. The
slave had been inoculated in Africa and told Mather that
the members of his tribe always protected themselves in that
manner against the dread disease. Mather issued an "Address to the Physicians of Boston" urging them to inoculate
their patients, and Boylston followed his advice. Instantly
there was an uproar. Inoculation, said its opponents, was an
un-Christian rite; probably with something of witchcraft in
it. Mobs attacked the homes of Mather and Boylston. The
clergy divided in a battle of pamphlets. The press took up
the fight. The *New England Courant,* recently established
by James Franklin, Benjamin's older brother, was particularly offensive in its attacks upon those who favored inoculation, so much so that Increase Mather publicly cancelled his
subscription, though he sent his grandson to quietly buy a
copy of the next issue, which latter fact Franklin duly publicized with the observation that subscriptions were cheaper
than single purchases.[26]

The lack of respect shown him in the battle for inoculation was a severe blow to the eighty-two-year-old Increase
Mather. The apostasy of Timothy Cutler the following year
(see page 371) completely broke the old man's spirit. He
took to his bed and within a few months was dead. Nor did
Cotton Mather long survive his father; in 1728 he too passed
to his last accounting; and thus ended a great, if not always
attractive, theological hierarchy.[27]

From the picture of Cotton Mather on page 435, we learn
much of the man and something of his times. In his features,
we sense the smug certainty that God was on his side and that
whatever he said or did was right; from his wig we gather
that he conformed in a measure to the prevailing fashion.

COTTON MATHER.

From the portrait by Peter Pelham.

Courtesy, American Antiquarian Society, Worcester, Mass.

435

This portrait was made by Peter Pelham, a Boston artist, as copy for an engraving which became widely distributed and is still the commonly accepted picture of Mather. Subsequently Pelham, who had learned his profession in England, engraved portraits of many other celebrated New Englanders. That of Timothy Cutler shown on page 372 of this volume, is from his hand. But art could not yet pay its way in America, and to supplement his income Pelham conducted a fashionable school in which, along with the three R's, dancing was taught. Agnes Surriage was one of his pupils.[28]

Another interesting portrait is that of Samuel Sewall on page 437. It was made in the 1720's when the Judge was over seventy years of age. We see no wig on Sewall's head. He wore his own hair. In fact, when wigs first came into vogue, and the minister of his church yielded to the prevailing fashion, Sewall, on a Lord's Day, betook himself to Benjamin Colman's somewhat unorthodox church on Brattle Street, thus to express his disapproval of his own minister's weakness. But the Judge did not take part in the battle over inoculation. One witch hunt had been enough for him. Or it may be that his thoughts were taken up with more personal matters. He was, at the time, a widower seeking a third wife. Cautiously, he had been paying court to Madam Katharine Winthrop, hoping to win her heart through gifts of religious books and half-pound boxes of candy, and to avoid her pointed suggestions that, if she married him, he would have to keep a coach and—Heaven defend him—wear a wig. When we look into those calculating old eyes, we can see why he and Madam Katharine failed to hit it off.[29]

Even in selecting an artist to paint his portrait, Sewall was conservative. He employed Nathaniel Emmons, a local lad of no great reputation. Most men of Sewall's eminence would have selected John Smibert, who had recently arrived in America with Dean Berkeley in the expectation of becoming Professor of Painting in the Indian college which the Dean planned to establish in Bermuda (see page 350). When that wild dream blew up, Smibert moved to Boston and shortly became the society artist of the city. But no more than Pelham could he make a living as a portrait painter. Ac-

SAMUEL SEWALL.

From the portrait by Nathaniel Emmons.

Courtesy, Massachusetts Historical Society, Boston.

cordingly, he opened a shop, where, in addition to his own work, he sold engraved prints "after the finest Pictures . . . done by Raphael, Michael Angelo, Poussin, Rubens and other the greatest Masters," thus introducing art to raw America. Perhaps the best example which we have of Smibert's own work is his portrait of William Pepperrell shown on page 420.[30]

But Boston did not have a monopoly on artists. "You see that originall," said the landlord of the Sign of the King's Arms at Perth Amboy, New Jersey, to Doctor Hamilton in 1744—pointing to a strange figure clothed in a loose woollen gown, a pair of thick worsted stockings without garters, and a greasy nightcap. "He is," continued the landlord, "an old batchellor, and it is his humor to walk the streets always in that dress. Tho he makes but a pitiful appearance, yet he is the proprietor of most of the houses in town. He is very rich, yet for all that, has no servant but milks his own cow, dresses his own vittles, and feeds his own poultry himself."[31]

The "originall" was John Watson. On page 439 is a reproduction of a portrait which he made of himself in 1720, when he was thirty-five years of age. Among his accounts, kept in an old arithmetic book, there stands the following: ". . . for painting in New York 1726 . . . Lewes Morris on pictor 3 o o." In other words, in 1726, for £3, Watson made a portrait of Lewis Morris, Lord of the Manor of Morrisania and Chief-justice of the Province of New York. Presumably it was the "pictor" shown on page 211. But we may assume that Watson did not lose on the transaction; he had been born in Scotland. Along with his portrait painting, and he had many well-to-do customers, he operated a print shop at Perth Amboy, he speculated in real estate, he loaned money, he imported and sold everything from hats, stockings and gloves to buttons and necklaces. No dancing lessons to simpering girls for this dour Scot.[32]

To these early "limners" we owe a deep debt. Out of their canvases or prints rise not only the faces of the men and women of the day, but also those details of costume which no words can describe. Most elusive and perhaps most talented among them was Robert Feke, born at Oyster Bay,

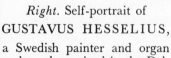

Left. Self-portrait of
JOHN WATSON
at age thirty-five.

Courtesy, Mr. Hall Park Mc-
Cullough, North Bennington,
Vt., and the American An-
tiquarian Society, Worcester,
Massachusetts.

Right. Self-portrait of
GUSTAVUS HESSELIUS,
a Swedish painter and organ
maker who arrived in the Delaware River region in 1711 and
made a number of well authen-
ticated portraits.

Courtesy, Pennsylvania Historical Society, Philadelphia.

Long Island, about 1705. During his youth and early manhood he had followed the sea—as a sailor. Where he learned to paint is a mystery. Doctor Hamilton met him at Newport in 1744 and called him a "most extraordinary genius . . . never having had any training." He had, said Hamilton, "exactly the phizz of a painter, having a long pale face, sharp nose, large eyes with which he looked upon you stedfastly, long curled black hair, a delicate white hand, and long fingers." His reputation was already well established. Within the next few years his brush placed him among the foremost of the early American artists, with commissions from people of wealth, taste and position in Newport, Boston and Philadelphia. Representative of his work is the portrait of William Bowdoin, of the New England merchant family, reproduced on page 441. This and a score of other superb portraits were completed in 1749 and 1750. And the latter year Feke vanishes from history.[33]

Unfortunately we have no information as to how these artists, with their paints and brushes and canvases and frames, travelled from city to city; probably they went by coastwise boats. But as the century wore along there was more and more overland travel, and intermittently, along the more travelled roads, efforts were made to provide public transportation. When Madam Knight journeyed westward from Boston in 1704 she had no alternative but to go on horseback. Seventeen years later, we find Peter Belton, a former post rider, announcing a weekly service between Boston and Newport carrying "Bundles of Goods, Merchandise, Books, Men, Women and Children, Money, &c." By the 1740's hired conveyances were common. One seen near Princeton, New Jersey, was thus described: "They travell high behind and low before, many of them running upon 4 wheels so that the horses bear no weight but only draw, and by this means they can travell att a great rate, perhaps 40 or 50 miles a day." Within a few years one James Wells was advertising through-trips between Philadelphia and New York —by boat up the Delaware and by stage across New Jersey.[34]

Coaches, privately owned or hackney, seldom went far from the streets of the cities. For short rides into the country

WILLIAM BOWDOIN.

From the portrait by Robert Feke.

Courtesy, The Bowdoin College Museum of Fine Arts, Brunswick, Me.

441

chairs or chaises (light two-wheeled vehicles usually drawn by a single horse) were popular. On roads where more power was required, the curricle, similar to the chaise but drawn by a team, was often used. Thus in 1759, Andrew Burnaby, an English visitor, on his way northward from Virginia, borrowed George Washington's curricle for the trip from Mount Vernon to Frederick, Maryland—and on the road ran into a strolling company of players. He took the opportunity to visit their theater, which, he tells us, "was a neat, convenient tobacco-house, well fitted up for the purpose." [35]

For long trips, however, horse and saddle remained the accepted mode of travel. When Doctor Hamilton started from Annapolis for New England in 1744, he was on horseback followed by his slave Dromo, also on horseback. Often he overtook or was overtaken by other horsemen who plodded along with him. The first leg of his route was through Baltimore and Wilmington to Philadelphia. From the latter city he followed the Delaware to the ferry opposite Trenton, crossed into Jersey, and continued to Perth Amboy where he ferried over to Staten Island, rode across to the Narrows, ferried over to Long Island, rode to Brooklyn and ferried to New York. That was the regular approach to the city from the southward. Newark Bay and the "meadows" barred the more direct presentday roads. And on leaving New York for the eastward Hamilton again crossed to Brooklyn and rode along the northern shore of Long Island—for a hundred miles —to the village of Southold where he crossed the Sound by boat to New London, Connecticut. From there he followed the well trodden Post Road to Newport and Boston. [36]

All along his route Hamilton found public houses where food and shelter were available. At the Susquehanna Ferry the boatman and his family were "att vittles . . . upon a homely dish of fish without any kind of sauce," when the doctor arrived. Graciously they invited him to join them, but his stomach was not equal to the offer. "They had," he said, "no cloth upon the table, and their mess was in a dirty, deep, wooden dish which they evacuated with their hands, cramming down skin, scales, and all." But this was an exception; from Philadelphia to Boston the inns were, on the whole, satisfactory and their gaily painted boards—Sign of the Half Moon and Heart (Huntington, Long Island), Sign of the White Horse (Newport, Rhode Island), Sign of the Dragon (Marblehead, Massachusetts) and many others—held out an acceptable welcome to. hungry man and beast.[37]

In 1745 William Logan and "Jemmy" Pemberton of Philadelphia had business in Georgia. Like Hamilton they went by horseback. Their route led southward to Cape Charles, Virginia, where, using tackle to hoist their horses aboard a sloop, they crossed the mouth of Chesapeake Bay to a point somewhat west of Norfolk—where they again took to the saddle. At Edenton, North Carolina, they sent their horses across the Chowan River on a makeshift ferry while they rowed over in a canoe. Passing through New Berne (Count Graffenried's old town) they went to Wilmington on the Cape Fear River—where the pirates formerly made their rendezvous (see page 310). There they gave up the notion of getting to Georgia on horseback—"impossible to get there by land, without expense danger & Fatigue," Logan recorded, and hired a boat.

Logan and Pemberton found occasional inns along their route, but not usually to their liking and worse as they advanced southward. In lower Delaware they had "a Tolerable bed" but a "very nasty room" and "vile chocolate." Between Edenton and Bath, in North Carolina, they were forced to put up at a "mean house," with "earthern floor," and "many air holes." For dinner they had "chickens boiled in very nasty manner," and they "slept poorly" on a "stinking ordinary Bed." Bad as these accommodations were, still they were symbols of white settlement where less than forty years earlier Lawson and Graffenried had found only a few Indians.[38]

Even more striking had been the changes in the area between New York and New Castle, Delaware. Where in 1664 Peter Alricks had found only a narrow path, a traveller of 1744 found "a very pleasant road" and many houses. At the falls of the Raritan was the "neat small city" of New Brunswick. At Princeton a village was growing up. Where in 1679 Jasper Danckaerts had seen only a few Swedish farm houses was the bustling city of Philadelphia. A similar transformation had taken place all up and down the coast. Most of the desirable tidewater land was in private possession. And still the population grew and the demand for land increased.[39]

In April, 1737, an advertisement appeared in the *Virginia Gazette:* "This is to give notice, That on the north side of the James River, near the Uppermost Landing, and a little below the Falls, is lately laid off . . . a Town called Richmond with streets 65 Feet wide in a pleasant and Healthy situation . . ." Lots were offered for sale on condition that the buyers would, within three years, build houses twenty-four feet long by sixteen feet wide fronting within five feet of the street. The advertisement was signed by William Byrd. The site was that of his father's old trading house. The result was the city of Richmond, today the capital of Virginia.[40]

Richmond was but one of many land schemes—promoted by individuals or by companies. Thousands of people who could not afford seaboard prices, or who simply yearned to move on, became ready customers for the new land. Other thousands—merchants, ministers, lawyers, college professors, people in all walks of life—people who had no thought of leaving their homes—bought and sold and traded in the shares of these land companies.[41]

The western push was on.

25

The Hinterland

WADING CREEKS, climbing over fall-
en trees, cutting a path through tangled
underbrush, some fifty or sixty people—men, women and children—were
pushing their way westward through
the foothills of the Catskill Mountains of New York in the
autumn of 1712. They were the vanguard of a much larger
group that in the following spring joined them on the fertile
lands of the Schoharie valley, thirty miles west of Albany.

To these people—Palatines they were commonly called—
the valley of the Schoharie was a "promised land," the end
of their long journey from their homes in Germany, from
their exile in England, from their voyage across the western
sea, from their servitude in the pine woods of Livingston
Manor. Part of that great mass of uprooted people from
whom Count Graffenried had recruited his colony at New
Berne (see pages 299–305), they had sailed from London
for New York—between three and four thousand of them—
only a few weeks after their fellow exiles had departed for
North Carolina. Their transportation to America was in-

tended to get them out of England; to make them self-sup-
porting; and to produce tar for the Royal navy. The tar was
to be made from pines that Livingston could well spare from
the broad acres of his manor—lying along the Hudson River,
above presentday Poughkeepsie; and until the project became profitable, the government was to feed and clothe the
Palatines. But the tar never did flow; the government declined to continue the support of its German wards; and in
1712 Governor Hunter of New York had no alternative to
bidding the Palatines take care of themselves. Most of them
scattered over the province wherever they could get jobs; the
remnant, under the belief that Schoharie had been promised
to them, emigrated, as we have seen, to that frontier valley.[1]

But not even Schoharie proved their "promised land"; it
had already been promised to others with more influence
among those who controlled New York politics. Nor would
the Palatines keep their farms as tenants. Some went deeper
into the New York hinterland where, at a place called German Flats—along the Mohawk River near where William
Johnson settled a few years later—they were given land to
the end that they might be a buffer against the French and
their Canadian Indians. Others dragged their few possessions
overland to one of the tributaries of the east fork of the Susquehanna River, made canoes and let the current guide them
to Pennsylvania. It was not a lonely trip. There was a considerable Indian village at Oquage, a few miles east of presentday Binghamton. At Binghamton itself was the important
village of Otseningo, inhabited by a mixed group of Onondaga and Shawnee Indians. Seventeen miles onward was
Owego, which town still retains the old Indian name. At the
spot now designated by the classical name of Athens—just
over the Pennsylvania line—stood the Indian village of Tioga.
Ten or twelve miles farther down, the canoes were abandoned for the overland path across country to the west branch
of the Susquehanna, where Madam Montour lived. She was
a French woman with a growing brood of half-breed children. Her village is commemorated by the modern town of
Montoursville. The next stopping place of importance was
Shamokin, at the forks of the Susquehanna (presentday Sun-

bury). This leg of the journey might be made by canoe, but from there onward the route to Tulpehocken, where many of the Schoharie people settled, was eastward over the Blue Mountains (see map page 449).[2]

Tulpehocken may, for all practical purposes, be identified with the area lying between the modern towns of Reading and Lebanon—still Indian land in the 1720's and very much in the hinterland of the province of Pennsylvania. Thither in 1729, as a late-migrating former resident of Schoharie, came Conrad Weiser with his wife and children. He had been a boy of fourteen when the Palatines arrived in New York. When the Livingston Manor experiment broke up he had been placed with the Mohawk Indians and had, as an adopted member of the nation, learned the Iroquois language. Later he had acquired a passable command of English.[3]

Weiser was thoroughly at home in the Tulpehocken region of Pennsylvania. His father-in-law had preceded him; all around him were German-speaking farmers; he was welcomed at the Lutheran church. Pennsylvania had from its beginning been a haven for unhappy Germans. We will recall the coming of the Frankfort and Crefeld people in 1683 (see page 102). A steady stream of other Germans had followed. In 1727, two years before Weiser came from Schoharie, James Logan, as land agent for the Young Proprietors (William Penn's sons), reported the arrival of fifteen hundred Palatines, direct from Europe.[4]

Almost as great as the German influx was the flood of settlers from northern Ireland, the so-called Scotch-Irish. In 1727 eight or nine shiploads arrived, and the number grew in the succeeding years. ". . . it looks as if Ireland is to send all her inhabitants hither," wrote Logan in 1729, adding, ". . . last week no less than six ships arrived, and every day two or three arrive also." The Scotch-Irish, like the Palatines, pushed past the settled coast line into the interior. Nor did they pay much respect to existing land titles, either proprietary or Indian. Where they saw unoccupied land that suited them, they took it. "It was," said they, "against the laws of God & Nature that so much land should be idle while so many Christians wanted it to labor on & to raise their bread." It is understandable why Logan, himself a Scot, looked upon the new Scottish immigrants as troublesome. Still, they settled farther into the hinterland than most of the Palatines would venture.[5]

The Scots were solidly Presbyterian. The Germans, on the other hand, represented many sects—Lutheran, Reformed, Dunkers, Mennonites, and fanatical dissenting groups within the sects.

Most spectacular of these odd religious variations was the community that gathered around Conrad Beissel, a mystically minded young German who arrived at Germantown, Pennsylvania, in 1720. It is probable that he came to America with the intention of joining the brotherhood established by Kelpius on Wissahickon Creek (see page 221), but that group had disappeared. He visited the Labadist colony at Bohemia Manor—fruit of Jasper Danckaert's trip to Maryland in 1679 (see pages 74 and 75), but found no comfort there. For a few years he acted as minister of a Dunker (Baptist) church at Conestoga, far out on the frontier, near the place where Lancaster, Pennsylvania, was coming into being. But none of these experiences satisfied Beissel's flaming mysticism, and about 1732 he took up the life of a hermit—in a cabin on Cocalico Creek, within a dozen miles of the Tulpehocken region where Conrad Weiser was just getting settled.[6]

Soon Beissel's spiritual quest attracted followers. Three young men, searching for salvation, joined him, and Beissel put them to clearing the land. Shortly two young women also applied for admission. That would have posed a problem for a more worldly soul, but not for Beissel: he had a Sister House built on the other side of the creek, and set them to work. More converts arrived, among them Maria Sauer, wife of Christopher Sauer, a Conestoga farmer who later, in Germantown, became the publisher of *Der Hoch-Deutsch Pennsylvanische Geschicht-Schreiber*. Beissel made Frau Sauer a prioress over the growing number of his female followers. More houses were built. More land was acquired. And Ephrata, as the Cocalico cloisters came to be known, prospered both physically and spiritually.[7]

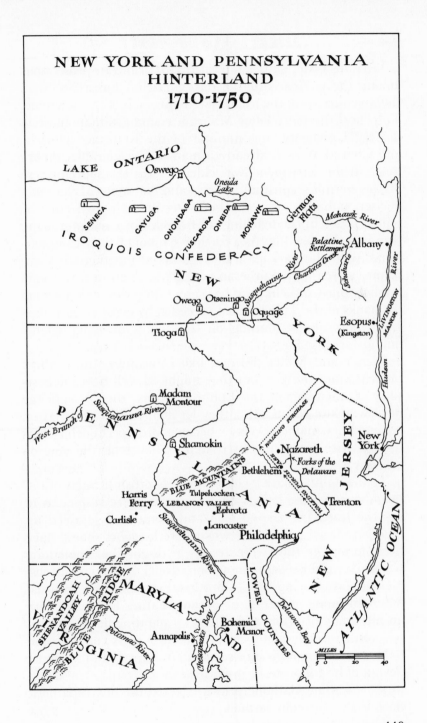

NEW YORK AND PENNSYLVANIA
HINTERLAND
1710·1750

LAKE ONTARIO

Oswego

Oneida Lake

SENECA CAYUGA ONONDAGA TUSCARORA ONEIDA MOHAWK

German Flats

Mohawk River

Palatine Settlement

Albany

I R O Q U O I S   C O N F E D E R A C Y

N E W

Susquehanna River

Charlotte Creek

Schoharie

Owego Otseningo

Oquage

Esopus (Kingston)

Y O R K

Livingston Manor

Hudson

Tioga

Madam Montour

West Branch of Susquehanna River

P E N N S Y L V A N I A

Shamokin

BLUE MOUNTAINS

Harris Ferry

Tulpehocken

LEBANON VALLEY

Ephrata

Carlisle

Lancaster

Philadelphia

Nazareth

Forks of the Delaware

Bethlehem

WALKING PURCHASE

NEW JERSEY

New York

Trenton

Susquehanna River

LOWER COUNTIES

Delaware Bay

ATLANTIC OCEAN

B L U E   R I D G E

SHENANDOAH VALLEY

VIRGINIA

M A R Y L A N D

Potomac River

Annapolis

Chesapeake Bay

Bohemia Manor

MILES
0   20   40

With his order thus established Beissel began proselyting among the members of the disorganized Dunker and Lutheran churches of the frontier settlements. In 1735 he visited Tulpehocken where Peter Miller, a young graduate of Heidelberg University, was minister of the Reformed church, and Conrad Weiser, already a man of considerable importance in the settlement, was elder. It was the supreme test of the hermit's spiritual power—and he won. Miller and Weiser, unhappy with the bickering in their own church, sensed peace in the teachings of Beissel. Both accepted baptism into the new life. As a further symbol of their complete break with the dark past they gathered together all their formerly treasured Lutheran books, put them in a pile and publicly burned them. And be it noted that this ceremony on the banks of the Tulpehocken preceded by eight years James Davenport's book burning on the shores of Long Island Sound (see page 379).[8]

Weiser and Miller did not, like Davenport, throw their breeches into the fire, but they might as well have done so since, as members of the Ephrata society, they wore long, narrow, white gowns. Also, they let their beards grow. They received new names: Weiser became Brother Enoch. They walked with slow, measured steps. They took the vow of celibacy.[9]

To the unimaginative German and Scottish farmers of the neighborhood, the goings on at Ephrata were suspicious to say the least. Unmarried men and women all jumbled up together; fasting monks; gowns where breeches should have been; probably they were Jesuits in disguise, or something worse. Nor did Beissel's innovations dispel the prevailing suspicions. From being simple Brother Friedsam (his spiritual name, meaning peaceful) he became Father Friedsam, with an hierarchy of priors and prioresses standing between himself and the lowly members. Not even prayers could ascend to Heaven without his intercession. For himself and the more devout of his followers he prescribed the tonsure. . . . "Croppies" (meaning Catholic priests), jeered the unsympathetic Scotch Presbyterian farmers.[10]

The daily routine at Ephrata was strict and austere. The

Brothers and Sisters arose early and worked late. There were midnight song services and frequent love feasts, including ceremonial foot-washings. Some of the Brothers worked in the fields or the mills; others engaged in craftsmanship—setting type, printing and binding books. The Sisters copied the musical scores of hymns—many of them composed by Beissel; did needlework, and painted pious mottoes in the bold German characters commonly known as *fraktur*. All worked for the society and all were supported by the society. There was no private property.[11]

Most members, upon entering the society, turned their existing property over to Beissel, but Conrad Weiser apparently kept title to his eight-hundred-acre farm and other fairly extensive property. Also, he appears to have spent a certain amount of time on his farm. And there temptation awaited him. Ann Eve, his good *hausfrau,* mother of his eight children, did not understand the blessings of spiritual peace—arrived at through celibacy and other means; she only knew that Brother Enoch was her Conrad—and Brother Enoch's celibacy evidently slipped a little; there was the usual addition to the Weiser family. Not even the device of making Ann Eve a member of the Ephrata society caused the vows of celibacy to operate; the Weiser family kept right on growing.[12]

Slowly Weiser's fundamental sanity reasserted itself. In 1743 or 1744 he cut off part of his long beard, discarded his gown and recognized the outside world by accepting an appointment as justice of the peace of Lancaster County. But Father Friedsam had a parting shot. Riding, horseback, along the road one day he and the former Brother Enoch met. Said Weiser, "I am amazed to see you on a horse when an ass was good enough for your Master." "Alas," Beissel replied, "all the asses have been made justices of the peace."[13]

Even before his essay into the realm of mysticism Weiser had been marked for public service. His knowledge of the Iroquois language and his tie of kinship with that Confederacy made him indispensable to the provincial authorities in carrying out a new and far-reaching Indian policy. With German and Scotch-Irish immigrants pouring into Pennsyl-

vania by the thousands the land office needed more land.
But no land could legally be opened for settlement until the
Indian title had been extinguished. That should have presented no great problem; the dwindling Delaware and the
restless Shawnee tribesmen were always ready to "drink"
their land, that is, to sell it for rum or for things that would
buy rum. Unfortunately they insisted on selling the same land
time after time—as often as they became thirsty. And there
was no central authority among them sufficient to compel
the petty chiefs to abide by their agreements. The only vestige
of Indian control over these troublesome natives resided in
the Iroquois who, by ancient conquest, had reduced them
to the status of "women." Ordinarily the Pennsylvanians
would have paid little attention to the Iroquois pretension,
but now, faced with the necessity of unclouded title to land,
James Logan seized upon the Indian interrelationship as a
basis for his own Indian policy. Pennsylvania would recognize the Iroquois lordship over the lesser tribes; the province
would settle all Indian affairs with the Iroquois; and, in return, the Iroquois would be called upon to force their subject peoples—Delawares, Shawnees and others—to accept and
live up to the agreements made.

In the autumn of 1731 a message went northward. Would
the Iroquois send "some of their wise old men of Authority"
to meet with their brothers of Pennsylvania? Since such an
invitation implied food, liquor and presents, "the wise old
men" readily accepted, and were generously entertained.
Conrad Weiser, himself Iroquois by adoption, acted as interpreter. Everything went off harmoniously. The visitors
were pleased with the assurance that at Philadelphia a fire
would always be burning where they and their brothers
of Pennsylvania could "sitt down . . . & take Council together." Incidentally, the Iroquois chiefs gave Pennsylvania
a quitclaim to the land lying in the Lebanon Valley; Conrad Weiser and his neighbors of Tulpehocken were assured
of legal titles to their farms."

The "fire" had been lighted. It remained to keep the road
between Philadelphia and the Iroquois Council house at
Onondaga free of briars and fallen trees, and that became

the responsibility of Conrad Weiser. He it was who, when important messages were to be delivered, followed the well-worn path over the mountains to Shamokin, up the west branch of the Susquehanna to Madam Montour's village, across country to the east branch, along it to Owego, and northward to Onondaga (presentday Syracuse, New York) —near two hundred miles as the crow flies, twice that as the path ran. Weiser it was who, when the visiting Iroquois delegations came down, met them at Shamokin or received them at Tulpehocken, and escorted them to Philadelphia—providing food for all, wagons for the lame, rum for the chiefs.[15]

The province, of course, footed the bill for entertainment as well as for the presents that the Indians always expected and always received. And James Logan, land agent for the Proprietors, saw to it that the province received its money's worth. Huge areas of land east and west of the Susquehanna River were cleared for settlement by the good will of the "wise old men of Authority." White men built their homes and cleared their farms ever deeper in the hinterland.[16]

It was an unusually large, and hungry, delegation of Iroquois that descended upon Weiser in the late spring of 1742. On their way to Philadelphia they stopped at "Stenton" for a visit with Logan. What his beautiful lawns and gardens must have looked like as the horde moved on may well be imagined. Ostensibly the Indians had come to the council fire for the purpose of collecting presents due on account of Susquehanna land. Logan, however, had an additional piece of business on the agenda—an Iroquois confirmation of the so-called Walking Purchase.[17]

This Walking Purchase went back to an agreement made between William Penn and the Delaware Indians in 1686. In return for certain payments Penn was to receive a strip of land along the Delaware River—starting opposite present-day Trenton, New Jersey, and extending northwesterly, *as far as a man could walk in a day and a half.* It is likely that both Penn and the Indians figured that such a walk would not exceed thirty or forty miles, and that the northern boundary would fall well short of the Forks of the Delaware— where the city of Easton stands today. The payment for the land had been made; the purchase had been confirmed two or three times by the Delawares; but the limits were so indefinite as to cause constant bickering between Indian claimants and white settlers. By 1735 it became evident that the only way to avoid a minor Indian war to have the purchase "walked"—and the Pennsylvania officials went about the affair in a businesslike manner. They surveyed the line to be walked; they had the underbrush cleared away; they hired a speedy walker; they provided horsemen to carry food and drink; and in the summer of 1737 the "walk" was made. As the first day wore along the Indians, struggling to keep up, became increasingly unhappy, ". . . you run," they said, "that's not fair, you was to Walk."

When the sun went down that first day the "walker" was almost at the Forks of the Delaware; at noon the next day he was twenty miles beyond; a total of sixty-four miles had been walked in the day and a half. All the desirable land at the Forks lay within the Purchase. Worse yet, from the Indians' point of view, the return line to the Delaware River —drawn at a right angle from the "walk"—reached around a bend in the river and took in land that the original grantors had never dreamed of including or had any right to include (see map on page 449).

Naturally the Delaware Indians were irritated; they even threatened to hold their homes by force. And it was to meet that threat that the Iroquois were gathered around the Philadelphia council fire in 1742. Solemnly Canasetego, head of the Iroquois delegation, examined the documents bearing on the Walking Purchase. Pontifically he delivered the verdict. "How come you," said he to the Delaware chiefs, "to take upon you to Sell Land at all. We conquer'd You. We made Women of you. You know you are Women and can no more sell Land than Women. Nor is it fit you should have the Power of Selling Lands since you would abuse it. This land that you claim is gone through Your Guts. You have been furnished with Cloaths and Meat and Drink by the Goods paid you for it and now you want it again like Children as you are . . ." There was much more but the gist of it was that Canasetego ordered the Delaware to get out of the Walking Purchase and do it quick.[18]

The Delaware dared not argue with their fierce overlords. They got out, but they left a few mangled white settlers behind them. Nor did they stay long at Shamokin where the Iroquois had told them to go. Most of them joined the wandering Shawnees already on the upper Ohio River, and there they listened with open ears to promises of revenge held out to them by the French traders and officers who dominated that region.[19]

But to the Penns it was clear that Logan's Indian policy had paid off. New settlers rushed into the Forks of the Delaware. The Moravians were already there—pacifistic refugees from war-torn Georgia (see pages 362 and 364). In 1741 they had bought land near the Forks where, at a place to which they gave the name of Bethlehem, Count Zinzendorf joined them on Christmas Eve of the same year. He had made the long trip from Saxony partly in the hope that he could unite the squabbling German sects into a single church, and partly with a view to establishing missions among the Indians. In neither project was he particularly successful. The only point on which the Lutherans, Dunkers, Mennonites and followers of Beissel would agree was that they would not agree with the Count. A trip into the Indian country turned out equally badly. Conrad Weiser, still wearing his Ephratan beard, was engaged as guide; and gaily, in the autumn of 1742, the expedition headed north and west over the mountains to Shamokin. In addition to Zinzendorf and Weiser there were in the party two men and two women, one of whom, Anna Nitschman, later became the Count's wife. They were equipped with saddle horses and pack horses. They had tents. There was even a small library of books strapped on the back of one of the horses. But the Indians proved to be less attractive than the Count had expected. They were, Zinzendorf discovered, "averse to wearing breeches." They did not want to be converted. They "showed no respect for his person"; they were given to "making fun of him"; they had no better manners than "to break wind in his presence"; in short they "did not know how to behave with a Reichs Count." Disillusioned, the Count returned to the settlements and early in 1743 sailed for Europe.[20]

Despite Zinzendorf's departure, or perhaps because of it,

the Moravian centers at Bethlehem and nearby Nazareth continued to grow in numbers and influence. By 1759, under the strict supervision of Bishop Spangenberg, they were operating more than two thousand acres of land; they had thousands of head of livestock; they had five mills, two inns and forty-eight farm buildings. There were seventeen Choir Houses, as they called the barrack-like buildings in which the people were housed; there were five schools and twenty buildings where various kinds of trades were carried on. As at Ephrata, all property was held on a communal basis. Marriage, however, was encouraged, though the children, at a tender age, were taken from their mothers and reared in a community nursery. As they grew older the boys and girls were placed in separate Choir Houses. Single men and single women lived in other Choir Houses; and there were appropriate Choir Houses for married men and women. Every detail of the lives of every member of the community was directed and supervised; they worked at the trades or tasks that they were told to work at; they loved and married the persons they were told to love and marry. Their reward was peace and an opportunity to adore their Saviour. Music played a great part in their lives. Hymns, in endless variations, were composed and sung.[21]

In addition to overseeing all the activities at Bethlehem and Nazareth, Bishop Spangenberg and his associates went up and down the back country preaching and missionizing among the German farmers who, having filled up the valleys of Pennsylvania, were pushing south and west into Virginia. The Shenandoah Valley particularly attracted the Germans, and it was proving much easier of access from the northward than through the pass in the Blue Ridge publicized by Spotswood and his Knights of the Golden Horseshoe (see page 280). From the Lebanon Valley of Pennsylvania to Harris Ferry (Harrisburg), down the level stretch where Carlisle, Chambersburg and Hagerstown stand today, across the Potomac and on southward—Route 11 as the modern motorist knows it—was a natural road.[22]

But the Blue Ridge was not the only barrier that stood between Virginia and the Shenandoah Valley. In 1722 Gov-

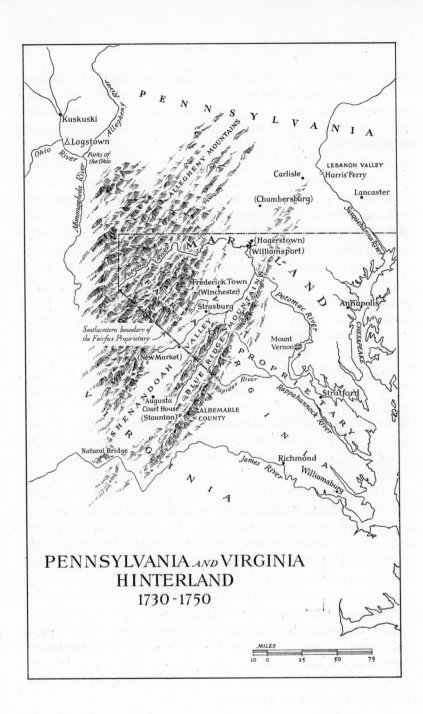

PENNSYLVANIA *and* VIRGINIA
HINTERLAND
1730-1750

MILES

10 0   25   50   75

ernor Spotswood, thinking of his iron mine and his land east
of the Ridge, had negotiated a treaty with the Iroquois Confederacy in which it was agreed that their warriors, when on
forays against the southern Indians, should pass to the westward of "the high Ridge of Mountains which extends all
along the Frontiers of Virginia." The result was that the
Shenandoah Valley, just west of the Ridge, became a main
highway for Iroquois bent on collecting Catawba scalps and
for Catawbas bent on collecting Iroquois scalps—time-hon-
ored pastimes which neither group was willing to forego, but
dangerous for white men whose hair might serve in a pinch.[23]

Another serious barrier to settlement in the Shenandoah
Valley was uncertainty regarding land titles. Did the land
come under the authority of Virginia or was it a part of the
Fairfax Proprietary? As will be recalled (page 394), Lord
Fairfax consistently claimed the utmost area specified in his
patent, namely, all the land between the Potomac and the
Rappahannock rivers—to their farthermost springs. If that
interpretation held, the northern part of the Valley lay within
the Northern Neck, and legal titles could be had only from
the Fairfax agent. The situation was one into which few responsible Virginians cared to venture. "King" Carter, secure
through his position as agent for Fairfax, took out patents for
a considerable acreage; some restless frontiersmen climbed
over the Ridge and built their cabins; but it remained for
Jost Hite, a Pennsylvania German, to become the first large-
scale land promoter in the Valley. In 1731 he acquired a
contract, issued under the authority of the Governor and
Council of Virginia rather than of Fairfax, by which he was
to receive one thousand acres of land for each family he settled in the Shenandoah. Within the next few years he brought
in ninety-four families, mostly Germans from Pennsylvania,
and seated them near the place that later came to be known
as Strasburg. For the moment Hite was the great landowner
of the Valley. But more prudent men awaited the outcome
of the suit which Lord Fairfax was steadily pressing before
the Privy Council in England.[24]

Meanwhile speculators were taking up large areas of land
in the uncontested southern part of the Valley, where Staun-

ton and Lexington stand today, and bringing in Scotch-Irish settlers by the hundreds.[25]

Then, in 1744, came the inevitable war with France—King George's War, it is usually called. While the French were scoring initial successes in Nova Scotia, and Governor Clinton, of New York, was rushing re-enforcements to Fort Oswego, the governors of Pennsylvania, Maryland and Virginia moved to protect their frontier settlements. As always, the Iroquois held the key to Indian action. If they sided with the French, the torch and the scalping knife would sweep through the entire back country; if they sided with the English, the French raiding parties could not penetrate to the western hinterland. It was, therefore, vitally important that the Iroquois be held to their traditional friendship; in particular, it was high time to settle an overdue bill presented by the Iroquois to Virginia and Maryland for land lying back of their frontiers. To be sure, the Iroquois had but a shadowy claim to the land in question, but things being as they were, it was better to pay up, and then, as Pennsylvania had done in similar cases, require the Iroquois to guarantee the title.[26]

Accordingly, an "enlarged" council fire was lighted at the frontier Pennsylvania town of Lancaster—a "lousy" place, infested with "German fleas and bugs," we are told—and thither travelled official delegations from Virginia and Maryland to meet with the chiefs of the Iroquois. Present as commissioners for Virginia were Thomas Lee and William Beverley, with several "Flaming fine gentlemen" in their train. Lee we have already met—as the master of "Stratford" and one-time agent for the Northern Neck (see pages 284 and 392). Beverley, too, we have met briefly; his birth, in 1698, had cost Ursula Byrd her life and had made a recluse of the able Robert Beverley (see pages 263 and 278). The Maryland commissioners were men of prominence in their province. Governor Thomas, of Pennsylvania, acted as host to the visitors.[27]

Most of these worthies were already at Lancaster when, on June 22, 1744, the chiefs of the Iroquois, "with their followers and attendants, to the number of 252, arrived in town." Witham Marshe, secretary to the Maryland commissioners, watched them come in. "They marched in very good order," he tells us, "with Cannasateego, one of the Onondaga chiefs at their head; who, when he came near to the courthouse wherein we were dining, sung, in the Indian language, a song, inviting us to a renewal of all treaties heretofore made, and that now to be made." Cannasateego will be identified as the chief who admonished the Delawares at Philadelphia in 1742.

The Iroquois had been escorted to Lancaster by Conrad Weiser, who, as Mr. Marshe discovered, was "highly esteemed" by them. In addition to serving as interpreter, Weiser saw to it that the visiting savages were fed and housed. On their arrival, he conducted them to "some vacant lots in the back part of the town, where sundry poles and boards were placed. Of these, and some boughs of trees, from the woods, the Indians made *wigwams,* or cabins, wherein they resided during the treaty."

The town was crowded with people: many were there on official business; others were there in the hope of profiting from the treaty; some were there just to see the fun. Madam Montour had come down with the Indians and was quite a social success. Another social event was a war dance in which the young bucks hopped, in "a frantic fashion," around a roaring fire (on a hot June night) howling "Yohoh! Bugh!" while three old men beat out the time on drums. Almost as good was a show put on by Governor Thomas. One evening, while at dinner with the commissioners and their secretaries, he spied two Germans passing by, one with a harp and the other with a fiddle. Come in and make music was the gubernatorial order, and the impromptu orchestra complied with such effect that Andrew Hamilton, of the first families of Philadelphia, began to jig. A young Iroquois buck joined in, and the dance was on. Even Conrad Weiser's toes must have twitched though he still had one foot in Ephrata and had cut off only a part of his beard. The Governor's parting present to the Indians was a promise that he would order the removal of the rest of Weiser's beard because it "frightened their Children." [28]

CONRAD WEISER.

Courtesy, Pennsylvania German Society, Philadelphia.

Leisurely the real business of the treaty got under way. There were speeches by the commissioners and by the chiefs, and then the Indians asked bluntly what Maryland and Virginia were prepared to pay. With little bickering the Maryland commissioners laid their offering on the table:—two hundred shirts, forty-seven guns, four dozen jew's-harps, etc., £220/15 in all. Maryland was buying good will only. Virginia, however, in addition to good will, was buying land, a vast, indefinite amount of it, and was proportionally cautious. Finally her commissioners opened their chests of goods and displayed a selection of knives, hatchets, blankets and other things dear to the heart of the Indian. Those goods "and Two Hundred Pounds in Gold, which lie on the Table, we will give you, our Brethren of the Six Nations," said the Virginians, "upon Condition that you immediately make a Deed recognizing the King's Right to all the Lands that are, or shall be, by his Majesty's appointment, in the Colony of Virginia."[29]

It was a tense moment. Back of these words—"all the Lands that are, or shall be . . . in the Colony of Virginia"—lay the royal patent of 1609 granting to the colony all the land lying "west and northwest" from its seaboard, a sizable piece of North America in much of which the authority of the Iroquois was non-existent. But the chiefs assented, with one qualification, namely that, in addition to the gold and the trade goods, they be given some rum to drink on the way home. This request the commissioners readily gratified, and thereafter the treaty moved smoothly forward: War parties would avoid the Shenandoah Valley; the Iroquois would keep their subject tribes from joining with the French; the covenant chain between the Iroquois and the English was made bright and strong. The final reading of the treaty was greeted by a series of guttural "Yo-hahs"* from the chiefs, and the meeting broke up in the best of humor.[30]

Lee and Beverley, veteran land speculators though they were, must have been a bit dazed as they rode homeward from Lancaster. The area they had opened for settlement was so vast that would-be colonizers scarcely knew where to

*Meaning, "It is well."

begin. Some asked for and secured grants in what is now western Pennsylvania; others located their lands even farther westward.[31]

There still remained the question as to how far Lord Fairfax's grant reached. In 1745 came the decision, direct from the King's Privy Council. Fairfax's claim was upheld in every detail. His southwestern boundary was a line from the headspring of the Rapidan branch of the Rappahannock to the headspring of the north branch of the Potomac. Unquestionably Jost Hite's land lay squarely within the Fairfax Proprietary. Hite was doomed to a lifetime of litigation; the Virginia Land Office was doomed to the loss of rich quitrents; but for the Washingtons, Lawrence and George, and for other friends of the Fairfax family, the decision meant first chance to secure choice parcels of valuable land. It was in the Fairfax Proprietary that George Washington, as a boy of sixteen, learned the mystery of surveying and earned enough money to begin buying land for himself. There, too, he made the shocking discovery that white human beings did not all speak the English language. He was with a surveying party. All day long the German settlers—men, women and children—had been watching the proceedings, and with good reason, since their farms were perhaps at stake. To young Washington they were "as ignorant a set of people as the Indians." His reason for so classifying them was, "They would never speak English but, when spoken to, they speak all Dutch." Tidewater was meeting the frontier.[32]

The official survey of Fairfax's southwestern boundary was made in 1746. Starting on the eastern shoulder of the Blue Ridge, the line crossed the Valley in a northwesterly direction, almost through the presentday town of New Market, and ended where southwestern Maryland now points into West Virginia. It was an interesting group of men who supervised and made this survey, who selected the starting and the stopping points, who dragged the instruments over mountains, across rivers and through tangles of laurel. Colonel William Fairfax, agent for the Proprietary, was there as a commissioner for Lord Fairfax. Colonel William Beverley, still thinking about his experiences at Lancaster, was there as a commissioner for Virginia. Thirty years had passed since as a boy, riding with the Knights of the Golden Horseshoe, he had first looked down from the Blue Ridge upon the Shenandoah Valley. Now, in addition to his official duties, he had a personal interest in the position of the Fairfax line; he owned thousands of acres in the southern end of the Valley—where the Scotch-Irish were making their settlements.[33]

Also in the party, associated with Beverley as a commissioner for Virginia, was Joshua Fry, formerly a professor of mathematics and natural philosophy at William and Mary College, but more recently a judge in the newly formed Albemarle County. And with Fry, as one of the surveyors, was Peter Jefferson. He, too, was from Albemarle where, in a very modest house, his little son Thomas was toddling about. Five years later Fry and Jefferson were to collaborate in making the first good map of Virginia.*[34]

Another of the surveyors was Thomas Lewis, a son of John Lewis, pioneer settler in the southern part of the Valley. John had come to the Shenandoah region in 1732 direct from Ireland. His best-known biography is the epitaph carved on his tombstone—high on a hillside overlooking the city of Staunton. It reads, in part, as follows:

> Here lies the remains of
> John Lewis
> who slew the Irish lord, settled Augusta County
> Located the town of Staunton
> and furnished five sons to fight the battles of the
> American Revolution

We can readily understand why a Scotch-Irish tenant would have slain his Irish landlord, and we can believe that Lewis did so. No one will question his claim regarding the town of Staunton. Also, that he gave five sons to the American Revolution is a matter of history. But that he settled Augusta County, Virginia, is a slight overstatement. Augusta County, formally constituted in 1745, was a very large county; it included presentday western Virginia, West Virginia, Ohio, Kentucky, Indiana, Illinois, Michigan, Wisconsin and parts

*The chapter-head decorations in the present volume are based upon the cartouche of the Fry and Jefferson map.

west, not even excluding, in the eyes of good Virginians, California. It had become thus extensive because of the cession made by the Iroquois at Lancaster in 1744.[35]

But large as Augusta County was, it still was not large enough for the restless land hunters who poured into it. Some, who could not afford the price of land in the Shenandoah Valley, pushed on southward, crossed to the easterly side of the Blue Ridge and settled—with or without a title—in the western part of Lord Granville's grant (see page 317 and map on page 471). Typical of these was the Boone family, among whom was a lad named Daniel.[36]

Others went still farther south into the hinterland of South Carolina, which colony had, for several years, been actively promoting such settlements. In 1730, to be exact, Governor Robert Johnson had initiated the creation of "townships," consisting of approximately twenty-thousand acres each, and so constituted as to create a small-farming, white, Protestant population in the regions lying back of the great slave-operated tidewater plantations. Settlers in these townships were given fifty acres for each member of the family, including servants and slaves; and further to encourage immigration the colony set aside, from the importation duty levied on negro slaves, a fund from which to pay the transportation of poor people and to provide them with tools and immediate subsistence. Under this arrangement thousands of Swiss and Germans, along with many Scotch-Irish, had poured into the new townships—Queensboro on the Peedee, Fredericksburg on the Wateree, Saxe Gotha where the Broad and the Saluda join to form the Congaree, and New Windsor on the Savannah, to mention but a few. The map on page 471 will help in locating them.[37]

New Windsor was laid out in the early 1730's. Only twenty-six families with British names took up land within the first few years. The real settlement resulted from a visit made in 1734, by the agent for a group of prospective Swiss immigrants. He had viewed each of the new townships, decided upon New Windsor, and entered into a contract to bring over a number of families—the colony providing food, tools and cattle sufficient to get the people started, and setting out the land without charge for surveying. Two years later the immigrants arrived, some fifty families, under the leadership of the Reverend Bartholomew Zouberbuhler, their minister, and John Tobler, former governor of the canton from which they came. Some succumbed to the change of climate, but the majority fitted into the life of the back country and within a generation were indistinguishable from their neighbors. Typical perhaps was Tobler's career. He operated a fair-sized farm; he opened a store at nearby Savannah Town; he invented a machine for shelling rice; he published an almanac; and when he died he left £83 in cash, almost £2,000 in bonds and mortgages, two negroes, two pictures, an organ, a flute, a clock, and a small library of German books.[38]

Saxe Gotha held attractions for traders as well as for farmers. Through it ran the trading path from Charleston to the Cherokee towns; from it branched a path to the Catawba towns. Even before the establishment of the township in 1733, Thomas Brown, a Scotch-Irishman, had been trading with the Catawbas and shortly set up a store near the forks of the Broad and the Saluda. Naturally, he and other speculators took up land in the new township, but, as in New Windsor, many of the actual tillers of the soil came from Switzerland and Germany—most of them assisted by the township bounty fund. And, like the settlers in New Windsor, the Saxe Gothans justified the assistance given them. A Charleston merchant, in 1733, testified that they were "industrious and settling apace." Fifteen years later, when Thomas Brown died, it was a former Swiss bounty settler, Herman Geiger, who bought his store. Soon, in addition to the regular business, Geiger was serving food and drink to travellers on the Cherokee trading path. When he died his estate, appraised at nearly £1,900, included nine negroes, a thousand pounds in accounts collectible, thirty-three horses, sixty cattle, seventy hogs, two four-horse wagons, a grist mill, a fanning mill, a saw mill, a trading boat, a book of sermons, a Bible, two decanters and twenty liquor glasses. The bounty boy had done all right.[39]

Sixty miles up the Saluda valley, northwesterly from Saxe Gotha, the Charleston-Cherokee path was joined by a path

coming up from Savannah Town and also heading for the
Cherokee country (see map on page 471). The junction was
known as Ninety-Six, that being its estimated distance, in
miles, from Keowee, the nearest of the Cherokee towns. The
location was an attractive one—either for trade or farming—
and in 1746 a group of speculators from Augusta County,
Virginia, had offered to bring in a large number of families,
provided Governor Glen would clear the title by purchase
from the Cherokee Indians.[40]

Unfortunately at this time, the Cherokee were not in exactly the humor to be approached on such a subject. For one
thing, they were just recovering from the communistic in-
doctrination of Christian Gottlieb Priber, one of those vision-
aries who thrives best in a primitive society. Priber, said to
have been born in Saxony not far from the home of Count
Zinzendorf, came to Georgia among the early immigrants
to that paradise of the philanthropists. Shortly he was in
South Carolina and in 1736 he turned up at the Cherokee
town of Tellico (whose ghost hovers over the presentday
motorist as he speeds southward from Knoxville, Tennessee
—across the T. V. A. bridge that spans the Little Tennessee
River—and onward toward Atlanta). There, at Tellico,
Priber shed his civilized garb, retaining only a shirt and flap,
cut his hair Indian fashion and mastered the Cherokee language. Having thus become one with the Indians he undertook to remake them. He made old chief Moytoy "Emperor"
and himself "Principal Secretary of State"; he proposed a
communistic form of society—all property, all wives, all children to be held in common; he insisted that the French
should be treated with as much kindness as the English; and,
worst of all, he advised against the sale of land to the ever
expanding English. It is not to be wondered that the Governor of South Carolina directed Ludovick Grant, a highly
respected trader in the Cherokee towns, to arrest Priber and
bring him down to Charleston. Grant, as he told the story,
did his best, but found that Priber was "well apprized of my
design and laughed at me, desiring me to try it, in so insolent
a manner that I could hardly bear with it; and I told him
that although I knew the Indians would not permit me to

Carry him down to be hanged, Yet could not find fault, I hoped, if I should throw him into the Fire. . . ." But Grant dared not do even that. Finally, in 1743, a band of Creek Indians, in the assurance of a reward from Oglethorpe, kidnapped the Principal Secretary of State, and sent him down to Georgia where he died under the rigors of philanthropic imprisonment.[41]

But Priber's teachings, though still fresh in their minds, were not the only deterrents to Cherokee compliancy in 1746. King George's war was in full swing. Many of the Shawnee and Delaware, booted out of Pennsylvania in 1742, had migrated to the upper Ohio region. They had carried with them no love for the grasping English and in their new homes had easily come under the influence of the French, which influence they extended southward along the Warriors Path (see maps on pages 471 and 478). The Cherokee were more afraid of their fierce northern visitors than they were of the Carolinians.[42]

As a matter of fact, the Assembly and Council of South Carolina, dominated as they were by the rich tidewater planters, had at the time little interest in frontier affairs or Indian policy. Governor Glen, on the other hand, had the vision to see that the contest for empire then being waged with France might well be won or lost in the Indian villages. Also, it may be that he visualized some personal profits in the Indian trade. In the spring of 1746, accompanied by two hundred and fifty armed horsemen, he set forth from Charleston for a series of visits with the Indians of the Carolina hinterland. Near Saxe Gotha he met the Catawbas and confirmed the long friendship between themselves and the English. Riding on westerly, he found the "Emperor" and other leading chiefs of the Cherokee encamped at Ninety-Six, and evidently won their confidence. Sixty miles to the southward, at Fort Moore, on the Savannah River, he held a conference with some of the head men of the Creeks.[43]

The Creeks proved a disappointment to the Governor. They liked to trade with the English at Savannah Town; they liked to trade at that new place called Augusta, on the westerly side of the river; but they saw no point in giving up any bargains offered at Fort Toulouse, the French trading post at the forks of the Alabama River. They were, they figured, "better supply'd with Goods when they lived well with both French and English."[44]

Nor did Glen have better luck in an attempt to lure the Choctaw trade away from the French. Red Shoe, who as we know (page 344) had a liking for English goods, promised his help, but when the long English pack-train, financed by Governor Glen, plodded into the Choctaw country it found no customers; the French saw to it that any Indian who ventured to trade with the Carolinians came to grief; Red Shoe was knocked in the head by his irate tribesmen.[45]

But with the Cherokees Governor Glen's blandishments paid off. In February, 1747, they deeded Ninety-Six to Carolina. Soon outfitting stores and places of entertainment were established at this strategic crossroads; soon traders in increasing number were pushing their pack-trains up the path to the Cherokee towns, and longer pack-trains, loaded with skins, were plodding down to Charleston. Soon the Cherokee were so tied by economic bonds to Carolina that the head men were demanding an English fort to protect them against possible French aggression. And in 1753, supposedly ninety-six miles, but in reality only about seventy miles up the path, right beside the Lower Cherokee town of Keowee, there arose Fort Prince George, bristling with cannon and garrisoned by English soldiers.[46]

When the Overhill Cherokee (those who lived over the mountains) saw the fort at Keowee they not unreasonably protested that it served little purpose. It was against the Overhill towns—Chota, Tellico and others—that the first blow from the French or the French Indians would fall; those towns, too, must have a fort if they were not to join the French. On July 2, 1755, a delegation from the Cherokee, seven hundred strong, met Governor Glen on the Saluda. Chief Attakullakulla, who as a boy, in 1730, had accompanied Sir Alexander Cuming to England (see pages 353–354), was their orator. "We, our wives and children, are all children of the great King George," said he. Opening a bag of earth and laying it at the Governor's feet, he said, "We freely surrender part of our possessions." Holding up a bow and arrow, he said, "These are all the arms we have for our defense . . .

Give us arms and we will go to war against the enemies of
the great King." The offer of the Cherokee, made there on
the Saluda River on July 2, 1755, was even more than the
imperialistically minded British Board of Trade could have
hoped for—though General Braddock could have used some
of those warriors on the Monongahela River a week later.
The following year Fort Loudoun was built—on the Little
Tennessee, practically beside Chota, chief town of the Over-
hills.[47]

By this treaty of the Saluda, South Carolina's presump-
tive frontier had been pushed beyond the mountains, and it
seemed high time. A growing population was looking for
new land. The townships had done their work. From them
as centers the farms had spread and met, and whereas in 1729
the population of the colony had consisted of ten thousand
whites and twenty thousand negro slaves, in 1759 it consisted of thirty-six thousand whites and fifty-five thousand
negro slaves. It was the back country, with its many small
farms and few plantations, that had wrought this transformation.[48]

The way of life in the back country was primitive even for
the well-to-do. Houses framed from hewn or sawed plank
were rare; glass for windows was even more rare. Also, houses
with more than one room were rare. Isaac Cloud's home on
the Little Saluda was probably typical; in its one room, on
a night in May, 1751, there lay down to sleep Isaac and
his wife, their two children, a hired man and two visiting
Shawnee Indians. The Indians and the hired man slept on
the floor.[49]

Corn was the staff of life. Pone and sow belly were standard menus. The land was suited to grain, but difficulties of
transportation made all heavy products valueless. Except
for the Cherokee Path there were no roads that would accommodate wagons, even if the settlers had possessed such
vehicles. Mostly it was subsistence farming with a few packs
of cowhides, or some cattle and hogs on the hoof, to exchange
for outside necessities.

With cowhides plentiful there was no lack of leather for
shoes and boots. Men's shirts and breeches were commonly
of the same material. One observer stated that the women

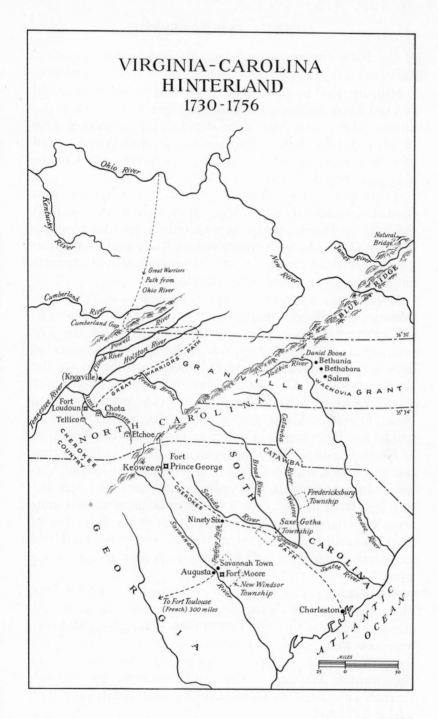

VIRGINIA-CAROLINA
HINTERLAND
1730-1756

Ohio River

Kentucky River

Great Warriors
Path from
Ohio River

New River

James River

Natural Bridge

Cumberland River

Cumberland Gap

Powell River

Holston River

Clinch River

Clinch River

BLUE RIDGE

36° 30'

(Knoxville)

Tennessee River

Fort Loudoun

Chota

Tellico

Etchoe

CHEROKEE COUNTRY

NORTH CAROLINA

GREAT WARRIORS PATH

French Broad

GRANVILLE

Daniel Boone

Yadkin River

Bethania
Bethabara
Salem

WACHOVIA GRANT

35° 34'

Keowee

Fort Prince George

SOUTH CAROLINA

Catawba River

CATAWBA

CHEROKEE

Saluda River

Ninety Six

Broad River

Wateree River

Fredericksburg Township

Saxe-Gotha Township

Pee Dee River

CAROLINA

Savannah River

Trading Path

Savannah Town

Augusta
Fort Moore
New Windsor Township

To Fort Toulouse
(French) 300 miles

GEORGIA

Santee River

Charleston

ATLANTIC OCEAN

MILES
25   0   50

of the back country were never clothed in more than "a shift and one thin petticoat."

Still, life had its pleasures. Rum the frontiersman would and did have. Tobacco, for smoking and chewing, was home grown. There were enough fiddles in every community to supply music for dances. John Tobler, at New Windsor, and Martin Friday, on the Congaree (near presentday Columbia), had organs.[50]

There were a few organized churches—Presbyterian and Baptist—but not enough to serve more than a small part of the country. Itinerant preachers visited the settlements occasionally. The Moravian missionaries from Bethlehem, following the road blazed by the Virginians, sought converts among the German-speaking people.[51]

It was probably from the reports of these wandering missionaries that Bishop Spangenberg got the idea of establishing a new Moravian center to the southward. In the late summer of 1752 he, with a few of his associates, rode, on horseback, from Bethlehem to Philadelphia and on down the Eastern Shore of Chesapeake Bay to Cape Charles where they crossed by boat to Norfolk and rode on to Edenton, North Carolina. There they met Lord Granville's agent. As will be recalled (page 317), Granville held the northern part of North Carolina under a proprietary grant similar to that under which Lord Fairfax held the Northern Neck of Virginia. In other words, Granville owned the land, and the proceeds from its sale as well as the subsequent annual quitrents went into his pocket. Like Fairfax or the Governor of South Carolina, he was interested in getting his land sold to permanent settlers, and had made an offer to the Moravians.[52]

Spangenberg and his party were there to consider the offer. Together with Granville's surveyor they rode westward, two hundred and fifty and more miles, looking for a location, and soil, that would suit them. On the watershed of the upper Yadkin River (see map page 471) they found what they wanted. The land was not all in one piece, but was sufficiently close together to meet their requirements—and they had it surveyed.[53]

The deal was completed in England—between Spangenberg, who sailed shortly after the survey was made, and Granville, who had never seen his American proprietary. For £500 cash and an annual quitrent of £148, 9 shillings, 2½ pence the Moravians acquired title to 98,985 acres of land. The new home was ready; it remained only to occupy it.[54]

The first settlers were selected from the single men at the Pennsylvania community—thirteen in all: a minister, a cook, a doctor, a carpenter, a gardener, a tailor and seven farmers. On October 8, 1753, they set out on foot, their horses and wagon having been sent ahead to Harris' Ferry (Harrisburg). Many of their brethren, also afoot, accompanied them on this first leg of the journey. At the ferry, the pioneers bade farewell to their friends, and turned southward through Carlisle, a small city of sixty houses. Forty miles farther south, where Hagerstown now stands, they found that the farmers were mostly Scotch-Irish, but as they entered the Shenandoah Valley the German language predominated. At Winchester, then called Frederick Town, they had to help the farmers thresh before they could buy oats for their horses. As they approached Augusta Court House (Staunton) the population again became Scotch-Irish. Near Natural Bridge, where the James River breaks through the Blue Ridge, they passed to the eastern side of the mountains and headed for the Yadkin. On November 17 they reached their destination and, like true Moravians, burst into song—

> We hold arrival Lovefeast here
> In Carolina land
> A Company of Brethren true,
> A little Pilgrim Band,
> Called by the Lord to be of those
> Who through the world go
> To bear Him witness everywhere
> And naught but Jesus know.[55]

Such was the founding of Bethabara in the region that came to be known as Wachovia. Two additional towns were shortly founded, Bethania and Salem, the latter of which today forms a part of the hustling city of Winston-Salem, North Carolina, fragrant with the weed despised by Zinzendorf.

26

Ohio

O N THE SAME DAY that the Moravian brethren arrived at Bethabara, namely, Saturday,
November 17, 1753, Major George Washington, Christopher Gist and five men, some
mounted, some afoot, with baggage horses and
lead horses, were trailing, single file, westward through the
Laurel Ridge in presentday southwestern Pennsylvania. For
three days they had not seen a human habitation. The fallen
leaves blotted out any evidence of previous travel. Only an
experienced woodsman such as Gist would have known they
were on the right path. The air was heavy with snow.

The party had started from the Ohio Company's trading
house at Wills Creek (Cumberland, Maryland) ; their destination was a French fort somewhere between the Forks of
the Ohio and Lake Erie. Major Washington was carrying
a letter from Governor Dinwiddie asking the commandant
of the fort by what authority he was there and suggesting
that he get out.[1]

In sending this letter, which had momentous consequences,
Dinwiddie was acting as Governor of Virginia, as spokesman

for the King of England, and as a stockholder in the Ohio Company of Virginia.

The Ohio Company was outwardly a commercial, speculative project. Apparently it originated in the ever-fertile mind of Thomas Lee, whom we will recall as the one-time agent for the Fairfax Proprietary and more recently as one of the commissioners at the Treaty of Lancaster (see pages 284 and 459). It may well be that the idea first occurred to Lee at Lancaster, when the Iroquois ceded their western lands to Virginia: ". . . all the Lands that are, or shall be . . . in the Colony of Virginia" were a lot of lands and held great possibilities of profit for those who had the courage to develop them. In addition there was the rich trade with the Indians who already lived on these lands.[2]

Few Virginians of the time, or Pennsylvanians either, believed that Pennsylvania's limits extended beyond the mountains; therefore all of that desirable region about the Forks of the Ohio and westward was, by virtue of the Virginia charter and the Treaty of Lancaster, a part of Virginia, to be exploited by Virginia. True, Virginia's line of settlement and of Indian trade had traditionally been to the southwestward rather than to the northwestward; true, for twenty years Pennsylvania traders had been working in the Ohio country; but now Virginia would claim its own.[3]

The potentialities of the Ohio trade may be estimated from the operations of George Croghan. He had come to America, from Ireland, in 1741—probably as a man in his middle twenties. Relatives already settled in Pennsylvania doubtless attracted him to that province, and shortly we find him established on a 350-acre tract of land between Harris' Ferry and Carlisle, squarely athwart not only the important southward road to the Shenandoah Valley but also the westward path along which traders travelled to the Ohio country. And it was the produce of the Indian trade rather than of the soil that interested Croghan. Log warehouses for the storage of skins, stables and forage for pack horses, made "Croghans" an important eastern terminus for the traders. Soon he was leading his own pack-trains over the mountains and establishing trading bases there. On the Youghiogheny River southeast of the Forks of the Ohio (see map page

479) he built storehouses, made canoes, planted corn fields, enclosed pastures for his horses—and probably kept a man in charge. On the Allegheny River, a few miles northeast of the Forks, and at Logstown, an important Indian town some fifteen miles beyond the Forks, he had even more extensive establishments.[4]

From these bases, Croghan and his men fared westward. They visited the Wyandot villages along the southern shore of Lake Erie—doing business within sight of the French trading post at Detroit, as the Governor of Canada complained to the Governor of New York. They displayed their array of bright-colored finery—far better and much cheaper than the French goods—almost at the gates of the French fort called Miami, on the Maumee River (see map on page 478). At the Indian town of Pickawillany, Croghan had a large stockaded warehouse. And at the Shawnee town of Sonioto, on the Scioto River, he operated a store and collected skins. All of this trade was at the expense of the French posts at Niagara, Detroit, Miami and Ouiatenon.[5]

At the height of his trading career Croghan probably had more than twenty-five men working for him as employees or associated traders. His pack-horses must have numbered at least two hundred. The goods that he offered his savage customers included guns, gunpowder, lead, flints, tomahawks, blankets, ribbons, women's stockings (red, yellow and green preferred), knives, needles, looking glasses, kettles, silver jewelry, and always rum. The packs that his long trains of horses brought back over the mountains contained mostly deer skins, destined for the English market.[6]

It was a far-flung business, geographically and financially. Croghan and his traders advanced goods to the Indians against the next year's batch of pelts. Shippen & Lawrence, merchants, of Philadelphia and Lancaster, advanced the goods to Croghan. And London merchants advanced them to Shippen & Lawrence. If a Miami Indian, out hunting north of Pickawillany, slipped on the bank of a creek with his gun cocked, the repercussion might be felt all the way to London.[7]

Such was the trade in which the Ohio Company of Virginia aspired to share. It seemed a strange business for

Thomas Lee, Lawrence Washington and other great planters and land speculators of the Northern Neck who constituted the majority membership. But there were other members to whom trading was the natural function of any company. Thomas Cresap, for one, had long been engaged in the Indian business. His home, far up the Potomac, was a fort, a store, and an inn, known to all the Indians who followed the north-south paths. Then there was John Hanbury, a London merchant; he was interested in selling goods to the Company for resale to the Indians. The objectives of the Company doubtless represented the diverse interests of the members. The Lees, Washingtons and their group hoped to profit by the ownership of land; Cresap and his friends hoped to profit by selling guns and blankets to the Indians; Hanbury expected to profit by selling guns and blankets to the Company.

In November, 1748, the American members of the Company petitioned Governor Gooch, of Virginia, for a grant of land west of the mountains. When he hesitated, fearing that such a move might impede the peace negotiations then going on with France, Hanbury laid a supporting petition directly before the Lords of Trade in London. The Company, he maintained, would strengthen the colonial frontier and bring great profit to English manufacturing through trade with the Indians.

But the Ohio Company needed no special help from a London merchant; bigger men than Hanbury were interested in it. In fact, the Lords of Trade, the Privy Council and the King himself evidently saw in it a vehicle for establishing England's claim to the region west of the mountains. Its proposal received prompt and careful study; the provisions were revised to meet the broad design of imperial England; and on July 13, 1749, the grant was made—by Governor Gooch acting upon detailed instructions from the Board of Trade. Two hundred thousand acres of land adjacent to the Ohio River were given at once, with the proviso that when a fort had been built and two hundred families settled on this land, the tract would be increased to five hundred thousand acres.[8]

Meanwhile the French had been watching England's western expansion with growing concern. The trading operations

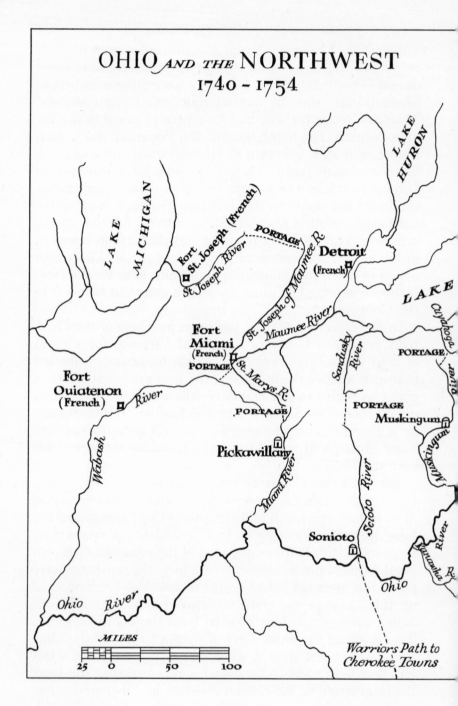

OHIO *AND THE* NORTHWEST
1740 ~ 1754

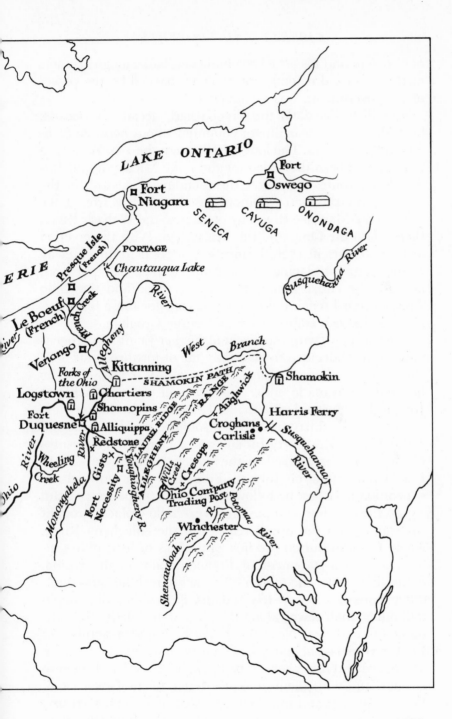

LAKE ONTARIO

Fort
Oswego

Fort
Niagara

SENECA   CAYUGA   ONONDAGA

ERIE

Presque Isle
(French)

PORTAGE

Chautauqua Lake

Susquehanna River

Le Boeuf
(French)

French Creek

River

River

West   Branch

Venango

Allegheny

Kittanning

SHAMOKIN PATH

Shamokin

Forks of
the Ohio

RANGE

Logstown

Chartiers

Shannopins

Aughwick

Harris Ferry

Fort
Duquesne

Alliquippa

Croghans

Carlisle

Redstone

LAUREL RIDGE

ALLEGHENY

Ohio River

Wheeling Creek

Fort
Gists

Necessity

Youghiogheny R.

Wills Creek

Cresaps

Susquehanna River

Monongahela River

Ohio Company
Trading Post

Potomac River

Winchester

Shenandoah

479

of Croghan and his associates had been bad enough; rumors of this proposed colonization scheme, backed by the power of the government, was a challenge.

As will be recalled, the French had, decade by decade, been shortening their line of communications between Canada and Louisiana. The long trip through the Fox-Wisconsin portage had been discarded for the Lake Michigan and Illinois River route, and, after the founding of Detroit in the early 1700's, the most commonly used route was from Lake Erie up the Maumee River, by portage to the Wabash River, thence into the Ohio and the Mississippi. With the erection of Fort Niagara in 1726, France seemingly held the gateway to the west. Interlacing rivers, connected by easy portages, brought the entire area between Lake Erie and the Ohio River within French dominance—except for those few troublesome English traders such as George Croghan.

Now, in 1749, with the threat of further English encroachment, France decided to place her line of fortified posts even closer to the mountains, and to warn off all trespassers. The first move was made under the direction of Captain Pierre Joseph de Celoron de Blainville. Leaving Montreal on June 15, 1749, with thirty-five French soldiers, one hundred and eighty Canadians, thirty Indians and a chaplain—in twenty-three canoes—he arrived at the portage from Lake Erie to Lake Chautauqua on July 16. From this point onward the expedition may best be followed on the map, pages 478 and 479. A little pulling and pushing over shallow places brought the canoes into the upper reaches of the Allegheny River. There Celoron buried the first of a series of lead plates inscribed with a statement of France's claim to the region. Somewhat below the mouth of French Creek he buried another plate. But he saw few Indians. Kittanning, Shannopin and other small towns along the river stood silent; their inhabitants had fled. Near the Forks he found a number of English traders, one party having a train of fifty horses with a hundred and fifty packs of peltry. Celoron ordered them to get out, and with them he sent a letter to the Governor of Pennsylvania protesting their presence in French territory.

At Logstown the flotilla was welcomed by a doubtful salute of musketry—too much lead flying around for comfort and too many warriors to make the use of force advisable. Still the head-men were inclined to be conciliatory up to the point of agreeing to throw out Croghan's traders. Prudently Celoron ordered his canoes into the water and floated on down the river. For more than two hundred miles there were no Indian towns of any importance, but three more lead plates were buried—one at the mouth of Wheeling Creek, one at the mouth of the Muskingum River and one at the mouth of the Kanawha.

The expedition approached Sonioto with well-founded caution. Scouting Shawnee warriors had made it plain that they wanted no French army in their midst. Only after considerable explanation were the canoes allowed to land at all, and then on the eastern side of the Scioto rather than at the town. Croghan's trading-house, overflowing with English goods, was in full view across the river, but Celoron did not dare attempt to plunder it, though he was under orders to do so. After three days of futile "talk," and with the Indians standing armed along the bank of the river to speed his departure, Celoron led his little navy on down the Ohio.

At the mouth of the Miami River he buried another lead plate and paddled upstream to Pickawillany—a new town made up mostly of Miami Indians who had moved away from the French fort on Maumee River in order to trade with the English. Their chief, called La Demoiselle by the French and Old Britain by the English, received the Celoron party courteously enough, but gave evasive answers when urged to return to his French allegiance.

From Pickawillany Celoron portaged across to the St. Marys River, called at Fort Miami, followed the Maumee easterly to Lake Erie and went back down the Lakes the way he had come. Except for planting the lead plates, a few of which were picked up by small boys many years later, the trip had been a failure. In his report Celoron summed up the Ohio situation: "All that I can say is that the tribes of those localities are very badly disposed toward the French and entirely devoted to the English." [9]

Had Celoron said that the Ohio Indians were entirely devoted to the English *traders* his statement would have been more nearly correct. As a matter of fact most of the Indians about the Forks of the Ohio had moved west to escape close contact with the English. In the region between the Forks and Lake Erie they had found a fair and uninhabited haven —uninhabited because eighty years earlier the Iroquois had exterminated the indigenous Erie Indians and turned their village sites into a hunting ground. Thither, as early as the 1730's had come a band of Delaware Indians, crowded out of Pennsylvania; they settled at Kittanning (see map page 479). A few years later, Peter Chartier, a French half-breed licensed by Pennsylvania to trade among the Shawnee Indians on the Susquehanna River, led his customers over the mountains; Chartiers Town, on the Allegheny River, was one of the results.[10]

As the English pressure increased in eastern Pennsylvania, a steady stream of dispossessed Delawares straggled up to Shamokin and then westward to the Ohio country. Venango, Shannopin and several other Delaware towns came into being along the Allegheny River.[11]

At the same time dissatisfied groups of Iroquois, generally referred to as Mingoes, began to drift into the area. "Queen" Alliquippa, an ancient Seneca squaw, ruled over one such town, on the Monongahela a few miles above the Forks. Logstown, occupied by Shawnees and Delawares as well as by Mingoes, was the council town of the region; there resided Tanacharison, sub-chief for the Iroquois Confederacy; there resided Scarouady, the Iroquois commissioner in authority over the Shawnees. However ineffectively its authority was exercised, the Onondaga Council House nevertheless claimed overlordship on the upper Ohio. And this was part of the vast region which, by the Treaty of Lancaster, Virginia believed she had purchased from the Iroquois. Virginia's title, however, despite anything that had been agreed upon by the chiefs from the Onondaga Council House, was not admitted by the Indians of the Forks. The white man's traders were welcome at the Ohio towns because they brought, strapped on the backs of their horses, goods that the Indians could not get at the French forts, or that, if they could get, cost many more skins. Naturally the Indians were entirely devoted to those Englishmen, but they were not devoted to Englishmen who wished to settle on their land.[12]

Nonetheless the Indian's land, in addition to his trade, was what the Ohio Company of Virginia had been promised and what its members wanted. And in pursuance of the various objectives specified in their grant, Lee and his fellow directors authorized Hanbury to send over an assortment of Indian trade goods. A piece of land, on the southern side of the Potomac, opposite Wills Creek, was purchased from Lord Fairfax, and a two-story log warehouse erected as the first of a chain of such depots between Virginia and the Ohio country. A couple of experienced Indian traders, one a former employee of George Croghan, were hired. And Christopher Gist was sent to explore and report on the land in the Ohio Valley.[13]

Gist, a native of Maryland, had failed in business and moved to western North Carolina. There, on the Yadkin River, not far from the Boones, he had taken up a farm and become a very able surveyor. His experience and abilities fitted the needs of the Ohio Company and he was offered, probably through the good offices of Thomas Cresap, a handsome fee for undertaking a preliminary survey of the Ohio country. Coming north he received his instructions and on the last day of October, 1750, started westward—from Cresaps' trading house on the Potomac. He had a few surveying instruments packed on one of his horses, and was accompanied by a young negro servant. His route was an old Indian path through the mountains. On November 19 he was at Shannopin Town, where he made some hasty surveys but dared not let the Indians catch him at it; they had discovered, back in the Walking Purchase (page 454), what happened when surveyors appeared.[14]

At Logstown the Indians were openly suspicious of Gist's mission and told him that if he had in mind making a settlement among them, they were sure he would "never go Home again Safe." Luck was with him, however; George Croghan, "a meer Idol" among the Indians, had just passed through; Gist told the Indians that he was a friend of the trader and hurried after him—across country toward Muskingum (see map on page 478). On the way he overtook one of the Virginia Company traders and they travelled on together. It was Friday, December 13, when they filed into the Wyandot village on the Muskingum to find the English flag flying over the chief's house and everybody greatly excited. Croghan was sending out messengers in every direction ordering his traders into town. Several had already been captured by the French and were, together with their packs of skins, on the way to Quebec rather than to Lancaster. Shippen & Lawrence were going to have difficulty meeting their commitments in London.[15]

Croghan doubtless realized that bankruptcy was staring him in the face, but he was making the present trip as an emissary of the Governor of Pennsylvania, and official business came first. He must visit each of the important towns, deliver presents from the Governor and make an appropriate good-will speech. The speeches, of course, had to be made in the Indians' own languages and since Croghan was not a particularly accomplished linguist, Andrew Montour, a son of Madam Montour, had accompanied him as interpreter and orator. Gist took advantage of Montour's fluency to invite the Indians to a council at Logstown where the King (meaning the Ohio Company) would be distributing presents—some moons hence.[16]

With these messages delivered, the ambassadors—Gist, Croghan, Montour and their entourage—rode southward through the snow (it was January, 1751) to Sonioto. Gist noted that it was a town of over a hundred houses, lying on both sides of the Ohio River. The welcome given the Englishmen was quite different from that extended to Celoron only a few months earlier. They were escorted to the townhouse—ninety feet long and roofed with bark—where Croghan distributed the presents and Montour, after his speech for the Governor of Pennsylvania, again extended the invitation from the Ohio Company: presents would be given at Logstown.[17]

From Sonioto the party turned northward—they were horseback—to Pickawillany. The route passed through "beautiful natural Meadows, covered with wild Rye, Blue Grass and clover" and abounded "with Turkeys, Deer, and Elks and most sorts of Game particularly Buffaloes, thirty or forty of which are frequently seen feeding in one meadow," reported Gist. Pickawillany consisted of four hundred families and was "daily increasing." Old Britain was very happy to see his English friends and, as at Muskingum and Sonioto, Montour made his speeches and invited the Indians to Logstown—while Croghan delivered a present of trade goods from the Governor of Pennsylvania.

Everything was going amicably when into the town stalked four Ottawa Indians carrying a French flag. They were there with a message from the King of France—accompanied by two small kegs of brandy and a roll of tobacco: Would the Pickawillians return to their former homes near the French fort? Old Britain's answer was a short refusal—and he walked out of the council house. His War Chief made the final answer. Speaking as though to the French themselves, he said: "Fathers, You desire that We may speak our Minds from Our Hearts which I am going to do; You have often desired that We should go home with You, but I tell you it is not Our Home, for We have made a Road as far as the Sea to the Sunrising, and we have been taken by the Hand by our Brothers the English, and the Six Nations, and the Delawares, Shannoahs [Shawnees], and Wyendotts and We assure You it is the Road we shall Go: and as You threaten us with War in the Spring We tell you that if You are angry we are ready to receive You, and resolve to die here before We will go to You; And that You may know that this is our Mind, we send you this String of black Wampum." Black wampum meant war.[18]

Gist continued his explorations almost to the Falls of the Ohio (Louisville). There he turned eastward and, by a circuitous route over the mountains, made his way back to Virginia—to find the affairs of the Ohio Company in a confused state. Thomas Lee was dead. Lawrence Washington was a sick man. There was no Governor. Gooch had resigned, but before doing so he had used his authority to create a competitor for the Ohio Company, known as the Loyal Land Company. Several of the more prominent members of the Ohio Company had transferred their support to the new company. And the remaining members were apparently ready to back down on their claim in the Ohio country. Whereas a year earlier they were prepared.to survey land as far down as the Mississippi, now they were interested only in the southeasterly side of the Ohio—which region Gist was again sent off to examine.[19]

But the Board of Trade and King George's advisors had not lost interest in the Ohio project. A new Governor was already on his way to Virginia who not only was himself a member of the Ohio Company but who carried instructions from the King directing him to advance the program of the Company. This new Governor was Robert Dinwiddie, formerly Surveyor-general of Customs for the southern part of America and a member of the Governor's Council in Virginia. A professional royal servant, he was naturally and sincerely a prerogative man.[20]

From the time of Dinwiddie's arrival in Virginia, late November, 1751, the affairs of the colony and the Ohio Company became, for all practical purposes, identical. Scarcely was the Governor through listening to the addresses of welcome before he was making plans for the all-important treaty at Logstown—the one to which Gist had been inviting the Indians and which was intended to clear the way for English settlement beyond the mountains. He directed that the presents for the Indians should be delivered into the hands of Thomas Cresap, and assured him that he had "the Success and Prosperity of the Ohio Company very much at Heart." He tried to hire Conrad Weiser to act as interpreter, and when that failed did hire Andrew Montour.[21]

The date set for the opening of the treaty was May 15, 1752. A commission, headed by Josiah Fry, whom we have already met at the survey of the Fairfax Line, was directed to deliver "His Majesty's Present to the Ohio Indians" and to "treat with the said Indians in order to confirm what was agreed upon at the Treaty of Lancaster, and to secure that Nation to the Interest of His Majesty and this Colony." It is to be noted that the treaty had ceased to be exclusively an affair of the Ohio Company; the presents were from the King, and the results were for the good of the colony.[22]

It was well past the middle of May, in fact it was the last day of May, 1752, when the Virginia commissioners, accompanied by Gist and Montour, with four canoe-loads of presents, arrived at Logstown. George Croghan and his one-time partner, William Trent, were already there—the former as representative of the Governor of Pennsylvania, and the latter in expectation of employment by the Ohio Company.

The presents—a selection from those goods sent over by John Hanbury—were distributed, with appropriate speeches by Montour, to all the chiefs, Delaware, Shawnee and Wyandot, as well as Mingo. But it was to Tanacharison, Scarouady and their fellow Mingoes—in other words, the Iroquois sub-chiefs—that the commissioners made their proposals. Would they accept the Treaty of Lancaster? The reply was that the Indians did not understand that that treaty had anything to do with land over the mountains. They were, however, entirely willing that the English should build a fort to protect them from the French. Did that mean, asked the commissioners, that a settlement might be made? No, it did not, replied Tanacharison; and preliminary attempts to change his mind only brought the answer that in such a matter the Onondaga Council would have to make the decision. After a private conference with Montour, however, and probably a promise of liberal compensation from Croghan's supply of rum, the old chief agreed that the Virginians might settle on the eastern side of the river.

Thus, on June 13, the treaty was made, written up and signed. The Mingo chiefs granted the Virginians the right to build a fort; the Treaty of Lancaster was ratified—for whatever that was worth to either the Virginians or the Indians; "And whereas his Majesty has a present Design of making a Settlement or Settlements of British Subjects on the southern or eastern Parts of the River Ohio, called otherwise the Allagany, We [Tanacharison and five other Iroquois chiefs] in Council . . . do give our consent thereto, & do further Promise that the said Settlement or Settlements shall be unmolested by us, and that we will, as far as in our power, assist and Protect the British subjects there inhabiting." [23]

And that settled it. The Treaty of Lancaster was law on the Ohio. Celoron's lead plates were just lead. No longer could the French capture George Croghan's pack trains, or make demands upon Old Britain and his Pickawillians. The commissioners started on their journey back to Virginia. Trent and Montour started westward to deliver Old Britain's share of the Logstown present. At Muskingum they heard bad news. A twenty-three-year-old French half-breed, Charles Michel de Langlade, from Michilimackinac, with two hundred Ottawa Indians at his back, had taken up Old Britain's challenge. Coming down the lakes, they had slipped through northern Ohio, and pounced upon the unsuspecting Pickawillians. The town had been captured; several Indians and one English trader had been killed; the warehouses had been pillaged of £3,000 worth of goods; Old Britain had been boiled and eaten. It was a fairly complete reply to that string of black wampum.[24]

The French gauntlet was down. Both sides realized that it would be picked up at the Forks of the Ohio, and the race was on for possession of that strategic point. All through the summer and autumn of 1752 and early spring of 1753, Gist and Cresap were busy laying out and improving a road from Wills Creek to the Monongahela River. Along this road, just west of the Chestnut Ridge, Gist established a small settlement. Where the road reached the river, and an open waterway to the Forks, a substantial warehouse, known as Redstone Fort, was built. Surveys were made for another warehouse or fort somewhere near the Forks. Soon Ohio Company pack-trains would be moving back and forth between Wills Creek and the Ohio country, and the forts would be so strong the French would not dare molest them. Everything was going fine.[25]

On the night of April 19, 1753, William Johnson was sleeping peacefully in his house along the Mohawk River in New York when, about midnight, a party of Indians "came whooping and hallowing in a frightfull manner." They had an urgent message. Some of their young men, out hunting near Lake Ontario, had seen large bodies of armed Frenchmen and Canadian Indians being assembled and suspected that they were to be sent against the Ohio Indians. Johnson wrote a hurried account of what he had heard and started a man on horseback for Albany—to get the story to Governor Clinton in New York.[26]

Twenty-five days later Lieutenant Holland, at Fort Oswego, had news: "I begg to inform your Excellency," he wrote to Governor Clinton, "that yesterday passed this place thirty odd French Canoes, part of an army consisting of six thousand French, besides 500 Indians, commanded by Monsieur Marrin designed for the River Ohio or Belle Riviere, which from what we can learn from a French man who stopped here as well as sundry accounts from the Indians, are to settle the limitts between us and they at Ohio and that they lay claim to all the Lands descending or terminating in the great Lake and that in case of opposition they are to support their Claim by Force of Arms & are to cause all the english whether Traders or others to quit them parts. . . ." [27]

While the lieutenant's report was speeding to New York and Virginia, the French armada—of a thousand men, not six thousand—was moving up Lake Ontario, across the Niagara Carrying Place, and into Lake Erie. At presentday Erie, Pennsylvania, the French engineers found a good harbor from which, over a road not more than ten miles long, cannon, supplies and baggage could be carried into French Creek, a tributary of the Allegheny River. Here was a natural connecting waterway, except for that one short portage, from the Atlantic to the Gulf of Mexico—and along it France would establish her boundary with the English colonies. A fort was built at Presque Isle, as the harbor on Lake Erie was called; a road was built from that place to the head of French Creek, and there another fort, named Le Boeuf, was built. At Venango, where French Creek flows into the Allegheny River, the engineers found a suitable building already erected —the trading house of John Frazier. They captured two of Frazier's men, ran up the French flag and moved in.

And then came fever, dysentery and other frontier ills. The men were too weak to work. Even Captain Marin sickened and died. Frost was in the air when his successor, Legardeur de Saint Pierre, arrived, and the decision was to go into winter quarters, which meant cutting wood and huddling around the fireplaces. [28]

Naturally a steady stream of reports regarding the French advance had poured into Governor Dinwiddie's offices, and been forwarded to the King's ministers in London. The seriousness with which England regarded the matter is evident from the fact that, in the late summer of 1753, a war ship, especially commissioned for the purpose, was sent hurrying across the Atlantic with instructions from the Earl of Holdernesse, Secretary of State, for Dinwiddie. He was "not to be the aggressor," but if he found anyone trespassing "within the undoubted limits of his majesty's province," he was first to require them to desist, and if they failed to do so, he was authorized "to repell force by force." It is to be noted that these instructions placed in Dinwiddie's hands the power to determine what were the "undoubted limits of his majesty's province," and when force should be repelled by force.[29]

The instructions reached Dinwiddie on October 21. No time was to be lost if a warning to the French were to be delivered before winter made the mountain paths impassable. The problem of a messenger was solved by the arrival in Williamsburg of young Major Washington. He offered to carry the Governor's letter to the French commander on the Ohio and bring back a reply. We have already seen him on his way (page 474).[30]

It did snow—was ankle deep when Washington and his men reached Gist's settlement, five miles northeast of present-day Uniontown, Pennsylvania. Five days later they were at Shannopin Town, near the Forks of the Ohio, where they swam their horses across the Allegheny and plodded on to Logstown. There they were delayed for six days while Tanacharison and the other chiefs protested their friendship for the English and boasted of what they would say to the French. Since Washington needed the Indians as guides and hoped that their presence would impress the French, he was forced to curb his impatience.

At last—it was the 30th of November—the party got under way, horseback, across country, headed for Venango. Tanacharison and three other Indians led the way. The distance was some seventy miles; the creeks were already high; there was constant rain; and it took four days to get there. The French officer in command received them with every courtesy but refused to accept Governor Dinwiddie's letter; it would have to be delivered to Captain Saint Pierre at Fort Le Boeuf, fifty miles farther on.

But the start was not to be made the next morning. For one thing rain fell in torrents; for another Tanacharison must needs go into council with the Delaware Indians who made up the village of Venango. They should break off friendly relations with the French, insisted Tanacharison; he should mind his own business was, in effect, the Delaware reply, which point of view the French commander so clarified by blandishments and brandy that the other Logstown Indians began to recognize it as reasonable.

Late in the day of December 6, accompanied by a French officer and four soldiers, the Washington party, including the Indians, started northward, up French Creek. The water was high, the horses were almost useless; time after time the men had to crawl over swollen streams on fallen trees; sometimes they had to make rafts. The sun had already set on December 11 when they waded across an arm of the Creek and entered Fort Le Boeuf.

The following morning Washington presented Dinwiddie's letter to Captain Saint Pierre. There were, of course, delays while the letter was being translated, while the French officers held a conference, and while a reply was being drafted. In the meantime, Washington sized up the fort and the French further corrupted his Indians. In fact, the Indians were so busy drinking brandy and receiving presents that they forgot the harsh words they had intended saying to their French Fathers, and it was only with the greatest difficulty that Washington persuaded them to accompany him back to Logstown.

With Saint Pierre's letter in his pocket, Washington, with Gist and the Logstown Indians, started southward on December 16—in canoes provided by their French hosts. The horses had been sent ahead to wait for them at Venango.

The Creek was rough; in places the ice was so thick the paddlers could not break their way through; sometimes they had to carry the canoes over bad spots. Nor were their troubles at an end when they met the horses at Venango. Forage had been scarce and the animals were too weak to carry both riders and baggage. Washington figured that he and Gist would make better time if they went ahead, afoot and alone. Accordingly, leaving the horse-train to follow at its own pace, they started off—wrapped in heavy coats, packs on their backs and guns in their hands. It was a dangerous venture and so proved. They were shot at by a hostile Indian; Washington was nearly drowned in rafting across the Allegheny River; Gist's fingers and toes were frost-bitten. On the Monongahela they found Frazier, the trader whose house the French were occupying at Venango, and secured riding horses from him. They made a social call on old Queen Alliquippa. On the second of January they were at Gist's settlement where they rested for a day. As they approached Wills Creek, on January 6, they met a pack-train of seventeen horses under the supervision of William Trent. The outfit belonged to the Ohio Company of Virginia and was carrying materials and stores for a fort at the Forks of the Ohio.[31]

On January 16, 1754, Major Washington arrived at Williamsburg and handed Captain Saint Pierre's letter to Governor Dinwiddie. Very graciously the French officer acknowledged receipt of the Governor's communication and stated that he was sending it to the Marquis DuQuesne, Governor of New France, for answer. But, continued the Captain, "As to the summons you sent me to retire, I do not think myself obliged to obey it. Whatever may be your instructions, I am here by virtue of the orders of my General; and I entreat you, Sir, not to doubt one moment, but that I am determined to conform myself to them with all the exactness and resolution which can be expected from the best of officers."[32]

And there was the situation—during those cold months of February and March, 1754. At Venango was the spearhead of the French army, somewhat shattered but still numbering some hundreds of men—reaching down from Canada, through Niagara, Presque Isle and Le Boeuf—ready to push forward, with the coming of spring, along the line of Celoron's lead plates. At the Forks of the Ohio, seventy miles from Venango, was William Trent, recently commissioned a captain by Governor Dinwiddie. With him, and also in the pay of the colony of Virginia, were between thirty and forty men—hewing logs and starting to build a fort, for the King of England and the Ohio Company of Virginia. Between this post and Virginia stood the Redstone warehouse where a few men were strengthening the walls, Gist's settlement where there were perhaps a dozen families, and Wills Creek where there may have been two or three men in charge— all employees of the Ohio Company.[33]

Governor Dinwiddie was fully aware that when the ice went out of the creeks the French intended to advance. Washington had told him of canoes being made ready at Le Boeuf;

Trent had passed along Indian accounts of French boastings. In January the Governor ordered the county lieutenants of the Shenandoah Valley to call out enough militiamen to provide Washington with a hundred men with whom he was to march to the support of Trent at the Forks.[34]

At the same time Dinwiddie asked the House of Burgesses for funds with which to pay and supply Washington's men; he wrote to the governors of the neighboring colonies asking them to join in "the common cause" by sending soldiers or supplies; he sent messages to the Cherokees and Catawbas inviting them to take part in expelling the Frenchmen; and he asked the British ministry for two or three of the independent companies of soldiers—not militia and not regular army, but enlisted men stationed in the colonies and at the call of the ministry for use where needed. The Burgesses, however, were skeptical both as to the advantages of and the title to the western lands; one member even got out an atlas and argued that the Ohio country actually belonged to the French. The neighboring governors failed to convince their assemblies of a "common cause" in the Ohio Company's venture. Governor Glen, of South Carolina, questioned Virginia's rights beyond the mountains. The Cherokees and Catawbas did nothing. And the dispatch of the independent companies, while approved, was, as always, tardy.[35]

Nor did the prospective militiamen from the western counties show any enthusiasm about saving the investments of the great men of the Northern Neck. In fact, their attitude was so antagonistic that the Governor cancelled the muster and called for volunteers—baiting the call with promises of Ohio land in addition to the regular wages. Even so, enlistments lagged. Only with the greatest difficulty was Washington able to get together enough men to make up two companies—and most of those enlisted because they needed shoes and shirts.[36]

It was the second day of April, 1754, when, with about one hundred and thirty men, Washington, now Colonel Washington, marched westerly from Alexandria, Virginia. At Winchester a few more men joined the little army, but a week was lost in an effort to collect enough wagons to carry the necessary supplies.

On April 19 the column was plodding up the Potomac, still some distance from Wills Creek, when a messenger came down the road asking for Colonel Washington. He had a letter from Captain Trent: The French were hourly expected at the Forks of the Ohio.

Three days later another messenger from the west was in Washington's camp. He was Edward Ward, late Ensign under Trent. The French had arrived at the Forks, and the fort was theirs.[37]

It had all happened on April 17. Around a bend of the Allegheny River west of Shannopin Town had come a vast fleet of canoes and batteaux. Eighteen pieces of artillery had been unloaded and brought to bear on the flimsy English fort. French soldiers—a thousand of them, Ward estimated —had climbed out of the canoes and formed a line just out of gunshot. The English had been ordered to depart or take the consequences. Trent happened to be away at just this time—looking for recruits, he said; getting a few packs of skins to safety, some suspected. In any case, Ward was in command. He had asked for time to consult a superior officer. The French had given him just one hour.

"Your undertaking," said the French officer, "has been concerted by none else than by a company who have more in view the advantage of a Trade than to endeavour to keep the Union and harmony which subsists between the Crowns of France and Great Britain." Nor, insisted the officer, was his demand upon the English garrison intended to disturb "the good harmony and friendship" existing between the two countries. Rather, it was necessary because of the "incontestable" fact that "the lands situated along Belle [Ohio] River belong to his Most Christian Majesty."

Ward had yielded—it was all he could do—and marched his men to the Ohio Company warehouse at Redstone. He himself was on his way to report to Governor Dinwiddie at Williamsburg. He handed Washington a letter from Tanacharison begging the English to send an army to oust the French.[38]

The situation posed a problem for the young Colonel. The fort that he was to have assisted had already fallen and was garrisoned by an enemy force so far in excess of his own that there was no possibility of immediate recapture. Washington held a council of war with his officers, and the decision was to push on as far as possible, perhaps to Redstone—making a road for future operations and showing the Indians that the English were still to be considered.

Thus for a month Washington's men dug out stumps, filled in holes, bridged deep gullies. Some additional soldiers joined his command; he received glowing promises of more to come. From the Indians and from traders hurrying eastward with their packs he heard stories of the French; they were building a new, and very strong, fort at the Forks—Fort DuQuesne they called it, in honor of their Governor.[39]

By the last week of May Washington was at the Great Meadows—just west of the Laurel Ridge—ten miles from Gist's settlement, which was occupied by a few friendly Indians—twenty-five miles from the Redstone warehouse, which had been left to its fate when Trent's men followed Ward down the road—fifty miles from Fort DuQuesne, where were perhaps six hundred French troops. Increasingly, Washington heard stories of French scouting expeditions. On the 24th he received a message from Tanacharison: The French were marching to "meat Miger Georg Wassionton." Later in the day a trader, making a belated exit from the west, told Washington he had seen two Frenchmen at Gist's and heard that a large party was on the march. On the 27th Gist himself came into camp and reported that fifty French had been at his settlement the day before, and that he had seen their tracks within five miles of Washington's camp. About eight o'clock that same evening there came another message from Tanacharison: He, with some of his followers, was on his way to join Washington, and had spotted the place where the French party was concealed. Without a moment's hesitation Washington took forty men and, guided by Tanacharison's messenger, set out to meet the Indians. It was pouring rain; the night was pitch dark; and the path was narrow. It was just getting light when the Virginians splashed into the Indian camp. Scouts were sent out to verify the position of the French; their hiding place was surrounded; the battle was short. Eleven French were killed, including the Sieur de Jumonville, commander of the party; there were twenty-one prisoners; the fate of the injured is evident from Washington's report to Dinwiddie; the Indians, he said, "served to knock the poor, unhappy wounded in the head, and bereiv'd them of their scalps." [40]

It was a decisive victory for the Virginians, except for one detail; the French claimed that they were on their way to Washington as an embassy, to warn him out of the Ohio country—much as, a few months earlier, he had gone to Fort LeBoeuf to warn the French away. Washington dismissed the French claims as baseless, and Dinwiddie supported him. Nonetheless, the affair created great excitement in Canada, and Jumonville's brother, Coulon de Villiers, came raging up the Lakes from Montreal to wreak vengeance on the Virginia Colonel. [41]

Washington fully expected a counterattack, and threw up a "palisado'd Fort" at Great Meadows. Its character may be judged from the fact that it was finished in five days. Still Washington believed it was strong enough to stand out against five hundred assailants. Re-enforcements, too, began coming in—additional Virginia troops, swivel guns and supplies. Even one of the independent companies, brought up from South Carolina, marched into the camp; but it brought trouble as well as help. Captain James Mackay, the officer in command, held his commission from the King, and he declined to take orders from a Virginia colonel. Furthermore, he would not let his men dig out stumps and make roads unless they got extra pay. The situation was impossible and, to avoid a complete breakdown in morale, Washington, on June 16, began moving his hardworking men westward toward Gist's settlement, partly with the idea of completing a road to the Ohio Company warehouse at Redstone, and partly to get away from Mackay. [42]

There, at Gist's, Washington was waited upon by delegates from the various Indian tribes—Mingoes, Delaware and Shawnees—whose towns lay close to the French fort at the Forks of the Ohio. What did he intend to do? This was what the Indians wanted to know. Support them against the French, he said—speaking through Croghan and Montour, both of whom were present as interpreters. With whom would they side, he asked? The Indians noted the absence of presents; they observed the lack of food, even for the soldiers; they doubtless knew, even as Washington did, that Croghan's horses were being used to pack pelts out of the country rather than to bring in flour for the army. Glumly, and without conviction, they expressed their friendship and walked out of the camp. Even old Tanacharison led his few followers back to the fort at Great Meadows, and made excuses when asked to return and help scout against the French.[43]

But Washington still had an intelligence service. From Logstown, late in June, came word that re-enforcements had just arrived at Fort DuQuesne—they were, of course, Coulon de Villiers and his Canadian Indians—and that several hundred French and Indians were ready to march against the English.[44]

At first Washington thought of making a stand at Gist's, and called Mackay to his assistance. But the lack of food— the men had been without bread and bacon for some time —convinced him that a retreat to Great Meadows and his "Palisado'd Fort"—now, with good reason, called Fort Necessity—was prudent. The distance was only about ten miles, but, not even by requisitioning the pack-train belonging to Croghan and Trent—and thus causing their goods and pelts to fall a prize to the French—were there enough horses to draw the ammunition and supplies. The heavy guns had to be dragged by the men—with Mackay's dandies looking on.[45]

If the wornout and hungry men expected to find bread and bacon awaiting them at Fort Necessity they were doomed to disappointment. What did await them when they arrived there on the first day of July, was still more work—strengthening the fort before the French arrived. Nor did they have long to wait.

During the night of July 2nd Tanacharison and the other friendly Indians, with their squaws and children, vanished.

On the morning of the 3rd there was an early alarm—a sentry shot in the leg. The soldiers stood to arms.

It began to rain. The trenches around the fort slowly filled with water.

About eleven o'clock there was a single musket shot, a

lull, and French soldiers filed out of the woods. Wild yells told of the presence of other foes—Ottawa, Abenaki, Nipissing.

The French did not rush the fort as Washington thought they would; rather they circled it, firing from any vantage point while the Virginians, crouched in their water-filled trenches returned the fire whenever a careless Frenchman raised his head too high.

All afternoon and well into the evening the battle kept up, as did the rain. The French attackers were, of course, soaked and their ammunition was running low. The English were in even deeper trouble; they were starved; their guns were foul; their trenches were awash; and many of the men were getting drunk. Washington refused one French offer of a parley, but when it was repeated he accepted. Out of approximately three hundred and fifty men he had twelve dead and forty-three wounded. The terms as finally agreed upon provided that the English should march out of the fort, with the honors of war, and return to their own country without insult from either the French or the Indians; that they might take their personal belongings with them; and that the prisoners captured by Washington in the Jumonville affair should be freed. As a guarantee of this last condition two of Washington's captains were to be left as hostages with the French. The articles of capitulation were written in French and translated for Washington by one of his captains who could speak the language. One word, however, was either incorrectly translated or its significance was missed by Washington. He was caused to admit that he had *assassinated* Jumonville, which unintentional statement was later made the most of both in Canada and in France.

The following morning, July 4, 1754, Washington and his men marched out of their fort—and continued easterly over Laurel Hill, over the Allegheny Ridge, to the waters that flow into the Atlantic.

The French, after destroying Fort Necessity, marched westerly—back to Fort DuQuesne—burning the buildings at Gist's and at Redstone on their way. There were none to contest their authority beyond the mountains.[46]

27

Colonial Union Fails

THERE WERE, of course, many varying comments on Washington's unsuccessful campaign against the French.

Said William Johnson, rising star of the Mohawk Valley, "I wish Washington had acted with prudence & Circumspection requisite in an officer of his Rank . . . he should rather have avoided an Engagement until our Troops were all Assembled . . ." And then, thinking of the scalping parties that would haunt the frontier, Johnson added, "I can without much of a Prophetick Spirit foresee the ruin of this country verry shortly without the imediate interposition of his Majesty & Parliament."[1]

The Earl of Albemarle, Commander-in-chief for North Britain, Ambassador Extraordinary to France, and titular Governor of Virginia (Dinwiddie holding the title of Lieutenant-governor), observed, "Washington and many such may have courage and resolution but they have no knowledge or experience in our profession; consequently there can be no dependence on them. Officers, and good ones, must be sent to discipline the militia and lead them on. . . ."[2]

499

Tanacharison, late headman at the Forks of the Ohio, spoke with somewhat more authority, though even he, as will be recalled, was not present at the Battle of Fort Necessity. Late in August, 1754, Conrad Weiser found the old chief near Harris's Ferry, Pennsylvania, "a little in Liquor," and together they travelled westward through the rugged mountains to Andrew Montour's place, where a number of refugee Indians—men, women and children—were eating Mrs. Andrew out of house and home. Two days more brought Weiser and Tanacharison to Aughwick (see map page 479), where Croghan, his Ohio warehouses a prey of the victorious French, had taken refuge from his Pennsylvania creditors. Despite his own troubles the trader was extending hospitality to the homeless Indians who thronged his place—giving them butter, milk and the run of his cornfield. The Indians were, not unnaturally, wavering in their friendship for the English; it might be better, they figured, to go back to Logstown and make their peace with the French. Weiser's mission, as representative of the Governor of Pennsylvania and with funds for the purchase of food and clothing, was to hold them fast to the English cause. Under the stimulus of better things to come Tanacharison became talkative and gave Weiser his professional opinion of the late campaign: ". . . the French had acted as great Cowards and the English as Fools," he said.[3]

Quite different from these critical comments was the judgment of Governor Dinwiddie, who had planned the campaign and who knew more about it than anyone else. At no time did he blame Washington or his men for the fiasco of Fort Necessity; on the contrary he consistently praised them as having done more than should have been expected of them. Had Maryland, Pennsylvania, New York and the Carolinas come to Virginia's aid, as they should have done, there would have been no defeat, Dinwiddie insisted. And he was right. The combined strength of the English colonies, if they had been able to act as a united body, exceeded anything that France could have brought against them. But the defense of the Ohio Company's fort had not struck the other colonies as a matter calling for united action; in fact, the colonies were not in the habit of interfering in each other's affairs. As individual, separate communities, loosely connected with the mother country, they had developed, and as such they were accustomed to act; nor, since the disastrous Dominion of New England (see pages 140–149), had the home government attempted to force them to act as a unit.[4]

But by 1753 it had become evident to the British ministry that a struggle was impending in which the combined strength of the colonies would be needed. The imperial ambitions of England and of France were moving toward collision on the Ohio River. Virginia was spearheading England's claim, but upon the result might depend the very existence of the other colonies. They should therefore, as the ministry viewed it, give aid and assistance to Virginia. Accordingly, on the same day that he directed Dinwiddie to repel force with force, the Earl of Holdernesse had sent a circular letter to the other governors directing them, as a particular charge from the King, to "keep up an exact correspondence" with each other, and in case of any hostile moves by the French to call their assemblies and lay before them "the necessity of a mutual assistance."[5]

In general, the governors had striven to follow the King's instructions, but, despite their showy titles, despite their close relations with the Board of Trade, despite their correspondence with members of the ministry, the governors had no real power. They could call up their assemblies and tell them what the King had said, but they could not compel the assemblies to vote the funds required to put the royal instructions into effect. And thus it was that, with the exception of North Carolina, not one of the colonies provided the assistance for which Dinwiddie asked.[6]

Still, some farsighted men in America as well as in England recognized the necessity of joint action. In May, 1754, for example, there appeared in Franklin's *Pennsylvania Gazette* a cartoon depicting a snake divided into several parts each named for one of the colonies. The caption read, "Join, or die." Elsewhere, throughout the colonies, able men weighed and considered America's future and, from suggestions of vague "mutual assistance," began to think in terms of a formal political union. Thus Governor Shirley of Massachusetts, in writing to Governor Benning Wentworth of New Hampshire regarding the possibilities of the Six Nations going over to the French, expanded the recommendations of the Secretary of State by saying, "How necessary then is that union of the English Colonies which the Earl of Holdernesse recommends to all his Majesty's Governours."[7]

And it was as an incident of a treaty with the Six Nations, held at the frontier town of Albany, that the first real attempt was made, by Americans, to create a union of all the American colonies. The strained relations with France made it imperative that the covenant chain between the Indians and the colonists be brightened by kind words and solid presents. In September, 1753, the Lords of Trade had instructed the Governor of New York to arrange for such a treaty and at the same time had requested the Governors of Virginia, Maryland, Pennsylvania, Massachusetts and the other northern colonies to send delegates—"men of Character, ability and integrity." And, added the Lords, the treaty should be conducted not as between the Indians and the separate colonies but as between the Indians and His Majesty. Again that idea of colonial unity.[8]

It was a picturesque assemblage that gathered at Albany in June, 1754. From the Mohawk castles had come old Hendrick and other leading chiefs. Onondagas, Oneidas, Cayugas, Senecas, and even the Tuscaroras, newcomers from Carolina (see pages 302–305), were represented. Tight lipped warriors and painted squaws strolled about and stared. William Johnson was there—both as a delegate for New York and as a friend of the Indians. From Massachusetts had come Thomas Hutchinson and other prominent men. Elisha Williams, late President of Yale College, was there as a delegate from Connecticut. Among the delegates from Pennsylvania were John Penn, a grandson of William Penn, and Benjamin Franklin.[9]

Conrad Weiser had come up with the Pennsylvania delegation. Ephraim Williams, destined to be the god-father of Williams College, had accompanied his cousin Elisha. Traders, bill collectors, brokers of good will—all were there.[10]

The usual speeches were made. Old Hendrick did most of the talking for the Indians. He reminded his English brothers that the land over which they and the French were quarrelling really belonged to the Six Nations. He pointed to the colonial muddling and incompetence. "Look," said he, "at the French, they are Men, they are fortifying everywhere —but, we are ashamed to say it—you are all like women, bare and open. . . ." Nonetheless, but without enthusiasm, he promised that the Six Nations would renew and brighten the Covenant Chain between themselves and their English brethren.[11]

While the formal speeches and agreements were taking place in the Court House, some less lofty deals were transpiring outside. One of the most spectacular was negotiated by John Lydius, a Dutch trader acting for the Susquehanna Land Company of Connecticut. Singly or in groups Lydius invited the chiefs to his house, treated them bountifully to liquor and got their marks on a deed to a vast area of land lying on the east branch of the Susquehanna River in present-day northern Pennsylvania—an area claimed by Connecticut under the provision of its charter which granted bounds from sea to sea. One of the witnesses of the deed was Ephraim Williams.[12]

This land purchase by the Susquehanna Company has gone down in history as a most outrageous piece of skulduggery, excoriated particularly by the Pennsylvania authorities. It is unquestionably true that the Connecticut speculators came to Albany with the intent of getting title to the land by any means necessary, but it is also likely that, after their arrival, they picked up some ideas from the procedure of that most astute of Indian agents, Conrad Weiser. He, too, was busy outside the Court House—not with rum, to be sure; rather with an equally potent form of persuasion sometimes called bribery. And from the Six Nations—for John Penn and his family, the Proprietors of Pennsylvania—Weiser bought, at a cost of £400, title to all the land south of the west branch of the Susquehanna, an area many times the size of the Connecticut purchase.[13]

Some of the delegates doubtless knew about and had a

hand in these questionable land deals. Others, such as Thomas Hutchinson, of Massachusetts, probably paid little attention to the Indian speeches, the haggling or the inevitable chicanery incident to the meeting. They were there for a more important purpose which appeared when, on June 24, a committee was appointed "to prepare and receive Plans and Schemes for the Union of the Colonies." Hutchinson and Benjamin Franklin, and perhaps some others, submitted plans which they had prepared. As promptly as possible the committee reported its findings and on the morning of the fourth day of July, at just the time that Washington and his bedraggled army were marching out of Fort Necessity, the delegates at Albany were debating the various proposals. In the end Franklin's plan, with some revisions, was approved. Under its provisions Parliament was to be petitioned to establish a General Government in which all the American colonies would be included but under which each colony would retain its existing form of government except insofar as the combined welfare took precedence. The union was to be administered by a President General and a Council of forty-eight members—the former appointed and supported by the Crown, the latter apportioned among the colonies on the basis of population and appointed by the assemblies of the respective colonies. This Grand Council was to be empowered to deal with the Indians, to raise and pay soldiers, to build forts and otherwise to protect the colonies. To meet the costs of its operations the General Government was to be authorized to levy such taxes or duties as in the case of each colony would be least oppressive.[14]

It seemed to be a workable plan, and was unanimously accepted by the delegates. But it did not appear so attractive to the people back home. Not a single assembly confirmed it, nor did the King exhibit any interest in it. Franklin tells us the reason. "The assemblies," said he, "did not adopt it, as they all thought there was too much *prerogative* in it, and in England it was judg'd to have too much of the *democratic*."[15]

Virginia had not been represented at the Albany Congress —the House of Burgesses refusing to vote the necessary funds.

Dinwiddie, however, read the Plan of Union with interest—
and then asked the King for regular troops, engineers and
supplies. After his recent experience he had little faith in
"mutual assistance." Nor did he see any likelihood of results
from allowing the colonies to tax themselves. ". . . these
obstinate People will grant Nothing," he said. A poll tax of
two shillings six pence, laid on all the colonists, from Maine
to Georgia, would, he reckoned, just about provide the
amount needed to defend them against the French; and time
after time, in letters to the King's ministers and the Lords
of Trade, he urged the imposition of such a tax.[16]

Horatio Sharpe, Governor of Maryland, agreed with Dinwiddie that the only feasible way to raise funds for colonial
defense was through a direct tax laid on the colonists by
Parliament. He saw no objection to a poll tax but as alterna-
tives suggested a duty on spirituous liquors or "a stamp duty
or something similar to it on deeds and writings."[17]

Shirley, too, as he observed the inactivity of the colonial
assemblies in the face of the French menace, came to the conclusion that whatever was to be done would have to be done
by compulsion from England; or, as he phrased it, Parliament would have to act "for the preservation of His Majesty's dominions upon this Continent, which the several Assemblies have in so great a measure abandon'd the defense
of, and thereby lay'd His Majesty's Government at home
under a necessity of taking care of it for the State, by suitable assessments upon the Colonies."[18]

The King had already acted. In the autumn of 1754 he
sent Dinwiddie £10,000 in specie for use in place of the
funds which the House of Burgesses had refused to appropriate. At about the same time he ordered two regiments
of regular troops to Virginia, and directed Dinwiddie and
Shirley to raise additional forces in their colonies. And, late
in December, General Edward Braddock, with a commission as Commander-in-chief of His Majesty's armed forces
in America, followed the transports westward across the
Atlantic.[19]

Colonial self-government had failed; prerogative would
lead the hosts of war, and the bill would come later.

28

"The King's regular and disciplin'd troops"

"ENERAL BRADDOCK arrived last night at Hampton. Being in a hurry, I cannot enlarge . . ." wrote·Governor Dinwiddie on the morning of February 20, 1755.[1]

And the Governor continued being in a hurry for the next six weeks—as did also General Braddock and his Quartermaster, Sir John St. Clair. Barrels of beef and pork were sent up to Alexandria where the troops were to be encamped. Bacon and butter were ordered in great quantities from the Shenandoah Valley. Wheat was bought from the Pennsylvania farmers, and arrangements made for having it bolted into flour and hauled to Wills Creek. Hundreds of head of beef cattle were engaged for delivery at the same place. Every wagon that could be had was requisitioned. Additional troops were recruited. St. Clair inspected the road westward from Winchester and exhausted a rich vocabulary on its deficiencies; he viewed the Appalachian Mountains —from a distance—and pronounced them a slight obstruction.[2]

About the middle of March the last of the troop transports arrived at Hampton Roads and proceeded up the Potomac to Alexandria. To the majority of the inhabitants of the provincial town the precise drills, the martial music, the scarlet coats were new, spectacular and impressive. Probably no one was aware that under many of those dazzling uniforms were men whose only claim to fame lay in the speed with which they had fled from a Scottish battlefield.³

Late in March the excitement at Alexandria was heightened by the arrival of Dinwiddie and Braddock, to be joined shortly by Governor Shirley of Massachusetts, Governor De Lancey of New York, Governor Morris of Pennsylvania and Governor Sharpe of Maryland. With De Lancey came William Johnson, unofficial spokesman for the Six Nations. Together the General and the Governors agreed upon ways of putting into effect a prepared plan of campaign. There were four main objectives. Braddock, with the regular troops, was to march over the mountains and expel the French from the Forks of the Ohio. Provincial troops were to capture Niagara; Shirley undertook that mission. Other provincial troops were to push the French out of Crown Point on Lake Champlain; that fell to Johnson to whom also was assigned the sole management of affairs having to do with the Six Nations—a hard blow for Conrad Weiser and Pennsylvania. The final objective, if time remained, was the recovery of some contested land in Nova Scotia, or Acadia as the French called it.⁴

With these details settled the Governors hurried home and Braddock returned to his preparations for taking Fort Du-Quesne. Some of the troops had already marched for Winchester, on the way to Wills Creek. Others had been sent to Frederick, Maryland, on the supposition that they might find a better road westward from that point. About April 20 Braddock himself rode to the Maryland town to see how things were going. He found neither provisions nor wagons nor a road and was in a most unpleasant humor when into town came Benjamin Franklin—ostensibly calling as Postmaster-general but in reality aiming to soften the General's wrath over Pennsylvania's refusal to appropriate funds for the campaign. Learning of the difficulty about horses and wagons, Franklin offered to procure from the Pennsylvania farmers one hundred and fifty wagons and fifteen hundred horses and have them delivered at Wills Creek the following month.[5]

This improved the General's humor but when Franklin ventured to suggest that the Indians fought differently from Europeans, Braddock waved his advice aside with the remark: "These savages may, indeed, be a formidable enemy to your raw American militia, but upon the king's regular and disciplin'd troops, sir, it is impossible they should make any impression."[6]

Lack of a road westward through Maryland could not, however, be waved aside and the General had to ferry his men back across the Potomac and follow Washington's old route from Winchester to Wills Creek, now coming to be known as Fort Cumberland. The barnlike structure—on the Maryland side of the river opposite the Ohio Company's warehouse—was a fort in name only and the other improvements were equally primitive. It was, however, the last remaining English base on the road to the Forks of the Ohio, and there the General remained from May 10 till June 7—waiting for his artillery, assembling supplies, improving the road.[7]

There were, in all and including teamsters, pack-horsemen and servants, somewhat over two thousand men at Fort Cumberland. The 44th Regiment consisted of 700 men; most of them were regular troops that had come over from England; some were veterans of Washington's expedition of 1754; some had been recruited at Alexandria. To the Regiment were attached an Independent Company from New York, a company of carpenters, two companies of Virginia Rangers and a company of Maryland Rangers—all under the command of Colonel Sir Peter Halkett. A similarly constituted Regiment, the 48th, was under the command of Colonel Thomas Dunbar.[8]

The General's immediate "family" consisted of his secretary, William Shirley, eldest son of the Governor of Massachusetts, and three aides-de-camp, Captain Robert Orme, Captain Roger Morris and George Washington. As a colonel of provincial troops Washington had resigned his commission rather than again be put in the situation which Captain

Mackay had posed for him in 1754. Both Dinwiddie and Braddock, however, wanted him in the expedition and when the General offered a position where rank would not operate, he gladly accepted. As an aide-de-camp he would have a first-hand opportunity to see how, in the words of the Earl of Albemarle, "officers, and good ones" succeeded where he, with "no knowledge or experience" in the profession of arms, had failed.[9]

Washington must have been grimly reminded of one of his own failures when he found at Fort Cumberland some fifty of the Indians—men, women and children—who had hung around Fort Necessity in 1754. They had been living at Aughwick and Croghan had brought them to the General as prospective scouts. Braddock tried hard to satisfy these strange recruits—he vaguely sensed their value—but he did not understand them, and when he found that little Bright Lightning and other Indian maidens were undermining the morale of his troops by their promiscuous popularity, he ordered the women back to Aughwick. Most of the Indian men escorted the squaws home—and failed to return.[10]

Nor did the thousand or so Catawbas and Cherokees promised by Governor Dinwiddie show up. As we know (page 469) the Cherokees had a previous invitation to meet Governor Glen on the Saluda River in South Carolina. But General Braddock knew nothing of this; there were many things having to do with frontier life of which he knew nothing.[11]

Late in May the wagons and horses promised by Franklin filed into Fort Cumberland—but the wagons came empty. Braddock had expected that they would pick up the flour that Dinwiddie had ordered from the farmers south of Carlisle (page 506) and blamed Cresap for the failure; also he blamed him for supplying bad beef. In fact, he blamed everybody for something—Dinwiddie and St. Clair included.[12]

Particularly, the road over the mountains irritated Braddock. St. Clair with a company of engineers was out in advance cutting a twelve-foot-wide path through the woods and filling in ditches, but the road-bed was still very bad when, on June 7th, Halkett marched with the 44th Regiment. Colonel Burton followed on the 8th with the independent

companies, the rangers and the artillery. On the 10th Colonel
Dunbar, with the 48th Regiment, brought up the rear. Progress was slow. Not only was the road soft but the loads were
too heavy for the horses. On the 11th a number of heavy
wagons and unnecessary cannon were sent back to Fort Cumberland. On the 15th the head of the army toiled over the
Allegheny Ridge—"a rocky ascent of more than two miles,
in many places extremely steep; its descent is very rugged
and almost perpendicular; in passing which we intirely de-
molished three wagons and shattered several," recorded Captain Orme.[13]

The next day the Captain noted that the horses were growing "every day fainter." The army had progressed only twenty-two miles in ten days. Laurel Hill and Chestnut Ridge lay
still ahead. Something had to be done. The decision was that
the General should push ahead with the best men, the strong-
est horses, the lightest wagons and a minimum of heavy guns,
while Colonel Dunbar would bring up the heavy wagon-
train and the remaining men at what speed he could.[14]

The reorganization was made and on the 19th the General
started forward—with approximately thirteen hundred men,
including four hundred engineers. On the 25th he passed the
charred remains of Fort Necessity. Five days later he crossed
the Youghiogheny River and, making a wide arc to the right,
was, on the night of July 8th, camped near the east bank of
the Monongahela River, twelve miles from Fort DuQuesne.
Two days more and the English flag would be flying over the
Fort—of that no one in Braddock's army had a doubt.[15]

Nor did the French and their Indian allies at the Fort have
any great confidence in their ability to successfully resist the
oncoming English force. They had known for weeks that the
blow was impending. Some re-enforcements, both white and
Indian, had been sent from Canada. Langlade and his wild
tribesmen from the west were there. Braddock's expedition
had been shadowed from the day it passed the Allegheny
Ridge. And the Indians were doubtful. They had never seen
a body of men move in such unison. They had no heart to
go up against cannon. When, on the evening of the 8th, the
French commandant suggested that they join in laying an

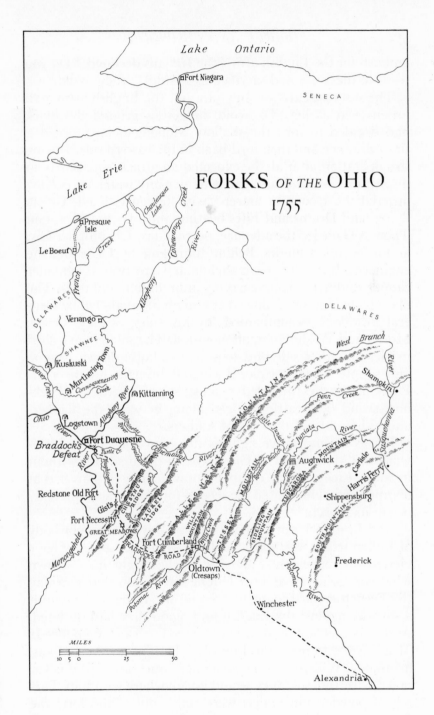

Lake   Ontario

⊡Fort Niagara

SENECA

Lake Erie

FORKS *of the* OHIO
1755

Chautauqua Lake

Conewango Creek

⊡Presque Isle

Le Boeuf ⊡

French Creek

Allegheny

DELAWARES

DELAWARES

Venango ⊡

West Branch

River

SHAWNEE

Beaver Creek

Shamokin
•

•Kuskuski

Murthering Town

Penn's Creek

⌂Connoquenessing Creek

⊡Kittanning

Allegheny River

Little Juniata

Juniata River

Ohio River

⌂Logstown

Braddock's Defeat

⊡Fort Duquesne

Turtle Cr.

Kiskiminetas River

Loyalhanna Cr.

Kiskiminetas River

Conemaugh River

MOUNTAINS

Juniata River

TUSSARORA MOUNTAIN

⌂ Aughwick

Carlisle
•

Harris Ferry
•

Redstone Old Fort ⊡

Youghiogheny River

River

CHESTNUT RIDGE

LAUREL RIDGE

ALLEGHENY

Raystown Branch

Shippensburg
•

Gist's

Fort Necessity ⊡

GREAT MEADOWS

WILLS MOUNTAIN

TUSSEY MOUNTAIN

SIDELING MOUNTAIN

SOUTH MOUNTAIN

Monongahela

Wills Creek

Fort Cumberland ⊡

BRADDOCK'S ROAD

Frederick
•

Potomac River

Oldtown
(Cresaps)

Potomac River

Winchester
•

MILES

10 5 0   25   50

Alexandria•

ambush for the English army, the Indians declined. "Do you want to die . . . and sacrifice us besides?" they asked.[16]

The sun rose early on July 9th, but the English army had arisen even earlier. To avoid dangerous ground Braddock had decided to ford the shallow Monongahela, proceed a short distance and then ford back to the eastern side. During this operation, if at all, he expected an attack and, partly to inspirit his own men and partly to awe any watching enemy, ordered the troops to march "with bayonets fixed, Colors flying, and Drums and Fifes beating and playing." Captain Thomas Gage led the advance, preceded by Christopher Gist and a few other guides. Behind him came St. Clair and the engineers. Immediately in their rear were two six-pounder cannon and five wagons carrying ammunition and tools. The main body of troops followed at a slight interval—led by General Braddock, accompanied by his aides, Shirley, Orme, Morris and Washington, all mounted. The soldiers marched in files on either side of a long line of horse-drawn cannon and supply wagons. Colonel Halkett brought up the rear. Flanking parties guarded against surprise attacks. Pack-horses and beef cattle trudged along between the flankers and either side of the files of soldiers.[17]

It was an impressive sight as the army moved slowly toward the Monongahela. Gage crossed the first ford without incident, except that a company of watching Indians fled at his approach. He secured the second ford, and the main body began its march.[18]

Had Braddock's army been equipped with a proper body of Indian scouts, the hostile Indians would not so easily have viewed his movements, and instead he might have known what was going on at Fort DuQuesne. Again that morning the French commandant had urged the Indians to attempt a surprise against the English and again they had declined. At that point Captain Beaujeu stepped forth and announced: "I am going to meet the English." Turning to the Indians, he asked, "Will you let me go alone?" Such an appeal never failed with Indians; they would go anywhere with him. Barrels of powder and bullets were rolled out of the fort; the savages—more than six hundred of them—crowded about, filled their pouches and, led by Beaujeu, plunged into the woods. With them went some thirty other French officers, one hundred regular soldiers and a hundred Canadians.[19]

Meanwhile Braddock had been deliberately, carefully, getting his men across the Monongahela. Hour after hour the columns had crept along or stood at ease while the engineers smoothed a grade or cut trees. It was two-thirty o'clock; the last of the rear had passed the second ford; the divisions were stretched out a mile or more through an open forest. The French had failed to strike at the fords; it was probable, thought Braddock, that they would attempt no resistance; it was more likely that a distant boom would signalize the destruction of the fort as the French fled before the invincible might of England's "regular and disciplin'd troops."[20]

Still there was no carelessness. The flanking parties were protecting the sides of the columns; Gage's men were guarding against any surprise from the front; when suddenly Gist and the guides came tumbling back into the advance and almost at the same moment there came into view, on the run, a swarm of French and Indians led by an officer almost as naked as the Indians. As he saw the English, the officer—it was Beaujeu—waved his arms to either side; the Indians separated, some to the right and some to the left of the English columns, and disappeared into the woods. Gage's men and the Canadians exchanged volleys; Beaujeu and other officers fell; and the Canadians fled. It appeared, even to the remaining French officers, to have been an easy victory for the English.[21]

The Indians, however, were yet to be heard from. No one saw them, but from behind trees and logs and stumps came puffs of smoke and reports of guns. Men began to fall while wild war whoops echoed through the forest. It was more than Gage's outposts could take and they fell back, becoming entangled in the main body of troops which Braddock was advancing to their support. At the same time the flanking companies ran in, further confusing the formations and exposing the entire line to the deadly fire of the Indians, who by this time were aware of their advantage and were making the most of it. Delawares who had lost their land in the Walking Purchase now howled and spat their revenge; Langlade's Ottawas from Michilimackinac, who had boiled Old Britain, whooped their certainty that they could boil Braddock. To the British regulars the shouts of the Indians were strange and terrifying. Trained to stand and deliver a volley, they saw nothing to shoot at; too cowardly to follow their officers against the hidden foes, they stood in huddled masses; too frightened and confused to know what they were doing, they fired, time after time, point blank into their own ranks. Braddock raged and shouted orders, but was scandalized at Washington's suggestion that the provincials be allowed to fight the Indians in their own way, from tree to tree.[22]

Heavier and heavier came the fire from the woods. The advance company was driven from its six-pounders, and no orders could prevail upon the men to recover them. Orders all too often found no officers left to execute them; mounted men had been easy targets for the Indians; officer after officer had been bowled from his horse. Shirley had been killed; Halkett had been killed; Orme, Morris, St. Clair had been wounded. Washington had twice had his mount shot from under him, but himself remained unscathed. Braddock, realizing that a retreat was probably inevitable, had just ordered the men to guard the wagons when a bullet crashed through his arm and pierced his lung.

Only those about him noticed the General's fall, but his order to protect the wagons was gradually obeyed. And those Pennsylvania-Dutch boys in charge of the wagons needed help. They had come to drive their horses for fifteen shillings a day as promised them by Franklin; they had not counted on being shot at or having to hold horses that were rearing with pain or fright. And this had now been going on for something like three hours.

Suddenly there came from the front and the left flank a particularly heavy rattle of muskets . . . Probably more Indians . . . With one accord, the regulars broke—for the ford of the Monongahela, for the road back over the mountains, for Virginia, for England, for safety from those unearthly yells and those unceasing bullets. Many threw away their guns and their coats in order to run faster. The drivers were close behind them; cutting their horses loose from the wagons, they hopped on their backs and joined the racing mob. Orders to stop, if given, meant nothing. As well have tried to stop "the wild bears of the mountains," said Washington.[23]

The General, helped into a wagon by Washington, was carried along with the rout. Only the dead, the seriously wounded or the slow of foot were left on the battlefield, where an orgy of murder and pillage was being enacted.

The Indians made no attempt to pursue the English beyond the ford of the Monongahela, and as evening approached, they began returning to Fort DuQuesne. Most of them carried scalps, still dripping with blood; many were loaded down with guns, coats and other loot; some drove in teams of horses, late the pride of Pennsylvania farmers. Most grim of the booty was a group of prisoners—ten or twelve—brought in naked, their faces blackened and their hands tied behind their backs. One by one they were fastened to a post on the bank of the Allegheny opposite the fort, gouged with fire brands, tortured in every way known to the ingenuity of an Indian, and finally burned. Far into the night the savages howled with joy as their victims howled with pain.[24]

Painful, too, was the flight of the defeated army. Many, already wounded, fainted or died along the road. Braddock, despite his wound, kept his faculties and when he saw there was no chance of rallying his men, ordered Washington to ride ahead, find Dunbar and have provisions and wagons sent to meet the fugitives. The young Virginian was just recovering from a severe attack of fever; he had been in the saddle for more than twelve hours; the night was black as pitch; the road unspeakably bad; but the following forenoon he staggered into Dunbar's camp, seven miles northwest of Great Meadows, forty miles from the fords of the Monongahela.[25]

News of the defeat had preceded Washington. Dunbar, fearful of his own safety, was on the point of retreat, but he obeyed orders. The wagons were sent; and by July 11 Braddock, with most of his survivors, arrived in camp. Sick as he was the General clung to his authority. By his orders unnecessary supplies were destroyed. All available horses were utilized for transporting the wounded, and on the 13th the retreat continued. A short distance down the road Braddock ordered Dunbar to take over the command. As the creaking wagons approached Great Meadows the General could stand the pain of travel no longer. The columns were halted and about nine o'clock that night he died.[26]

And there, at Great Meadows, General Braddock was buried—in such a way that no trophy-hunting Indian might possibly find the place. Squarely in the middle of the road, at the head of the columns, he was lowered to rest with such honors as the army could bestow. Then Dunbar snapped the order: March! Over the freshly turned earth passed the foot troops, the wagons and the horses. Not even the rear guard knew when it passed the grave. Nor does any man today know its exact location. It was not far from the ruins of Fort Necessity. Probably the great National Road to the West, built in the early 1800's ran over the spot. Route 40 of today, with its countless thousands of hurrying automobiles, goes over or near it.[27]

"March!" . . . and Braddock's broken army plodded eastward over Laurel Hill, over the Allegheny Ridge. The flag of France still waved beyond the mountains.

29

Committees of Correspondence

WHEN THE first account of Braddock's defeat reached Williamsburg, Dinwiddie refused to believe it. Hardly more was he prepared to believe the news that came to him shortly from Fort Cumberland; Dunbar was marching his survivors to Philadelphia and going into winter quarters—in August. With the western road left thus unprotected, it was a certainty that bands of hostile Indians would swarm into the back country of Virginia.[1]

Governor Shirley was at Albany, New York, preparing for his campaign against Niagara, when word reached him of the defeat on the Monongahela. By Braddock's death he became commander-in-chief of the military forces in America. But he failed in his own assignment—the capture of Niagara. Nor did William Johnson expel the French from Crown Point, though in successfully defending his camp against attack at Lake George, he won the only laurels of the year, in recognition of which the King made him a baronet.[2]

No honor flowed from the British conquest in Nova Scotia and the dispersal of the Acadians. Whatever the verdict of history, it has been lost in Evangeline's sad cry, echoing through the forest primeval, "O Gabriel! O my beloved."

Thus ingloriously ended the ambitious plans for 1755—with stalemate in the north and with the Indians killing, scalping and burning along the western frontier from Staunton in the Shenandoah Valley of Virginia to Tulpehocken in Pennsylvania.[3]

For two years the war—made official in 1756 by formal declarations—became a series of minor attacks and counterattacks, while the major strength of both England and France was concentrated on the struggle in Europe, commonly called the Seven Years' War. Shirley, having failed as a successful commander-in-chief, was superseded by Lord Loudoun, who in turn was superseded by James Abercromby. With little to show on the credit side, the colonies lost Oswego in 1756 and Lake George in 1757. And still the Indians, urged on from Fort DuQuesne and Quebec, raided and killed along the frontiers.

Few regular troops were provided for the American colonies; England was more concerned with warding off a possible French invasion of her own shores. For such armies as they raised, the American commanders were largely dependent upon action by the assemblies of the various colonies, some of which would and some of which would not vote their quotas. And almost invariably in sending men and supplies the assemblies also sent commissioners to oversee and control their soldiers in the camps or their goods in the commissary depots. Thus there might be five or six different groups supervising what should have been a unified effort. Ruefully the Earl of Loudoun remarked, "I wish to God you could persuade your people to go all one way."

Each season inexperienced men—farmers, mechanics, clerks—would be called together, on short enlistments, marched off under equally inexperienced captains to encampments where little or no provision had been made for feeding or housing them, and in which no idea of sanitation existed. Dysentery and other diseases would naturally appear and carry off more men than were lost in battle. And then the campaign would collapse and the men, those who had survived, would straggle home. Naturally, the French, with a strong force of regular troops and with the Indians as their allies, could ravage the back country almost at will.

But in 1757 the odds shifted. France was becoming weaker while in England foreign affairs had come under the capable, energetic hands of William Pitt. No longer was the war in America to be one simply of driving the French back; it was to be a war to drive them out of America; America was to be British.

The colonies were spurred on to raise more men. Arms, provisions, and additional regulars were sent by England. The incompetent Abercromby, called "Mrs. Nabbycromby" after a crushing defeat at Ticonderoga, was replaced by Jeffery Amherst. And soon Pitt's "system" began to show results. In August, 1758, Fort Frontenac fell to a bold attack by the provincial troops, thus cutting the French supply line to Niagara and Fort DuQuesne. Three months later General Forbes, pushing westward across Pennsylvania, forced the evacuation of DuQuesne. And in July, 1759, Niagara fell an easy prey to Sir William Johnson. At practically the same time Amherst's overpowering approach to Ticonderoga compelled the French to give up that strategic spot.

Quebec, the symbol of French power in America, was already under attack, and as autumn turned the leaves to red and gold the English forces closed in on the doomed citadel. Its fate was sealed on the Plains of Abraham in September, 1759. Montreal fell the following year and by the terms of capitulation, confirmed in the treaty of peace signed at Paris in 1763, Canada and much of Louisiana became British.'

The loss of Canada by France, and its acquisition by England, did not loom as important in 1763 as it did later. Many Englishmen felt that, economically, it would be better to hold the six-hundred-and-nineteen-square-mile sugar-producing island of Guadeloupe in the Lesser Antilles and return Canada to France. Politically, too, there were misgivings as to what the older English colonies would do if wholly freed from the danger of French attack. Said the Duke of Bedford,

"I don't know whether the neighborhood of the French to our North American colonies was not the greatest security for their dependence on the mother country, which I believe will be slighted by them when their apprehension of the French is removed." Others expressed similar misgivings.[5]

To counteract these fears, Benjamin Franklin, at the time living in London, stepped into the discussion with a pamphlet entitled *Interest of Great Britain Considered with Regard to Her Colonies* in which he showed that there was nothing to worry about. "Their jealousy of each other," he said, "is so great that however necessary an union of the colonies has long been, for their common defence and security against their enemies, and how sensible soever each colony has been of that necessity, yet they have never been able to effect such an union among themselves, nor even to agree in requesting the mother country to establish it for them. Nothing but the immediate command of the crown has been able to produce even the imperfect union but lately seen there, of the forces of some colonies. If they could not agree to unite for their defence against the *French* and *Indians,* who were perpetually harassing their settlements, burning their villages, and murdering their people; can it reasonably be supposed their is any danger of their uniting against their own nation, which protects and encourages them, with which they have so many connections and ties of blood, interest and affection and which 'tis well known they all love much more than they love one another? In short, there are so many causes that must operate to prevent it, that I will venture to say, an union amongst them for such a purpose is not merely improbable, it is impossible . . ."[6]

English diplomacy sided with Franklin and it was Canada and the West that England demanded and retained at the Treaty of Paris. The price of conquest had, however, been high. England's national debt, that comfortable economic device initiated in the days of King William (see page 161), had doubled between 1756 and 1763. The colonies, too, were heavily saddled with war debts despite the fact that many of their expenses had been refunded by the British Treasury.[7]

Nor was the expense at an end. Hardly had English garrisons replaced the French at Detroit and Michilimackinac before a widespread Indian conspiracy was formed against them. In the spring of 1763 the savages struck. Presque Isle, Le Boeuf, Venango, Miami and all the smaller western posts fell before the well planned onslaught. Only Detroit, Niagara and Fort Pitt (formerly DuQuesne) held out. The persistence with which Pontiac, an Ottawa chief, led the attack against Detroit caused his name to be attached to the entire outbreak—Pontiac's Conspiracy, it was generally called.[8]

Gradually the Indians were brought to terms, but it was evident that for years to come, an army would be needed in the west, partly to protect the whites against predatory Indians, and partly to protect the Indians against predatory whites. The cost would be large, perhaps £200,000, perhaps more, annually. To the taxpayers of England, and to the British ministry, it seemed only reasonable that the American colonies should bear a part of this burden.[9]

The first approach to the problem was an oblique one. Duties on goods and commodities imported into the colonies were, by an act of Parliament, so increased, revised and supervised that a substantial revenue might be expected. Seemingly no new principle was involved; the colonists had long been accustomed to paying duties prescribed by Parliament through the trade and navigation acts. There was, however, a very real difference between those earlier acts and the act of 1764. The duties assessed under the navigation acts were primarily for the purpose of regulating trade; the duties assessed under the new act were frankly for the purpose of raising revenue, and thus came to be taxation. Also, as it happened, the new duties bore harshly on New England imports—particularly on the ever essential molasses from the West Indian islands. Instantly the merchants of Massachusetts, Rhode Island and eastern Connecticut rose in protest. To be taxed without their own consent was contrary to their rights as Englishmen, they insisted; and not being represented in Parliament, they had not given their consent to this act. James Otis, as spokesman for the New Englanders, justified resistance to the act on the ground that it was an innovation, an invasion of the liberties of the colonists, and thus unconstitutional. Natural rights, he held, took precedence over acts of Parliament. "An act against the Constitution," he said, "is void." [10]

By "the Constitution" Otis meant that vast body of established rights, privileges and customs which make up the English Constitution. And in contending that this "constitution" took precedence over statute law, which is to say Parliamentary law, he was but stating a fact accepted by a generation of Americans suckled on the common law of England. Christopher Gadsden, South Carolina merchant and planter, expressed the same idea in another way when he said, ". . . we should all endeavor to stand upon the broad and common ground of those natural and inherent rights that we all feel and know, as men and as descendants of Englishmen, we have a right to." [11]

So commonly accepted was the theory of natural rights that the Massachusetts Assembly adopted it as a platform on which to oppose Parliamentary taxation. And to the end that the colonies might present a solid front, Otis was made chairman of a committee to inform the assemblies of the other colonies regarding the position taken by Massachusetts. Committees of Correspondence for the purpose of keeping in touch with officials in England had long existed, but a committee created specifically to bring about closer relations among the colonies was, like Parliamentary taxation, an innovation—and a long step in the direction of colonial union. This much had the first attempt to tax the colonists accomplished. [12]

Sons of Liberty

B UT THE BRITISH TREASURY still needed money
—in addition to all that the new customs duties
might bring in. And despite colonial objections or
theorizing, some additional source of revenue had
to be tapped. The responsibility for deciding what
that source should be fell upon George Grenville, newly installed Chancellor of the Exchequer and First Lord of the
Treasury of England. One of the least objectionable of the
various taxes imposed by Parliament upon the people of
England—and it had been in use there for seventy years—
was the one already suggested by Governor Sharpe (see page
505), namely a stamp tax on legal documents, newspapers,
almanacs and such. In the autumn of 1763 word reached
America that Grenville was considering the extension of this
stamp tax to the colonies. With one accord, the colonial
assemblies directed their London agents to protest.[1]

Grenville listened patiently to the addresses of the agents,
among whom were Benjamin Franklin, acting for Pennsylvania, and Jared Ingersoll, acting for Connecticut. When
they had finished he asked what they could suggest instead

of the stamp tax. And all that they could suggest, or that the colonies would have supported them in suggesting, was that the various assemblies should appropriate, upon request, their pro rata share of the money needed. Grenville doubtless recalled how the assemblies of Maryland, Pennsylvania and the other colonies had failed Virginia in 1754 and 1755. He may have remembered Dinwiddie's complaint: ". . . these obstinate People will grant Nothing." In any case his decision was for a tax that the colonists would have to pay, rather than for a request which the assemblies might or might not honor.[2]

And there, face to face, stood two irreconcilable political concepts—the ancient English custom of a free gift to the King versus a recent and alien idea that the King might take what he needed. Not in the amount but in the manner in which the money was to be raised stood a political principle that could, and did, amaze and mystify the British ministry; that could, and did, shatter the prophecies of so keen an American observer as Franklin.

Nor in refusing to be taxed by Parliament were the colonists being merely captious. A very real principle was involved, a principle as old as the colonies themselves. In the charters authorizing the first overseas settlements the colonists had been guaranteed all the liberties, franchises and immunities of Englishmen. As each new colony came into being the King had either directed, authorized or encouraged the creation of representative assemblies—elected by the freemen and endowed with a limited power of government within their respective colonies. Slowly but inevitably the assemblies had extended their power.

Subsequently, and markedly from the later years of the seventeenth century, the mother country sought to bring the colonies to a great dependence upon the King. Charters were broken, proprietaries were recovered. By the 1760's only Connecticut and Rhode Island retained the full right of self-government. In Maryland, Pennsylvania and Delaware the proprietors still named the governors but their appointees had to be approved by the King. New Hampshire, Massachusetts, New York, New Jersey, Virginia, North Carolina,

South Carolina and Georgia were royal colonies; the King appointed the governors.

Nonetheless, in all the colonies—royal, proprietary and corporate—the assemblies continued to control the internal aspects of their respective governments. This they did by their power over the public purse. Without the approval of the assemblies, expressed in appropriations, money was not available for any public purposes, even for the payment of the governors' salaries.

Such was the situation in 1764. But if, through a stamp tax or any other Parliamentary tax, the King were enabled to extract from the colonists, and hold in his hands, the money traditionally appropriated by the assemblies, then, with that money, the King could pay the salaries of the governors and other officials, could pay the costs of a military establishment (perhaps to be used against themselves), and in short, could so fund all the public expenses that the governors would be under no compulsion to call their assemblies into session. Thus representative government would lapse, and, as James Otis tellingly phrased it, *"If we are not represented, we are slaves."* [3]

Oblivious of the issue involved, or of its seriousness, Grenville, in February, 1765, laid the so-called stamp act before the House of Commons and asked for its passage. Among those who spoke in its favor was Charles Townshend, who as a later Chancellor of the Exchequer was to attempt to fasten even more severe measures upon the Americans. Said he, ". . . will these Americans, Children planted by our Care, nourished up by our Indulgence untill they are grown to a Degree of Strength & Opulence, and protected by our Arms, will they grudge to contribute their mite to releive us from the heavy weight of that burden which we lie under?"

The answer came quickly—from Colonel Isaac Barre, a member of the House who had lived in America and knew the people: "They planted by your Care? No! your Oppressions planted em in America . . . They nourished up by *your* indulgence? they grew by your neglect of Em:—as soon as you began to care about Em, that Care was Exercised in sending persons to rule over Em . . . to Spy out their Lyberty misrepresent their Actions & to prey upon Em; men whose behaviour on many Occasions has caused the Blood of those Sons of Liberty to recoil within them . . . They protected by *your* arms? they have nobly taken up Arms in your defense, have Exerted a Valour amidst their constant & Laborious industry for the defence of a Country, whose frontier, while drench'd in blood, its interior Parts have yielded all its little Savings to your Emolument. . . ."

There was much more, all of which Jared Ingersoll, agent for Connecticut, jotted down and sent home, where the term "Sons of Liberty" so appealed to the people that under that name they began forming local political societies pledged to oppose the stamp act.[4]

Meanwhile Grenville's bill had easily passed a final vote in a half-empty House of Commons, and the Treasury began looking about for suitable men to act as stamp distributors in the various American colonies. Franklin, still not liking the act but convinced that it was inevitable, recommended one of his friends for the job in Pennsylvania. Andrew Oliver, a member of the Governor's Council and Secretary of the Colony of Massachusetts, accepted the position of distributor for his colony. Jared Ingersoll made no question of the propriety of serving for Connecticut. None of these men, and few other of the prominent colonials, thought that there would be more than passing objection to the stamps.[5]

The first shock to their complacency came from Virginia. The General Assembly was in session. There was much unhappy conversation about the newly passed Stamp Act, but none of the influential tidewater leaders did anything. Finally, on May 29, young Patrick Henry, a new member and from the back country, offered a series of seven resolutions, the substance of which was summed up in: "Resolved, Therefore that the general assembly of this colony have the sole right and power to lay taxes and impositions upon the inhabitants of this colony, and that every attempt to vest such power in any person or persons whatsoever other than the general assembly aforesaid, has a manifest tendency to destroy British as well as American freedom."

In urging his resolutions upon the Assembly Henry is said

to have become rhetorical: "Cæsar had his Brutus—Charles the first his Cromwell—and George the Third . . ." at which point the Speaker of the House cried, "Treason, Treason," while the young burgess continued, ". . . may profit by their example."

On May 30, amid scenes of great excitement, five of the resolutions were approved. The next issue of the Virginia *Gazette* carried the text of the "Resolves." They were copied by other newspapers in other colonies, and, in the words of Thomas Hutchinson, who was very much in a position to know, "had a tendency to bring on those acts of violence which soon after were committed in Boston."[6]

Jared Ingersoll, on his way home from England, landed at Boston on July 28, 1765. He was, of course, known as the prospective stamp distributor for Connecticut and was observed to be often in the company of Andrew Oliver, the prospective distributor for Massachusetts. The Boston *Gazette* came out with some uncomplimentary remarks about stamp masters. And on the morning of August 14 a stuffed figure labelled "Distributor of Stamps" was found hanging from a great elm tree—known as the Liberty Tree—under which the members of that new society, the Sons of Liberty, were accustomed to meet.

Crowds soon gathered. The Governor called his Council together and considered removing the offensive effigy, but thought better of it. Toward evening a well organized group, doubtless Sons of Liberty, lowered the effigy from the tree and, forming a procession, carried it to the Town House where the Governor and his Council were still in session. Behind this somewhat orderly group came a mob of several thousand men who tore down a house that Oliver was having built for a stamp office, and then, still unsatisfied, marched to his home, broke in the doors and windows, smashed up the furniture and milled around until midnight.[7]

The next day Oliver resigned as stamp distributor, and that night the Sons of Liberty made a big bonfire in his honor. When news of these doings reached New York the distributor for that city was, as he expressed it, "Threaten'd with Mr. Olivers Fate if not Worse," and he hastily resigned. Other distributors in other colonies did likewise for similar reasons.[8]

Oliver's "fate" had irritated Thomas Hutchinson, that outstanding prerogative man, Lieutenant-governor and Chief-justice of Massachusetts, who lived in the big house with the King's arms over every window. He had suggested doing something to preserve order and was generally believed to be sympathetic to the Stamp Act. On the night of August 26 a mob gathered before his house. As he and his family fled, just in time, through the back door, the mob smashed in at the front entrance. Beautiful furniture was broken; tapestries and paintings were ruined; silver was trampled under foot; irreplaceable manuscripts which Hutchinson had collected for use in his *History of the Colony of Massachusets-Bay* were scattered in the muddy streets. The interior of the house was a complete wreck. Probably the rioters went farther than was intended, but there can be little doubt that their action was prompted by a well organized group.[9]

While these events were transpiring elsewhere, Jared Ingersoll arrived home—at the town of New Haven in Connecticut Colony—and discovered that he, too, was an extremely unpopular person. He was castigated in the newspapers. He was threatened by the Sons of Liberty who, as will be recalled, had taken their name from the report of Barre's speech sent to Connecticut by Ingersoll himself. In town after town, he was hanged and burned in effigy. At New London, famous for its shows since the days when James Davenport almost burned his breeches (page 379), the people outdid themselves. From a special gallows erected in the center of town dangled an effigy of Ingersoll with a devil peeping over his shoulder and a copy of the Stamp Act pinned to his breast. As the crowd gathered, consisting of people "of all Professions and Denominations," the figure was pulled from the gallows, mounted on a pole and paraded through the streets, while bugles screamed, drums beat and cannon roared. Finally, the figure was again suspended on the gallows and burned. Even the little children pointed to the effigy and cried, "There hangs a Traitor," and "There's an Enemy of his Country." In a speech made at the gallows one of the leaders suggested that the people ". . . ask him [Ingersoll] peaceably to resign it, and if he refuses to, use him in such a manner, that he will be glad to do anything for a quiet life." [10]

About the middle of September, Ingersoll "received repeated and undoubted Intelligence of a Design formed by a great Number of People in the eastern Parts of the Colony to come and obtain" his resignation. These "people" were, of course, the Sons of Liberty and, as the General Assembly was meeting at Hartford on the 19th of the month, Ingersoll decided to forestall his unwelcome visitors by making a report to the legislature and letting that body decide what course he should pursue. Accordingly, on the morning of the 18th he started from New Haven for Hartford, together with the Governor and several members of the Assembly. All were on horseback. About eighteen miles up the road they met two horsemen, armed with long white sticks, who stated that they were part of a large number of men on their way to pay Ingersoll a call. When Governor Fitch directed one of them to tell his friends to go back home, the man bluntly informed him "that they lookt upon this as the Cause of the People, & that they did not intend to take Directions about it from any Body."

Thus put in his place, the Governor rode on to Hartford while Ingersoll stopped at a tavern to send some messages: one, to tell the oncoming Sons of Liberty that they would find him at Hartford, rather than at New Haven; another to his family at New Haven directing them to barricade the house.

The next morning Ingersoll started on toward Hartford. As he neared Wethersfield he met four or five horsemen who turned and rode with him. "About half a Mile further," as he told the story, "we met another Party of about Thirty whom I accosted, and who turned and went on in the same Manner. We rode a little further and met the main Body, who, I judge, were about Five Hundred Men, all on Horseback, and having white Staves, as before described. They were preceded by three Trumpets; next followed two Persons dressed in red, with laced Hats, then the rest, two abreast. Some others, I think, were in red, being, I suppose, Militia Officers. They opened and received me; and then all went forward until we came into the main Street in the Town of Wethersfield. . . ."

There the horsemen formed a circle with Ingersoll inside. To his inquiry as to what they wanted, they answered that they wanted him to resign his Office of Stamp Distributor. When he explained that he was on his way to Hartford to ask the sense of the Governor and Assembly, they replied, "Here is the Sense of the Government, and no Man shall exercise that Office." When he pointed out that they represented only a part of the colony, he was told, "It don't signify to parly—here is a great many People waiting and you must resign." To his query as to what would happen if he refused, the answer was, *"Your Fate."*

While this was going on several Assemblymen, on their way to Hartford, stopped to watch. Ingersoll called to them that he was being held a prisoner and asked them to assist him, but when they attempted to argue with the crowd, they were advised that "they had better go along to the Assembly where they might possibly be wanted."

After being held for about three hours and upon being pointedly told that the men were getting out of hand, Ingersoll yielded and wrote out a resignation. His captors read it, did not like it and wrote out a form of their own, which Ingersoll signed.

"When I had done," Ingersoll tells us, "a Person who stood near me, told me to give Liberty and Property, with three Cheers, which I did, throwing up my Hat into the Air*; this was followed by loud Huzzas; and then the People many of them were pleased to take me by the Hand and tell me I was restored to their former Friendship. I then went with two or three more to a neighbouring house, where we dined.

"I was then told the Company expected to wait on me into Hartford, where they expected I should publish my Declaration again. . . . We accordingly mounted, I believe by this Time to the Number of near one Thousand and rode

---

* "Liberty and Property" was the watchword of the Sons of Liberty and was properly followed by three cheers and the throwing of one's hat into the air. Some say that Ingersoll gave an added touch by throwing his wig as well as his hat into the air.

into Hartford,* the Assembly then sitting. They dismounted opposite the Assembly House, and about twenty Yards from it. Some of them conducted me into an adjoining Tavern, while the main Body drew up Four abreast and marched in Form around the Court House, preceded by three Trumpets sounding; then formed into a Semi-circle at the door of the Tavern. I was then directed to go down and read the Paper I had signed, and which I did within the Presence and Hearing of the Assembly; and only added that I wisht the Consequences of this Day's Transaction might be happy. This was succeeded with Liberty and Property and three Cheers; soon after which the People began to draw off, and I suppose went Home." [11]

Similar scenes, sometimes even more violent, took place in New York, in South Carolina—wherever an attempt was made to distribute the tax stamps. The uniformity of the demonstrations—meetings under Liberty Trees, parades with effigies of the stamp-masters hung on poles, assaults upon the homes of suspects—indicated a close connection among the leaders of the movement. [12]

---

*The story goes that one of the men asked Ingersoll, who was riding a white horse, how it felt to be attended by such a retinue. His reply was that it gave him a clearer idea than ever before "of that passage in Revelations which described Death on a pale horse and Hell following him."

31

The Road to Union

FOR A FULL CENTURY England had been striving to establish a measure of unity among her widely diverse American colonies—to draw them into and make them a workable part of the British Empire.

The Navigation Acts had been moves in that direction. The Vice-admiralty Courts had been created to further serve that purpose. The extinction of the corporate and proprietary charters and the substitution of royal control were parts of the same general pattern. The formation of the Dominion of New England in 1686 had been intended as a preliminary to placing all the colonies under a single royal governor. The Albany Congress of 1754 was expected to initiate at least a military union.

But the idea of colonial union had failed to take root. Each colony had clung to its own individuality (see page 501). None had seen an advantage in becoming a part of a general group. All had been content to remain children of Mother England, upon whose people and institutions they had looked with genuine affection.

In 1765, however, at the very time that Jared Ingersoll

was being forced to resign his job as distributor of stamps, twenty-seven delegates from nine of the colonies were preparing to meet in New York—not at the suggestion of the British ministry, but rather at the call of the Massachusetts Assembly—not to carry out the wishes of the King and Parliament, but rather to resist them. In short, the purpose of the meeting was to consider the Stamp Act, to express the attitude of the colonies toward it, and to work for its repeal. In a Declaration of Rights the delegates set forth that the colonists were "entitled to the inherent rights and privileges" of English-born subjects of England; that no taxes should be imposed upon them but by their own consent, given personally, or by their representatives; that since they could not be represented in Parliament, due to distance, the only representatives they could have were those in their colonial assemblies; that they never had been, or constitutionally could be, taxed by any other authority. In petitions to the King and the Houses of Parliament they repeated their claim to the "inherent rights and liberties" of Englishmen.[1]

Inherent rights and liberties—the rights of Englishmen— liberty and property! Over and over, far back in English history, far back in colonial history (see pages 141, 263), these and similar expressions occur and recur. These rights and liberties were the very substance of the English constitution, not to be violated by anyone. There were personal rights and liberties; there were economic rights and liberties; there were political rights and liberties; and the colonists insisted, on sound constitutional grounds, that all these rights and liberties were as common to Englishmen born in the colonies as to Englishmen born in England.

In many ways, however, Englishmen in America and Englishmen in England had drifted apart. In England the dead weight of poverty and debt, the piling up of hired workmen in cities, the loss of touch with the land, had made the common people less jealous of their personal rights, less interested in their economic rights; often they were without political rights. In America, on the other hand, the very conditions of life—elbow room, opportunity, land almost for the asking —had bred a democracy that the native Englishmen could not understand—a democracy that was adding new rights to those encompassed within the English constitution.

For one thing, the native-born American was becoming conscious, perhaps self-conscious, of a difference between himself and those born in England. As early as 1701 Governor Nicholson had, as we know (page 260), noted that the "natives" had an "aversion to others, calling them strangers." Fifteen years later, we find Spotswood (page 286) setting forth that the native-born "looked upon all persons not born in the Country as forreigners."

Along with this nativism, the American had developed a marked touchiness. This was well illustrated in the brawl between Robert Mason and Thomas Wiggins (page 115). Where Mason made his mistake was in taking Wiggins by the arm to hurry him out of the house. Americans did not like being pushed around—as Mason might have figured out as he lay sprawled on the hot coals in the fireplace. Or again, take the case of Governor Dudley and the teamster (page 180). Unquestionably it was the Governor's manner—more English than the English—that irked the man and brought the reply, "I am as good flesh and blood as you . . . you may goe out of the way." Native-born Americans were not going to be put off the road even by a governor.

Almost equally touchy were the Americans in the matter of political rights. As early as the 1670's the Massachusetts magistrates were contending that acts of Parliament did not extend to America (see page 107). In 1695 we find a New Yorker complaining of Governor Fletcher's "insolent" attitude toward the provincial assembly, which body the people looked upon as the guardian of their "libertys and propertys." Also, we will recall Samuel Jennings' lecture of 1707 to Lord Cornbury: "We cannot," he said, "but be very uneasy when we find by these new methods of Government our Liberties and Properties so much shaken that no man can say he is Master of either. . . ." And when, in 1754, Governor Dinwiddie told the Virginia House of Burgesses that their failure to grant money might cause the people to lose "the Liberties, Properties, and the pure Religion that they enjoyed," he was pointedly informed that they, the Burgesses, were the "faithful Guardians" of those rights and privileges.[2]

In fact, as we have seen (pages 421–423), the colonial assemblies had, over a long period of years, been assuming the real power of government in the various colonies and leaving to the royal governors but a semblance of authority. And in this the assemblies had the hearty support of the great majority of the colonists—who had faith and confidence in their own representatives but progressively less in those who represented the British government. They had watched British muddling in King George's War—while they, themselves, had captured Louisburg. They had seen Braddock beaten by a handful of naked Indians; "This Whole transaction," said Benjamin Franklin, "gave us Americans the first suspicion that our exalted ideas of the prowess of the British regulars had not been well founded." Others, particularly the American contingent at Cartagena, had previously made the same discovery.[3]

Unfortunately, too many of the British officers who served in America during the French and Indian War were of a type that did not understand the native Americans. Too often they had only contempt for the "farmer" officers of the provincial troops. Too often they went blandly ahead with affairs that vitally concerned the Americans without so much as asking their advice. And too often the result was failure. By the time the war was over Englishmen from England were commonly being referred to by the Americans as "foreigners."[4]

Thus, in 1760, we find the American colonists claiming all the rights and privileges of the British constitution; we find them insisting upon governing themselves through their own assemblies and inclined to ignore the King's prerogative or the power of Parliament; we find them touchy and sensitive to what they considered social and political slights; and we find them bitter toward and suspicious of British officialdom.

At just that time a new King, George the Third, ascended the throne of England—intent upon regaining the authority which his grandfather and great-grandfather had lost to Parliament. By adroit use of the patronage at his disposal he soon brought Parliament to almost complete dependence upon the royal prerogative. What his ministers asked for, Parliament granted. And among the objectives for which he strove was one requiring the American colonies to help carry the burden of imperial control. His was the order—get money from the Americans—that caused Grenville to place the Stamp Act before Parliament. His was the order that caused Parliament, in approving the Stamp Act, so to by-pass and ignore the colonial assemblies that they must ultimately wither and die, and with them the liberties of the colonists.

Suddenly, it seemed, all the old ties of blood, of culture, of trade, between America and England snapped. All the accumulated dislikes and grievances of Americans against Englishmen became concentrated in fury against the action of Parliament. All the differences between the colonies faded into insignificance as against the danger from England. Christopher Gadsden, back in Charleston, South Carolina, from the Stamp Act Congress, expressed the current thinking. "There ought," he said, "to be no New England men, no New York, &c. . . . but all of us Americans."[5]

Even as Gadsden made his statement, committees of correspondence—with their well-publicized "resolves"—were strengthening the colonial assemblies in their decisions to stand fast, and to stand together, in resistance to the objectionable British acts.

At the same time, societies of the Sons of Liberty—organized within existing clubs and fraternal groups—were fostering a sense of unity among the farmers, mechanics and others who would provide the manpower for revolution.

In the struggle to preserve their liberties and properties the colonists had found the road to union.

Bibliography

IN general the reference numbers are placed at the end of the paragraph concerned. In some cases, where several paragraphs are plainly derived from, or supported by, the same source or sources, the reference numbers are placed at the end of the last paragraph bearing on the subject. Where a short title seems sufficient, the full title and description are nevertheless given the first time the citation appears, and the statement is made that thereafter the short title, as identified, will be used. The full title and description, however, are repeated the first time the citation appears in each subsequent chapter section.

CHAPTER 1. BIRTH OF AN EMPIRE

1. *Documents relative to the Colonial History of the State of New York,* Vol. II (Albany, 1858), 433–434—hereafter cited as *N. Y. Col. Doc.*
2. *Ibid.,* Vol. II, 69, Vol. III (Albany, 1853), 73, 82–83, 345–346; Brodhead, John R., *History of the State of New York,* Vol. II (New York, 1871), 15–51.
3. Calder, Isabel M., "The Earl of Stirling and the Colonization of Long Island," in *Essays in Colonial History Presented to Charles McLean Andrews* (New Haven, 1931), 74–95; Andrews, Charles M., *The Colonial Period of American History,* Vol. III (New Haven, 1937), 58, note 1; Thorpe, F. N., *The Federal and State Constitutions,* Vol. 3 (Washington, 1909), 1637–1640.
4. Andrews, Charles M., *The Colonial Period of American History,* Vol. IV (New Haven, 1938), 50–84; *N. Y. Col. Doc.,* Vol. III, 44–46.
5. Fernow, B., ed., *Documents Relating to the History of the Dutch and Swedish Settlements on the Delaware River,* being Vol. XII of *N. Y. Col. Doc.* (Albany, 1877), 357; Brodhead, John R., *History of the State of New York,* Vol. I (New York, 1853), 697; *Dictionary of American History,* Vol. I (New York, 1940), 19; Andrews, Charles M., *The Colonial Period of American History,* Vol. III, 52–53, Vol. IV, 151; Bruce, Philip A., *Economic History of Virginia in the Seventeenth Century,* Vol. II (New York, 1895), 77, 84.
6. Andrews, Charles M., *The Colonial Period of American History,* Vol. III, 53–63; *N. Y. Col. Doc.,* Vol. III, 63.
7. Coleman, R. V., *The First Frontier* (New York, 1948), 77.
8. Williamson, William D., *History of the State of Maine,* Vol. I (Hallowell, 1832), 240–242, 245–253, 328–333, 407–408; *Dictionary of American History,* Vol. IV (New York, 1940), 239–240.
9. Coleman, R. V., *The First Frontier,* 306–317.
10. *Ibid.,* 303–306.
11. *Ibid.,* 306, 315.

12. *Ibid.*, 210–211, 366; *Dictionary of American History,* Vol. IV, 111–112.

13. Coleman, R. V., *The First Frontier,* 393–394.

14. Thorpe, F. N., *The Federal and State Constitutions,* Vol. 3, 1637–1640.

15. *N. Y. Col. Doc.,* Vol. III, 339–340, 342–346.

16. Campbell, Charles, *History of the Colony and Ancient Dominion of Virginia* (Philadelphia, 1860), 245–248; Bruce, Philip A., *Economic History of Virginia in the Seventeenth Century,* Vol. I (New York, 1895), 401, 567–570; Freeman, Douglas S., *George Washington,* Vol I (New York, 1948), 447–456; Beverley, Robert, *History and Present State of Virginia* (Chapel Hill, 1947), 92–94.

17. Coleman, R. V., *The First Frontier,* 214; Andrews, Charles M., *The Colonial Period of American History,* Vol. III, 182–192; Thorpe, F. N., *The Federal and State Constitutions,* Vol. 5, 2743–2753.

18. Andrews, Charles M., *The Colonial Period of American History,* Vol. III, 102–104.

19. *N. Y. Col. Doc.,* Vol. III, 74–77; Brodhead, John R., *History of the State of New York,* Vol. II (New York, 1871), 67–74; Andrews, Charles M., *The Colonial Period of American History,* Vol. III, 109–110.

20. Andrews, Charles M., *The Colonial Period of American History,* Vol. III, 106, 109; *N. Y. Col. Doc.,* Vol. III, 67–68.

21. *N. Y. Col. Doc.,* Vol. III, 106.

22. Lee, F. B., *New Jersey as a Colony and as a State,* Vol. I (New York, 1902), 114–115; Brodhead, John R., *History of the State of New York,* Vol. II, 49; *Dictionary of American History,* Vol. IV, 1i; Andrews, Charles M., *Colonial Period of American History,* Vol. III, 141–150; Whitehead, William A., *East Jersey under the Proprietary Governments* (New York, 1846), 37–40; Whitehead, William A., ed., *Documents relating to the Colonial History of the State of New Jersey,* Vol. I (Newark, 1880), 8–14, 43–46, 58–61, Vol. II, 328.

23. Whitehead, William A., *East Jersey under the Proprietary Governments,* 30–32; Brodhead, John R., *History of the State of New York,* 81–83.

24. Whitehead, William A., *East Jersey under the Proprietary Governments,* 36; Brodhead, John R., *History of the State of New York,* 81–86.

25. South Carolina Historical Society, *Collections,* Vol. V, 33–46; Whitehead, William A., *Documents relating to the Colonial History of the State of New Jersey,* Vol. I, 28–43; Andrews, Charles M., *Colonial Period of American History,* Vol. III, 140.

26. Whitehead, William A., ed., *Documents relating to the Colonial History of the State of New Jersey,* Vol. I, 106; Whitehead, William A., *East Jersey under the Proprietary Governments,* 41–46; New Jersey Historical Society, *Collections,* Vol. VI (Newark, 1864), 1–2.

CHAPTER 2. THE KING SPEAKS

1. *Documents relative to the Colonial History of the State of New York,* Vol. III (Albany, 1853), 64–65—hereafter cited as *N. Y. Col. Doc.;* Coleman, R. V., *The First Frontier* (New York, 1948), 157–158, 174, 202, 362.

2. Trumbull, J. Hammond, ed., *The Public Records of the Colony of Connecticut, 1636–1665* (Hartford, 1850), 433, 435; Massachusetts His-

torical Society, *Collections,* Fourth Series, Vol. VII (Boston, 1865), 311; Brodhead, John R., *History of the State of New York,* Vol. II (New York, 1871), 53–56.

3. *N. Y. Col. Doc.,* Vol. III, 83, 93, 96–97; Hutchinson, [Thomas,] *History of the Colony of Massachusets-Bay,* Vol. I (Boston, 1764), 233–234, 249–250; Coleman, R. V., *The First Frontier* (New York, 1948), 304–306, 315–317, 320–321, 351–352, 389–392, 405.

4. *N. Y. Col. Doc.,* Vol. III, 93–96; Shurtleff, N. B., ed., *Records of the Governor and Company of the Massachusetts Bay in New England,* Vol. IV, Part II (Boston, 1854), 157–235, 274–275, 318, 327–328—hereafter cited as *Mass. Col. Rec.;* Hutchinson, [Thomas,] *History of the Colony of Massachusets-Bay,* Vol. I (Boston, 1764), 235–249.

5. *Mass. Col. Rec.,* Vol. IV., Pt. II, 248–251, 265–273; Bouton, Nathaniel, ed., *Documents and Records relating to the Province of New-Hampshire,* Vol. I (Concord, 1867), 256–258, 270–280; *N. Y. Col. Doc.,* Vol. III, 101–102.

6. Libby, Charles T., ed., *Province and Court Records of Maine,* Vol. I (Portland, 1928), 200–219; Williamson, William D., *History of the State of Maine,* Vol. I (Hallowell, 1832), 411–420; *Mass. Col. Rec.,* Vol. IV, Pt. II, 243–245.

7. *Mass. Col. Rec.,* Vol. IV, Pt. II, 236–247.

8. *Mass. Col. Rec.,* Vol. IV, Pt. II, 248–252, 278–279; *N. Y. Col. Doc.,* Vol. III, 106–108; Hutchinson, [Thomas,] *History of Massachusets-Bay,* Vol. I (Boston, 1764), 547–548.

9. Libby, Charles T., ed., *Province and Court Records of Maine,* Vol. I (Portland, 1928), 301–303.

10. *Ibid.,* 263–264.

11. *Ibid.,* 266.

12. *Ibid.,* 328.

13. *Ibid.,* 267.

14. *Ibid.,* 282, 289, 300.

15. Williamson, William D., *History of the State of Maine,* Vol. I (Hallowell, 1832), 427–429; *N. Y. Col. Doc.,* Vol. III, 101.

16. *Mass. Col. Rec.,* Vol. IV, Pt. II, 368, 370–373, 401–404; Williamson, William D., *History of the State of Maine,* Vol. I (Hallowell, 1832), 431–437; Josselyn, John, *An Account of Two Voyages to New England* (Boston, 1865), 151.

CHAPTER 3. CAROLINA

1. South Carolina Historical Society, *Collections,* Vol. V, being The Shaftesbury Papers (Richmond, 1897), 188, 190, 198—hereafter cited as S. C. Hist. Soc., *Col.*

2. Thorpe, Francis N., *The Federal and State Constitutions,* Vol. V (Washington, 1909), 2743–2771.

3. S. C. Hist. Soc., *Col.,* Vol. V, 53–81; Andrews, Charles M., *Colonial Period of American History,* Vol. III (New Haven, 1937), 192–199.

4. S. C. Hist. Soc., *Col.,* Vol. V, 137–145, 156, 190–191; *Dictionary of American Biography,* Vol. XX (New York, 1936), 508–509.

5. S. C. Hist. Soc., *Col.,* Vol. V, 56, 133–158.

6. *Ibid.,* 160–165, 217–220.

7. *Ibid.*, 165–168, 175, 210.
8. *Ibid.*, 174–176, 188, 196–197, 210.
9. *Ibid.*, 164, 169–171.
10. *Ibid.*, 178, 203, 215–216; McCrady, Edward, *History of South Carolina under the Proprietary Government, 1670–1719* (New York, 1897), 120–121.
11. S. C. Hist. Soc., *Col.*, Vol. V, 173–181.
12. *Ibid.*, 179, 182, 189, 193, 196–197, 203, 212, 297.
13. *Ibid.*, 179, 183, 187, 191, 194–195, 203.
14. *Ibid.*, 198; "Treaty of Madrid," *Dictionary of American History,* Vol. III (New York, 1940), 322.
15. S. C. Hist. Soc., *Col.*, Vol. V, 93–117.
16. *Ibid.*, 95–100, 110–111, 120, 177, 203–204; Andrews, Charles M., *Colonial Period of American History,* Vol. III (New Haven, 1937), 212–222.
17. S. C. Hist Soc., *Col.*, Vol. V, 121, 469.
18. *Ibid.*, 311, 315.
19. *Ibid.*, 32, 39.
20. *Ibid.*, 125–127, 193, 269, 284.
21. *Ibid.*, 186–187, 191–192, 194.
22. *Ibid.*, 163, 180, 193, 203, 215, 228, 272, 297, 299.
23. *Ibid.*, 210–213, 271–274, 282.
24. *Ibid.*, 171, 203, 235, 275, 282, 297; *Dictionary of American Biography,* Vol. XX (New York, 1936), 11–12.

CHAPTER 4. NEW FRANCE

1. Kellogg, Louise Phelps, *French Regime in Wisconsin and the Northwest* (Madison, 1925), 80–100; Buck, Solon J. and Elizabeth H., *Planting of Civilization in Western Pennsylvania* (Pittsburgh, 1939), 22–25.
2. Brodhead, John R., *History of the State of New York,* Vol. II (New York, 1871), 100–102; *Documents relative to the Colonial History of the State of New York,* Vol. III (Albany, 1853), 121–125—hereafter cited as *N. Y. Col. Doc.*
3. Brodhead, John R., *History of the State of New York,* Vol. II, 102–104; *N. Y. Col. Doc.*, Vol. III, 118–119; Parkman, Francis, *Old Regime in Canada,* Vol. I (Frontenac Edition, New York, 1915), 246–250.
4. *N. Y. Col. Doc.*, Vol. III, 126–127.
5. *Ibid.*, 135; Parkman, Francis, *Old Regime in Canada,* Vol. I, 252–267; Brodhead, John R., *History of the State of New York* (New York, 1871), Vol. II, 114–120.
6. Kellogg, Louise Phelps, *French Regime in Wisconsin and the Northwest* (Madison, 1925), 101–178.
7. Parkman, Francis, *La Salle and the Discovery of the Great West* (Frontenac Edition, New York, 1915), 52; Kellogg, Louise Phelps, *French Regime in Wisconsin and the Northwest,* 89.
8. Kellogg, Louise Phelps, *French Regime in Wisconsin and the Northwest,* 131, 158–159.
9. *Ibid.*, 131, 137, 155, 157–158.
10. Parkman, Francis, *La Salle and the Discovery of the Great West* (Frontenac Edition, New York, 1915), 48–56.
11. *Ibid.*, 57–60; Kellogg, Louise Phelps, ed., *Early Narratives of the North-*

west (New York, 1917), 227–228; *Dictionary of American Biography*, Vol. XII (New York, 1933), 394–395.

12. Kellogg, Louise Phelps, ed., *Early Narratives of the Northwest* (New York, 1917), 227–229.

13. *Ibid.*, 229–236.

14. *Ibid.*, 236–256.

15. *Ibid.*, 257; Parkman, Francis, *La Salle and the Discovery of the Great West* (Frontenac Edition, New York, 1915), 74–77.

16. *Ibid.*, 85–96.

CHAPTER 5. A DUTCH INTERLUDE

1. Brodhead, John R., *History of the State of New York*, Vol. II (New York, 1871), 200.

2. *Ibid.*, 205–206.

3. *Ibid.*, 206–207, 234.

4. *Ibid.*, 209–244; Whitehead, William A., ed., *Documents relating to the Colonial History of the State of New Jersey*, Vol. I (Newark, 1880), 122–138; *Documents relative to the Colonial History of the State of New-York*, Vol. II (Albany, 1858), 571–707.

5. Brodhead, John R., *History of the State of New York*, Vol. II (New York, 1871), 244–259; *Documents relative to the Colonial History of the State of New-York*, Vol. II (Albany, 1858), 707–740; Vol. III (Albany, 1853), 215–222.

CHAPTER 6. KING PHILIP

1. Shurtleff, N. B., ed., *Records of the Governor and Company of the Massachusetts Bay*, Vol. IV, Part II (Boston, 1854), 519.

2. *Ibid.*, 566; *Ibid.*, Vol. V, 16–20; Williamson, William D., *History of the State of Maine*, Vol. I (Hallowell, 1832), 441–445.

3. *Documents relative to the Colonial History of the State of New York*, Vol. IX (Albany, 1855), 119; Parkman, Francis, *Count Frontenac and New France under Louis XIV* (Frontenac Edition, New York, 1915), 359; Williamson, William D., *History of the State of Maine*, Vol. I, 536–537; Brodhead, John R., *History of the State of New York*, Vol. II (New York, 1871), 310.

4. Coleman, R. V., *First Frontier* (New York, 1948), 340, 357–360, 393–396.

5. *Documents relative to the Colonial History of the State of New York*, Vol. III (Albany, 1853), 97.

6. *Dictionary of American Biography*, Vol. XII (New York, 1933), 380–381; Arnold, Samuel G., *History of the State of Rhode Island*, Vol. I (Providence, 1899), 387–390.

7. Lincoln, Charles H., ed., *Narratives of the Indian Wars, 1675–1699* (New York, 1913), 25–26; Hubbard, William, *Narrative of the Indian Wars* (Boston, 1775), 49–50; Arnold, Samuel G., *History of the State of Rhode Island*, Vol. I, 390–393; *Dictionary of American Biography*, Vol. III (New York, 1929), 479; *Ibid.*, Vol. XII (New York, 1933), 589–590.

8. Hutchinson, [Thomas,] *History of the Colony of Massachusets-Bay*,

[Vol. I] (Boston, 1764), 276–290; Arnold, Samuel G., *History of the State of Rhode Island*, Vol. I, 391–398; Lincoln, Charles H., ed., *Narratives of the Indian Wars*, 7–13, 26–31.

9. Lincoln, Charles H., ed., *Narratives of the Indian Wars*, 13, 30, 34, 39, 47; Hutchinson, [Thomas,] *History of the Colony of Massachusets-Bay*, [Vol. I,] 291–297; Arnold, Samuel G., *History of the State of Rhode Island*, Vol. I, 399–401.

10. Williamson, William D., *History of the State of Maine*, Vol. I, 518–553; Coleman, R. V., *First Frontier*, 200.

11. Hutchinson, [Thomas,] *History of the Colony of Massachusets-Bay*, [Vol. I,] 298; Pulsifer, David, ed., *Records of the Colony of New Plymouth*, Vol. X, being *Acts of the Commissioners of the United Colonies of New England*, Vol. II (Boston, 1859), 357–365.

12. Arnold, Samuel G., *History of the State of Rhode Island*, Vol. I, 401, 408–409.

13. *Ibid.*, 401.

14. Hutchinson, [Thomas,] *History of the Colony of Massachusets-Bay*, Vol. I, 299–307; Arnold, Samuel G., *History of the State of Rhode Island*, Vol. I, 405–407; Lincoln, Charles H., *Narratives of the Indian Wars*, 56–68.

15. Lincoln, Charles H., ed., *Narratives of the Indian Wars*, 112–167.

16. *Dictionary of American Biography*, Vol. III (New York, 1929), 479.

17. *Dictionary of American Biography*, Vol. XIV (New York, 1934), 534; Lincoln, Charles H., ed., *Narratives of the Indian Wars*, 41, 105; Hutchinson, [Thomas,] *History of the Colony of Massachusets-Bay*, Vol. I, 307.

18. Lincoln, Charles H., ed., *Narratives of the Indian Wars*, 4, 13, 16; Hutchinson, [Thomas,] *History of the Colony of Massachusets-Bay*, [Vol. I,] 307; Coleman, R. V., *First Frontier*, 340.

19. Toppan, Robert N., ed., *Edward Randolph*, Vol. I (Boston, 1898), 52; *Ibid.*, Vol. II, 192–194, 196–199.

20. *Ibid.*, Vol. II, 216–217.

21. *Ibid.*, 192–194.

22. *Ibid.*, 217.

CHAPTER 7. LOW PRICES–HIGH TAXES

1. Beverley, Robert, *History and Present State of Virginia*, Edited by Louis B. Wright (Chapel Hill, 1947), 70–71.

2. Andrews, Charles M., ed., *Narratives of the Insurrections, 1675–1690* (New York, 1915), 11–12, 113 note 4; Andrews, Charles M., *Colonial Period in American History*, Vol. II (New Haven, 1936), 340; Henning, W. W., *Statutes at Large*, Vol. II (New York, 1823), 280.

3. Bruce, P. A., *Institutional History of Virginia in the Seventeenth Century*, Vol. II (New York, 1910), 264.

4. Campell, Charles, *History of the Colony and Ancient Dominion of Virginia* (Philadelphia, 1860), 274–276; Freeman, Douglas S., *George Washington*, Vol. I (New York, 1948), 447–465.

5. Beverley, Robert, *History and Present State of Virginia*, Edited by Louis B. Wright, 75–76.

6. *Ibid.*, 78; Andrews, Charles M., ed., *Narratives of the Insurrections*, 20, 105–110.

7. Andrews, Charles M., ed., *Narratives of the Insurrections*, 109–112.

8. *Ibid.*, 112–115.

9. *Ibid.*, 116–117.

10. *Ibid.*, 117–128.

11. *Ibid.*, 35, 128–136.

12. *Ibid.*, 6–7, 61, 136–139, 145.

13. *Ibid.*, 36–39, 139–140; Campbell, Charles, *History of the Colony and Ancient Dominion of Virginia*, 315–318.

14. McIlwaine, H. R., ed., *Minutes of the Council and General Court of Colonial Virginia, 1622–1632, 1670–1676* (Richmond, 1924), 454–461; Campbell, Charles, *History of the Colony and Ancient Dominion of Virginia*, 313–321; Andrews, Charles M., ed., *Narratives of the Insurrections*, 40.

15. Beverley, Robert, *History and Present State of Virginia*, Edited by Louis B. Wright, 84–86.

16. Andrews, Charles M., ed., *Narratives of the Insurrections*, 36; Andrews, Charles M., *Colonial Period of American History*, Vol. II, 338–341.

17. *Dictionary of American Biography*, Vol. III (New York, 1929), 427.

18. *Maryland Archives*, Vol. XV (Baltimore, 1896), 127–128; Andrews, Charles M., *Colonial Period of American History*, Vol. II, 343–344.

19. Andrews, Charles M., ed., *Narratives of the Insurrections*, 145, 159; South Carolina Historical Society, *Collections*, Vol. V (Richmond, 1897), 274, 424–425, 430–hereafter cited as S. C. Hist. Soc., *Col.*

20. Andrews, Charles M., ed., *Narratives of the Insurrections*, 145–146, 158; Toppan, R. N., ed., *Edward Randolph*, Vol. II (Boston, 1898), 249–250.

21. Andrews, Charles M., ed., *Narratives of the Insurrections*, 149–152.

22. *Ibid.*, 150–160; Saunders, William L., ed., *Colonial Records of North Carolina*, Vol. I (Raleigh, 1886), 256–261.

23. Andrews, Charles M., ed., *Narratives of the Insurrections*, 152, 161–164.

24. [Rivers, William J.], *A Sketch of the History of South Carolina* (Charleston, 1856), 109, 111, 114–115; McCrady, Edward, *History of South Carolina under the Proprietary Government* (New York, 1897), 190.

25. S. C. Hist. Soc., *Col.*, Vol. V, 456–462.

26. *Ibid.*, 462; [Rivers, William J.], *A Sketch of the History of South Carolina*, 388–390.

27. Crane, Verner W., *The Southern Frontier, 1670–1732* (Durham, 1928), 19–21; [Rivers, William J.], *A Sketch of the History of South Carolina*, 127–129, 393.

28. [Rivers, William J.], *A Sketch of the History of South Carolina*, 115, 129–130; McCrady, Edward, *History of South Carolina under the Proprietary Government*, 182.

CHAPTER 8. QUAKERS

1. Whitehead, William A., ed., *Documents relating to the Colonial History of the State of New Jersey*, Vol. I (Newark, 1880), 209; Andrews, Charles M., *Colonial Period of American History*, Vol. III (New Haven, 1937), 151–152.

2. Andrews, Charles M., *Colonial Period of American History*, Vol. III, 138–150; Lee, Francis B., *New Jersey as a Colony and as a State*, Vol. I (New York, 1902), 135–138.
3. Brodhead, John R., *History of the State of New York*, Vol. II (New York, 1871), 270.
4. *Ibid.*, 301–302; Lee, F. B., *New Jersey as a Colony and as a State*, Vol. I, 145–146; Andrews, Charles M., *Colonial Period of American History*, Vol. III, 152, 163–166.
5. *Dictionary of American Biography*, Vol. XIV (New York, 1934), 433–434.
6. *Dictionary of American History*, Vol. II (New York, 1940), 182, article on "East Jersey."
7. Fernow, B., ed., *Documents relating to the History of the Dutch and Swedish Settlements on the Delaware River*, being Vol. XII of the *N. Y. Col. Doc.* (Albany, 1877), 559, 565–567, 568–569; Brodhead, John R., *History of the State of New York*, Vol. II, 302.
8. Whitehead, William A., ed., *Documents relating to the Colonial History of the State of New Jersey*, Vol. I, 241–270.
9. *Ibid.*, 241–244; Andrews, Charles M., Colonial Period of American History, Vol. III, 166–167.
10. Fernow, B., ed., *Documents relative to the History of the Dutch and Swedish Settlements on the Delaware River*, 579–580; Brodhead, John R., *History of the State of New York*, Vol. II, 305–306; Andrews, Charles M., *Colonial Period of American History*, Vol. III, 166–167.
11. *Documents relative to the Colonial History of the State of New-York*, Vol. III (Albany, 1853), 240; Brodhead, John R., *History of the State of New York*, Vol. II, 332–334; James, B. B., and Jameson, J. F., eds., *Journal of Jasper Danckaerts* (New York, 1913), 239–244.
12. Whitehead, William A., ed., *Documents relating to the Colonial History of the State of New Jersey*, Vol. I, 303–304, 314–315; Andrews, Charles M., *Colonial Period of American History*, Vol. III, 157–158; Brodhead, John R., *History of the State of New York*, Vol. II, 333–334.
13. James, B. B., and Jameson, J. F., eds., *Journal of Jasper Danckaerts*, 3–42.
14. *Ibid.*, 43–50, 62.
15. *Ibid.*, 45–47.
16. *Ibid.*, 50–54, 61, 83.
17. *Ibid.*, 57–62.
18. *Ibid.*, 64–67.
19. *Ibid.*, 80.
20. *Ibid.*, 91–97.
21. *Ibid.*, 97–98.
22. *Ibid.*, 99.
23. *Ibid.*, 100–107.
24. *Ibid.*, 109–115.
25. Coleman, R. V., *First Frontier* (New York, 1948), 384–385; *Dictionary of American Biography*, Vol. VIII (New York, 1932), 592.
26. James, B. B., and Jameson, J. F., eds., *Journal of Jasper Danckaerts*, xx–xxv, 115.
27. *Ibid.*, 196–197.
28. *Ibid.*, 198, 216–217.

CHAPTER 9. LA SALLE

1. See page 38; Brodhead, John R., *History of the State of New York,* Vol. II (New York, 1871), 404–405.
2. Parkman, Francis, *La Salle and the Discovery of the Great West* (Frontenac Edition, New York, 1915), 99–102, 120–121—hereafter cited as Parkman, *La Salle.*
3. *Ibid.,* 122–130.
4. *Ibid.,* 130–142.
5. *Ibid.,* 127–130, 137–143.
6. *Ibid.,* 144–146.
7. *Ibid.,* 140–141, 146–154; Shea, J. G., ed., *Discovery and Exploration of the Mississippi Valley* (Albany, 1903), 95–96—hereafter cited as Shea, *Discovery.*
8. Parkman, *LaSalle,* 154; Shea, *Discovery,* 96.
9. Parkman, *LaSalle,* 154–156; Kellogg, Louise P., *Early Narratives of the Northwest, 1634–1699* (New York, 1917), 288—hereafter cited as Kellogg, *Northwest.*
10. Parkman, *LaSalle,* 156–163; Kellogg, *Northwest,* 288; Shea, *Discovery,* 97; Cox, I. J., *The Journeys of Rene Robert Cavelier, Sieur de La Salle,* Vol I (New York, 1905), 79–81.
11. Parkman, *La Salle,* 163–168; Kellogg, *Northwest,* 289; Shea, *Discovery,* 97–98.
12. Kellogg, *Northwest,* 289; Shea, *Discovery,* 98; Parkman, *La Salle,* 170–172.
13. Shea, *Discovery,* 98–100; Parkman, *La Salle,* 172–179; Kellogg, *Northwest,* 289; Cox, I. J., *The Journeys of Rene Robert Cavelier, Sieur de La Salle,* 82–83.
14. Kellogg, *Northwest,* 289; Parkman, *La Salle,* 180–181; Shea, *Discovery,* 100, 155.
15. Parkman, *La Salle,* 185–187; Shea, *Discovery,* 101, 111; Kellogg, *Northwest,* 290.
16. Parkman, *La Salle,* 187–194; Kellogg,, *Northwest,* 290.
17. Parkman, *La Salle,* 194–198.
18. Parkman, *La Salle,* 199–201, 216–218; Kellogg, *Northwest,* 290; Shea, *Discovery,* 153–154.
19. Shea, *Discovery,* 155.
20. Shea, *Discovery,* 111–149; Parkman, *La Salle,* 242–281; Kellogg, *Northwest,* 331–333.
21. Parkman, *La Salle,* 199–203.
22. Alvord, C. W., *The Illinois Country, 1673–1818,* being Vol. I of the Centennial History of Illinois (Springfield, 1920), 84–86; Hanna, Charles A. *The Wilderness Trail,* Vol I (New York, 1911), 158.
23. Parkman, *La Salle,* 223–238; Kellogg, *Northwest,* 291–296; Shea, *Discovery,* 159–164.
24. Parkman, *La Salle,* 203–215, 236; Shea, *Discovery,* 165–166.
25. Parkman, *La Salle,* 283–291.
26. Parkman, *La Salle,* 293–312; Kellogg, *Northwest,* 297–305; Shea, *Discovery,* 169–188; French, B. F., ed., *Historical Collections of Louisiana and Florida, Second Series* (New York, 1875), 17–27.

CHAPTER 10. PENNSYLVANIA

1. Whitehead, William A., ed., *Documents relating to the Colonial History of the State of New Jersey,* Vol. I (Newark, 1880), 337–345, 347–348, 366–373, 383–394; Andrews, Charles M., *Colonial Period of American History,* Vol. III (New Haven, 1937), 154, 158, 164–165, 168–169; Brodhead, John R., *History of the State of New York,* Vol. II (New York, 1871), 341–342, 368.
2. Fisher, S. G., *The True William Penn* (Philadelphia, 1900), 197–203; Andrews, Charles M., *Colonial Period of American History,* Vol. III, 277–278; Shepherd, W. R., *History of the Proprietary Government in Pennsylvania* (New York, 1896), 176.
3. Thorpe, F. N., ed., *Federal and State Constitutions,* Vol. V (Washington, 1909), 3035–3044; Andrews, Charles M., *Colonial Period of American History,* Vol. III, 278–285; Toppan, R. N., ed., *Edward Randolph,* Vol. I (Boston, 1898), 129–130, 178–179.
4. Vulliamy, C. E., *William Penn* (New York, 1934), 156.
5. Thorpe, F. N., ed., *Federal and State Constitutions,* Vol. V, 3036; Mathews, E. B., *Map and Map-Makers of Maryland* (Baltimore, 1898), 376–378.
6. Myers, A. C., ed., *Narratives of Early Pennsylvania, West New Jersey and Delaware* (New York, 1912), 200, 202—hereafter cited as Myers, *Narratives;* Shepherd, W. R., *History of the Proprietary Government in Pennsylvania,* 176.
7. Myers, *Narratives,* 202–215.
8. Andrews, Charles M., *Colonial Period of American History,* Vol. III, 289; Myers, *Narratives,* 219–220, 240, n. 1.
9. Thorpe, F. N., ed., *Federal and State Constitutions,* Vol. V, 3045.
10. Myers, *Narratives,* 219–220; Shepherd, W. R., *History of the Proprietary Government in Pennsylvania,* 19.
11. Thorpe, F. N., ed., *Federal and State Constitutions,* Vol. V, 3052–3059.
12. *Ibid.,* 3059–3063.
13. Andrews, Charles M., *Colonial Period of American History,* Vol. III, 292–295; *Colonial Documents relative to the History of the State of New-York,* Vol. III (Albany, 1853), 247.
14. Winsor, Justin, *Narrative and Critical History of America,* Vol. III (Boston, 1884), 480–482; Fisher, S. G., *The True William Penn,* 229–230; *Dictionary of American History,* Vol. V (New York, 1940), 433; *Dictionary of American Biography,* Vol. XIII (New York, 1934), 155; Myers, *Narratives,* 221, 240–241.
15. Winsor, Justin, *Narrative and Critical History of America,* Vol. III, 482; Vulliamy, C. E., *William Penn,* 168–173; Deed Record G., p. 410, also B. 9, pp. 407–412, of New Castle County, Delaware, Book B; Hazard, Samuel, *Annals of Pennsylvania, 1609–1682* (Philadelphia, 1850), 596–607.
16. Andrews, Charles M., *Colonial Period of American History,* Vol. III, 297–298; Shepherd, W. R., *History of the Proprietary Government in Pennsylvania,* 242–243; Fisher, S. G., *The True William Penn,* 230–231; Winsor, Justin, *Narrative and Critical History of America,* Vol. III, 485–488.

17. Andrews, Charles M., *Colonial Period of American History*, Vol. II (New Haven, 1936), 360; Winsor, Justin, *Narrative and Critical History of America*, Vol. III, 488.

18. Shepherd, W. R., *History of the Proprietary Government in Pennsylvania*, 19; Myers, *Narratives*, 237–238, 251.

19. Myers, *Narratives*, 239–244.

20. Egle, W. H., ed., *Minutes of the Board of Property of the Province of Pennsylvania*, Vol. I (Harrisburg, 1893), 3–4; Vulliamy, C. E., *William Penn*, 168; Fisher, S. G., *The True William Penn*, 238–239; Myers, *Narratives*, 221, 247–254; Winsor, Justin, *Narrative and Critical History of America*, Vol. III, 491.

21. Myers, *Narratives*, 229, 239–242; Winsor, Justin, *Narrative and Critical History of America*, Vol. III, 491.

22. Myers, *Narratives*, 227–229, 250; Winsor, Justin, *Narrative and Critical History of America*, Vol. III, 492–493.

23. Winsor, Justin, *Narrative and Critical History of America*, Vol. III, 491–492; Whitehead, William A., *East Jersey under the Proprietary Governments* (New York, 1846), 108.

24. Winsor, Justin, *Narrative and Critical History of America*, Vol. III, 492.

25. Learned, M. D., *Life of Francis Daniel Pastorius* (Philadelphia, 1908), 212–213.

26. *Ibid.*, 109–129.

27. *Ibid.*, 117, 122–134.

28. Shepherd, W. R., *History of the Proprietary Government in Pennsylvania*, 243–247; Winsor, Justin, *Narrative and Critical History of America*, Vol. III, 485–486.

29. Myers, *Narratives*, 260–261.

30. Vulliamy, C. E., *William Penn*, 194–195; Neill, Edward D., *Terra Mariæ* (Philadelphia, 1867), 166–167.

31. Neill, Edward D., *Terra Mariæ*, 167–168.

32. *Ibid.*, 168–169; Andrews, Charles M., *Colonial Period of American History*, Vol. II, 358–359.

33. Mereness, N. D., *Maryland as a Proprietary Province* (New York, 1901), 32–33; Andrews, Charles M., *Colonial Period of American History*, Vol. II, 359–362.

CHAPTER 11. *QUO WARRANTO*

1. Andrews, Charles M., *British Committees, Commissions, and Councils of Trade and Plantations, 1622–1675* (Baltimore, 1908); *Dictionary of American History*, Vol. I (New York, 1940), 206–207, article on "Boards of Trade and Plantations," and Vol. III (New York, 1940), 301–302, article on "Lords of Trade and Plantation"; Andrews, Charles M., *Colonial Period of American History*, Vol. IV (New Haven, 1938), 55–59; Toppan, R. N., ed., *Edward Randolph*, Vol. I (Boston, 1898), 46–51—hereafter cited as *Randolph*.

2. Andrews, Charles M., *Colonial Period of American History*, Vol. IV, 12–21; *Dictionary of American History*, Vol. IV, 73–74, article on "Navigation Acts"; Grant, W. L., and Munro, James, eds., *Acts of the Privy Council of England*, Colonial Series, Vol. I (1908), 49.

3. Shurtleff, N. B., ed., *Records of the Governor and Company of the Massachusetts Bay*, Vol. V (Boston, 1854), 200—hereafter cited as *Mass. Col. Rec.*

4. *Randolph*, Vol. II, 206, 209, 219, 248–250.

5. *Ibid.*, Vol. I, 74–82; Vol. II, 265–277; *Mass. Col. Rec.*, Vol. V, 99–100, 106–116; Hutchinson, [Thomas], *History of the Colony of Massachusets-Bay*, Vol. I (Boston, 1764), 311–312; Hammond, I. W., ed., *New Hampshire State Papers*, Vol. XVII (Manchester, 1889), 529–531.

6. *Randolph*, Vol. I, 82; *Mass. Col. Rec.*, Vol. V, 156.

7. *Documentary History of the State of Maine*, Vol. VII (Portland, 1901), 343–356.

8. *Randolph*, Vol. I, 92–104, 117; Vol. II, 289–298; Vol. III, 4–5.

9. *Ibid.*, Vol. I, 115–120, 228; Vol. III, 47–52.

10. *Ibid.*, Vol. I, 121–124; Vol. III. 56–66.

11. *Ibid.*, Vol. III, 56, 104–109; Hammond, I. W., ed., *New Hampshire State Papers*, Vol. XVII, 524–528, 587; Bouton, Nathaniel, ed., *Documents and Records relating to the Province of New-Hampshire*, Vol. I (Concord, 1867), 373–413.

12. *Randolph*, Vol. III, 70–76.

13. *Ibid.*, Vol. I, 140–150; Vol. III, 89–103, 110–113.

14. Hammond, I. W., ed., *New Hampshire State Papers*, Vol. XVII, 549, 559–562; Bouton, N., ed., *Documents and Records relating to the Province of New-Hampshire*, Vol. I, 420–421, 433–443; *Randolph*, Vol. I, 147, 180.

15. *Randolph*, Vol. I, 151–162; Vol. III, 126–128.

16. *Ibid.*, Vol. I, 157, 179; Vol. III, 207–208; *Mass. Col. Rec.*, Vol. V., 346–349.

17. Coleman, R. V., *The First Frontier* (New York, 1948), 164, 232–235, 242–244; *Randolph*, Vol. I, 198.

18. Massachusetts Historical Society, *Collections*, Fourth Series, Vol. VIII (Boston, 1868), 495; American Antiquarian Society, *Transactions and Collections*, Vol. III (1857), 134–135.

19. *Randolph*, Vol. I, 196–206, 209.

20. Massachusetts Historical Society, *Collections*, Third Series, Vol. I, 74–81.

21. *Randolph*, Vol. I, 215–216, 237, 242; *Mass. Col. Rec.*, Vol. V, 430, 451.

22. *Randolph*, Vol. I, 244, 257–264; Vol. IV, 51–58.

23. *Mass. Col. Rec.*, Vol. V, 466–517.

24. *Randolph*, Vol. I, 250.

25. *Ibid.*, Vol. I, 256–265; *Dictionary of American History*, Vol. IV, 98, article on "Dominion of New England."

26. Bouton, N., ed., *Documents and Records relating to the Province of New-Hampshire*, Vol. I, 468–471, 474–498, 502–504, 508–515, 556.

27. Hammond, I. W., ed., *New Hampshire Provincial Papers*, Vol. XVII, 584–602; Bouton, N., ed., *Documents and Records relating to the Province of New-Hampshire*, Vol. I, 556–562, 569–573.

28. Bouton, N., ed., *Documents and Records relating to the Province of New-Hampshire*, Vol. I, 578–582.

29. *Randolph*, Vol. I, 274–275.

30. *Ibid.*, Vol. I, 266; *Mass. Col. Rec.*, Vol. V, 77; *Dictionary of American Biography*, Vol. V (New York, 1930), 481–483; Coleman, R. V., *The First Frontier*, 363.

31. *Randolph*, Vol. I, 275–278; Vol. IV, 74–75, 78; 80–84; *Mass. Col. Rec.*, Vol. V, 515–516; Massachusetts Historical Society, *Collections*, Fifth Series, Vol. V (Boston, 1878), 138–139.

32. Hutchinson, [Thomas], *History of the Colony of Massachusets-Bay*, Vol. I, 355–357; *Randolph*, Vol. I, 283–284; Massachusetts Historical Society, *Collections*, Fifth Series, Vol. V, 139–158.

33. *Randolph*, Vol. I, 258, 287–288, 290, 296–297; Vol. IV, 78–79; Trumbull, J. H., *The Public Records of the Colony of Connecticut, 1678–1689* (Hartford, 1859), 207–213, 349–377.

34. *Dictionary of American Biography*, Vol. I (New York, 1928), 300–301; *Dictionary of American History*, Vol. IV, 98, article on "Dominion of New England," Bartlett, J. R., ed., *Records of the Colony of Rhode Island and Providence Plantations*, Vol. III (Providence, 1858), 212–218; *Documentary History of the State of Maine*, Vol. VII (Portland, 1901), 369–373.

35. *Randolph*, Vol. II, 6; Massachusetts Historical Society, *Collections*, Fifth Series, Vol. V (Boston, 1878), 159.

36. *Randolph*, Vol. II, 7; Massachusetts Historical Society, *Collections*, Fifth Series, Vol. V, 159–162.

CHAPTER 12. ALONG THE TRADING PATHS

1. Saunders, William L., ed., *Colonial Records of North Carolina*, Vol. I (Raleigh, 1886), 353; [Rivers, W. J.], *Sketch of the History of South Carolina* (Charleston, 1856), 148–150; McCrady, Edward, *History of South Carolina under the Proprietary Government* (New York, 1897), 213–214.

2. Salley, Jr., A. S., ed., *Narratives of Early Carolina* (New York, 1911), 181–187—hereafter cited as Salley, *Carolina;* Andrews, Charles M., *Colonial Period of American History*, Vol. III (New Haven, 1937), 224–226.

3. Salley, *Carolina*, 182–183; Crane, Verner W., *The Southern Frontier, 1670–1732* (Durham, 1928), 19–21, 139–140; Swanton, John R., *Indians of the Southeastern United States* (Washington, 1946), 184.

4. Crane, V. W., *Southern Frontier*, 34; McCrady, E., *History of South Carolina under the Proprietary Government*, 195–197, 214–216; Insh, G. P., *Scottish Colonial Schemes, 1620–1686* (Glasgow, 1922), 186–211.

5. Coleman, R. V., *The First Frontier* (New York, 1948), 31–33; McCrady, E., *History of South Carolina under the Proprietary Government*, 203, 214–216; Crane, V. W., *Southern Frontier*, 28–31.

6. Insh, G. P., *Scottish Colonial Schemes, 1620–1686*, 210–211.

7. Crane, V. W., *Southern Frontier*, 33–36; Lanning, John Tate, *The Spanish Missions of Georgia* (Chapel Hill, 1935), 172–181.

8. *Dictionary of American History*, Vol. III (New York, 1940), 260, article on "Lederer's Exploring Expeditions."

9. *Virginia Magazine of History and Biography*, Vol. XXIV (Richmond, 1916), 228–231, 351–359, Vol. XXV (Richmond, 1917), 51–52.

10. Brodhead, John R., *History of the State of New York*, Vol. I (New York, 1871), 396–398.

11. *Ibid.*, 397; *Documents relative to the Colonial History of the State of New-York*, Vol. IV (Albany, 1855), 670–671.

12. Brodhead, John R., *History of the State of New York*, 397, 403; *Docu-*

ments relative to the Colonial History of the State of New-York, Vol.
III (Albany, 1853), 417.

13. Brodhead, John R., *History of the State of New York*, 404.
14. *Ibid.*, 476–478; Kellogg, Louise P., ed., *Early Narratives of the North-west, 1634–1699* (New York, 1917), 308–309.
15. Brodhead, John R., *History of the State of New York*, 470–483; Kellogg, L. P., ed., *Early Narratives of the Northwest*, 310–311.

CHAPTER 13.   TEXAS

1. Parkman, Francis, *La Salle and the Discovery of the Great West* (Frontenac Edition, New York, 1915), 313–327, 342–350—hereafter cited as Parkman, *La Salle*.
2. *Ibid.*, 351–366; Cox, I. J., ed., *The Journeys of Rene Robert Cavelier, Sieur de LaSalle*, Vol. II (New York, 1906), 1–4—hereafter cited as Cox, *LaSalle*.
3. Cox, *LaSalle*, Vol. II, 4–57.
4. Parkman, *La Salle*, 375–377.
5. *Ibid.*, 391–397; Cox, *LaSalle*, Vol. II, 57–68.
6. Cox, *LaSalle*, Vol. II, 53–55, 57–60, 72; Parkman, *La Salle*, 396.
7. Parkman, *La Salle*, 363, 396, 400–401, 420–421, 448.
8. *Ibid.*, 399, 409; Cox, *LaSalle*, Vol. II, 71, 73, 98.
9. Cox, *LaSalle*, Vol. II, 71–72, 84, 87; Parkman, *La Salle*, 395–415.
10. Kellogg, Louise Phelps, ed., *Early Narratives of the Northwest, 1634–1699* (New York, 1917), 307–308.
11. Cox, *LaSalle*, Vol. II, 87–99.
12. *Ibid.*, Vol. II, 92, 99–122.
13. *Ibid.*, Vol. II, 123–128; Parkman, *La Salle*, 420–432.
14. Cox, *LaSalle*, Vol. II, 130–168.
15. *Ibid.*, 168–189; Swanton, John R., *The Indians of the Southeastern United States* (Washington, 1946), 98–100.
16. Cox, LaSalle, Vol. II, 189–200.
17. *Ibid.*, 200–233; Kellogg, Louise P., ed., *Early Narratives of the Northwest*, 311; Parkman, *La Salle*, 456–463.
18. Kellogg, Louise P., ed., *Early Narratives of the Northwest*, 311–321.
19. Bolton, H. E., ed., *Spanish Exploration in the Southwest, 1542–1706* (New York, 1916), 348—hereafter cited as Bolton, *Southwest;* Parkman, *La Salle*, 414.
20. Hackett, C. W., *Revolt of the Pueblo Indians of New Mexico and Otermin's Attempted Reconquest, 1680–1682*, Vol. I (Albuquerque, 1942), xix–xxiii.
21. *Ibid.*, Vol. I, 5–7.
22. *Ibid.*, Vol. I, xxxvii–liii, 13, Vol. II, 239.
23. *Ibid.*, Vol. I, lxv–lxvii, 12–19.
24. *Ibid.*, Vol. I, 19–23.
25. *Ibid.*, Vol. I, lxvii–lxxviii, 26–28.
26. *Ibid.*, Vol. I, lxxix–cxli.
27. Hodge, F. W., ed., *Handbook of American Indians North of Mexico*, Vol. I (Washington, 1907), 636; Bolton, *Southwest*, 314–317, 320–343.
28. Bolton, *Southwest*, 347–348.
29. *Ibid.*, 353–362, 388–399.

30. *Ibid.,* 363–364, 402–403; Cox, *LaSalle,* Vol. II, 149.
31. Bolton, *Southwest,* 368–387, 405–423.

CHAPTER 14. REVOLUTION

1. Toppan, R. N., ed., *Edward Randolph,* Vol. IV (Boston, 1899), 264–265–hereafter cited as *Randolph;* Andrews, Charles M., *Narratives of the Insurrections, 1675–1690* (New York, 1915), 175–176–hereafter cited as Andrews, *Insurrections.*
2. Barnes, Viola F., *Dominion of New England* (New Haven, 1923), 86–90–hereafter cited as Barnes, *Dominion;* Andrews, *Insurrections,* 178; *Randolph,* Vol. IV, 171–182.
3. Bates, A. C., *Charter of Connecticut* (Hartford, 1932), 28–38; Trumbull, J. H., ed., *Public Records of the Colony of Connecticut, 1678–1689* (Hartford, 1859), 229–hereafter cited as *Conn. Col. Rec.*
4. Bates, A. C., *Charter of Connecticut,* 38–39; *Conn. Col. Rec., 1678–1689,* 248–249.
5. Bates, A. C., *Charter of Connecticut,* 40–44; Trumbull, Benjamin, *History of Connecticut,* Vol. I (New Haven, 1818), 371–372.
6. Brodhead, John R., *History of the State of New York,* Vol. II (New York, 1871), 463, 465, 469–472, 499–502–hereafter cited as Brodhead, *New York; Conn. Col. Rec., 1678–1689,* 366–367, 382; *Documents relative to the Colonial History of the State of New-York,* Vol. III (Albany, 1853), 537–542–hereafter cited as *N. Y. Col. Doc.*
7. *N. Y. Col. Doc.,* Vol. III, 543–549; Hutchinson, [Thomas,] *History of the Colony of Massachusets-Bay,* [Vol. I] (Boston, 1764), 353–354; Andrews, *Insurrections,* 180, 241; Barnes, *Dominion,* 73.
8. Andrews, *Insurrections,* 177, 241.
9. Hutchinson, [Thomas,] *History of the Colony of Massachusets-Bay,* [Vol. I,] 359–360; Barnes, *Dominion,* 171–211; *Randolph,* Vol. II, 60–62, Vol. IV, 171; Andrews, *Insurrections,* 179–180, 244–246.
10. *Dictionary of American Biography,* Vol. XII (New York, 1933), 391; Murdock, K. B., *Increase Mather* (Cambridge, 1925), 185–189.
11. *N. Y. Col. Doc.,* Vol. III, 567; Parkman, Francis, *Count Frontenac and New France Under Louis XIV* (Frontenac Edition, New York, 1915), 360–363.
12. Parkman, Francis, *Count Frontenac and New France Under Louis XIV,* 363; *N. Y. Col. Doc.,* Vol. III, 571; Williamson, W. B., *History of the State of Maine,* Vol. I (Hallowell, 1832), 587.
13. Brodhead, *New York,* Vol. II, 518; Williamson, W. D., *History of the State of Maine,* Vol. I, 607–610; Hutchinson, [Thomas,] *History of the Colony of Massachusets-Bay,* [Vol. I,] 364–365; Barnes, *Dominion,* 225–227; Andrews, *Insurrections,* 247.
14. Barnes, *Dominion,* 227–228; Winsor, Justin, *The Memorial History of Boston,* Vol. II (Boston, 1881), 12; Hutchinson, [Thomas,] *History of the Colony of Massachusets-Bay,* [Vol. I,] 370–371.
15. *Randolph,* Vol. II, 83–84; Whitmore, W. H., ed., *The Andros Tracts,* Vol. I (Boston, 1868), 75–76, note 23.
16. *N. Y. Col. Doc.,* Vol. III, 591, 660.
17. Cross, A. L., *History of England and Greater Britain* (New York, 1914), 576–584; Bryant, Arthur, *Samuel Pepys, The Saviour of the Navy* (Cambridge, 1939), 295–301.

18. *Randolph*, Vol. II, 89; Vol. IV, 277; Hutchinson, [Thomas,] *History of the Colony of Massachusets-Bay*, [Vol. I,] 372–373.

19. Murdock, K. B., *Increase Mather*; 190–215; Adams, James Truslow, *Founding of New England* (Boston, 1921), 431–432; Barnes, *Dominion*, 231–237; Andrews, *Insurrections*, 277.

20. Barnes, *Dominion*, 238–240; Brodhead, *New York*, Vol. II, 556–557; *Randolph*, Vol. II, 87; *N. Y. Col. Doc.*, Vol. IX (Albany, 1855), 404–408.

21. *Randolph*, Vol. II, 87–88, Vol. IV, 271–272, 277–278; Andrews, *Insurrections*, 186–190, 199–200, 215–216, 232–233.

22. Hutchinson, [Thomas,] *History of the Colony of Massachusets-Bay*, [Vol. I,] 377–378; Andrews, *Insurrections*, 202, 232.

23. Andrews, *Insurrections*, 188, 202; Barnes, *Dominion*, 244; *Randolph*, Vol. IV, 272.

24. Andrews, *Insurrections*, 174, 189–190, 203–240, 216–217; *Randolph*, Vol. II, 104, 115, Vol. V, 20–21; Barnes, *Dominion*, 244.

25. Barnes, *Dominion*, 244–247, 254.

26. Murdock, K. B., *Increase Mather*, 219–220; Fortescue, J. W., ed., *Calendar of State Papers, Colonial Series, America and West Indies, 1689–1692*, Vol. 13 (London, 1901), §332.

27. *Conn. Col. Rec., 1678–1689*, 250; Arnold, S. G., *History of the State of Rhode Island*, Vol. I (Providence, 1899), 512–513.

28. Brodhead, *New York*, Vol. II, 557, 561, 565.

29. *Ibid.*, 563, 566–571; *N. Y. Col. Doc.*, Vol. III, 590–604, 609.

30. Brodhead, *New York*, Vol. II, 564–576; *N. Y. Col. Doc.*, Vol. III, 614–616.

31. Brodhead, *New York*, Vol. II, 594–595; Andrews, *Narratives*, 324.

32. Andrews, *Insurrections*, 301–314; Winsor, Justin, *Narrative and Critical History of America*, Vol. III (Boston, 1884), 550–552; Mereness, N. D., *Maryland as a Proprietary Province* (New York, 1901), 38–41; *Dictionary of American Biography*, Vol. IV (New York, 1930), 369.

33. Barnes, *Dominion*, 265–267; *Randolph*, Vol. II, 121–126.

34. Barnes, *Dominion*, 268; Mereness, N. D., *Maryland as a Proprietary Province*, 42.

35. Vulliamy, C. E., *William Penn* (New York, 1934), 225–233; Fisher, S. C., *The True William Penn* (Philadelphia, 1899), 309–332.

36. Hutchinson, [Thomas,] *History of the Colony of Massachusets-Bay*, [Vol. I,] 390, 405–411; Thorpe, F. N., *Federal and State Constitutions*, etc., Vol. III (Washington, 1909), 1870–1886.

37. *N. Y. Col. Doc.*, Vol. IX, 404–408.

38. *N. Y. Col. Doc.*, Vol. III, 623–629; Brodhead, *New York*, Vol. II, 594.

39. Brodhead, *New York*, Vol. II, 595–616; *N. Y. Col. Doc.*, Vol. III, 731–733; Andrews, Charles M., *Colonial Period of American History*, Vol. III (New Haven, 1937), 130–132; Andrews, *Insurrections*, 320–354.

40. Brodhead, *New York*, Vol. II, 616–617; Massachusetts Historical Society, *Collections*, Fifth Series, Vol. V (Boston, 1878), 317–319.

41. Brodhead, *New York*, Vol. II, 619–623; *Dictionary of American Biography*, Vol. XI (New York, 1933), 156–157; *N. Y. Col. Doc.*, Vol. III, 636–648, 727, 743, 748–749.

42. Brodhead, *New York*, 631–636; *N. Y. Col. Doc.*, Vol. III, 759–760.

43. Brodhead, *New York*, Vol. II, 636–638; *N. Y. Col. Doc.*, Vol. III, 760, 767, 794.

44. Brodhead, *New York,* Vol. II, 638–640.
45. *Ibid.,* Vol. II, 648–649; *Dictionary of American Biography,* Vol. XI, 156–157; *N. Y. Col. Doc.,* Vol. III, 794.

CHAPTER 15. THE VISIBLE AND THE INVISIBLE WORLD

1. Winsor, Justin, *Narrative and Critical History of America,* Vol. V (Boston, 1887), 92; Winsor, Justin, *Memorial History of Boston,* Vol. I (Boston, 1880), 206–208.
2. Winsor, Justin, *Memorial History of Boston,* Vol. I, 201, 213–214.
3. *Dictionary of American Biography,* Vol. XVI (New York, 1935), 610–612; Vol. XVIII (New York, 1936), 113–114.
4. Weeden, W. B., *Economic and Social History of New England, 1620–1789,* Vol. I (Boston, 1890), 302–303; Adams, James Truslow, *Provincial Society* (New York, 1927), 113–116.
5. Massachusetts Historical Society, *Collections,* Second Series, Vol. II (Boston, 1814), 97–124.
6. Mass. Hist. Soc., *Col.,* Fifth Series, Vol. V (Boston, 1878), 282–288.
7. Cross, A. L., *History of England and Greater Britain* (New York, 1914), 637–638.
8. Bouton, Nathaniel, ed., *Documents and Records relating to the Province of New-Hampshire,* Vol. II (Manchester, 1868), 46–55; Williamson, W. D., *History of the State of Maine,* Vol. I (Hallowell, 1832), 609–613—hereafter cited as Williamson, *Maine.*
9. Mass. Hist. Soc., *Col.,* Fifth Series, Vol. V, 311.
10. Parkman, Francis, *Count Frontenac and New France Under Louis XIV* (Frontenac Edition, New York, 1915), 218–228—hereafter cited as Parkman, *Frontenac;* Brodhead, John R., *History of the State of New York,* Vol. II (New York, 1871), 606–609—hereafter cited as Brodhead, *New York.*
11. Mass. Hist. Soc., *Col.,* Fifth Series, Vol. V, 315–317.
12. Parkman, *Frontenac,* 246–252; Fortesque, J. W., ed., *Calendar of State Papers,* Colonial Series, America and West Indies, 1689–1692, Vol. 13 (London, 1901), 275–276; *Dictionary of American Biography,* Vol. XIV (New York, 1934), 551–552.
13. Williamson, *Maine,* Vol. I, 619–622; Parkman, *Frontenac,* 239–245.
14. Brodhead, *New York,* Vol. II, 617–623; Parkman, *Frontenac,* 274–292; Hutchinson, [Thomas,] *History of the Colony of Massachusets-Bay,* [Vol. I,] (Boston, 1764), 402—hereafter cited as Hutchinson, *Massachusets;* Williamson, *Maine,* Vol. I, 625–640.
15. Whitmore, W. H., ed., *Andros Tracts,* Vol. III (Boston, 1874), 53; Burr, G. L., ed., *Narratives of the Witchcraft Cases, 1648–1706,* 12–13, 95—hereafter cited as Burr, *Witchcraft.*
16. Burr, *Witchcraft,* 8–38.
17. *Ibid.,* 15.
18. *Ibid.,* 93–143.
19. *Ibid.,* 99–124.
20. Hutchinson, *Massachusets,* [Vol. II,] 22–26; Burr, *Witchcraft,* 343–344.
21. Mass. Hist. Soc., *Col.,* Fifth Series, Vol. V, 358.
22. Burr, *Witchcraft,* 344–356; Hutchinson, *Massachusets,* Vol. II, 27–50.
23. Burr, *Witchcraft,* 356–376.

24. *Ibid.*, 360, 366–367, 373; Mass. Hist. Soc., *Col.,* Fifth Series, Vol. V, 363.
25. Hutchinson, *Massachusets,* Vol. II, 31.
26. Burr, *Witchcraft,* 261–262.
27. *Ibid.*, 209–251.
28. *Ibid.*, 196–202.
29. *Ibid,* 374–375, 387–388; Mass. Hist. Soc., *Col.,* Fifth Series, Vol. V, 445.
30. Burr, *Witchcraft,* 293–294, 296–393.
31. *Ibid.*, 293–294.
32. Winsor, Justin, *Narrative and Critical History of America,* Vol. V (Boston, 1887), 92–93; *Dictionary of American Biography,* Vol. XII (New York, 1933), 393; Adams, James Truslow, *Provincial Society, 1690–1763* (New York, 1927), 19–21; Wertenbaker, T. J., *The First Americans, 1607–1690* (New York, 1927), 196–197; Winship, George P., ed., *Boston in 1682 and 1699: A Trip to New England by Edward Ward, and a Letter from New England by J. W.* (Providence, 1905), 54–55.
33. Mass. Hist. Soc., *Col.,* Fifth Series, Vol. V, 492, 498.
34. Bouton, Nathaniel, ed., *Documents and Records relating to the Province of New-Hampshire,* Vol. II, 124–129; Hutchinson, *Massachusets,* Vol. II, 82.
35. Williamson, *Maine,* Vol. I, 635, 643–644, 650.
36. Lincoln, C. H., ed., *Narratives of the Indian Wars, 1675–1699* (New York, 1913), 263–266.
37. Parkman, Francis, *A Half-Century of Conflict,* Vol. I (Frontenac Edition, New York, 1915), 55–91.
38. *Documents relative to the Colonial History of the State of New York,* Vol. IV (Albany, 1854), 790; Weeden, W. B., *Economic and Social History of New England,* Vol. I, (Boston, 1890), 363–364; Andrews, C. M., *Colonial Period of American History,* Vol. IV (New Haven, 1938), 178–271.
39. *Dictionary of American Biography,* Vol. XIV (New York, 1934), 551–552, Vol. XVIII (New York, 1936), 113–114; Winsor, Justin, *Narrative and Critical History of America,* Vol. V (Boston, 1887), 93–103.
40. Winsor, Justin, *Narrative and Critical History of America,* Vol. V, 103–105; *Dictionary of American Biography,* Vol. V (New York, 1930), 481–483; Mass. Hist. Soc., *Col.,* Fifth Series, Vol. VI (Boston, 1879), 58.
41. Massachusetts Historical Society, *Collections,* Fifth Series, Vol. VI (Boston, 1879), 144 and note 1.
42. Trumbull, Benjamin, *History of Connecticut,* Vol. I (New Haven, 1818), 407–418; Arnold, S. G., *History of the State of Rhode Island and Providence Plantations,* Vol. II (Providence, 1899), 16–23, 30.
43. *Dictionary of American History,* Vol. IV (New York, 1940), 321; *Dictionary of American Biography,* Vol. VIII (New York, 1932), 180–181.
44. *The Private Journal of a Journey from Boston to New York in the Year 1704.* Kept by Madam Knight (Albany, 1865), 19–58.

CHAPTER 16. PATENTS AND PIRATES

1. *The Private Journal of a Journey from Boston to New York in the Year 1704.* Kept by Madam Knight (Albany, 1865), 60–63, 74—hereafter cited as Knight, *Journey.*

2. Knight, *Journey*, 63, 73–74; Fox, Dixon Ryan, *Caleb Heathcote* (New York, 1926), 96–117, 201–202, 214–215—hereafter cited as Fox, *Heathcote*.

3. Knight, *Journey*, 63; Bolton, Robert, *History of the Several Towns, Manors, and Patents of the County of Westchester*, Vol. I (New York, 1881), 581–595; *Dictionary of American Biography*, Vol. VI (New York, 1931), 262–263.

4. Hall, E. H., *Philipse Manor Hall* (New York, 1912), 66, 71–73.

5. Knight, *Journey*, 70; Valentine, David T., *History of the City of New York* (New York, 1853), 68–69; *Documents relative to the Colonial History of the State of New-York*, Vol. IV (Albany, 1854), 400–401, 620–621—hereafter cited as *N. Y. Col. Doc.*

6. Miller, John, *New-York Considered and Improved, 1695*. With Introduction and Notes by V. H. Paltsits (Cleveland, 1903), see Map; Knight, *Journey*, 68; Fox, *Heathcote*, 211–212; Stokes, I. N. Phelps, *The Iconography of Manhattan Island*, Vol. I (New York, 1915), 183; Dix, Morgan, *History of the Parish of Trinity Church in the City of New York* (New York, 1898), Vol. I, 89; *N. Y. Col. Doc.*, Vol. IV, 327.

7. *N. Y. Col Doc.*, Vol. III (Albany, 1853), 821; Fox, *Heathcote*, 198–199; *Dictionary of American Biography*, Vol. XIX (New York, 1936), 259; Dix, Morgan, *History of the Parish of Trinity Church in the City of New York*, Vol. I, 90.

8. Stokes, I. N. Phelps, *Iconography of Manhattan Island*, Vol. I, 183, 186; Hall, E. G., *Philipse Manor Hall*, 51–52; *N. Y. Col. Doc.*, Vol. IV, 329, 388; Miller, John, *New York Considered and Improved, 1695*, With Introduction and Notes by V. H. Paltsits, Map; Valentine, D. T., *History of the City of New York*, 214–215.

9. Knight, *Journey*, 66–69.

10. *Ibid.*, 70–71.

11. *N. Y. Col. Doc.*, Vol. IV, 420; Stokes, I. N. Phelps, *Iconography of Manhattan Island*, Vol. I, 187; *Dictionary of American Biography*, Vol. VII (New York, 1931), 475–476.

12. *N. Y. Col. Doc.*, Vol. III, 624.

13. *Ibid.*, Vol. III, 846–847, Vol. IV, 53, 55, 84.

14. *N. Y. Col. Doc.*, Vol. III, 827–833, 856–860, Vol. IV, 33–34.

15. *N. Y. Col. Doc.*, Vol. III, 838, 855–856, Vol. IV, 29–31.

16. Trumbull, Benjamin, *History of Connecticut*, Vol. I (New Haven, 1818), 390–395; Hoadley, C. J., ed., *Public Records of the Colqny of Connecticut, 1689–1706* (Hartford, 1868), 111–117; *N. Y. Col. Doc.*, Vol. IV, 31, 56, 58–59, 69–74, 84.

17. *N. Y. Col. Doc.*, Vol. IV, 16–19, 85–92.

18. *Ibid.*, 320; Fox, *Heathcote*, 11–12.

19. Hall, E. H., *Philipse Manor Hall*, 72–73.

20. *N. Y. Col. Doc.*, Vol. IV, 384, 391–393.

21. *Ibid.*, Vol. IV, 327, 330, 384, 391–392, 397, 472–473, 535, 822–823, Vol. V, 283; Fox, *Heathcote*, 71; Winsor, Justin, *Narrative and Critical History of America*, Vol. V (New York, 1887), 236–237 (Map); *Dictionary of American History*, Vol. II (New York, 1940), 419.

22. *N. Y. Col. Doc.*, Vol. IV, 791.

23. *Ibid.*, Vol. IV, 274, 304, 323, 412–413, 433, 532; Fortescue, J. W., ed., *Calendar of State Papers*, Colonial Series, Vol. XV, America and West

Indies (London, 1904), 260, 262; Toppan, R. N., ed., *Edward Randolph,* Vol. V (Providence, 1899), 185–188.

24. *N. Y. Col. Doc.,* Vol. IV, 223, 274, 307, 433, 459–460, 469; Fortescue, J. W., ed., *Calendar of State Papers,* Colonial Series, Vol. XV, America and West Indies (London, 1904), 260.

25. *N. Y. Col. Doc.,* Vol. IV, 385–386, 479.

26. *Ibid.,* Vol. IV, 307, 387, 433, 481.

27. *Ibid.,* Vol. IV, 826.

28. *Ibid.,* Vol. IV, 266–273, 411, 415.

29. *Ibid.,* Vol. IV, 413.

30. *Dictionary of American Biography,* Vol. X (New York, 1933), 367–369, Vol. XI (New York, 1933), 318–319; *N. Y. Col. Doc.,* Vol. IV, 251.

31. *N. Y. Col. Doc.,* Vol. IV, 762–765; *Dictionary of American Biography,* Vol. X, 368.

32. *N. Y. Col. Doc.* Vol. IV, 275.

33. *Ibid.,* Vol. IV, 583–584.

34. *Dictionary of American Biography,* Vol. X, 368–369.

35. *N. Y. Col. Doc.,* Vol. IV, 532.

36. Whitehead, W. A., ed., *Documents relating to the Colonial History of the State of New Jersey,* Vol. II (Newark, 1881), 277–293–hereafter cited as *N. J. Archives; N. Y. Col. Doc.,* Vol. IV, 532, 542, 551, 584, 1135; Adams, James Truslow, *Provincial Society, 1690–1763* (New York, 1927), 72–73.

37. *N. Y. Col. Doc.,* Vol. IV, 528, 666, 855, 887, 1069–1070, 1112, Vol. VI (Albany, 1855), 851, Vol. VII (Albany, 1856), 576; *Dictionary of American History,* Vol. III (New York, 1940), 200, 285, Vol. V (New York, 1940), 426.

38. *N. Y. Col. Doc.,* Vol. V (Albany, 1855), 38; 111; *Dictionary of American Biography,* Vol. IV (New York, 1930), 441–442; *N. J. Archives,* Vol. III (Newark, 1881), 179, 207–211.

39. *N. Y. Col. Doc.,* Vol. IV, 1070; *N. J. Archives,* Vol. II, 87, 93, 489–500, 506–536.

40. Andrews, Charles M., *Colonial Period of American History,* Vol. III (New Haven, 1937), 171–174; *N. J. Archives,* Vol. XXI (Paterson, 1899), 315–316.

41. Andrews, Charles M., *Colonial Period of American History,* Vol. III, 171–173; *Pennsylvania Magazine of History and Biography,* Vol. VII (Philadelphia, 1883), 327–331; *N. Y. Col. Doc.,* Vol. III, 838–839, Vol. IV, 397, 532; *N. J. Archives,* Vol. II, 41–72, 97–99, 305, Vol. XXI, 315–317.

42. Thomas, Gabriel, *An Historical Description of the Province and Country of West-New-Jersey in America* (London, 1698), 15–20, 26–29; Lee, F. B., *New Jersey,* Vol. I (New York, 1902), 352–353.

43. *N. J. Archives,* Vol. II, 270, 322–327.

44. Whitehead, W. A., *East Jersey under the Proprietary Governments* (New York, 1846), 165, 302–hereafter cited as Whitehead, *East Jersey;* Thomas, Gabriel, *West-New-Jersey,* 32.

45. Whitehead, *East Jersey,* 271; *Dictionary of American Biography,* Vol. XIII (New York, 1934), 213–214.

46. Whitehead, *East Jersey,* 279; Whitehead, W. A., *Contributions to the Early History of Perth Amboy* (New York, 1856), 9.

47. Whitehead, W. A., *Contributions to the Early History of Perth Amboy*, 7–9; Whitehead, *East Jersey*, 108, 281–283; *N. J. Archives*, Vol. II, 312; *Minutes of The Board of Proprietors of the Eastern Division of New Jersey from 1685 to 1705* (Perth Amboy, 1949), 47; *Journal of the Procedure of the Governor and Council of the Province of East New Jersey* (Jersey City, 1872), 118–119.

48. Whitehead, W. A., *Contributions to the Early History of Perth Amboy*, 12–49; Whitehead, *East Jersey*, 88–122; Andrews, Charles M., *Colonial Period of American History*, Vol. III, 154; *Journal of the Procedure of the Governor and Council of the Province of East New Jersey*, 144; *Dictionary of American Biography*, Vol. VIII (New York, 1932), 180–181.

49. *N. J. Archives*, Vol. II, 28.

50. *Dictionary of American History*, Vol. IV (New York, 1940), 321.

51. Andrews, Charles M., *Colonial Period of American History*, Vol. III, 176–177.

52. *Ibid.*, 160–163, 180–181 note; Whitehead, *East Jersey*, 137–139; *N. J. Archives*, Vol. I (Newark, 1880), 540, Vol. II, 174–175, 177–185, 311–313; *N. Y. Col. Doc.*, Vol. IV, 438–439, 546–547, 719, 777, 817.

53. Andrews, Charles M., *Colonial Period of American History*, Vol. III, 176–177; *Dictionary of American Biography*, Vol. II (New York, 1929), 36–37; *N. J. Archives*, Vol. II, 301, 348.

54. *N. J. Archives*, Vol. II, 313–315.

55. *Ibid.*, Vol. II, 333–334.

56. *Ibid.*, Vol. II, 327–331.

57. *Ibid.*, Vol. II, 344–353, 380–384, 387–390, 394–462, 489–500.

58. *N. J. Archives*, Vol. III (Newark, 1881), 173–180; Lee, F. B., *New Jersey*, Vol. I, 212–213; *Dictionary of American Biography*, Vol. IV (New York, 1930), 441–442.

59. *N. Y. Col. Doc.*, Vol. V, 18–19, 33–38.

60. *N. J. Archives*, Vol. II, 517; Andrews, Charles M., *Colonial Period of American History*, Vol. III, 178–179; *Minutes of the Board of Proprietors of the Eastern Division of New Jersey from 1685 to 1705*, vii-xi; Fisher, E. J., *New Jersey as a Royal Province* (New York, 1911), 171–209.

61. *N. Y. Col. Doc.*, Vol. V, 705.

CHAPTER 17. BROTHERLY LOVE

1. Pound, Arthur, *The Penns of Pennsylvania and England* (New York, 1932), 215.

2. *Minutes of the Provincial Council of Pennsylvania*, Vol. I (Philadelphia, 1852), 135–137—hereafter cited as *Pa. Col. Rec.*

3. Andrews, Charles M., *Colonial Period of American History*, Vol. III (New Haven, 1937), 308–311; *Pa. Col. Rec.*, Vol. I, 244; *Dictionary of American Biography*, Vol. XI (New York, 1933), 329–330, 334–335; Pound, Arthur, *The Penns of Pennsylvania and England*, 217.

4. *Pa. Col. Rec.*, Vol. I, 317; Andrews, Charles M., *Colonial Period of American History*, Vol. III, 309–312; Shepherd, W. R., *History of Proprietary Government in Pennsylvania* (New York, 1896), 499—hereafter cited as Shepherd, *Pennsylvania;* Fortescue, J. W., ed., *Cal-*

endar of State Papers, Colonial Series, Vol. 13, America and West Indies, 1689–1692 (London, 1901), 390, 525.

5. *Dictionary of American Biography,* Vol. X (New York, 1933), 289–290.

6. *Dictionary of American Biography,* Vol. II (New York, 1929), 563–564.

7. *Pa. Col. Rec.,* Vol. I, 352–357; *Documents relative to the Colonial History of the State of New-York,* Vol. IV (Albany, 1854), 35, 56—hereafter cited as *N. Y. Col. Doc.;* Shepherd, *Pennsylvania,* 499–500; *Votes of Assembly, Pennsylvania Archives,* Eighth Series, Vol. I (1931 reprint), 160.

8. *N. Y. Col. Doc.,* Vol. IV, 52, 108–109; Proud, Robert, *History of Pennsylvania,* Vol. I (Philadelphia, 1797), 403–404; Shepherd, *Pennsylvania,* 500; *Pa. Col. Rec.,* Vol. I, 472–475.

9. *Dictionary of American Biography,* Vol. X, 312–313.

10. Fisher, S. G., *Pennsylvania, Colony and Commonwealth* (Philadelphia, 1896), 22–24; *N. Y. Col. Doc.,* Vol. IV, 296–297.

11. Toppan, R. N., ed., *Edward Randolph,* Vol. V (Boston, 1899), 107–116—hereafter cited as *Randolph.*

12. *Randolph,* Vol. II, 143–150; McCrady, Edward, *History of South Carolina under the Proprietary Government* (New York, 1897), 202–204; South Carolina Historical Society, *Collections,* Vol. I (Charleston, 1857), 127.

13. Fortescue, J. W., ed., *Calendar of State Papers,* Colonial Series, Vol. XVI, America and West Indies, 1697–1698 (London, 1905), 483–484; *Pa. Col. Rec.,* Vol. I, 603.

14. *Randolph,* Vol. V, 174, 214, 301.

15. *Randolph,* Vol. V, 169–182; *Pa. Col. Rec.,* Vol. I, 580; Whitehead, W. A., ed., *Documents relating to the Colonial History of the State of New Jersey,* Vol. II (Newark, 1881), 280–281; Fortescue, J. W., ed., *Calendar of State Papers,* Colonial Series, Vol. XV, American and West Indies, 1696–1697 (London, 1904), 262–264; *N. Y. Col. Doc.,* Vol. IV, 542–543.

16. Buck, W. J., *William Penn in America* (Philadelphia, 1888), 224; Fisher, S. G., *The True William Penn* (Philadelphia, 1899), 347–349; *Dictionary of American Biography,* Vol. XI (New York, 1933), 360–362; Bigelow, John, *Autobiography of Benjamin Franklin* (Philadelphia, 1868), 269–270.

17. Thomas, Gabriel, *An Historical and Geographical Account of the Province and County of Pensilvania* (London, 1698), 5–8, 20–22, 28–45.

18. *Ibid.,* 38; Armstrong, Edward, ed., *Correspondence between William Penn and James Logan,* Vol. II (Philadelphia, 1872), 22, 203—cited hereafter as *Penn-Logan.*

19. Fisher, S. G., *The True William Penn,* 349–352.

20. *Ibid.,* 353; *Penn-Logan,* Vol. I (Philadelphia, 1870), 62–64.

21. *Penn-Logan,* Vol. I, 40, 62–64, 79.

22. Fisher, S. G., *The True William Penn,* 353–354.

23. *Penn-Logan,* Vol. I, 42, Vol. II (Philadelphia, 1872), 231–232.

24. *Penn-Logan,* Vol. I, 5, 7, 8, 13, 14.

25. *Ibid.,* Vol. I, 4, 14, 15, 56, 114, 149.

26. Vulliamy, C. E., *William Penn* (New York, 1934), 267–268.

27. *Penn-Logan*, Vol. I, 18; *Pa. Col. Rec.*, Vol. I, 602–604; *Dictionary of American Biography*, Vol. XI, 329.

28. Andrews, Charles M., *Colonial Period of American History*, Vol. III, 319; *Pa. Col. Rec.*, Vol. I, 596–597, 613, Vol. II (Philadelphia, 1852)·, 56–60; *Penn-Logan*, Vol. I, 150.

29. Shepherd, *Pennsylvania*, 56–59; *Penn-Logan*, Vol. I, 9–10; Egle, W. H., ed., *Minutes of the Board of Property of the Province of Pennsylvania*, Vol. I (Harrisburg, 1893), 185–192.

30. *Randolph*, Vol. V, 263–274; *Penn-Logan*, Vol. I, 17, 78, 379–380; Shepherd, *Pennsylvania*, 506–507.

31. *Dictionary of American Biography*, Vol. VIII, 181, Vol. XI, 361; *Penn-Logan*, Vol. I, 7, 56, 59–61, 66, 78–79; Fisher, S. G., *The True William Penn*, 357–358.

32. *Penn-Logan*, 55, 112, 147, 166–167, 188, 257.

33. *Dictionary of American Biography*, Vol. X, 290; *Dictionary of American History*, Vol. II (New York, 1940), 402.

34. Fox, D. R., *Caleb Heathcote* (New York, 1926), 213–215.

35. *Penn-Logan*, Vol. I, 81, 179, 185.

36. *Ibid.*, 173, 186, 206–207.

37. *Ibid.*, 208–209; Vulliamy, C. E., *William Penn*, 169; Myers, A. C., *Narratives of Early Pennsylvania, West Jersey and Delaware* (New York, 1912), 261.

38. Neill, Edward D., "Memoir of John Evans" in *New-England Historical and Genealogical Register*, Vol. XXVI (Boston, 1872), 421–422; Vulliamy, C. E., *William Penn*, 277–278; *Penn-Logan*, Vol. I, 206–209, 211, 265–267, 300, 315, 318, 320, 322, 326; *Dictionary of American Biography*, Vol. XIII (New York, 1934), 553–554.

39. *Penn-Logan*, Vol. I, 354–355, 369.

40. *Ibid.*, Vol. I, 22, 270, 283, 285; Vol. II, 137–138; *Pa. Col. Rec.*, Vol. II 60; Andrews, Charles M., *Colonial Period of American History*, Vol. III, 321–325.

41. *Penn-Logan*, Vol. I, 360–361, 376, Vol. II, 37.

42. Myers, A. C., *Narratives of Early Pennsylvania, West New Jersey and Delaware*, 215; *Penn-Logan*, Vol. II, 37–39, 41–43, 52–53, 61–62, 93–96, 100–101.

43. *Penn-Logan*, Vol. II, 100–101, 108–109, 148–149, 156, 162–164, 167–169, 174–179, 198, 200–201, 209–210, 223, 228, 234, 237–238, 243, 246–252, 255–257, 262–263, 267–269, 272–274, 288, 292, 305–306; Shepherd, *Pennsylvania*, 184–198.

44. *Penn-Logan*, Vol. II, 137–140, 156, 167–169, 190, 225, 269, 348–349, 428, 435–436; Vulliamy, C. E., *William Penn*, 286–290; Shepherd, *Pennsylvania*, 198–200; *Dictionary of American Biography*, Vol. XIV (New York, 1934), 437.

45. *Dictionary of American Biography*, Vol. XI, 360–361, Vol. XIII, 553–554, Vol. XIV, 430–433; *Penn-Logan*, Vol. I, 11; Pound, Arthur, *The Penns of Pennsylvania and England*, 234–235.

CHAPTER 18. TOBACCO

1. Wright, L. B., and Tinling, Marion, eds., *The Secret Diary of William Byrd of Westover, 1709–1712* (Richmond, 1941), 47–52—hereafter cited as Byrd, *Diary*, I.

2. *Dictionary of American Biography,* Vol. III (New York, 1929), 383–384; Bassett, J. S., *The Writings of "Colonel William Byrd of Westover in Virginia Esqr."* (New York, 1901), xvi, xxix.

3. *Virginia Magazine of History and Biography,* Vol. XXIV (Richmond, 1916), 228—hereafter cited as *Va. Mag.*

4. *Ibid.,* Vol. XXIV, 232, 359.

5. *Ibid.,* Vol. XXV (Richmond, 1917), 50–52.

6. *Ibid.,* Vol. XXV, 43–45, 50–52, 131–132, 134, 136–137.

7. Bruce, P. A., *Economic History of Virginia in the Seventeenth Century,* Vol. II (New York, 1935), 82–84—hereafter cited as Bruce, *Economic; Va. Mag.,* Vol. XXIV, 232.

8. *Va. Mag.,* Vol. XXV, 133–134.

9. Brock, R. A., ed., *The Official Letters of Alexander Spotswood,* Vol. I (Richmond, 1882), 52—hereafter cited as *Spotswood;* Bruce, *Economic,* Vol. II, 82–93, 108.

10. Coleman, R. V., *The First Frontier* (New York, 1948), 270.

11. *Va. Mag.,* Vol. XXV, 359, 363, Vol. XXVI (Richmond, 1918), 20–21, 132, 247–250, 388.

12. *Va. Mag.,* Vol. XXVI, 129, 390–391.

13. *Ibid.,* Vol. XXVI, 128–129, 131.

14. *Dictionary of American Biography,* Vol. I (New York, 1929), 233, Vol. II (New York, 1929), 383–384, Vol. III (New York, 1929), 541–542, Vol. VI (New York, 1931), 438–439; Campbell, Charles, *History of the Colony and Ancient Dominion of Virginia* (Philadelphia, 1860), 344.

15. Bruce, *Economic,* Vol. I, 567–570; Beverley, Robert, *History and Present State of Virginia,* Edited with an Introduction by Louis B. Wright (Chapel Hill, 1947), 92–94—hereafter cited as Beverley, *Virginia;* Freeman, Douglas S., *George Washington,* Vol. I (New York, 1948), 447–487.

16. Freeman, Douglas S., *George Washington,* Vol. I, 487–488; Beverley, *Virginia,* 94.

17. *Dictionary of American Biography,* Vol. VI, 438–439; *Va. Mag.,* Vol. I (Richmond, 1893), 37–38, 45, 51, 108.

18. *Va. Mag.,* Vol. I, 17–26, 39, 120–121.

19. *Ibid.,* Vol. I, 395.

20. *Ibid.,* Vol. I, 395–396, Vol. VII (Richmond, 1899), 199.

21. *Ibid.,* Vol. II (Richmond, 1895), 265, 269.

22. *Ibid.,* Vol. II, 373, Vol. III (Richmond, 1895), 9.

23. Beverley, *Virginia,* 95–99; Bruce, P. A., *Institutional History of Virginia in the Seventeenth Century* (New York, 1910), Vol. I, 350, Vol. II, 496–498—hereafter cited as Bruce, *Institutional.*

24. Beverley, *Virginia,* 98–99; Bruce, *Institutional,* Vol. I, 380–386; *Dictionary of American Biography,* Vol. II, 335–337.

25. Bruce, *Institutional,* Vol. I, 387–389; Beverley, *Virginia,* 99–100; Campbell, Charles, *History of the Colony and Ancient Dominion of Virginia,* 346.

26. Bruce, *Institutional,* Vol. I, 390–401; Beverley, *Virginia,* 98–99.

27. *Dictionary of American Biography,* Vol. I, 300–301, Vol. XIII (New York, 1934), 499–501.

28. Mereness, N. D., *Maryland as a Proprietary Province* (New York,

1901), 42; *Dictionary of American Biography*, Vol. IV (New York, 1930), 369, 430; Armstrong, Edward, ed., *Correspondence between William Penn and James Logan*, Vol. II (Philadelphia, 1872), 51.

29. Toppan, R. N., ed., *Edward Randolph*, Vol. II (Boston, 1898), 138–143, Vol. V (Boston, 1899), 74–75, 77–80, 88–91.

30. Coleman, R. V., *The First Frontier*, 286–290; *Maryland Archives*, Vol. XX (Baltimore, 1900), 35; *Dictionary of American Biography*, Vol. XIII, 500.

31. Cook, Eben, Gent., *The Sot-weed Factor* (London, 1708), from Shea, *Early Southern Tracts*, No. II (1865), 5, 6, 8, 9, 16, 21, 23.

32. *Dictionary of American Biography*, Vol. XIII, 500; *Maryland Archives*, Vol. XX, 122, 126, 130, 173, 176, 181, 250, 453, 487, 489, 491, 492.

33. *Maryland Archives*, Vol. XIX, 435–440.

34. *Maryland Archives*, Vol. XX, 493, 511, 561–564.

35. Steiner, B. C., "Rev. Thomas Bray and His American Libraries" in *American Historical Review* (Oct. 1896), 59–75.

36. Bruce, *Institutional*, Vol. I, 130 note 1; Campbell, Charles, *History of the Colony and Ancient Dominion of Virginia*, 356–357; *Dictionary of American Biography*, Vol. II, 336.

37. Bruce, *Institutional*, Vol. I, 107, Vol. II, 457–459; Bruce, *Economic*, Vol. II, 562.

38. Bruce, *Economic*, Vol. II, 563–564.

39. Bruce, *Institutional*, Vol. II, 459–461; Beverley, *Virginia*, 105.

40. Beverley, *Virginia*, 105.

41. Bruce, *Institutional*, Vol. I, 398–401; *Va. Mag.*, Vol. VI (Richmond, 1898), 69–70.

42. *Va. Mag.*, Vol. VI, 70.

43. Bassett, John S., *The Writings of "Colonel William Byrd of Westover in Virginia, Esqr,"* xii.

44. Toppan, R. N., ed., *Edward Randolph*, Vol. V, 230–287.

45. *Ibid.*, Vol. II, 181–182, Vol. V, 291.

46. Flippin, P. S., *The Royal Government in Virginia, 1624–1775* (New York, 1919), 114.

47. Beverley, *Virginia*, xv.

48. *Ibid.*, 106–107.

49. *Dictionary of American Biography*, Vol. II, 233, Vol. XIII, 500–501; Andrews, Charles M., *Colonial Period of American History*, Vol. IV (New Haven, 1938), 292; *Spotswood*, Vol. II, 243; Andrews, M. P., *Virginia, The Old Dominion* (New York, 1937), 179; Flippin, P. S., *Royal Government in Virginia, 1624–1775*, 61–62, 116–118; Campbell, Charles, *Colony and Ancient Dominion of Virginia*, 375–377.

50. Bruce, *Institutional*, Vol. II, 407–416; *Spotswood*, Vol. II, 1–2.

51. Bruce, *Institutional*, Vol. II, 358–390.

52. Beverley, *Virginia*, 249; Bruce, *Economic*, Vol. I, 562; Byrd, *Diary*, I, ix.

53. Bruce, *Institutional*, Vol. II, 575–580; Byrd, *Diary*, I, 368; *Spotswood*, Vol. II, 247.

54. Bruce, *Institutional*, Vol. II, 534–574; Woodfin, Maude H., ed., *Another Secret Diary of William Byrd of Westover, 1739–1741* (Richmond, 1942), 323; *Spotswood*, Vol. II (Richmond, 1885), 140.

55. Bruce, *Institutional*, Vol. II, 584–587; Beverley, *Virginia*, 250–251;

Andrews, Charles M., *Colonial Period of American History*, Vol. IV, 119.

56. Bruce, *Economic*, Vol. I, 457; Byrd, *Diary*, I, 443; Wright, L. B., ed., *Letters of Robert Carter, 1720–1727* (San Marino, 1940), 22, note 37 —hereafter cited as *Carter Letters*.

57. Byrd, *Diary*, I, *passim*.

58. *Ibid.*, 84, 127, 204, 221, 295, 316, 400, 405, 464, 494, 502, 562, 573, and *passim*.

59. *Ibid.*, 468, 502, 550, and *passim*.

60. *Ibid.*, 34, 61, 227, 276, 351, 363, and *passim*.

61. *Ibid.*, 527–528.

62. Beverley, *Virginia*, 272.

63. Byrd, *Diary*, I, 148, 412, 540; Bruce, *Economic*, Vol. II, 121–122.

64. Byrd, *Diary*, I, 277–315, 550, 584–586, and *passim*.

65. *Ibid.*, 41, 50, 60–61, 69, 126, 129, 133, 144, 196, 213, 222, 310, 363–365, 460, 497, 503, 568, and *passim*.

66. *Ibid.*, 369–374, 385–386.

67. *Ibid.*, 159, 167, 374.

68. *Dictionary of American Biography*, Vol. XVII (New York, 1935), 467–469; *Spotswood*, Vol. I, 1–13; Byrd, *Diary*, I, 194–195, 244–253, 255–271, and *passim*.

69. Byrd, *Diary*, I, 296–300, 330–337, 426–445, and *passim*.

70. *Dictionary of American Biography*, Vol. II, 336.

71. *Spotswood*, Vol. I, 10, 52, Vol. II, 8, 66–67; Byrd, *Diary*, I, 259.

72. Campbell, Charles, *History of the Colony and Ancient Dominion of Virginia*, 376; Winsor, Justin, *Narrative and Critical History of America*, Vol. V (Boston, 1887), 279; Byrd, *Diary*, I, 11, 45, 98; *Spotswood*, Vol. I, 4.

73. *Spotswood*, Vol. I, 103, 156–157; Byrd, *Diary*, I, 194, 335, 340, 343, 474, 561.

74. Byrd, *Diary*, I, 508; *Spotswood*, I, 122, 174; Bruce, *Institutional*, Vol. I, 396–397.

75. *Spotswood*, Vol. II, 88–92, 94, 144–150, 194–196; Dodson, Leonidas, *Alexander Spotswood* (Philadelphia, 1932), 70–98.

76. Todd, V. H., *Christoph von Graffenried's Account of the Founding of New Bern* (Raleigh, 1920), 92, 224, 257–259; *Spotswood*, Vol. I, 20–21, 168, Vol. II, 70–71, 95–96, 217–218.

77. Maury, Ann, *Memoirs of a Huguenot Family* (New York, 1853), 262–264—hereafter cited as Maury; *Carter Letters*, 54.

78. *Dictionary of American Biography*, Vol. II, 233; Beverley, *Virginia*, xiv–xxxiv; Maury, 265–268.

79. *Spotswood*, Vol. I, 40, Vol. II, 149; Maury, 266, 281–283.

80. Maury, 283–289.

81. Jones, Hugh, *The Present State of Virginia* (London, 1924), 14; *Documents relative to the Colonial History of the State of New-York*, Vol. V (Albany, 1885), 677.

82. *Dictionary of American Biography*, Vol. XVII, 467–469; *Spotswood*, Vol. II, 187–238, 263; Dodson, Leonidas, *Alexander Spotswood*, 257.

83. Woodfin, Maude H., ed., *Another Secret Diary of William Byrd of Westover, 1739–1741*, xxi–xxii; *Spotswood*, Vol. II, 152, 174, 188, 278, 304, 306–307, and *passim*.

84. *Carter Letters,* 30.
85. *Ibid.,* 2, 5–6, 19, 22 note 37, 36, 46–48, 74–75; Bruce, *Economic,* Vol. I, 433–442; *Va. Mag.,* Vol. XXVI, 247.
86. *Carter Letters,* 10, 13, 40–43, 48, 50, and *passim.*
87. *Ibid.,* 11.
88. *Ibid.,* vii–viii, 60–61–63–64; *Dictionary of American Biography,* Vol. III, 541–542; Freeman, Douglas S., *George Washington,* Vol. I (New York, 1948), 492–494.
89. *Carter Letters,* 4, 7.
90. *Ibid.,* 12, 25–26.
91. *Ibid.,* 25, 34–35, 37.
92. *Documents relative to the Colonial History of the State of New-York,* Vol. V, 671–672. Interestingly enough, when the treaty was finished, Spotswood took from his own breast "a golden Horse Shoe" and presented it to the Iroquois spokesman as a pass to be presented when the Indians might have legitimate reason to cross the Blue Ridge into Virginia (*Ibid.,* 677).
93. Dodson, Leonidas, *Alexander Spotswood,* 200–201, 270–274.
94. *Spotswood,* Vol. II, 153.
95. Jones, Hugh, *The Present State of Virginia,* 58; Dodson, Leonidas, *Alexander Spotswood,* 277–298.
96. Freeman, Douglas S., *George Washington,* Vol. I, 37–47.

CHAPTER 19. SKINS AND SLAVES

1. Nicholson, Watson, *Anthony Aston, Stroller and Adventurer* (South Haven, 1920), 58–59.
2. *Dictionary of American Biography,* Vol. XIII (1934), 127–128; [Rivers, W. J.], *A Sketch of the History of South Carolina* (Charleston, 1856), 456–hereafter cited as Rivers; McCrady, Edward, *History of South Carolina under the Proprietary Government, 1670–1719* (New York, 1897), 378–380–hereafter cited as McCrady, I.
3. McCrady, I, 380–382; Lanning, J. T., *The Spanish Missions of Georgia* (Chapel Hill, 1935), 227–228; Crane, Verner W., *The Southern Frontier* (Durham, 1928), 76–77–hereafter cited as Crane; Salley, Alexander S., Jr., ed., *Narratives of Early Carolina, 1650–1708* (New York, 1911), 342–344–hereafter cited as Salley, *Early Carolina.*
4. Crane, 78–80; Lanning, J. T., *Spanish Missions in Georgia,* 186–187; *Dictionary of American History,* Vol. I (New York, 1940), 88 (Apalache Massacre), 144 (Ayuable, Battle of).
5. Crane, 80; Rivers, 209–213; McCrady, I, 396–400; *Documents relative to the Colonial History of the State of New-York,* Vol. IV (Albany, 1854), 1088–1089.
6. McCrady, I, 268–401; Toppan, R. N., ed., *Edward Randolph,* Vol. V (Boston, 1899), 268–271.
7. McCrady, I, 315, 341–342; Lawson, John, *A New Voyage to Carolina* (London, 1709), 2–hereafter cited as Lawson.
8. McCrady, I, 349–350; Salley, *Early Carolina,* 289, 292, 310; Lawson, 4; Andrews, Charles M., *Colonial Period of American History,* Vol. IV (New Haven, 1938), 95–98.
9. McCrady, I, 345; Salley, *Early Carolina,* 290; Lawson, 5.

10. Rivers, 447; McCrady, I, 238–239, 263–264; Lawson, 12, 14.
11. McCrady, I, 320; *Dictionary of American Biography,* Vol. XII (New York, 1933), 234.
12. McCrady, I, 326–327, 345; Crane, 89, 163.
13. Swanton, John R., *The Indians of the Southeastern United States* (Washington, 1946), 208–211; Crane, 81.
14. Crane, 36, 44–45, 132.
15. *Ibid.,* 133–135.
16. *Ibid.,* 95–96, 133–136.
17. *Ibid.,* 42–44, 129–130, 132–133; Williams, Samuel Cole, *Dawn of Tennessee Valley and Tennessee History* (Johnson City, 1937), 22–23.
18. Crane, 332.
19. *Ibid.,* 110–111, 328.
20. *Ibid.,* 112–114, 182.
21. *Ibid.,* 154–155; Lawson, 6–13.
22. Lawson, 14–41.
23. *Ibid.,* 42–59; Crane, 328.
24. Lawson, 80–90; *Dictionary of American Biography,* Vol. X (New York, 1933), 57–58.
25. Todd, V. H., ed., *Christoph von Graffenried's Account of the Founding of New Bern* (Raleigh, 1920), 33–34, 364, 376, 386—hereafter cited as Todd; Armstrong, Edward, *Correspondence between William Penn and James Logan,* Vol. II (Philadelphia, 1872), 295, 315, 341—hereafter cited as *Penn-Logan.*
26. Todd, 43–49.
27. Todd, 45–46, 49, 225–226.
28. *Ibid.,* 46, 48, 226–228, 283, 377–378; Saunders, W. L., ed., *Colonial Records of North Carolina,* Vol. I (Raleigh, 1886), 774–775—hereafter cited as *N. C. Col. Rec.;* Brock, R. A., ed., *The Official Letters of Alexander Spotswood,* Vol. I (Richmond, 1882), 81–86, 91–96, 100–102, 107–109—hereafter cited as *Spotswood.*
29. *N. C. Col. Rec.,* Vol. I, 763–772, 774–775.
30. Todd, 306–320.
31. Todd, 275, 373–375.
32. Todd, 263–271.
33. *N. C. Col. Rec.,* Vol. I, 825–829; *Spotswood,* Vol. I, 116–118.
34. *Spotswood,* Vol. I, 121–127, 134–138; Todd, 282; Wright, L. B., and Tinling, Marion, *The Secret Diary of William Byrd of Westover,* 1709–1712 (Richmond, 1941), 418–425.
35. McCrady, I, 498–503; Crane, 159–160; *Spotswood,* Vol. I, 170–171.
36. McCrady, I, 525–526; *Spotswood,* Vol. II (Richmond, 1885), 2–7.
37. Swanton, John R., *The Indians of the Southeastern United States,* 199.
38. Todd, 88–90, 98–99, 257–259, 383–386; *Penn-Logan,* Vol. II, 341.
39. Salley, A. S., Jr., ed., *Journal of the Commissioners of the Indian Trade of South Carolina* (Columbia, 1926), 4.
40. *Ibid.,* 33–34.
41. *Ibid.,* 9–13, 17–19, 39–47.
42. *Ibid.,* 10, 13–14, 22.
43. *Ibid.,* 15, 27, 30–32, 35, 48–49.
44. McCrady, I, 533–536; Crane, 167–170.
45. Crane, 169–179; McCrady, I, 534–537.

46. Crane, 179–183.
47. *Spotswood,* Vol. II, 111–112, 119, 125, 136; Crane, 173–179, 183.
48. Crane, 167, 328.
49. *Ibid.,* 206, 224; *Documents relative to the Colonial History of the State of New-York,* Vol. V (Albany, 1855), 432–433; *Spotswood,* Vol. II, 119–122.
50. Crane, 207–208; McCrady, I, 538–544; Rivers, 270–278.
51. Hughson, S. C., "The Carolina Pirates and Colonial Commerce, 1670–1740" in *Johns Hopkins University Studies in Historical and Political Science,* Twelfth Series, Vol. XII (Baltimore, 1894), 59–72—hereafter cited as Hughson.
52. *Dictionary of American Biography,* Vol. VI (New York, 1931), 16; Hughson, 74–88.
53. Hughson, 88–111.
54. *Ibid.,* 73–75, 79; *N. C. Col. Rec.,* Vol. II (Raleigh, 1886), 342–344.
55. Hughson, 76–77, 83; *Spotswood,* II, 272–275, 305–306; *N. C. Col. Rec.,* Vol. II, 343–344.
56. Hughson, 113–134.
57. McCrady, I, 539–540, 626–629; South-Carolina Historical Society, *Collections,* Vol. I (Charleston, 1857), 170–171; Crane, 215; Rivers, 292–293.
58. Rivers, 296–299.
59. *Ibid.,* 299–301.
60. *Ibid.,* 297–309; McCrady, I, 645–654.
61. Rivers, 309–310; McCrady, I, 655–658.
62. McCrady, I, 663–664.
63. *Ibid.,* 665–666; Crane, 219–220; South-Carolina Historical Society, *Collections,* Vol. I, 172.
64. *Dictionary of American Biography,* Vol. IX (New York, 1932), 401–403, Vol. XIII, 499–501.
65. Andrews, M. P., *Virginia, The Old Dominion,* 173; Massachusetts Historical Society, *Collections,* Fifth Series, Vol. VI (Boston, 1879), 422–423.
66. Crane, 60–62, 229, 235, 250–251, 283; *Dictionary of American Biography,* Vol. XIII, 499–501.
67. McCrady, I, 677–680; Crane, 288–290; South Carolina Historical Society, *Collections,* Vol. I, 172.
68. McCrady, I, 679–680; North Carolina Historical Society, *The James Sprunt Historical Publications,* Vol. 13, No. 1 (Durham, 1913), 35–56.
69. *Dictionary of American History* (New York, 1940), Vol. I, 41 (Alamance, Battle of), Vol. II, 412 (Granville Grant).

CHAPTER 20. LOUISIANA

1. South Carolina Historical Society, *Collections,* Vol. II (Charleston, 1858), 144–145; Crane, Verner W., *The Southern Frontier, 1670–1732* (Durham, 1928), 235–236—hereafter cited as Crane.
2. Rowland, Dunbar, and Sanders, A. G., eds., *Mississippi Provincial Archives, 1701–1729,* French Dominion, Vol. II (Jackson, 1929), 267–271—hereafter cited as *Miss. Archives, 1701–1729.*
3. *Dictionary of American Biography,* Vol. II (New York, 1929), 250–

252, Vol. IX (New York, 1932), 455–457; Thwaites, R. G., *France in America, 1497–1763* (New York, 1907), 73; Gayarre, Charles, *History of Louisiana: The French Domination,* Vol. I (New York, 1867), 36–38—hereafter cited as Gayarre I.

4. Parkman, Francis, *A Half-Century of Conflict,* Vol. I (Frontenac Edition, New York, 1915), 300–301—hereafter cited as Parkman, *Conflict;* Alford, C. W., *The Illinois Country, 1673–1818* (Springfield, 1920), 127–128—hereafter cited as Alford, *Illinois;* Gayarre I, 38–40.

5. *Miss. Archives, 1701–1729,* 9–18.

6. Alvord, C. W., and Carter, C. E., eds., *The New Regime, 1765–1767* (Springfield, 1916), 415–417; Alford, *Illinois,* 124–128; *Dictionary of American Biography,* Vol. IV (New York, 1930), 484–485; Parkman, *Conflict,* Vol. I, 302–303; Crane, 50–57; McCrady, Edward, *History of South Carolina under the Proprietary Government, 1670–1719* (New York, 1897), 54–56.

7. *Dictionary of American Biography,* Vol. XI (New York, 1933), 191–192; Kellogg, Louise Phelps, *The French Regime in Wisconsin and the Northwest* (Madison, 1925), 251–252, 274–275—hereafter cited as Kellogg, *French Regime; Miss. Archives, 1701–1729,* 12–13; Parkman, *Conflict,* Vol. II, 348–353.

8. *Documents relative to the Colonial History of the State of New-York,* Vol. IX (Albany, 1855), 712—hereafter cited as *N. Y. Col. Doc.; Miss. Archives, 1701–1729,* 12–13.

9. *Miss. Archives, 1701–1729,* 14–15; *N. Y. Col. Doc.,* Vol. IX, 712.

10. Alford, *Illinois,* 98–110, 128; *Miss. Archives, 1701–1729,* 16–17; *N. Y. Col. Doc.,* Vol. IX, 453, 494; Kellogg, *French Regime,* 250.

11. Kellogg, *French Regime,* 250–251; *N. Y. Col. Doc.,* Vol. IX, 568–569.

12. Kellogg, *French Regime,* 257–261; Alford, *Illinois,* 107–109.

13. *N. Y. Col. Doc.,* Vol. IX, 673.

14. Kellogg, *French Regime,* 269–270; Alford, *Illinois,* 112.

15. Kellogg, *French Regime,* 271–272; Alford, *Illinois,* 112–114; *Dictionary of American Biography,* Vol. III (New York, 1929), 397–398.

16. Alford, *Illinois,* 113–114; Parkman, *Conflict,* Vol. I, 22–33.

17. Kellogg, *French Regime,* 271–272; Wisconsin State Historical Society, *Collections,* Vol. XVI (Madison, 1902), 221–227.

18. Alford, *Illinois,* 131–132; Crane, 45, 65–67.

19. Alford, *Illinois,* 137–141; *Dictionary of American History* (New York, 1940), Vol. I, 266–267 (Cahokia), Vol. III, 199–200 (Kaskaskia).

20. *Miss. Archives, 1701–1729,* 18–20; Rowland, Dunbar, and Sanders, A. G., eds., *Mississippi Provincial Archives, 1704–1743,* French Dominion, Vol. III (Jackson, 1932), 18–29—hereafter cited as *Miss. Archives, 1704–1743;* Crane, 67–68.

21. Crane, 45, 68–69.

22. *Ibid.,* 69–70.

23. *Ibid.,* 83–86; *Miss. Archives, 1704–1743,* 26, 490; *Dictionary of American Biography,* Vol. IX, 455–457, Vol. XVIII (New York, 1936), 587–588.

24. *Miss. Archives, 1701–1729,* 21, 41, 56; *Miss. Archives, 1704–1743,* 28, 35, 490.

25. *Miss. Archives, 1704–1743,* 136–137; Crane, 85–86.

26. *Miss. Archives, 1701–1729,* 23, 28, 45; *Miss. Archives, 1704–1743,* 47.

27. Parkman, *Conflict*, Vol. I, 308–310; *Miss. Archives, 1701–1729*, 28, 32, 57, 167; *Miss. Archives, 1704–1743*, 24.
28. *Miss. Archives, 1701–1729*, 211–212.
29. *Miss. Archives, 1704–1743*, 79–80, 108.
30. Parkman, *Conflict*, Vol. I, 307–310; Gayarre I, 116–125; *Miss. Archives, 1704–1743*, 76–110; *Dictionary of American Biography*, Vol. III (New York, 1929), 397–398.
31. Alford, *Illinois*, 142–145; Parkman, *Conflict*, Vol. I, 309–315; *Miss. Archives, 1701–1729*, 74–236; *Miss. Archives, 1704–1743*, 173–223; Gayarre I, 103–114.
32. *Dictionary of American Biography*, Vol. XVI (New York, 1935), 295–296; Gayarre I, 165–182.
33. Espinosa, J. Manuel, *First Expedition of Vargas into New Mexico, 1692* (Albuquerque, 1940), 16–19, 27–42, 59–83, 120–133, 187–204, 256–260, and *passim*.
34. *Dictionary of American Biography*, Vol. X (New York, 1933), 419–420; Chapman, C. E., *A History of California: The Spanish Period* (New York, 1921), 190–191.
35. *Dictionary of American Biography*, Vol. XVI, 295–296; *Dictionary of American History*, Vol. III, 302 (Los Adaes), Vol. V, 23 (San Antonio Missions).
36. *Miss. Archives, 1701–1729*, 182; Alford, *Illinois*, 145.
37. *Dictionary of American History*, Vol. III, 421 ("Mississippi Bubble"); Parkman, *Conflict*, Vol. I, 315–319; Gayarre I, 191–213.
38. *Miss. Archives, 1704–1743*, 224–230; Crane, 256.
39. *Miss. Archives, 1704–1743*, 229; *Miss Archives, 1701–1729;* 256; Winsor, Justin, *Narrative and Critical History of America*, Vol. V (Boston, 1887), 35–36—hereafter cited as Winsor; Gayarre I, 234–235.
40. Gayarre I, 242; Winsor, Vol. V, 35–36; Alford, *Illinois*, 150–153; *Dictionary of American History*, Vol. I, 106 (Arkansas, French Post and Mission at).
41. *Miss. Archives, 1704–1743*, 491–492; *Miss. Archives, 1701–1729*, 254; Crane, 229, 235–237.
42. Crane, 239–249, 262–263.
43. *Missouri Historical Review*, Vol. XLIII (Jan., 1949), 115–116; *Dictionary of American Biography*, Vol. II, 482–483.
44. Kansas State Historical Society, *Collections*, Vol. XI (Topeka, 1910), 397–423.
45. *Miss. Archives, 1701–1729*, 275; Wisconsin State Historical Society, *Collections*, Vol. XVI, 413–414.
46. Gayarre I, 217–232.
47. *Dictionary of American History*, Vol. II, 67 (Côte des Allemands); *Miss. Archives, 1701–1729*, 465.
48. Parkman, *Conflict*, Vol. I, 317; *Miss. Archives, 1701–1729*, 274–275.
49. *Dictionary of American History*, Vol. I, 321 (Casket Girls); Gayarre I, 390.
50. Parkman, *Conflict*, Vol. I, 319; Winsor, Vol. V, 49; *Miss. Archives, 1701–1729*, 369–370, 403, 428–429, 661–664.
51. Alford, *Illinois*, 154, 159; *Miss. Archives, 1701–1729*, 275, 404, 496.
52. *Miss. Archives, 1701–1729*, 428, 461; Alford, *Illinois*, 156; *Dictionary of American Biography*, Vol. II, 482–483; *Dictionary of American His-*

tory, Vol. IV, 188 (Fort Orleans) ; Parkman, *Conflict,* Vol. I, 361–362.

53. *Dictionary of American Biography,* Vol. II, 250–253; *Miss. Archives, 1704–1743,* 452, 455, 494, 499–539.

54. Crane, 269–270.

55. *Ibid.,* 270–272.

56. Rowland, Dunbar, and Sanders, A. G., eds., *Mississippi Provincial Archives, 1729–1740* (Jackson, 1927), 34–hereafter cited as *Miss. Archives, 1729–1740.*

57. *Ibid.,* 33.

58. *Ibid.,* 36; Crane, 273–274.

59. Swanton, John R., *The Indians of the Southeastern United States* (Washington, 1946), 158–161, 649–650, 661–662, 679–680.

60. *Miss. Archives, 1704–1743,* 360–370, 512–513; *Miss. Archives, 1727–1740,* 54–61; Winsor, Vol. V, 46–48; *Dictionary of American History,* Vol. IV, 57; Gayarre I, 396–416.

61. *Miss. Archives, 1729–1740,* 61–81; 167; Parkman, *Conflict,* Vol. I, 320–321.

62. Alford, *Illinois,* 167; Parkman, *Conflict,* Vol. I, 322.

63. *Miss. Archives, 1704–1743,* 540–556; *Miss. Archives, 1729–1740,* 193.

64. *Miss. Archives, 1729–1740,* 193.

CHAPTER 21. THE PHILANTHROPISTS FOUND A COLONY

1. Coulter, E. Merton, *A Short History of Georgia* (Chapel Hill, 1933), 23–hereafter cited as Coulter;. Winsor, Justin, *Narrative and Critical History of America,* Vol. V (Boston, 1887), 367–372–hereafter cited as Winsor; Jones, C. C., *History of Georgia,* Vol. I (Boston, 1883), 132–145–hereafter cited as Jones.

2. *Dictionary of American Biography,* Vol. II (New York, 1929), 610–611.

3. *Dictionary of National Biography,* Vol. IV (London, 1885), 348–356.

4. American Antiquarian Society, *Proceedings,* New Series, Vol. VIII (Worcester, 1893), 109–110; Berkeley, George, *Alciphron, or the Minute Philosopher,* in Seven Dialogues (New Haven, 1803); Arnold, S. G., *History of the State of Rhode Island and Providence Plantation,* Vol. II (Providence, 1899), 99–100.

5. Crane, Verner W., *The Southern Frontier, 1670–1732* (Durham, 1928), 307–308–hereafter cited as Crane.

6. *Dictionary of American Biography,* Vol. IV (New York, 1930), 434–435; American Antiquarian Society, *Proceedings,* New Series, Vol. VIII, 133–148.

7. *Dictionary of American History* (New York, 1940), Vol. IV, 269 (Pietism); Sweet, W. W., *Religion in Colonial America* (New York, 1943), 210–212, 223–228.

8. *Dictionary of American History,* Vol. IV, 22 (Moravians).

9. *Dictionary of American Biography,* Vol. XVII (New York, 1935), 428–429; *The Encyclopaedia Britannica,* Eleventh Edition, Vol. XXV (New York, 1911), 593–594.

10. Whitehead, John, *Life of the Rev. John Wesley,* Vol. I (Boston, 1844), 71–77, 257–308; *The Encyclopaedia Britannica,* Eleventh Edition, Vol. XXVIII, 527–529.

11. Crane, 310–313.

12. *Ibid.*, 306, 320; *Dictionary of American Biography*, Vol. II, 610–611; Coulter, 15.

13. Crane, 210–213, 283–287.

14. *Ibid.*, 294–297.

15. *Dictionary of American Biography*, Vol. IV (New York, 1930), 591–592; Crane, 276–280, 294–302.

16. Crane, 320–325; Coulter, 15–18; Thorpe, F. N., ed., *Federal and State Constitutions, Colonial Charters, and other Organic Laws*, Vol. II (Washington, 1909), 765–777.

17. Winsor, Vol. V, 361–366; Coulter, 18–19; Jones, Vol. I, 96–105.

18. Coulter, 20–23; Jones, Vol. I, 113–120; *The Colonial Records of the State of Georgia*, Vol. I (Atlanta, 1904), 127, 130–131, 133–135—hereafter cited as *Ga. Col. Rec.;* Georgia Historical Society, *Collections*, Vol. II (Savannah, 1842), 40.

19. Winsor, Vol. V, 372; Jones, Vol. I, 106–112; Coulter, 51–56; *Ga. Col. Rec.*, Vol. I, 198, 216.

20. Winsor, Vol. V, 372–374; Coulter, 24–25; *Dictionary of American Biography*, Vol. II, 425–426.

21. Winsor, Vol. V, 375–376; Jones, Vol. I, 174–186; Coulter, 30–31; *Ga. Col. Rec.*, Vol. I, 177, 184–185.

22. Coulter, 31–32; Winsor, Vol. V, 376–377.

23. Coulter, 25–26, 52–54.

24. *Ibid.*, 32; *Ga. Col. Rec.*, Vol. I, 160, 234; Jones, Vol. I, 202–207; Winsor, Vol. V, 377; Winchester, C. T., *Life of John Wesley* (New York, 1906), 41.

25. Coulter, 32–35; Jones, Vol. I, 225–237; *Ga. Col. Rec.*, Vol. I, 234.

26. Coulter, 35–37; Jones, Vol. I, 238–256.

27. Whitehead, John, *Life of the Rev. John Wesley*, Vol. I, 77–95; Bailey, A. E., *The Gospel in Hymns* (New York, 1950), 82–102.

28. Whitehead, John, *Life of the Rev. John Wesley*, Vol. II, 5–39; Parker, P. L., ed., *The Heart of John Wesley's Journals* (New York, n. d.), 17–27; Winchester, C. T., *Life of John Wesley*, 48–50.

29. *Dictionary of American Biography*, Vol. VIII (New York, 1932), 68–70, Vol. XX (New York, 1936), 124–129; Coulter, 67.

30. Coulter, 32, 39, 53, 74.

31. *Ibid.*, 26.

32. *Ibid.*, 41–44; Winsor, Vol. V, 381–385; *Dictionary of American History*, Vol. III, 173; Jones, Vol. I, 326–334.

33. Coulter, 45–48; *Dictionary of American History*, Vol. I, 202–203; Jones, Vol. I, 344–360.

34. *Dictionary of American Biography*, Vol. XIV (New York, 1934), 1–3; Coulter, 70.

35. Coulter, 26, 61–65; Jones, Vol. I, 418–428.

36. Coulter, 61–62.

37. Winsor, Vol. V, 387; Coulter, 62–65; *Dictionary of American Biography*, Vol. VIII, 69.

38. Winsor, Vol. V, 387–388; Coulter, 65–66.

39. Coulter, 58–59, 74; Jones, Vol. I, 429–434.

40. Coulter, 61–62, 66; Jones, Vol. I, 380–399.

41. Jones, Vol. I, 450–467; Winsor, Vol. V, 389.

CHAPTER 22. AN ANGRY GOD

1. [Dwight, Sereno Edwards, ed.,] The Works of President Edwards (New York, 1829), Vol. VII, 58, 168–169–hereafter cited as Edwards, *Works.*
2. *A Faithful Narrative of the Surprizing Work of God in the Conversion of Many Hundred Souls in Northampton and the Neighboring Towns and Villages of New-Hampshire in New England.* In a Letter to the Rev'd Dr. Benjamin Colman of Boston. Written by the Reverend Mr. Edwards, Minister of Northampton, on Nov. 6, 1736 (London, 1738), 4–5, 14, 105–116.
3. Sweet, W. W., *Religion in Colonial America* (New York, 1943), 282–284–hereafter cited as Sweet; *Dictionary of American Biography,* Vol. VI (New York, 1931), 30–37; Edwards, *Works,* Vol. I, 120–125, Vol. IV, 75–280; Walker, Williston, *The Creeds and Platforms of Congregationalism* (New York, 1893), 194–237.
4. Coleman, R. V., *The First Frontier* (New York, 1948), 328–330, 355–356, 363; *Dictionary of American History* (New York, 1940), Vol. III, 5–6; *Dictionary of American Biography,* Vol. IV (New York, 1930), 311, Vol. XVIII (New York, 1936), 59–60; Walker, Williston, *The Creeds and Platforms of Congregationalism,* 238–300.
5. Sweet, 113–115; *Dictionary of American History,* Vol. V, 37; Wendell, Barrett, *Cotton Mather* (Cambridge, 1926), 266–269; Murdock, K. B., *Increase Mather* (Cambridge, 1926), 382.
6. Fox, Dixon Ryan, *Caleb Heathcote* (New York, 1926), 243–258.
7. Sweet, 49–51; *Dictionary of American Biography,* Vol. V (New York, 1930), 14–15, Vol. VIII (New York, 1932), 491–492, Vol. X (New York, 1933), 118–119.
8. Sweet, 50–51; Murdock, K. B., *Increase Mather,* 387; *Dictionary of American Biography,* Vol. V, 14–15, Vol. X, 118–119.
9. Sweet, 274–275; *Dictionary of American Biography,* Vol. VII (New York, 1931), 17–18.
10. *Dictionary of American Biography,* Vol. XVIII (New York, 1936), 366–370; Sweet, 250–270; Ford, H. J., *The Scotch-Irish in America* (Princeton, 1915), 249–290.
11. *Dictionary of American Biography,* Vol. XVIII, 366–367.
12. Edwards, *Works,* Vol. I, 120–170, Vol. VII, 168; *Dictionary of American Biography,* Vol. VI, 30–33; Sparks, Jared, ed., *Library of American Biography,* Vol. VIII, being the Lives of Jonathan Edwards and David Brainerd (New York, 1856), 58–69, 81–88.
13. *Dictionary of American Biography,* Vol. XX (New York, 1936), 124–129.
14. *Ibid.,* Vol. XX, 126; Bigelow, John, ed., *Autobiography of Benjamin Franklin* (Philadelphia, 1868), 251–258.
15. *Dictionary of American Biography,* Vol. XVIII, 367.
16. *Dictionary of American Biography,* Vol. XX, 126–127 (Note that date in line 8, col. 2, page 126, should read 1740); Edwards, *Works,* Vol. I, 146–147; Walker, G. L., *Some Aspects of the Religious Life of New England, with Special Reference to Congregationalists* (1897), 89–92.
17. *Dictionary of American Biography,* Vol. XVIII, 367.
18. Chauncy, Charles, *Seasonable Thoughts on the State of Religion in*

New England (Boston, 1744), 4–5.

19. *Ibid.*, 106.
20. *Ibid.*, 98–99; Trumbull, Benjamin, *History of Connecticut,* Vol. II (New Haven, 1818), 160–162, 167–168.
21. *Dictionary of American Biography,* Vol. V (New York, 1930), 84–85; Bridenbaugh, Carl, *Gentleman's Progress, The Itinerarium of Dr. Alexander Hamilton, 1744* (Chapel Hill, 1948), 161—hereafter cited as *Hamilton.*
22. Campbell, Charles, *History of the Colony and Ancient Dominion of Virginia* (Philadelphia, 1860), 442–443; *Hamilton,* 8–9, 22, 117, 120; Bigelow, John, ed., *Autobiography of Benjamin Franklin,* 255–256.
23. *Hamilton,* 123, 163, 167.
24. *Ibid.*, 102, 118–119; Tolles, F. B., *Meeting House and Counting House* (Chapel Hill, 1948), 141–143.
25. Purefoy, G. W., *History of the Sandy Creek Baptist Association* (New York, 1859), 45; Sweet, 277.
26. *Official Register of Princeton University,* Vol. XLI (Princeton, 1949), 90–92; *Dictionary of American Biography,* Vol. V, 301–302.
27. *Dictionary of American Biography,* Vol. III (New York, 1929), 313–314; Hamilton, 122.
28. Massachusetts Historical Society, *Proceedings,* Second Series, Vol. VII (Boston, 1892), 340; Hoadley, Charles J., ed., *Public Records of the Colony of Connecticut, 1751–1757* (Hartford, 1877), 217–218; *The Wolcott Papers,* being Connecticut Historical Society, *Collections,* Vol. XVI (Hartford, 1916), 375–377.
29. *Official Register of Princeton University,* Vol. XLI, 92; *Dictionary of American Biography,* Vol. VI, 35–38.
30. Burnaby, Andrew, *Travels through the Middle Settlements in North-America* (London, 1775), 55.
31. *Dictionary of American Biography,* Vol. X, 118–119; *Documents relative to the Colonial History of the State of New-York,* Vol. VI (Albany, 1885), 849–850.

CHAPTER 23. ABLE MEN AND FINE HOMES

1. *Dictionary of American Biography,* Vol. VI (New York, 1931), 585–598; *Dictionary of American History,* Vol. IV (New York, 1940), 246, 307; Bigelow, John, ed., *Autobiography of Benjamin Franklin* (Philadelphia, 1868), 168–170, 193–194, 206–207.
2. Bigelow, John, ed., *Autobiography of Benjamin Franklin,* 260–263; *Dictionary of American History,* Vol. I (New York, 1940), 64.
3. Bigelow, John, ed., *Autobiography of Benjamin Franklin,* 330–336; Dictionary of American Biography, Vol. VI, 588–589.
4. *Dictionary of American Biography,* Vol. XI, 360–362; Tolles, F. B., *Meeting House and Counting House* (Chapel Hill, 1948), 147.
5. Earnest, Ernest, *John and William Bartram* (Philadelphia, 1940), 22–43, 76–80.
6. *Dictionary of American History,* Vol. V (New York, 1940), 513; *Dictionary of American Biography,* Vol. II (New York, 1929), 564, Vol. V (New York, 1930), 212, Vol. VIII (New York, 1932), 181–182, Vol. XIII (New York, 1934), 214, Vol. XX (New York, 1936), 648–649;

Documents relative to the Colonial History of the State of New York,
Vol. V (Albany, 1855), 942–955; Massachusetts Historical Society,
Proceedings, Second Series, Vol. VII (Boston, 1892), 342.

7. Woodfin, Maude H., ed., *Another Secret Diary of William Byrd of
Westover, 1739–1741* (Richmond, 1942), xxi–xxxi, 415–443.

8. *Ibid.,* xxxviii; Waterman, T. T., *Mansions of Virginia, 1706–1776*
(Chapel Hill, 1946), 145–168, 413, 423.

9. Waterman, T. T., *Mansions of Virginia,* 92–102, 423; Freeman, Douglas
S., *George Washington,* Vol. I (New York, 1948), 90–91, 492–494.

10. Waterman, T. T., *Mansions of Virginia,* 110, 136–138, 420; Farish,
H. D., ed., *Journal & Letters of Philip Vickers Fithian* (Williamsburg,
1943), 58–59, 106–109.

11. Freeman, Douglas S., *George Washington,* Vol. I, 481, 489–491, 499–
510; Wayland, John W., ed., *The Fairfax Line, Thomas Lewis's Journal
of 1746* (New Market, 1925), 1–85.

12. Waterman, T. T., *Mansions of Virginia,* 330–332.

13. Freeman, Douglas S., *George Washington,* Vol. I, 52–53, 73–75.

14. *Ibid.,* Vol. I, 67–77.

15. *Ibid.,* Vol. I, 264, Vol. II, 1–3.

16. *Ibid.,* Vol. I, 141–142; Campbell, Charles, *History of the Colony and
Ancient Dominion of Virginia* (Philadelphia, 1860), 418; *A Dialogue
Between Thomas Sweet-Scented, William Oronoco,* etc., by a Sincere
Lover of Virginia (Williamsburg, 1732).

17. *Dictionary of American History,* Vol. IV (New York, 1940), 480;
Ramsay, David, *History of South Carolina,* Vol. II (Charleston, 1809),
201, 205–207; Andrews, Charles M., *Colonial Period of American History,* Vol. IV (New Haven, 1938), 95–98; Ravenel, Harriott H., *Eliza
Pinckney* (New York, 1896), 19—hereafter cited as Ravenel.

18. Ravenel, 7, 102–107; Ramsay, David, *History of South Carolina,* Vol.
II, 209–212; Meriwether, R. L., *Expansion of South Carolina, 1729–
1765* (Kingsport, 1940), 167.

19. Donnan, Elizabeth, "The Slave Trade into South Carolina before the
Revolution," in *American Historical Review,* Vol. XXXIII, 804–828.

20. *Dictionary of American Biography,* Vol. XI (New York, 1933), 32–35.

21. *Ibid.,* Vol. XII (New York, 1933), 234–235; *South Carolina Historical
and Genealogical Magazine,* Vol. XVIII (1917), 12–14—hereafter cited
as *S. C. Hist. & Gen. Mag.*

22. *S. C. Hist. & Gen. Mag.,* Vol. XX (1919), 57–63, 118–141, 204–212,
256–259, Vol. XXI (1920), 10–23, 59–61.

23. Ravenel, 101–102, 110–112; *S. C. Hist. & Gen. Mag.,* Vol. XX, Map
opp. p. 3; Earnest, Ernest, *John and William Bartram,* 55, 82; *Dictionary of American Biography,* Vol. VII (New York, 1931), 131–132.

24. Ravenel, 126–128.

25. *Ibid.,* 120–121.

26. *S. C. Hist. & Gen. Mag.,* Vol. XX, 76–78.

27. *Ibid.,* Vol. XX, 9–12.

28. *Ibid.,* 91–94; Lockwood, Alice G. B., ed., *Gardens of Colony and State*
(New York, 1934), 220.

29. Ravenel, 53–54.

30. Andrews, Charles M., *Colonial Period of American History,* Vol. IV,
247–249; *American Historical Review,* Vol. II (1897), 229–240; Bouton,

N., ed., *Documents and Records relating to the Province of New-Hampshire,* Vol. IV (Manchester, 1870), 833, Vol. V (Nashua, 1871), 19–hereafter cited as *N. H. Prov. Papers.*

31. *N. H. Prov. Papers,* Vol. IV, 678; Massachusetts Historical Society, *Collections,* Sixth Series, Vol. VII (Boston, 1894), 80–85.

32. Connecticut Historical Society, *Collections,* Vol. XVII (Hartford, 1918), 1–2.

33. *New-England Historical and Genealogical Register,* Vol. XXIV (Boston, 1870), 52; *N. H. Prov. Papers,* Vol. IV, 851.

34. Adams, N., *Annals of Portsmouth* (Portsmouth, 1825), 173–175; Massachusetts Historical Society, *Collections,* Sixth Series, Vol. VII, 320, 431, 434.

35. *N. H. Prov. Papers,* Vol. IV, 833–865, Vol. V, 921–925.

36. *Ibid.,* Vol. IV, 568, 836, Vol. V, 595–596.

37. Hammond, Otis G., *The Mason Title and Its Relations to New Hampshire and Massachusetts* (Worcester, 1916), 11–12–hereafter cited as Hammond, *Mason Title;* Batchellor, A. S., ed., *Documents Relating to the Masonian Patent,* being *Masonian Papers,* Vol. III (Concord, 1896), 177–193–hereafter cited as *N. H. State Papers,* Vol. XXIX.

38. Hammond, *Mason Title,* 12–13; *N. H. State Papers,* Vol. XXIX, 193–196.

39. Massachusetts Historical Society, *Collections,* Sixth Series, Vol. VII, 402; *Dictionary of American Biography,* Vol. II (New York, 1929), 144, Vol. XVII (New York, 1935), 120–122, Vol. XIX (New York, 1936), 653–654.

40. *N. H. Prov. Papers,* Vol. V, 596.

41. *Ibid.,* Vol. V, 87, 591–596, 793, 822–826, 833–835; *N. H. State Papers,* Vol. XXIX, 213–217.

42. *N. H. State Papers,* Vol. XXVI, being *Town Charters,* Vol. III (Concord, 1895), vi, 99–102, and *passim;* Hammond, *Mason Title,* 16–17.

43. *Dictionary of American Biography,* Vol. XIX, 654; Connecticut Historical Society, *Collections,* Vol. XVI (Hartford, 1916), 313; Adams, James Truslow, *Revolutionary New England* (Boston, 1923), 257.

44. Brewster, C. W., *Rambles about Portsmouth* (Portsmouth, 1859), 98–100; Drake, S. A., *Nooks and Corners of the New England Coast* (New York, 1875), 202–206.

45. Longfellow, Henry, *Complete Poetical Works,* Household Edition (Boston, 1882, 1883), 283–286, "Lady Wentworth"; Brewster, C. W., *Rambles about Portsmouth,* 101–102.

46. Nason, Elias, *Sir Charles Henry Frankland* (Albany, 1865), 22–74; *Dictionary of American Biography,* Vol. VI (New York, 1931), 585; Winsor, Justin, *Memorial History of Boston,* Vol. II (Boston, 1881), 525–526.

47. *Dictionary of American Biography,* Vol. IX (New York, 1932), 439–443; Winsor, Justin, *Memorial History of Boston,* Vol. II, 523–528; Teele, A. K., ed., *History of Milton, Mass., 1640 to 1887* (Boston, 1887), 135–136; Weeden, W. B., *Economic and Social History of New England* (Boston, 1891), 531–532.

48. *Dictionary of American Biography,* Vol. II, 498–501, Vol. VI, 262–263, Vol. IX, 439–443.

49. Andrews, Charles M., *Colonial Period of American History,* Vol. IV,

242–243, 267; *Dictionary of American History*, Vol. IV, 6, Vol. V, 296–297; Weeden, W. B., *Economic and Social History of New England*, Vol. II, 459.

50. Lossing, Benson J., ed., *The American Historical Record,* Vol. I (Philadelphia, 1872) , 318–340.

51. *Dictionary of American Biography*, Vol. XV (New York, 1935) , 444–445; *The Company of the Redwood Library and Athenaeum, Charter and Amendments—By-laws* (Newport, 1937) , 3–8; Lockwood, Alice G. B., ed., *Gardens of Colony and State* (New York, 1931) , 204, 220–221.

52. *Dictionary of American Biography,* Vol. XVIII (New York, 1936) , 18–21.

53. Lockwood, Alice G. B., ed., *Gardens of Colony and State* (New York, 1931) , 217.

54. *Ibid.*, 208–211; Bridenbaugh, Carl, ed., *Gentleman's Progress, the Itinerarium of Dr. Alexander Hamilton, 1744* (Chapel Hill, 1948) , 103—hereafter cited as *Hamilton.*

55. *Hamilton,* 53; Hall, E. H., *Philipse Manor Hall at Yonkers, N. Y.* (New York, 1912) , 108–110.

56. Bolton, Robert, *History of . . . County of Westchester,* Vol. I (New York, 1881) , 98–99, 734–735; *Dictionary of American Biography,* Vol. V, 212–213, Vol. XI, 318–320.

57. *Dictionary of American Biography,* Vol. XIX, 485–487; *New-York Gazette,* July 19–26, 1731.

58. Pound, Arthur, *Johnson of the Mohawks* (New York, 1930) , 21–32; *Hamilton,* 85.

59. *Dictionary of American History*, Vol. III, 304; *Dictionary of American Biography*, Vol. XIV (New York, 1934) , 456–457, Vol. XVII, 120–122, Vol. XIX, 486; Winsor, Justin, *Narrative and Critical History of America,* Vol. V (Boston, 1887) , 410–412; Pound, Arthur, *Johnson of the Mohawks,* 77.

60. *Documents relating to the Colonial History of the State of New-York,* Vol. VI (Albany, 1855) , 419, 432—hereafter cited as *N. Y. Col. Doc.;* Pound, Arthur, *Johnson of the Mohawks,* 100–117; Sullivan, James, ed., *The Papers of Sir William Johnson,* Vol. I (Albany, 1921) , 59–202.

61. *N. Y. Col. Doc.,* Vol. V (Albany, 1855) , 805, Vol. VI, 424, 428, 433–437, 474–476.

62. Hutchinson, [Thomas,] *History of the Province of Massachusets-Bay,* Vol. II (Boston, 1767) , 149, 151–152, 370–373; Adams, James Truslow, *Revolutionary New England,* 132–137; Smith, W. Roy, *South Carolina as a Royal Province, 1719–1776* (New York, 1903) , 82; Brock, R. A., ed., *Official Records of Robert Dinwiddie,* Vol. I (Richmond, 1883) , 100–101.

63. *Massachusetts Gazette & Boston Weekly News-Letter,* Mar. 8, 1770.

64. *N. Y. Col. Doc.,* Vol. IV (Albany, 1854) , 298; *N. H. Prov. Papers,* Vol. IV, 843; Lonn, Ella, *Colonial Agents of the Southern Colonies* (Chapel Hill, 1945) , 3–52, 248–269, and *passim.*

CHAPTER 24. PEOPLE

1. Burnaby, Andrew, *Travels through the Middle Settlements in North-America in the years 1759 and 1760* (London, 1775) , 83–84.

2. Stiles, H. R., *Bundling; Its Origin, Progress and Decline* (Albany, 1871),
   passim.
3. "Diary of Joshua Hempstead," in New London County Historical
   Society, *Collections,* Vol. I (New London, 1901), 267.
4. New Hampshire Historical Society, *Collections,* Vol. 9 (Concord, 1889),
   123–191.
5. Massachusetts Historical Society, *Proceedings,* Second Series, Vol. VII
   (Boston, 1892), 344–345–hereafter cited as Mass. Hist. Soc., *Proc.*
6. Bridenbaugh, Carl, ed., *Gentleman's Progress, The Itinerarium of Dr.
   Alexander Hamilton, 1744* (Chapel Hill, 1948), 99–102 and notes 217–
   220–hereafter cited as *Hamilton;* Rhode Island Historical Society,
   Collections, Vol. XXII, 41–45.
7. Mass. Hist. Soc., *Proc.,* First Series, Vol. V (Boston, 1862), 108–126;
   New England Historical and Genealogical Register, Vol. XXIV (Boston, 1870), 50–63–hereafter cited as *N. E. Hist. & Geneal. Reg.*
8. *N. E. Hist. & Geneal. Reg.,* Vol. XXIV, 53.
9. Mass. Hist. Soc., *Proc.,* First Series, Vol. V, 124.
10. *Ibid.,* 124; *Hamilton,* 139 and note 311.
11. Mass. Hist. Soc., *Proc.,* First Series, Vol. V, 124.
12. *Hamilton,* 146; Burnaby, Andrew, *Travels through the Middle Settle-
    ments in North-America,* 21.
13. *Hamilton,* 42–43, 45, 88, 116, 151, 175.
14. *Ibid.,* xvi.
15. *Dictionary of American Biography,* Vol. I (New York, 1928), 95–101.
16. Weeden, W. B., *Economic and Social History of New England, 1620–
    1789,* Vol. I (Boston, 1890), 75, Vol. II (Boston, 1890), 514, here-
    after cited as Weeden; *Dictionary of American History,* Vol. V (New
    York, 1940), 287–288; Lincoln, Charles H., ed., *Correspondence of
    William Shirley,* Vol. I (New York, 1912), 418–hereafter cited as
    Shirley.
17. *Shirley,* Vol. I, 412–419; Hutchinson, [Thomas,] *History of the Prov-
    ince of Massachusets-Bay,* [Vol. II,] (Boston, 1767), 430–435–hereafter
    cited as Hutchinson.
18. Hutchinson, [Vol. II,] 392–393; Weeden, Vol. II, 473–491; *Hamilton,*
    146, 170; Mass. Hist. Soc., *Proc.,* First Series, Vol. V, 123–124.
19. Hutchinson, [Vol. II] 393–396, 436–440; Weeden, Vol. II, 675; Adams,
    James Truslow, *Revolutionary New England* (Boston, 1923), 190–191.
20. *Dictionary of American Biography,* Vol. I, 95.
21. Wright, Louis B., and Tinling, Marion, eds., *Secret Diary of William
    Byrd of Westover, 1709–1712* (Richmond, 1941), 75; Brock, R. A., ed.,
    Official Records of Robert Dinwiddie, Vol. I (Richmond, 1883), 30.
22. Rhode Island Historical Society, *Collections,* Vol. VIII (1893), 112–
    113.
23. *Hamilton,* 43, 139, 186; Freeman, Douglas S., *George Washington,*
    Vol. I (New York, 1948), 192.
24. *Hamilton,* xii–xiii; *Dictionary of American Biography,* Vol. II (New
    York, 1929), 433–434, Vol. VIII (New York, 1932), 170–171; Bigelow,
    John, ed., *Autobiography of Benjamin Franklin* (Philadelphia, 1868),
    281–284.
25. *Dictionary of American Biography,* Vol. II, 535–536, Vol. III (New

York, 1930), 286–287, Vol. VII (New York, 1931), 132–133; Glenn, T. A., *Some Colonial Mansions* (Philadelphia, 1899), 380–382.

26. *Dictionary of American Biography*, Vol. VI (New York, 1931), 599, Vol. XII (New York, 1933), 388; Wendell, Barrett, *Cotton Mather* (Cambridge, 1926), 273–281.

27. Murdock, K. B., *Increase Mather* (Cambridge, 1926), 385–388.

28. *Dictionary of American Biography*, Vol. XIV (New York, 1934), 409; Nason, Elias, *Sir Charles Henry Frankland* (Albany, 1865), 26.

29. Mass. Hist. Soc., *Col.*, Fifth Series, Vol. VI (Boston, 1879), 48–49.

30. Fielding, Mantle, *Dictionary of American Painters, Sculptors and Engravers* (New York, 1945), 112; *New England Quarterly*, Vol. VIII (1935), 14–28, being "Mr. Smibert Shows His Pictures, March, 1730," by Henry Wilder Foote; *Dictionary of American Biography*, Vol. XVII (New York, 1935), 228–230.

31. *Hamilton*, 38.

32. American Antiquarian Society, *Proceedings* (October, 1940, Worcester), being "John Watson, Painter, Merchant and Capitalist of New Jersey, 1685–1768" by John Hill Logan.

33. Foote, Henry Wilder, *Robert Feke, Colonial Portrait Painter* (Cambridge, 1930); Morgan, John Hill, *Early American Painters* (New York, 1921), 46; *Dictionary of American Biography*, Vol. VI, 312–313; *Hamilton*, 102.

34. *Boston News Letter*, April 17–24, 1721; *Hamilton*, 35; Adams, James Truslow, *Provincial Society, 1690–1763* (New York, 1927), 301.

35. Burnaby, Andrew, *Travels through the Middle Settlements*, 37.

36. *Hamilton*, 3–106.

37. *Ibid.*, 8, and *passim*.

38. *Pennsylvania Magazine of History and Biography*, Vol. XXXVI (Philadelphia, 1912), 1–16, 162–164.

39. *Hamilton*, 30–38.

40. *The Virginia Gazette*, April 15–April 22, 1737.

41. *Dictionary of American History*, Vol. II, 424–425 (Greenbriar Land Company), Vol. III, 311 (Loyal Land Company), Vol. IV, 163 (Ohio Company of Virginia). Northward the Masonian Proprietors of New Hampshire (see pages 407–408) were making grants by the score, many of them west of the Connecticut River in territory claimed by New York. Byrd, Julian P., "The Susquehanna Company," in *Dictionary of American History*, Vol. V, 211; Dexter, F. B., ed., *Literary Diary of Ezra Stiles*, Vol. I (New York, 1901), 434, 436, 660; Adams, James Truslow, *Revolutionary New England*, 263.

CHAPTER 25. THE HINTERLAND

1. Wallace, Paul A. W., *Conrad Weiser* (Philadelphia, 1945), 3–16, hereafter cited as Wallace; *Documents relative to the Colonial History of the State of New-York*, Vol. V (Albany, 1855), 112–113, 117–122, 160–161, and *passim*—hereafter cited as *N. Y. Col. Doc.*

2. *N. Y. Col. Doc.*, Vol. V, 575; Wallace, 78, 86; Halsey, F. W., ed., *A Tour of Four Great Rivers* (New York, 1906), liii–liv, 64–69.

3. Wallace, 17–33; *Dictionary of American Biography*, Vol. XIX (New York, 1936), 614–615.

4. Wallace, 35–39; *Pennsylvania Archives,* Second Series, Vol. VII (Harrisburg, 1878), 96–97.
5. *Pennsylvania Archives,* Second Series, Vol. VII, 96–97; Ford, H. J., *Scotch-Irish in America* (Princeton, 1915), 264–265; Hanna, C. A., *The Scotch-Irish,* Vol. II (New York, 1902), 63.
6. Klein, W. C., *Johann Conrad Beissel* (Philadelphia, 1942), 34–80, 116.
7. *Ibid.,* 70, 81–82; *Dictionary of American Biography,* Vol. XVII (New York, 1935), 415–416; Wallace, 51–52.
8. Wallace, 57–61; Klein, W. C., *Johann Conrad Beissel,* 82–87.
9. Acrelius, Israel, *History of New Sweden* (Translated by W. M. Reynolds, Philadelphia, 1874), 376; Klein, W. C., *Johann Conrad Beissel,* 87; Wallace, 60–63.
10. Wallace, 104, 107.
11. Acrelius, Israel, *History of New Sweden,* 373–401; Aurand, A. Monroe, *Historical Account of the Ephrata Cloister and the Seventh Baptist Society* (Harrisburg, 1940), 3–15; Klein, W. C., *Johann Conrad Beissel,* 108–150.
12. Wallace, 61, 63.
13. *Ibid.,* 108–115, 174.
14. *Ibid.,* 39–49.
15. *Ibid.,* 65–94.
16. *Ibid.,* 95, 100; Shepherd, W. R., *History of Proprietary Government in Pennsylvania* (New York, 1896), 98–100—hereafter cited as Shepherd, Pennsylvania.
17. Wallace, 125–129.
18. *Ibid.,* 96–99, 129–131; Shepherd, *Pennsylvania,* 100–103.
19. Shepherd, *Pennsylvania,* 102–103; Wallace, 99–100.
20. Wallace, 118–124, 133–144; Sweet, W. W., *Religion in Colonial America* (New York, 1943), 223–225; *Dictionary of American Biography,* Vol. XX (New York, 1936), 657–658.
21. Sweet, W. W., *Religion in Colonial America,* 225–227.
22. *Virginia Magazine of History and Biography,* Vol. XI (Richmond, 1903), 235–236, 3721375, Vol. XII (Richmond, 1904), ·55–61—hereafter cited as *Va. Mag.*
23. *N. Y. Col. Doc.,* Vol. V, 669–677.
24. Bruce, P. A., *History of Virginia,* Vol. I (Chicago and New York, 1924), 315–317; *Dictionary of American Biography,* Vol. IX (New York, 1932), 80; *Va. Mag.,* Vol. XIII (Richmond, 1905–6), 133–134, 286–288; Freeman, Douglas S., *George Washington,* Vol. I (New York, 1948), 186–188.
25. *Va. Mag.,* Vol. XIII, 113–138, 295–297; Campbell, Charles, *History and Ancient Dominion of Virginia* (Philadelphia, 1860), 427–432.
26. *N. Y. Col. Doc.,* Vol. VI (Albany, 1855), 254; Colden, Cadwallader, *History of the Five Nations of Canada* (London, 1747), 91—hereafter cited as Colden, *Five Nations.*
27. Colden, *Five Nations,* 87–152; Massachusetts Historical Society, *Collections,* First Series, Vol. VII (Boston, 1801), 178—hereafter cited as Mass. Hist. Soc., *Col.,* First Series, Vol. VII; Wallace, 184.
28. Mass. Hist. Soc., *Col.,* First Series, Vol. VII, 171–201; Colden, *Five Nations,* 151.
29. Colden, *Five Nations,* 87–152.

30. *Ibid.*, 136, 144, 148, 151; *Va. Mag.*, Vol. XIII, 141–142; Wallace, 184–194.

31. *Dictionary of American Biography*, Vol. III, 311 (Loyal Land Company), Vol. IV, 163 (Ohio Company of Virginia).

32. Freeman, Douglas S., *George Washington*, Vol. I, 188–189, 221, 509–510; *Dictionary of American Biography*, Vol. IX, 80.

33. Wayland, J. W., *The Fairfax Line: Thomas Lewis's Journal of 1746* (New Market, 1925), 1–85; Gordon, Armistead C., *In the Picturesque Shenandoah Valley* (Richmond, 1930), 115.

34. *Dictionary of American Biography*, Vol. VII (New York, 1931), 48–49.

35. *Va. Mag.*, Vol. XIII, 138; for confirmation of his memory of the inscription on John Lewis' tomb, the author is indebted to Mrs. J. D. Perry, Staunton Public Library, Staunton, Virginia; *Dictionary of American History*, Vol. I, 138–139 (Augusta County, Va.).

36. *Dictionary of American Biography*, Vol. II (New York, 1929), 441–442.

37. Crane, Verner W., *The Southern Frontier, 1670–1732*, 292–294; Meriwether, Robert L., *Expansion of South Carolina, 1729–1765* (Kingsport, 1940), 17–25–hereafter cited as Meriwether; McCrady, Edward, *History of South Carolina under the Royal Government, 1719–1776* New York, 1899), 121–142.

38. Meriwether, 66–69; *Journal of Southern History*, Vol. V (February, 1939), 83–97.

39. Meriwether, 53–65.

40. *Ibid.*, 117–125.

41. Williams, Samuel Cole, *Dawn of Tennessee Valley and Tennessee History* (Johnson City, 1937), 101–113; Brown, John P., *Old Frontiers* (Kingsport, 1938), 50–52; *Dictionary of American Biography*, Vol. XV (New York, 1935), 210.

42. Meriwether, 198.

43. *Ibid.*, 193–194.

44. *Ibid.*, 190.

45. *Ibid.*, 195–197.

46. *Ibid.*, 124, 195, 206–208; McCrady, Edward, *History of South Carolina under the Royal Government, 1719–1726*, 306–308.

47. Williams, Samuel Cole, *Dawn of Tennessee Valley and Tennessee History*, 184–194; Brown, John P., *Old Frontiers*, 52, 54–55, 61–77; Meriwether, 208–210.

48. Brock, R. A., ed., *Official Records of Robert Dinwiddie*, Vol. II (Richmond, 1884), 202–203; Meriwether, 160.

49. Meriwether, 122, 165.

50. *Ibid.*, 160–184.

51. *Ibid.*, 180; *Va. Mag.*, Vol. XI, 235–236, 372–375, Vol. XII, 55–61.

52. Fries, Adelaide L., ed., *Records of the Moravians in North America*, Vol. I (Raleigh, 1922), 14–15, 28–64–hereafter cited as *Moravian Rec.*; Coulter, E. Merton, "The Granville District" in *The James Sprunt Historical Publications*, Vol. 13 (North Carolina Historical Society), 35–56.

53. *Moravian Rec.*, Vol. I, 28–64.

54. *Ibid.*, Vol. I, 65–66.

55. *Ibid.*, 73–80.

CHAPTER 26. OHIO

1. Fitzpatrick, John C., *The Diaries of George Washington, 1748–1799,* Vol. I (Boston, 1925), 43–hereafter cited as *Washington Diaries;* Massachusetts Historical Society, *Collections,* Third Series, Vol. V (Boston, 1836), 102, being Gist's Journal–hereafter cited as Mass. Hist. Soc., *Col.*

2. Bailey, K. P., *The Ohio Company of Virginia* (Glendale, 1939), 19–31, 39, 147–150–hereafter cited as Bailey.

3. Brock, R. A., ed., *Official Records of Robert Dinwiddie,* Vol. I (Richmond, 1883), 96, 118–hereafter cited as *Dinwiddie;* Bailey, 106; Wallace, Paul A. W., *Conrad Weiser* (Philadelphia, 1945), 47–48; Hanna, C. A., *The Wilderness Trail,* Vol. I (New York, 1911), 168.

4. Volwiler, A. T., *George Croghan and the Westward Movement, 1741–1782* (Cleveland, 1926), 23, 32–39–hereafter cited as Volwiler, *Croghan; Dictionary of American Biography,* Vol. IV (New York, 1930), 556–557.

5. Volwiler, *Croghan,* 34–37; *Documents relative to the Colonial History of the State of New-York,* Vol. VI (Albany, 1855), 733–hereafter cited at *N. Y. Col. Doc.;* Thwaites, R. G., ed., *Collections of the State Historical Society of Wisconsin,* Vol. XVIII (Madison, 1908), 12.

6. Volwiler, *Croghan,* 30.

7. *Ibid.,* 30–31, 40–43; Nixon, L. L., *James Burd* (Philadelphia, 1941), 15–16; Hanna, C. A., *The Wilderness Trail,* Vol. I, 5.

8. Bailey, 24–60.

9. Thwaites, R. G., ed., *Collections of the State Historical Society of Wisconsin,* Vol. XVIII, 36–58; Thwaites, R. G., ed., *The Jesuit Relations and Allied Documents,* Vol. LXIX (Cleveland, 1900), 150–199; *Dictionary of American History,* Vol. I (New York, 1940), 330.

10. Buck, Solon J., and Elizabeth H., *The Planting of Civilization in Western Pennsylvania* (Pittsburgh, 1939), 24–30; Thwaites, R. G., ed., *Collections of the State Historical Society of Wisconsin,* Vol. XVII (Madison, 1906), 331, 448; Thwaites, R. G., *Jesuit Relations and Allied Documents,* Vol. LXIX, 25 note 18; Hanna, C. A., *Wilderness Trail,* Vol. I, 311, 355.

11. Buck, Solon and Elizabeth H., *Planting of Civilization in Western Pennsylvania,* 29; Hanna, C. A., *Wilderness Trail,* Vol. I, 290–314, 352–356.

12. Buck, Solon and Elizabeth H., *Planting of Civilization in Western Pennsylvania,* 27–30; Hanna, C. A., *Wilderness* Trail, Vol. I, 269–273, 289–314, 352–383; Wallace, Paul A. W., *Conrad Weiser,* 259.

13. Bailey, 63–82.

14. *Dictionary of American Biography,* Vol. VII (New York, 1931), 323–324; Bailey, 85–96; Summers, Lewis P., *Annals of Southwest Virginia, 1769–1800* (Abingdon, 1929), 27–29–hereafter cited as Summers, *Annals.*

15. Summers, *Annals,* 29–32; Volwiler, *Croghan,* 71–72.

16. Volwiler, *Croghan,* 71–72; Summers, *Annals,* 32–36.

17. Summers, *Annals,* 36–40.

18. *Ibid.,* 40–46; *N. Y. Col. Doc.,* Vol. VII (Albany, 1856), 266–271.

19. Summers, *Annals,* 47–57; Bailey, 64–68, 79–82, 95–96, 147.
20. Bailey, 147–151; *Dictionary of American Biography,* Vol. V (New York, 1930), 316–317.
21. *Dinwiddie,* Vol. I, 6–19.
22. *Ibid.,* 7–11; *Virginia Magazine of History and Biography,* Vol. XIII (Richmond, 1905–1906), 143–152.
23. *Virginia Magazine of History and Biography,* Vol. XIII, 154–174; Volwiler, *Croghan,* 44, 77–78; Bailey, 135–137; *Dictionary of American Biography,* Vol. XVIII (New York, 1936), 638–639.
24. *Virginia Magazine of History and Biography,* Vol. XIII, 152–154; Volwiler, *Croghan,* 77–79; Thwaites, R. G., ed., *Collections of the State Historical Society of Wisconsin,* Vol. XVIII, 128–129; *Dictionary of American Biography,* Vol. V, 216–217; Hanna, C. A., *Wilderness Trail,* Vol. II, 291–292.
25. Bailey, 152–157; *N. Y. Col. Doc.,* Vol. VI, 599–600, 730.
26. *N. Y. Col. Doc.,* Vol. VI, 778–779.
27. *Ibid.,* Vol. VI, 780.
28. *Ibid.,* 835–837; Parkman, Francis, *Montcalm and Wolfe,* Vol. I (Frontenac Edition, New York, 1915), 90–93, 133–137; Bailey, 174–175; *Dictionary of American History,* Vol. IV, 359 (Venango).
29. *Dinwiddie,* Vol. I, 39–40; Bailey, 201–203 note 486; *N. Y. Col. Doc.,* Vol. VI, 794–795.
30. Freeman, Douglas S., *George Washington,* Vol. I (New York, 1948), 274–276–hereafter cited as Freeman, *Washington.*
31. *Washington Diaries,* Vol. I, 44–67; Mass. Hist. Soc., *Col.,* Third Series, Vol. V, 102–108, being Gist's Journal.
32. *Washington Diaries,* Vol. I, 67; Freeman, *Washington,* Vol. I, 325.
33. Parkman, Francis, *Montcalm and Wolfe,* Vol. I, 136; *N. Y. Col. Doc.,* Vol. VII, 269; *Dinwiddie,* Vol. I, 55–57; Bailey, 191–193; Freeman, *Washington,* Vol. I, 329, 337.
34. *Dinwiddie,* Vol. I, 48–63; *N. Y. Col. Doc.,* Vol. VI, 827; *Washington Diaries,* Vol. I, 73; Freeman, *Washington,* Vol. I, 329.
35. Freeman, *Washington,* Vol. I, 329–333; *Dinwiddie,* Vol. I, 52, 60–91, 93–99, 102–103, 375; Bailey, 205–208.
36. *Dinwiddie,* Vol. I, 82, 92; Freeman, *Washington,* Vol. I, 330–334.
37. *Washington Diaries,* Vol. I, 73–75; Freeman, *Washington,* Vol. I, 343–350.
38. *Washington Diaries,* Vol. I, 75–78; Freeman, *Washington,* Vol. I, 350–353; Bailey, 192–197; *N. Y. Col. Doc.,* Vol. VI, 840–842.
39. *Washington Diaries,* 76–85; Freeman, *Washington,* Vol. I, 353–368.
40. *Washington Diaries,* Vol. I, 84–88; Freeman, *Washington,* Vol. I, 368–377; *Dinwiddie,* Vol. I, 174–192.
41. *Dinwiddie,* Vol. I, 180, 202; Parkman, Francis, *Montcalm and Wolfe,* Vol. I, 153–156, 159; *Washington Diaries,* Vol. I, 88–89; Freeman, *Washington,* Vol. I, 374–376.
42. *Dinwiddie,* Vol. I, 181–182, 185, 190, 192–193, 197–200; *Washington Diaries,* Vol. I, 90–92; Freeman, *Washington,* Vol. I, 379–391.
43. *Washington Diaries,* Vol. I, 93–101; Freeman, *Washington,* Vol. I, 391–394; *Dinwiddie,* Vol. I, 220; Volwiler, *Croghan,* 85–87; Sullivan, James, ed., *Papers of Sir William Johnson,* Vol. I (Albany, 1921), 496–497.

44. Freeman, *Washington*, Vol. I, 396; Parkman, Francis, *Montcalm and Wolfe*, Vol. I, 159–161.

45. *The Maryland Gazette*, Thursday, August 29, 1754; Freeman, *Washington*, Vol. I, 397–400; Volwiler, *Croghan*, 87; Sullivan, James, ed., *Papers of Sir William Johnson*, Vol. I, 497.

46. *The Maryland Gazette*, Thursday, August 29, 1754; Freeman, *Washington*, Vol. I, 400–415; *Dinwiddie*, Vol. I, 239–250; Parkman, Francis, *Montcalm and Wolfe*, Vol. I, 159–167; Gipson, Lawrence H., *The Great War for the Empire: The Years of Defeat, 1754–1757* (New York, 1946), 38–43.

CHAPTER 27. COLONIAL UNION FAILS

1. *Papers of Sir William Johnson*, Vol. I (Albany, 1921), 410—hereafter cited *Johnson Papers*.

2. Freeman, Douglas S., *George Washington*, Vol. I (New York, 1948), 423–424.

3. Wallace, Paul A. W., *Conrad Weiser* (Philadelphia, 1945), 365–373; hereafter cited as Wallace.

4. Brock, R. A., ed., *Official Records of Robert Dinwiddie*, Vol. I (Richmond, 1883), 235–260, 334—hereafter cited as *Dinwiddie; Documents relative to the Colonial History of the State of New-York*, Vol. VI (Albany, 1855), 838—hereafter cited as *N. Y. Col. Doc.*

5. *N. Y. Col. Doc.*, Vol. VI, 794–795.

6. *Dinwiddie*, Vol. I, 119–130, 339, 344.

7. *The Pennsylvania Gazette*, May 9, 1754; Bouton, Nathaniel, ed., *Documents and Records relative to the Province of New-Hampshire*, Vol. VI (Manchester, 1872), 279.

8. *N. Y. Col. Doc.*, Vol. VI, 800–802; Lincoln, C. H., ed., *Correspondence of William Shirley*, Vol. II (New York, 1912), 40–46—hereafter cited as *Shirley*.

9. *N. Y. Col. Doc.*, Vol. VI, 853–892; for Elisha Williams see *Dictionary of American Biography*, Vol. XX (New York, 1936), 256–257.

10. Wallace, 356–357; for Ephraim Williams see *Dictionary of American Biography*, Vol. XX, 259.

11. *N. Y. Col. Doc.*, Vol. VI, 869–870.

12. *Dictionary of American History* (New York, 1940), Vol. II, 24 (Connecticut's Western Lands), Vol. V, 211 (Susquehanna Company); *Wolcott Papers in Collections of the Connecticut Historical Society*, Vol. XVI (Hartford, 1916), 428–429, 435; *Johnson Papers*, Vol. I, 398–401, 405, 440–441, Vol. IX (Albany, 1939), 199–200; Wallace, 361.

13. Wallace, 350–360.

14. *N. Y. Col. Doc.*, Vol. VI, 860, 875, 889–891; Bigelow, John, *Autobiography of Benjamin Franklin* (Philadelphia, 1868), 294–296; *Fitch Papers in Collections of the Connecticut Historical Society*, Vol. XVII (Hartford, 1918), 19–29; Hutchinson, [Thomas,] *History of the Province of Massachusetts Bay*, Vol. III (London, 1828), 19–23; Gipson, L. H., "Thomas Hutchinson and the Framing of the Albany Plan of Union, 1754," in *The Pennsylvania Magazine of History and Biography*, January, 1950.

15. Hutchinson, [Thomas,] *History of the Province of Massachusetts Bay*,

Vol. III, 23; Bigelow, John, ed., *Autobiography of Benjamin Franklin*, 295; Shirley, Vol. II, 111–118.

16. *Dinwiddie*, Vol. I, 81, 241, 249–254, 282–284, 311.

17. *Correspondence of Governor Horatio Sharpe*, Vol. I, in *Archives of Maryland*, Vol. VI (Baltimore, 1888), 99.

18. *Shirley*, Vol. II, 124.

19. *Dinwiddie*, Vol. I, 353, 392–422, 511; *Shirley*, Vol. II, 118 note; *N. Y. Col. Doc.*, Vol. VI, 915–916.

CHAPTER 28. "THE KING'S REGULAR AND DISCIPLIN'D TROOPS"

1. Brock, R. A., ed., *Official Records of Robert Dinwiddie*, Vol. I (Richmond, 1883), 511—hereafter cited as Dinwiddie.

2. Sargent, Winthrop, *The History of an Expedition against Fort Duquesne in 1755* (Philadelphia, 1855), 287—hereafter cited as Sargent; *Dinwiddie*, Vol. I, 519–523, Vol. II, 3; Freeman, Douglas S., *George Washington*, Vol. II (New York, 1948), 10–11, 21–22—hereafter cited as Freeman, *Washington*.

3. *Dinwiddie*, Vol. II, 4; Freeman, *Washington*, Vol. II, 20; Sargent, 290.

4. Sargent, 300; *Documents relative to the Colonial History of the State of New-York*, VI (Albany, 1855), 920–922, 942—hereafter cited as *N. Y. Col. Doc.*; *Dinwiddie*, Vol. II, 15–18; Sullivan, James, *Papers of Sir William Johnson*, Vol. I (Albany, 1921), 465–475—hereafter cited as *Johnson Papers;* Lincoln, C. H., ed., *Correspondence of William Shirley*, Vol. II (New York, 1912), 158–164, 195–205—hereafter cited *Shirley;* Freeman, *Washington*, Vol. II, 23–25; Wallace, Paul A. W., *Conrad Weiser* (Philadelphia, 1945), 381.

5. *Shirley*, Vol. II, 173, 198–205; Freeman, *Washington*, Vol. II, 26; Sargent, 298–299, 307–309; Bigelow, John, ed., *Autobiography of Benjamin Franklin* (Philadelphia, 1868), 302–309.

6. Bigelow, John, ed., *Autobiography of Benjamin Franklin*, 310–311.

7. Sargent, 309, 368–373; Freeman, *Washington*, Vol. II, 33–34.

8. Sargent, 327–329; Freeman, *Washington*, Vol. II, 20.

9. Freeman, *Washington*, Vol. I, 440–445, Vol. II, 11–19; *Dictionary of American Biography*, Vol. XIII (New York, 1934), 226, for Roger Morris.

10. Sargent, 309, 374–375, 378–379, 407–408; Volwiler, A. T., *George Croghan and the Westward Movement, 1741–1782* (Cleveland, 1926), 94–97.

11. *Dinwiddie*, Vol. I, 514, 524, Vol. II, 27, 77, 125; Sargent, 314–315.

12. Sargent, 312–313, 377; Freeman, *Washington*, Vol. II, 44–45.

13. Freeman, *Washington*, Vol. II, 47–51; Sargent, 322, 326, 331–335, 380–382.

14. Sargent, 335–336, 383–384.

15. Sargent, 336–352, 384; Freeman, *Washington*, Vol. II, 61; Gipson, Lawrence H., *The Great War for the Empire: The Years of Defeat, 1754–1757* (New York, 1946), 82–86—hereafter cited as Gipson, *1754–1757*.

16. *N. Y. Col. Doc.*, Vol. X (Albany, 1858), 303–304; Parkman, Francis, *Montcalm and Wolfe*, Vol. I (Frontenac Edition, New York, 1915),

218–219–hereafter cited as Parkman, *Montcalm and Wolfe;* Gipson, *1754–1757,* 86–91.

17. Sargent, 384–385; *Shirley,* Vol. II, 207–209; Freeman, *Washington,* Vol. II, 64–66; Parkman, *Montcalm and Wolfe,* Vol. I, 220–222 and map; Gipson, *1754–1757,* 92–95, and Map.

18. Sargent, 354, 384; Freeman, *Washington,* Vol. II, 64–67.

19. "Remarkable Occurrences in the Life and Travels of Colonel James South" in *Mirror of Olden Time Border Life,* J. Pritts, Compiler (Abingdon, 1849), 387–388; Parkman, *Montcalm and Wolfe,* Vol. I, 218–219; Gipson, *1754–1757,* 91–92; *N. Y. Col. Doc.,* Vol. X, 303–304.

20. Sargent, 353–354; Freeman, *Washington,* Vol. II, 67–68.

21. Sargent, 354, 387; *Shirley,* Vol. II, 207–209; Freeman, *Washington,* Vol. II, 68–69; *N. Y. Col. Doc.,* Vol. X, 303–304; Gipson, *1754–1757,* 92–94.

22. Sargent, 354–355; *Shirley,* Vol. II, 311–313; Freeman, *Washington,* Vol. II, 72; Fitzpatrick, John C., ed., *The Writings of George Washington,* Vol. I (Washington, 1931), 149–150; Pargellis, Stanley, ed., *Military Affairs in North America* (New York, 1936), 106–107, 111.

23. Sargent, 355–356; *Shirley,* Vol. II, 312; Fitzpatrick, John C., ed., *The Writings of George Washington,* Vol. I, 149–150; Freeman, *Washington,* Vol. II, 75–76; Pargellis, Stanley, ed., *Military Affairs in North America,* 107.

24. Freeman, *Washington,* Vol. II, 76–78; Pritts, J., Compiler, *Mirror of Olden Time Border Life,* 388.

25. Freeman, *Washington,* Vol. II, 78–80.

26. Sargent, 357, 388; *The Pennsylvania Gazette,* August 28, 1755; Freeman, *Washington,* Vol. II, 80–82.

27. Sargent, 388; Freeman, *Washington,* Vol. II, 82–83.

CHAPTER 29. COMMITTEES OF CORRESPONDENCE

1. Brock, R. A., ed., *Official Records of Robert Dinwiddie,* Vol. II (Richmond, 1884), 99, 113–114, 117–hereafter cited as *Dinwiddie;* Lincoln, C. H., ed., *Correspondence of William Shirley,* Vol. II (New York, 1912), 211–213–hereafter cited as *Shirley.*

2. *Shirley,* Vol. II, 209–210, 241–242; *Dictionary of American Biography,* Vol. X (New York, 1933), 124–128, Vol. XVII (New York, 1935), 120–122; *Documents relative to the Colonial History of the State of New York,* Vol. VI (Albany, 1853), 1020–hereafter cited as *N. Y. Col. Doc.*

3. *Dinwiddie,* Vol. II, 109, 320, and *passim;* Freeman, Douglas S., *George Washington,* Vol. II (New York, 1948), 115–156; Wallace, Paul A. W., *Conrad Weiser* (Philadelphia, 1945), 395–552.

4. Parkman, Francis, *Montcalm and Wolfe,* Vol. III (Frontenac Edition, New York, 1915), 102–254; *N. Y. Col. Doc.,* Vol. VII (Albany, 1856), 75, 345.

5. Corbett, Julian S., *England in the Seven Years' War,* Vol. II (London, 1907), 173; Hutchinson, [Thomas,] *History of the Province of Massachusetts Bay,* Vol. III (London, 1828), 100–102–hereafter cited as Hutchinson; Linde, Jonathan, *Three Letters to Dr. Price Containing Remarks on His Observations on the Nature of Civil Liberty, etc.* (London, 1776), 136–137.

6. *The Interest of Great Britain Considered with Regard to Her Colonies and the Acquisitions of Canada and Guadaloupe* (London, 1760), 41.
7. Channing, Edward, *A History of the United States,* Vol. III (New York, 1912), 29–35; Trumbull, Benjamin, *History of Connecticut,* Vol. II (New Haven, 1818), 466; Hutchinson, Vol. III, 37, 111; Flippin, P. S., *The Royal Government in Virginia, 1624–1775* (New York, 1919), 298–300; Parkman, Francis, *Montcalm and Wolfe,* Vol. II, 290–292; *N. Y. Col. Doc.,* Vol. VII, 1–2; Lonn, Ella, *Colonial Agents of the Southern Colonies* (Chapel Hill, 1945), 194–195, 337–338.
8. *Dictionary of American History,* Vol. IV (New York, 1940), 305–306.
9. Channing, Edward, *History of the United States,* Vol. III, 36 note 2; *Dictionary of American History,* Vol. V (New York, 1940), 154; *Papers of the New Haven Colony Historical Society,* Vol. IX (New Haven, 1918), 230.
10. Hutchinson, Vol. III, 107–114; *Dictionary of American Biography,* Vol. XIV (New York, 1934), 101–105; Adams, C. F., ed., *The Works of John Adams,* Vol. II (Boston, 1850), 522, Vol. X (Boston, 1856), 247; Sparks, Jared, ed., *Library of American Biography,* Second Series, Vol. II (Boston, 1844), 97–112; Frothingham, Richard, *The Rise of the Republic of the United States* (Boston, 1872), 168–170; Otis, James, *The Rights of the British Colonies, Asserted and proved* (Boston, 1764).
11. Gibbes, R. W., ed., *Documentary History of the American Revolution, 1764–1776* (New York, 1855), 8; *Dictionary of American Biography,* Vol. VII (New York, 1931), 82–83.
12. Hutchinson, Vol. III, 110; *Dictionary of American Biography,* Vol. XIV, 103.

CHAPTER 30. SONS OF LIBERTY

1. Gipson, Lawrence H., *Jared Ingersoll* (New Haven, 1920), 116–118—hereafter cited as Gipson, *Ingersoll;* Lonn, Ella, *Colonial Agents of the Southern Colonies* (Chapel Hill, 1945), 338–341.
2. *Papers of the New Haven Colony Historical Society,* Vol. IX (New Haven, 1918), 312–313, 335–336—hereafter cited as *N. H. C. H. S. Papers;* Brock, R. A., ed., *Official Records of Robert Dinwiddie,* Vol. I (Richmond, 1883), 250.
3. *N. H. C. H. S. Papers,* Vol. IX, 313; Hutchinson, [Thomas,] *History of the Province of Massachusetts Bay,* Vol. III (London, 1828), 112—hereafter cited as Hutchinson.
4. Gipson, *Ingersoll,* 139–141; *N. H. C. H. S. Papers,* Vol. IX, 183, 309–311; *Newport Mercury,* Monday, May 27, 1765.
5. Gipson, *Ingersoll,* 145–147.
6. *Dictionary of American Biography,* Vol. VIII (New York, 1932), 554–559; Campbell, Charles, *History of the Colony and Ancient Dominion of Virginia* (Philadelphia, 1860), 540–543; Wirt, William, *Sketches of the Life and Character of Patrick Henry* (Philadelphia, 1836), 74–83; Hutchinson, Vol. III, 119.
7. Gipson, *Ingersoll,* 153; Hutchinson, Vol. III, 120–121.
8. Hutchinson, 121–122; *N. H. C. H. S. Papers,* Vol. IX, 328–329; Gip-

son, *Ingersoll*, 166–167; Abbott, Wilbur C., *New York in the American Revolution* (New York, 1929), 38–40.

9. Hutchinson, Vol. III, 124–126; *New-England Historical & Genealogical Register*, Vol. XXXII ·(Boston, 1878), 268–269.

10. Gipson, *Ingersoll*, 153–169.

11. *N. H. C. H. S. Papers*, Vol. IX, 341–349.

12. *Collections of the New York Historical Society*, for the Year 1877 (New York, 1878), 54–63, for the Year 1881 (New York, 1882), 336–337; McCrady, Edward, *History of South Carolina under the Royal Government, 1719–1776* (New York, 1899), 563–572.

CHAPTER 31. THE ROAD TO UNION

1. *Journal of the First Congress of the American Colonies, in opposition to the Tyrannical Acts of the British Parliament held at New-York, October 7, 1765* (New York, 1845), 27–41.

2. *Documents relative to the Colonial History of the State of New-York*, Vol. IV (Albany, 1854), 223; Brock, R. A., *Official Records of Robert Dinwiddie*, Vol. I (Richmond, 1883), 356–359.

3. Bigelow, John, *Autobiography of Benjamin Franklin* (Philadelphia, 1868), 313.

4. Parkman, Francis, *Montcalm and Wolfe*, Vol. II (Frontenac Edition, New York, 1915), 325–326; Gipson, L. H., *Jared Ingersoll* (New Haven, 1920), 151.

5. Gibbes, R. W., ed., *Documentary History of the American Revolution, 1764–1776* (New York, 1855), 8.

Index

A

Abenaki Indians, 144, 172–173, 498
Abercorn, Ga., 362
Abercromby, James, 518–519
Abickaws, 343
Acadia, 507, 518
Accokeek Creek iron mines, 286, 395
Acoma, N. M., 331, 334
Acts of Trade. *See* Navigation laws
Adams, Samuel, 429–432
Agents, Colonial, 406, 422–423, 523, 526
Alamance, battle of the, 317
Alamo, The, 335
Albany, Fort, 4, 10, 31, 32, 34, 38, 41, 65, 75–77, 85, 124, 126, 142, 145, 153–154, 162–164, 195, 205, 285, 488, 502–504, 517
Albany Congress, 502–504
Albemarle, Earl of, 499
Albemarle County, Va., 464
Albemarle Point, (S. C.), 24
Albemarle Settlements, (N. C.), 10, 30, 56, 61, 62, 64, 298
Alciphron, 350
Alexander, Wampanoag chief, 45, 51
Alexandria, Va., 493, 506–508
Allegheny River, 489–491, 494, 515
Allen, James, 157
Allen, John, 116
Alliquippa, "Queen," 479, 482, 492
Allouez, Father Claude Jean, 35
Almanacs, 385–386
Alricks, Peter, 1, 2, 10, 41, 74, 236
Altamaha River, 318, 338, 358, 362
American Philosophical Society, 386
Amherst, Jeffery, 519
Amsterdam, Fort, 41
Anaya, Cristobal de, 136
Andrews, Joan, 18
Androboros, 315
Andros, Edmund, 42, 68, 69, 70, 94, 118, 140–149, 151, 251, 256–257
Anglican Church. *See* Church of England

Ann Arundel Town. *See* Annapolis
Annapolis, Md., 253, 255, 429, 442
Anne, Queen of England, 216, 300
Anne, The, 356
Apache Indians, 137
Apalache, 121–122, 288, 297, 306, 328
Arabian gold, 201, 205
Archibeque, Captain Juan de, 339–340. *See also* L'Archeveque, Jean
Arkansas River 36, 90, 129, 134, 326–337, 340–341
Arlington, Earl of, 57, 60
Ashley Barony, 64
Ashley River, 24, 66, 290, 292, 396, 398, 401
"Ashley Wood and Jerico," 401
Assemblies, growing power of, 422–423, 522–525, 534–536
Aston, Anthony, 287–288
Attakullakulla, Chief, 469–470
Augusta, Ga., 362, 365
Augusta County, Va., 464–465, 467
Augusta Court House. *See* Staunton, Va.
Augwick (Pa.), 500, 509
Awakening, The Great, 367–382, 384, 433
Ayubale, Mission of, 288
Azilia, Margravate of, 353

B

Bacon, Nathaniel, 58, 59, 60
Baker, Ebenezer, his wife, 168
Ball, Joseph, 396
Baltimore, Lord, 8, 60, 61, 75, 96, 98, 100, 103–104, 113, 140, 147, 151–152, 217, 252–253, 255–256, 281
Baltimore, Md., 442
Baptists, 12, 380, 427, 472
Barbados, 9, 22, 23, 28, 29, 64, 71–72, 101, 120, 210, 212, 228, 244, 247, 282, 295, 413
Barefoot, Walter, 114–115

Barnwell, John, 292, 304, 314–315, 338

Barre, Col. Isaac, 525–526, 528

Bartlet, Phebe, 368

Bartram, John, 387–388, 399

Basse, Jeremiah, 210, 214–215

Bath, N. C., 298, 311

Bathurst, Sir Francis, 358

Baylor, John, 278

Beadon, Stephen, 307

Beaujeu, Capt. Daniel Lienard de, 512–513

Bedford, Duke of, 519–520

Beebee, Samuel, 426

Beissel, Conrad, 448, 450–451, 455

Belcher, Jonathan, 381, 405–406

Bellingham, Gov. Richard, 16

Bellomont, Earl of, 178, 180, 188, 190, 202–206, 214, 423

Bellomont, Lady, 205

"Belmont," 399

Belton, Peter, 440

"Belvoir," 394–395

"Berkeley," 391–392, 393 (exterior view)

Berkeley, George, 348, 350, 374, 427, 436

Berkeley, John, Lord, 9, 12, 13, 67, 207

Berkeley, Sir William, 9, 58, 59, 60, 65, 122, 124

Bermuda, 23, 26

Bethabara, N. C., 471, 473

Bethania, N. C., 471, 473

Bethesda Orphanage, 362, 364, 374

Bethlehem, Pa., 455–456, 472

Beverley, Robert, 246, 258, 260, 262–263, 269, 278, 279, 459

Beverley, William, 278, 459, 462–464

Bienville, Jean Baptiste le Moyne, Sieur de, 320–322, 327–330, 336, 338, 341–343, 345–346

"Big Knife," or "Long Knife," 125, 285

Biloxi, 320–323

Blackamore, Rev. Arthur, 274, 276

"Black-Beard." *See* Teach, Capt.

Blackwell, John, 218–219

Blair, Rev. James, 251, 256–257, 263, 272, 274, 281, 285, 423

Blathwayt, William, 263

Bloody Marsh, battle of, 363–364

Blue Ridge, 280, 456, 458, 463–465, 473

Board of Trade, 178, 180, 214, 216, 260–263, 280, 290, 309, 315, 317, 354, 423, 477, 486, 501–502, 505. *See* also Lords of Trade

Bohemia Manor, 75

Boisbriant, Pierre Duque, Sieur de, 337, 340

Bolzius, John Martin, 357, 365

Bond, Captain, 320

Bond, Dr. Thomas, 433

Bonnet, Stede, 310–311

Bonython, Eleanor, 19

Bonython, John, 19

Book burning, 379, 450

Book selling, 158, 160, 220

Boone, Daniel, 465

Bosomworth, Thomas, 366

Boston, 16, 52–53, 109, 112, 116–118, 144, 147–148, 157–158, 160–163, 170, 181, 205, 373, 375–376, 410, 427–431, 433–438, 440, 442, 527–528

Boston *Gazette,* 527

Boston Post Road, 181–188, 442

Boudinot, Elias, 154, 206–207

Bourgmont, Etienne Venyard, Sieur de, 339, 342

Bowdoin, James, 412

Bowdoin, William, 440, 441 (portrait)

Bowery, The, 188, 192

Boyle, Robert, 276

Boylston, Zabdiel, 434

Braddock, General Edward, 470, 505, 506–516, 517, 535

Bradford, William, printer, 220, 315, 388, 419

Bradstreet, Madam, 162

Bradstreet, Simon, 116, 118, 148–149, 161, 164

Brand, Captain Ellis, 312

Bray, Associates of Doctor, 353–354, 357, 366

Bray, Rev. Thomas, 256, 348, 350–351, 352–353, 380

Brayne, Capt. Henry, 29

Breaster, Francis, 18

Bridges, John, 206

Bright Lightning, a Mingo maiden, 509

Broad Arrow, 22, 404–405

Broadway, N. Y., 72, 190, 192

Brodnax, Mrs., 244

Bronck, Jonas, 212

Brooke, Chidley, 196

Brooklyn, N. Y., 41, 72, 154

Brown, Daniel, 371

Brown, Thomas, 466

Brown University, 384
Bruton Parish (Va.), 272
Buffalo and buffalo hides, 129, 137, 322, 342, 484
Bundling, 425–426
Burlington, N. J., 70, 74, 101, 181, 208, 216–217, 228–229
Burnaby, Rev. Andrew, 429, 442
Burr, Aaron, 381–382
Burton, Col. Ralph, 509
Burwell, Miss Martha, 315–316
"Bush Hill," 388, 390
Byrd, Evelyn, 266
Byrd, Mrs. William, II (Lucy Parke), 268, 271
Byrd, Ursula, 278, 459
Byrd, William, I, 124, 241–246, 251, 260, 298
Byrd, William, II, 240–241, 245–246, 264–266, 267 (portrait), 268–276, 280–281, 304, 350, 390–391, 393, 423–424, 432, 444
Byllinge, Edward, 67, 68, 208

C

Cadillac, Antoine de la Mothe, 325–326, 330, 332, 335–336
Cahokia Indians, 327
Cahokia settlement, 327, 331
Calef, Robert, 171
California, 335
Calvert, Cecilius, Second Lord Baltimore, 96
Calvert, Charles, Third Lord Baltimore, 61, 96
Calvert, Leonard, 253
Cambridge Synod of 1648, 116, 368
Canada, 32, 34, 38, 78, 161, 163–164, 172–176, 338, 519–520. *See also* New France
Canasetego, or Cannasateego, Iroquois chief, 454, 460
Canonchet, Narragansett chief, 45, 48, 52
Cape Fear Settlement, 22, 23, 30
Carbajal, Augustine de, 136
Cardross, Lord, 121
Carlisle, Pa., 473, 475, 509
Carolina, 9, 10, 21–30, 64–66, 119–122, 230, 261, 276–277, 287–317, 320, 322, 326–329, 336, 338, 343–344, 353. *See also* South Carolina; North Carolina
Carolina, The 23, 24, 26, 29

Carpenter, Samuel, 103, 226, 227, 234
Carr, John, 41
Carter, John, 284–285
Carter, Robert ("King Carter"), 246, 260, 272, 280–282, 283 (portrait), 284–285, 391–394, 423, 458
Carter, Robert, Junior, 392, 394
Carter, Samuel, 215
Carter, The, 282
Carteret, Sir George, 9, 12, 13, 67, 68, 69, 207
Carteret, James, 68, 73
Carteret, Lord, 309–310, 316–317, 356. *See also* Granville Grant
Carteret, Philip, 13, 67, 68, 69, 94
Casimir, Fort, 2
Casket Girls, 341
Cassiques, 27
Cataraqui, 38, 40
Catawba Indians, 295, 297–298, 304, 308, 458, 466, 471, 493, 509
Cattle, 135, 210, 212–213, 290, 292, 466, 470
Cavelier, Abbé Jean, 127–128, 130–132
Cayuga Indians, 31, 32, 38, 125, 305, 502
Celoron de Blainville, Pierre Joseph de, 480–481, 484, 487
Cenis Indians, 129–134, 138
Chambly, Fort, 32
Champlain, Lake, 31, 32, 34, 153, 162–163, 174, 195, 507
Charles II, King of England, 4, 8–10, 16, 17, 20, 53, 55, 57, 106, 107–108, 110–113, 246, 317
Charleston (or Charles Town), S. C., 24, 26, 28–30, 64, 66, 119–122, 287–292, 295, 304–306, 308–312, 314, 322, 326, 328, 336, 343, 354, 356, 396, 398–399, 466
Charlevoix, Father Pierre, 340
Charter Oak, 142
Charter of Privileges (Pennsylvania), 229–230, 233, 236
Chartier, Peter, 482
Chartiers Town, 482
Chartres, Fort de, 331, 337, 340–341
Chassin, Sieur, 341
Chauncy, Charles, 378
Cherokee Indians, 294, 298, 304, 308, 322, 342–343, 353–354, 365, 466–467, 469–471, 493, 509
Cherokee Trading Path, 353, 466, 470

Chicago Portage, 31, 36, 38, 86, 89, 133, 337
Chickasaw Indians, 294, 296, 326–327, 329, 344–346
Choctaw Indians, 294, 296, 308, 327–329, 336, 342–346, 469
Choir Houses, 456
Chota, Cherokee town, 308, 469–471
Christ-Anna, 277, 285, 297, 308
Church of England, 15, 16, 17, 108, 112, 117, 140, 149, 158, 188, 190, 232–233, 256, 285, 351–352, 368, 370–371, 373–374, 380, 382, 384, 427
Claggett, William, 427
Clinton, Gov. George, 421, 429, 459, 488
Clothing and Costume, 55, 180, 192, 228–229, 254, 260, 302, 379, 427, 434, 436, 438, 470–472, 529
Cloud, Isaac, 470
Clubs, political, 429
Clubs, social, 429
Coates, Capt. Edward, 202
Cocalico Creek. See Ephrata
Colden, Cadwallader, 421–422, 434
Cole, Nathan, 375–376
Colleges, 158, 160, 171, 184, 190, 250–251, 255, 257–258, 272, 274, 276, 304, 369, 370–371, 373, 381–382, 384, 387, 464
Colleton, Sir John, 9, 22, 23, 29
Collins, Henry, 414
Collinson, Peter, 386, 388
Colman, Benjamin, 370, 379, 436
Columbia University. See King's College
Comanche Indians, 342
Commissioners of Indian Trade (South Carolina), 306–307
Committees of Correspondence, 423, 522, 536
Compagnie de l'Occident, 336
Compagnie des Indies, 336–337, 341–344
Compton, Henry, 351
"Concessions and Agreement" of Carolina and New Jersey, 13
"Concessions and Agreement" of New Jersey, 67
"Concessions and Agreements" of West Jersey, 69–70
Concord, N. H., 426–427
Congaree (S. C.), 472
Congregationalists, 13, 14, 112, 117, 157–158, 164, 171–172, 201, 351,

367–368, 370–371, 373, 375, 381–382, 427
Connecticut, 4, 8, 13, 15, 42, 44, 48, 113, 117–118, 141–142, 149, 152, 154, 180–181, 183–187, 195, 202, 230, 261, 366, 370–371, 373, 375–376, 382, 426, 502–503, 521, 523–524, 526–531
Constitution, British, 522
Coode, John, 151, 252, 255, 257
Cooper, Anthony Ashley, 9, 24, 28, 29. See also Shaftesbury, Lord
Cooper River, 24, 66, 290, 396, 398–399
Copley, Lionel, 252
Coram, Thomas, 350–351, 354
Corey, Giles, 167, 171
Corey, Goodwife, 167
Cornbury, Lady, 206
Cornbury, Lord, 206–207, 216–217
"Corotoman," 392
Cortlandt Manor, 418
Cosby, William, 388, 390, 419
Côte des Allemands, 341
Cotton, Goodwife, 114
Cotton, John, 166
Council for New England, 7, 8, 108, 406
Council of Trade and Plantations, 106
Coureurs de bois, 78, 321–325, 332, 339, 342
Couture, Jean, 129, 134, 294, 322, 326
Covenant chain, 125, 145, 196, 285, 503
Coweta, 121–123, 294, 296, 308, 343
Coxe, Doctor Daniel, 208, 320–321
Cranfield, Edward, 111, 114
Creek Indians, 121, 294, 296, 304, 306, 308–309, 336, 342–343, 347, 365–366
Cresap, Thomas, 477, 483, 486, 488, 509
Crevecœur, Fort, 83, 84, 85, 88
Croghan, George, 475–476, 480–481, 483–487, 496–497, 500, 509
Crosley, Joss, 306
"Crowfield," 403
Crown Point, 507, 517
Crozat, Antoine, 330, 332, 336
Culpeper, John, 61, 62, 64
Culpeper, Thomas, Lord, 57, 60, 246
Cumberland, Fort, 508–510, 517
Cumberland Island, 360
Cuming, Sir Alexander, 353–354, 469

Cusseta, Creek town, 296, 306
Customs duties, 4, 6, 70, 95, 104, 106, 109–111, 122, 176, 203, 222, 224, 252, 261, 289, 410, 521, 523
Cutler, Timothy, 371, 372 (portrait), 373, 376, 434, 436
Cutt, John, 109
Cutt, Mrs. John, 172

D

Danckaerts, Jasper, 70–76, 217
Danforth, Thomas, 117
Daniel House, 159 (Kitchen)
Davenport, James, 378–379, 450
Davenport, John, 184
Davies, Samuel, 382
Dawkins, William, 282, 284
Debt, public, 161, 164, 431, 520
Deerfield, Mass., 46, 174–176, 289
De Lancey, James, 388, 418–419, 422, 429, 507
De Lancey, Stephen, 205–206, 208, 418–419
De Lancey, Susannah, 419
Delaware, Falls of, 1, 73, 102, 210, 217. *See also* Trenton, N. J.
Delaware, Lower Counties on the, 9, 93, 98, 100, 101, 104, 117, 236–237, 261, 366, 524
Delaware Indians, 452–455, 482, 485, 487, 490, 496, 513–514
De Leon, Alonso, 137–139, 339
Dellius, Godfrey, 200
"Democratic, too much of the," 504
Denonville, Marquis de, 126
De Sauvole de la Villantray, 320, 322
Des Plaines River, 36, 82, 86
Detroit, 81, 126, 325–326, 330, 337–338, 476, 521
Devil, The, 166–168, 379
Diaz, Melchior, 335
Dickinson, Jonathan, 381
Dinwiddie, Governor Robert, 422, 432, 474, 486, 489–494, 495, 499–501, 505, 506–507, 509, 517, 524, 534
Dockwra, William, 213
Dolphin, The, 222, 224
Dominion of New England, 118, 141–149, 151, 207–208
Dongan, Governor Thomas, 124–125, 140
Dorchester, S. C., 292
Dover, N. H., 161

Downe, Richard, 18
Downing, Emanuel, 53
Doz, Andrew, 101
"Drayton Hall," 401, 402 (exterior and interior views), 403
Drummond, William, 60
Drunkenness, 18, 73, 272, 274, 301, 304, 429, 432–433, 498, 500
Dubois, Catherine, 154
Dudley, Joseph, 115–118, 141, 148, 151, 155, 179 (portrait), 180–181, 261, 422, 534
Dudley, Thomas 113, 116–117
Duhaut, 128, 130–132
Duluth (Daniel Greysolon, Sieur Duluth), 85, 126, 321
Dunbar, David, Surveyor-General of the King's Woods, 404
Dunbar, Col. Thomas, 508, 510, 515–516, 517
Dunkers, 448, 450, 455
Dunton, John, 158, 160
Du Quesne, Fort, 495, 497–498, 507, 510, 512, 515, 518–519. *See also* Pitt, Fort
Du Quesne de Menneville, Marquis, 492, 495
Dustin, Hannah, 173
Dutch, 1–6, 10, 12, 15, 40–42, 71–72, 124, 149, 162, 190, 194, 198, 373
Dutch Reformed Church, 72, 190, 373
Dutch West India Company, 2, 6
Duties. *See* Customs duties

E

East India Company, 204–205
East Jersey, 69, 70, 73, 93, 94, 117, 142, 152, 195, 200–202, 207, 209–217, 230, 232, 261. *See also* New Jersey
Eaton, Theophilus, 184
Ebenezer, Ga., 357
Eden, Charles, 310–311
Edenton, N. C., 310, 443, 472
Edwards, Jonathan, 367–368, 369 (portrait), 374–375, 381–382
Electricity, 386–387
Elizabethtown, N. J., 13, 41, 70, 212–213, 215, 381
El Paso, New Mexico, 135–137, 332, 334, 339
El Quartelejo, 340
Emmons, Nathaniel, 436, 437

Engel, Christen, 301
English Turn, 321
Enoch, Brother. *See* Weiser, Conrad
Ephrata (Pa.), 448–451, 455, 460
Erie Indians, 31, 482
Esopus (Kingston), N. Y., 75
Evans, Captain John, 198, 206
Evans, John, Deputy-Governor of Pennsylvania, 233–234, 299
Every, Captain, 225

F

Fairfax, Anne ("Nancy"), 394–395
Fairfax, Catherine, Lady, 246
Fairfax, Thomas, Lord, 394, 458, 463, 483
Fairfax, Col. William, 394, 463
Fairfax Proprietary, 217, 392, 457–458, 463
"Fairhill," 227, 389 (exterior view)
Faneuil, Peter, 188, 412
Feke, Robert, 438, 440, 441
Fenwick, James, 67, 68, 69, 94
Fish, 7, 17, 20, 176, 412
Fitch, Gov. Thomas, 529
Fitzhugh, William, 246–247, 248 (portrait), 249–250, 258, 260, 284
Five Nations. *See* 304–305 for change of name from Five Nations to Six Nations, but all references will be found under "Iroquois"
Fletcher, Gov. Benjamin, 190, 192, 195–196, 198, 200–204, 206, 212, 220, 234, 534
Florida, 21, 22, 24, 120–122, 287–289, 292, 309, 320, 327–328, 338, 360, 362–364
Flower, Enoch, 102
Fontaine, John, 277–280
Food, 29, 92, 115, 131, 139, 161–162, 172, 187, 192, 210, 225, 228, 253, 268, 427, 442–443
Forbes, Gen. John, 519
Ford, Philip, 236–237
Fort. *See* under identifying name of fort
Foundling Hospital of London, 351
Fox Indians, 322, 326
Fox-Wisconsin Waterway, 36, 84, 322, 337–338
Frame of Government (Pennsylvania), 97, 103, 229
Franchise, 13, 14, 27, 60, 61, 69, 97, 172, 263, 430

Franciscan Missionaries, 21, 81, 84, 121, 135, 288
Frankland, Sir Charles, 410, 412
Franklin, Benjamin, 375, 380, 384–387, 423, 433, 501–502, 504, 507–509, 520, 523–524, 526, 535
Franklin, James, 434
Frazier, John, Carolina trader, 307
Frazier, John, trader at Forks of Ohio, 489, 491–492
Frederica, Ga., 360, 362–363
Frederick, Md., 442, 507–508
Frederick Town (Winchester), Va., 473, 493, 507–508
Fredericksburg Township (S. C.), 465
Free Society of Traders, 97, 98, 101, 103
"Freedom," 526
Frelinghuysen, Theodorus Jacobus, 373–374
French and Indian War, 506–519, 535
French Creek, 489
Friday, Martin, 472
Friedsam, Father. *See* Beissel, Conrad
Frontenac, Fort, 39, 77, 78, 79, 83, 85, 88, 126, 326, 421, 519
Frontenac, Louis de Buade, Count de, 35, 38, 40, 77, 78, 86, 162–163, 324
Fry, Joshua, 464, 486
Frye, Deacon, his wife, 168
"Fundamentall Constitutions" of Carolina, 27
Fur trade, 7, 31, 58, 77, 79, 81, 86, 88, 124, 126, 142, 144, 242, 271, 277, 298, 322–324, 339, 342, 365. *See also* Skin trade; Indian trade
Furniture. *See* Household goods

G

Gadsden, Christopher, 522, 536
Gage, Capt. Thomas, 512–513
Garcia, Alonso, 135–136
Garden, Dr. Alexander, 399, 434
Gardens, 388, 390–391, 394, 399, 401, 403, 410, 412, 414, 416
Geiger, Herman, 466
George, Capt. John, 116, 148
George, Lake, 517–518
George I, King of England, 315
George II, King of England, 353, 486
George III, King of England, 535

Georgia, 347–348, 353–366, 455, 467, 525

German Flats, 446

German Reformed Church, 448, 450

Germanna, 277–279, 285–286, 305

Germans, 102, 277–278, 286, 299, 305, 337, 341, 357–358, 445–452, 456, 458, 460, 463, 465–466, 472–473. *See also* Palatines

Germantown, Pa., 102, 225, 448

Gillam, Zachariah, 62, 64

Gilliard, Philip, 306

Gilman, Samuel, 404

Gist, Christopher, 474, 483–486, 488, 490–492, 495, 512–513

Gist's Settlement, 488, 490, 492, 495–498

Glen, Gov. James, 422, 467, 469, 493, 509

Goelet, Francis, 427

Golden Horseshoe, Knights of the, 280, 337, 456, 464

Gooch, Gov. William, 477, 485

Goodwin children, 166, 167

Goose Creek (S. C.), 291, 293, 403

Gorges, Sir Ferdinando (the elder), 7, 17

Gorges, Sir Ferdinando (the younger), 17, 55, 107–108

Gowanus, N. Y., 72

Graeme, Thomas, 434

Graffenried, Baron Christoph von, 277, 299–303, 305

Graham, James, 194, 212

Grant, Ludovick, 467

Granville Grant, 317, 465, 471–473

Great Awakening. *See* Awakening, Great

Great Meadows, 495, 497, 515–516

Great Nine Partners Patent, 200, 206

Great Swamp Fight, 48, 49

Great Warriors Path, 471

Green Bay, 34, 36, 81, 84, 85, 86, 337, 340

Grenville, George, 523–526, 536

Grible, Elias, 18

Griffin, The, 81, 83

Groton, Mass., 172

Guadeloupe, 519

Guilford, Conn., 184–185

H

Habersham, James, 362, 365

Habersham & Harris, 365

Hadley, Mass., 46

Halfway Covenant, 368

Halkett, Sir Peter, 508–509, 512, 514

Hamilton, Dr. Alexander, 416, 428–429, 433, 438, 440, 442

Hamilton, Andrew, Governor of East Jersey, 181, 213–215, 232–233

Hamilton, Andrew, Philadelphia lawyer, 388, 390

Hamilton, Andrew, present at Treaty of Lancaster, 460

Hamilton, George. *See* Earl of Orkney

Hanbury, John, 477, 483, 487

Harlem (N. Y.), 73, 188

Harris Ferry (Harrisburg), Pa., 456, 473, 475, 500

Harrison, Benjamin, 391

Hartford, Conn., 15, 529–531

Harvard College, 158, 160, 171, 190, 370, 382, 387, 429

Haverhill, Mass., 173

Head rights, 244, 268

Heathcote, Anne, 418

Heathcote, Caleb, 187–188, 190, 198, 199 (portrait), 200, 202, 224, 233, 309, 348, 370–371

Hell, 367, 374, 378–379, 531 (note)

Hempstead, Joshua, 426

Hendrick, Mohawk chief, 502–503

Hennepin, Father Louis, 79, 83, 84, 85, 320–321

Henry, Patrick, 526–527

Hermann, Augustine, 74–75, 96

Hermann, Ephraim, 73, 74, 98, 236

Hesselius, Gustavus, 439 (self-portrait)

Hester, The, 214–215

Hidalgo, Pedro, 135

Hiens, 128, 130–132, 134, 138

Hilton, Martha, 408, 410

Hinckley, Thomas, 116

Hinnoyossa, Alexander, 1, 2

History of the Colony of Massachusets-Bay, 410, 528

Hite, Jost, 458, 463

Hoch-Deutsch Pennsylvanische Geschicht-Schreiber, 448

Hog, Seabank, 114

Holdernesse, Earl of, 489, 501–502

Holland, Lieut. Hitchen, 488

Holme, Thomas, 97, 100

Holy Experiment, 94, 97

Holy Family, Mission of, 326–327

Hopkey, "Sophy," 360, 362

Hospital, public, 433

Household goods and furniture, 18, 187, 206, 226, 245, 247, 249–250, 258, 278, 400–401

Houses, 18, 29, 66, 72, 74, 84, 90, 101, 115, 131, 138, 159, 177, 185, 187, 193, 201, 210, 225–228, 245, 247, 249, 257, 266, 272–275, 290, 298, 387–395, 398–403, 408–412, 414–418, 470, 484

Howard, Lord, of Effingham, 124–125, 250

Huguenots, 188, 277, 290, 292

Hull, John, 112, 158

Hungarian Club, 429

Hunter, Gov. Robert, 315, 446

Huron Indians, 31, 325

Hutchinson, Anne, 412

Hutchinson, Thomas, 410, 411 (views of homes in Boston and in Milton), 412, 423–424, 432, 502, 504, 527–528

I

Iberville, Pierre le Moyne, Sieur de, 162, 172–173, 318, 319 (portrait), 320, 325–328

Illinois Country, 126–127, 130–132, 134, 323, 326–327, 342

Illinois Indians, 82, 83, 84, 86, 88

Illinois River, 36, 82, 83, 84, 85, 86, 88

Immaculate Conception, Mission of, 326

Impressment, 430–431

Indian captivity (Mrs. Rowland-son), 150–152

Indian Slavery. *See* Slavery, Indian

Indian Trade, 28, 31, 58, 65, 66, 77, 79, 81, 86, 88, 120–122, 124, 126, 137, 142, 144, 242, 271, 277, 292, 294–295, 298, 306–307, 327–329, 336, 343–344, 365, 468–469, 475–477, 480–482. *See also* Fur Trade; Skin Trade

Indians. *See* under name of nation or tribe

Indians, Education of, 276–277, 304, 350, 374

Indigo, 342, 397–398, 400–401

Inflation, 431–432

Ingersoll, Jared, 523, 526–531

Ingoldesby, Major Richard, 155

Inner Light, 219, 254

Inns, 428–429, 438, 442–443, 456

Inoculation, 434, 436

Ipswich Protest, 141

Iron industry, 286, 395, 458

Iroquois, The, 12, 31–34, 38, 40, 41, 77, 79, 82, 85, 86, 88, 124–127, 142, 162–163, 196, 277, 285, 305, 323, 326, 421, 447, 451–455, 458–462, 465, 475, 482, 485, 487, 502–503, 507

Isleta, N. M., 13, 136

J

Jacob, The, 202

James, Falls of the, 58, 124, 246, 264, 269

James II, King of England, 104, 113, 140, 144–146, 147, 149, 151, 153, 219, 221. *See also* York, Duke of

Jamestown, Va., 59, 257

Jefferson, Peter, 464

Jenkins' Ear, War of, 363

Jennings, Samuel, 210, 216–217, 228–229

Jesuit Bark (Quinine), 271, 279

Jesuit Missionaries, 34, 35, 81, 85, 335

"Jesus, Lover of My Soul," 360

Johnson, Fort (Charleston, S. C.), 289

Johnson, Sir Nathaniel, 288, 290

Johnson, Robert, 310, 312, 314, 465

Johnson, Samuel, 371, 373, 382, 384

Johnson, William, merchant of Newport, 413

Johnson, William, of New York, 419, 421, 445, 488, 499, 502, 507, 517, 519

"Join or die," 501

Jolliet, Louis, 35, 36, 38, 40, 337

Josephs Town, Ga., 362

Joutel, Henri, 128–132

Jumano Indians, 133, 137

Jumonville, Sieur de, 495, 498

Junto, The, 386

K

Kankakee River, 82, 86

Kaskaskia Indians, 326

Kaskaskia settlement, 327, 331, 337

Kayoderosseras Patent, 206

Keith, George, 219–220, 232–233

Kelpius, Johann, 221, 448

Kent, The, 69–70
Keowee Town, 353, 471, 467, 469
Kiawah, 24
Kidd, Capt. William, 190, 203–206, 225, 418
King George, Fort, 338
King George's War, 419, 459, 535
King William's School, 254–255
King's Bridge (N. Y.), 188, 189, 198
King's College (Columbia University), 384
King's Province, 45, 113, 118
King's Woods, Surveyor General of, 404, 408
Kino, Father Eusebio Francisco, 335
Kittanning, 480, 482
Knight, Madam Sarah, 181–192, 213, 440
Knight, Judge Tobias, 311–312

L

Labadists, 75–76, 448
La Demoiselle. *See* Old Britain
La Forest, Francois Daupin de, 323–324
La Grange, Monsieur de, 71–72
Lake. *See* under identifying name of lake
Lake Erie-Lake Chautauqua Portage, 480
"Lake Farm," 400
La Motte, Fort, 34
Lancaster, Mass., 50
Lancaster, Pa., Treaty of, 459–462, 465, 475, 482, 486–487
Land Bank of Massachusetts, 431–432
Land tenure, 27–28, 57, 67–69, 94, 97, 102, 110–111, 143, 200, 208, 210, 217, 244, 252, 317, 356–357, 407
Landgraves, 27
Langlade, Charles Michel de, 487–488, 510, 514
L'Archeveque, Jean, 130, 138. *See also* Archibeque, Captain Juan de
La Salle, Robert Cavelier, Sieur de, 78–92, 127–131, 134, 137, 320–321, 332, 337, 339
Laurel Hill, 474, 495, 498, 510, 516
Laurens, Henry, 398
Law, John, 336–337, 340–341
Lawson, John, 290, 295, 298–303
Lead mines, 342

Lebanon Valley, 456
Le Boeuf, Fort, 479, 489–490, 492, 511, 521
Lederer, John, 124
Lee, Thomas, 284, 392, 459, 462, 475, 477, 483, 485
Le Fevre, Rev. Tanaquil, 274, 276
Leighton, William, 18
Leisler, Jacob, 150–151, 153–156, 163, 188, 194–195, 198
Le Sueur, Madam, 330
Le Sueur, Pierre, 321–322, 326
Leverett, Gov. John, 53, 54 (portrait), 55
Lewis, John, 464
Lewis, Thomas, 464
L'Huillier, Fort, 322
Liberties as Englishmen, 141, 216, 263, 521, 524, 533–534, 536. *See also* Rights as Englishmen
Liberty and Property, 216, 530–531, 534, 536
Liberty Trees, 527–531
Libraries, parochial, 256, 348
Libraries, private, 158, 266, 387, 390, 455, 466
Libraries, subscription, 386, 414
Library Company of Philadelphia, 386, 388
Lindsay, David, 413
Liotot, a surgeon, 128, 130, 132
Literary and Philosophical Society (Newport), 350, 374, 414, 429
Little Hunting Creek Plantation, 395
Little Nine Partners Patent, 206
Livingston, Robert, 203–205
Livingston, Robert R. 418
Livingston Manor, 418, 445–447
Lloyd, David, 219, 224, 229–230, 234, 236
Lloyd, Thomas, 218–220
Locke, John, 27, 348
"Log College," 373, 380–381
Logan, James, 225, 227–230, 232–234, 235 (portrait), 236, 239, 387–389, 447, 452–453, 455
Logan, William, 443
Logstown, 457, 476, 479, 480, 482–487, 490–491, 497, 500
Logstown, Treaty of (1752), 486–487
Long Island (N. Y.), 4, 12, 15, 72, 442
Long Warrior of Tennessee, 343
Lords of Trade, 94, 95, 104–114, 116,

118, 141–142, 151–153, 195, 202–203, 216, 219–221, 225, 230, 232, 252, 423. *See also* Board of Trade
Los Adaes, 335, 338
Loudoun, Fort (on the Little Tennessee, 470–471
Loudoun, Lord, 518
Louis, Fort (Mobile), 317, 330
Louisburg, French fortress, 419, 421, 432, 535
Louisiana, 91–92, 288, 309, 318–323, 325–332, 335–347, 519
Lovelace, Gov. Francis, 40, 41
Loyal, Fort, 163
Loyal Factor, The, 224
Loyal Land Company, 485
Lucas, Eliza. *See* Eliza Lucas Pinckney
Lumber, 64, 342, 403–405, 408, 412
Lutherans, 357, 447–448, 455
Lydius, John, 503
Lynn, Ann, 19

M

Macarty, Cornelius, 307
MacGregorie, Maj. Patrick, 126, 155
Mackay, Capt. James, 496–497, 509
Madagascar trade, 201, 203, 205–206, 396, 418
Maine 7, 15, 16, 17, 18, 19, 20, 46, 48, 55, 106–108, 113, 118, 144–145, 147, 153, 173, 325, 403, 405
"Malbone," 416
Malbone, Godfrey, 414, 416
Manhattan Island, N. Y., 72–73, 188, 194
Manigault, Gabriel, 292, 398–399
Manigault, Judith, 292
Manning, Capt. John, 40, 41
Marest, Father Gabriel, 326
Marin, Capt., 488–489
Markham, William, 96, 97, 221–222, 224–225
Marquette, Father Jacques, 34, 35, 36, 38, 337
Marshe, Witham, 460
Mary, Queen of England, 195
Maryland, 8, 56, 60, 61, 74–75, 96, 98–104, 125, 151–152, 154, 195, 230, 240, 251–257, 261, 271, 281, 366, 459–462, 500, 502, 507–508, 524
Mason, Capt. John, 7, 405
Mason, John Tufton, 405–407

Mason, Robert, 55, 107–111, 114–117, 534
Masonian Proprietors, 406–407
Massachusetts, 7, 8, 14, 15, 16, 17, 20, 43–53, 106–118, 140–149, 151–154, 157–181, 195–196, 202, 366, 405–407, 410–413, 422, 430–433, 502, 504, 521–522, 524, 526–528, 533–534
Massanet, Father Damian, 139, 332
Massasoit, 45
Masts, 16, 20, 108, 403–404, 427
Matheos, Antonio, 121–122
Mather, Cotton, 157–158, 161, 163, 166, 168, 170–171, 370, 379, 434, 435 (portrait), 436
Mather, Increase, 144, 147, 149, 157, 163–164, 165 (portrait), 170–171, 190, 434
Mather, Mrs., 162
Mather, Richard, 157
Maumee River, 326, 476, 480–481
Maumee-Wabash Portage, 338, 480
Maverick, Samuel, 14, 15, 16
Medical school, 433
Membre, Father Zenobius, 84, 88, 90, 91, 127, 129–130
Mennonites, 448, 455
"Mepkin," 398
Merrimac River, 7, 17, 43, 405–406
Methodists, 352, 362
Mexia, Capt. Alonso Dias, 288
Mexico, trade with, 332–336
Miami, Fort, 476, 478, 481, 521
Miami Indians, 88, 326, 476, 481
Miamis, Fort (on St. Joseph River), 81, 83, 84, 86, 88
Michel, Franz Louis, 299, 301–302, 305
Michilimackinac, 34, 35, 81, 82, 84, 85, 126, 322–323, 325–326, 487, 514, 521
Middleton, Edward, 293
Middletown, N. J., 12, 210, 214, 216
Milborne, Jacob, 155–156
Milk for Babes, 166
Miller, Peter, 450
Miller, Thomas, 62, 64
Milwaukee, 81
Mingoes, 482, 487, 496
Minquez, Father Juan, 339
Miranda, Father Angel de, 288
Mississippi, Discovery of the, 36–38, 88, 90–92, 127–128, 320–321
"Mississippi Bubble," 336, 340–341

Mobile, 288, 294, 308, 318, 327–328, 330, 335, 343
Mohawk Indians, 31, 32, 34, 38, 51, 125, 305, 421, 447, 502
Mohican Indians, 52
Molasses, 412–414, 521
Moll, John, 74, 98, 236
Mompesson, Roger, 234
Monmouth, Duke of, 113, 146
Monmouth Purchase, 12, 210, 212, 215
Monongahela River, 470, 488, 510, 512–515, 517
Monterey, Calif., 335
Montgomery, Sir Robert, 353
Montour, Andrew, 484–487, 496, 500
Montour, Madam, 446, 453, 460, 484
Montreal, 162, 174, 195, 323–324, 496, 519
Moodey, Joshua, 157, 161, 166
Moodey, Mrs. Joshua, 162
Moore, Gov. James, 287–289, 293, 322, 328
Moore, James, Junior 304, 314
Moravians, 351–352, 358, 362–364, 455–456, 472–473
More, Nicholas, 98, 103, 218
More Wonders of the Invisible World, 171
Morgan, Francis, 19
Morgan, William, 426
Morris, Lewis, 194, 207, 211 (portrait), 212, 216–217, 315, 388, 390, 438
Morris, Robert Hunter, 507
Morris, Capt. Roger, 508, 512, 514
Morrisania Manor, 194, 212
Mount Hope, 46, 52
"Mount Vernon," 395, 442
Moytoy, "Emperor," 467
Muirson, Rev. George, 370–371
Musgrove, Capt. John, 306, 347
Musgrove, Mary, 347, 366
Muskingum, Wyandot village, 478, 483–484, 487

N

Nairne, Thomas, 292, 307–308
Narragansett Indians, 45, 48, 50, 53
Nassau Hall, 382, 383 (view)
Natchez Indians, 344–346
Natchitoches, 332, 335, 337–338
Nativism, 534–535
Natural rights, 522

Navigation laws, 4, 9, 53, 62, 71, 106–110, 176, 181, 203, 230, 289–290, 396, 521
Nazareth, Pa., 456
Neale, Thomas, 213–214
Necessity, Fort, 496–498, 500, 504, 509–510, 516
Negro slavery. *See* Slavery, Negro
New Amstel, 1, 2, 6
New Amsterdam, 1, 2, 4, 6, 12
New Berne, N. C., 300, 305, 443
New Castle, Del., 2, 10, 74, 93, 95, 98, 101, 181, 224, 236, 252
New England Courant, 434
New France, 31–39, 77–92, 125–126, 160–164, 323–327, 337–338, 474, 480–482, 485, 487–498, 510–516. *See also* Canada; Louisiana
New Hampshire, 7, 15, 16, 20, 55, 106–111, 113–115, 118, 152, 161, 172, 178, 180, 202, 366, 403–410, 502, 524
New Haven, Conn., 15, 181, 184–186, 371, 528–529
New Haven Colony, 13
New Inverness, Ga., 362–363
New Jersey, 12, 13, 41, 67–70, 73, 102, 142, 180, 195, 200, 202, 207–208, 210–217, 232–233, 261, 366, 373, 375, 380–382, 524. *See also* East Jersey *and* West Jersey
New Jersey, College of, 381–382, 383 (view)
New Light, 379–382, 433
New London, Conn., 181, 183, 379, 426, 442, 528
New Mexico, 135–137, 332–335, 339–340
New Netherland, 2–4, 6, 10, 41, 42
New Orleans, 336–337, 341
New Rochelle, N. Y., 188, 412
New Utrecht, N. Y., 41
New Windsor Township (S. C.), 465–466, 472
New York, 4, 10, 12, 15, 71–73, 75–77, 124–125, 142, 149–150, 153–156, 180–181, 187–208, 214–217, 220–222, 225, 265, 366, 375, 388, 390, 416–422, 429, 442, 445–446, 488, 500, 502–504, 524, 527, 531, 534
New York Gazette, 388, 419
New-York Weekly Journal, 388
Newark, N. J., 13, 14, 210, 214–215, 381

Newport, R. I., 154, 350, 380, 413–
416, 427, 429, 440, 442–443
Niagara, 79–81, 126, 326, 476, 480,
507, 517, 519, 521
Nicholas, Alexander, 307
Nicholson, Francis, 145–146, 149–
150, 250–252, 254–255, 257, 260–
263, 315–316, 318, 338, 348, 534
Nicolls, Richard, 6, 10, 12, 14–16, 20
Nicolls Commission, 14–17, 44, 105
Nika, Shawnee hunter, 129–130
Ninety-Six, 467, 469
Nipissing Indians, 498
Nitschman, Anna, 455
No Cross, No Crown, 68
"Nomini Hall," 392, 394
Norris, Isaac, 227, 234, 236, 239, 389
Norristown, Pa., 234
North Carolina, 276–277, 298–305,
307, 311, 316–317, 366, 465, 472–
473, 500–501, 524. *See also* Caro-
lina
Northampton, Mass., 367, 374–375,
382
Northern Neck, 9, 57, 246–247, 281–
284, 392, 394, 458, 493
Nova Scotia, 152
Nutter, Anthony, 115

O

Ocracoke Inlet, 312
Oglethorpe, James Edward, 347–
348, 350, 352, 354, 356–357, 358,
360, 363–364, 366
Ohio, Forks of the, 474–476, 480,
482, 488, 490, 492–494, 496, 507–
508
Ohio Company of Virginia, 475–
477, 483–486, 494, 500
Ohio Company's Trading House,
474, 483, 508
Ohio Country, 475–495, 480–494, 501
Old Britain, 481, 484–485, 487–488,
514
Oliver, Andrew, 526–528
Onanguisset, Potawatomi chief, 324
Oneida Indians, 31, 32, 38, 125, 305,
502
Onondaga Council House, 452–453,
482, 487
Onondaga Indians, 31, 32, 38, 125,
305, 446, 502
Oquage, 446

Orange, Fort, 4. *See also* Albany,
Fort
Orkney, Earl of, 263, 271
Orkney, Lady, 271
Orleans, Fort, 342
Orme, Capt. Robert, 508, 510, 512,
514
Orvietan, 85
Osgood, Mary, 168, 170
Oswego, Fort (N. Y.), 421, 459, 488,
518
Otermin, Antonio de, 135–136
Otis, James, 521–522
Otseningo, 446
Ottawa Indians, 485, 488, 498, 514
Ouiatenon, Fort, 338, 476, 478
Outreouati, chief, 125
Overhill Towns (Cherokee), 308,
354, 469–470
Owego, 446, 453
Oyster Point, 66

P

Palatines, 300–301, 303, 305, 445–
447. *See also* Germans
Paper money, 164, 431–432
Paris, Peace of, 519–520
Parmiter, Thomas, 307
Parthenia, 228
Paschall, Thomas, 101
Pastorius, Francis Daniel, 102
Pawnee Indians, 339–340
Pecos, N. M., 331, 334
Pelham, Peter, 372, 435, 436
Pemaquid, Me., 7, 20, 44, 48, 144–
146, 161, 163, 172–173
Pemberton, James, 443
Penn, Hannah, 225–226, 228, 237,
238 (portrait), 239
Penn, John, son of the Proprietor,
226, 237, 239
Penn, John, grandson of the Pro-
prietor, 502–503
Penn, Letitia, 225, 228
Penn, Richard, 237
Penn, Thomas, 237
Penn, William, Proprietor of Penn-
sylvania, 68, 69, 93–104, 113, 140,
147, 151–152, 195, 217–219, 221,
225–239, 261, 299, 305, 453
Penn, William, Junior, 233–234, 237
Pennsbury, 226, 228–230, 232
Pennsylvania, 93–104, 152, 195–196,
207, 218–239, 261, 362, 364, 366,

373, 385–390, 446–456, 459–463, 474–476, 480, 482, 484–486, 500, 502, 507, 518–519, 523–524, 526
Pennsylvania, University of, 384
Pennsylvania Gazette, 385, 501
Pensacola, 320, 327–328, 338, 343
Pentegoet, Fort, 44, 144–145
Pepperrell, William, 419, 420 (portrait), 421, 438
Pequot Indians, 52
Perier, Governor, 343–344
Perry, Micajah, 241, 263, 276, 282, 284, 391. *See also* Perry & Lane
Perry & Lane, 241–242, 244–245, 251, 263–264. *See also* Perry, Micajah
Perth, Earl of, 212
Perth Amboy, N. J., 102, 181, 212–217, 438, 442
Philadelphia, Pa., 100–103, 181, 210, 222, 224–226, 228, 233–234, 239, 374–375, 385–386, 388, 390, 440, 442–443, 452–453
Philip, "King," 45–52
Philipsborough, Manor of, 188, 198, 418
Philipsborough Manor House, 416, 417 (exterior and interior), 418
Philipse, Adolphus, 198, 203, 429
Philipse, Frederick, 71, 188, 198, 203, 416
Philipse, Frederick, Second Lord of the Manor of Philipsborough, 416
Philipse, Margaret, 71, 188, 416
Phips, Sir William, 163–164, 170, 178, 179 (portrait), 196, 325
Physical Club (Boston), 429
Pickawillany village, 476, 478, 481, 484–485, 487–488
Pierson, Abraham, 184
Pietism, 351–352, 358, 373
Pight, John, 306
Pigot, George, 371
Pima Indians, 335
Pimitoui, 323, 326–327
Pinckney, Charles, 397, 399
Pinckney, Eliza Lucas, 397, 399–400, 403
Pine Tree Shillings, 15, 112
Pio, Father Juan, 135
Pirates, 200–206, 224–225, 230, 310–312
Pitch, 290
Pitt, Fort, 521. *See also* Du Quesne, Fort
Pitt, William, 519
Plains of Abraham, 519

Platte River, 339–340
Plays and players, 287, 315, 442
Plymouth Colony, 8, 15, 45, 48, 52, 113, 118, 152, 154
Pocotaligo, 307
Pontiac's Conspiracy, 521
Poor Richard's Almanac, 385–386
Port Royal (Carolina), 12, 23, 24, 120, 122, 288, 292, 307–308, 356
Port Royal (Nova Scotia), 163, 172, 325
Port Royal, The, 23
Portrait painters, 434–440
Portsmouth, N. H., 172, 181
Postal service, 40, 101–102, 181, 183, 213–214, 507
Potawatomi Village, 86
Pratt, William, 282
Praying Indians, 46
Prentis, Thomas, 426
Prerogative, 180, 421–423, 432, 486, 504–505, 535
Presbyterians, 368, 373–374, 380–382, 448, 450, 472
President, The, 144
Presque Isle, 489, 492, 521
Pressing to death, 167–168
Preston, Samuel, 234
Priber, Christian Gottlieb, 467–468
Prince George, Fort, 469
Princeton, N. J., 381, 443
Princeton University. *See* College of New Jersey
Principo Iron Works, 286
Printing, 158, 220, 385, 387
Protestant Association of Maryland, 151, 252
Prudhomme, Fort, 90
Pueblo Revolt, 135–137, 332–334
Punishments, physical, 18–19, 60, 156, 167–168, 268, 270, 311
Purchase, Thomas, and Mrs. Purchase, 46
Purry, Jean Pierre, 353, 362

Q

Quakers, 12, 67–70, 73, 74, 93, 94, 102, 196, 207–208, 210, 218–220, 225, 229, 232–234, 236–237, 254, 256, 380, 427
"Quarters" (for negroes), 249, 266
Quary, Robert, 120, 217, 222–223, 225, 229–230, 232–233, 236, 261–262

Quebec, 31, 154, 163–164, 172, 323–324, 518–519
Queen Anne's War, 173–176, 287, 328. *See also* Anne, Queen of England
Queensboro Township (S. C.), 465
Quidah, The, 204–205
Quitrents, 8, 12, 13, 28, 96, 109–110, 114, 143, 200, 203, 210, 215, 217, 230, 232, 246, 251–252, 264–265, 268
Quo Warranto, 104, 108–113, 117, 119, 141, 151

R

Ramon, Manuela Sanchez, 332, 335
Randolph, Edward, 53, 55, 106–112, 114–117, 143–144, 148, 151, 176, 178, 203, 222, 224, 230, 252, 255, 260–261, 289
Ratcliff, The Rev. Robert, 117
Red Shoe, of Cushtusha Town, 344, 469
Redstone, Fort, 488, 492, 494–496, 498
Redwood, Abraham, 414
Redwood Library, 414, 415 (view)
Reformed Churches. *See* Dutch Reformed Church; German Reformed Church
Renault, Philippe Francois, 342
Rents. *See* Quitrents
Representation, 107, 141, 194, 264, 422, 524–525, 533, 536
"Republican way of Thinking," 422–424
Rhett, Col. William, 311
Rhode Island, 8, 15, 44, 45, 48, 52, 113, 117–118, 149, 152, 154, 180–181, 201–202, 230, 261, 350, 366, 413–416, 427, 521, 524
Rice, 290, 342, 365, 396–398, 400–401, 466
Richardson, Samuel, 218
Richmond, Va., 444
Rights as Englishmen, 141, 263, 521, 522, 533–535. *See also* Liberties as Englishmen
Rosalie, Fort, 345
Rose, The, 116, 144, 148
Rouville, Hertel de, 173–176, 289
Rowlandson, Mrs. Joseph, 50–52
Royal African Company, 6, 242, 244
Royal Society of London, 386–387

Rum, 279, 306, 357, 364–365, 412–414, 452–453, 462, 472, 503
Ryswick, Treaty of, 173

S

Sabbath, The, 426–427, 433
St. Antoine, Fort, 323
St. Augustine, Florida, 21, 22, 26, 121, 287–289, 309, 360, 362–364
Saint-Castin, Baron de, 144–145, 172–173
St. Catherine (French Louisiana), 345
St. Catherines, or Katherines, Island, 24, 366
St. Clair, Sir John, 506, 509, 512, 514
St. Croix River, 6, 7, 20
St. Denis, Louis Juchereau de, 332, 335, 338
St. Esprit, Mission du, 34
St. Francis Xavier, Mission of, 34, 35, 84
St. George, Fort, 360
St. Ignace, Mission of, 35, 36, 81, 326
St. John's College, 255
St. Joseph, Fort, 323
St. Joseph River, 81, 82, 86
St. Louis, Fort (on Illinois River), 126–127, 134, 323
St. Louis of Texas, 128, 134, 137–138
Saint-Lusson, Daumont de, 34, 35
St. Mary's, Md., 252–253, 257
Saint Pierre, Legardeur de, 489–492
St. Simon, Fort, 360
St. Simons Island, 358, 363
St. Theresa, Fort, 32
Salem, Mass., 107, 159, 160, 167–168, 176
Salem, N. J., 68, 210
Salem, N. C., 471, 473
Salem witchcraft trials, 167–170
Salmon Falls, N. H., 162
Saluda, Treaty of the, 469–470, 509
Salzburgers, 357
San Antonio mission, 335
San Francisco de los Neches, 335
San Francisco de los Texas (or Tejas), 139, 332
San Juan Bautista, 332, 335
San Luis, presidio of, 288
San Marco, Fort (St. Augustine), 288, 363
San Xavier del Bac, 335
Sanderson, The, 413–414

Sandford, Robert, 22, 24
Sandford, William, 215
Sangre de Cristo Pass, 339
Santa Fe, N. M., 135–136, 334, 339–340
Santo Domingo, N. M., 136, 334
Sauer, Christopher, 448
Sauer, Marie, 448
Sault Ste. Marie, 34, 35, 323
Savacola, Mission of, 121
Savannah, Ga., 355 (view), 356-358, 360, 362, 365–366, 375
Savannah Town, 292, 294, 322, 336, 353, 362, 466–467
Saxe Gotha Township (S. C.), 465–466
Saybrook Platform of 1708, 370
Sayle, William, 23, 29, 30
Scalp bounties, 173
Scarouady, Mingo sub-chief, 482, 487
Scarsdale, Manor of, 187, 233, 309
Schenectady, N. Y., 32, 162
Schoharie Valley, 445–447
Schools, 102, 277, 436, 456
Schuyler, Peter, 196, 197 (portrait), 200
Scotch, 120–122, 207, 212–213, 225, 252, 357, 362–363, 433
Scotch-Irish, 373, 447–448, 450–452, 459, 464–466, 473
Searles, Robert, 21, 22
Selyns, Domine, 156
Seneca Indians, 31, 32, 38, 79, 125–126, 305, 482, 502
Servants, 27, 28, 29, 212, 228, 254, 258, 265–266, 268–269, 272, 358
Seven Years' War. *See* French and Indian War
Seventh-Day Baptist, 233
Sewall, Mrs. Samuel, 162
Sewall, Samuel, 116, 118, 145, 153, 158, 160–162, 167, 170, 172, 180, 316, 436, 437 (portrait)
Shackamaxon, Treaty of, 100
Shaftesbury, Earl of, 64, 66, 106, 119. *See also* Anthony Ashley Cooper
Shamokin, 446, 453, 455, 479, 482
Shannopin Town, 479, 480, 482–483, 490, 494
Sharpe, Horatio, 505, 507, 523
Shawnee Indians, 65, 88, 120, 446, 452, 455, 470, 476, 481–482, 485, 487, 496
Shelly, Capt. Giles, 205–206, 225
Shenandoah Valley, 280, 456–459, 462–464, 473, 475, 493, 506, 518

Shippen & Lawrence, 476, 484
Shipping, 107, 176, 412–414
Shirley, Gov. William, 406, 419, 430–432, 502, 505, 507, 517–518
Shirley, William, Junior, 508, 512, 514
Short, Mercy, 168
Shrewsbury, Duke of, 204–205
Shrewsbury, N. J., 12, 41, 210, 214, 216
Silk culture, 290, 342
"Silk Hope," 290, 398–399
Sioux Indians, 84, 85, 320, 322
Six Nations. *See* 304–305 for change of name from that of Five Nations, but all references will be found under "Iroquois."
Skin trade, 28, 65, 66, 120–122, 124, 137, 292, 294–295, 298, 306–307, 328, 332, 336, 365, 475–476, 480. *See also* Fur trade; Indian trade
Slate-roof House, 227 (view), 239
Slavery, Indian, 46, 53, 120, 161, 287–289, 292, 295, 298, 304–308, 327–330, 343–344, 397
Slavery, Negro, 1, 2, 6, 27, 64, 75, 107, 194, 203, 212, 228, 240–249, 258, 265–271, 278, 282, 286, 292, 295, 329, 341, 348, 357, 364–365, 392, 395, 397–398, 400, 410, 412–414, 418, 426–428, 434, 442, 466, 470
Sloughter, Henry, 153, 155–156, 194, 219
Sluyter, Peter, 70–76
Smallpox, 72, 163, 244, 434
Smibert, John, 420, 436–438
Smuggling, 6, 188, 413
Society for the Propagation of the Gospel in Foreign Parts, 232–233, 256, 276, 300, 316, 348, 370–371, 373, 380, 382, 384
Solebay, H. M. S., 419
Sonioto, Shawnee village, 476, 478, 481, 484
Sons of Liberty, 526–531, 536
South Carolina, 287–298, 303–318, 322, 326–329, 336, 338, 343–344, 353, 354, 356, 365–366, 396–403, 422, 465–472, 500, 525, 531. *See also* Carolina.
Southampton, L. I., 42
Southold, L. I., 42
Sowl, Andrew, 220
Spangenberg, August Gottlieb, 352, 358, 360, 362, 456, 472–473

Spanish Florida, 21, 22, 24, 26, 120–122, 287–289, 309, 320, 327–328, 338, 360, 362–364

Spotswood, Alexander, 263, 271–272, 273 (portrait), 274–277, 279–281, 285–286, 303–305, 308, 311, 337, 423, 456, 458, 534

Springfield, Mass., 46

Stacey, Mahlon, 217

Staked Plains, 137

Stamp Act Congress, 533, 536

Stamp tax, 505, 523, 524–531, 536

Starr, Comfort, House, 185 (exterior and interior views)

Start, John, 18

Starved Rock, 323

Staunton, Va., 464, 473, 518

Stebbins, Benoni, house, 174, 177 (view)

"Stenton," 239, 387–388, 389 (exterior view), 453

Stiles, Ezra, 381, 390, 414, 415 (portrait), 427

Stoddard, Solomon, 368

Stoll, Joost, 150

Story, Enoch, 234

Stoughton, William, 153, 158, 161–162, 167, 169 (portrait), 170, 178, 180

Strasburg, Va., 458

"Stratford," 392

Stratford, Conn., 371, 373

Stuart's Town, 120–121

Stuyvesant, Peter, 188

Surriage, Agnes, 410, 436

Susquehanna Land Company, 503

Susquehannock Indians, 124

Swansea, 46

Swedes, 2, 74, 96, 98, 100

Swiss, 277, 299–301, 303, 305, 353, 465–466

T

Taensa Villages, 90, 91, 134

Talbot, George, 103–104

Tamerlane, Penn's stallion, 228

Tanacharison, Mingo sub-chief, 482, 487, 490, 494–495, 497, 500

Taos, N. M., 135

Tar, 290, 446

Tatham, John, 210

Taxes, 57, 60, 61, 141, 172, 258, 262, 264–265, 505, 521–522, 523–525, 533

Teach, Capt. ("Black-Beard"), 310–312, 313 (picture)

Tegantouki, Seneca chief, 86

Tellico, 467, 469, 471

Tennent, Gilbert, 373–379, 381–382

Tennent, William, 373, 381

Tesuque, pueblo, 135

Tew, Capt., 201

Texas, 128–132, 137–139, 320, 332, 338

Thomas, Gabriel, 226

Thomas, Gov. George, 459–460

Thomlinson, John, 406, 423

Three Brothers, The, 23, 24, 26

Ticonderoga, 519

Tioga, 446

Tithables, 265–266

Tobacco, 4, 5, 6, 9, 56, 60, 62, 106, 240–245, 247, 249, 253, 263–266, 269–270, 280–284, 342, 390–392, 395–396, 472

Tobacco fleet, 240–242, 270, 282

Tobler, John, 466, 472

Tomo Chichi, Chief, 347–348, 349 (portrait), 356–357

Tonti, Henri de, 79, 83, 84, 85, 86, 87 (portrait), 88, 90, 91, 126–127, 129–130, 134, 138, 320, 323–324, 327–328

Tony, Byrd's Indian trader, 271, 302

Toulouse, Fort, 296, 309, 331, 336–337, 342

Townshend, Charles, 525

Townships, of South Carolina, 465–466, 470

Trade. *See* Lords of Trade; Board of Trade

Trade laws. *See* Navigation laws

Travel, 73–76, 153–154, 160, 181–190, 228, 272, 277–280, 427; 440–443, 472–473, 474, 480–481, 483–485

Treat, Robert, 142

Trent, William, Philadelphia merchant, 217, 227, 234

Trent, William, fur trader, 486–487, 492–494, 497

Trenton, N. J., 217

Triangular Trade, 413–414

Trinity Church (N. Y.), 190, 203, 384

Trout, William, 222

Tuesday Club, The Ancient and Honorable, 429

Tulpehocken (Pa.), 447–448, 450, 452–453, 518

Turf and twig, 34, 98, 469
Turk's Head Inn, 172
Tuscarora Indians, 276, 297–298, 301–305, 307, 502
Tuskenehaus, Creek Indian, 306
Tyler, Goody, 168

U

Unitas Fratrum. See Moravians
United Colonies of New England, 44, 45, 48
Urmston, Rev. John, 300–301

V

Van Cortlandt, Stephanus, 419
Van Cortlandt Manor, 418
Vanderspeigel, John, 190
Van Rensselaer, Manor of, 418
Vargas, Diego de, 333 (portrait), 334, 339
Vehicles, 162, 180, 190, 192, 201, 228, 428, 440, 442, 507, 510, 514–515
Venango, 479, 482, 489–492, 511, 521
Vesey, William, 190, 191 (portrait)
Vice-Admiralty Courts, 176, 222, 224, 261, 311
Villazur, Don Pedro de, 339–340
Villiers, Coulon de, 496–497
Virginia, 9, 21, 56–60, 106, 111, 122–125, 195, 240–251, 255–286, 302–303, 305, 308, 366, 382, 390–396, 422, 456–465, 474–475, 477, 482–483, 485–498, 501–502, 504–505, 517–518, 524, 526–527
Virginia Gazette, 444, 527
Virginia Indian Company, 276–277, 280, 308
Voyageurs, 325–326

W

Wachovia, 471, 473
Wadsworth, Capt., of Hartford, 142
Waldron, Maj. Richard, 161
Walker, Timothy, 426–427
Walking Purchase, 453–454, 513–514
Wall Street, N. Y., 72
Wampanoag Indians, 45, 48
Ward, Ensign Edward, 494
Warren, Capt. Peter, 418–419, 421
Warriors Path. *See* Great Warriors Path

Warwick, Earl of, 200
Washington, Augustine, 286, 395
Washington, George, 286, 395, 442, 463, 474, 490–498, 499–500, 504, 508–509, 512, 514–515
Washington, Lawrence, 395, 463, 477, 485
Watson, John, 211, 438, 439 (self-portrait)
Wawayanda Patent, 206
Weiser, Ann Eve, 451
Weiser, Conrad, 447–448, 450–453, 455, 460, 461 (portrait), 486, 500, 502–503, 507
Welch, Thomas, 329
Welcome, The, 98
Wells, James, 440
Welsh, 98
Wendell, Jacob, 428
Wentworth, Benning, 404–410, 502
Wentworth, Mark Hunking, 408
Wentworth Hall, 408, 409 (interior detail), 410
Wesley, Charles, 352, 358, 360
Wesley, John, 352, 358, 360, 362
West, Capt. Joseph, 23, 29, 64, 66
West Jersey, 69, 70, 73, 74, 93, 94, 117, 142, 152, 195, 200, 202, 207–210, 216–217, 230, 232, 261. *See also* New Jersey
West Jersey Society, 208, 210
Westo Indians, 63, 65–66, 119–120, 123, 292, 362
Westover (Va.), 240–241, 243, 245–246, 264, 266–271, 390–392, 393 (exterior view)
Wethersfield, Conn., 15, 142, 529–530
Whipping Post Club, 429
Whipple House, 159 (view)
White, Goody, 19
Whitefield, George, 362, 364–365, 374–376, 377 (portrait), 380–382
Whitmore, Daniel, 404
Wicaco village, 100
Wiggins, Thomas, 115, 534
Wigs, 180, 228, 302, 434, 436
Wilkins, "Billy," 268
Willard, Samuel, 118, 157, 161, 166, 170
William, Fort (Cumberland Island), 360
William and Mary, King and Queen of England, 147, 148, 150, 154, 160
William and Mary College, 251, 257–

258, 272, 274, 276, 304, 382, 387, 464
William of Orange, 140–141, 145–146. *See also* William III, King of England
William III, King of England, 147, 149, 150–151, 153, 161, 164, 257, 320–321. *See also* William of Orange
Williams, Elisha, 502
Williams, Ephraim, 502–503
Williams, Eunice, 176
Williams, John, family, 174
Williams, Roger, 44, 48
Williamsburg, Va., 257, 271–276, 338, 490, 492, 494, 517
Williamson, Mr., of Savannah, 360
Wills Creek, 474, 483, 488, 492, 494, 506, 508
Winchester, Va. *See* Frederick Town
Winslow, Edward, 45
Winslow, Josiah, 45, 47 (portrait)
Winston-Salem, N. C., 473
Winthrop, Fitz-John, 163–164
Winthrop, Gov. John, 113, 116, 157
Winthrop, John, The Younger, 15
Winthrop, Madam Katharine, 436
Wise, John, 141
Witchcraft, 164–171, 436
Wonders of the Invisible World, 170
Woodward, Henry, 22, 23, 26, 28, 64, 65, 66, 120–122

Wragg, Samuel, 397
Wright, John, 306–307
Wyandot Indians, 476, 483, 485, 487

Y

Yadkin River, 472–473, 483
Yale College, 184, 371, 372 (view), 381–382, 387, 502
Yamacraw Indians, 356
Yamasee Indians, 288, 292, 297, 304, 306–309, 336, 342
Yellow fever, 328–329
York, Duke of, 93, 94, 96, 98, 104, 113. *See also* James II, King of England
York, Proprietary of the Duke of, 4–6, 8, 10, 15, 20, 42, 43, 44, 67, 68, 70, 207
Young, Rowland, 18
"Young Proprietors" of Pennsylvania, 239, 447, 455

Z

Zenger Libel Trial, 388, 390
Zinzendorf, Nicolaus Ludwig, Count von, 351–352, 358, 455, 473
Zouberbuhler, Rev. Bartholomew, 466
Zuni, N. M., 133, 135, 331